# ACT for Gender Identity

*of related interest*

**Theorizing Transgender Identity for Clinical Practice**
**A New Model for Understanding Gender**
*S.J. Langer*
ISBN 978 1 78592 765 2
eISBN 978 1 78450 642 1

**Counselling Skills for Working with Gender Diversity and Identity**
*Michael Beattie and Penny Lenihan with Robin Dundas*
ISBN 978 1 78592 741 6
eISBN 978 1 78450 481 6

**Sex, Sexuality, and Trans Identities**
**Clinical Guidance for Psychotherapists and Counselors**
*Edited by Gary J. Jacobson, LCSW and Jan C. Niemira, LCSW and Karalyn Violeta, LCSW*
*Foreword by Kate Bornstein and Barbara Carrellas*
ISBN 978 1 78592 617 4
eISBN 978 1 78592 618 1

**Improving Services for Transgender and Gender Variant Youth**
**Research, Policy and Practice for Health and Social Care Professionals**
*Tiffany Jones*
ISBN 978 1 78592 425 5
eISBN 978 1 78450 789 3

**Person-Centred Counselling for Trans and Gender Diverse People**
**A Practical Guide**
*Sam Hope*
ISBN 978 1 78592 542 9
eISBN 978 1 78450 937 8

# ACT *for* Gender Identity

*The Comprehensive Guide*

ALEX STITT, LMHC

Jessica Kingsley Publishers
London and Philadelphia

First published in 2020
by Jessica Kingsley Publishers
73 Collier Street
London N1 9BE, UK
and
400 Market Street, Suite 400
Philadelphia, PA 19106, USA

*www.jkp.com*



**Library of Congress Cataloging in Publication Data**
A CIP catalog record for this book is available from the Library of Congress

**British Library Cataloguing in Publication Data**
A CIP catalogue record for this book is available from the British Library

ISBN 978 1 78592 799 7
eISBN 978 1 78450 812 8

Printed and bound in the United States

# Contents

# 1

# Introduction

## *Storm Cloud Butterflies*

To be *fierce* is to be proud of yourself in the face of adversity.

To be *fabulous* is to inspire others by being exactly who you are.

Accepting our gender in a world of prejudice, heterosexism, cissexism, and transphobia often feels like a butterfly trying to glide through a rain storm. Having come so far and transformed so much, navigating life's maelstrom feels overwhelming. Despair is common, and loneliness doubly so. Outrage is understandable, and the torrential shame is blown on gusts of fear and bias.

Take heart that the world is changing. The 2016 census performed by UCLA's prestigious Williams Institute found that, in less than a decade, the number of transgender Americans had doubled from 0.3 percent to 0.6 percent (Flores *et al.*, 2016c). That's approximately 1.4 million remarkable human beings. Of course, 700,000 transgender individuals didn't suddenly materialize out of thin air. We were always here, but after decades of advocacy, social education, hard-won political battles, fallen friends, gained allies, and massive changes in the field of mental health, the chrysalis finally cracked. The youth of America are finding more liberty to express themselves, while those who have spent their lives hidden are beginning to emerge with both community support and even community celebration.

The change from *gender identity disorder* to *gender dysphoria* in the American Psychiatric Association's *Diagnostic and Statistical Manual of Mental Disorders* (DSM) 5th edition (2013) attested to the realization that the brunt of mental health issues facing transgender individuals—from post-traumatic stress disorder (PTSD) to anxiety, self-harm, substance abuse, eating disorders, and suicidal ideation—do not derive from having a transgender identity. A healthy community, embodied by unconditional acceptance, cultivates healthy identity constructs.

Quelle surprise. On the other hand, a society comprised of deleterious homogeny, where uniqueness is quashed and children are made to feel like pariahs, has only one outcome: a hateful downpour.

Following suit, the World Health Organization (WHO) depathologized gender variance in their 2018 revision of the *International Classification of Diseases* (ICD-11). Removing gender variance as a disorder, the ICD-11 still includes *gender incongruence* as a diagnosis, as therapy is still beneficial to individuals seeking self-actualization, and many nations around the world require a diagnosis in order to provide therapeutic or medical assistance.

We know that storms do not subside quickly, and that the dangers facing trans populations remain all too real. The extensive 2011 National Transgender Discrimination Survey found that 46 percent of trans men and 42 percent of trans women attempt suicide, with increased risks amongst individuals who are differently abled, who have mental health conditions, or who are HIV positive (Grant *et al.*, 2011; Haas, Rodgers, and Herman, 2014). Echoing this dark fact, the 2015 US Transgender Survey, produced by the National Center for Transgender Equality, found that 40 percent of trans individuals had attempted suicide in their lifetime (James *et al.*, 2016). This same survey underlined how 47 percent of the trans population had been sexually assaulted in their lifetime, with 46 percent of respondents being verbally harassed, and 9 percent being physically assaulted in the last year alone.

So how can you, as a mental health practitioner, possibly aid a population so targeted by prejudice, misconception, and hateful propaganda? What can you provide when the courageous advocate—who's been fighting the good fight since they were old enough to realize they were different—breaks down because they feel so utterly overcome? How can you aid gender variant people fatigued by the armor they've worn for so long? Or help the genderqueer teen exhausted from correcting pronouns? Or the trans man angry at their family's disapproval? Or the genderfluid person's shapeshifting anxiety?

While cognitive behavioral therapy (CBT) and person-centered therapy (PCT) have certainly helped clients manage an array of gender-related issues to various degrees of success, many mental health practitioners working with transgender clients often pine for something more. Ideally a shift in society or a calm in the storm would be nice, yet when this is not available in the immediate future the need for a specialized therapeutic modality becomes clear.

Gender affirmative therapy requires practitioners to not only take a deep look at themselves and their own conceptualization of gender, but to adopt values that empower the full range of gender identity, expression, and experience (Ali, 2014; Ansara, 2010; Carroll, Gilroy, and Ryan, 2002; Livingstone, 2010; Raj, 2002). A trans-positive therapist needs to take into account the role of systematic oppression and social alienation in order to conceptualize autoplastic and alloplastic treatment plans. By affirming the client's autonomy, you can shed the expectations and role impositions of gender binary from the therapeutic relationship, yet this is only possible if you monitor the role gender plays in both transference and countertransference. This may require you to familiarize yourself, not merely with the new, ever growing terms applied to gender identity and gender pronouns, but with the field of queer theory (Frank and Cannon, 2010). Evolving from post-structural feminism, queer theory highlights how gender is a core component to identity, without ascribing to inflexible norms and expectations (Gamson, 2000). When you no longer presume there is a binary of black and white, you are free to see a rainbow continuum.

*Gender variance*, in this text, describes the complete array of possible gender identities, as not all outside the binary identify as *transgender*, for a myriad of personal and cultural reasons. A wider umbrella, gender variance encompasses a range of gender constructs including, but not limited to, post-op, pre-op, and non-op male-to-female (MTF) and female-to-male (FTM) people, trans men and trans women who do not seek complete transition, as well as genderqueer, genderfluid, agender and third gender individuals (Andre and Guitierrez, 2010; Ettner, 1999; Kusalik 2010; Luengsuraswat, 2010; Mallon, 2009). Gender variance can also include binary and nonbinary cisgender people whose gender expression exceeds their cultural gender norms, which in turn can make them targets for abuse (Devor, 1989; Lucal, 1999). These include transvestites, drag artists, and queer identities that identify with their anatomic sex while bending, blurring, or breaking their gender role.

With such a diverse array of people, many therapists strive to be trans positive by increasing their awareness of psychosocial issues facing the gender variant demographic and by continuing their development in multicultural competency. Yet literature providing an actual therapeutic modality is scarce. In other words, while therapists may be able to conceptualize the issues at hand, and validate the struggle, they're not always certain how to help. In recent years, the popularity of Acceptance and Commitment Therapy (ACT) has steadily been on the rise, due in part to its wide applicability, and how ACT combines elements of Skinnerian contextualism with mindfulness practices akin to many Eastern philosophies including Zen Buddhism. ACT is unique in its focus, as it encourages us to accept our complete emotional experience without the pitfalls of avoidance or maladaptive coping mechanisms. Subsequently, ACT is an ideal mode of therapy for developing and affirming gender identity and emotional resilience.

Steven Hayes, the founder of ACT and celebrated author of *Get out of Your Mind and into Your Life: The New Acceptance and Commitment Therapy* (Hayes and Smith, 2005), presents six ACT precepts easily adapted to gender affirmative therapy:

1. *Acceptance*: Relinquishing avoidance strategies to accept our emotions allows gender variant individuals to come to terms with the full experience of who we are. This is a vital step as many of us endure closeted or compartmentalized periods of our life as a maladaptive survival mechanism. Furthermore, attempts to ignore or power through macro-, meso-, and microaggressions can have a detrimental effect on both physical and mental health (Roland and Burlew, 2017).

2. *Cognitive defusion*: Understanding cognitive–emotional fusion (being at the mercy of our thoughts and feelings) and cognitive–emotional defusion (being able to take a step back to allow for calm objectivity) allows us to move from emotional reactivity to living a proactive, self-actualized life. Shifting our relationship with our thoughts to observe cognitions and emotions without judgment is a key step when coming to terms with both who we are and how we feel.

3. *Being present*: Implementing mindfulness in the here and now helps to cultivate direct contact with our senses and our environment. In doing so, past trauma and intrusive thoughts are able to enter the mind and dissipate via meditative practice.

4. *Self-as-context*: Utilizing perspective-taking and metaphors, ACT develops an understanding of how language forms our locus of perspective (here vs. there, now vs. then, I vs. you). By increasing our mental flexibility and recognizing how we naturally develop a multifaceted identity—inclusive but not limited to our gender—we are able to develop emotional and psychosocial adaptability.

5. *Values*: Developing awareness around our values in order to make healthy, proactive life choices helps us nurture our self-knowledge and personal pride in order to combat internalized homophobia and transphobia. While validating gender identity is integral, validating our core value construct is both clarifying and empowering.

6. *Committed action*: Making active steps to embody our value constructs in order to maintain a healthy identity has always been the most difficult and ultimately most rewarding step of the coming-out and self-affirmation process. This stage of ACT is most akin to other behavioral modalities, as it requires measurable, concrete steps to shifting behavior.

How we cope with the hardships of the outside world is, was, and will always be the source of both our pain and our victory, our despair and our passion. Indeed, with the client on the couch, it becomes clear that both the storm and that courageous butterfly exist together within them, with every original hope and internalized fear. Uniquely, ACT provides a route through this inner storm, useful to any practitioner striving to help gender variant clients come to terms with both identity and emotional acceptance.

As a nonbinary person and a licensed mental health professional, I must own my bias, and explain the grammatical voice of this text. Like so many outside of the statistical bell curve, I have been the misunderstood child, and the distraught teen, and the fatigued adult sat across from bewildered therapists who didn't know what to do with me. Yet like so many therapists, I also endorse the restorative power of relational connection, and have learned a great deal of humility from my turn in the clinician's chair. Empathizing with both, I hope to challenge how we think about the therapeutic relationship by reconstructing the conversation, yet to do so I had to make a very personal linguistic choice. I am a person before an occupation, so instead of writing as a clinician for clinicians, I nest my professional insight within my experience as a gender minority, aligning my voice with those of the clients.

To conceptualize the sheer diversity of gender, we will periodically meander through culturally contextual case vignettes, using *they*, *them*, and *their* unless pronouns are specified. Yet when authors sit the reader apart from the subject for too long, relatability is often sacrificed for objectivity. In research literature, transgender and nonbinary identities are often treated as a peculiar novelty, regarding *those* people and *their* experience over there. This language of distinction inadvertently creates a false divide from that of the reader, contributing to unnecessary frames of opposition. For this reason, much of this book is written in the first-person plural, so that *we* can understand each other, *together*.

Since this is a clinical guide, *you* will be distinguished only when we need to address *your* role as the clinician, or to focus your attention on your personal experience. Admittedly, your therapeutic role does set you apart— not because of your gender— but because you are the second half of our wonderful conversation. As ACT encourages us to hold ideas loosely by challenging rigid constructs and absolute thinking, we may shake things up a bit, allowing us to be as radically different as we are universally similar. Side by side, we will complete exercises together, and from time to time we'll let you know what kind of questions may be helpful to ask, or what you may need to be mindful of in such delicate situations. This inclusive writing style may be natural for some and awkward for others, as clinicians are rarely instructed by clients.

Language most certainly influences our perception, but it does not determine our existence, it only describes it. Too often, gender development is conceptualized on a fixed track, from boys to men or girls to women, framing our language in rigid terms of normalcy and homogeny (Nagoshi and Brzuzy, 2010). Yet our experiences are as diverse as our identities, and we all explore and re-explore gender at our own pace. Exceeding physical presentation and personal pronouns, gender impacts our entire construct of self—personally, intellectually, socially, academically, occupationally, and spiritually. Who are we? What is our relationship with our body? How do we move through this world? How do we express ourselves? No matter the answer, the question is relatable to all, marking all responses as meaningful, and therefore worthy of compassion and empathy.

Gender identity actualization is not a solely transgender experience, yet for cisgender individuals (male men and female women) who may have taken their gender identity for granted, it may be difficult to examine. So, let us begin here with a tentative, delicate feeling as hopeful as it is nervous. All too often, we enter session hoping to banish anxiety once and for all! This, ACT observes, is the agenda of emotional control in action. Ironic process dictates that the more we try to duck and dodge the rain, the more we seem to get wet, which is to say, the more we try to get rid of our emotions, the more emotions are brought to the forefront of our attention (Wegner, 1994; Wegner *et al.*, 1987; Wenzlaff and Wegner, 2000). Unable to eradicate our feelings, we may begin to loathe them, reject them, even fear them, leading to depression and anxiety. At this point, we often experience two gut responses. The first is a knot, signaling that we're in over our head—that the storm has become too great. The second is a prelude to this knot, a fluttering in our stomach best described as trepidatious butterflies.

Though beautiful and transformational, butterflies are so often associated with anxiety, as the precursor of a panic attack or something to avoid. But what if those very same butterflies were actually our fragile courage? What if those butterflies were our call to action? Evidence that we have taken one step past our comfort zone? One step closer to authenticity? If you have ever felt those vulnerable butterflies in your tummy at the thought of disclosing some personal truth—even if only for an instant— then you might understand some small glimmer of what it's like for a trans person to speak proudly amidst a thunderous storm of self-doubt.

ACT has proven to be efficacious for the treatment of anxiety (Forsyth and Eifert, 2016), depression (Strosahl and Robinson, 2017), PTSD (Walser and Westrup, 2007), disordered eating (Sandoz, Wilson, and Dufrene, 2010), body image (Sandoz and Dufrene, 2013), suicide prevention (Barnes *et al.* 2017), substance abuse (Batten and Hayes, 2005), and grief (Speedlin *et al.*, 2016)—all substantial issues confronting sexual and gender minorities. As there is little research currently available applying ACT techniques to Lesbian, Gay, Bisexual, Transgender and Queer (LGBTQ) populations, this text is best used as an adjunct to pre-existing workbooks, rather than as a complete treatment plan. Unlike other ACT books that address a specific mental health issue, *ACT for Gender Identity* is a trouble-shooting resource to help ACT practitioners work with a vast multicultural demographic of gender minorities. As the first ACT text written specifically for gender variant populations, there are many complex issues to cover, from the intersectionality of culture, sexuality, and gender, to the impact of oppression on mental health, to the unique experiential milestones gender variant people encounter over the lifespan. As a form of gender-affirmative therapy, *ACT for Gender Identity* follows the World Professional Association for Transgender Health (WPATH, 2011) *Standards of Care for the Health of Transsexual, Transgender, and Gender Nonconforming People*, Volume 7. These adapted ACT techniques, when taken in conjunction with WPATH's standards of care, can help ACT practitioners work with a population for whom acceptance means so much.

Mindful sensory awareness and emotional acceptance can provide a powerful, transformational experience, yet therapeutically they're only the beginning. To cover the broad array of intersecting life issues, *ACT for Gender Identity* is sectioned into Awareness, Acceptance, Actualization, Adaptation, and Affirmation. ACT aficionados already familiar with mindful awareness, emotional acceptance, and value-congruent self-actualization, may already be wondering why it's relevant to include Adaptation and Affirmation. The answer is perhaps more easily understood by those who have delved into the transformative aspects of gender identity. Consider that much of the LGBTQ community have sought acceptance for centuries, only to receive varying degrees of tolerance in differing social contexts. Yet tolerance isn't acceptance, and acceptance isn't a finish line. For oppressed social micro-groups, self-acceptance is an imperative for survival. Accepting ourselves, we can then actualize our values to live a full and meaningful life. Yet we must also accept what we have no control over, and how often our inability to govern the external leads us to micromanage the internal. ACT usually remedies this by identifying value-congruent and value-incongruent behavior, but when working with a population impacted by minority stress, trauma, and social exclusion, it becomes clear how social oppression can split our self-concept, and with it our value construct. Definitive core values become more difficult to identify, as we are divided between *survival values* and *self-actualization values*, both of which are equally significant.

In Adaptation, we revisit many of the common mental health issues gender variant people report, placing self-harm and substance abuse, body image, anxiety, PTSD, depression and suicidal ideation, in the context of our adaptive or maladaptive coping mechanisms. In Affirmation, we explore the ecological reciprocity we have with our social, academic, occupational, romantic, and familial relationships over the lifespan. Gender affirmative ACT does not encourage us to accept intolerance, but to accept the valid emotional reaction to intolerance, defuse from the internalization of discrimination, and act on our values. We are not crazy for being angry, nor insane for feeling lonely, nor broken for feeling sad. Our tears are always worth their salt. On realizing this, it becomes easier to affirm our personal, social, and experiential identity even in moments of stress.

To practice gender affirmative therapy, you, as a clinician, are required to examine and question your own conceptualization of sexuality and gender. Rooting out the common myths and misconceptions perpetuated by heterosexism and cissexism entails a deep examination of what you believe about yourself as a man or woman or genderqueer or genderless person in contemporary society. This is no small or simple task, so be kind to yourself, and develop a healthy self-care routine as you challenge your respective assumptions of self, society, and professional competency.

If you're not a mental health practitioner and you picked up this book out of sheer curiosity, or perhaps as a bold self-help guide, then be encouraged to continue reading, and to expand your knowledge of both gender and ACT beyond the covers of this book, as neither subject can be grasped in a single text. There's always more to learn! Yet if you do find yourself struggling with your emotions, especially those arising from your personal gender identity, then you're encouraged to seek out an ally, a community, and a truly competent therapist. Between you and me, there are many compassionate therapists with golden hearts and true intentions, yet empathy without understanding can often feel like being handed an umbrella underwater or a snorkel in the rain. It takes a while to find the right therapist, and you may need to try a few before you feel comfortable being yourself. This is known as *goodness of fit* in the therapeutic relationship. It is often said that one can only take a person as far as they've gone themselves, which is why working with a transgender or nonbinary therapist is recommended, whenever possible. However, do not assume that cisgender therapists are wholly incapable of aiding your process, as many go to great lengths to educate themselves. The fact is no one will ever be you, or truly understand your uniqueness—an existential point every human being can relate to regardless of sex, sexuality, or gender. Test them if you have to! Keep those therapists on their toes! But don't go it alone.

And to those precious few LGBTQ individuals entering the field of psychology, know that the butterfly effect is often misunderstood.

Meteorologist and pioneering chaos theorist Edward Lorenz once asked if the flap of a butterfly's wings in Brazil would set off a hurricane in Texas. Pop culture adores the idea that a small ripple can cause a great effect, but that wasn't Lorenz's point. He was far more concerned with the fallibility of predictability. The truth is, a butterfly cannot power a tornado any more than a singular human being can end prejudice outright. Additionally, while a butterfly may contribute to the initial conditions causing a hurricane, the lack of a butterfly may equally contribute to the initial conditions causing the hurricane. One can never really know. So, do we give up to random chance? Do we put aside our committed action? No. You see, Lorenz never postulated the impact of 1.4 million butterflies flying together.

Keep your wings bright. We need you now more than ever.

# 2

# Gender Affirmative ACT

Picture a butterfly in a spiderweb. If asked to describe the web, we might say it's delicate, or pentagonal in shape, though its layered intricacy would be difficult to put into words. Now describe the butterfly. We might observe its color, but the complex patterns dotting and circling each delicate wing would be just as hard to explain. Right away we see the distress, as our beautiful butterfly is trapped in something complex and not of its own making, yet to understand the struggle requires great attention. We all understand webs and butterflies in their simplicity, yet the moment we try to describe them, and the moment they interact, their intricacy becomes too much to describe.

When we were born, we were only our *somatic self*, laughing, crying, and reacting to our immediate sensory experiences. We would clench our little fists, and pout our little mouths, and furrow our foreheads in surprise, existing solely in the present without words or meaning attached. As our prefrontal cortex connected the dots, we began to label our experiences, turning phonetic sound into meaning. Developing our ability to speak, we also developed our ability for symbolic thought, at which point we became aware of our first imaginary friend, the cognitive shadow that is our *thinking self*. Our chatty inner monologue has been talking to us ever since we were toddlers. Our thinking self talks so much we often believe everything it says. We may even overidentify with the thinking self, becoming disconnected from what our bodies tell us. As we grew, we were socialized to tell stories about who and what we are in order to explain our actions and even our existence, forming our *conceptual self* (Luoma and Villatte, 2012).

This is why, even within our mind, it often seems like *me*, *myself*, and *I* are in hot debate, as what *I feel*, what *I think*, and what *I am* do not always align. Our compassion wants to free the somatic butterfly, but the more it fights with the conceptual web, the more it alerts our thinking spider. Panic, anxiety, depression, grief, and trauma cause the butterfly to get stuck all the more, making us victims of ourselves twice over as that cognitive arachnid—our overactive, analytical mind—attacks our emotional reaction with venomous judgment. Yet there's someone else here, too, watching the whole scene unfold. As we imagine this in our mind's eye, we can visualize the butterfly, the web, and the spider, as *I feel*, *I think*, and *I am* become secondary to *I observe*. Our *observational self* experiences our somatic, bodily sensations, as well as our analysis and our criticism of it, without getting all tangled up. As we learn to notice our thoughts and feelings in the present moment, ACT then asks us to notice who is noticing (Harris, 2009a; Hoare, McIlveen, and Hamilton, 2012). Stepping back from our existential urgency, we mindfully expand our awareness to see ourselves in a larger context.

The mind–body connection can be tenuous for the gender explorative just starting out, as part of self-actualization is a negotiation between our conceptual self and our physical form. Certainly, gender affects and is affected by our cognitive process, yet to fully understand the breakdown of integrated functioning that occurs in gender dysphoria and internalized cissexism—and to fully recognize the intuitive nature of gender—*ACT for Gender Identity* introduces the *somatic self*. Differentiated from our inner monologue, the somatic self accounts for our gut response and our intuition, as it's that innocent, emotive part of us that feels without words, and it is that innocent, emotive part of us that feels our gender. Our consciousness alternates perspective between the *participant* riding life's rollercoaster, the *participant observer* riding the rollercoaster while thinking about the experience, and the *observer* assessing the rollercoaster from the outside (Strosahl and Robinson, 2017). Our somatic self, therefore, is wholly participatory, though as silent as the observational self. It's our fists gripping the ride, and our pounding heart, and our shaking knees, and before all that it was the anticipatory excitement that led us to this rollercoaster over that one. Our somatic self is not a creature of choice or deliberation, as it operates on appetitive instinct, including our impulse to run, jump, sing, dance, express, and play. How these behaviors are labeled and gendered comes later, when our thinking self, guided by social constructs, and the somatic self, guided by intuitive senses, collaborate to form our conceptual self. We were, after all, rambunctious before they called us boyish, and graceful before they called us girly.

Anyone who's ever questioned their gender is striving to decipher who they are from the web of gender norms, yet it gets so confusing when it's so delicate and stuck together. Gender affirmative ACT explores gender in all dimensions of our somatic, thinking, conceptual and observational self. How do we feel our gender in our bodies? What do we think of gender as it liberates and limits us? How do we conceptualize our gender identity? And what do we observe within ourselves as all these facets of ourselves interact?

ACT is a deeply fitting therapeutic approach for working with gender minorities as it begins by challenging the *assumption of healthy normality* (Hayes, Strosahl, and Wilson, 2012; Wilson and Murrell, 2004). In simple terms, the medical model presents our natural state as healthy and free of ailment and disease. Adopting this same assumption, mental health was presented idyllically as an intrinsic state of happiness, connection, and peace, free of emotional unrest or mental distortion (Hayes *et al.*, 2012). This placed anyone with a history of stress, worry, or trauma outside the scope of normality, in particular pathologizing gender minorities as paraphilic and neurotic. When the assumption of healthy normality is applied to a demographic population, a dangerous power differential is introduced, separating the ideal from the deviant, as those who deviate are presumed unhealthy, unfit, or unnatural. ACT overturns the idea that psychological dysfunction stems solely from abnormality. Of course, there are unique neurological and psychosocial cases compromising mental health, but by and large the ubiquity of human suffering indicates how common emotional unrest and mental distortions really are (Hayes *et al.*, 2012). The *assumption of destructive normality*, therefore, observes how it's our typical everyday emotional processes, mental machinations, and linguistic learning that leads to creating, exacerbating, or amplifying our dysfunction (Hayes *et al.*, 2012; Wilson and Murrell, 2004). Review the amount of prejudice, violence, conflict, divorce, suicidal ideation, midlife crisis, and overall stress, in conjunction with the lifetime incidence of mental health disorder, and it becomes clear that psychological distress is in no way abnormal (Hayes, Pistorello, and Biglan, 2008). Bright, brilliant, capable people can fall into grief, despair, and uncertainty. Strong, passionate, motivated people can be undermined by their own driving attitude. Intelligent, creative, and curious people can become derelict in their genius. For gender minorities, ACT recognizes how a very natural process of self-identification and social performance becomes arrested by rigid and limiting social scripts, resulting in deleterious psychosocial consequences.

Everyone in this world develops and self-actualizes their own respective gender identity, their relational frames having formed patterns of thought called *gender schemas*. Some men define themselves through brute strength, others through intellect. Some men aspire to leadership and legacy, others to art and creativity. Some men pride their cold wit, others nurture their compassion. Likewise, some women define themselves through brute strength, others through intellect. Some women aspire to leadership and legacy, others to art and creativity. Some women pride their cold wit, others nurture their compassion. If they were all to meet, they might disagree on what it means to be a man or woman, yet none of them are wrong. Their wings and webs are their own, as are their critical spiders.

As a form of gender affirmative therapy, ACT explores gender ecologically, recognizing how internal cognitive frames, language structure and social performance affect and are affected by our external environment. Perhaps more than any other application of ACT, gender affirmative ACT encourages clinicians to become active advocates, provide psychoeducation, and maintain a network of community resources. Gender affirmative therapists often engage in community outreach for this reason, creating safe spaces while advocating for gender appropriate healthcare. For ACT clinicians working with a disenfranchised and often invisible minority, this socially holistic approach is a prerequisite, as value-congruent actions become stifled when options are limited. In this way, gender affirmative ACT clinicians help us challenge internal blocks while simultaneously challenging society's external barricades.

## Gender and relational frame theory

We all have our own beliefs about what it means to be masculine, feminine, a man, or a woman, just as many have nuanced beliefs about what it means to be androgynous, fluid, or completely agender. We may even have some ideas about how our gender came to be in the first place. Perhaps we feel gender is intrinsic, neurological, or biogenic— that we were born this way! Perhaps our gender development felt like a discovery process, unveiling, unfolding, and evolving over time. We may feel that gender is socially constructed, like a kind of performance we picked up from familial behavior or cultural expectation. We may feel like our gender identity, or at the very least our gender expression, developed in reaction to life's demands—that we had to be masculine or feminine to defend ourselves, blend in, or even to distance ourselves from something harmful. We may feel that aspects of our gender development involved all of the above, or we may take umbrage at the very idea that gender is either inherent or learned.

All of these beliefs are included as part of our gender schema. As subtext to our origin story, our beliefs influence how we perceive ourselves in relation to the world around us. Much like our captured butterfly, it can be difficult to discern the delicate wings of personal identity from the social web. Are they different? Are they the same? Only we will know for certain, though we may befuddle ourselves should we forget we're both the spider and the butterfly. Stress arises when we develop inflexible parameters for our gender identity that either limit us from meeting our needs or put us in conflict or competition with others. Additional stress arises when gender constructs that are not our own, or that we do not agree with, are projected onto us. Should we internalize these projections, we often feel a sense of dissonance between *who we are* and *who we're supposed to be*. Discerning between them means unpacking our gender schemas, one relational frame at a time.

ACT is built on a foundation of relational frame theory (RFT), which states that everything we know is framed in relation to everything else (Hayes *et al.*, 2006). These conceptual relationships allow us to make inferences without ever having to be told. Just as *front* implies *back* and *up* implies *down*, our thoughts link together in a web of association. Yet this complicated world is filled with abstract concepts branching off in all kinds of directions. If ideas are treated as malleable, flexible, and expandable patterns, then we can grow in response to diverse new people, places, and contextual circumstances. A rigid mind, by contrast, rejects notions that don't match up with its preformed associations, maintaining bias, prejudice, all-or-nothing terminology, absolute language, and emotionally based reasoning. To recognize the nuance in RFT, a person may, hypothetically, have a very flexible open-minded view of race, but a very rigid view of gender. Another person may have a very flexible, adaptable understanding of gender, but still preach sexuality as binary. Another person may have a very flexible understanding of human beings on the whole but restrict themselves with self-imprisoning limitations. In this latter example, their cognitive associations with *humanity*, as a concept, branch off into *creativity*, *innovation*, *freedom*, and *autonomy*, yet their associations with *self* branch off into *pathetic*, *incapable*, *helpless*, and *lost*.

Stress, trauma, and even personal growth can sometimes bring our otherwise unchecked or unnoticed inflexiblity to our awareness, in the same way that we're not aware of our national bias until we leave our country, or fail to recognize racism in our homogenous community, or don't realize how self-deprecating we are until a friend points it out. Mental rigidity is sadly commonplace, leading us to maintain unhealthy patterns and boring routines. Even when we're not dysregulated or dysfunctional, we may feel dissatisfied, disinterested, disaffected, disrespected, displeased, and disconnected, yet carry on without changing anything. Recognizing a pattern, after all, does not change the pattern, which is why ACT progresses from mindfully observing our thoughts to committing to value-congruent action.

Playing with word associations is a fun way to demonstrate the semantic network of our relational frames. Try asking someone to close their eyes and say—as fast as they can—the first thought that pops to mind when they hear the word *red*. Maybe they responded with *fire* or *apple* or *blue*. Follow up on their answer. If they said *fire*, what's the first thing that comes to mind when they hear *fire*? *Fireman*. What's the first thing that comes to mind when they hear *fireman*? *Siren*. And when they hear *siren*? *Odysseus*. And when they hear Odysseus? *Greek*. And when they hear *Greek*? *Tzatziki*. And when they hear *Tzatziki*? *Cucumber*. And when they hear *cucumber*? *Green*.

While the color red can branch off into an infinite possibility of associations, human beings do not have an infinite capacity to contain them all. Indeed, we create very individual and very personal semantic networks, relating ideas to each other in formations we're not always aware of. In this example, we could have never predicted that the pattern would take us from fire to a Greek legend to lunch and back to a color again. To test flexibility, ask them to try again, using *red* as the same starter word. Perhaps, this time, *red* will launch off into *stop-signs*, or *lava*, or *blood*, or *love*. Who knows? Some, however, may automatically jump back to their original answer, finding that *red* has a strong personal association, in this example, with fire. An inflexible imagination may not be able to pull anything else to mind. Closing their eyes, the word *red* automatically sparks flames. Likewise, those trapped in perceptual loops may find themselves going in circles. Red may remind them of green, and green reminds them of red, and red reminds them of green, and round and round they go. Relational frames, however, are often far more complicated than simple word associations, as each idea contains within it a set of literal and abstract associations that influence, restrict, or permit our behaviors, opinions, and personal insights.

Learning to speak, we quickly learned to categorize, labeling ourselves in context to our environment. Our *hierarchical frame*, for example, states that *this subject* fits into *that box* because of certain attributes. If we say "ice cream is sweet" and "ice cream is a dessert" we understand "dessert is sweet" without ever being told, yet we also understand more (Hayes *et al.*, 2012). With only two points of information, we also infer that "dessert is ice cream," that "sweet is ice cream," and that "sweet is dessert" (see Figure 2.1). Critical thinkers will spot a problem here, as not every dessert is ice cream, not everything sweet is ice cream, and not everything sweet is dessert; but try telling that to a four-year-old oversimplifying their sweet tooth.

**Figure 2.1** *Hierarchical ice cream*

When gender is conceptualized in a hierarchical frame, our perspectives of sex (males and females) binds to performative social roles and cultural expectations. Children often maintain this viewpoint, not yet understanding the nuances of gender expression. They may adamantly believe that girls have long hair. Therefore, if a child has long hair, that child is a girl (see Figure 2.2).

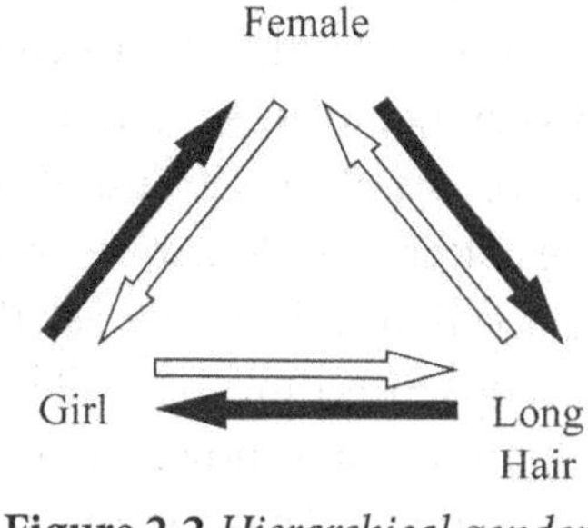


**Figure 2.2** *Hierarchical gender*

The reason gender variance is such a difficult topic for some to grasp is because our identities disrupt the presumed relational frame established by the cultural majority. In this case, a person can no longer presume that "females are girls," or that "females have long hair," meaning they can no longer derive that "long hair means they're a girl," or any of the reversed assumptions, including "long hair means they're female," "girls have long hair," and "girls are female." Having challenged the quick and simple rule, we expand into contextual thinking.

Another fun way to introduce hierarchical frames of gender is to go to the zoo. Anthropomorphizing animals, we'll project masculine strength onto the muscular bison and feminine grace onto the feline, yet neither strength nor grace have anything to do with sex or gender directly. Just ask the female bison or the male cat. To practice mental flexibility in our symbolic thought, let's take an inventory of our animalistic anima and animus archetypes. What animals do we associate with masculinity or femininity? Then reverse the sex, imagining elegantly male swans and weathered female alligators. Our tendency to gender animals and sort them into symbolically hierarchical categories is actually quite remarkable, even if verging on silly. When a golden retriever runs up with a stick in its mouth, people will instinctively say "good boy," having associated slovenly playfulness with boyishness. The dog doesn't care, it just wants you to throw the stick, but then its owner walks up, sheepishly correcting that their dog is actually a girl—as if the frame of distinction actually matters to the dog, still wagging its tail furiously in anticipation of the stick. Owners can be quite fastidious about the correct gendering of their pets, which speaks loudly to how gender visibility and power dynamics shape human lives. And things become more complicated if it's a French dog, as certain Latin-based languages gender nouns, casually referring to *le chien* in the masculine even if she's female.

Every culture has its own hierarchical gender frames, associating and labeling certain behaviors and characteristics to indicate boy, girl, man, and woman. Given the influence of testosterone and estrogen on both the body and the psyche, such frames are often founded in phenotypes and levels of aggression, nurturance, and emotionality (Archer, 1991; Slabbekoorn *et al.*, 2001). There is a reason why the spider web is patterned as it is. Yet gender variant people, depending on our culture of origin, often fall outside of the hierarchical framework by looking and behaving differently from our culture's respective gender norms. And that's just the beginning! Banding together, outliers, subcultures, and countercultures then form their own hierarchical gender framework, generating all new stereotypes. Lesbians have butch haircuts. Jane has a butch haircut. Therefore, Jane is a lesbian. Of course, we all see how inaccurate this is, yet even the LGBTQ community can get stuck in its own web.

Hierarchical frames break down in real-world settings, as even terms like *man* and *woman* cannot be taken for granted (see Table 2.1). If we were to collect together a truly diverse sample of human beings and ask the men to stand on one side of the room and the women to stand on the other, we'd discover that even the gender binary isn't a binary experience as many who identify as being a man or a woman took unique life paths to get there.

**Table 2.1 Expanding gender labels**

| I am a man | I am a woman |
|---|---|
| Cisgender man: Born male, identifies as a man. "I am a man." | Cisgender woman: Born female, identifies as a woman. "I am a woman." |
| Cisgender intersex man: Born intersex, identifies as a man. "I am a man." | Cisgender intersex woman: Born intersex, identifies as a woman. "I am a woman." |
| Transsexual man: Born female, identifies as a man. May identify as FtM, or may downplay their transgender identity. "I am a man. I was always a man." | Transsexual woman: Born male, identifies as a woman. May identify as MtF, or may downplay their transgender identity. "I am a woman. I was always a woman." |
| Transgender man: Born female, identifies as a transgender man. May identify as FtM to maintain their transgender identity. "I am a man. I am a trans man." | Transgender woman: Born male, identifies as a transgender woman. May identify as MtF to maintain their transgender identity. "I am a woman. I am a trans woman." |

As life experience isn't equatable to a label, mindfully exploring gender doesn't mean analyzing or categorizing it. After all, stating *I am a man* or *I am a woman* either expresses very little or presumptuously implies a great deal, depending on who we're talking to and what mood we're in. Yet everyone uses categories as mental shortcuts to convey and communicate who we are. Quite innocently, we develop this kind of base labeling through *coordination frames.*

When we were tiny tots, our parents asked, "Where's teddy?" Pointing at our teddy-bear would cause our parents to nod and smile approvingly, and we liked approval. Learning to read and write, we discovered that seeing the letters t-e-d-d-y and saying "teddy" was also correct and worthy of praise. Not only this, but saying "teddy" and writing t-e-d-d-y were equally valuable, demonstrating how a verbal relation in one direction both predicts and reinforces our learning of it in the other direction (Hayes *et al.*, 2012). In this way, language prepped us to see entity as a symbolic label, a symbolic label as an oral label, and an oral label as an entity (Hayes *et al.*, 2012). In other words, our teddy, and the spoken word "teddy" and the written word t-e-d-d-y, are all representative of the same thing (see Figure 2.3). Our coordination frames also allow us to grasp synonyms, as a child will know which toy to pick up, whether we ask them to get their *teddy* or their *bear*. Problematically, coordination frames can lead us to believe things are the same, even when they're not. So we developed *distinction frames*, allowing us to differentiate, when we're older, between a bear (teddy), a bear (grizzly), and a bear (a full-bodied gay man) (see Figure 2.4). They're still all bears, but only one's going to slip us a phone number.

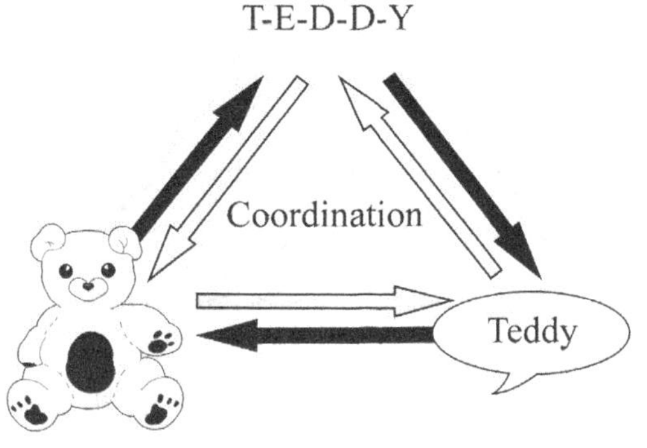


**Figure 2.3** *Frame of coordination*

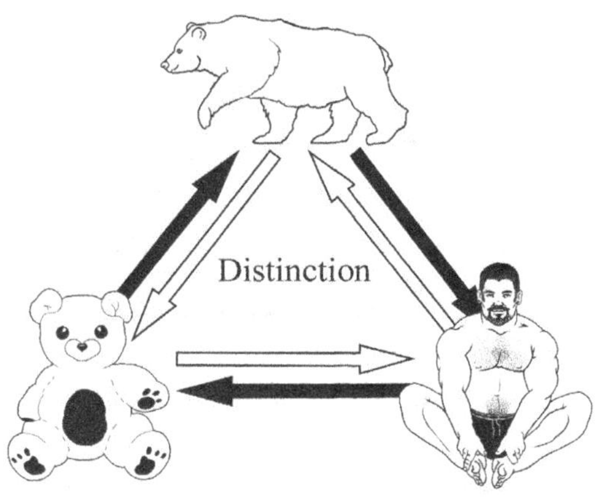


**Figure 2.4** *Frame of distinction*

As we become socially conscious, we quickly develop *comparison frames*, observing that Lien is stronger than Suzy, but Suzy is stronger than Danny. With only two comparisons to reference, our mind fills in the blank, inferring six relationships (see Figure 2.5). If Suzy is stronger than Danny, but Lien is stronger than Suzy, then Lien is also stronger than Danny. Not only this, but we also know Danny is weaker than Suzy and Lien, and Suzy is weaker than Lien, respectively. Antonyms have a funny way of coloring our perspective of ourselves and others, as measuring our aspirational strength feels better than measuring our deficient weakness. Being pretty in our own right is lovely, yet being *prettier* is comparative, as it denotes someone else is uglier. Being smart is a wonderful quality, yet being *smarter* insinuates someone else is more stupid. Being masculine is descriptive, yet being *manlier* is competitive. Being feminine is also descriptive, yet being *womanlier* feels like quantifying a quality, as it implies someone can be more or less of a woman.

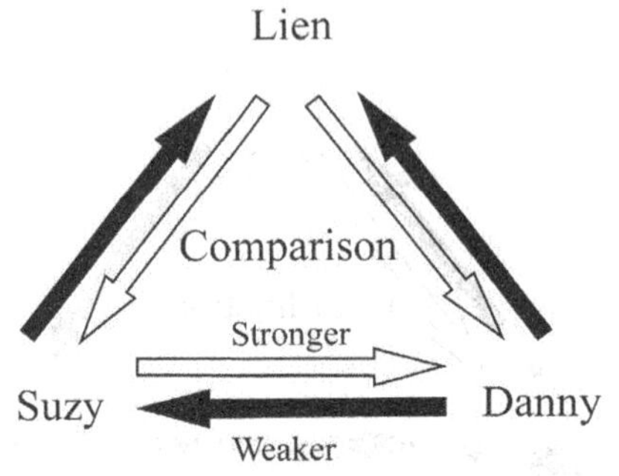


**Figure 2.5** *Frame of comparison*

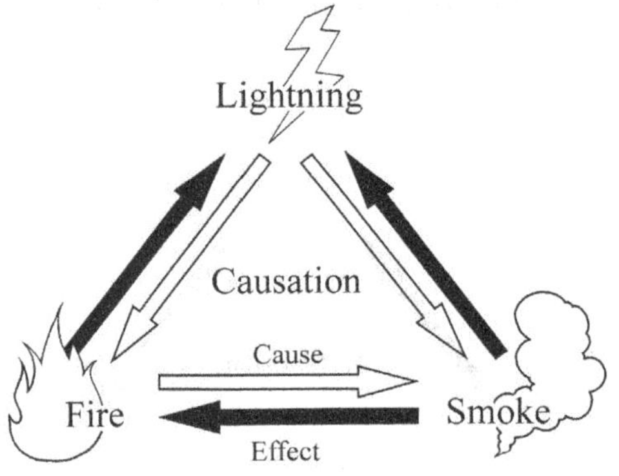


**Figure 2.6** *Frame of causation*

To engage and operate the world around us, frames of *causality* help us understand cause and effect. By knowing that lightning causes fire and that fire causes smoke, we further understand how one is the effect of the other, allowing for deduction should smoke rise in the forest on a stormy day (see Figure 2.6). Fusing to frames of causality, however, can prompt us to make false connections and believe erroneous deductions. In social situations, we may feel unable to move on or let go of our thinking without a clear and evident answer, prompting us to jump to conclusions, mistake correlation for causation, or generate blame. As gender is so morphous and diverse, such causal frames can hinder gender exploration, as those who urgently need an answer will often favor an unhealthy explanation over the unknown. Gender is undoubtedly complex, but we'll blame ourselves, or point at childhood development, pathology, society, genetics, evolution, reincarnation, metaphysics, and even God to account for our uniqueness. It's one thing to hold these explanations loosely, like curious puzzles to play with, but when we fuse to causality we grip these puzzles for dear life. We may grip our causations so tightly we may feel affronted by explanations we don't agree with. Very quickly, we begin measuring ourselves against black-and-white *oppositional frames* of thought, wanting things to be as simple as big or small (see Figure 2.7). Feverishly trying to determine if we're good or bad, a saint or a sinner, normal or weird, straight or gay, hot or not, right or wrong, we may start seeing opposites where they don't exist.

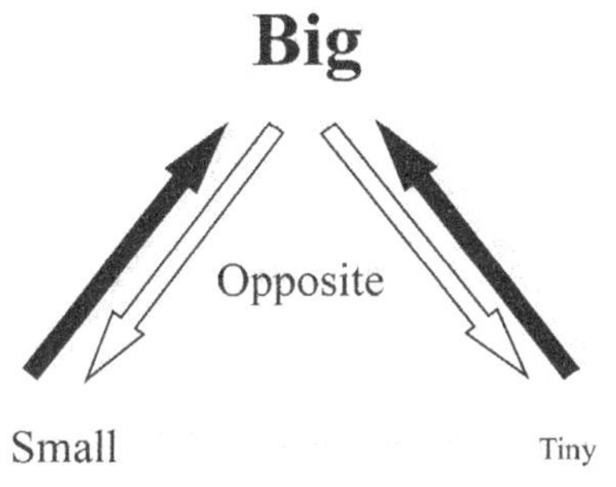


**Figure 2.7** *Frame of opposition*

In ACT, mindfulness, acceptance, and defusion are introduced to lessen the pressure and urgency coupled to our thoughts and perceptions, thereby allowing us to act with perspective and clarity. Instead of trying to cope or adjust a psychological issue, ACT redefines control and experiential avoidance as the problem, focusing on a descriptive life experience over personal assessment, and transcended awareness over symptom-focused management (Hayes, 2004; Hayes and Smith, 2005; Orsillo *et al.*, 2004). This is no simple task, for while we can disempower these rigid frames, we can't banish them from our mind—especially when they're anchored to socially prevalent gender roles, norms, and expectations. Still, as we begin to see ourselves in the context of our total life experience, many oppositional frames we thought were factual turn to smoke.

Just for fun, ask a random group of adults to shout out the opposite of *cat*. They'll probably yell *dog*. What's the opposite of *lemon*? *Lime*. What's the opposite of *man*? *Woman*. These are, of course, false. The opposite of *cat* is anti-cat, which doesn't exist because cats don't have opposites. What has two ears, two eyes, a nose, a mouth, sharp incisors, four paws, a tail, is covered in fur, sits on their hind quarters, and is kept as a pet? Cat? Dog? Both? On close inspection cats and dogs are actually quite similar. What's a zesty, bitter, tropical citrus fruit that's good for both cooking and martinis? It seems lemons and limes are quite similar too. Far more similar than the fabled anti-lemon, which grows in reverse on an anti-tree in a magically opposite dimension.

Naturally, there are enormous differences between cats and dogs, lemons and limes, but the oppositional associations ingrained in us as we grow often result in many false dichotomies. Just to illustrate this social construct, some adults may shout that the opposite of *cat* is *mouse*, as our cartoons demand one hits the other with a frying pan. Presented so simply, it takes very little for people to undo the myth that men and women are antithetical to each other. There are certainly opposites in this world, including hot and cold, up and down, big and small, empty and full, front and back, but the majority of life isn't so polarized, and we often generate great obstacles for ourselves when we treat it like it is.

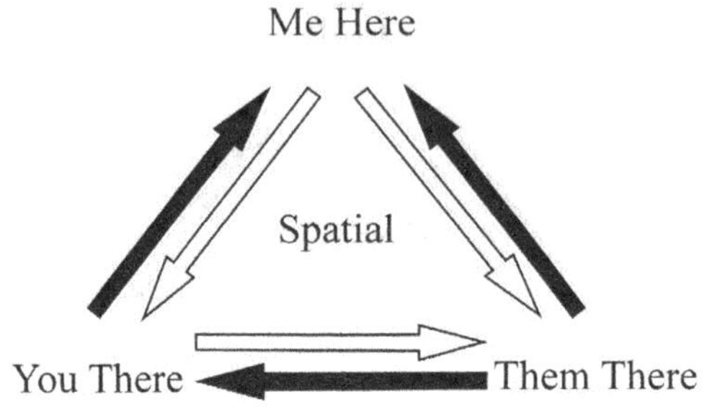


**Figure 2.8** *Spatial frame*

Taking a step back to see our *spatial frames*, we can understand ourselves in dimensional space, recognizing how objects exist physically in proximity to each other. Recognizing how you stand closer to me, and farther from them, also denotes how I am standing closer to you and, correspondingly, farther from them, as well (see Figure 2.8). This may not imply anything, per se, yet when we begin to explore gendered body language, personal space, and nonverbal communication, we find all manner of beliefs and behavioral roles encoded into spatial frames. Who is allowed into our personal bubble, and why? In Western cultures, men may take up more public space, yet are deemed threatening when they stand in close proximity, whereas women take up less public space, but are encouraged to stand close to each other.

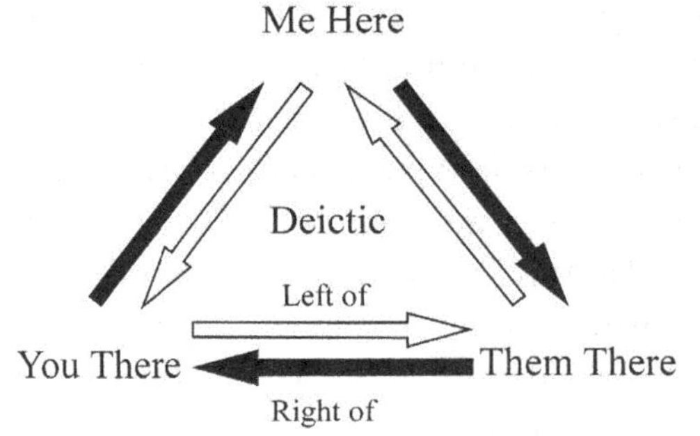


**Figure 2.9** *Deictic frame*

So, if our spatial frame considers how we exist in relation to *here* and *there*, *this* and *that*, and our *temporal* frame shows how we exist in relation to our *past*, *present*, and *future*, our *deictic* frame observes the existing relation between *self* and *other*. Deictically, that which is *me, here*, and *now*, stands apart from *you, there*, and *then* (Polk *et al*., 2016). While deictic frames often contain a spatial and temporal deixis, our deictic frame is not as measurable as space or time, relating instead to our perspective (see Figure 2.9). The phrase "the front of the building to my left" contains within it a spatial frame pertaining to the building (its front), and a spatial and deictic frame pertaining to me (my left). Unlike other frames, this personal deictic has no specific counterpart. In oppositional frames, big formally relates to small. In comparison frames, a leopard is like a cheetah. But a personal deictic conveys our relation to time, place, and situation, which is highly important when we're trying to differentiate between self and other. In English, we verbally swing between first person (I did…), second person (you did…), and third person (he/she/they did…). Note how gender pronouns, and all of their encoded meaning, pop up in the third person as a means of delineating self from other. Grammatically, they and them are used as a third person plural (they did it together), or as third person singular (they did it alone). Third person singular has been used historically when the gender is unknown, unassumed, or irrelevant to the subject. Yet in recent history, some gender variant people have claimed the third person singular (they did…) as a gender free (agender), gender dynamic (genderqueer), or gender-multiple (genderfluid) pronoun. While calling a person they, instead of he or she is a very simple concept, some people really struggle to adjust linguistically. While lack of exposure to gender variant people certainly contributes to this, even people within the transgender community can sometimes stumble with they as a pronoun because of how persistent binary relational language can be. It can be difficult for some to adjust, since saying "look at them over there" could refer to a nonbinary person standing in the corner, a group of people standing in corner, or just for fun, a group of nonbinary people standing in the corner.

Applying deictic context to our aforementioned hierarchy of female girls with long hair, we understand how this association may have existed *then* and *there* in *their* culture, perhaps in a bygone era, but not *here* and *now* in *our* culture. In the context of contemporary Western society, we understand that some females grow up to be men, that girls can have short hair, and that long hair does not signify sex or gender.

Whether we accept our gender identity or not, we still interact with the literal *other*, including friends, family, community, work colleagues, and religious congregations, who interpret our identity as much as they project onto it. For gender variant people there is frequently a distinction between our gender identity, our presenting identity, and our perceived identity (Lucal, 1999). These intersecting facets of self can even compete for dominance in our own head, creating false paradigms of self vs. true self as we fuse with gendered rules and restrictions so as not to jeopardize our wellbeing, our family, our relationships, or our careers.

As natural storytellers, *self* interacts with *other* through narration. In our mind, this transforms us into a character, as we describe our role, history, and personal attributes in simplified terms (Hayes *et al.*, 2012). This mental construct backed up by our anecdotal life experience is our aforementioned conceptual self boiled down to its essence. Reducing our multifaceted complexity, we'll describe ourselves in near absolute terms for the sake of telling a cohesive story (Luoma and Villatte, 2012). We'll say, "I am good," "I am stupid," "I am anxious," or "I am compassionate," holding up reasons and past experiences to justify our thinking. This conceptual self can be very powerful should we feel empowered, or very destructive should we highlight nothing but our flaws. In either case, ACT helps us remember that we are more than our story by mindfully engaging with the world around us.

At first glance, our spatial and temporal frames may seem to have little influence on gender—especially for those with cisgender privilege whose expression thereof may not change between where they are now, or three feet to the left, or four hundred miles away. Yet where *here* is can certainly impact the transparency of gender and expression. If *here* is validating and *there* is threatening, our journey from here to there can influence how we walk and talk and present ourselves. By expanding awareness, we start to recognize how our context-dependent gender rules are preserved by social groups and encoded into the social spaces they inhabit. This is one reason why we will dress up to go out to a fancy restaurant, even if we're not expecting to meet anyone, as the physical location is encoded with a socioeconomic expectation. Sexism, cissexism, and racism are built into many social spaces, forcing many of us to dress down in order to be "appropriate." Code-switching is a common experience for multilingual, multinational, and ethnically diverse individuals operating in a variety of social spaces and power dynamics. Verbal colloquialisms, body language, even expression of humor and temperament can switch and adapt to multiple social environments, and also to the geographic locations where these interactions are expected to take place. Consider the strict social regulation expected in academia, or the racist dress codes at certain job sites, or the performance expectations of patriarchal professionalism demanded at work, even when no one is around, as if being ourselves might cause us to be expelled, written-up, or fired. Nostalgia presents another unique example of how a geographic place can be encoded with social scripts, as visiting our old stomping grounds can bring back old body language and ways of talking. Walking through our teenage neighborhood can literally stroll us down memory lane, accessing identity scripts we may not have performed in years. Code-switching and behavioral memory can also apply to our gender expression, as we may internalize social rules, or generate our own, to maintain comfort or safety.

> "I can be myself at home, but when I go to the store I always dress down."
>
> "I'm a woman, but everyone at work knows me as Charlie. I like being Charlie, but if we're being honest, I'm definitely not Charlie."
>
> "You could say I'm genderqueer, but that just means waitresses call me Sir, and waiters call me Miss."

Add a temporal deixis and gender changes with time. To make this relatable, cisgender people have a chronologically transgender experience. That may sound odd but remember that the gender construct for a little girl is very different from that of a grown woman. Kate Bornstein once noted in her memoir, *A Queer and Pleasant Danger*, how boy and man are two separate gender constructs (Bornstein, 2012). Cherishing boys and girls as distinct genders from men and women, with distinct body maps and socially performative scripts, is so commonplace we barely give it any thought. When we lump sex and gender together, we create a dichotomy—males here, females there, regardless of age—yet how often have we encountered adult boys who never grew up or adolescent women forced into mental maturity before their bodies physiologically caught up? Puberty is, in itself, an uncomfortable gender transition, demanding us to morph and adapt our social interactions, and our relationship with our body as our bodies change. It's for this reason that the same ACT techniques introduced for transgender and nonbinary people can also help self-identified cisgender people questioning their own gender schemas, gender role, and gender identity. Majority aside, this temporal gender transition is made even more dynamic for gender variant people, as our former self may have had a completely different physical sex and form. This can make our relationship with former, present, and future self quite unique. We may connect with our childhood or feel estranged from it entirely. We may look forward to our future self, or fear either the known or unknown we may become.

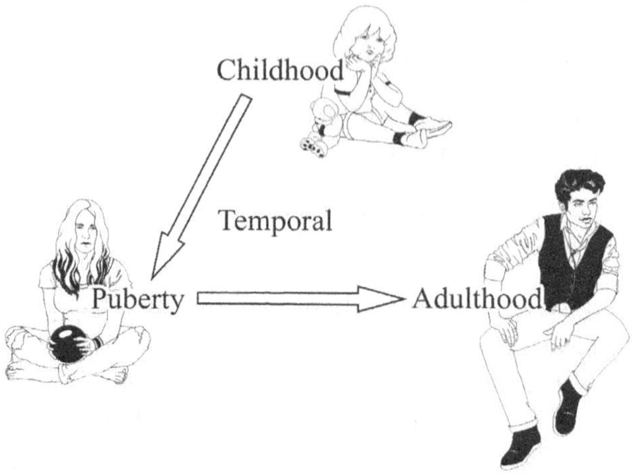


**Figure 2.10** *Temporal frame*

As all these frames pattern together our gender schemas, it becomes apparent how our use of language shapes so much of our perception. From an evolutionary standpoint this is advantageous, as memory and imagination—which greatly rely on these frames of perception—allow us to learn and adapt in the wake of a stimulus while also preparing for the next. Memory and imagination can also hold us captive, and even bully us. We might recoil when asked to imagine the death of someone we love, since our instinct to avoid death leads us to avoid all thoughts of it, too—a cognitive strategy that has no survival value (Wilson and Murrell, 2004). In ACT, such avoidance is a natural product of our relational learning, and a big problem as it also leads us to avoid distressing thoughts as if they're actually real (Wilson and Murrell, 2004). We'll panic at the prospect of something scary, and ball our fists at the memory of our pain, and so lose sight of *what is* in the dread of *what could be* or the trauma of *what was.*

This is most apparent when we talk to memory ghosts, arguing with people long passed as if they're still here, or when we project onto others like involuntary role play, slipping into "what you said when you hurt me" as if, for a moment, whoever we were talking to transformed into our father, brother, sister, mother, ex-lover, or negligent school teacher. Applying "if ____ then ____" allows us to generate rules to achieve what we want (Hayes *et al.*, 2008). "If I dress up, then I get attention." It also allows us to generate rules to rationalize or avoid what we don't want. "If I dress up, then I get unwanted attention." It also allows us to justify avoidance. "If I don't go out, then I won't be embarrassed." It also allows us to generate false truths and superstitions, pulling from the confirmation bias of our prior experiences. "If I wear my lucky shirt, I'll get lucky tonight!" Inevitably, our verbal constructs frame the world in which we live, accounting for a wide assortment of social expectations and eccentric behaviors (Hayes *et al.*, 2008). Living in this verbally structured world is what ACT calls *cognitive fusion*, as our thoughts now attempt to shape our experience through our narration of them (Hayes, 2004; Hayes *et al.*, 2008, 2012; Wilson and Murrell, 2004). These rigid mental frames are also evident when we say "I can't" do something. Should we believe *men are powerful* and *men wear pants*, then the phrase "I'm the man who wears the pants in this house" makes the prospect of a summer dress sacrilege, "I can't wear that, I'm a man!" Should we believe *women are sexy* and *women wear makeup*, then the phrase "I have to put my face on," denotes a natural look has no identity, "I can't go out looking like this!" By and large, our relational frames work insomuch as we live our lives even if our thoughts aren't accurate and our behaviors are limited by these created scripts. Yet sometimes our relational frames can't adapt to the broader, complex world around us, and our linguistic loopholes can't excuse or evade our emotions, at which point our perceptions, beliefs, cognitions, and behaviors become unworkable.

## Gender and functional contextualism

Gender exploration can feel as liberating as it can feel paralyzing, as the well-defined road has to come to an end and we find ourselves staring at the forest. Without a preformed trail, this could go anywhere. So how do we know which way to go?

Functional contextualism is the core of ACT. It is not a compass to guide us through this wilderness, or a map, or even a GPS. It is the entirety of the wilderness, including the compass, and the map, and the GPS, and even ourselves in it. It's only when we're attentive to its entirety that we can explore the wilderness effectively; otherwise we would just amble around the woods trying to read a map without ever looking up. This holistic perspective makes functional contextualism an excellent approach for gender affirmative therapy as it takes in the totality of our lived experience.

Functional contextualism is built on four pillars: *wholeness*, *context*, *truth*, and *goals*. In ACT, we learn to see an event by exploring the multiple cognitive, emotional, and social consequences of behavior as they're experienced both internally and externally (Hayes *et al.*, 2012). *Wholeness*, therefore, recognizes that we are the adventurer, and the wilderness, and the web, and the spider, and the butterfly. In this way, our gender is as much a private experience, as it is a somatic feeling in our body, as it is a social performance, as it is a sociopolitical position, as it is a symbolic archetype, as it is a labeled stereotype. Though asking us to clarify which dimensions we're frustrated with can be a useful way of checking the "all or nothing" trap, ACT focuses on the inclusive whole, as one aspect of gender cannot be surgically removed from the rest. Instead of focusing on or distinguishing a perceived problem area, the expansive language practiced in ACT approaches our experience as a whole. This subtle yet powerful difference allows us to identify the different dimensions of our gender, while making room for all of them, thereby reducing our internal sense of pressure.

The second pillar is *context*, as slowly but surely our frames integrate with each other, allowing us to function organically in our environment, with our environment, and in response to our environment. Without context we would obey our relational frames like badly programmed robots, repeating protocols without deviation regardless of the circumstance. Perceiving context allows us to give the appropriate response to the appropriate stimuli. Context also allows us to see exception, variance, divergence, distinction, and all manner of diversity. No two men, women, genderqueer, or agender people are the same. Expressions of respect and love differ from culture to culture, as do expressions of masculinity, femininity, and androgyny. Likewise, expression of gender can change in different social settings as we swap our ball gowns for battle armor, just as they can change over time with our evolving social roles and social status.

Taking a pluralistic view presents a fluid spectrum of gender identities which blend and morph into each other over the lifespan, ACT clinicians learn to view clients in context of our gender schema as well as the ecological context of our lives (Ekins and King, 1998; Fassinger and Arseneau, 2007; Monro, 2007; Tando, 2016). This includes understanding and conceptualizing the evolving depth and breadth of our gender labels, as well as our personal relationship with gender as an experience. For some:

- Gender may remain fixed.
- Gender may transition from one identity to another.
- Gender may incorporate the experience of transition into identity.
- Gender may downplay the experience of transition altogether.
- Gender may blur masculine and feminine to create blended androgyny.
- Gender may combine masculine and feminine to create dichotomized androgyny.
- Gender may alternate between two or more gender identities contextually or over time.
- Gender may be neutralized, negating gender, or the prioritization of gender, as a part of identity.

Recognizing this relationship within ourselves is usually what leads people to resonate with certain concrete, fluid, binary, or nonbinary gender constructs.

For those outside the LGBTQ community, queer language can feel confusing, as very different people may use the same label with very different interpretations (Fassinger and Arseneau, 2007). As such, pay close attention to the cultural, generational, and personal context we present ourselves in. To hammer this home, there is no "correct" gender relationship. Some strictly defined gender constructs may actually work very well for us in certain situations, but cause us to get hung up in others. Some fluidly defined gender constructs may also work very well for us, until we begin to feel nebulous and indecisive. It all depends on context.

This leads us to functional contextualism's third pillar, *truth*. Taking a pragmatic approach, ACT doesn't pursue a singular concrete truth, admitting that truth is subjective (Hayes *et al.*, 2012). Truth be told, the abstract concept of *truth* as a demand for consistency can become an obstacle, like a philosopher unable to act without righteous piety, or a guru too busy pondering what reality is to escape the burning house (Hayes *et al.*, 2012). Applying this to gender, we quickly find that our self-defined gender identity is neither healthy nor unhealthy, problematic nor beneficial, nor is one label any more or less correct than others.

When we attempt to meet the internal or external demand for consistency, we quickly limit our beliefs of what we can or can't do. A cisgender man, a genderqueer butch, and a transsexual woman can all follow their respective stereotypes right off a cliff, engaging in unhealthy, unproductive, or counterintuitive behavior should they feel obligated or pressured to perform a certain role. Releasing our charge to find the singular, penultimate truth high atop the mountain allows us to come back to the present moment, adapt to our situation, and find a workable route to that which is most important to us (Hayes *et al.*, 2012). And if what's most important to us is discerning the truth—albeit our gender or our sexuality—then take heart in *the hero's journey*. Gender exploration is a long look in the mirror—a form of admission and acceptance for what is, not an external adventure. The hero's journey shows this every time, as our protagonist realizes they had the answer all along but didn't know it until they stopped looking. Isn't that right, Dorothy?

Yes, there are verifiable facts in this world, and ACT as a therapeutic practice grounds itself in functional contextualism's fourth pillar, *goals*. As the truth debate quickly sidelines the therapeutic process—as there is no essentialist ontology that proves our gender, let alone what our gender definitively means—functional contextualism favors practical workability (Hayes *et al.*, 2012). Maintaining a holistic perspective of ourselves in the context of our experiential reality, we can begin to identify our value constructs, which in turn provide a path to our personal goals. In the wilderness, we go downhill to find the river, recognizing that we're thirsty and water flows downhill. Likewise, the late afternoon sun informs us to gather firewood before dark to save us from the oncoming cold.

For those exploring and actualizing gender, practical workability highlights the unmet needs to find safe, manageable routes to emotional acceptance, psychological stability, and social support. In a real-world scenario, telling a transgender person that our first priority is to *come out* might very well put us in harm's way. It is not your task, as a clinician, to coax out disclosure, any more than it is your task to help a butterfly emerge from its chrysalis (Ali, 2014; Rachlin and Lev, 2013). Doing so may actually damage the butterfly's wings. Being so goal-focused, either as a client or clinician, can certainly be useful but it can also get in the way (Hayes *et al.*, 2012). The impatient, goal-focused mind demands an outcome just as the problem-solving mind demands a problem to solve. If left unchecked, this can lead to future-tripping, past-tripping, literal thinking, or an overly critical and judgmental perspective. Our relationship to value-based action can be strengthened and clarified by assessing the workability of our goal (Hayes *et al.*, 2012). For example, "ending anxiety" or "overcoming depression" demand to eradicate psychological distress, which is an unworkable goal! On the other hand, goals like "speaking up when I'm nervous" or "making sure to eat even when my mood ruins my appetite" demonstrate courage and commitment in the action.

A trans-positive, gender affirmative approach ecologically recognizes how gender minorities affect and are affected by our environment, bringing to the foreground deep questions regarding our locus of control (Lev, 2004; Mallon, 2009; Riley, Wong, and Sitharthan, 2011; Stitt, 2014). When our personal goals center on willingness, acceptance, advocacy, self-worth, or personal resilience, you can help us establish our social support networks and LGBTQ connections, while assessing and navigating any potential familial, community, or religious conflicts we may have (Ali, 2014; Devor, 2004; Lev, 2007; Rachlin and Lev, 2013; Singh, Hays, and Watson, 2011; Strosahl and Robinson, 2017). Moving away from abstract ideals, such goals are set and measured pragmatically. Our goal, for example, may be to courageously open up about our gender, and though it's certainly courageous to come out during the middle of a Klan rally, it might not be practical unless we have a lot of back-up. We may state that we "don't want to be afraid" when we disclose to our parents, yet this assumes we can control our feelings. A value-guided approach would be to disclose to allies we already trust to establish a support network, and practice accepting and defusing from anxiety. Accepting emotions as they are reinforces our desire for courageous transparency while progressively working up to parental disclosure.

Unlike other therapeutic modalities that strive to reconstruct or deconstruct a client's relational frame or distorted mindset, ACT doesn't attempt to re-order how one thinks in order to live a healthy, productive life (Blackledge, 2015; Hayes *et al.*, 2012). Instead, ACT accepts these frames as they exist in our head, however rigid and critical they may be, without conceding to them. We can accept a dog barking on a chain without leaning forward to let it bite us. We can even accept a dog barking on a chain and take three steps back. In ACT, the process of disempowering our cognitions and their convincing need to do, fix, or say something to amend our feelings is called *defusion*.

Defusion, contrary to what many hope for, isn't a cerebral way to control or eradicate our thoughts and feelings (Harris, 2008). Indeed, anyone trying to use mindfulness to rid themselves of anxiety or intrusive thoughts will probably feel incredibly anxious about their intrusive thoughts (Harris, 2008). If anything, defusion takes a level of *willingness* to sit with our discomfort—the very opposite of avoidance! Defusion allows us to feel unpleasant emotions without judging ourselves unnecessarily for them. With this clarity, we can ask our thoughts a simple question, *Is this helpful?* (Harris, 2008).

One of the most classic of all ACT exercises directs us to cup both hands an inch or two in front of our face. Our hands represent all the thoughts and feelings we focus on or fight with. Sure, we may be vaguely aware of our surroundings, but we can't see anything with our hands in front of our face. Then, little by little, as we slowly lower our hands, we become aware of the whole world around us. We're still aware of those thoughts and feelings, just as we're still aware of our hands now resting on our lap, but now there's so much more to see and engage (Harris, 2009a).

There are many defusion techniques we'll explore throughout this book, all of which aid in expanding our perception. When we're no longer trying to run, hide, or control our thoughts and feelings, we begin to see them in context, as part of an experiential whole. In this way, it becomes easier to accept that we are not defined by our self-deprecating mantras, controlled by our limiting beliefs, or at the mercy of our emotional process. So defused, functional contextualism engages our whole sensory awareness, to initiate creative and value-congruent ways to express exactly who we are. As a byproduct of this mental flexibility, we often feel less polarized in our relationship with gender, and far less pressure to fit certain categories of behavior unless we genuinely want to.

## Translating gender

If gender is so individuated and diversely multicultural, how can you ever prepare to work with such a vast and dynamic population? How can we talk about a subject when every member of the conversation is using words differently? If a client tells you they see magenta, and another sees indigo, and another sees violet, we're still fundamentally in a purple area. But what happens when you see purple but we adamantly claim it's red? The answer: Listen and work with us in that paradigm, as we're going to see the world in a uniquely beautiful way, and also struggle with traffic lights. This is not a foreign concept, as we translate foreign languages all the time, though we may need time to discern meaning, and may lose a little in translation. Indeed, the very act of talking about gender is an exercise in mental flexibility.

To proceed, we're going to cover some commonly used terms and identity constructs that will be useful to us throughout the coming chapters, without holding on to any of them dogmatically. We can begin by recognizing sex, gender identity, and gender expression as separate constructs intersecting with each other at dynamic points in a person's life (Benson, 2013; Bolich, 2007; Diamond, 2002, 2010; Nagoshi, Brzuzy, and Terrell, 2012). Each construct brings with it a whole array of labels, which take on different meanings for each respective person, to such extent that some may identify with more than one, or feel labels are inadequate (Monro, 2007; Valentine, 2007). Clients and clinicians may disagree with the terms as they're defined here, and that's the whole wonderful point!

## *Sex*

Sex is a genetic and anatomical classification of male, female, and intersex. An intersex individual is defined as a person born with a physiological condition exceeding the parameters of male and female. Considering chromosomal, hormonal, and genital factors, approximately 1.7 percent of children born have an intersex condition (Blackless *et al.*, 2000). Notably, while some of these individuals do incorporate their intersex condition as part of their identity, many intersex individuals are unaware of their condition until much later in life (Turner, 1999). Since unaligned designations are socially uncommon, parents of intersex children are frequently advised to raise the child as either a boy or girl, though an increasing number of intersex individuals are adopting neutral or genderqueer identity constructs as they grow older (Diamond and Sigmundson, 1997; Dreger, 2000). In the past, the medical community conceptualized intersex conditions as deviations from a presumed norm, yet the Intersex Movement advocates an expanded view of anatomic sex, allowing for the inclusion of a third sex identity (Preves, 2002, 2003; Turner, 1999). Because of the range of congenital and morphological conditions, independent third sex identity formation requires a lot more research to be fully understood.

## *Gender identity*

*Gender identity* refers to our relationship with our internal body map, encapsulating how we wish to be recognized via names, pronouns, gender roles, and so much more (Zandvliet, 2000). Queer theorists often joke that our sex is between our legs and our gender is between our ears, and said so plainly it's easy to grasp the difference. This has led many postmodern thinkers to view gender as a socially constructed performance. While ACT doesn't concern itself with ontology, ontology does present us with personal conundrums. For example, if gender variance is treated as solely conceptual then it becomes all too easy to relocate to the pile of disordered thinking or the heap of social trend. For this reason, when we're first exploring the edge of gender, we may hyperfocus on validity, wondering aloud if we're transgender, or doubting ourselves as neurotic, or accusing ourselves of being crazy. If gender is treated as a solely mental phenomenon, then it becomes as elusive as an idea, and it is ever so hard to trust something as ephemeral as an idea.

Sex identity and gender identity are often conflated, treated synonymously, or granted varying degrees of legitimacy. As *transsexual*, as a term, transitions sex and *transgender* transitions gender, society deems one a transition of the physical body and the other a transition of the abstract mind. This creates the false premise that the former is more "real" than the latter because of its physicality. This premise is present in essentialist literature striving to define typologies for what is a "true transsexual" for medical purposes. Instead of exploring gender as an adjective, such language presents *transsexual* as a noun, like an object or a thing that either is, or is not. Cisgender people also conflate sex and gender, using male and man or female and woman interchangeably. With all these divisions we begin presuming the opposite of a lemon is a lime, and place cisgender people opposite gender variant people, and in turn transsexual narratives opposite transgender narratives. This is not accidental, for while transsexual women received much of the medical intrigue over the past hundred years, those who identify as transsexual often suffer a form of social erasure in contemporary postmodern conversations seeking to blur or erase socially constructed categories. The pushback against the medical model not only pushed back against doctors and gatekeeping psychiatrists, but also their patients.

Stepping back, we see that mind and body are clearly inseparable, and that it's our language of the issue that structures our conceptualization of self and describes our relationship with our body. Though language and social construct are massively influential and at times detrimental to our relationship with our body, they cannot birth this relationship. We do not become men by writing "I'm a man" a hundred times on a chalkboard. We do not become women by spending every day in a dress. Parents have tried to shape their children's gender behavior to no avail, and conversion therapists have tried to suppress gender variant inclinations to great detriment. When a cisgender script is forced on someone it does not fit, it generates intense internal dissonance. This is also true when gender variant scripts are forced, as well, like when nonbinary people feel pressured to follow a transnormative script, transgender people are pressured to follow a transsexual script, or transsexual people feel pressured to follow a nonbinary script.

The linguistic distinction between sex and gender is not erroneous as they are not synonymous, yet neither are they parsed so easily. Sex is most certainly anatomical, yet with it there is a mental experience, as the endocrine system can also influence our mood and attitude. Gender is most certainly experienced mentally, yet with it there is a physical experience, as we do not think our gender into being, we *feel it*.

As gender desires actualization in physical form, our *gender expression* manifests the non-physical through body language, fashion, and even physical transition (Zandvliet, 2000). Working backwards, expression reflects conceptualization, yet what is this conceptualization based on? Regardless of whether gender is or is not socially constructed or how any of this conundrum came to be, what mechanism alerts us to identify with any given gender construct? In other words, we can imagine all kinds of gender identities and gender roles, but how do we know which is ours?

Our use of language and pattern recognition provides us context, yet pattern recognition is secondary to sensory input. We don't *think* emotions, we *feel* them somatically in our body, then label, categorize, and interpret them in our mind, then perform them socially by either unintentionally blurting out our feelings, or through deliberately expressive acts. This process of sensing, decoding, interpreting, recoding, and expressing can all happen in the blink of an eye, being so fast we're barely aware of it. In fact, we go to therapy to slow the whole process down just to better understand ourselves and our emotional response systems. When gender variant people articulate how we *know* our gender identity, it's often described in *feeling* terms. There's often an intrinsically felt sense of *resonance* and *dissonance*—a bodily comfort and discomfort—which the mind then labels, categorizes, and interprets. Depending on our ability to reconcile this somatic self with our conceptual self, we either suppress our desire to perform and express our gender, or we come out. Dynamically, gender identity is a felt somatic experience within the body, an intrapersonal experience within the mind, and a socially performative experience engaging the world around us.

For those who grew up with just pink or blue, a comprehensive range of genders can be tough to fathom. Where once there were two buckets of paint, there are now 20. Where once there were 20 buckets of paint, they're now poured out onto the floor, swirling together, with the buckets discarded. So, let's explore where all the colors mix. *Liminality* is the place between places—the limbo neither here nor there, making a liminal identity outside of, or in between, social convention (Denticel and Dietert, 2015). This includes pink with blue polka-dots, blue with pink stripes, half blue and half pink, a mixed shade of purple, and neon green. Even the literature is tricky to sift through, as there is no singular representation or definition for even the most commonly held gender labels. Accepting this, and the variety of interpretations each label can have, it's still important to understand the fundamentals of *cisgender*, *transgender*, *transsexual*, and *nonbinary* constructs including *genderqueer*, *genderfluid*, *agender*, and *third gender* people.

## Cisgender

*Cisgender* individuals, including the majority of male men and female women, feel that their anatomic sex aligns with their gender identity. While the term cisgender originated as a way of developing a gender continuum, some argue this can only be accomplished if we remove cisgender as a concept of normativity (Aultman, 2014; Enke, 2013). Since cisgender people are the vast majority, this is difficult to accomplish, yet it's not impossible, especially when we observe how cisgender identities are not uniform, but multicultural. Cisgender constructs of man and woman undergo dramatic changes across ethnic, racial, national, and socioeconomic cultures, presenting not only different values, beliefs, and power dynamics but even different standards of beauty, body language, and expressive behavior. We can assume all birds in an aviary are pigeons, but a true ornithologist studies the wild and how vibrantly diverse plumage can be.

Recognizing the intersection of gender identity, gender expression, and sexual orientation yields dynamic gender nonconformity that breaks from cisnormative expectations whilst walking the line of cisgender privilege. Essentially, when cisgender people don't adhere to a gender binary, they challenge what it means to be a male man or a female woman. Some identify as queer, the most notable of which being butches, bois, bears, femmes, kings and queens (Mellman, 2017). Not all who align with these labels identify as cisgender, either, as queer identities often deconstruct the boundaries of gender and sexuality. For example, let's have a cocktail at a gay bar. In our flirtatious chats we'll find quite a variety, all of whom identify as male, and all of whom identify as men, some far more masculine or feminine than others. Yet even if we compare three effeminate gay men of equal age, each has a different take on their gender identity. The first says boldly that he's an effeminate cisgender male. The second calls himself queer, deliberately blurring the line of what it means to be cisgender. The third spiritually identifies as a gay man with a woman's soul, acknowledging their cisgender status and privilege while recognizing something more. Comparably, the distinction between trans men and butch (female-bodied people with archetypally masculine traits) relies on the individual's conceptualization of self, more so than any discernable category of image or behavior (Beemyn and Rankin, 2011; Devor, 1989; Halberstam, 1998; Inness, 1997; Rubin, 1992; Valentine, 2007). The larger takeaway here is that not all who identify as cisgender are cisnormative, and that not all who are gender nonconforming identify as transgender.

## Transgender and transsexual

So, what's the difference between transgender and transsexual? In essence, the *trans* in *transgender* refers to those who transform, transcend, or transmute gender, whereas the *trans* in *transsexual* refers to those who seek to transition anatomic sex. Of course, these terms are not mutually exclusive, and classifiers based on behavior wash out in diverse, real-world demographics like vague lines drawn in sand. Yet the distinction is needed to address the diversity of perspective, as many transsexual people are very clear that it's not their gender being changed, but their anatomic sex (Kotula, 2002). Utilize self-referential language as there is no singular transgender or transsexual narrative. Gender labels are not clean categories and may overlap in a kaleidoscope of terms. One person may identify as a "transgender transsexual", another may identify as one but not the other, while a third may completely reject both (Fassinger and Arseneau, 2007; Gamson, 2000; Nagoshi and Brzuzy, 2010).

Even the definition of *transgender* differs depending on who you're talking to. For some it's an umbrella for everyone who's not cisgender, which some would argue it's more of a vague political classifier if anything, and for others it's a far more personal identity, claimed as a way of validating their liminality (Lev and Sennott, 2012; Serano, 2016). In this way, you may work with a transsexual client who identifies as a man, a transsexual client who identifies as a trans man, or a transgender client who identifies as trans-masculine.

While open to interpretation, those who elect *transgender* as a primary identifier tend to be sociogenic and nonbinary in their self-construct, leading to selective use of hormone replacement therapy (HRT), body modification, and social presentation (Finn and Dell, 1999; Halberstam, 2005; Raj, 2002; Richards *et al.*, 2016; Riley *et al.*, 2011). By contrast, those who actively favor *transsexual* as a label tend to, but do not always, identify with a biogenic, binary self-construct, leading them to pursue varying degrees of transition, from HRT to sex reassignment surgery (SRS) (Finn and Dell, 1999; Raj, 2002). In other words, knowing themselves to be a man or woman, transsexual people self-actualize to become such. Colloquially, and somewhat problematically, the medical language of transition tends to be described as a transsexual experience. Even *sex reassignment surgery* implies an emphasis on sex, reassigning the male to female or vice versa. Yet there are a whole range of gender identities outside of the binary scope undergoing medical procedures to self-actualize. To this end, *gender alignment surgery* is a broader and more apropos term to describe the full range of medical procedures available, including SRS.

As a historical point of fascination for researchers, most literature hyperfocuses on the transsexual experience, specifically a linear MtF path to transition. Marginalization and discrimination often center around issues of legitimacy, calling into question who is a "real" man or woman, elevating issues of *passability*—defined as the ability to blend in with cisnormative people—and overall social acceptance to a point of safety. Held at proverbial and even literal gunpoint, individuals who are read as transgender or nonbinary face higher rates of discrimination and violence than those who are either passable or inconspicuously queer (Beemyn and Rankin, 2011; Miller and Grollman, 2015; White and Goldberg, 2006). Passability, also known as readability, can be a point of frustration, aspiration, dismissal, and desire, depending on the client's perspective of transition, or pre-existing sex phenotypes if the gender a person presents isn't the gender perceived. An MtF woman may be femme-presenting, but encounters ridicule if they're not perceived as such. Some develop fierce emotional resilience to handle this, others develop strict rules of behavioral expression in order to be read, others dress down, presenting femininity a piece at a time as HRT and gender alignment surgery help them feel more comfortable with their bodies. Some stay in the closet for years.

When we reject the pressure to conform, pass, or hide, and create safe, comfortable places to express who we are, a broad range of transgender and transsexual identities appear, each at various stages of personal growth. A trans person may be in a stage of pre-transition, transition, or post-transition at the onset of therapy, though transition status does not determine their gender identity (Hird, 2002; Nagoshi and Brzuzy, 2010). They may still define themselves as a transsexual person even if they haven't undergone, or never plan to undergo any operative procedures. Conversely, a person may completely transition, yet reject the transsexual label altogether. Observably, the preference for terminology is often a generational marker, as many transitioning pioneers proudly came out as transsexual in the 1960s and 1970s, whereas millennials and post-millennials tend to favor broader, less binary terms like transgender or gender variant.

## Nonbinary

Returning to our gender nonconforming crew, the term *nonbinary* rejects the very assumption of gender as a dichotomy, which is noteworthy as some gender variant people actually do endorse this binary (Losty and O'Connor, 2018; Richards *et al.*, 2016). Colloquially, *nonbinary* has been adopted as a cultural viewpoint ("I don't believe in gender dichotomy") and also may frequently be employed as a gender label ("I am outside of the gender dichotomy") (Losty and O'Connor, 2018; McQueen, 2011). This can make things confusing, as there are both binary and nonbinary trans people, depending on culture, and even binary and nonbinary cisgender people, the latter most often found in the LGB community. For clarity, this text honors nonbinary as a gender identity outside of a dichotomous gender construct, as this term is often used by people who do not fit the presented masculine/feminine, man/women, male/female paradigm.

Approximately one-third of trans people identify as nonbinary, though they've only recently begun to receive social recognition even within the trans community (Matsuno and Budge, 2017; Otis, 2015; Richards *et al.*, 2016). In Israel, 35 percent of 2225 trans people surveyed identified as nonbinary (Joel *et al.*, 2014). In Scotland, 29 percent of 794 trans people identified with nonbinary, genderqueer, genderfluid, no gender, or other (McNeil *et al.*, 2012). In the USA, 13 percent of 6450 trans people identified with a "gender not listed here," with many write-ins describing themselves as genderqueer, pangender, transgenderist, twidget, birl, OtherWise or third gender (Grant *et al.*, 2011; Harrison, Grant, and Herman, 2012).

## Genderqueer

To delineate, nonbinary trans people tend to favor the terms *genderqueer* or *pangender*, though there is no singular nonbinary label or narrative (Harrison *et al.*, 2012). Genderqueer individuals often describe themselves as a mix or unification of masculine and feminine qualities and characteristics. Some feel like an androgynous blend, while others celebrate dichotomy by juxtaposing male and female phenotypes (Denticel and Dietert, 2015; Devor, 1989; Ekins and King, 1998, 1999; Israel and Tarver II, 1997; Nestle, Howell, and Wilchens, 2002; Otis, 2015). Being gender nonconforming means throwing off the rules, making labels nebulous playthings at best, and many genderqueer individuals may also identify as genderfluid and vice versa. Others, however, may perceive clear distinctions between them, conceptualizing genderqueer as a separate construct. More poignantly, some genderqueer people describe transgressing gender, transmuting gender, or even transcending the limits of gender.

## Genderfluid

*Genderfluid* or *bigender* individuals are *polygender*, meaning they have two or more gender identities that they oscillate between (Bockting, Knudson, and Goldberg, 2006; Ekins and King, 1998; Lev, 2004; Richards *et al.*, 2016; Sell, 2001). Genderfluidity is interpreted very differently by people, as some may shift between essentialist gender categories, like dipping into two separate buckets of paint, while others may feel their singular identity is a malleable mix of gender constructs, like one bucket with multiple colors swirling in it (Nagoshi and Brzuzy, 2010). Some may shift throughout a day, alternating genders contextually to fit place or company. Some hold one identity but simply shift their gender, and with it the filter through which they see and interact with the world (Case and Ramachandran, 2012). Others may feel the need to have several names to account for their shifts in form. Other genderfluid individuals may shift gradually over weeks, months, or even years, their gender independent of context but still morphous (Bockting *et al.*, 2006). Some may even report a sense of control, being able to access their various gender forms at will. Others may report no sense of control, feeling as if they shift genders organically and uncontrollably. Some may cycle gender identities, alternating between being a man, a woman, and being androgynous, just as some may cycle between the importance of passability and transgender visibility (Bockting *et al.*, 2006; Case and Ramachandran, 2012). Others may find they never return to a former gender, but identify with the term *genderfluid* as they continue to change throughout their life, having lived, for example, as a man, then a woman, then a genderqueer person.

## Agender

Agender individuals include anyone who doesn't identify with gender. They do not feel they are a man or a woman or any of the aforementioned gender constructs. Some may identify loosely with a genderqueer label, but differ in that they feel without gender, rather than being an androgynous blend (Denticel and Dietert, 2015; Ekins and King, 1999; Richards *et al.*, 2016). Agender individuals are also diverse in their experience and expression of gender neutralization. Some may feel like gender is a socially external phenomena that was not, or did not, integrate into their internal concept of self. They may describe feeling like they have no gender. Others may acknowledge their physical sex or gender role performance but find their identity schema eclipses their gender schema. Some may express a cursory acknowledgement of their sex or gender, loosely identifying with particular pronouns, but only to navigate social convention. Others still may say that their agender identity is not a lack of gender, but the expression of a "different" or "third" gender with minimal phenotypic traits. Some agender people may even pursue surgical means of gender nullification, including mastectomy, hysterectomy, nipple removal or castration (Johnson and Irwig, 2014; Vale *et al.*, 2010).

## Third gender

*Third gender* refers to cultures that exceed a gender binary, and who may or may not identify with the Western transgender or homosexual label depending on the cultural or individual interpretation thereof. Third gender identities are distinct paradigms intersecting both gender and sexuality into a person's social and communal role (Valentine, 2007). Indigenous Hawaiians, for example, distinguish *Wahine* (woman), *Kane* (man), and *Māhū* (in the middle) (Bolich, 2007; Matzner, 2001). The term *Fakaleiti* in Tonga and the *Fa'afafine* in Samoa roughly translate to "in the manner of women," observing a specific cultural practice in which certain boys are raised to adhere to female social and behavioral roles (Agoramoothy and Hsu, 2014; Bolich, 2007; Matzner, 2001; Roen, 2010; Sell, 2001). In India, the *Hijra* initiate a diverse array of people, including a minority of intersex individuals who fall outside of the male/female and/or man/woman paradigm (Bolich, 2007;

Brill and Kenney, 2016; Reddy, 2005). Observably, while some may identify as transgender, other *Hijra* undergo ceremonial castration (Agoramoothy and Hsu, 2014; Reddy, 2005; Sell, 2001). However, it may be inaccurate to describe the *Hijra* and *Kothi* of India within the Western conceptualization of transgender, which may ultimately be too limiting in scope and definition (Monro, 2007; Reddy, 2005). Likewise, the presence of third gender identities outside of the transgender construct is documented in 155 indigenous North American tribes (Devor, 1989; Roscoe, 1998; Sell, 2001). Challengingly, the term *third gender* is a Western construct used to describe genders that do not fit into Western paradigms (Towle and Morgan, 2006). Yet another taxonomical umbrella, the term *third gender* often leads to a romantic and almost primordial view of indigenous practices, glazing over their place in contemporary society (Towle and Morgan, 2006). In this text, *third gender* is not used as a generalization of identity or culture, but to identify when a specific cultural group has three or more socially recognized gender constructs.

A side note must be made for internet gender culture. Various online forums list hundreds of self-defined genders. Often, these labels explore pangender and polygender variables, such as the contexts in which gender expression may shift. These include transitional factors like time of day and lunar calendars, mirroring or reacting to the genders of those we're in proximity to, and numeric recognition of how many gender identities we have. Obscure gender constructs, especially those that fluctuate between several genders over short periods of time, may correspond to emotional instability, an unstable gender identity, or may simply reflect the language of an online cultural epoch. The popularity of certain gender terms is observably geographic and generational, so familiarize yourself with our use of language as it develops (Carroll *et al.*, 2002; Singh and Burnes, 2010; Smith, Shin, and Officer, 2012). The internet is, after all, an invisible country with its own cultural norms.

Understandably, it can be difficult for practitioners to track the ever expanding and ever fluctuating range of gender labels, leading to inadvertent micro-invalidations (Smith *et al.*, 2012). To wrap your head around the fundamentals, many of these terms are subcategorical observations of gender identity as they intersect with gender expression. For example, if we report living as a man by daylight and a woman by moonlight, we're still undergoing a polygender experience with two separate identity constructs. Perhaps this nocturnal association was conditioned over time, and perhaps our gender identity may break from this pattern when we feel emotionally integrated, but such unique gender profiles are so rare and so individuated no assumption can be made. Our terminology and use of labels are not to be dismissed, however, as they represent our personal, cultural, and spiritual interpretation of gender.

## *Gender expression*

Gender expression regards the masculinity, femininity, androgyny, or neutrality of our presentation. For example, a cisgender man may present as extremely feminine and yet identify as a man. Likewise, a cisgender woman may adhere to stereotypically masculine mannerisms while wearing stereotypically masculine clothes, and yet identify as a woman.

What constitutes masculine or feminine, however, differs from culture to culture, and even generation to generation. Compare dancers around the world and notice how Spanish Flamenco, Russian Hopak, and Afro-Brazilian Capoeira all celebrate masculinity in dance, whereas many Caucasian Americans look suspiciously at dancing boys, calling into question their masculinity and sexuality (Holdsworth, 2013; Risner, 2009). In cisnormative circles, gender expression can be presented as a spectrum from the hypermasculine to the hyperfeminine. Yet when we don't presume dichotomy, and take into account androgyny and gender neutrality, gender expression becomes more of a cultural performance than a declarative expression of sex.

Certain individuals may have a gender expressive identity independent of their actual gender identity. Drag artists are the most famous for this. Some adopt cross-dressing as a performative lifestyle while still identifying as cisgender, while other drag artists identify as nonbinary leaning into trans-masculine and trans-feminine identities departing from the norms associated with their anatomic sex. Consider, for example, a cisgender woman who presents hypermasculine behavior, fashion, and body language and is also very connected to being a female woman. Even though she is trans-masculine in expression, she also celebrates, appreciates, and aligns with being a female woman. Some may use the term *trans-masculine* interchangeably to describe their gender expression and their gender identity. Another woman may, alternatively, remove the "masculine" association built in, nullifying the gendered association, and reclassify the traits as *butch* (Halberstam, 1998; Inness, 1997). Now consider a self-identified cisgender woman who goes to gay clubs—not dressed up as a drag king, but as a hyperfeminine drag queen. As a unique form of hyperfantastical gender expression, crossover is not a prerequisite, and from time to time we may encounter drag queens with massive wigs and padded bras who are biologically female (Dalton, 2010).

Trying to account for cross-gender expression, people often presume it's a gay phenomenon, and not without reason. Drag culture has been at the heart of the gay community even before the great Widow Norton, José Sarria, graced San Francisco's Black Cat Bar in the 1950s. In fact, the heyday of female impersonation was arguably the vaudeville era, continuing the long-held stereotype correlating male effeminacy and theater. Even now, the majority of drag performers, specifically female impersonators, are gay (Taylor and Rupp, 2004). Outside of this flamboyant contingency, however, it's a very different story.

In Japan, boys cross-dressing as women, *Otoko-no ko*, had a mainstream revival in Tokyo's maid cafés; while in New York, men spirit themselves away to *Miss Vera's Finishing School for Boys Who Want to Be Girls* (Bodarky, 2017; Clegg, 2014). These cross-dressing men, who were often raised in strict gender paradigms, are not intrinsically gay. In fact, collected data has found that most cross-dressers and self-identified transvestites, outside of the drag scene, are heterosexual men (Bullough and Bullough, 1997; Docter and Fleming, 2001; Docter and Prince, 1997).

Taking all of this in, one can start to see how cross-gender expression is not only true for cisgender individuals, but actually quite common. Think of all the stereotypic social niches there are in Western society, from tomboys to jane-girls, from butch women to femme men. Yet if this is true for cisgender people, then cross-gender expression must also be true for transgender individuals. Trans women can be rough and tumble tomboys, trans men can present as effeminate, and all things in between.

## Translating sexuality

As sexual orientation is often expressed through gender expressive means, it is not uncommon for people to first question sexuality or explore gender in sexually expressive terms (Bockting *et al.*, 2006). The reverse is also common, as the majority of gender explorative youth later re-identify as gender-playful and gender-expansive lesbian, gay, bisexual, pansexual, or asexual identities without identifying as transgender (Drummond *et al.*, 2008; Green, 1987; Wallien and Cohen-Kettenis, 2008). Certainly, gender and sexuality are intimate lovers, yet all too often people make assumptions about one because of the other.

Hierarchical frames of sexuality are naively formulaic. *My gender identity* plus *my partner's gender identity* equals my sexuality. We know this isn't true, but our child-like pragmatism likes to put things in boxes. Man plus man equals gay. Man plus woman equals straight. Woman plus woman equals lesbian, and so on. As for bisexuals and pansexuals? They're told to "pick a side," and asexuals just haven't found the "right one" yet. It's through this mathematical oversimplification that many first conceptualize sexual orientation as children and adolescents. It's tidy, concrete, and so rigid some people never get past it, even in the LGBTQ community.

Globally, expression of sexual identity is incredibly diverse, with a great deal of leeway when it comes to personal interpretation, as all genders engage in an array of sexual behavior, receptive and insertive sex, and erotic touch (Bockting *et al.*, 2006; Lev and Sennott, 2012). Therein lies the beauty. To grasp the full gamut, sexuality and gender are best recognized as two independent yet intersecting facets of identity (Belawski and Sojka, 2014; Chavez-Korell and Lorah, 2007;

Devor 2002; Lombardi, 2001). Looking deeper, our sexual schema is subdivided into personal scripts, all layered and interwoven with each other. Our intrapsychic scripts include attraction, fantasy, and arousal, our interpersonal scripts regard our beliefs and behaviors pertaining to sexual and affectional interactions, and our cultural scripts contain all the heteronormative and homonormative imprints we may or may not embrace (Fabbre, 2014; Mellman, 2017). For those unfamiliar with LGBTQ social stressors, *homonormativity* includes the ideologies and social norms of a gay sub-majority primarily, but not exclusively, marketed by and for white gay metropolitan men.

We naturally fuse and defuse from these scripts depending on their level of influence and urgency in our lives, and how much our differing scripts align or conflict with each other. Our intrapsychic script may not, for example, align with our interpersonal or cultural script, in the same away that a woman isn't a lesbian just because she fantasizes about having sex with another woman. It doesn't even mean she's bisexual, or pansexual, as her fantasies have little bearing on her identity. She may just be curious. If her interpersonal script starts to shift and she begins to desire an affectionate relationship with a woman, then perhaps a sexual identity is forming. Dissonance occurs whenever these scripts are at odds with each other, which is tricky enough before bringing gender into the mix.

When the gender binary is no longer presumed, because our gender is in transition or our gender does not fit a binary, then the limits of vocabulary must be expanded. As all these labels are too subjective, some researchers have divorced attraction from identity by employing terms like androphilia (attraction to males/masculinity), gynephilia (attraction to females/femininity), ambiphilia (attraction to both), and panphilia (attractions beyond the gender binary) (Diamond, 2010; LeVay, 1993; Serano, 2010). Although far more apt as they convey attraction independent of our physical body or gender identity, these terms have a certain clinical lilt. Even saying them aloud feels like reading from a textbook. They have no social norms attributed to them, no inferred status symbols, and no rules of behavior. They're as dimensional as north, south, east, and west. They're just a compass. Yet in complex moments when we feel lost, a compass may be all we need. Straight, gay, lesbian, bisexual—all are loaded with assumptions and bias. Further neologisms are required to clarify gynandromorphophilic attractions cisgender people have for gender variant individuals, yet what a mouthful that is to say (Blanchard and Collins, 1993; Corsini, 2002; Diamond, 2010; Serano, 2010; Weinberg and Williams, 2010). This sterile language may never catch on, but it can be beneficial when we want to explore the recipe of attraction without all the additives.

Trying to impose what is definitively straight, gay, or bisexual to a population already outside of the bell curve leads to all kinds of contradictions in research. Researchers used to say trans men are primarily attracted to cis women (Devor,

1993, 1997; Pauly, 1998), and while this was certainly true of those surveyed, it discounted trans gay men (Bockting, Benner, and Coleman, 2009; Schleifer, 2006; Sevelius, 2009; Zandvliet, 2000). Observably, trans men—and indeed any gender variant person—may identify as gay, bisexual, pansexual, straight, asexual, or queer, and maintain committed relationships with both cis men and women, trans men and trans women, or really anyone (Beemyn and Rankin, 2011; Brown, 2010; Hines, 2006; Joslin-Roher and Wheeler, 2009; Lev and Sennott, 2012; Meier *et al.* 2013; Mellman, 2017; Pfeffer, 2008).

Taking this a step further, we may find ourselves crossing thresholds of sexuality our PE teacher never talked about in health class. As sexuality intersects with gender, subtle changes can crop up that we may not—or could not—have anticipated prior to transition. When we don't feel we can be open about these multifaceted parts of us, the shadow of secrecy looms over our relationships, undermining communication and sexual negotiation, and even increasing risk of sexually transmitted diseases (STDs) like HIV (Bauer *et al.*, 2013; Iantaffi and Bockting, 2011; Mellman, 2017; Sevelius, 2009).When we begin to challenge this secrecy, and accept both curiosity and confusion, some unique narratives can emerge, accounting for the highs, lows, and social complexity of *transitional sexuality*, *fluid sexuality*, *dynamic sexuality*, and *asexuality*.

## *Transitional sexuality*

People who do not identify as bi or pan may find their sexual identity relabeled as they transition. Consider a once heterosexual man who transitioned into a lesbian, or a once self-identified lesbian who transitioned into a heterosexual man. Respectively, their gynophilic attraction to women remains constant. The only thing that changed was the label, the social classifier, and with it a whole world of social interactions. For some, this isn't a change at all because they may have already identified as such long before transition. Yet for others, this new classification can feel as dramatic as moving to a new country with whole new social norms. Even if we always dreamed of moving to Uganda, nothing could quite prepare us for actually moving there. Even if we had always identified as a lesbian, it's quite powerful to attend Womenfest in Key West, the Dinah in Palm Springs, or to find our way to the Eressos International Women's festival on the Greek island of Lesbos.

One may not realize the unspoken intrapsychic, interpersonal, or cultural implications, expectations, or losses of transition. The aforementioned trans woman and her wife must now navigate what it means to be externally labeled as a lesbian couple, whether or not they personally identify with this label. Likewise, a trans man who lived in the lesbian community for much of their adult life may feel a sense of distance or even conflict with the community now that they're perceived externally as a man (Joslin-Roher and Wheeler, 2009; Rubin, 1992). Respectively, each may be introduced to gender norms they had been unaware of, due to limited access to the community pre-transition. It is, after all, one thing to transition into a man, and another to transition into a man of a certain sexuality, social scene, lifestyle, or social class. Comparably, it is one thing to transition into a majority of heteronormative women where one's queerness is erased, and quite another to transition into a lesbian community with creative and expressive outlets reflective of their social experience as a sexual minority (Joslin-Roher and Wheeler, 2009).

How to manage gender dysphoria, transition, and gender nonconformity in a sexual relationship depends largely on our reservation. The frank may explore sex openly with their partner, negotiating sexual and affectional touch of every kind, while the discreet may need your therapeutic help to navigate this topic, especially if discussing anatomy they don't connect to (Bockting *et al.*, 2006; Hill-Meyer and Scarborough, 2014). Sexual acceptance can also have a huge impact on sexual drive, for when gender is accepted and adored in the bedroom, libido begins to flourish, especially for natal males embodying a femme persona (Lev and Sennott, 2012).

As we all have phallic structures (penis/clitoris), soft tissue (scrotum/labia), pelvic muscles, perineum and rectal sensitivity, many re-conceptualize their genitalia and with it the how-to guide of sexual play (Hill-Meyer and Scarborough, 2014). Trans men and trans-masculine people may describe having a "dickclit" or refer to and treat their clitoris as a "dick" or "cock," or relabel their vagina "front-hole," or use strap-ons and packers to actualize their "phantom penis" (Bockting *et al.*, 2006; Hill-Meyer and Scarborough, 2014; Kotula, 2002). Trans women and trans-feminine people may or may not include their penis, or may simulate vaginal play, or relabel their anus as a vagina (Hill-Meyer and Scarborough, 2014). Most importantly, how we play with our body, and what body parts we do or do not enjoy stimulating, has no bearing on our gender identity (Hill-Meyer and Scarborough, 2014).

Like many aspects of transition, sex and sexuality can be an exciting affirmation of our developing identity, and a nerve-racking experience as well. We may disdain feeling naive or new, or tackle in-group–out-group concerns, especially if we've encountered rejection, exclusion, or attempts to delegitimize our sexuality on the basis of our gender.

## *Fluid sexuality*

Sexuality can be an ongoing process that changes across the lifespan. The word *can* is central here, as some individuals are set in aspects of their sexual identity, while others are far more fluid (Bockting *et al.*, 2006; Daskalos, 1998; Diamond, 2005; Kinnish, Strassberg, and Turner, 2005). Cisgender longitudinal studies claim that women, whether they identify as bi, lesbian, or straight, are more likely to have a fluid relationship with their sexual orientation than bi, gay, or straight men (Daskalos, 1998; Kinnish *et al.*, 2005; Mock and Eibach, 2012). There are also cases of MtF clients who reported their sexual orientation shifting during transition, which some of them personally attributed to HRT, and cases of MtE (male-to-eunuch) individuals who found their sexual orientation changed after voluntary castration (Bockting *et al.*, 2006; Brett, Roberts, and Johnson, 2007; Daskalos, 1998; Israel and Tarver II, 1997). Though hormone regimens can certainly affect sexual drive, there is no standing evidence that hormones can change sexual orientation. It is possible that reducing testosterone reduced levels of aggression they had previously associated with heteronormative behavior and heterosexual identity, just as it's possible that self-actualization allowed them to defuse from sexual suppression or repression.

When we, as gender variant people, find our sexual orientation shifting, it may be because of a corresponding shift in how we see ourselves, how people interact with us differently, and how comfortable we are engaging in new kinds of relationships (Hill-Meyer and Scarborough, 2014). Bisexual erasure may also factor when sexualities appear to "emerge," as bisexuals can struggle to preserve identity over time. The myth of the non-committal bisexual stems from a false stereotype assuming that if a person is attracted to both men and women then they can't be monogamous. It also presents the bogus notion that bisexuals can't "commit" to a sexual orientation and are just denying their homosexuality. Though surveyed bisexual populations report monogamy as more of a sacrifice than straight, gay, or lesbian populations, they tended toward traditional monogamous relationship dynamics (Mark, Rosenkrantz, and Kerner, 2014). Understanding this, bisexuals in long-term relationships may re-identify as gay or straight to build connection, fit in, or camouflage for safety and social convenience.

> "This is the eighth dinner party in a row that I've had to explain that just cause I'm bi doesn't mean I'm unsatisfied with my marriage."

> "I never really thought of myself as bisexual. I mean, I was always curious about men, but I knew I wasn't gay, so I wrote it off as a phase."

While few studies have researched the sexual fluidity of gender variant populations, polygender/genderfluid individuals may relate either a stable or fluid sexuality. Those with a stable sexuality may, for example, feel their bisexuality or pansexuality remains constant regardless of their gender or the labels thereof. These scenarios can play out romantically, provided all partners understand and accept their genderfluidity, and are capable of having a relationship with a person with two or more presentations: "My lover is both a straight man and a lesbian." While the attraction remains constant, sexually navigating shifts in gender necessitates clear communication, as the genderfluid person may express themselves differently. Body language may change, along with voice, fashion, grooming habits, and even recreational interests. If, however, the polygender body maps aren't so compartmentalized, gender expression may only shift minimally, perhaps only changing a few general aspects of outward presentation. This is not, however, to be taken lightly, as small outward changes may reflect a deep internal change inexpressible through simple words or actions.

Interest in sexual initiation, frequency, intensity, positioning, and power dynamics may also shift. For example, though lesbians and heterosexual men are both aroused by women, a polygender person who identifies as both a lesbian and a heterosexual man may have encoded each sexuality construct with different approaches to sexual acts and expression. More than just a change in preference for stereotypic sexual behavior, activities that they adored in one gender state may no longer feel *right* in another. Desire for sexual penetration can pull a 180. They may even change how they kiss a person.

Provided a polygender person can express these shifts effectively, and provided their romantic partner can recognize and respect this while also meeting their own personal needs, the relationship can blossom. Imagine a flower with flexible petals folding and unfolding on a stable and committed stem. One old trick is to designate a nonverbal flag associated with a specific gender expression, albeit a necklace, a hat, a color-coded wardrobe, or even a hairstyle.

Yet what about fluid changes in sexual orientation? In the last example the genderfluid person maintained an attraction for women, regardless of gender. Now consider a genderfluid person with distinct sexual orientations interwoven with their compartmentalized gender schemas.

Meet Kay. They work at the library when they're not busking with an accordion on the weekends. They're also a physiological female genderfluid person. Looking back at their life, Kay seems to shift gender presentation several times a year. In your first session they presented as a lesbian. As the year went on, they began referring to themselves as a gay man attracted to men, with no interest in women. A few months later, they're a lesbian again. In short, Kay's not in the closet, or going through phases of denial. They simply have two different genders with two different sexualities. Having independent sexual orientations is not comparable to bisexuality, which assumes a stable attraction to both sexes, though some may use the term loosely to make it easier for others to understand. For Kay, their sexuality is state dependent. They're both a gay woman and a gay man. If they're strictly monogamous, this can be difficult, but not impossible, yet a great deal of reciprocal acceptance is required to ensure that all needs are being met for each partner. Some alleviate the tension of having two sexual orientations by finding a partner who is also capable of shifting gender states, or by having polyamorous or polysexual relationships.

## *Dynamic sexuality*

Genderqueer and agender people often have unique sexual identities, quite apart from both the heteronormative and homonormative understanding of sex and attraction. It's not uncommon for genderqueer and agender individuals to identify as bi, pan, or asexual, yet some may navigate nomenclature that doesn't fit (Denticel and Dietert, 2015). If a genderqueer person develops a crush on a man or a woman, are they gay or straight? Here, the rudimentary math of sexuality breaks down in glorious failure, as algebra usually does when based on genitals. They may say, "I'm attracted to men," or "I'm attracted to women," or "I like both," just to make it easier for whoever they're talking to.

Xander, our local bartender, was having a really good night. They've found a cute guy, had a great date, and brought him home. Upfront, the guy seems open minded, and they spent the whole evening talking about gender and what it's like for Xander to be genderqueer. Yay! No more closets to come out of! Then they fell into bed, and everything's going great…until he started treating Xander's female body like a woman, throwing the moment right out the window.

For some transitioning and genderfluid people there are unspoken binary acts that can help validate gender. These kinds of romantic and coital behaviors generate a gendered form of sexual energy. Hinduism aligns this in Kundalini yoga, Hawaiians feel it in their *mana*, and the Taoists call it *yin* and *yang*. This energy has little to do with sexual position, who's on top or bottom, or sexual power dynamics like who's dominant or submissive—though they can certainly influence the outcome! Rather, this energy manifests in how we treat each other, how we touch, and even perceive each other. It is, perhaps, a delicate subject for nonbinary individuals as we teach lovers how to have sex, not with a man or woman, but with us as a unique person. We may love penetrative sex or find it confusing and somehow undermining of our identity, requiring us to expand into other arenas of sexual play. We may give but not receive, or vice versa, or be completely asexual and not even go there.

Developing a personally dynamic sexual expression takes time and research, albeit through conversation, literature, pornography, or sexual experimentation. Again, while this is true for all people of all genders, gender variant people are trailblazers in this area whether we like it or not. Innovating sexuality, especially as it corresponds to an atypical gender identity, needs a lot of self-forgiveness and personal permission-giving. When there is no manual, we have to try a lot to figure it out.

## *Asexuality*

Not only do some gender variant people identify as asexual, historically asexuality was once presumed an aspect of transsexuality when clinicians first observed gender dysphoric nonsexuality (Bockting *et al.*, 2006; Lev and Sennott, 2012). Abstaining from sex or feeling nonsexual because one is incongruent with their anatomy is not intrinsically synonymous with asexuality, as sexual attraction for others remains, albeit inaccessible. Asexuality, by contrast, doesn't prioritize sexual attraction, yet this doesn't always equate to an absence of sexual desire, as some asexuals may seek sexual stimulation both alone or with a partner (Bogaert, 2015). The difference here is that asexuals have a low or absent sexual attraction to others (Bogaert, 2015; Scherrer, 2008; Steelman and Hertlein, 2016). Some asexuals do not engage in sexual play at all, while others may engage in sexual play as a form of mutual masturbation, or maintain physically intimate nonsexual relationships (Belawski and Sojka, 2014; Bogaert, 2015; Hill-Meyer and Scarborough, 2014).

Socially, asexuals live in a world where the majority of the population is hyperfocused to the point of seeming brainwashed. Not only is sexuality everywhere, seeping into every social setting, many people can't even believe a person is nonsexual (Gressgård, 2013; Scherrer, 2008). Even therapists and medical practitioners will accuse asexuals of having a hypoactive sexual desire disorder (Bogaert, 2015; Gressgård, 2013; Steelman and Hertlein, 2016). Asexuals are frequently accused of "not knowing what they want," or "just not having a good experience yet," or are promised that one day "they'll figure out their sexuality." Much like bisexual erasure, asexual erasure minimizes a nonsexual orientation, presuming all people must fundamentally have some sexual attraction, that one day they'll "pick a side" or "figure it out."

Gender variant asexuals may also face the double-whammy of existing in an overly sexualized world that also fetishizes their gender. Eroticized for thousands of years, the bordello of sexual fantasy is the one place cisgender society seems to permit gender variance—which is doubly annoying if we're nonsexual to begin with! Asexuality doesn't omit relationships, unless one is also aromantic—at which point it's the single-life. This can make dating a bit more of an interview process, scanning for communication skills, open-mindedness, and acceptance of both gender variance *and* nonsexuality. A tall order, for sure! Despite fusing with rationale, stating that it's easier not to date, or that being single is fine, affectional loneliness can be a very real problem. Asexuals of all genders may at times labor to hold their boundaries, feeling like they have to concede to sex in order to keep a relationship, a dilemma which can further compromise esteem and self-worth.

To evade the perils of self-doubt, and the comparison to heteronormative and homonormative expectations, we must collectively adjust the conversation. Recognizing that our attraction is not dependent on our form can provide a great deal of liberty, as it removes power from labels defined from external sources. In other words, *my sexuality is mine, it isn't defined by whose hand I'm holding.* It is also imperative that you make no assumptions about our sexuality, albeit our sexual orientation or our sexual behavior, as doing so creates unnecessary barriers in session (Lev and Sennott, 2012).

## Translating intersectionality

Trying to puzzle out our multifaceted identity can feel overwhelming, especially for the young and disenfranchised. Consider all the continuums of sex, gender, gender expression, and even sexual orientation that not only layer over each other but intersect with degrees of marginalization and privilege (Risman, 2004; Sennott, 2011). Just ask an upper-class teenage African American what it means to be a woman, and compare her answer with a lower-class, Native American woman rendered disabled in her old age. The similarities in their answer will be as powerful as their cultural and personal differences. Socioeconomic status, ethnicity, education, ability, religion, body type, and age weave into our construct of gender and yet exist independently of it (Risman, 2004; Senott, 2011). The pattern, prioritization, equilibration, or compartmentalization of these dimensions—along with many others—form a complex identity schema unique to the individual.

When these complex dimensions harmonize, we feel empowered in our wholeness, and proud of our unique individuality. Yet it can take a long time to get to this point, especially for those who belong to more than one marginalized group. Cultures clash within us as different aspects of identity fight for priority in every situational context. Oppressed here and privileged there, a minority in this community and a majority in that, we feel layer upon layer of social implications like a stained-glass ceiling.

Stand too close and the colorful glass has pattern but no cohesion, as every cut shard appears independent of the next. Step back and all the shapes lock together into an image of who we are, yet still our parts remain as segmented as the glass, cohesive, but not integrated, with a shard of red here and a cut of green there. We need to take one more step back. As the sunlight shines, the stained glass projects an image onto the floor. The colors emanate and blend with each other, maintaining form and distinction while glowing in unity. Every shard of glass is a dimension of our ethnicity, race, ability, nationality, spirituality, community, or family. The whole stained-glass image shows how these identities intersect, yet we transcend our patterns. It's not until the light of our personal identity—our unique personality, our core values, and our genuine gender— shines through that our colorful diversity truly integrates and illuminates.

Stained-glass ceilings, however, are still glass ceilings, as the external world uses our diversity as barriers against us. What we are most proud of can be held in front of us as a blockade, insinuating that our strengths are a shortcoming or our history a hindrance. LGBTQ history is fraught with divisions tearing the rainbow apart along racial, ethnic, spiritual, political, and even gendered lines.

How many times did it feel like marching in this protest meant we couldn't be seen walking in that parade? How many times did it feel like aligning with this side of the family pitted us against another? Fear of exclusion can lead us to hide, compartmentalize, or even feel like we're betraying both ourselves and our community simultaneously, and in more ways than one. We're not just talking about marginality here. We're talking about having margins on each side of the proverbial page. We're even talking about being marginalized in the margin, when we're pushed to the edge of the edge. Imagine getting through a whole day without a transphobic encounter, only to find there's no wheelchair ramp at the LGBTQ resource center, and you're a self-identified pangender paraplegic. Imagine being supported in school for being out and proud, only to find everyone goes quiet when you say "Black Lives Matter," as if your gender is more accepted than your African ancestry. Imagine having a bustling Cuban community, with friends and family who love and adore you, provided you never bring up that time you stole your sister's quinceañera dress. The tensions are real, as is our internal dissonance.

Rather than tear ourselves between one facet of our identity over another equally fundamental facet of who we are, ACT allows us to sit with complexity. This means also sitting with all the emotions whirling therein. In therapy, we learn to lean back from the dysfunctional web of thoughts and maladaptive behaviors generated by internal dissonance and encounters with discrimination (Burdge, 2007; Maguen, Shipherd, and Harris, 2005). Counting our blessings with our scars, our experience with privilege may internally clash with our experiences of oppression. We may find ourselves simultaneously belonging to demographic majorities and minorities with varying degrees of visibility and empowerment. Or we may find ourselves completely outside major arenas of privilege, sans voice or even recognition. Reconciling our multiple dimensions requires a level of self-awareness, as that which we take pride in can also be a source of shame and self-doubt. Yet our complexity can actually be a source of both mental flexibility and personal resilience, as we can draw on so many dimensions of self without being trapped into a singular "I am" statement (Nagoshi and Brzuzy, 2010; Risman, 2004). Seeing this, we can build coalitions of diversity without stripping down who we are or shoving ourselves into overtly rigid definitions.

There is far too much to cover in a single chapter to prepare you for working with the full breadth of multicultural gender issues. Certainly, a gender specialist's education is never done, as we're all lifelong students and tenured teachers in the school of humanity. As such, go beyond this text to read up on gender as it pertains to *racial discrimination and empowerment*, perspectives on *ethnocultural gender legitimacy, mimicry, and otherness*, issues facing *differently abled visibility*; and how *spiritual rejection and incorporation* factor over our lives.

## *Racial discrimination and empowerment*

In the USA the trans population is mostly comprised of trans people of color, many of whom contend with pressure both within their racial and ethnic community, alongside the added disempowerment of being a racial and ethnic minority (Conron *et al.*, 2012; Flores, Brown, and Herman, 2016a; James *et al.*, 2016). An emotional undertaking on its own, gender exploration and self-actualization is made exponentially more difficult when the outside world kicks up dirt at the base of one's family tree.

Gender privilege is a sexist and cissexist power imbalance weighted all the more by racially gendered stereotypes. For example, as Asian men are typecast as passive and African American men are typecast as aggressive, trans men of color actualizing their masculinity also find their interactions with others—in particular with employers—influenced and impeded by these stereotypes (Schilt, 2010). We do not merely become men or women or nonbinary, we actualize our gender in the context of our racial and ethnocultural experience. Racism, sexism, and cissexism indicate a pattern of rigid relational frames, yet the expression and consequence of such rigid psychosocial structures are not analogous (Butler, 1993). The history cultivating each is respectively complex, and trying to capture the sociopolitical, geopolitical, and psychosocial impact of each is impossible to do in a single text. Treating racism, sexism, and cissexism as equivalent underestimates the very specific psychological weapons each wields against the individual. That said, the intersection of race and gender identity can be a source of deep value constructs and personal meaning, even when under attack.

Recognizing how gender minorities are recurrent targets for discrimination, a 2011 survey of over 6000 transgender Americans found that trans people of color, in particular Black, Latino, Native American, and multiracial respondents, experienced two to three times the rate of sexual and physical assault in the workplace than transgender white people (Grant *et al.*, 2011). In schools, 83 percent of multiracial students reported harassment and bullying, 45 percent of which involved physical assault. This same survey found that 24 percent of trans American Indians reported sexual assault, a daunting number echoed by 18 percent of multiracial, 17 percent of Asian, and 15 percent of Black respondents (Grant *et al.*, 2011). The digital news company, Mic, compiled a comprehensive database of all known transgender homicides in the USA between 2010 and 2016 using data from the National Coalition of Anti-Violence Programs (NCAVP) (Talusan *et al.*, 2017). Disturbingly, 72 percent of trans homicide victims were Black femme or Black trans women (Talusan *et al.*, 2017).

Poverty is disproportionately rampant amongst trans people of color, as racial privilege and socioeconomic class are literally redlined together. Combine this historical and systematic racism with gender discrimination against transgender employment, and the loud bang that follows is the sound of opportunity slamming the door shut. Left in the cold, we see the blue lights flash. Amongst the general population, 2.7 percent of the USA—approximately 1 out of every 37 adults—are dealing with some form of correctional supervision, either in prison or by working their way through the system (Kaeble and Glaze, 2016). In the trans community that number skyrockets to 16 percent—approximately 6 out of every 37 transgender adults have to work their way through the system (Grant *et al.*, 2011). Of that 16 percent, 47 percent are African American, and 30 percent are Native American (Grant *et al.*, 2011).

Being targeted by law enforcement for being a racial minority and then further scrutinized for being transgender is painfully common (Mogul, Ritchie, and Whitlock, 2011). In prison settings, transgender people are often assaulted directly by prison personnel, or left to fend for themselves against violent inmates (Mogul *et al.*, 2011; Stotzer, 2014). To add insult to injury, and injury to injury, the Movement Advancement Project (2016), working in conjunction with the Center for American Progress, found that transgender people assigned intolerant probation workers have been charged for violating parole for wearing gender congruent clothes, or having these clothes taken away in mandatory residential re-entry programs.

If one has questionable citizenship, life can take a frightening turn. Trans immigrants may hold off on transition, needing all their paperwork to match, or find they have to simplify their identity for government officials unfamiliar with transgender identities—let alone racially diverse transgender identities (Kourbatova and Redfield, 2014). These literal culture clashes mean that racially diverse trans immigrants are more likely to be picked up by law enforcement on false pretenses, and then to be subjected to harassment, isolation, and abuse while being detained by immigration offices (Harmon, 2012; Kourbatova and Redfield, 2014; Ziegler and Rasul, 2014). To illustrate the absurd cruelty of intolerance, innocent transgender Latina women—profiled and accused of "loitering for the purpose of prostitution" by the New York Police Department's stop-and-frisk policy—were being cuffed just for carrying condoms (Kourbatova and Redfield, 2014).

Though ACT defuses from intrusive thoughts, many cognitions are anchored to the very real concerns and dangers facing gender variant people, especially gender variant people of color (Maguen *et al.*, 2005). The emotional depletion and psychological fatigue resulting from compounded micro-, meso-, and macroaggressions against sexual, gender, disability, and racial minorities is defined here as *minority stress* (Hendricks and Testa, 2012; Nodin *et al.*, 2015). Social, educational, occupational, and health resources can help lift minorities up, yet minority stress isn't a symptom set one can simply alleviate. Indeed, every social, educational, and occupational arena contains its own potential for minority stress.

Experiences with neglect, cruelty, and injustice can shape our outlook on life and expectation of the future, and generate negative self-talk. To cope, overcome, or avoid such pervasive stress, we may advocate, protest, and rebel against social norms, or else camouflage or code-switch to operate safely around the majority. As excess time may be spent having to consider the performative script of the oppressive majority, meeting a clinician who recognizes the power differential and fluidly understands our respective language can be a powerful experience. Since familial systems and ethnocultural demographics express emotions differently—and therefore cope with minority stress differently—clinicians are encouraged to take a holistic approach to communication. This includes studying the diversity of emotive expression, including body language (kinesics), the utilization of physical space (proxemics), verbal speech (linguistics), and even the aspects of spoken language that exceed words (paralinguistics), including the use of pauses and inflections.

Dimensions of racial and gender inequality have uniquely different influences and causal mechanisms within every social, political, and socioeconomic tier that differ in every nation in respect to their history of power imbalance (Risman, 2004). When working with gender variant people of color, it's useful to take a *both/and* perspective to address the distinct issues facing *both* racial inequality and gender inequality, respectively, *and* how they intersect personally, socially, and occupationally (Risman, 2004). Having shouldered through racial oppression, some people may downplay gender issues, or vice versa. Having felt isolated by their community, some may dismiss danger, overestimating or underestimating their ability to handle conflict.

This is where community connection and social activism with gender variant people of color can help a person take that broad step from self-acceptance to self-empowerment (Pflum *et al.*, 2015; Singh and McKleroy, 2011). Connecting with the broader LGBTQ community, the queer community, and even the sex-positive community can be incredibly validating, as is connecting with cisgender people of color who accept gender variance, yet connecting with a gender variant person who shares our racial or ethnic background allows for a nuanced depth of recognition and personal validity (Singh and McKleroy, 2011; Ziegler and Rasul, 2014). Such interactions create a heartfelt opportunity to see and be seen by one who mirrors our own strengths, struggles, questions, and curiosities in a way that few can truly fathom (Devor, 2004). Some trans people of color find this mirroring in socially organized programs like Community Kinship, Life, or the Audre Lorde Project in New York, or through spiritual organizations like TransFaith in Color (Singh and McKleroy, 2011; Ziegler and Rasul, 2014). The National Confederacy of Two Spirit Organizations and the Northeast Two Spirit Society developed a comprehensive list of Native American two-spirit organizations, from the Bay Area American Indian Two Spirits (BAAITS.org) to the Dancing To Eagle Spirit

Society (DancingToEagleSpiritSociety.org) in Vancouver, to the 2 Spirited People of the 1st Nations (2Spirits.com) in Toronto (Pruden, 2013). As it's sometimes difficult to find racial connections even within the LGBTQ community, the internet becomes a powerful tool to find and connect with people as unique as oneself, and can even be employed in session to search out websites and online forums (Devor, 2004; Lev, 2007; Singh, 2013; Ziegler and Rasul, 2014). These include the Trans People of Color Coalition (TPOCC), Asian Pacific Islander Women and Transgender community, Queer Women of Color Media, bklyn boihood, BlackTranmen.org, and BlackTransWomen.org (Ziegler and Rasul, 2014). When belonging within a community is fostered, it's only natural to engage in social activism to advocate, uplift, and protect that community. For gender variant people of color, practicing self-advocacy and social activism to vocalize their lived experience, defend their rights, and challenge sexism, cissexism, and heterosexism, has proven time and again to increase resilience in response to stress (Singh 2013; Singh, Hays and Watson 2011; Nodin *et al.*, 2015).

It is not enough to be visible or tolerated in therapeutic settings, and though demonstrations of respect are validating they are still the bare minimum. When it comes to empowering a human being, social acceptance is felt when we know we are recognized, and recognition is only felt when we know we are understood. This is a tall order on an existential level, for how do we know if we're ever understood? And by proxy, how do we know if our integrated identity is ever accepted? We may reduce the need for acceptance and social approval by developing a defensive stance in public spaces. Some may state, "I don't need other people to understand me" or "I've gotten by on my own, I don't need anyone." When our personal needs are not met, we figure out how to survive without them. Yet a therapeutic safe space can provide an empowering opportunity to elevate our narrative and accept the emotional gravity of our experience. By actively listening, affirming our identity, and acknowledging points of privilege, power imbalance, and oppression where they exist, you can help strengthen our voice by underlining the personal value constructs present in our hopes, fears, agency, and conflict (Ali, 2014; Burdge, 2007; Reck, 2009; Reicherzer and Spillman, 2012; Singh, 2013; Singh and McKleroy, 2011; Ziegler and Rasul, 2014).

## *Ethnocultural gender legitimacy, mimicry, and otherness*

Most assumptions made about transgender and transsexual people stem from generalizations borne of white hegemony, rarely considering the perspective of trans Africans, trans Arabs, trans Asians, ad cultural infinitum (Halberstam, 2005; Hanssmann, Morrison, and Russian, 2008). This is very evident in the LGBTQ community when Western individualism—rebelliously chanting "We're here. We're queer. Get used to it!"—encounters Eastern collectivism, which deeply values family and integration. The Out and Proud model is specific to a cultural group, yet may not be efficacious for Asian, Filipino, Pacific Islanders, or even family oriented Hispanic cultures, and tribally oriented Native American cultures requiring a broader, family system approach to disclosure. The Out and Proud model also doesn't account for empowering gender via acts of modesty. This is most clear when people mistakenly assume hijabs are symbols of sexist oppression, minimizing the cultural and personal significance to the Muslim women wearing them. Furthermore, constructs of transgenderism are not uniform. Not only do masculine and feminine binaries differ and expand from culture to culture, so too do dimensions of *legitimacy*, *mimicry*, and *otherness*.

As culture shapes language, so too does language shape self-construct. Accordingly, the term *real* is emotionally charged for gender minorities as it questions our legitimacy (Nestle *et al.*, 2002). Sadly, this is exactly what some have to contend with as they navigate both their own ethnocultural community and oppressive cultures outside of it (Mallon, 2009; Nagoshi and Brzuzy, 2010; Reicherzer and Spillman, 2012; Zandvliet, 2000). As all people who exist are *real* and are therefore capable of *authenticity*, defined here as transparent self-congruence, such terms are reserved for personal self-acceptance as only the individual can discern whether or not they feel real or authentic within themselves.

*Legitimacy*, by contrast, refers specifically to when a person's gender is appraised and sanctioned within a culture. The etymology of legitimacy is fitting here, as historically it refers to the degree to which someone is recognized by law as belonging to a family. Some cultures make room for gender variance and so legitimize our existence; others simply do not, and only tolerate our presence like derelict children. Legitimacy also differs from validity and acceptance as both a trans woman and a drag queen have *valid* identities independent of what their communities think or believe, just as each is capable of being accepted.

Even socially liberal Western cultures, seeing a trans woman standing next to a drag queen, view one as a definitive woman and the other as an emulative one. A presumptuous frame in the back of the mind fuses to the idea that the first is somehow more legitimate than the second, even if both are accepted. In some Middle Eastern Islamic traditions, the *Mukhannath*—trans women—are separated into two types: one whose effeminacy is innate and therefore free of blame, and the other whose effeminacy is adopted for immoral purposes (Rowson, 1991). This odd dimension of *legitimacy* and *mimicry*, of definitive and emulative, appears in cultures throughout the world, yet it's not neatly divided. Zoom in on the American drag scene and we'll find, very quickly, that different ethnic cultures treat cross-dressing with different degrees of legitimacy and mimicry. Cross-dressing as a behavior can be a grand show on a glittering runway, like an act of make-believe, or a core part of our personal or spiritual identity—depending largely on the drag queen's ethnocultural perspective of gender (Taylor and Rupp,

2004). Depending on the tradition, gender mimicry can be a point of shame, honor, or both, since cultural attitudes are rarely uniform in any community.

We can have a valid and accepted identity as a gender mimic, even if neither we nor our culture legitimize us as a man or woman. American drag queens celebrate this fact by affronting cisgender norms wherever possible. Their stage personas are often foul-mouthed, competitive, temperamental extensions of masculinity dolled up in exaggerated femininity, more over-the-top than an operatic diva (Taylor and Rupp, 2004). Scoffing at the binary, they may discard any need for social legitimacy. Other cultures may, in turn, legitimize the act of mimicry itself. Examples of sanctioned gender play set within strict cultural parameters include the Japanese *Otoko-no ko* and the Kabuki *Onnagata* practice, and the female impersonators of China's Peking Opera. A community can accept these identities as valid, and even celebrate them, yet treat these same identities as fictional characters rather than extensions of the actors themselves. Off stage, those who are seen as *mimics* are highly susceptible to dehumanization and violence, especially when the dominant culture views them as frauds, tricksters, and charlatans (Bettcher, 2007; Schilt and Westbrook, 2009; Yep, 2003).

In some parts of the world, gender mimicry can be a form of social survival, at which point terms like transgender, transsexual, or transvestite do not accurately convey the impetus behind a person's cross-dressing behavior. The *Bacha Posh* in Afghanistan and the *Burrnesha* in Albania are both examples of biological females who adopt masculine identities in order to access education, work, and social empowerment (Becatoros, 2008; Qadiry, 2012). Yet it would also be inaccurate to describe these identities as just a "disguise," as their masculinity can integrate into their identity or, in some cases, was already present before they adopted the social role.

Culturally sanctioned legitimacy is an issue for every gender variant identity. Transgender people can find their perceived legitimacy is contextual, as different social and ethnic groups treat them differently. Patriarchal cultures emphasizing hypermasculinity, including some Latino and African American communities, may attempt to delegitimize trans women or male effeminacy, while trans men may be ignored as non-existent (Eligon, 2017; He, 2016). However, cultural perspectives on gender, and therefore a culture's relationship with gender variance, is highly complex, intersecting familial values with religious, socioeconomic, and sociopolitical identities. A massive international study ranking openness and acceptance of transgender people found that 74.7 percent of Argentinians, 72.6 percent of Mexicans, 71.6 percent of Indians, 70 percent of Peruvians, and 67.2 percent of Brazilians were in support of transsexual people being able to attain SRS (Flores, Brown, and Park, 2016b). Comparatively, of the 2115 murders of trans people recorded internationally between 2008 and 2016, 78 percent took place in Central and South America, with 257 in Mexico and 868 in Brazil alone

(He, 2016; TGEU, 2018). Sitting with the weight of this, any inference would be a surface scratch. What we do know is that, all over the world, cultural gender binaries generate great social influence, making conformity to gender roles a deep cause for celebration, and gender nonconformity a cause for condemnation.

To make the subject even more confusing, some cultures will "accept" trans people without viewing them as legitimate. Pathologizing *transsexualism* as a mental health disorder is a potential example of this, yet so too are cultures that "love the sinner but not the sin" or are prepared to accept their new daughter—if *and only if* they fully transition. This is where *otherness* plays a part, especially in nonbinary cultures, or cultures that contain gender-nonconformity. Otherness is the degree to which a person's gender can individuate from the majority rule while still retaining legitimacy. Even in Western drag culture, some cross-dress to be emulative of men or women, while some go to extravagant lengths to be something above and beyond—something *other*. When otherness is not legitimized within a culture, the gender is seen as performative—like an art form, a theater act, or a sexual fetish. When otherness is legitimized within a culture, space is made for gender diversity (Denticel and Dietert, 2015).

How strict is the binary, and does our ethnic culture permit genders outside of man and woman? For example, European cross-dressing behavior typically emulates the binary gender norms, whereas the *Hijra* in India are not particularly regarded as men or women (Bolich, 2007; Ettner, 1999; Reddy, 2005; Sell, 2001). In Tanzania and Kenya, the Swahili language doesn't indicate gender through pronouns, making the cross-dressing *Mashoga* a unique example of how homosexual identities and gender identities blend as they intersect social power dynamics (Murray and Roscoe, 1998). Identifying each other through feminine nicknames, the *Mashoga* blur what Americans would divide as gay, transgender, and even third gender (Murray and Roscoe, 1998). This intersection of sexual orientation and gender identity is also dynamic amongst the *Sistergirls* and *Brotherboys* of Australia, who live either partially or completely as the opposite sex (Smith *et al.*, 2014). The *Metis* in Nepal, *Acault* in Myanmar, *Fa'afafine* in Samoa, *Fakaleiti* in Tonga, and *Māhū* in Hawaii all reflect cultural legitimization of otherness (Bolich, 2007; Coleman, Colgan, and Gooren, 1992; Ettner, 1999). Uniquely, the Bugis people of Sulawesi, an island in Indonesia, identify five genders, including the *Oroané* (masculine males), *Makkunrai* (feminine females), *Calai* (masculine females), *Calabai* (feminine males), and the spiritual *Bissu* (all gender) (Bolich, 2007; Davies, 2007). These are not bygone cultures, to look back on with awe, but living identities currently discerning how to operate in, around, and outside of contemporary globalization (Towle and Morgan, 2006). To that end, cultural legitimacy isn't always synonymous with social legitimacy, as indigenous cultural identities are often lost in contemporary communities—

which is to say the cultural script exists but may be ignored or even disrespected by those estranged from their heritage.

With such a diverse array of cultural, multicultural, and multi-local identities, you can help affirm identity by decolonizing gender (Zandvliet, 2000). Actualizing gender identity doesn't mean forgoing ethnocultural identity, nor does it demand adherence to the gender norms broadcast by the dominant culture (Zandvliet, 2000). In session, help clients actively monitor internalized racism, ethnocentrism, cissexism, and any judgments stemming from a culturally oppressive hegemony. Help them listen for it in their own use of language, as beliefs are often tuned into judgments and rules broadcast by an imposing, if not totally oppressive, culture. ACT introduces intrusive thoughts as an annoying radio that's impossible to turn off, plays only bad news 24/7, and seems to get louder when we try to ignore it (Hayes and Smith, 2005; Harris, 2008). To adapt this metaphor to gender colonization, imagine being forced to listen to the worst music station ever. Try asking: What's your least favorite music genre? Maybe it's country, or opera, or mass-marketed pop music, or polka. What's the worst thing to listen to, and what would it be like if that's all the stereo would ever play? Although it's cathartic to shout at the speakers, and even make fun of how bad it is, someone else's song keeps playing in our head. Even if we hate it, we'll wind up singing along to the catchy earworm. Humming along with lyrics we find insipid, tapping our feet to boring rhythms, we can feel so immersed in this terrible music we may begin to forget that there was ever another song.

Acceptance isn't about conceding or submitting to transphobia, racism, or ethnocentrism, as each are worth challenging in all their forms; yet long after we put out a forest fire, the earth is still scorched. Long after the bigots are chased away, that incessant radio still plays on, drowning out the good music in the next room. Defusion and mindful expansion, in this case, help clients dance through a house filled with multiple radios, stereos, and sound systems, each playing a different song or music genre. We can't turn any of them off, but we can find our own rhythm, knowing that between songs we might still hear that old radio playing its terrible tune behind us. Knowing that we're not beholden to the broadcast, intrusive thoughts can become faded background noise, making it easier to invest in culturally reaffirming practices. That doesn't mean we won't encounter others blasting obnoxious music in our ears, but claiming personal agency in an oppressive world also means claiming personal agency in our mind.

There are so many narratives with deep cultural roots, including but not limited to: transsexualism as a transition to inclusion; transgenderism as a celebration of otherness; cultures of gender mimicry; cultures of gender subversion; and shamanistic cultures of gender transcendence. Racially and ethnically diverse clients may even clash with their own understanding of gender, as their cultural heritage encounters contemporary feminism and Western queer identity. Finding contemporary labels limiting, some may hold on to their heritage, or reconnect with their estranged roots, or integrate their ethnicity as part of a multifaceted whole, or seek to redefine how their ethnicity intersects with gender, or even step away from their cultural traditions if they don't reflect the transitional path they feel within themselves (Monro, 2007; Roen, 2010; Towle and Morgan, 2006).

### *Differently abled visibility*

Under-represented, trans people who are differently abled or neurodiverse rarely encounter communities or social opportunities that allow them to fully integrate their identity. There may be social events for people with autism, and transgender pride events, yet socially visible scenes, media, or representations for trans people with autism are few and far between (Ware and Marshall, 2014). This can lead to a kind of double invisibility, as if only a certain aspect of their identity can be recognized at any time (Abbott and Burns, 2007; Ballan, Romanelli, and Harper IV, 2011). This is especially true for individuals with invisible health differences, including Ehlers-Danlos syndrome, Crohns, multiple sclerosis, epilepsy, and narcolepsy to name a few. For individuals with intellectual differences like Down syndrome, Fragile X syndrome, and developmental delays, and for individuals with physical differences like cerebral palsy, muscular dystrophy, spina bifida, spinal cord injury, or dwarfism, their gender can often feel neglected by society. As archetypes of masculinity and femininity generate body stereotypes, the public eye glosses over bodies that exist outside of these stereotypes. Likewise, there's a pervasive myth that people who are differently abled are non-sexual, a concept which is not only false, but attempts to further nullify sexual and gender identity. The thought that a quadriplegic person is not only sexual, but a lesbian trans woman, would never cross the mind of someone who only sees their wheelchair.

*Ableism* is the systematic oppression and exclusion of people who are differently abled (Levi, 2006). Eugenics is the most nefarious example, yet ableism crops up quite insidiously in everyday situations by slapping on a label, undermining a person's self-determination, lowering expectations which in turn lower their expectations of self, or by attempting to "normalize" a person rather than working with their difference (Levi, 2006). An example of this latter point can include forcing oral language on a deaf child, believing it will help them more than learning American Sign Language (ASL). Similarly, trans people with sensory differences, including blindness and deafness, may find their liminality intensified through isolation and social negligence. *Audism*, for example, is the exclusion of the Deaf, intersecting both ableism and linguicism as they face prejudice around their difference as well as unique forms of prejudice around their language.

When working with trans people who are differently abled, validating their relationship with resilience, self-empowerment, and interdependence can help them affirm their unique personal and communal value (Ballan *et al.*, 2011). Using the internet to find people with similar life experiences, helping them build their community and even meet online friends in person, can both expand their social support network and deepen their relationships (Ballan *et al.*, 2011; Devor, 2004; Lev, 2007; Ware and Marshall, 2014). Outside of these online connections, encouraging clients to share stories in both social and professional settings creates opportunities to integrate their identity through personable connection and social recognition (Ballan *et al.*, 2011).

## *Spiritual rejection and incorporation*

Spirituality and the pursuit of higher meaning is an intimate journey, especially if our life experience challenges so many assumptions of the physical flesh and bone. What it means to be man or woman, or something more or something separate or something other, is an existential question tantamount to what it means to be human. Encountering the specter of gender dysphoria, some may pray for their transgender feelings to go away, and feel disheartened, disillusioned, or betrayed when they remain (Bockting *et al.*, 2006). In this same vein, gender transition makes one very aware of impermanence, severance, and change, bringing some to question the very nature of consciousness and soul. Even traumas and hardship bring one to ponder trust, faith, and forgiveness.

As an example, the 2015 US Transgender Survey found that 25 percent of Middle Eastern respondents, 18 percent of American Indian, 15 percent of Black, 12 percent of Latino, 12 percent of Asian (including Japanese, Chinese, and Korean) and 14 percent of multiracial respondents had run away from home. Of those who had been rejected by their spiritual community, many struggled to find a trans-positive church, temple, or synagogue (Whittle, Turner, and Al-Alami, 2007). American Indians (54%) were most likely to find a welcoming spiritual community, with Latinos (37%) and Asians (34%) struggling the most. This same survey found that 63 percent of gender variant respondents had a spiritual or religious identity, while 37 percent did not. In the breakdown, 21 percent followed Christianity, 22 percent identified as atheist, 23 percent pondered agnosticism, 9 percent practiced paganism, 6 percent meditated on Buddhism, 4 percent practiced Judaism, 4 percent asserted they were secular humanists, and 4 percent identified as Wiccan, while 1 percent identified as Druidic, Hindu, Muslim, Native American Traditionalists, Polytheists, and Taoist, respectively.

Despite the stigma found within many Abrahamic interpretations of faith, there are many spiritual practices that accept gender variant people, though we may have to search to find an open denomination or cobble together an eclectic practice of our own (Coleman, Colgan, and Gooren, 1992; Kidd and Witten, 2008; Porter, Ronneberg, and Witten, 2013; Smith and Horne, 2007; Witten and Eyler, 2012). Earth-based spirituality including shamanism, Wicca and Druidry, alongside contemporary Pagan eclecticism including the Radical Faeries, can also provide a spiritually holistic path for gender variant people (Sell, 2001; Smith and Horne, 2007; Witten, 2015). Many Earth-based spiritualities adhere to themes of interconnection and transformation, providing transgender representation in nature allegories, narrative myths, and a pantheon of deities.

Sadly, of 28,000 transgender people surveyed, 18 percent had been rejected from aspects of their spiritual community in the past year (James *et al.*, 2016). The percentage was higher for African Americans, 25 percent of whom had conflicts with their congregation, and skyrocketed to 40 percent for gender variant Asians (James *et al.*, 2016). Genderqueer, genderfluid, and agender identities also encounter conflict with, and even excommunication from, rigidly binary religions (Bockting *et al.*, 2006; Witten, 2015).

In particular, gender variant Christians attending conservative congregations may feel pressured to conceal their gender identity to avoid conflict and excommunication, or to safeguard their family's community standing (Green, 2012; Yarhouse and Carrs, 2012). Fortunately, various denominations belonging to the United Church of Christ, the United Methodist Church, the Church of England, the Episcopal Church, the North American Catholic Church, and the Lutheran Church have adopted nondiscrimination canons, opened their congregations, and in some cases even permitted trans people to be ordained. Likewise, non-denominational Jewish organizations, including the LGBTQ advocacy group Keshet, help schools to accommodate gender variant kids (Borschel-Dan, 2015). This echoes the sentiment of transgender inclusion upheld by resolutions published by the Reconstructionist Rabbinical Association (JTA, 2017), the Union for Reform Judaism (URJ, 2015), and the conservative Rabbinical Assembly (RA, 2016).

In Islamic circles, attitudes regarding gender variance differ greatly. In Malaysia, some Muslim trans women, the *Mak Nyahs*, will forgo SRS so they can transition back into a man before death just to receive their burial rights (Koon Teh, 2001; Witten, 2015). Perhaps, of all the bizarre advocates in history, the Ayatollah Khomeini issued a fatwa in the 1980s encouraging SRS for trans women after being beseeched by Maryam Hatoon Molkara, a trans-rights activist who had been forcibly institutionalized in the 1970s and injected with testosterone against her will (Tait, 2005). Since Molkara's efforts, Iran now provides financial assistance to those seeking transition, making Iran second only to Thailand in its number of annual SRS operations (Alipour, 2016; Barford, 2008).

Gender variance is historically recognized within Hindu and Buddhist culture, from the *Kathoey* in Thailand, to the *Acaults* in Myanmar, to the *Hijra* in India, though social inclusion is rare (Agoramoorthy and Hsu, 2014; Bolich, 2007; Coleman, Colgan, and Gooren, 1992; Monro, 2007; Reddy, 2005). In India, transgender people are restricted in their right to marry, adopt children, or even gain healthcare, with only 25 percent of transgender people having a national ID card (Agoramoorthy and Hsu, 2014; Brill and Kenney, 2016). Even so, Hinduism as a faith presents many gender expansive deities and ceremonies, including the blended unification of Shiva and Durga called Ardhanarisvara, and the goddess of cross-dressing Sri Bhagaveti-devi who is celebrated in her annual gender bending festival, Chamaya-vilakku (Agoramoorthy and Hsu, 2014; Witten, 2015). Buddhism also theologically accounts for gender variance, yet in some beliefs it's deemed a form of karmic debt to be pitied (Witten, 2015).

As secular Westerners cast skepticism on spiritual emergence, often narrowing their eyes at those who speak of visions, gender variant individuals are subjected to multiple tiers of doubt, as both their gender and their spirituality is scrutinized as evidence of mental illness (Lev, 2004). In one interview, discussing spirituality with 30 self-identified third gender individuals, 93 percent felt they'd had a deep, transcendent experience, even leading to paranormal abilities (Sell, 2001). This is only outlandish if one presumes all spiritual practice equates with mental illness. The ability to talk with god, sit with ancestors, commune with nature, heal through prayer, astral project, and receive visions through dreams are commonly practiced throughout the world. As we test the boundaries of gender, and therefore the mind–body relationship, it's only natural to explore the historic role of gender in shamanism and spiritual practice. In contemporary societies that do not value visible manifestations of liminality—of the threshold experience between and outside of man and woman, life and death, ground and sky—the natural perspective gained from being a gender variant person is deemed odd, oracular, or mad. It seems like more are concerned by Zeus' bleeding ax wound than by the newborn Athena who just stepped out of his skull.

Spirituality unpacks every dimension of self in relationship to life, family, community, nature, god, and the universe. Unfortunately, dogmatic scripts can also fuse shame with inarguable justifications, as there are plenty of doctrines to flagellate ourselves with. ACT works within our spiritual beliefs, while tactfully utilizing the values intrinsic therein to alleviate dissonance. As a clinician, build your theological competency and flex your philosophical agility. Debate, or even well-framed presentations of your spiritual perspective, isn't typically useful. Feeling imposed upon, we may just dig our heels in further, or simply quit the therapeutic relationship. Not only this, but many religions, including some chapters of Christianity, have a skeptical view of psychology, viewing therapy as a danger to faith (Ord, 2014; Soheilian and Inman, 2009). ACT can be presented as a spiritually safe modality as it does not interrogate faith, serving instead to explore our rule-governed behavior and the weight of self-critical judgment in our lives (Ord, 2014). Fortunately, many faiths still value the power of questions. After thousands of years, rabbis still pore over the Talmud, Christians still compare and contrast the Old Testament with the New, Buddhists still ponder Zen koans, and pagans still explore the intricacies of totemic worship. As Kenneth Pargament (2007) observed in his book *Spiritually Integrated Psychotherapy: Understanding and Addressing the Sacred*, this permits us to explore three dimensions of spirituality pertinent to our psychological health: *transcendence*, *boundlessness*, and *interconnectedness*.

In a spiritual context, transcendence is an expansion of self (Pargament, 2007). Gender variant people often turn to spirituality to rise above the sea of labels, boxes, binaries, and social categories, which is itself a process of defusion (Nieuwsma Walser, and Hayes, 2016). By developing a diverse range of meditative practices in touch with these traditional and spiritual perspectives, you can help strengthen and augment mindfulness with our pre-existing cultural practice (Witten, 2015). Observing how our present-based experience contains within it both past and future, just as *here* includes within it the idea of *there*, cultivates an expanded sense of boundlessness (Nieuwsma *et al.*, 2016; Pargament, 2007). Within this boundlessness we find interconnection, as "you" and "I" are relational to each other, a felt experience all the more powerful for those with similar histories of isolation, alienation, and community rejection (Nieuwsma *et al.*, 2016). We can demonstrate this by leaning in close to each other and seeing our reflection in each other's eyes.

ACT asks clinicians to be anthropological advocates, validating our cultural identity in all its dimensions. Inclusion can so easily mutate into assimilation, unless tactful care is taken to recognize and affirm intersectionality. After all, any town or city is a series of concentric circles, some visible, some invisible, looping and rotating through each other. The more preconceived notions of the world you challenge within yourself, the more interconnected these circles become, and the more invisible minorities come into view.

## The mindful clinician

To work effectively with such a diverse demographic means challenging every "common sense" idea regarding gender (Chavez-Korell and Johnson, 2010; Goethals and Schweibert, 2005). Biases accrue, big and small, in countless facets of our daily lives that we're not even aware of. Should we adhere to rigid hierarchies, we become preoccupied with essentialist taxonomies trying to discern what is or is not a "real" man or woman, and even what is or is not a "true" transsexual (Nestle *et al.*, 2002). This forced binary has led many gender variant people to feel pressured into seeking HRT or SRS, unnecessarily focusing on a post-op or pre-op status by conforming to a socially endorsed transsexual script (Nagoshi,

Brzuzy, and Terrell, 2012; Siebler, 2012). Even empathic clinicians trying to help a client accept their identity as a lesbian, or a trans man, or a gay man, or a trans woman, may inadvertently reinforce the gender binary or a rigid, narrow view presuming all gender variant people are the same (Benson, 2013; Mizock and Lundquist, 2016).

It is not a therapist's place to diagnose or label gender, or attempt to change our gender schema, or impose values on us. Doing so can be confusing if we're still figuring it out for ourselves. In this sense *what* and *who* we are must be figured out independently of the therapeutic practitioner. Psychoeducation is certainly beneficial, as is an introduction to gender variant community, role models, literature, and media. Talking about the depth of gender in a safe setting is also a great way to build comfort with what can be a highly uncomfortable topic, but you cannot determine our gender for us—even if that's what we're requesting you to do! Some clients may outright ask: "Do you think I'm ____?" If you get caught up in trying to answer—even for their benefit—then you're trying to fix what was never a problem and solve what was never a riddle. Furthermore, you may be neglecting the emotional fusion in the question, and the client's potential issues with indecision, self-admission, or the unknown.

Swinging the pendulum too far in the other direction, clinicians who claim to be "objective observers" or "detached mirrors" may fail to examine what intersex and gender variant narratives evoke within their own internal process, in turn neglecting how their privilege, bias, and emotional transference enters into the session (Lev, 2004; Quinodoz 1998; Williams, 2002). Likewise, therapists who feign to progressively "treat everyone the same regardless of gender" or "rule out" gender as an issue may be avoiding the subject due to their own lack of training in this area (Mizock and Lundquist, 2016). Too often, clinicians market themselves to gender minorities out of the genuine desire to help this population, but a college course in gender studies or multicultural counseling doesn't equate with competency (Benson, 2013; Bess and Staab, 2009). Even at the graduate level, where students might just cover the theoretical framework, few students come away with sufficient training to work with gender variant populations (Bess and Staab, 2009; Bidell, 2012; Chavez-Korrell and Lorah, 2007; Fassinger and Arseneau, 2007; Feinberg, 2001; Frank and Cannon, 2010; Gainor, 2000; Israel and Tarver II, 1997; Lev, 2004). Anyone can find a coffee shop, but finding a real barista is a different matter. Likewise, finding a queer-friendly practitioner isn't too difficult, but compassion and competency aren't synonyms. LGBTQ clients are recommended to shop around in order to find a therapist who actually knows more than the primary colors of the rainbow. After all, just because a therapist lists a demographic on their website as a population they work with, it doesn't mean they have the tools or experience to be effective.

Continuously monitoring for your own hang-ups and mental rigidity, the mindful therapist understands that competency is active, not static. As a gender specialist you must therefore take time to explore yourself and your own ongoing journey (Bess and Staab, 2009; Goethals and Schweibert, 2005; Nadal, Skolnik, and Wong, 2012). Do the work. *Your work*. Having read every queer book in the great rainbow library, accept that knowledge is outdated the moment it went into print. Every generation, in every corner of the world, personalizes their own understanding and expression of gender, just as you did. The question is, are you aware of your gender epoch? Developing competency in this area demands admitting your own bias, questioning your own schemas, catching your own blind spots, and even monitoring your own cisnormative language—even if you happen to be gender variant yourself (Benson, 2013; Bockting *et al*., 2006; Chavez-Korell and Lorah, 2007; Lev and Sennott, 2012; Livingstone, 2010).

Have you ever noticed your nonverbal cues in the presence of men or women? And are you aware of how they change in androgynous company? Or how they change around people who share your gender? Once more, if your first response is to say "I treat all my clients the same," then you may be tuning out your own intrinsic privilege. And if, through sheer diligence you *are* treating all clients the same, are you also tuning out individuality? Therapists who operate from a "one-size-fits-all" perspective are, in effect, minimizing the unique personal and social needs of gender variant clients.

There is no shame in acknowledging that we, as human beings, have a diverse array of responses to a diverse array of people. Inflections, intonations, and body language all modify in response to age, sex, and gender, making it a counselor's responsibility to be aware of yourself in your own body! Study the norms of cultural kinesics, the role of body posture and eye contact, and be mindful of your own communication patterns. Set yourself a few therapeutic challenges to practice privately in your day-to-day life.

- Do you feel differently when approaching men or women?
- Do you make more declarative statements around men or women?
- Count how many questions you ask men or women in a group.
- Do you express more doubt when men or women share a story?
- Do you feel more guarded around men or women?
- How do you posture yourself in the company of men or women, and does this change if you're around men *and* women?
- Do you knowingly or unknowingly adjust these behaviors around senior citizens?

- Do you notice your behaviors change around men or women of different race or ethnicity?
- Do your attitudes and behaviors change around boys and girls, and does your attitude change based on how they act or how they look?
- Monitor how often you do or do not play into presumed gender roles. When bringing food to a potluck, do you automatically hand it to the woman of the house? Do you hand meat to men, assuming they barbecue? How often do you ask women for directions? How often do you ask men to babysit?

As an exercise, try mapping your own gender schema by writing down the first adjectives and associations that come to mind (see Table 2.2). Be as honest as you can with yourself by penciling in your first response, even if you don't necessarily agree with it. We tend to have more than one mind about these matters.

**Table 2.2 Gender associations**

| | |
|---|---|
| Men | are |
| | have to |
| | do |
| | do not |
| | become |
| | create |
| | behave |
| Women | are |
| | have to |
| | do |
| | do not |
| | become |
| | create |
| | behave |

Some find mapping their gender schema quite surprising, even cringe-worthy, depending on their associations. Sweeping generalizations demonstrate bias, and few people—let alone clinicians—like to admit their prejudiced viewpoints. Relational frame theory demonstrates how no one is immune to bias as we operate from presupposition, inferring connections where there may be none, so let's be honest about that. Our use of language is categorical, yet presupposition is distinct from prejudice in that presupposition is flexible while prejudice is not. Presupposition can be challenged and adapted by gathering knowledge from our present-based awareness to provide us context, whereas prejudice is to literally prejudge—to project preformed ideas. So have a look at your binary schema for a second. Typically, ACT doesn't bother quantifying thoughts or feelings as measuring them is like taking a tape measure to a tiger—knowing it's 10 feet long neglects its teeth and claws, instincts, and primal needs. Yet let's do exactly that. Let's take a tape measure to a tiger and give each presupposition or prejudiced thought about gender a percentage for how much you believe that statement is true. Really sit with this. If you wrote "Men are *brave*," how central, how important, or how often do they have to be Herculean, in your opinion: 90 percent of the time? 60 percent of the time? If you wrote "Women create *life*," how central is it for a woman to embody the Gaia/Madonna archetype? It may seem odd to rank, as it is odd to take a tape measure to a tiger, but how important is it that a woman creates life? Is it 70 percent or 80 percent of her power or purpose, in your perspective? Should you resist generalization, answer solely for yourself. How definitive are these factors to you? Little details like this accrue, as they demonstrate deliberate mindfulness and action on your part, and how attentive to gender issues you are. Sensitize yourself as you navigate this binary of men and women, because we're about to go beyond it.

Create space from criticism or the desire to deny bias. All of us grew up with gendered generalizations, assumptions, and expectations further warped by outdated cultural stereotypes presented through television and media. To challenge your own bias, you must first own them. This is your own personal gender schema. If you do not like it, or feel trapped by it, then you may appreciate the steps taken to defuse from these persistent ideas. If you're aligned with your beliefs of gender, then know where you stand, yet do not impose your viewpoint on a client. In Jungian terms, this is the face of your anima and animus. It is not wrong or incorrect, but it only applies to one person in this world: you.

Now try filling in another set, but this time let's see how you conceptualize gender diversity (see Table 2.3).

**Table 2.3 Gender variant associations**

| | |
|---|---|
| Trans men | are |
| | have to |
| | do |
| | do not |
| | become |
| | create |
| | behave |
| Trans women | are |
| | have to |
| | do |
| | do not |
| | become |
| | create |
| | behave |
| Genderqueer people | are |
| | have to |
| | do |
| | do not |
| | become |
| | create |
| | behave |
| Agender people | are |
| | have to |
| | do |
| | do not |
| | become |
| | create |
| | behave |

| | | |
|---|---|---|
| Genderfluid people | are | |
| | have to | |
| | do | |
| | do not | |
| | become | |
| | create | |
| | behave | |
| Third gender people | are | |
| | have to | |
| | do | |
| | do not | |
| | become | |
| | create | |
| | behave | |

Since no group is so easily definable, anything you wrote is probably a generalization and therefore a stereotype, even if it's complimentary. No doubt there will be a lot of assumptions and myths to debunk and defuse from. If, however, describing gender variance was difficult, you may be faced with one of two potential learning curves. If you felt resistant to make generalizations at all—knowing ahead of time that they'd be an instant stereotype—good on you! Just keep in mind that playing the diplomat can be a way of avoiding the discomfort of personal growth by abstaining from controversy. Abstaining from generalization doesn't mean you're free of bias, it just means you may struggle to admit your bias, even to yourself. On the flip side, if you struggled to fill in the blanks because nothing came to mind, then you may need to explore gender dynamics outside of your own. Additionally, if you feel uncomfortable talking about sex or gender, then work with a gender specialist to come to terms with this before ever working with a gender variant client, as your discomfort will contribute to an oppressive therapeutic relationship (Lev and Sennott, 2012).

If this experience felt like an uncomfortable trap where you're damned if you do and damned if you don't, then you're getting a glimmer of what it's like to be a gender variant person sifting through our own social stereotypes and internalized assumptions. Kudos for examining your own bias. Fortunately, presupposition can change through experience, education, and mindfulness. This can be a humbling journey, but know that even educated and experienced clinicians may still be influenced by hierarchical thinking. We all take categorical shortcuts, leading us to fall back into subtle gender norms or commonly held queer narratives. Be patient and forgiving of yourself, and role model this for clients. Questioning every assumption you ever made about masculinity, femininity, and the nature of androgyny is not easy. Nor is understanding the full extent of how your cultural identity, your privilege, your gender expression, and even the salience of your identity formed who you are (Chavez-Korell and Johnson, 2010). Competency is not a diploma or a finish line, but an ongoing process marking one milestone after the next.

If you're not familiar with gender variant history, take a deep dive. A queer knowledge base is invaluable, as it can help frame our ongoing obstacles while also spotlighting potential role models (Carroll *et al.*, 2002; Singh and Burnes, 2010). Listen to Laura Jane Grace wail in her punk band Against Me, or Lucas Silvera of The Cliks, or trans soul singer Shia Diamond, or listen to the gentle warble of Anohni, formerly of Antony and the Johnsons. Rewind the tape and watch Parinya "Nong Toom" Charoenphol become Thailand's champion *Kathoey* (third gender) kickboxer (Westbrook, 2016). Read Christine Jorgensen's autobiography and learn how her publicized SRS gave hope to so many, including the future showgirl Coccinelle (Jorgensen, 1968; Meyerowitz, 2002). Listen to Billy Tipton dance his fingers across the piano, or Willmer "Little Ax" Broadnax belt gospel. Imagine Roberta Cowell rocketing from race car driver, to WWII fighter pilot, to Britain's first trans woman to have a sex change. Marvel at Gerd Gottlieb's Art Deco portrait of her husband—né wife—Lili Elbe. Picture Jack Bee Garland serving in the US military in the Pacific, only to be found out, booted off the boat, smuggled back in by his fellow soldiers, and allowed to work as an interpreter in the Philippines (Meyerowitz, 2002; Sullivan, 1990). Read about We'wha of the Zuni people, who was quite possibly the first *Lhamana* (two-spirit) person to shake hands with a US president, Grover Cleveland, in 1886 (Roscoe, 1991). Then read the first written cross-dressing testimonial in Europe, when François Timoléon, abbé de Choisy attended the Papal inaugural ball in 1676 as a woman, having spent much of his childhood dressed as a girl (Scott, 1973). Do we have to be a queer encyclopedia? No, but as gender variant people have always existed, there's a whole history to catch up on, including some very dark times that could impact your sessions in a very real way.

Contemporary clinicians have taken strides to normalize therapy as a holistic health process, yet the mental health field remains in the shadow of a very grim history associating gender variance with psychological disorder. Sadly, we weren't respected within our own developmental parameters, but as deviations from cisgender development—neurotic detours needing to be put back on track. Only a few short decades ago electroshock and lobotomization were implemented as conversion therapy for LGBTQ individuals (Meyerowitz, 2002). Since then, these treatments have been rebuked, refuted, rebuffed, and rejected by the American

Counseling Association (ACA), the American Psychiatric Association (APA), the American Medical Association (AMA), the American Academy of Pediatrics (AAP), and—it goes without saying—the Association for Lesbian, Gay, Bisexual and Transgender Issues in Counseling (ALGBTIC) (Gorenberg, 2011; Mallory, Brown, and Conron, 2018).

The Williams Institute estimates that 20,000 LGBTQ teens in the USA, age 13 to 17, have received conversion therapy from licensed practitioners in states which have not yet banned this practice, while 57,000 teens have received similar treatments from religious organizations (Mallory *et al.*, 2018). The Trevor Project's 2019 National Survey on LGBTQ Youth Mental Health found that, of 25,896 respondents, two out of three young people had someone in their life try to talk them out of their sexual or gender identity, and that kids who had been subjected to conversion therapy were twice as likely to attempt suicide. Specifically, 57 percent of gender variant kids subjected to conversion therapy had attempted suicide in the last year, alone (The Trevor Project, 2019). And that's only the kids in the USA. Take this alongside how rapidly the mental health field has evolved in recent years, and it's easy to empathize with those who still feel unclear about what contemporary treatment for gender-related issues even entails.

Uncertain, with shifty eyes and nervous body language, we may sit on the couch assessing you as much as you're assessing us. Know that poor interactions with cisgender therapists, operating from a stance of privilege and bias, have proved to be so detrimental that we may not seek out therapy when we need it most (Bess and Staab, 2009; Bockting *et al.*, 2004, 2006; Carroll *et al.*, 2002; Maguen *et al.*, 2005; Poteat, German, and Kerrigan, 2013; Shipherd, Green, and Abramovitz, 2010). Sincerely safe spaces to express and emote, stewarded by a person who truly understands what we're going through, are a rarity for our 0.6 percent minority. This is especially true for those in the early stages of gender identity actualization, and those who feel they have to front a "put-together" persona so as not to be read as "unstable."

To make things worse, misdiagnosis is disturbingly common for many trans clients prior to coming out (Glavinic, 2010; Lev, 2004). Unable to voice our gender even to our therapists, we may be inaccurately tagged with bipolar disorder, attention deficit hyperactivity disorder (ADHD), and even schizophrenia (Glavinic, 2010). Subjected to medications and treatments that eventually failed because they didn't address the unspoken or underlying issue, we may re-enter therapy years later with a very critical view of both therapists and the therapeutic experience (Poteat *et al.*, 2013).

Unlike transphobia, which is blatantly easy to spot, noticing cisgenderism takes keen self-awareness. Clinicians commonly overemphasize or underestimate the role of gender when working with gender variant clients (Mizock and Lundquist, 2016). This same phenomenon pops up with overly excitable allies who, in their desire to be the super-advocate, inadvertently tokenize their minority friends by reducing us to a single-topic issue. Even well-intentioned therapists can be limited by their lack of exposure, making them oblivious of the power dynamic occurring in session.

When surveyed, gender variant individuals often have a positive attitude toward therapy, seeking out therapists for personal growth reasons entirely independent of gender (ALGBTIC, 2009; Benson, 2013; Rachlin, 2002; Sheerin, 2009). Aware that competence is a scarcity, we may anticipate that health providers simply won't meet our gender-related needs, so even if we like you we may hold back, or turn to a gender specialist as needed (Benson, 2013; Chavez-Korell and Lorah, 2007; Lev, 2004; Poteat *et al.*, 2013; Rachlin, 2002; Raj, 2002; Sheerin, 2009; Shipherd *et al.*, 2010).When specialists are unavailable, we may sigh a heavy sigh, as now we may feel like we have to educate the so-called professional (Mizock and Lundquist, 2016; Sheerin, 2009). This is exceptionally true for nonbinary and gender nonconforming individuals, as counselors are rarely equipped to work with genderqueer, genderfluid, agender, or third gender people whose therapeutic needs differ from trans people in transition on several fronts. As these clients are probably not pursuing transition or passability, therapy often includes coping with marginalization, discrimination, feelings of erasure, nonentity, and invisibility, resulting in compassion fatigue from having to negotiate their existence with the world (Denticel and Dietert, 2015; Mallon, 2009; Miller and Grollman, 2015; Nodin *et al.*, 2015; Richards *et al.*, 2016; Riley *et al.*, 2011; Witten, 2015).

Ideally, gender variant clients would do well to find a gender variant therapist, but as transgender and nonbinary clinicians are so few in number and so high in demand, cisgender clinicians will need to develop very tactful ways of illustrating their understanding. This is a unique challenge, emphasizing the need to familiarize yourself with the themes, customs, and concepts that your clients operate within. Understanding and authenticity are essential.

Be hopeful. If we walk into your office of our own volition, then we're actively pursuing therapy, even if we don't initially trust your competency—or even the therapeutic process! Do not, however, overestimate yourself. If you have not worked with gender variant clients, address this during the informed consent overview in your first session. It may be a complete non-issue for some clients still willing to proceed, but others may need more gender competent care. Refer as needed, seek consultation often, and continue developing your skillset (ALGBTIC, 2009). That means consuming literature critically, though you're going to need more than your textbooks! Become active in your community. Go volunteer with LGBTQ organizations. Find an LGBTQ mentor. Talk long into the night. Be a part of a living history. Doing so will not only increase your exposure, and therefore understanding of the population, it will also let you be known. Word-of-mouth is how many clients find a gender affirmative therapist (Benson, 2013; Bess and Staab, 2009).

### *Safe space, building rapport, and introducing ACT*

Look around your office. It's a room like any other, but does anything let prospective clients know we're in a truly safe space? Are there any books on the shelf relating to queer theory or gender identity? Are there any transgender brochures available? Any inclusive posters or safe space stickers? If you're a sand-tray therapist, does your collection of toys include androgynous archetypes as well as anima and animus figures? If you're a play therapist, is your collection of dolls and puppets all binary boys and girls or is there wiggle room?

Scan through your intake paperwork. Is it gender inclusive or gender absent? Having no gender-related content is not inclusive, after all, it's just omission. Your paperwork asks for a name, but are you asking for our legal name for insurance reasons or our preferred name? And is there room for both or are you making us choose? Do you ask us to check a box for male or female and did you intend to inquire about our anatomic sex? If you have gender boxes, are there more than two, or is it just *man*, *woman*, and *other*? Does your paperwork cover preferred pronouns? Do you have an anti-discrimination statement committed to affirming gender, or is it just an open-ended statement for the whole LGBTQ community, with the T and the Q tacked on as an afterthought? Little details like this accrue, as they demonstrate deliberate mindfulness and action on your part (Ali, 2014; Benson, 2013; Bockting *et al.*, 2006; Goethals and Schweibert, 2005; Mizock and Lewis, 2008; Singh and McKleroy, 2011).

Emphasizing confidentiality as sacred during the informed consent process is not only the first step to building rapport, but the first step to helping us feel genuinely safe. Know that the questioning and closeted may not come out right away, using the first sessions to assess your competency, credibility, and emotional understanding. Should we reveal, during the first session or later on down the road, that we're seeking an assessment for HRT or gender alignment surgery, then patiently walk through the protocol to clear up any misconceptions (ALGBTIC, 2009; Bockting *et al.*, 2004, 2006; WPATH, 2011). Make it clear that any evaluations for HRT or gender alignment surgery are not based on our passability or conformity to a gender role, image, or stereotype, but on our ability to actualize our authentic gender identity, our emotional resilience, and psychosocial adjustment (Bockting *et al.*, 2004; Lev, 2004; WPATH, 2011; Zandvliet, 2000).

When encountering *all* new clients, gender neutral pronouns (they/them/theirs) are encouraged if we have yet to identify our gender directly (Mizock and Lewis, 2008). And while you're at it, you may want to hang up cordial terms like

"Sir," "Mr.," "Miss" and "Ma'am," until you know what gender you're validating, or feel free to throw them out, altogether (Burdge, 2007; Nagoshi and Brzuzy, 2010). Someone may outwardly appear cisgender, yet visual cues are a poor measure of identity. A client may walk into your office with physically male phenotypes and expressively masculine clothes, knowing all too well they're a woman on the inside. Another client may regale you with a story about how they were born female and have been taking testosterone for years. Another seemingly male client may identify as genderqueer, regardless of their fashion. Another may walk into your office, revealing they're an MtF transsexual "dressing down" in stereotypically masculine clothes so as not to be harassed. Another client may walk into your office as a man in one session and walk in as a woman the next.

All these clients may be mislabeled "cisgender" when their external expression is viewed through a cisnormative lens. If you refer to them with male pronouns (he/him/his), the process or disclosure is further exacerbated by the process of contradiction. In other words, they not only have to come out, they have to correct your assumptions about them. Confident or well-guarded clients may think nothing of this, having corrected multiple people in any given week. Yet others may feel awkward, desiring to establish pronouns while being too shy to request them, or else feel nervous about correcting people in positions of power—including therapists, teachers, and social workers.

In conversation, gender neutral pronouns act as a place-holder until we disclose our preference. It is often quite acceptable to ask us our pronouns, but the phraseology necessitates tact. *What are your pronouns?* or *What pronouns do you go by?* summon a quick, factual response. Whereas *Do you go by male or female pronouns?* assumes a binary, which not everyone fits into.

Gender neutral pronouns are also useful when first exploring our relationship status. Asking a boy if they have a girlfriend, or a girl if they have a boyfriend, presumes they're heterosexual. Asking *Do you have a boyfriend or a girlfriend?* once again presumes we're limited to a binary, but also implies we're limited to monogamy. We may have genderqueer, genderfluid or agender partners, and some of us may have more than one. For most cisgender heterosexuals, this seemingly innocuous question takes no effort to answer, but if we have a gender dynamic relationship we may or may not feel ready to out ourselves or our partner. Additionally, asking genderqueer, genderfluid, or agender people *Do you have a boyfriend or girlfriend?* can force honest yet ambiguous answers:

*"Sometimes."*

*"My girlfriend is my boyfriend."*

*"I have a partner."*

*"I am in a relationship."*

*"We're queer."*

Those in gender dynamic relationships receive a lot of quizzical looks and raised eyebrows when we're honest. Some people glaze over our response, or blink, or cringe, or become so fascinated by our relationships that they bombard us with a queer quiz:

"How does that work?"
"Who's the husband/wife?"
"Who's the top/bottom?"
"How do you even have sex?"
"How do you manage?"
"Isn't it weird/stressful?"

A conscientious use of language not only circumvents all this by keeping all possibilities open, it can also validate our identity and relationship dynamic before it's even stated (Benson, 2013; Chavez-Korell and Lorah, 2007; Livingstone, 2010). *Are you seeing anyone?* and *What's intimacy like in your life?* are broad, open-ended explorations allowing us to fill in the blanks as we feel comfortable. Those who do not use gender neutral language may not even realize it's being implemented in session; others may be very appreciative. In any case, building rapport requires being conscious of both your overt statements and covert inferences. When both are encoded with acceptance, patience, and safety, you demonstrate that you genuinely care.

To validate our right to express ourselves, our personal agency, and to balance the power differential, the first sessions may resemble a more client-centered approach. Cultivating rapport through unconditional positive regard creates a judgment-free safe zone for us to proceed at a comfortable pace of self-disclosure (Lev, 2004; Livingstone, 2008, 2010; Reicherzer, Patton and Glowiak, 2011; Riley *et al.*, 2011). Likewise, taking extra time in the initial sessions—even running out the clock at the end of the day—will help us feel a genuine acceptance and personal investment (Mizock and Lewis, 2008). While there's certainly an art to balancing professional role and personal disclosure, open authenticity on the clinician's part can help a prospective client understand your therapeutic approach, level of open-mindedness, familiarity with LGBTQ issues, and most importantly your ability to connect in a meaningful way. After wading through well-intentioned but naive allies, after feeling alone in a crowded room, we're often searching for someone who not only sees us for our whole self, but someone who can also aid our growth through mutual empathy and a felt emotional connection (Miller, 1986; Jordan, 1991).

Having held back for years, we may have never felt it appropriate or even possible to share the full extent of our life experience with anyone. Even if we've had support, we may have omitted the personal highs and lows if we felt our allies couldn't relate. This message of self-censorship often stems from the assumption that others won't understand us, or from stunted experiences when our vulnerability felt invalidated (Poteat *et al.*, 2013). Even if we're bold and outspoken, we may have private, compartmentalized topics we deem too nuanced or too fragile to share aloud. Such topics may include our views on gender, but extend far beyond to include relational frameworks, irrational fears, unspoken aspirations, and unprocessed life experiences.

Clients want to be able to jump in knowing that our gender is already validated without having to educate our therapist (Benson, 2013). That said, if you do genuinely need to look something up, clients can find it refreshing when you educate yourself without burdening us to explain (Ali, 2014; Benson, 2013; Goethals and Schweibert, 2005). Read that book title or check out that online resource we mentioned. Watch that movie we related to, check out a queer news source, and spend as much time familiarizing yourself with the new colloquialisms as you do the empirical research. It's all meaningful.

You will flub. Rapport will be strained. Even therapists who have worked in the field for years will accidentally mess up a pronoun (Lev and Sennott, 2012). It happens! Especially if you've worked with a client pre-transition and have habituated yourself through repetition to use an old name, or when a client has yet to come out and is therefore operating both public and private names and pronouns (Bockting *et al.*, 2004; Richmond, Burnes and Carroll, 2012). You're human. You will make mistakes. Just be conscious that this error, when deliberate or perceived as deliberate, can be tantamount to abuse, especially from a trusted authority figure (Ansara, 2010, 2015). Clients rarely bring up these issues, downplaying the importance of pronoun use as a social survival tactic, so don't assume that you're in the clear just because we never corrected you (Ansara, 2010). For some clients it may be a small mistake easily forgiven with a shrug of the shoulders, but others may feel deeply wounded. You can help us express our feelings of betrayal with pronoun misuse in the therapeutic relationship by destigmatizing the conversation, role modeling relational honesty, and repairing trust (Lev and Sennott, 2012). A large part of this is addressing the mistake without stealing too much attention to yourself, as it's not about you or how "good" you are most of the time. Don't start in just because you're aware of your own mistake, as calling out how you're actively challenging your own privilege can actually come across as disconcerting, making any apology awkward. Always ask yourself: *Am I apologizing for my benefit or theirs*? Sincerity is essential, yet sincerity must also be coupled with conscientiousness.

Whatever you do, do not turn your mistake back on us! Too many clinicians have tried to account for pronoun flubs by saying they only got a pronoun wrong because we "don't feel" like a man or woman, or because we "don't have the mannerisms," or even because they doubted the depth or seriousness of our gender identity (Ansara, 2010). You made a mistake, so own it. It's a quick correction, and you've probably had years of practice already! Remember when that person in the park corrected you on the sex of their dog? You didn't argue. You just switched pronouns in two seconds flat. Easy-peasy.

If you use the wrong pronoun, there are two dynamics to think through. The first is the need for sincerity, since a sincere apology can bridge moments of broken rapport. If we have never experienced someone genuinely apologizing for gender neglect, having a therapist request forgiveness can demonstrate a rare level of compassion. Or not. The second thing to consider is the emotional exhaustion of over-apology. Some of us may be bombarded by apologies all day long from kind yet oblivious people, making you just one more flubber in a long line of flubbers, bunglers, and botchers. Even little *I'm sorry* statements intentionally or unintentionally seek pardon from us. Imagine how many times people have accidentally trodden on our identity and asked for clemency. If you can see how exhausting it is to continuously pardon other people's gender gaffes and social faux pas, then you can see how necessary these subtle adjustments in language are.

Rather than apologize, adjust. Self-correction demonstrates that you're not perfect but capable of amending your practice without expending our valuable energy.

*You were talking about your partner. She—I mean he—said he's moving soon, right?*

Sure, we may roll our eyes at you, but provided you caught yourself, and bring your attention back to our emotional process rather than your own, we'll most likely give you a pass. Unless, of course, you keep making the same mistake. At which point, seek consultation with a trained gender specialist, as self-awareness is a prerequisite for building a strong therapeutic relationship with gender variant clients (Lev and Sennott, 2012). You may have a block in your own schema or be projecting something irrelevant onto our process. But consultation comes later. You're still in session and we're uncomfortable because you messed up again. If you're tactful, it's possible to use this error, at least the first time, to address our relationship with our feelings while simultaneously role modeling emotional language.

*Right now, I'm really aware that I got your pronoun wrong three times today. I feel embarrassed and apologetic because I really respect you. I'm also curious how you feel when people get your pronouns wrong like that?*

Conversations of this kind call for great care and are only worth engaging if it's apparent we need to address it. Rolling our eyes, looking down or away, crossing our legs, squaring our jaw, clenching our fists, giving an exacerbated sigh, or even shrinking back into a flat affect, may signal a need to address the interaction, or signal our desire to drop it! Presume nothing and ask directly, acknowledging that doing so will certainly involve leaning into the discomfort. If the invitation to explore this area is not accepted, do not push the issue.

As time goes on, it's okay to return to pronouns as a topic, especially if we're still experimenting with our identity. Our confidence may have shifted with our identifiers. Because re-asking us about our pronouns can give us pause—it's often best to follow our lead with explorative, affirmative, non-threatening questions.

*You mentioned using gender plural pronouns for the past six months, how's that been going for you?*

*I noticed you smiled when you started talking about your boss finally using male pronouns. Would you like to talk about that?*

In any therapeutic relationship there's a dance between how much a client will explore and is desiring to explore. This dissonance between what is discussed and what is desired to be discussed may represent a negative belief construct we have fused with. It will take time for us to discern what we're willing to address, providing plenty of opportunity to build rapport and practice mindful contact with our senses.

If we adamantly know our gender identity or sexual orientation, then we have already established our conceptual self. Because both gender identity and sexual orientation can change over the lifespan, validate, and affirm our self-awareness, not just our gender.

*You really know yourself.*

*I admire your self-awareness.*

*A lot of clients I know fight with this, but you have it down.*

Questioned, belittled, and undermined by the intolerant, we may enter therapy questioning, belittling, and undermining ourselves. This does not, however, imply our gender identity is unstable. Hostile experiences may have left us feeling raw and defensive. Be careful, therefore, of the word *seem*. While *You really know yourself* is an affirmation, *You seem to really know yourself* is a doubt in disguise.

ACT often uses metaphor to exemplify themes and concepts we may be struggling with, and to also provide the felt understanding we're searching for. The power of a metaphor relies on its ability to accurately capture our experience, as a well-crafted metaphor can contain within it both an explicit and implicit level of understanding. No matter how wild, or bizarre, volatile, or extreme a person's experience may be, it is still possible to connect with, relate to, and understand the fundamental emotions therein. Some of the classic ACT metaphors, including *the passengers on a bus,* can help demonstrate your comprehension of intrusive thoughts (Hayes *et al.*, 2012). Imagine driving a bus full of people—each one a thought, idea, expectation, daydream, or memory. They're all here, the babe of beautyism, the biker of anxiety, the grandmother of guilt, the teenager of depression, even the bigot of internalized transphobia. They can't cross the yellow line on the floor separating the passengers from the driver, so they're stuck in the back, unable to interrupt our driving. They can get loud sometimes, and they can be really convincing, but you're the driver behind the wheel. If we listen to them, we might stop the bus and not go anywhere, or drive off a cliff, or drive in circles, or drive without ever getting gas. Fortunately, they're not in charge, and despite their complaints, threats, groans, and seductive whispers, they never will be. The problem is, if we try to ignore them by closing our eyes, we'll crash the bus. If we spend all our energy trying to argue with them, we'll get exhausted and fall asleep while driving. So, what can we do? Our task is to acknowledge they're in the back while simultaneously keeping our eyes on the road, expanding our attention as needed.

ACT is often the refuge for clients who have already tried structured therapeutic modalities, but didn't find the control strategies—like thought-stopping in rational emotive behavior therapy (REBT), positive thinking in CBT, or distraction in dialectical behavior therapy (DBT)—to be particularly beneficial (Harris, 2008). ACT doesn't try to stop, redirect, or distract us from our thoughts. Instead, ACT expands awareness to allow for mental flexibility, emotional acceptance, and personal agency even when our thoughts or feelings are difficult (Hayes, 2004). Early sessions will contain a lot of permission-giving by simply holding space for us to express and emote as needed. Track cognitive–emotional fusion, control strategies, and areas of personal avoidance we may struggle with, and jot them down.

ACT differs from the client-centered approach in that it is far more psychoeducational and instructional in later sessions. However, if we haven't established trust in your therapeutic knowledge base, there is no moving forward. Attempts to present ACT techniques, even seemingly gentle mindfulness activities, might be met with resistance if we believe you don't understand us or our circumstances. We might concede that these techniques work well for other people, but we're the exception. And you know what? We might be right. If your first thought is to provide a body-dysmorphic client with a mind–body breathing exercise, that client might just shut down. If you champion value-congruent behavior but fail to take into account the social or even physical risks of doing so, you might set a client up to be a target. If a client comes out to you and, as a helpful advocate, you begin offering transition options right off the bat, then you might be reducing them to a single issue. Slow down. Listen. Reflect what you hear. Let us truly know we're both heard and understood. Any struggle we may be going through is worth validating, as is the sex or gender identity we present (Raj, 2002; Reicherzer *et al.*, 2011). It's not your task to cross-examine us.

As sessions progress, you can become more directive, yet it's important to hold space. One of the most subtle and subversive ways cisgender bias can impact therapy is through haste and over-direction. Yes, ACT is psychoeducational, introducing terms like *fusion* and *defusion* while teaching clients mindfulness exercises and helping us to expand our emotional vocabulary, but don't leap in trying to be another expert in our lives! Enough people have probably told us what to do, what to be, what to wear, how to act, and what to hide. We may even push back against mindfulness activities, thinking you don't know how hard it is to let the proverbial leaf float away on the stream. Be tactful. Slow down. Build rapport.

As gender variant communities tend to be both small and sparse, the gender affirmative approach encourages interactions outside of the session (Singh and McKleroy, 2011; Smith *et al.*, 2012). Conserving a healthy professional boundary is ethically evident in any therapeutic practice, yet we need to know you won't turn your back on us in public and that you're open to relating to us outside the confines of the office (Livingstone, 2008). Some professionals hold strict boundaries with their clientele, turning encounters outside of the office into a friendly *Hello, and I'll see you later!* If you've ever been on the receiving end of this, you may have noticed how detached professionalism can read as emotional distance—because it is. The clinician is taking emotional space from the client, which is both fair and healthy, but don't ghost us! If we struggle with isolation and alienation, we may interpret this as evidence of insincerity.

As a therapist beginning to invest in your local LGBTQ community, you may need to get used to orbiting in the same social scene as your clients. Chances are you will not only move in the same circles, but also have some of the same social connections. This is exceptionally true in rural areas with very small LGBTQ communities. Rather than shy away from this, engage us should we engage you. Put the ball in our court. Obviously, confidentiality is sacred, and everything shared in session stays in session, but interactions outside of the office invest in both rapport and understanding.

Be conscious of how "out" we are, and your own reputation too. Some clients may not want to associate with you in public if people know you're the counselor with the rainbow flag. Likewise, when interacting with clients outside of the office it is imperative to be aware of which pronouns to use when encountering third parties, as we may not have disclosed our gender to others (Bockting *et al.*, 2004; Feinberg, 2001; Richmond *et al.*, 2012). Back in session, you can help discreet clients by exploring online resources, reading material, and how to connect with the LGBTQ community (Lev, 2009).

As is already evident, working with gender variant populations is all relative. Herein lies the benefit of ACT, which asks us to mindfully expand awareness to observe our internal process, and practice mental flexibility with value-congruent action (Hayes, 2004; Hayes and Smith, 2005). Defusing from hard rules, strict categories and, in the case of clinicians, overly formulaic treatment plans, allows us to be truly present with each other, and therefore attentive to the emotional process. In the end, however, it is the relational action of transparency, demonstrated by gender affirmative curiosity, that demonstrates you're not beholden to a preformed script, and that you're truly interested in our personal life experience (Lev and Sennott, 2012; Malpas, 2006).

# 3

# Awareness

If you've ever been to a pride parade—waving rainbow flags and riding fabulous floats—you may have encountered opposition. Amidst all the smiles and social support, there's usually one gruff person with a megaphone blasting their dogmatic view that we're all going to hell. We can argue with them, but our chances of changing their mind are about as thin as their chances of shouting the gay away. They're critical, cynical, pessimistic, and rude. They also thrive on attention, and the more we give them, the closer we are to their booming megaphone. Yes, we can engage them—sacrificing time and energy so they don't hassle anyone else—but if we argue for too long, we'll end up missing the whole parade. So, we decide to walk away, but that's a loud megaphone and they keep following the parade, so we really can't ignore them. When we try, we just get more upset when they shout their rhetoric over the crowd. A deep, vigilant part of us can't help but keep an eye on this potential danger. Shaking our head, we start to believe the whole parade is ruined because of one loud voice—until a friend makes a joke, and a cute fairy in rainbow wings glides by, and glitter rains down like confetti. Then something quite natural happens. Even though we're aware of the protestor, and can hear them from time to time, we expand our awareness to observe the whole parade. We see everyone, and we hear everything, including the dissenter tagging along behind. We feel the solidarity and the comfort, *because* we also feel the doubt, and we may even laugh as the Sisters of Perpetual Indulgence engage the megaphone, or brandish megaphones of their own.

Like our parade protestor, doubts and fears creep into our mind, citing dogmatic rules, reasons, judgments, and role expectations. Intrusive thoughts leap out at every cynical opportunity. Fears, worries, oppression, internalized sexism, cissexism, homophobia, transphobia, and racism all linger, loiter, and invade our consciousness. It is no mystery why so many try so hard to avoid thinking about them, yet the more we try to put them out of our mind, the more prevalent they become, a tedious experience called *ironic process* (Wegner, 1994). Ruminating on gender as it relates to our conceptual self, ruminating on our angst, obstacles, worries, and traumas, we may try and suppress our thoughts, feelings, and even our memories, only to have them backfire (Strosahl and Robinson, 2017). Indeed, the more we try to suppress negative thoughts, feelings, and memories, the more likely we are to recall them, which is why the anxious, depressed, and traumatized are so quick to recall terrible life experiences and hold a negatively biased slant (Dagleish and Yiend, 2006; Strosahl and Robinson, 2017). However, because the boomerang only comes back after suppression's short-term utility—meaning we think it worked because throwing the boomerang got it away from us—we continue our avoidance patterns, thinking we just have to throw it harder next time it comes around (Gold and Wegner, 1995; Gross, 2002; Hayes, *et al.*, 2012; Orsillo et al., 2004). For gender variant people—especially those just coming to terms with gender or those struggling with self-worth—just the prospect of introspection may feel daunting. Right away, we find an impasse to mindfulness, as the mind feels so full.

Resistance is not always intentional. Doubt is often reactionary. Fear is impulsive. Cynicism strikes like lightning. Memories can feel blocked. Indeed, those with a history of depression or trauma often report feeling like their brain is sluggish and their memories are elusive. This may be due, in part, to how thought suppression consumes our cognitive resources, impairing our working and autobiographical memory during these attempted periods of emotional regulation (Dagleish and Yiend, 2006; Gross, 2002; Luoma and Villatte, 2012; Morin and Hamper, 2012). Additionally, many LGBTQ advocates may resist therapeutic techniques, having fought so hard for so long that they believe even therapy must be a kind of battle against their inner demons—and at times it can certainly feel like it! Skeptical fisticuffs of this kind cannot be disarmed through discussion, yet steady rapport building can build enough trust to introduce nonthreatening mindfulness experiences, progressively defusing from fight or flight cognitions. Many cognitive behavioral approaches attempt to alter attention by homing in on a specific response to a specific stimulus, by noticing and then attempting to attenuate anxiety, or anger, or so forth (Orsillo *et al.*, 2004). ACT goes the other way, by broadening attentional focus to observe a transcendent sense of self larger than any transient, momentary experience (Hayes, 2004; Hayes and Smith, 2005; Orsillo *et al.*, 2004).

Instead of eradicating or even distracting ourselves from these arduous mental megaphones shouting at our personal parade, ACT makes room for them while increasing contact with our entire self-as-context. Taking in the larger experience, we can recognize how we're not limited to any singular internal or external stimulus. This means learning how to expand our internal awareness to observe our thoughts and make contact with our feelings (Harris, 2008). Increasing our metacognitive awareness, we begin to decenter our thoughts, making room for multiple ideas, insights, and imaginings, which we then practice disidentifying from, allowing our internal stimuli to exist as mental experiences instead of aspects of who we are (Orsillo *et al.*, 2004; Teasdale *et al.*, 2002). We can also use our sensory contact with the present moment to describe our context without getting hitched to past comparisons, future expectations, or how things "should be" (Luoma and Villatte, 2012). In this way, mindful awareness is a distinct practice from mental self-monitoring, as observation accepts emotions as they're noticed in our lived experience, whereas analysis seeks out flaws to fix, keeping us in pursuit of our problems.

If we hate the protestor, we focus too much on him, and so relinquish our power. If we believe the protestor, we feel ashamed, and implode on ourselves. Crestfallen, we may frown as we just want our pain to end, yet our emotions are innocent in all of this. Sadness, anger, and fear are not villains in this story. They're more like scared kids, running away from or standing up to the mean megaphone. Trying to make our distress *go away* is like pointing at a crying child and yelling "Stop it!" Yes, we might startle them, but they'll keep balling their eyes out. Can you picture your four-year-old self, fumbling and stumbling up to you, hands shaking and eyes watering? What would you do? Would you push them away? Tell them to just ignore it? Tell them to toughen up, kid, 'cause it's a cold hard world? And if you answered yes, are you willing to try self-compassion, even if it means feeling the tears?

Even if we feel stuck in our lives, our emotional process, or believe we're locked into maladaptive coping mechanisms like self-harm, substance abuse, and sexual impulsivity—our willingness to help ourselves can still ring true (Batten and Hayes, 2005; Hayes *et al.*, 2008). Even if we don't know how to help ourselves yet, we can still validate our desire to learn, for no matter how forlorn, defeated, or hopeless we feel, we still made it through the parades and the protestors to get here.

## Gender fusion and the agenda of emotional control

ACT presents psychological distress as a form of cognitive–emotional inflexibility called *cognitive fusion* (Hayes, 2004). Overidentifying with our thoughts and feelings, fusion quite literally implies melting, as we melt into our language, confusing our identity with our personal narrative, and our existence with our experience of it (Walser and Westrup, 2007). Not wanting to succumb to this, we start to fight our thoughts and feelings. In ACT, the *agenda of emotional control* describes our attempts to escape or marshal our feelings, especially when we view them as limitations and flaws. Ever since we were children, we were taught to contain our feelings. If we had stage fright, we were told there was nothing to fear; when we grazed our knees, we were told there was nothing to cry about; and when we hit puberty, the general advice was not to think about our anxiety, as if feeling these feelings is as detrimental as the circumstances that elicited them (Wilson and Murrell, 2004). Eventually we start avoiding people, places, and situations that cause us discomfort, or distract ourselves from, or completely suppress unwanted thoughts and feelings (Harris, 2008). In moderation, experiential avoidance isn't necessarily an issue, provided it is deliberate, time-limited, and serving a function, like finding ways to bide time and distract from worry as we wait for urgent news (Wilson and Murrell, 2004). But when we constantly control or avoid our thoughts and feelings, we soon find ourselves arguing with ourselves, as if somehow we can beat our mind into submission, swallow our tears, or hide behind a happy mask (Harris, 2008). Failing this, we'll bully ourselves into a different emotion, judging ourselves so harshly we'll feel guilty for being angry or pathetic for being sad (Harris, 2008). And if that doesn't work? We'll zone out, go numb, and have another drink (Harris, 2008). No one ever said these were good ideas, but when we insist on controlling our feelings, we feel like there's no other choice. Of course, all our control tactics only add to our distress through ironic process.

See that purple-haired femme kid catching the bus? That's Sean. A rebellious genderqueer teenager, Sean's heading to a rough part of town, bravely proclaiming "I can handle it" while hiding a knife in their coat. Fused with bold confidence, they're obeying the loud and proud "never-say-die" rule adopted by so many young queer warriors. Not wanting to feel their own fear, Sean puffs out their chest, yet the knife in their pocket is the sharp reminder of their fear, even if they won't admit it. In this case, Sean is mistaking bravado for pride, and arrogance for confidence. After all, even if Sean can handle a dangerous situation, do they really need to? Either way, braving the rough part of town isn't Sean's problem.

No longer a flexible value, Sean's courage has become a rigid rule, making it hard to conceptualize alternatives, and making Sean too stubborn to consider them even if they could. Sean's avoiding their fear, yet even behind their brave mask they're pre-emptively waiting for something to go wrong. Fortunately, all Sean encounters today are a few bratty kids staring and pointing at their outfit. Shrugging them off, Sean says, "I don't let it get to me." The positive intent is not to let the ogling curiosity of kids disrupt their day, and to perhaps even revel in it a little, as it can be fun to introduce kids to a rainbow world. Besides which, being fortified enough to brush off a child's idle comment is typically a healthy boundary. Yet the mantra "I don't let it get to me" is akin to saying, "I feel, but I refuse to acknowledge my feelings."

Rather than come to terms with the difficult thoughts and emotions we've fused to, the agenda of emotional control prefers to avoid any situation, person, or stimulus that may prompt the thought or feeling to begin with. Upsetting topic? Don't talk about it. Tense situation? Don't go near it. Controversy on TV?

Change the channel. We can continue in this fashion for years until that fateful day when we reach the limits of our control or avoidance, at which point our resilience might be so low our stress levels go through the roof. In fact, people who habitually avoid experiences respond more intensely to situations, illustrating increased sensitivity and reduced stress tolerance (Hayes and Smith, 2005; Sloan, 2004). What started as a fear of one's ex generalized into an anxiety around all men or women. What started as a mild pet peeve has progressed into absolute intolerance. Or worse! Having controlled all the external factors, we realize that we're distressed by our own somatic emotional process—that we're distressed by feeling *feelings*. Soon we're afraid of being afraid, or angry at ourselves for feeling angry, or lamenting existence because we feel sad!

To a healthy extent, we will cry when we're sad and laugh when we're happy. But have we ever laughed so hard that when we tried to calm down and keep a straight face, we busted up laughing more? What did we do? We probably became mindful of our body, took a deep breath, exhaled, and tried to let out the giggles—which only made us giggle more! That's the fun side of fusion, and a great way of illustrating how hard it can be to take mental space and calm down when we're stuck in a certain frame of mind.

Anger, sadness, fear, and all those emotions labeled as "negative" aren't intrinsically bad or problematic unless we get stuck in them. Consider a trans person accosted at a grocery store by a random stranger, causing them to feel scared and angry. Perhaps they find safety, or put the stranger in their place, or walk away, or flip them off. All are valid responses spurred by the heat of the moment, and their feelings of anger and fear may actually be a useful extension of that fight or flight response. But when the immediate danger is gone, they may still feel a lurking paranoia, or a lingering rage, or a wallowing depression.

Fusion is only problematic when thoughts or emotions prevent us from living a full and healthy life (Harris, 2008). Emotions can take on a sense of immediacy and desperate urgency, hijacking our attention. Sadness triggers thoughts of hopelessness, guilt writes an epitaph of worthlessness, and anger boils into hatred. Racing thoughts, perseverance, obsessive thinking, and self-deprecation all reflect how our thoughts fuse to our feelings.

Consider this same trans person second-guessing their return to the store. Worry sets in. Maybe they'll be accosted by another stranger, or the same stranger, or get judged by the cashier who saw the incident go down. Fused to worry, they might shop during the late hours of the evening, just to avoid bumping into anyone, or go to the store only when there are plenty of witnesses, or start shopping online so as not to risk it.

There are a lot of terrifying macroaggressions facing gender minorities, including violence, hostility, sexual assault, and any direct attempt to physically, emotionally, socially, or occupationally harm someone because of their gender

(Roland and Burlew, 2017). Yet there are, perhaps, infinitely more mesoaggressions and microaggressions occurring in number and frequency that we internalize and fuse with, reinforcing our self-doubt and self-deprecation.

Mesoaggressions include systematic discrimination, like rules denying access to public spaces, legislation disqualifying a person from adopting children or getting married based on their gender, to even the lack of anti-discrimination laws—when the system ignores gender issues entirely (Roland and Burlew, 2017). Microaggressions include every small, invalidating slash or cut, whether it was intentional or not. In fact, incorrect pronouns, misidentifying sexual orientation, or assumptions based on gender stereotypes hurt all the more when uttered from oblivious allies and unaware friends (Chang and Chung, 2015; Nadal *et al.*, 2015; Roland and Burlew, 2017). Assuming all transgender narratives are the same, denying gender bias, passively disapproving gender variance or assuming it's a mental health issue, adheres to the cisnormative binary at the cost of minimizing other genders. Likewise, letting offensive or incorrect terminology slip into the conversation, implying threat, denying bodily privacy by being overly hyperfocused on anatomy, or fetishizing gender variance as "exotic," are all clear microaggressions which—if left unchecked—can become macroaggresions (Chang and Chung, 2015; Nadal *et al.*, 2012, 2015).

In traumatic situations the fusion process is evident, but with so many small and systematic transgressions stacked up over a lifetime, gender fusion can be quite subtle. Our gender schemas are heavily influenced by our culture of origin, our concrete or relativistic view of the world, our experience in the coming out process, and our personal locus of control, responsibility, and self-acceptance. When our gender schemas become rigid, our identity becomes locked in place, reducing adaptability and emotional resilience. Unable to cry, even when they need to, the masculine can find their archetypal strength working against them. The rugged individual can feel too proud to ask for help. Unable to shout out, even when they need to, the feminine can contend with internalized disempowerment. How often do the nurturing define themselves through self-sacrifice, and so struggle to hold boundaries, or fear they're *not good enough*? Feeling excluded, the androgynous and nonbinary can fuse with alienation, feeling like they have to work twice as hard, or keep everything in, just to be treated as equals. After all, even genuinely happy smiles can become masks for our fret and worry when we hide behind them.

Most of the time we're unaware of the social behaviors fused with our gender identity, until we find ourselves boxed in to a performative role, or clashing with an expected norm, or holding ourselves to a standard we never agreed to. Noticing this, the first steps toward mindful self-awareness occur quite early in the therapeutic process, when we voice our distress, discomfort, or internal dissonance. Even if we don't fully understand the core of our issues, we're aware of how "stuck" we feel. In ACT terminology, the flexibility or inflexibility of our cognitions or gender schemas reflect the degree to which our personal beliefs have fused to *rules*, *reasons*, *judgments*, and *social roles*.

### *Fusing with rules*

Intersecting cultures give us all kinds of gender rules to live by, which we then synthesize into our own personal beliefs of what men, women, and nonbinary people can and cannot do. Rule-governed thinking makes life a transactional series of "should," "must," "ought to," and "have to" statements, obeying rules in order to be safe, seen, attractive, or accepted. These rules are often as serious as they are absurd. If you want to be seen as masculine, you have to have *this* haircut, because if you have *that other* haircut you'll be read as butch. If you want to be seen as feminine, you have to talk, walk, and act like *this*. But don't tell people you dressed down while traveling, because they'll think you're in the closet again. And don't wear a skirt if you're a genderqueer female, because your allies will think you're a girl again. And a *real* woman wouldn't be caught dead in *that*. And you have to look androgynous if you're genderqueer.

The gendered strata of rule-governed behavior are dizzying. The heteronormative and homonormative expectations of sexual orientation rely heavily on the cisnormative expectation that males must be men and females must be women. And that's only the first layer! Challenging this, we then contend with *transnormative* expectations in order to be nonverbally identified as an "out" trans person, and *queer-normative* expectations that call for dismissing binary culture. Just to illustrate how complex this gets, transgender people sometimes get rejected by other transgender people who don't feel they're *transgender enough* because they live by a different set of gendered rules. In turn, people in transition who minimize their trans identity may turn passability into a binding *I should* statement, the inflexible law of gender-land dictating how to be read as a cis man or woman.

Passability can also feel like the magic key to recognition and social acceptance especially when there's a risk of harm or intolerance. For some in transition, the first time they pass as a man or woman without anyone realizing they're gender variant can feel like a dream come true. Some can find healthy ways to balance their identity with social gender norms, yet the rules can stack up. Behavior and body language, may start to feel like they have to be exhaustively measured and performed, with great social risk if one doesn't pass. The topic of passability has a lot of tension in the trans community, as some feel it's a necessary step, while others feel it reinforces gender stereotypes and erases the trans identity. Likewise, some body types and facial forms are more "passable" than others who do not have this privilege (Mallon, 2009). In session, let's track how tyrannical our rules of passability may be, and the degree of stress they cause us. Quite naturally, we may feel a powerful sense of ease and comfort when we no longer pressure ourselves to pass (Spade, 2006; Zandvliet, 2000).

When mapping a gender schema, we start to hear rules in statements beginning with:

- I have to____________________
- I always____________________
- Boys don't____________________
- It's important to____________________
- Girls are supposed to____________________
- Women always have to____________________
- It's up to the man to____________________
- My mom always said____________________
- Dad taught me to____________________

A trans man, adhering to the threadbare stereotype of stoic masculinity, may state, "I don't talk about my problems. It's a guy thing." A trans woman, fusing with the image conscious trends of beautyism, may state, "Women are supposed to shave their legs." If these ideas serve them, and they're capable of talking about their issues when they need to, or going without shaving without distress, then there's no problem. If, however, breaking from these rules generates disproportionate levels of emotional turmoil, then they may need to practice some mental flexibility.

## *Fusing with reason*

Gripping to rationality we fuse with reason, yet our reasoning is not always reasonable. We may attest that we're "just being realistic" when in actuality we're being cynical. Falling back to cyclical thinking, we may justify ourselves while simultaneously dismissing new information, or we may fuse to emotional reasoning, tossing out deductive logic altogether. In the early stages of gender actualization, reasons are often presented as conditional statements camouflaged as questions.

> "If I know I'm a woman, and I like other women, does that mean I'm a lesbian?"
>
> "I've been out as a trans man for ten years now, but sometimes, on occasion, I'll wear a skirt. I mean...does wearing a skirt make me less of a man?"

These can often be explored by having the client repeat their own question as an *if...then* statement, thereby allowing them to formulate their own answer.

> "*If* I'm a woman who likes women, *then* I'm a lesbian. Well, no, that's not really true, 'cause I'm into men too. So, does that mean I'm bisexual?"

> "*If* I wear a skirt, *then* I'm less of a man. No. I mean I know that's not true. But I still feel like it is."

If...then statements don't always provide clarity, especially if we genuinely believe our emotionally based reasoning. So fused, we make very assertive statements, grounded in the certainty of our own misery.

> "I'm not pretty enough to be a girl."

> "I'm not tough enough to be a man."

> "Society doesn't accept genderqueer people, so I don't have a chance."

Reinforced by hard life lessons we may cite bullying, sexual harassment, and trauma to defend why we continue caging, hiding, or harming ourselves. With such evidence, our reasons are inarguable, and those who try to prove us wrong "just don't understand." We may refuse to come out of the closet, having already experienced very real and disastrous consequences. We may hesitate to enter into new relationships, alluding to heartbreaks from the past. The maladaptive construct here is overgeneralization, since we expect things to turn out "just like last time."

The reality of minority stress is undebatable, and outside attempts to disprove our reason-governed thinking may come across as invalidating. The question, of course, is how often these reasons get in our way, stop us in our tracks, or justify unhealthy behaviors like self-harm and substance abuse. Fusing with reason is like believing the mirage of an oasis in the desert. We cannot deny the desert exists, or the very real dangers of sandstorms and dehydration, but if we can't expand our perception and see past the mirage, we'll never find shade or water.

Trying to point out a mirage is useless if a part of us wants the oasis to be real; at which point, any therapist who tries to dismiss our prior reasoning will get dusted off with all the other naysayers. Inevitably, whether or not our reasoning is based on facts or fears, the defusion process is the same. Mirages naturally dissipate when we stop fixating on them and start focusing on the desert itself. In kind, our fixated, absolute-thinking lessens when we breathe and take a moment to observe ideas as thoughts, and only thoughts, backdropped against the context of our life.

### *Fusing with judgment*

Having built a trap with rules and baited it with reasons, we catch ourselves in judgment. Judgmental language is addictive in a world of uncertainty and endless possibility, as it creates false certainty with bold exclamation marks. What may have begun with mild loneliness turns into doubt and negative self-labeling—"I'm worthless, I'm pathetic, I'm disgusting, I'm alone, no one loves me!" Internalizing sexism, cisgenderism, cissexism, and transphobia, we continuously compare ourselves to the de facto global majority, and so disempower ourselves.

*Patriarchal sexism* systematically favors masculinity over femininity, which justifies itself by generating *oppositional sexism*—the belief that male and female are rigid, inflexible, and mutually exclusive categories (Serano, 2016). When we fuse with this dichotomous thinking, we compartmentalize who we are, often judging our feminine qualities as inferior, or aspiring only to stereotypically male virtues. In a similar vein, *cisgenderism* operates either knowingly or unknowingly from a position of cisgender privilege, often neglecting, ignoring, dismissing, rejecting, or disempowering gender variant identities (Ansara, 2015). Viewing cisgender as "normal," anyone outside of this paradigm is judged as odd or unnatural.

Taking this a step further, *cissexism* views gender variant identities as inherently inferior, treating us with hostility, disgust, and violence (Johnson, 2013; Serano, 2016). Examples include: dismissing our names or gender identity; deliberately or accidentally misgendering us; taking photographs without permission; exploiting discrepant social, sexual, or legal power dynamics; or deliberately excluding us from social organizations, public events, or potential employment opportunities. Sexism and cissexism reduce a person's individual identity to their gender, neglecting all other facets of our being until we're little more than a body to be objectified or ridiculed (LeMaster, 2018). When we internalize this, we too begin to limit our perception of self. As the aggressor only sees us in context of our gender, our gender becomes the point of focus.

Cissexism is typically used synonymously with transphobia, yet the former is institutionally systemic. Rooted in sexism, *transphobia* describes the unhealthy mental schemas contributing to both cisgenderism and cissexism, including a person's emotional insecurities and moral indignation, mistrust and dehumanization of gender minorities (Benson, 2013; Bettcher, 2007; Johnson, 2013; Serano, 2016; Whittle, *et al.*, 2007). In ACT terms, transphobia is a fusion to unhealthy hierarchical cognitions. Just as sexism is the product of misogynistic thinking, cissexism is the product of transphobic thinking. Yet where is the phobia? Where is the fear? Gender constructs become rigid and brittle when they're encoded with moral scripts, which is why aggressors often justify their violence toward gender minorities as a pre-emptive defense of their worldview. Like paranoid guard dogs, they bark and snarl even when no one's trying to harm them.

Internalizing macro-, meso-, and microaggressions, we fuse with monstrous mantras, believing negative self-assessments that aren't even true. We underestimate ourselves—"I can't deal with this!" Or undercut ourselves—"Every time someone gives me a compliment I cringe, 'cause it just shows they don't know how fucked up I am." As the pendulum swings, this judgmental mindset can also be turned on others, creating unhealthy and unrealistic bias on our part. We may begin to blame the cisgender, heterosexual, vanilla majority, and even other members of the LGBTQ community, projecting our own anxiety, bias, and prejudice. Playing the blame game, we feel there has to be a winner and a loser, an in-group and an out-group, a self in battle with the other, because if it's not their fault, then it has to be our fault, and if it's not our fault, then it has to be their fault.

In reality, we are not all blameless. Sometimes, there's very real fault to be had. That's inarguable. Yet gender variant individuals frequently contend with unwarranted guilt and shame, ruthlessly critiquing ourselves for surviving or even just existing. If we cannot see the positive intent driving our maladaptive behavior, we may judge ourselves harshly, and then judge ourselves for judging ourselves.

### *Fusing with roles*

If rules dictate behavior for specific situations, then a role is a typecast characterization, taking all those rules and scripting them into a pseudo-identity. There are many types of role we can fuse with. In the family, parents stuck in their role can infantilize their adult kids, just as easily as their adult kids can fall back into adolescent habits whenever they're around their parents. Developmentally, some people never grow out of being the baby of the family, while some adults fused to maturity refuse to play silly games. Occupationally, some teachers can't stop teaching even when they're out of the classroom, just as some therapists find themselves counseling people at the bar even when they don't mean to. Roles mark our status and utility in any family or community; yet when we fuse to roles, we hyperfocus on one facet of a multifaceted whole, potentially compromising our adaptability. Struggling to exist outside of situations designed for that role, we perpetuate the part, even generating conflict when that role is not called for. Having spent years living up to role expectations, pleasing others, and making them proud, we may feel like we lost ourselves somewhere, having sacrificed our personal needs on the altar of social belonging.

*Social roles* form organically as a survival mechanism, fitting us into niche positions within our respective communities. Yet when we fuse with these constructs, we can begin to feel stereotyped. The joker feels compelled to joke. The intellectual feels compelled to answer. The empath feels compelled to help their friends. As we don't want to betray our social strengths, we get stuck "playing the part." So, the joker is never taken seriously, and the intellectual overthinks their problems, and the empath loses their boundaries. Clearly, we're favoring our demeanor over our nature in order to be accepted.

*Gender roles* include a broad subset of social performances assigned to our gender identity by our culture. Unlike social roles, gender roles hierarchically imply a sex or gender identity by associating specific, if stereotypic, value-guided behavior (Bolich, 2007). A 20-something with a scruffy moustache feeding a baby is presumed to be the father, as we assume they're a man, assume they're nurturing, and triangulate an inference. It may sound simple, but gender roles are supplanted should we not fit the gender or respective role. If this 20-something is actually a trans-masculine woman, a self-identified bearded lady proud of both her moustache and her femininity, then *father* is rejected, often with deep social repercussions. If a cissexist society cannot glaze over or ignore gender nonconformity, then it will often attempt to discredit our social power. If this fails, the society may even attack us physically in an attempt to defend its traditional gender roles from being adapted, changed, or warped.

But let's say this 20-something is actually a cisgender, male, baby-daddy. If being a man is a gender identity originating from within, then fatherhood is a role if—and only if—it's accepted and incorporated. Plenty of men have kids but walked away from being a father. Vice versa, plenty of men never had kids but stepped into a paternal role. To add yet another layer of complexity, national, ethnic, and generational cultures define gender roles differently, challenging us to suss through the relationship between social performance and social power (Bolich, 2007). What it means to be a matriarch or patriarch depends greatly on how our familial cultures integrate or diverge from the gendered expectations of the cultural majority. When it comes to being a parent, our relational frames are evident in our use of language. We may encode subtle inflections of power, affection, and formality between *Dad*, *Daddy*, *Pa*, and *Father*, as well as *Mom*, *Mommy*, *Ma*, and *Mother*. These intonations may be highly personal, yet social constructs, even outdated and vestigial ones, can influence how we talk and think about parenting. In Western patriarchies, Bobby is introduced before Susy, yet mother colloquially precedes father. "This is my Dad and Mom" may sound clunky in contrast to "This is my Mom and Dad." While we can take a deep dive into the history of linguistic sexism, the larger point is how gender roles influence social priority. Both patriarchal and matriarchal cultures place phenomenal importance on motherhood, but for arguably different reasons. Patriarchies prioritize heirs, thereby valuing mothers as a route to sons, whereas matriarchies focus on the woman in question, often honoring motherhood as a rite of passage or pinnacle life experience.

If our family belongs to a matriarchal culture or subculture, the divergent gender roles providing women autonomy, initiative, and social movement may clash with patriarchal systems. Likewise, in gender variant or simply egalitarian families, terms like Mom and Dad may take on far more flexible definitions, focusing on acts of nurturance and compassion over acts of authority and submission. Yet when gender variant people enter into parental roles, they often find the binary looming even in their own thoughts. Even Mom and Dad is a binary. Fortunately, love finds a way, and nonbinary families have cultivated all kinds of endearing terms including Zaza, Baba, Bibi, and Maddy.

Undeniable social and political limitations oppress gender variant people, and in particular gender variant people of color, from every angle. Yet the most treacherous limitations are those we impose on ourselves. All populations grapple with the agenda of emotional control, yet gender variant people may exert considerable time and effort into control tactics, given how many social spheres judge, criticize, and condemn who we are. Focusing on literal safety, some begin to feel like queer survivalists, constantly having to identify safe zones, assess self-defense options, and scan the scene for allies and enemies just to ask where the bathroom is! Massive amounts of time and energy may be spent on physical presentation and social strategies, compartmentalizing whole communities around who knows what. The avoidant may even minimize their social footprint in a sad attempt to disappear from the public eye. The prospect of giving up these control strategies may not only be frightening, but in some cases impractical. A distinction must be made between control strategies designed to preserve personal safety, and control strategies avoiding emotional process, as fusion occurs in each respectively and also in their overlap.

Therapeutic troubleshooting demands that you, as the clinician, think on your feet, as no manualized treatment plan can prepare you for how obstinate, complex, and clever fusion can be. Rather than argue, or try and *think* a way out, defusion exercises reduce the power these rules, reasons, judgments, and roles have over behavior.

ACT exercises demonstrate our ability and personal power to fuse and entangle our thoughts and emotions, and to defuse and detangle our thoughts and emotions. This ability to fuse and defuse is practiced throughout the therapeutic relationships through visualization exercises, mindfulness practices, and perception taking exercises. In the long term, defusion can help us expand our awareness, come to accept our personal truth, and actualize both our identity and a healthy lifestyle to match. In the beginning, however, defusion exercises can grant us intrapsychic agency by playing with internal volume and proximity, recognizing context, and experimenting with imagination.

## Defusion exercise: **Internal volume and proximity**

The observational self isn't a helpless member of the audience watching the show unfold—it's the playhouse technician. We may dream of being directors, commanding every thought and feeling that crosses the stage, but our internal actors ad lib half the time anyway. There's a script of beliefs and social schemas they keep referring back to, but then they seem to improvise. Making up spontaneous ideas, our thoughts can be hilarious, witty, clever, stupid, and periodically terrifying. No, we can't direct our thoughts and feelings, but we can control the audio and the lighting, focusing and refocusing our attention accordingly.

Screaming inside our head is a great example. Think of something absurd. *I hate penguins*. Then, with our eyes closed, scream *I hate penguins* as loud as possible on the inside. Keep screaming it. Now, without saying anything, mentally whisper *I hate penguins...*

Alright, we have now mastered internal volume. Playing with our internal volume demonstrates how the intensity of a thought can fluctuate inside our mind. A single thought can take center stage, and while we were internally screaming *I hate penguins* it was hard to think about anything else. Our other cognitions didn't disappear, but for a moment our penguin hatred stole the microphone. But what about when our hatred for penguins is really insistent? Imagine what it would be like to have someone, standing point blank, whispering in our ear, over and over again, *I hate penguins, I hate penguins, I really, really hate Emperor Penguins. They think they're so fancy in their tuxedos. Snooty upper-class birds won't even fly.* It would get pretty annoying. *I hate penguins.* All day long, everything we would try to do would be punctuated by this incessant whisper. Try imagining someone—paradoxically dressed in a penguin costume—whispering their anti-penguin agenda right next to us. Now, imagine them whispering ten steps away. We can still hear them, but the distance makes things muffled, and their Styrofoam beak doesn't help either. Now imagine them 30 feet off. We can see them whispering, but we can't really hear them. Now imagine them standing a mile away, still whispering. We know exactly what they're saying, but they're so far away they're inaudible. The thought still exists, they're never completely out of sight, but the moment we think it, the moment we realize they're still whispering *I hate penguins*, it's like they teleported right next to us again. Damn ironic process! What cruel Sisyphean curse is this? There are multiple meditations envisioning our thoughts as a leaf floating away on a stream, or as sand pouring through an hourglass, but there are always more leaves, and the hourglass can be turned over. Practicing our ability to create internal mental space makes this cyclical process of cognitive awareness and releasing defusion easier, and potentially faster, reducing the duration of distressing episodes.

Only a rare few actually hate penguins. Those who don't may laugh, or even feel guilty for hating the cute little birds. This illustrates how we can be hijacked by thoughts we don't actually believe. If we're depressed we may promptly point out that, unlike our false penguin animosity, we *actually do* hate ourselves, and that we *actually believe* what our self-deprecation tells us. Should we hold this belief, we may struggle to list what we like in this world, and asking us to name something we love is a great way to get us to look at the floor. Instead, be specific. *Like* and *love* are vague, abstract concepts dismantled quickly by anxiety, depression, and self-loathing, but kittens, puppies, and penguins are much easier to imagine.

This time, we're not going to scream in our head, we're going to sing in our head. We're going to sing, in the style of our favorite genre how much we love kittens, puppies, or penguins. *I love kittens. I love kittens, I love kittens and kittens, hooray. I love puppies, I love puppies, I love puppies and puppies today. I love penguins, I love penguins, I love penguins and penguins I say!* The rhythm doesn't matter. It doesn't even have to rhyme. We can even belt it like an opera singer or wail it like we're in a Norwegian death metal band. Notice any bodily changes as we rock out in our head. Did we smile? Giggle? Did we smirk a little? Did we call ourselves stupid for even trying? Did we think the whole exercise was stupid? Whatever we notice is fine, as each random thought, no matter how awkward, bashful, silly, cynical, or bold, adds to the actors on our mental stage. They were always there, but with our attention routed to the one player in a penguin suit, we neglected them. When we say we hate ourselves, we're forgoing every facet of who we are, including the part of us that smiles at mental kittens. By playing with internal volume and internal proximity, we can disempower our tedious, self-deprecating penguin, expanding our awareness to free the rest of the cast.

## Defusion exercise: **I'm having the thought**

Our language is littered with personal laws. Just count how often you say, *I always, I never, I have to, I must, I cannot, I wouldn't, I couldn't, I shouldn't.* What follows after these statements is often a rule that governs our conduct, by stopping us, blocking us, or forcing us to behave in ways we don't always desire or agree with. They may even have guided us for so long we can't imagine going against them, preferring the rule over the discomfort of breaking the rule. These rules can even shape how we see ourselves, to such an extent we may overidentify with the struggle. We may proclaim, *I am worthless. I am pathetic. I am unlovable.* Said so absolutely, it seems impossible to deny. We may as well be trying to move a mountain. So, let's stop trying to move the mountain! At its base, Everest towers over us, but what would happen if we stepped back a bit? From only a few miles away, we can see Everest still looming over the Himalayas, but relative size makes it appear somehow smaller, as if we could hold it in our hand. It is possible to accomplish this with our intrusive inner monologue, but instead of adding miles, we're going to add words.

Russ Harris presented the "I'm Having a Thought" exercise in his book *ACT Made Simple* (2009a), to show how adding context can help zoom out, expand, and defuse from absolute thinking. In the case of this unlovable mantra, repeat:

> "I am unlovable. I am unlovable. I am unlovable."

Now repeat:

> "I think I am unlovable."

The second statement transitioned us from a fact (I am) to an idea (I think I am). The next step in ACT is to notice the noticer, by including oneself in context, after which we can expand the context. Repeat:

> "This is me, having the thought that I am unlovable."
>
> "This is me, sitting in a room, having the thought that I am unlovable."
>
> "This is me, sitting in a room, on the third floor, having the thought that I am unlovable."
>
> "This is me, sitting in a room, on the third floor, in downtown Chicago, having the thought that I'm unlovable."
>
> "This is me, sitting in a room, on the third floor, in downtown Chicago, in the state of Illinois, having the thought that I am unlovable."
>
> "This is me, sitting in a room, on the third floor, in downtown Chicago, in the state of Illinois, in the middle of America, having the thought that I am unlovable."
>
> "This is me, sitting in a room, on the third floor, in downtown Chicago, in the state of Illinois, in the middle of America, on a planet hurtling around the sun, having the thought that I am unlovable."
>
> "This is me, sitting in a room, on the third floor, in downtown Chicago, in the state of Illinois, in the middle of America, on a planet hurtling around the sun, in a solar system swirling in the Milky Way, having the thought that I am unlovable."

Clients may scoff and laugh and say, "I get it, I get it!" But the exercise has two aspects. The first demonstrates how the more cognitions we add to a chained sequence of thought, the less emotionally raw it feels, challenging our all-encompassing absolutism. The second aspect expands awareness to see ourselves in the context of our life. A part of us may still believe that we're absolutely unlovable, but a few awkward, funny sentences later and we're also aware of a cosmic, bird's eye view. Remember not to debate the idea, or even counter it. We're not trying to feel loved or disprove our unlovability. We're trying to buffer enough space from this melancholy thought to expand awareness. Everest is still standing, after all, but now we can see all of the Himalayas.

## Defusion exercise: **Personify the distress**

From an evolutionary perspective, doubt is a great asset. Doubt made sure we didn't jump the ravine, or eat that poison berry, or trust the man with the big smile swaggering with an even bigger club. Doubt analyzes, questions, and inquires. It's the brainchild of our neocortex, scrutinizing our emotional limbic system and marshaling our reptilian impulsivity. Yet when we fuse with doubt, it seats itself on a skeptical throne, becoming a tyrannical cynic. Like a despot building vainglorious propaganda, cynicism pretends it is critical thinking, in the same way pessimists regularly proclaim they're realists. When encountering this kind of mental resistance, it's worth illustrating how analysis is observational, thoughtful, and constructive, while cynicism judgmentally spits on prototypes that don't work. Convincingly cautious, this cynical tyrant reminds us how dangerous the world is and how fragile we are. Doubt once kept us safe. Now it assures us that it's better to stay in and binge-watch TV than go out and make an attempt at life. It's always safer in bed.

A great way to practice defusion is to personify this inner monologue, thereby individuating our maladaptive thoughts, dysfunctional belief constructs, and scathing cynicism (Strosahl and Robinson, 2017). Those of us who've internalized our snarky bullies and disappointing parents might already have an internal personification, or we may need to imagine our self-deprecating thoughts as a manipulative character, whether that's Rumpelstiltskin, Ursula, or Severus Snape. Giving potentially scary or unsettling thoughts a quirky nickname allows us to experience them differently, as even the darkest thoughts become humorous when they're cartoonishly exaggerated (Strosahl and Robinson, 2017).

List some common self-deprecating thoughts, then imagine them in that character's voice. Now, let's deflate that power, by imagining our cynical tyrant sucking on a helium balloon. Give them a cartoon voice. Every time they say something, make it silly and squeaky. And if that doesn't last, as helium does wear off, imagine them shrinking, their voice becoming shriller and shriller. They're not going anywhere. They're just getting smaller and smaller.

Why can't we just squash them? Good question. Because we have to save them. Our cynical tyrant is that desperate, misguided part of us still holding on to the agenda of emotional control. As already noted, doubt has its place, just not at the center of everything; and with the tyrant dethroned, we can expand our awareness to focus on what's really important.

## Mindfulness and the observational self

Beginning on a cognitive-behavioral mountainside, ACT cultivated an existential, humanistic Zen garden. Through mindfulness, ACT helps us grow an awareness of awareness, so that we become conscious of our own consciousness. ACT presents two being states: the *thinking self*, fusing thoughts to feelings, and the *observational self*, objectively defusing thoughts from feelings (Harris, 2009a).

The thinking self is our whirring prefrontal cortex. Our internal monologue, neurologists have observed, lights up the left inferior frontal gyrus, including Broca's area, which has been linked to language processing and our semantic network—the very patterns that associate our relational frames (Devlin, Matthews, and Rushworth, 2003; Dronkers *et al.*, 2007; Morin and Hamper, 2012). Working collaboratively with the left posterior inferior frontal gyrus to articulate verbally, these facets of our brain play a huge role in encoding and decoding information, and decoding further, as is the case when we say something aloud and understand it on a deeper level. Encoding our meaning into sound, we then decode the sound, and derive new meaning. This ability to hear ourselves and process our own communication is the foundation of talk therapy. Many of us have no doubt had the moment when something feels more real now that we say it aloud. Many of us have also shared aloud, only to realize how dumb it sounds. If our conceptual self is our character, then our thinking self is our unreliable narrator.

Assuming happiness is the ultimate goal, the thinking self strives to ignore or control distressing emotions, or situations that cause distressing emotion (Harris 2009a; Hayes and Smith 2005). For many gender variant people, our thinking self has been a hypervigilant survivalist keeping us alive, or a ruminating problem solver trying to find some way to end our painful problems. Monitoring the exits, sitting closest to the door, carrying spare clothes in the car, our thinking self tries to problem solve. It'll even convince us that the best thing to do is bury our feelings. Disliking uncomfortable emotions, the thinking self tries to think its way out, and when it can't do that? It justifies having another drink, or cutting out of work, or cutting a thigh just to feel, or blaming others, or—in the most extreme case—what to write on our suicide note. Anything to escape or avoid emotional distress.

If we can hear our inner monologue, the question is: Who's listening? If we see pictures in our mind, the question is: Who's watching? That part of us, witnessing our own thoughts and feelings, is the observational self. When we visualize a guided meditation, or imagine an image, or recall a memory, it's the part of us that takes it all in. ACT presents the observational self as a form of transcendent self-awareness connecting with the various dynamics of who we are and how we feel (Sandoz *et al.*, 2010).

Yet the observational self isn't a passive observer. By being present with our thoughts and feelings, the observational self can expand our awareness to perceive who we are and how we feel in the context of our current circumstance. Preoccupied, the thinking self ruminates on the past, anticipates the future, or else judges the present, whereas the observational self focuses on what is, recognizing thoughts as mere thoughts, and emotions as passing experiences (Harris, 2008; Hayes and Smith, 2005).

In gender affirmative ACT, specifically, we also observe a third being state called the somatic self. Typically, the somatic self and the thinking self not only intersect, they fuse together operating as one, clenching our fists when we think angry thoughts and vice versa. These being states are not separate modes of consciousness but distinct focal points of mental awareness drawing our attention to our inner monologue or our physiological reaction. Presented as such, the somatic self includes our sensory awareness, how we feel in our body, as well as our linguistic and paralinguistic communication. Now, many people trust their gut, recognizing feelings of tightness or nausea when we betray our values or feel them being encroached upon. Headaches, stomach aches, irritable bowels, shaky hands, a crack in the voice, all indicate the presence of emotions, as they correspond to our actions and behavior. Yet our somatic responses are not always accurate, having been sensitized by trauma or misled by stimuli—including our cognitive fusion. If the thinking self is an unreliable narrator, then the somatic self is an unreliable audience. Quite literally, we watch scary movies and feel our heart jump in our chest, not because we mentally believe we're being attacked by monsters, but because the somatic self reacts to the noise, rhythm, and imagery. We know it's a movie. We even tell ourselves, "It's just a movie," because we know that guy is going to get killed the moment he opens the door! But the anticipation builds up, and right when he says, "The coast's clear," a claw rips him into the darkness and we spill popcorn all over our lap! We knew it was coming. The thinking self gave it a thumbs down for being a cliché, and we know it's not real, but our adrenalin spikes anyway.

Different cultures trust and distrust the somatic self to varying degrees, as it's also the source of our sexual and affectional orientation, along with all appetitive instincts. Arousal is reactive, not deliberate. When we trust our instincts, we hold the somatic self in high regard, knowing that experience comes before language and meaning (Gendlin, 1962). Essentially, we sense our existence before we make sense of our existence. The vessel of our body existed before we ever learned language or formed our conceptual or thinking self (Forsyth and Eifert, 2016). For gender variant people, this somatic self also accounts for our intrinsic sense of gender, experienced not through words, but through a sensation referred to here as *resonance*.

Our somatic self is our bodily, nonverbal awareness, which is very distinct from anatomic sex. This is most evident when working with gender variant people, as some of us are physically present and connected with our bodily experience, even if we're not aligned with our sex phenotypes or gender identity.

> "Transition wasn't a big deal for me. I'm just me with more estrogen. I still play lacrosse, I still take my dog for a walk, I still go swimming with my friends."

> "After my mastectomy I definitely felt more comfortable with my body, and sometimes I judge how I look—but my body's my temple, you know? My temple just got renovated, that's all."

Despite the claims of many psychiatric institutions, gender dysphoria is not the defining, penultimate feature of being transgender, transsexual, or gender nonconforming (WPATH, 2011). Clearly, many gender variant people have little to no symptoms of gender dysphoria, especially once they've transitioned, and should not be deemed gender dysphoric (Bockting *et al.*, 2006). Yet when the thinking self becomes incongruent with the somatic self, the relationship between conscious thought and physical body becomes tenuous. Misaligned, the body can feel foreign, dysphoric, and even dangerous. No longer in the relational category of *self*, the body and all its processes are put in the surreal category of *other*. Normalizing this, how many times have we felt dissonance between our thinking self and the gut response of our somatic self? Those with gender dysphoria often find the thinking self individuates from the body, leading to negative self-labeling or depersonalization. The thinking self can even abuse the somatic self through criticism, outright rejection, or neglect—ridiculing how we feel and what we resonate with.

> "I literally feel like I'm walking a tightrope. I'm okay, provided I don't look down; 'cause the moment I look down, I see a body that isn't mine. It's nothing like what I see in my head. So, I spend most of my day looking straight ahead...like I'm literally walking a tightrope."

> "Everything is wrong. *Everything*. I'm disgusted with myself. Last week I punched a mirror. I didn't mean to. I just saw my face and got really mad."

Engaging the observational self serves a double function for gender dysphoric clients, as it creates mental space from distress while simultaneously helping to reintegrate our divided sense of self. As mindfulness is intrinsically somatic, the more we connect with our awareness and defuse from our intrusive thoughts, the more our body can become an ally, even if our anatomic sex isn't congruent with our gender.

Mindfulness exercises increase our ability to shift perspective, transcending from a rigid, singular viewpoint to an integrated, multifaceted whole (Sandoz *et al.*, 2010). Yet when we're still unfolding our gender identity, practicing mindful self-awareness can be fraught with confusion and internal conflict (Lev, 2004). If our relationship with our body is dynamic, dissonant, or both, mindfulness practices can feel physically and emotionally uncomfortable. As a clinician, you can validate the struggle by normalizing and even frontloading clients about it ahead of time. Let us know that we're not trying to be meditative gurus on the mountain of inner peace. If anything, we're being mindful of the discomfort when it arises too, simultaneously recognizing somatic, intrapsychic, familial, or spiritual obstacles alongside our physical senses.

Mindfulness is not the act of "clearing one's mind" or "trying not to think," which is equivalent to cognitive suppression, nor is it a form of hypnosis trying to make us cluck like a chicken (Hayes and Smith, 2005; Walser and Westrup, 2007). Instead, mindfulness is an expansion of our internal and external awareness that regulates our body through breath work and creates space in our perception to allow all experiences to exist (Harris, 2008, 2009a). We don't have to believe, agree, or even trust our thoughts or feelings to allow them to exist. Instead, we're giving them permission to exist in our consciousness while continuing to expand our awareness.

Mindfulness also varies from perceptual multitasking to mindful wholeness. We often bounce our attention from this, to that, and back again, honing our focus from our breathing, to our thought, to our breathing, to another thought. This can be frustrating, especially if we want to focus on one more than the other. We may even judge ourselves for not being able to let a thought go, or not being able to sit still, or because we're easily distracted. Many mindfulness practices begin with perceptual multitasking, in the same way that meditations may draw our awareness from our toes to our ankles, to our legs, to our torso, to our chest, to our shoulders, to our neck, to our head. Yet the function isn't to exist as our toes, and then exist as our ankles, and to then exist as our legs, and so on. The function is to bring all of our body into our awareness, with our comfort and discomfort existing together. We can practice this by literally seeing the forest for the trees.

Stand in the park and look at a tree. Notice how it sways or stays perfectly still. Notice how healthy or unhealthy it looks. Notice its colors, its number of branches, its shadow on the ground. Then look at another tree. Notice all the differences and similarities. Then notice a third tree. Then come back to the first again. This is perceptual multitasking. Now, let's settle our eyes, and look at all three simultaneously. Notice how they all sway together in the breeze, and how all the shadows are cast in the same direction, and how all of them are contrasted against the sky. It may be hard to hold this perspective for long, as curiosity naturally hones our attention, and that's okay. Permit focus, but every now and then try being mindful of the whole.

When working with gender variant people, you may feel in over your head should the very technique you hoped would put us at ease suddenly triggers anxiety. ACT practitioners are all too aware of how clients resist and avoid mindfulness practices, but gender presents a unique challenge. Mindfulness exercises can be calming, but in ACT their primary purpose is to expand our mental, emotional, and physical awareness. That said, if we haven't come to terms with who we are, gender can feel like an intimidating catalyst to hide from. If we're at odds with our body, mindfulness can inadvertently zoom in on our discomfort. If we have experienced oppression and trauma in response to our identity, mindfulness may rattle some of the locked doors in our mind. Pay close attention, therefore, to how you phrase guided exercises. Consider the very different responses that could be elicited should you ask:

*How does your hand feel?*
*How do you feel about your hand?*
*How do you feel about feeling your hand?*

Initially, mindfulness activities can feel quite sectional, focusing on our neglected emotional state, checking in with our body, purveying judgments, or sitting with our identity constructs. As we become more adept at recognizing the overlap between cognitions, emotions, and somatic cues, a holistic integration begins to occur as we move from mindful multitasking to mindful wholeness. This is also true when first exploring gender. As it's a complex issue, we naturally section gender into subjects, yet the more we understand, the more intersectional and contextual we realize our gender is. Mindfully exploring gender is the process of understanding our very personal conceptualization and experience of gender in a variety of different situations and relationships. Intrapersonally, this includes our respective *dissonance*, *resonance*, and *gender stability* as well as our *somatic*, *emotional*, and *social* mindfulness.

## *Mindful dissonance*

Comparison is both common and natural. Many therapists strive to get clients not to compare themselves to others to no avail, as we can't be conscientious without also being socially conscious. Comparison is the axis of emulation, aspiration, compassion, charity, and competition. We compare ourselves to each other to find how we connect and where we belong, observing difference between us and both cisgender and gender variant people (Devor, 2004). Yet when we dwell on differences over similarities, we feel like pariahs and outcasts, which is why comparison gets such a bad name.

Accepting our differences without judgment can be exceptionally difficult for such a small, dynamic minority. We can't help but compare ourselves to the majority! Then we judge ourselves for comparing ourselves, and then judge ourselves for judging ourselves, and then compare ourselves to other people's judgments! What a mess. Yet what would happen if we stopped fighting the act of comparison or the denial of difference, and utilized our comparison to validate our difference?

When we don't fit the gender norms projected onto our birth sex, we begin to feel a strange, tugging experience—a sense of difference, as we realize that the interests and concerns of our peers do not reflect our own (Devor, 2004). Some may label it early, recognizing the gender conundrum even as children, yet others may feel this intrinsic dissimilarity long before realizing it has anything to do with gender. Maybe we struggled to connect with others, or struggled to play the game, or felt fraudulent for doing so even if we were good at it. Maybe we went through the motions, not knowing why we felt strange, or what this discordant strife and disequilibrium amounted to. In session, mindfully explore any dissonance we may have between self and others, and even self and self, without forcing a label on it.

The gender dysphoric mindset may not know our gender, even when we're overcome by a pervasive sense of otherness. We may enter therapy without any gender pretext, reporting that we feel something is wrong, off, weird, or different. Some may suspect gender is a component, but spend each session exploring other areas of life as a means of emotional avoidance. Sessions may feel like they're circling an unspoken issue, even if we don't appear "afraid" or "scared of going there." As an emotional defense, we may consistently state "I don't know" to even rudimentary questions, fusing to our own obliviousness so as not to go too deep. More so than ever, proceed at our pace as the gender dysphoric mindset will remain lost even if a concept is brought to our attention, meaning attempts to point out the issue may elicit pushback, resistance, denial, dismissal, or just plain confusion. If we feel bewildered, giving us a map of the wilderness only makes us feel more bewildered, especially if we don't know how to read cartography or have no point of reference. Be patient, and we will find our bearings, though we may need to circle our cognitions a few times over the course of several sessions to get there.

If these feelings are frequent, track the situations in which they emerge. In each situation, are there any precursory thoughts or events? What emotions do we feel when we compare ourselves to others, and what language do we use to do so? Interpersonal dissonance can feel like a reservation around others—a kind of hesitancy, reluctance, or flat-out refusal to join in gender normative behavior. Anecdotal stories illustrating this sense of otherness or estrangement may help expand our concept of self.

As we internalize social norms and expectations, we soon generate intrapersonal gender dissonance. We may feel as if we're arguing with ourselves about who we're supposed to be or how we're supposed to behave. While we may not yet know who or what we want to be, our socialization has taught us who and what we're not. If we recognize our gender dysphoria, we may also feel unlike others in either the cisgender or transgender community, especially if our experiences differ from the medically advertised transsexual narrative. Some of us may respond to the unknown with tongue-in-cheek humor, identifying ourselves as an MtWTF (Male-to-What-The-Fuck) or FtWTF (Female-to-What-The-FUCK). Some may be label-phobic, which is fine until we feel ill-defined, or jealous of those who seem to "fit in" or "know themselves so well." Perhaps this felt yet unnamed difference will emerge as a particular identity, sexuality, or expression, or something entirely unrelated to sex or gender! A pervading sense of disappointment may emerge alongside feelings of inadequacy, impotence, or powerlessness. Ruminating on our dissonance, we may express anguish, frustration, or grief, even if we don't know how to articulate or familiarize ourselves with our uniqueness. This dissonance can feel exhausting if we don't know who or what we are, since frames of distinction only show us our differences and dissimilarities. Fortunately, learning how to accept these differences allows us to be what we are, and not what we're not, even if we don't have a direct parallel to compare ourselves with (Hayes and Smith, 2005).

## Mindfulness exercise: **Interpretation**

To really fuse with our *I should* statements, we can envision people we admire, look up to, or want to be like. We can even compare ourselves to people who just seem to have it easier than us in their daily lives. Take a moment to feel the social pressure, the reluctance, the procrastination, the envy, the desire. We tend to smile when we think about all we could be, yet sigh when we think about all we should be, as the latter carries the brunt of obligation, expectation, and performative assessment. Make a column of *I should* statements and see what comes up (see Table 3.1). I should be *strong*. I should be *elegant*. I should be *beautiful*. I should be *a leader*. I should be more *kind*. I should be more *generous*. I should be more *healthy*. I should be more *patient*. Now draw three more columns.

ACT doesn't attempt to restructure thought or convince us that we shouldn't make so many *I should* statements. Our natural frames of comparison are only problematic when we get stuck in them, so ACT practices mental flexibility. Many times we have a visceral reaction to words and labels because we feel there's only one rigid interpretation of them. By recognizing different, contextual definitions we progressively disempower the *I should* statement (see Table 3.1). We may not identify with any of our final answers and that's okay. If we do, more power to us! But if we don't, recap how the exercise is to practice thinking outside of the rigid all-or-nothing box.

**Table 3.1 Interpreting *I should***

| I should be | Which means | And also means | And also means |
|---|---|---|---|
| Strong | Being physically tough | Being emotionally tough | Enduring a lot |
| Elegant | Being graceful | Being beautiful | Being well liked |
| Beautiful | Having sex appeal | Being confident | Being beloved |
| A leader | Being confident | Delegating | Role modeling |
| More kind | Being compassionate | Being friendly | Socializing |
| More generous | Being giving | Being charitable | Being helpful |
| More healthy | Being fit | Being athletic | Playing sports |
| More patient | Being tolerant | Being attentive | Caring to listen |

Follow-up questions can help build mental resources to call on later, or to tease apart the difference between a capability and an identity. *When have you endured a lot? When have you been well liked or felt confident in your body? Or been a role model? Or been friendly?* We are capable of embodying and exercising these characteristics even if we don't identify with them, which is why we can perform a courageous act without ever *feeling brave*, or get all the answers right and still *feel stupid*, or be the boss and *feel like an imposter*. Conversely, we may recognize and even embrace a characteristic but find no satisfaction in it. For example, while we may have the *ability* to be elegant, any felt dissonance within our elegant performance may illustrate that it's a social ideal and not a personal value.

Values, abilities, and characteristics are often so loaded into societal gender norms and expectations that people have a hard time viewing them separately. Empowering our ability to discern multiple interpretations of each value, whether we align with it or not, increases mental flexibility by increasing our awareness of experiential diversity. There are many ways to be strong, beautiful, intelligent, and many ways to be a leader. By actively exploring the diversity of each respective trait, we may find one that we align with, allowing us to fulfill our obligation to our *I should* statement. Conversely, we may find another quality we align with, allowing us to reject the *I should* statement altogether in favor of characteristics we can truly stand behind. But how do we find an alternative?

## Mindfulness exercise: **Antonym and alternative**

This exercise is very similar to the last one in that it also lists *I should* statements, before asking us to identify the antonym, if we want to identify with the antonym, and an alternative we prefer to be or become (see Table 3.2). The exercise can help us spot our own black and white, polarizing mentality in order to describe an identity we desire to actualize independent of the dichotomy.

**Table 3.2 Antonym and alternative**

| I should be | Antonym | I identify with | Alternative |
|---|---|---|---|
| Strong | Weak | No | Gentle |
| Elegant | Clumsy | No, but I feel I am | Coordinated |
| Beautiful | Ugly | No | Well groomed |
| Kind | Cruel | No, but I fear I am | Patient |

Our *I should* statements translate directly into *I'm not* statements, as the language implies not only the comparison, but the recognition of difference. *I should be strong* either admits that *I'm not strong* or *I don't believe I am*. We could pump iron, but we don't because another part of us doesn't adhere to this standard or value this quality, even when pressured to do so. This can lead to resenting ourselves and potential self-sabotage. Exploring possible alternatives allows us to imagine another way to be that is more desirable to us personally, even if we do not feel it's attainable yet. Self-actualization is vital, but gender identity is not a fix-it problem requiring instant action, and we, as the client, are still building our self-awareness.

## *Mindful resonance*

Resonance is a sensation of curiosity, connection, kinship, and attunement with a person, place, or stimulus. Having compared ourselves to others, we may feel alien, singular, and foreign even to ourselves. Exploring the edges of our comfort zone, or even the edge of our known reality we serendipitously encounter something or someone that we resonate with. Socially, this phenomenon is most observable in children. Perhaps little Johnny or Susy met a police officer and spent the next week running around playing cops and robbers. Perhaps 14-year-old Elijah went to their first emo show, and in less than a month has converted his wardrobe to fit the music scene. Perhaps Mark read the name Lilian and felt a kinship with it. Whatever the case, the encounter has opened a door and now nothing's quite the same.

But is a person's gender so impressionable as to be influenced by a random encounter? No. Gender identity and sexual orientation aren't contagious. If they were, the world would be a lot more fabulous. Yet as we develop our identity, the acknowledgement of our difference builds like potential energy. It can start small at first, even nonverbally, without internal cognition. Before thought comes reaction. Eyes linger. Attention stays. A young male may glimpse a woman and feel something not akin to attraction per se, but vicarious curiosity. A young female might see an openly transgender person and follow them with her eyes, or avert her gaze so as not to stare—ironically validating their interest by trying to deny it! Does this mean everyone who's stared at a transgender person, or feels a vicarious appreciation of the opposite sex, is a budding transsexual person themselves? Not at all. There is a distinction between external curiosity and internal resonance.

So, does that imply someone who feels cross-gender resonance is inherently transgender? Of course not. Perhaps they resonate with the person's expression, vibrancy, openness, or courage. Perhaps they admire the androgyny, or femininity, or masculinity. Perhaps they like the color of their high heels. Diehard LGBTQ allies often report a kinship with the community even as cisgender heterosexuals, since many have had friends or family members who are LGBTQ. Some of these allies may resonate on a more personal level, connecting with themes of uniqueness and difference in their own lives.

Gender resonance is powerful and persistent, as it sings everywhere. Reading gender variant books, watching characters on TV, poring through blogs and online forums assemble both knowledge and affinity. Connection with the LGBTQ community plays a big part, as meeting others with similar narratives allows us to find information and compare in a new way (Lev, 2004). Encountering likeness permits the normalization and humanization of self and others, increasing gender variant acceptance and personal resilience (Pflum *et al.*, 2015). It's this somatic feeling that guides us like a compass to gender labels, and modes of expression, and even to our chosen names.

As nonbinary role models are rare in the West, we spotlight fictional characters and gender-bending celebrities. From the boy players swooning as Shakespeare's Juliet, to Vaudeville's female impersonators, to burlesque and Broadway, theater has always been a haven for the gender ambiguous, selling packed auditoriums for *Victor/Victoria* and *La Cage aux Folles*. A similar history is observable in Japan's Takarazuka Revue, an all-female troupe founded in 1913 (Nakamura and Matsuo, 2003). The androgynous actresses of the Takarazuka Revue so inspired famed manga artist Osamu Tezuka that he drew *Princess Knight*, the fanciful tale of Princess Sapphire, bestowed at birth with the blue heart of a boy and the pink heart of a girl (Nakamura and Matsuo, 2003). Japan's fascination with androgyny is interwoven throughout shoujo manga and anime, a dramatic and romantic sub-genre specifically marketed to young girls. Examples include the gender swapping of *Ranma ½*, the princely-girl archetypes in *Ouran High School Host Club* and *Gekkan Shoujo Nozaki-kun*, and the gender dysphoria present in *Hourou Musuko*.

In the Western music scene, glam rock warped gender norms as early as the Cockettes in the late 1960s, followed by David Bowie, The New York Dolls, Prince, and Grace Jones. Soon, the post-feminist punk scene dived into androgyny shaved-head-first, battling sexism and cissexism on every front—leading to queer feminist punk, post-punk, Goth and Indie-folk music scenes. Not long thereafter, the rise of internet culture allowed millions at home to experiment—not only with cross-sex identity personas but with androgynous online avatars unrestrained by dichotomy.

Yet resonance isn't quelled by censorship, no matter how many books, albums, wigs, or makeup kits are thrown in the trash. As the trans community was historically marginalized by a cissexist majority safeguarding the children against gender subversive encounters, many personal stories of resonance focus less on our rare queer encounters and more on our resonance with the opposite sex. Originally benign thoughts like "That dress looks pretty" evolve into "I wish I could wear it" into "I wonder how I would look in it?" Should our feelings be normalized through exposure to gender-positive communities, they may flourish. Should our feelings be suppressed, the resonance remains, albeit polluted by a layer of internalized cissexism.

Genderqueer, genderfluid, and agender individuals also encounter resonance, often from nonbinary encounters scattered between social scenes, art forms, or gender bending aesthetics when direct role models are not available (Devor, 1989; Losty and O'Connor, 2018; McQueen, 2011). Even small encounters with androgyny sing. A haircut, or an outfit, or even the stride in a person's gait can provide a rapt sense of wonderment, like a foreshadowed connection or an adumbrated epiphany. We may not know what it means, but the androgynous, fluid, or genderless imprint hits home.

Before we admit our gender, we first begin to spot these points of resonance within ourselves, even if we haven't determined what they mean. Perhaps they don't amount to anything gender related. Perhaps these feelings of resonance are simply that—feelings of kinship. Only we can individually figure that out, and there's no rush to do so.

Elevating appreciation, moments of resonance hone our focus. Whatever the subject or stimuli, they preoccupy our attention so wholly that we might even forget what we're doing. Momentary interactions may leave us reeling for days, thinking, visualizing, wondering, and pondering. It's often hard to admit our resonance out loud, especially in societies that dismiss or mock vulnerability. How often have you asked someone for their favorite song, only to have them sidestep the answer? How often do you guard your own answer by claiming, "Oh, I listen to everything," instead of revealing your tracklist? Sometimes, being asked what our *favorite* band is, or our *favorite* song, can feel paralyzing, because the word *favorite* feels so loaded and absolute. Context can fix this easily, as it's so much easier to share our favorite song of the week, or the song we've been listening to today, or the song that's currently on repeat on our tracklist. But when we feel self-concious, any curiosity around our *favorite* sensory experiences can feel like a trap. Our agenda of emotional control supersedes vulnerability, as it's not the song we're worried will be judged, but our deep resonance with it.

If it's pertinent to get the ball rolling, you can role model emotional enthusiasm for your client by sharing vulnerable "I like" statements of your own, demonstrating times you felt resonance in your life. These can include moments of epiphany, clarity, recognition, and belonging in the wake of emotional hardship—those special, formative moments when you felt aligned with your life. If you opt to disclose a personal memory for the sake of role modeling resonance, exemplify the emotion felt within the body over the content of the narrative. It's rarely useful to compare stories, as a client's rigid frames of distinction may cynically pick apart how our lives are different from your attempt to relate. Instead, describing resonance as it is felt in the body normalizes and validates the somatic experience, from which we can make our own connections.

Yet resonance can be a two-way street, as it shares the contextual heart song from self to other. It's common to feel exposed, embarrassed, or ashamed after sharing a resonant moment if there's no connection made after a deep disclosure. Should we share a resonant moment of our own, you can show vulnerable solidarity through authentic curiosity and empathic mirroring. This can also be achieved in Gestalt fashion by describing what *you feel* in response to *our narrative* in present time—but only if it is appropriate to do so and if we're receptive to this communication. Don't be afraid to ask if we are, as questions convey the desire for caring consent. Remember, you're not sharing your opinions, or judgments, or burdening us with emotional labor. Instead, you're sharing when *our* expression caused *your* chest to tighten. Describe how you paused, or leaned forward, or furrowed your forehead. Both Gestalt and somatic therapy employ this as a means of role modeling, and of strengthening the therapeutic bond. In ACT, a therapist reflecting on their own emotional response role models how to accept feelings without being overcome by them. In turn, such reflection is a powerful tool in gender affirmative therapy as it conveys your investment in your client to us directly.

In the same way a yawn can set off a sleepy wave through an entire room, the mirror neurons of a listener can match the brain pattern of the storyteller. In therapy, both clinician and client pick up on subconscious cues, emotive expressions, and social idiosyncrasies, contributing to a somatic feeling of empathy, as our neural pathways emulate each other and in turn shift our body language, emotionality, and sensory experience (Gallese, Eagle, and Migone, 2007). This accounts for the amazing charge felt in therapeutic sessions, in those moments when a clinician and client are truly present with each other. Understanding and compassion combined still do not equate with empathy. A person feels truly *met* when two bodies resonate with each other. This form of mutual resonance is known in psychoanalytic and transpersonal therapeutic circles as *attunement* (Gallese *et al.*, 2007).

A word to the wise: clinicians can become addicted to resonance. As such moments of therapeutic attunement are powerful—affecting both clinician and client—therapists can inaccurately "measure" the client's progress by this connection, or lack thereof. Clinicians will say things like "I feel like I'm not getting through to them" or "I feel like they have a wall and they're not letting me in." Such thoughts illustrate the clinician's desire to resonate, as it's the desire to "get through" or be "let in" that obfuscates objectivity. Clients may gain a lot from a therapeutic relationship without ever resonating with the clinician, and that's perfectly acceptable. If, as a clinician, you notice this desire within yourself, then you're encouraged to seek out consultation so as not to place undue pressure on our process.

As previously mentioned, resonance is a two-way street, and clients are often fused to frames of distinction. Such frames may restrict our vulnerability, since we may feel too guarded to open up or too alien to connect, especially with a cisgender therapist! The process of humanizing the self progressively allows us to humanize the other, so that over time we begin to connect and even resonate with a diverse array of people. Yet we may not be in that headspace at the beginning of a therapeutic relationship. If we express a desire to move through scripts of isolation and alienation, then community contact is encouraged. For LGBTQ people coming out, it's often these first encounters with others like us that foster a mirrored sense of resonance (Devor, 2004; Lev, 2007; Pflum *et al.*, 2015). Knowing that people like us see themselves in our eyes is an invaluable experience like no other, as it shows that we're neither alone in spirit, feeling, thought, or form (Devor, 2004; Walch *et al.*, 2012).

## Mindfulness exercise: **A day in the life**

Whenever we close our eyes, our hearing picks up. Every immediate, nearby noise comes to our attention, but then we notice the background—the constant, ever-present sounds we had tuned out. Adjusting, we might then catch something unique— a sound so fleeting we didn't even register it. Maybe a bird call or a distant conversation. The *A day in the life* exercise is a very similar process, but instead of a sound we're looking for a feeling in our body.

With eyes closed, recount a recent moment of resonance. Maybe we resonated with a person passing on the street, or a cartoon character on TV, or the heroine in a novel, or the lyrics of a song. Hold that resonance in mind, then rewind the clock. Start at the start, at the very beginning of the day when we got out of bed. How did we feel? Walk through the daily routine. Was this a normal day, or was this something different? Spare no detail. Maybe we were on our way to work when we saw someone walking down the street. Or maybe our friend came over and showed us a movie. Or maybe we were flipping through books online and came across one in the preview we would have never picked up in the store.

What was our initial impression? Surprise, confusion, curiosity, uncertainty? Take time to describe each of the five senses. What did we see, or hear, or smell, or touch, or even taste in that moment? Something caught us—a unique feeling in our body, perhaps in our hands, or chest, or stomach. Perhaps we noticed we hadn't blinked in a while, or that our cheeks had turned a little red.

What came to mind in that moment? Did we avert our eyes or open an incognito page on our browser, or did we feel excited and want to find out more? How long ago did all this happen? What did we do next? Were we still thinking about it, or did we try not to think about it, or did we turn the page and just go about our day? When did we think about it later on? Did we share that moment with anyone, or keep it to ourselves? Or is it only coming back to our attention now that we're thinking of it? As we describe all this, what do we feel in our body, right here, right now? What emotions are coming up in this moment?

This exercise conversationally explores how moments of resonance, especially when they pertain to gender, have a way of rippling throughout our day. Sometimes there are precursive events that build up the moment, in the same way we can be super-appreciative to see a good friend after evading a bad enemy. Sometimes, points of resonance are unexpected, appearing in glorious fashion. Sometimes they last only a second or two, sometimes they last for days, and sometimes they leave a lingering afterglow as we muse about our literal muses.

## Mindfulness exercise: **Daydream**

After years of having fingers snapped in front of us to pay attention, someone asking about our daydreams can be quite surprising. Isolation, alienation, and gender dysphoria can lead us to fantasize a great deal, to such an extent that we may feel like we daydream too much. Fantasists may revel in their intricate imaginings to fulfill unmet needs, yet others may dismiss daydreams as silly or not worth talking about. When asked, a far-off look may come over us, or we may avert our eyes, or fail to remember any of our daydreams at all, having shrugged them off entirely.

People often associate the act of daydreaming with being in a negative mood, as we often drift into our head during unpleasant chores. In these moments we may distract ourselves through fantasy, or find ourselves visualizing our frustrations, brooding over dark and unpleasant thoughts (Killingsworth and Gilbert, 2010). Yet not all daydreams are created equal. Daydreaming falls into three general styles. Positive, constructive daydreaming includes the deliberate act of planning, fantasizing, and wondering; guilty dysphoric daydreaming causes us to spiral into guilt, hostility, and fear of failure; and poor attentional control includes the fleeting, random daydreams that pop in and out of our heads (Giambra, 1980, 1989, 1995; Huba, Aneshensel, and Singer, 1981; Huba and Tanaka, 1983; McMillan, Kaufman, and Singer, 2013; Singer, 1975; Singer and Antrobus, 1970; Singer and Schonbar, 1961). Research has even found that daydreams about social interactions, especially with those closest to us, elevate our happiness, which in turn aids mental flexibility and potentially our creative process (Jampole, Mathews and Konopak, 1994; Jampole *et al.*, 1991; Poerio *et al.*, 2015; Zedelius and Schooler, 2015).

ACT utilizes daydreaming through metaphor as well as fusion and defusion exercises. To fuse, ACT may ask us to remember or imagine an upsetting moment. In this case, however, we're going to fuse with resonance through creative fantasy. Engaging in positive, constructive daydreaming allows for internal exploration, which can increase mental flexibility by activating our imagination. Constructive daydreaming is also a form of emotional permission-giving, as we permit our resonant desires, hopes, and aspirations to exist in fantasy.

There are two aspects of daydreams to be mindful of. The first is the restrictive anchors tying us down—the judgments we can practice defusing from. Imagine Michelangelo locking the door of the Sistine Chapel so no one could ever see his paintings? Imagine if Jimi Hendrix had never got on stage? Imagine if Beyoncé only sang under her breath? Giving ourselves permission to share our daydreams is an act of personal acceptance.

The second aspect to be mindful of is the emotional content of the daydream itself. Even the most fantastic imagining has, at its core, an emotional truth—a desire to play the hero, or exact revenge, or to find true love, or to follow curiosity to the farthest edges of the universe. Warmth, belonging, hope, wonder, awe, gentleness, validity, honor, dignity, fame, glamor, and love shape our fantasies, as do pain, sorrow, loss, anger, and vindication, though we can't always identify them directly—or hesitate to admit them when we do.

Some respond well to open questions like *What do you daydream about?* Or *When your mind wanders, where does it go?* Yet some may need more direct questions, like *Have you ever fantasized about being someone else? If you could set the fashion, what would you wear? What's something you've wanted to do but never dared to? If you had a billion dollars, what would you spend it on? If you were a shapeshifter but could only transform into three different people, what forms would you take? If you had a pair of wings, how big would they be and what would they look like? Have you ever fantasized about your ideal partner? What are they like?*

As we explore the narrative, bring awareness to our emotions. What do we feel right now as we share? What's the most exciting, strange, or unique part in all this? How long have we had this dream?

Daydreams about being another sex or gender don't indicate that we're transgender if we're cis, or cisgender if we're trans. This is not to say that daydreams are empty vehicles, as they can be the precursor of transition or life change, but not necessarily so. This mostly depends on the frequency of the daydream and the intensity of resonance felt in it. Cross-sex or cross-gender personas are often prime examples of how value constructs and personality characteristics become interwoven into a gender schema. Fantasy allows us to easily access anima and animus archetypes without commitment. Having a male or female avatar in a role-playing game doesn't mean we want a sex change. The novelist does not intrinsically desire to become their heroes or villains, though they may connect with their characters' emotional motives. Observing this, our daydreams can teach us a great deal about how we feel, how we feel about ourselves, and how we feel about gender on the whole.

### *Somatic mindfulness*

Hold a cup of ice. Feel the cold. The mind, being lightning fast, will hurriedly discern whether we like or dislike the chill at our fingertips, but before we can judge the cold, we first have to be aware of it. A unique exercise is to hold a warm cup of tea in one hand, and a cold cup of ice in the other. Again, the mind will start comparing the two, but slow everything down! Just feel the warmth in one palm and the chill in the other, existing simultaneously. Our internal process is actually quite similar, as we so often generate dissonance by applying oppositional judgments to our sensory experiences. Let those thoughts drift, and just try focusing our attention from the warm hand, to the cool hand, and back again.

ACT presents mindfulness techniques as a way of exploring our physical awareness, calling to attention where in our bodies we feel tight, loose, sore, achy, light, heavy, constricted, relaxed, and comfortable (Hayes and Smith, 2005). Our somatic experience of gender goes beyond socially performative body language, to include the physicality of emotions related to our gender experience. We may feel dissonance as a churning knot in our stomach when we embody something fraudulent, or we may feel resonance as a warm glow when we're called by our actualized name for the very first time. Hands may tremble in fear, elation, or both. We may hold our breath when something resonates, or literally bite our tongue when we're too scared to correct pronouns.

The performative nature of gender is best described as gender expression and gender role, and in our first experiments they can be quite archetypal, not because we endorse the perpetuation of stereotypic behavior, but because we may feel resonance in the performance. This is where gender meets our conceptual self. Cisgender, transgender, and nonbinary people alike can get stuck in these conceptualized performances, fusing with various rules of behavior that are also quite physical.

On the bus we notice Helen reducing her physical space as Henry sprawls his legs—*manspreading*. Helen feels like she can't be so bold as to assert her body language, and the very thought of doing so makes her laugh bashfully. Yet our manspreader Henry is also trapped, as the very prospect of delicate poise feels like a threat to his masculinity.

Three seats down we see Sean again, our local genderqueer tough kid. They slouch a lot because they try not to think about body language or anything somatic. Sean's also riding with Sam, who presents as a girl, currently, as only Sean knows Sam is a closeted trans man. Sam has a different problem, which may be difficult to grasp for those who've never felt dissonant with their anatomic sex, or those like Sean who either avoid or feel indifferent to body language. Misaligned with their sex, Sam feels a bodily restriction not unlike claustrophobia, as if whole dimensions of physical movement and ambulatory behavior are impossible. Sam feels trapped in their body and their body language, yet unlike cisgender Helen and Henry, Sam's deep desire to express himself in his body carries with it huge emotional consequences.

Defusing from these scripted gender performances allows us to hold our conceptual self loosely in our mind. Yet we cannot defuse from the affective signals of our somatic self, as both emotions and our experience of gender exist as physical cues within the body. ACT has brought our observational awareness to our somatic experience many times before, through breathing exercises, body scans, and descriptions of our sensory experience. Classically, ACT uses our somatic awareness to expand us beyond our conceptual and thinking self. For those experiencing gender dysphoria, the conceptual self and the thinking self can, at times, become dissonant with our somatic experiences to varying degrees. As gender is a felt experience, an intrapsychic conceptualization of self, and a series of socially performed scripts, it does not exist in any singular dimension of our mind–body experience. Indeed, all three are needed to formulate and operate a healthy gender construct, just as all three can bicker and argue in moments of cognitive dissonance. Cognitive–emotional fusion heavily contributes to these moments of conflict, especially if the rules and assessment practices we've fused have no room for our conceptual self. When we feel different from the cultural gender script, the thinking self will proceed to roll up the script and bop us on the nose with it. This can create a dizzying scenario should we feel we have two or more conceptual selves sparring with each other, one based on who we are and the other based on who we "should be."

When sex is treated as anatomically real and gender is treated as psychologically abstract, they become unnecessary opposites dichotomously removed from each other, at which point we begin to view gender as our conceptual self and no more. This reallocates gender to a mental self-image issue, and while self-image is certainly part of our internal body map, a map is just a representation of the terrain. A map can be torn up, redrawn, and discarded. The terrain cannot. If gender was solely conceptual, then we could simply re-conceptualize ourselves. Sadly, some conversion therapists still believe this, and work overtime like cartographers trying to move mountains to match their maps. Naturally, our mental terrain does change, and our conceptual self does change over the lifespan, especially for genderfluid people, yet it's not the cartographer that's responsible for growth, and any dynamite they apply can be incredibly destructive.

Examining our amazing neuroplasticity, we observe how the mind and body are not separate organizations, in the same way that an idea is a cognitive experience generated by an undeniably physical network of firing neurons. ACT delineates our conceptual, thinking, somatic, and observational selves as a way of building awareness of each respective area and disidentifying and decentralizing any singular one, since they work together as a collective whole. While we are most familiar with our conceptual and thinking selves as they rely on language and the schemas constructed from our relational frames, our somatic self operates on nonverbal instinct, supplying the nigh indescribable sense of dissonance and resonance experienced by so many gender variant people.

Beneath all our socially performed scripts of gender is a somatic actor feeling the performance in every part of the body. At the very core of a person's identity is a certain sine qua non, an essence, a relationship with the physical being so difficult to put into words (Forsyth and Eifert, 2016). Strip away the layered strata of social norms, gendered expectations, and rule-governed behavior—set aside all the over-thinking and social analysis—and we are left with a very intimate relationship between self and body. Our personal awareness of our gender is a physical one.

Queer theorists and gender researchers will argue the origin of these feelings until the end of time or the discovery of telepathy, whichever comes first. Perhaps it's genetic, or accrued behaviorism, but in session the *why* doesn't really matter too much, even if your clients are preoccupied with the answer. By redirecting to *what is*, we can mindfully explore the felt experience of gender as it appears in our bodies. ACT encourages safe and healthy self-experimentation as we adjust and actualize our identity, as there are a lot of gender performances to play with. Hours will be spent at home playing with hair, makeup, eyebrow plucking, shaving, not shaving, growing hair out, trying on clothes, learning how to walk, the whole kit-and-caboodle. A genuinely trusted therapist can provide a client with further space to experiment, and this can be a fun, if emotionally charged, process we'll return to again as we move to self-actualization.

## Mindfulness exercise: **Sensory awareness**

In ACT, mindfulness of the body is used to ground us in the present, but when we feel discrepant with our anatomic sex and its phenotypes, such exercises can feel daunting, to say the least. Gender dysphoria can manifest as whole-body discomfort, or become localized to a specific area of our anatomy, such as our face, chest, or genitals. Intrusive thoughts can judge the size of our feet or the coarseness of our hair follicles, or make us think we look like our mom or dad when we smile. Likewise, mindfulness exercises focusing on physical touch may be distressing if we have largely ignored our bodily experience.

Imagine trying to mindfully eat while having a painful cavity. The more mindful we are of what we're eating, the more we're painfully aware of our toothache. Similarly, we may be directed to do something with our hands, only to get preoccupied by how big, small, masculine, or feminine our hands are. Going beyond judgment and negative assessment, we may feel completely disconnected, as though our hands belong to someone else, and we're just operating them. Ironic process at its worst, our gender dysphoria may become most apparent, and therefore distressing, when clinicians encourage us to reconnect with our bodies.

To add injury to intrusiveness, body pain is not only an analogous experience, but in some cases a literal one. Trans-masculine chest bindings can bruise when done incorrectly, or lead to rashes and yeast infections under the breast when the skin can't breathe. Trans-feminine tucking can cause chafing and, in a few cases, urinary trauma. On the whole, gender variant people rarely bring up the pinching discomfort of tape, bandages, layered sports-bras, tight underwear, lopsided packers, form-fitting shapewear, or whatever homemade DIY solutions we've found to change our silhouette. Nor are we always forthcoming about the cuts, scrapes, and bruises caused by self-harm, bullying, or partner abuse. If this is the case, mind-body exercises designed to help us relax can inadvertently become explorations of guilt and shame.

Instead of avoiding this mind-body contention, sensory mindfulness can slowly work up to our sense of touch in order to practice more physical mindfulness activities. The easiest sense to connect with is often our sight, as it focuses on the world outside of our bodies. To begin, let's stare out the window and name ten things we can see that are physically moving, from the leaves rustling in the trees to the cars driving by. Accomplishing this, let's name ten things we can see that are perfectly still, from the rocks on the ground to the buildings across the street. If possible, pick up an object—something natural like a leaf or a piece of bark—and name ten colors in that one object. Even a dead leaf will contain various shades of tan, red, brown, and black. It's okay if we don't have an artist's vocabulary. Just notice all the different hues and shades, from brown, to darker brown, to muddy brown, to black, to reddish brown.

Now let's close our eyes and listen to the world around us. What are ten sounds we can hear? If it's quiet, open the window. Are there birds? Cars? Wind? Let's take time to describe how far away they are and how loud, or low, or shrill each sound is. As the clinician, don't lead or point out what can be heard. Just wait, and let us expand our auditory awareness. Searching for noises, some of us may strain to hear, while others might slowly realize the sound of our own breath, or even our own heartbeat.

Taste and smell are an excellent sensory interim, as they slowly introduce tangible interactions, connecting the external with the internal. Bring some food to session and practice mindful eating (Strosahl and Robinson, 2017). Perhaps choose something aromatic and stimulating like a strawberry or a grape. To begin, let's take our time to really observe it. Feel it in our fingers, inspect it closely, and smell how sweet, or tangy, or flowery it is. Then place it on the tongue and explore it without chewing. Does it feel smooth, or rough, or bumpy? What happens when we slowly bite down? Does the flavor change? Taste and smell exercises are generally easy, yet intrusive thoughts can still crop up, especially if we judge our metabolism, body image, diet, or even the physical act of eating.

Now, let's try engaging our physical awareness. A nonthreatening way to do this is to let us lead by naming ten things we are physically touching. This little modicum of control may allow us to avoid certain parts of our anatomy, and for the time being that's okay. If we need a little help, ask us to notice the inside of our sock with our toes (a mostly gender-neutral body part). If we continue to get stuck, try noticing external stimuli, like the temperature or the breeze.

Contacting the five senses to explore the external world can progressively build our willingness to increase contact—not with the incongruent anatomy, per se, but with the emotional discomfort and distress associated with it. When we have practiced this introductory somatic mindfulness, more explicit awareness can be brought to the physical body and any emotionally charged cognitions connected with it. Building awareness around the five senses also permits us to interact with our body in a non-gendered way. With such pressure around gendered beauty and physicality, being able to smell a strawberry and feel the sun on our cheeks reminds us that all the gendered questions and criticisms are secondary to a purely sensory experience.

## Mindfulness exercise: **Contextual body language**

Let's try some sitting positions. Posturing can be really insightful or really silly, so let's feel the feelings, laugh if it seems funny, and attune to the physical sensations as much as possible. First, let's take note of how we're naturally sitting. Where is our center of gravity? What do we notice in our body, our legs, our hands, or our back? What emotion do we have in this position? Is it comfortable or not? How would we describe this body language?

Now try an experiment. Let's sit poised with both knees together, both ankles together, on the edge of the seat (see Figure 3.1, left). When do we ever sit like this? Is it comfortable or not? Stay poised with knees touching but let's spread our ankles apart so that our legs are akimbo (see Figure 3.1, right). When do people sit like this? How does it feel?

**Figure 3.1** *Sitting straight and akimbo*

Now lean into the seat and throw one arm over the back of it, so that we're expanding our shoulders as wide as they can go. Let's tip our chin down and sprawl our legs apart (see Figure 3.2, left). When might we sit like this? Does it feel comfortable or not? Do we ever sit like this? How would we describe this posture? Next, try sitting up straight, one leg crossed neatly over the other, with our hands folded on our lap. Retract everything in so that we take up as little width as possible (see Figure 3.2, right). When might we sit like this? Does this feel natural or not?

**Figure 3.2** *Sitting expanded and retracted*

From here, let's hang our head and lean forward with both hands flattened between our knees. This will probably close the space between our arms and cause our shoulders to rise a little (see Figure 3.3, left). Ever seen someone sit like this? What feelings arise in this position? To compare, let's stay leaning forward, but let's open our legs again so that our elbows rest on our knees and our hands clasp together (see Figure 3.3, right). Do we ever sit like this? What emotions can we feel in this position?

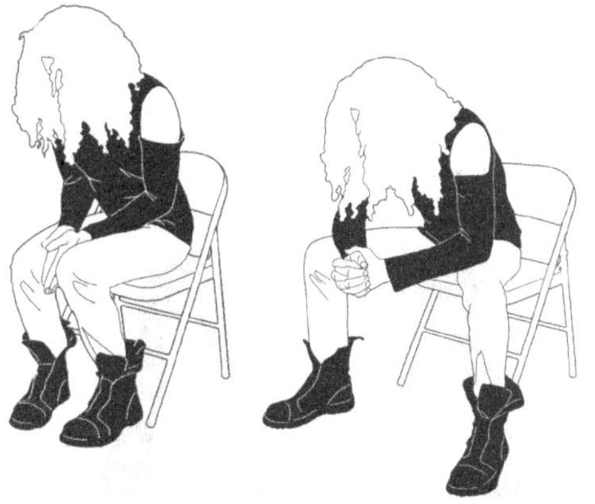

**Figure 3.3** *Sitting tight and clamped*

It is, perhaps, very easy to take these postures and camp them between masculine and feminine, yet this exercise can enlighten us to several unique aspects of our gender schema. The first is our emotional reactivity to these gender performances. All we're doing is sitting, but some of us react adversely to certain positions, or laugh awkwardly, or rest comfortably, or shrug them off with indifference, depending, that is, on our level of security with our own body and gender. Performative exercises like this can also help identify our sense of resonance to gender expression, as certain postures feel far more natural or even desirable than others. Some may say, "I always want to sit like this, but I'm worried people will think I'm a _____." Demonstrating our expectation of external judgment, of being labeled a sissy or butch, we reveal the conflict between our desire for authenticity and our fear of persecution. Note these areas of internalized cissexism and transphobia as areas to defuse from later.

As the clinician, implement gender neutral language in this exercise. It's perfectly acceptable for clients to gender their own body language as they see fit, but first provide an unlabeled opportunity. This exercise is easily undermined by gendered instructions. Telling a client to "sit like a little girl" or "sit like a tough guy," may fuse them to their judgments. Likewise, when you gender adjectives, you betray the judgment-free atmosphere of the session by revealing a biased assessment of gender.

Moving forward, let's try some power-poses, exploring with the same curiosity as before. Let's stand with our hands on our hips, with our feet firmly planted on the ground (see Figure 3.4, left). Then stand with our hands up high, as if we're trying to touch the ceiling (see Figure 3.4, right). Is this comfortable or not? Some may find power-poses to be exactly as they promised, *empowering*. Yet others, especially those who are self-conscious of their torso, may actually feel vulnerable and exposed in this position.

**Figure 3.4** *Standing power-pose*

There's a lot of different emotions encoded into our stance, so let's compare this with standing with our arms crossed and our knees locked. Holding this new position, let's really tighten our arms so that they press into our body (see Figure 3.5, left). What feelings emerge in this stance? When might we cross ourselves off like this? Let's take a minute to unfold and shake this feeling out, before trying the next one. This time, let's stand with both hands behind our head and one hip cocked to the side (see Figure 3.5, right). What does this feel like? Can we remember a time when we held this pose?

**Figure 3.5** *Standing locked and cocked*

Not all stances are dramatic and powerful. To diversify our body language, let's try some gentler poses. By standing with one leg crossed behind the other, with our hands behind our back, let's see what it's like to have our limbs behind us, leaving our front open (see Figure 3.6, left). Now, let's stand with both hands on our heart, letting our feet fall wherever they may (see Figure 3.6, center). How do these two stances compare? For our last position, let's stand with our knees together as we hug our tummy (see Figure 3.6, right). The same exploratory questions apply. What do we feel in these positions? Do we ever stand like this at home? Do any of these poses feel natural?

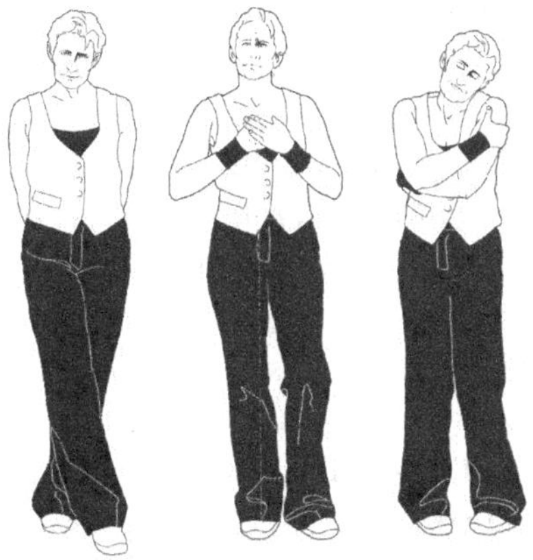

**Figure 3.6** *Standing gently and warmly*

As a complex, nonverbal system of communication, society affixes all kinds of gendered connotations to body language. How trapped we feel within our body language, however, is determined not by the action of movement, but by the litany of beliefs we have around the movement.

For those who are differently abled, these exercises can be easily adapted, depending on capability. If we can use our arms, try experimenting with closed fists and limp wrists, or by throwing out a shaka, or a pair of rock-n-roll devil horns, or even the Queen's wave. Another option is to experiment with facial expressions, like squaring the jaw or lowering eyebrows. Try looking "tough" or looking "shy" but clinicians should be cautious of gendered terms like "girly," "boyish," "manly," or "feminine." For the sake of mindfulness, focus on gender neutral descriptions, providing space for the client to gender their adjectives as desired (Mizock and Lewis, 2008). Anyone can be tough, shy, angry, sad, elegant, proud, noble, scared, thoughtful, curious, infatuated, or puzzled—yet not every gender rule gives permission to show it.

### *Emotional mindfulness*

At first glance, only happiness is "good" because it's fun and pleasurable, while all other emotions are "bad" because they're tumultuous and uncomfortable (Harris, 2009a; Hayes and Smith, 2005). If our hedonistic appraisal sees no worth in emotion—endorsing only pleasure and comfort—then we'll neurotically blame ourselves for feeling anger, sadness, grief, fear, or jealousy. We may slump on the couch, lamenting that there's something wrong with us because we couldn't keep our feelings under control, or because we shouldn't feel this way about something so small, or because—having avoided emotions for so long—we lacked the words to describe how we feel.

Even in our language, the majority of our feelings are treated as a kind of stigma. When asked how we're feeling, the only "socially acceptable" response is to give a passive, nondescript remark like "I'm fine" or "I'm good." As an awareness exercise, ask us to spend a day just counting how many people respond with quick, monosyllabic answers even in moments of distress. Or take a pen and mark our hand every time we respond passively with "fine" or "good" or "alright." Playing down emotional content is exceptionally common in Western youth culture, where the image of cool stoicism devolved into depressed apathy. Understanding this opaque language system as a defense mechanism evading vulnerability, "I'm fine" or "I'm good" translates to "I have emotions, but I'll deal with them and I don't want you to doubt or worry about me." When understood as a social mechanism, "I'm fine" or "I'm good" translates to "I want to share, but I don't know if you actually care or if you're asking out of social obligation." How many of us are just waiting for someone to press our answers. "Seriously though, how are you really feeling?" How many of us are afraid of the very same question, trying to avoid the answer and all the emotions loaded with it?

Early on in the therapeutic relationship, inquire what would happen if we chucked terms like *good* and *bad*, *positive* and *negative* right out the window. Just tacking "I feel" onto a word or statement doesn't make it an emotion. Arguably, "I feel good" is not an emotion, it's an assessment—at best a vague, nondescript placeholder for an emotion we dare not name. When we're no longer summarizing life with short, monosyllabic answers, we may feel a number of emotions we would typically dismiss. Sure, we're frustrated, mildly annoyed, but why talk about it? Sure, we're a little sad, maybe even bored, but why bring it up? We may even feel emotions that seemingly contradict other emotions. We may feel sad about this but glad about that. We may love someone and feel angry with them, at the same time. Life isn't so neat and tidy as we'd like it to be.

ACT focuses on describing thoughts and feelings over assessing or measuring them (Hayes and Smith, 2005). Because of this, emotional mindfulness often resembles permission-giving, as we slowly relinquish our judgment of our feelings to be truly aware of them. This is poignant as not all emotions are clear. Our experience of feelings is often muddied by sleep deprivation, hunger, unresolved issues, and our own secondary emotional process, like when we feel guilty about feeling angry, or angry about feeling hurt (Hayes *et al.*, 2012; Orsillo *et al.*, 2004; Plutchik, 1991). Validating our feelings exactly as they are is difficult, as there are a myriad of personal and social stressors prompting our feelings to exist in tandem, paradox, and contradiction. Learning how to identify our feelings through nonverbal cues, and by expanding our emotional vocabulary, aids in both meta-awareness and cognitive defusion, as we challenge judgmental emotional assessment and our overgeneralizing vocabulary.

## Mindfulness exercise: **Painting rainbows**

Struggling to express our feelings, we may repeat the same adjectives over and over: "I feel annoyed;" "I feel frustrated;" "I feel angry;" "I feel sad;" "I feel anxious." Likening this to art, our first paint set as kids was a pack of primary colors, but now that we're older we're learning about turquoise, and magenta, and navy blue. Expanding our emotional vocabulary is the art of combining yellow, blue, and red to create a whole rainbow of emotional experience, which is a great reason to crack out the old paint sets in session. Grab a brush, some spare paper, and let's paint some rainbows! This exercise can be a visualization, but literally playing with paint is a great tangible metaphor.

First, label each color with a familiar emotion. Red, happy. Blue, sad. Green, guilt. Yellow, fear. Everyone will allocate a different color to a different feeling, with many unique associations to explore. Now, there are two ways to paint a rainbow. One is to keep the colors separated, and the other is to let them blend. As we become increasingly more aware of our emotions, we start to notice that some feelings separate and blend too. When emotions separate, they become compartmentalized, which is to say we feel happy about this *and* sad about that, like a swathe of red next to a swathe of blue. A blend is to say our happiness and sadness have mixed together into a new feeling, a kind of purple in need of a name. Ever cried at a wedding? Ever gushed at a goodbye party? Combine red happy and blue sad and we'll feel a sappy purple spectrum, all tender and bittersweet.

If anger is red and joy is yellow, then what is orange? Joyous anger? What would we call that? Malevolence, vengeance, sadism, competitiveness, assertiveness, or even primal carnality could all be shades of orange. Since this is a psychoeducational exercise, brainstorm as many answers as possible. For example, happiness and sadness can paint a scene of whimsical nostalgia or homesick grief, depending on the interpretation. Happiness and fear can paint giddy, excited nervousness, verging on awe and wonderment, or—depending on the shade of fear—it can be a muddy kind of mania. Fear and sadness can paint despair or rejection. Fear and anger can paint repulsion or defiant courage!

Like any artist, we progress from primary and secondary to tertiary colors. What is the emotional equivalent of vermillion, violet, teal, chartreuse, and amber? Have we ever felt ennui, melancholy, triumph, relief, dismay, or pity? Pick up an emotional vocabulary chart or diagram to practice expanding and articulating the nuances of emotion. Note that this isn't an age-dependent exercise. Many adults have spent decades minimizing feelings down to the bare essentials of black or white, good or bad, awesome or shitty.

Having accrued a whole color palette, we can now paint a rainbow of our entire contextual experience. When recalling a distressing memory, are the emotions clearly partitioned or do they blend together? Sometimes, when we feel cynical, we may reject emotions, proclaiming that nothing makes us feel happy, or that we don't get angry. Instead of debating over linguistic definitions, we can explore with colors. When was the last time we felt red? When have we felt that fiery orange? Have we ever felt cool blue? Sometimes, we can fuse so tightly to an emotion we may believe we can only feel one at a time, yet a brief interview expanding our awareness often shows how there's more than just our anger, sadness, and pain. Being emotionally single-minded may initially seem easier, but such rigid focus makes it hard to exist in a personal and social sphere. By practicing emotional awareness, it becomes progressively easier to defuse from a singular, emotionally obsessive viewpoint. It's also a great way to decorate the office with rainbows.

## Mindfulness exercise: **Yes, and...**

In acting class the first rule of improvisation is "Yes and..." Any time a skit is met with "Yes, but..." the actors get stuck as the creative free-flow gets stifled by unnecessary contradiction. When we stifle ourselves, we very quickly narrow our perception, limiting our attention to only one or two feelings. We may even acknowledge an emotion, and use our "Yes, but..." to launch back into our reasons, explanations, and justifications. We use "Yes, but..." to give control back to our thinking self, at which point the improvisational scene is hijacked by an old, previously rehearsed script. Imagine going to a comedy show and having someone on stage steal the spotlight with a dark Shakespeare monologue. It doesn't matter if it's well performed, it's old, scripted, depressing, and kind of boring.

The *Yes and...* exercise is a simple, effective way to expand every somatic, cognitive, and emotional awareness we have, even outside of a session. Our inner monologue may lament how tired we feel this morning. Yes, and...? We also feel kind of relieved that we didn't get stuck in traffic. Yes, and...? We feel uncertain about how we should feel. Yes, and...? We feel hungry and our knee hurts. Yes, and...? And we feel frustration and regret because our knee hurts after taking the stairs. Yes, and...? We feel a little proud of ourselves for not taking the elevator.

Another way to do this is the *Get off our but* exercise, replacing every self-referential use of the word "but" with "and" (Hayes and Smith, 2005). For example, we may feel happy today *but* we have to go to work. Catching this, we can feel happy today *and* go to work.

As fusion leads to fixation, we naturally focus on what we're most fused with. For example, when asked to explore fear, we may identify synonyms or other emotions that feel equally daunting. The old colloquialism "On the one hand_____, on the other hand _____" is another *Yes, and...* approach. To troubleshoot hyperfocus, we can list five related feelings on one hand before expanding our attention to five unrelated feelings on the other. So, if we feel anxious, worried, frightened, cautious, and uncertain about work, what other dimensions of work elicit an emotional response? How do we feel about our co-workers, or the end of the work week, or what we'll spend our paycheck on? Having an emo chart is handy and can help expand vocabulary while also reinforcing that you, as the clinician, are not looking for a specific response. Trying to be chipper, we may assume we have to present a handful of positive emotions to counter the first hand, but this is not the case. On the one hand we may be worried about work because of job performance; on the other hand we may feel bored, frustrated, annoyed, concerned, and perplexed by our co-workers—all of which are meaningful emotions distinct from our original worry. This may seem doubly overwhelming, but we're just beginning to expand. To be playful, we can keep checking hands, imagining ourselves with multiple arms like Hindu deities, or we can play an emotionally elaborate game of heads-shoulders-knees-and-toes. On one shoulder _____, on the other shoulder_____. On one knee, _____, on the other knee_____. On one foot_____, on the other foot _____. Keep exploring multiple contexts in the same setting. There are a lot of stimuli at work, with many interactions, events, situations, and corresponding feelings.

If we get stuck, staring blankly at the emo chart or shrugging our shoulders at every *Yes, and...*, we can explore how we feel about our feelings. Exploring our secondary emotional process deepens our understanding, as we may feel apathetic about our anxiety or exhausted by our anger. Over time, *Yes, and...* cultivates mental flexibility by allowing our observational self to broaden its emotional awareness, noticing the diversity of feelings, as well as our dynamic relationships with each other. We may, for example, respect our co-worker and feel intimidated by our boss, enjoy our smoke break and be tired on Monday, feel nervous about the new position, and feel glad for making friends.

## Mindfulness exercise: **Pizza words**

Draw a large circle with a line down the middle of it. Ever have a pizza with two different toppings? Maybe vegetarian on one half, peperoni on the other? Let's imagine our favorite kind of pizza on one half. How would we describe it? *Tasty.* Write that in the circle. We're going to make a pizza out of words. How else would we describe a tasty pizza? We might call it *good, fine, okay, alright, amazing, wonderful, delicious, excellent, brilliant,* or *outstanding*! We might even call it *the best damn pizza in the world.*

Now let's take a slice from the other side. We were trying to be polite, ordering some other toppings for someone else, but this is the worst pizza ever. *Yuck.* Picture the worst pizza topping imaginable. How would we describe it? *Disgusting, nasty, bad, terrible.* Write those words down in the other half of the pizza. Now imagine it's been sitting in the fridge for days and it's starting to go off. How would we describe it then? *Wretched, vile, awful, shitty*—maybe even *fucked up* (see Figure 3.7)!

Problematically, pizza happens to be one of the most addicting junk foods on the planet. We tell ourselves we'll never order from that pizzeria again but we already know that's a lie. Even if we don't eat out, we know one of our friends is going to come over with a pizza on Saturday, and we'll be right back to where we started.

**Figure 3.7** *Judgmental pizza*

Reviewing the words on this split pizza, what do they all have in common? Half of them are decent, half of them are completely messed up, and all of them are judgments. Judgment words are the junk food of language. They're satisfying and life-affirming to say, and they're alright in moderation, but a diet of pizza words leaves us feeling pretty disgusting. And if someone asks us how we feel? We'll reach for another slice!

Quick arbitrary answers for quick arbitrary questions have conditioned many of us to respond to emotional inquiry with: "I'm good," "I'm okay," "I'm fine," or "I'm shitty." We cut the content short when we're unsure of who actually cares about the answer, or we cut the content short because we're avoiding our internal world, or we cut the content short because we don't want others to worry, judge, or second guess our capability in some way. Yes, we'll share pizza words with everyone, yet if we're alone, we run the risk of eating it all by ourself, restricting our emotional communication.

Young people in particular may protest that "good" and "bad" are emotions, but that's just the junk food talking. *Good* and *bad* are assessments, broad classifications of our emotions without actually expressing what those feelings really are. If someone says they're good, we have no idea if they're happy, excited, eager, jubilant, or ecstatic. If someone says they're bad, we have no idea if they're sad, angry, grieving, lost, confused, or numb. In summary, if we can use it to describe a pizza, it's not an emotion.

Try taking a diet from pizza words for a week, or even just in session. Make the office free of junk-food. It's not easy, even for clinicians, to omit judgment-oriented language. Like any diet, the trick is to find a healthy balance. If a therapist forbade us from eating pizza ever again, we might get up and walk out the door. Much like the *Yes, and...* approach, we're expanding on our judgments, and even using them as a reminder to check our emotions, in the same way that pizza for lunch can remind us to have a healthier dinner. Make a pact that every time we notice ourselves using a pizza word, we'll also express three emotions. "How was this exercise? It was fine I guess...and it was fun, but awkward and silly, too."

## *Social mindfulness*

Infants have no concept of gender, yet the world insists on gendering babies based on sex. From the get-go, the agency of understanding our gender lay with someone else, whether our parents, siblings, or community (Wight, 2011). Little girls dressed in pink stereotypes grow into teenage women bombarded by beautyism, who in turn grow into women sifting through familial, occupational, moral, and sexual pressures, who in turn grow into older women struggling with social invisibility. Little boys dressed in blue stereotypes grow into teenage men bombarded with toxic masculinity, who in turn grow into men sifting through uniquely different but equally subversive sets of familial, occupational, moral, and sexual pressures, who in turn grow into older men struggling with social impotence. These are not exclusively cisgender narratives, as some trans people have felt very similar, if not identical, pressures. However, being in transition can heighten these performance expectations and the perceived risks and consequences around them, while the gender nonconforming may feel relentlessly bombarded by social expectations they do not, cannot, or will not live up to.

Add to this the social imposition and performance expectation of being gender variant. When defined in terms of deviance, trans identities are politicized as a threatening transgression against gender norms (McQueen, 2011). And if we're not cast as the villain in modern media, then we're cast as the victim (Reitz, 2017). In 2012, the Gay and Lesbian Alliance Against Defamation (GLAAD) released a decade-long review of television and film representation, recognizing that trans characters were presented as victims in 40 percent of the plotlines, sex workers in 20 percent of the plotlines, and villains in 21 percent of the stories (GLAAD, 2012). Even the image of transsexualism is shaped by televised binaries, to such an extent that gender variant people will say to other gender variant people, "You don't look trans" or "I would have never known you were transgender."

As an empowerment process, self-actualization reclaims personal agency. This can be a frustrating task if our community doesn't receive or validate our gender. Here we are, doing all this personal work to understand ourselves, and having finally figured it out—having finally aligned with who we are—the world shrugs us off and spits at our feet. Even the LGBTQ community isn't always friendly, as the LGB can distance themselves from the T and Q. The benefits of gender variant community exposure are well documented, but nonbinary genderqueer, genderfluid, and agender people can feel excluded in the transgender community (Budge, Rossman, and Howard, 2014). Trying twice as hard to get people to receive us, we present our *positive face*, or else we turn our back and act like we don't care, presenting our *negative face* (Tracy, 1990; Wight 2011). Uniquely, both positive and negative faces are modes of social performance adhering to both personal and social scripts.

Beneath all the argued rhetoric and identity politics of gender is a social interaction. In a single conversation, each person projects onto the other their expectation and conceptualization of that person's gender, influencing their behavior toward them. On top of this, each person presents their own "gender performance" through verbal and nonverbal means (Butler 1990, 1993; Wight, 2011). Such performances aren't reductionist, by any means, as every intonation, paralinguistic pause, and posturing encapsulates a long history of cultural factors (Wight, 2011). Each society builds its gender roles and gender rules, which we either ascribe to or dissent from—yet even dissent is a performative act of rebellion. As an exercise, social mindfulness explores how conscious we are of our social behaviors, if we're being deliberate or reactionary, and how influenced we are by external perspectives.

## Mindfulness exercise: **Social belief inventory**

Gender variant people are often subjected to a lot of ignorant questions. A lot. A ridiculous amount. No facet of our lives goes unscrutinized at some point by someone wanting to know if we did, didn't, or are planning to have surgery, or how we have sex, or where we buy our clothes, or how our relationships work, and so on. Not only this, but cisgender people often look to gender variant people to be ambassadors to the realm of sex and gender. Some of us may happily take on the role of sex educator, gender advocate, and even queer confessional, yet some may feel annoyed by every misinformed cisgender person shopping for a private sexologist.

"When I meet a trans person, how should I ____?"

"Is it inappropriate to say ____?"

"Does wearing ____ make me ____?"

"If I do ____ does that make me ____?"

"How is one supposed to be transgender?"

"Can you tell someone's trans by how they look?"

"How are trans people supposed to behave?"

"How are trans people supposed to sound?"

"How do you let people know you're transgender?"

When asked any of these questions, we may sigh or roll our eyes, or answer as politely as we can, or flip you off. The answer to each question is utterly subjective and absolutely relative. As LGBTQ individuals straddle multiple communities, questions about our social beliefs can also give us pause. Which society are you talking about, here? Have we integrated our communities, or do we keep them separate? Be specific when exploring these themes, identifying respective social groups should they be explored.

*How do you feel when you hear the word transgender and you're by yourself? Do your feelings change when you hear that word around your family?*

*How do you believe the cisgender majority views transgender people?*

*How do you believe the local LGBTQ community views transgender people?*

*How does your church/synagogue/mosque address gender identity?*

Questions of this kind can bring up areas of fusion within our belief system, as our answer, no matter how accurate and insightful it may be, still falls into the scope of generalization. Likewise, our investment in other people's beliefs can also reinforce unhealthy behaviors that no longer serve us. Explore this by asking:

*What do people say to you that's insulting?*

*What do you believe other people think it's insulting to say?*

*Do you think there's a social role for transgender people in the cisgender world?*

*Is it the same role that cisgender people currently project onto you?*

*Do you think there's a social role for transgender people in the LGBTQ community?*

*Is it the same role that the LGBTQ community currently projects onto you?*

*Do you believe society allows transgender people to show their feelings?*

*Do you feel society has a certain expectation around how transgender people are supposed to look or sound?*

Bristled responses like "I don't care what other people think," though potentially or partially true, also convey fortified independence. In other words: "I want you to see that I don't care about what you see." Just as those who dissent from society are still a part of society, we cannot, no matter how hard we try, exist in a vacuum.

While sometimes difficult, taking a belief inventory can reveal how we view our community and overall society, alongside the messages we have received from it. Even if we actively rebel against them, the pressure remains; and given the dilemma of ironic process, we may still fuse with beliefs we don't even believe in.

## Mindfulness exercise: **Trans gazing**

*Trans gazing* is a mindfulness exercise best facilitated in trans empowerment groups. Ideally, trans gazing is led by a gender variant therapeutic practitioner or community role model intimately familiar with feminist and queer theory, as well as transgender subjectivity and identity politics (LeMaster, 2018; Stryker and Bettcher, 2016). Essentially, trans gazing is a public field trip with a safe cohort of openly gender variant individuals one can rely on for both social support and surrogate mindfulness (LeMaster, 2018). This exercise may be too much for clients who have not yet come out. However, undertaking such a field trip may provide a safety-in-numbers experience with known and trusted allies. For obvious reasons, in vivo experiences of this kind must be assessed on a case by case basis.

As a facilitator, select a high visibility area to enter and leave together, allowing for both a briefing and debriefing, while simultaneously ensuring client protection. While it's recommended to select a safe location, safety is not always a measurable factor, as we never know what potential encounters may occur on a field trip. Frontload everyone that this is a real-world scenario. It's not about exposure, or building stress tolerance, and we can leave whenever we want. Instead, this is a mindfulness exercise, as we're going to see who sees us.

Trans gazing watches the watcher (LeMaster, 2018). In a public space, we help each other take note of who's looking or staring. What expressions do people make? Does age play a factor? Are children curious? Do the elderly frown? Do people smile in support? Do people deliberately try not to look? Perhaps go to a coffee shop or a restaurant together. How does the server respond? Are they trying extra hard to be indifferent? Do they make a deliberate point of using pronouns, or do they not? Or do they reject our pronouns outright?

As we gaze at the gazers, explore in group discussion what feelings emerge during this process. Explore why we feel individuals react the way they do, or how we feel others see us. Are we being perceived as perverts or deviants, or are we being seen as courageous and brave? Do we feel like we're all being lumped together as a group or, depending on the diversity of the participants, do we feel people are reacting to us differently as trans men, trans women, or nonbinary people (LeMaster, 2018)? Do we feel invisible or highly visible? Do we feel race or cultural identity is a factor? Do we experience moments of affirmation or is it all rejection?

Be aware that verbal assaults may occur on outings like this; as such it's critical for facilitators to watch the watchers watching the watchers (LeMaster, 2018). As a mental health practitioner your primary duty is looking after the safety and wellbeing of your clients, which requires vigilance in a moving, social environment. A debrief session after the outing provides us an opportunity to process any emotions, observations, or responses we had, while also providing the facilitator a pre-directed action plan should escalation arise in either the clients individually, the clients as a group, or the environment as a whole.

This exercise is best facilitated by gender variant individuals familiar and sensitive to the experience, as this is a situation requiring both credibility and social role modeling. If the facilitator is gender variant, they may feel some of their own emotional process, requiring the practitioner to practice in-the-moment mindfulness (LeMaster, 2018). As a group activity, it's advisable to have a co-facilitator, to increase both physical and emotional safety and awareness for all participants, including the facilitator.

# 4

# Acceptance

*Acceptance* is a powerful word loaded with hopes and fears, questions, and caveats. Even when we need to change a facet of our life, we must first accept that we need a change (Blackledge and Hayes, 2001; Hayes and Smith, 2005). On realizing our gender, we may go public very quickly, or take years before finally admitting it (Devor, 2004). However, whenever, and wherever it happens, albeit with a best friend or alone in the mirror, finally admitting our gender is a huge step toward acceptance. Relief, concern, wonder, dread, hope, worry—it all floods forward as we sit with the implications this newfound acceptance will have on our personal, social, familial, and professional life (Devor, 2004). At this point, acceptance takes on a sudden shadow. When first presented as a therapeutic practice, clients may baulk, interpreting acceptance as defeat:

> "Am I supposed to accept that my parents will disown me?"
>
> "Am I supposed to accept that there's nothing I can do?"
>
> "Am I supposed to accept my body or my gender?"

To clarify, ACT doesn't encourage cutters to accept self-harm, but to accept the struggle they have with relinquishing control (Zettle, 2007). ACT doesn't aid alcoholics to accept solely addiction, but to accept the floating feelings they've tried so hard to drown, and the grief that comes with giving up the bottle (Hayes and Smith, 2005). ACT doesn't aid the socially anxious to accept retreat, but to accept the somatic feelings that arise in public situations (Forsyth and Eifert, 2016). For gender variant clients, ACT does not advocate helplessness, nor acceptance of a cissexist society. Quite the opposite.

By reclaiming value-congruent self-efficacy, we can take action, channeling our energy where it's most needed. Yet first we have to acknowledge what's out of our control, including our emotional response to social prejudice. We can't pretend everything's okay, nor can we selectively choose our emotions. To accept who we are is to also accept how we feel in the world we live. For some, this may look like setting boundaries, using our voice, and advocating for our needs. For others, this means ending our subscription to Bullshit Magazine. We may have to leave behind unhealthy relationship dynamics we've endured for years. Don't mistake this for avoidance. It may seem contradictory, but when we sidestep an abusive situation we're accepting the pain associated with it (Hayes and Smith, 2005). We're not tolerating it, or making excuses for it, or repeating history.

By mindfully exploring what brought us to therapy, you can gauge our *willingness* to help ourselves (Hayes and Smith, 2005). Willingness is the power of choice, smack dab at the crossroad of here and now. To differentiate, willpower is a finite resource. Those with ADHD can "force" themselves to pay attention just as the depressed can sometimes marshal willpower to keep themselves standing, but stubborn endurance isn't sustainable. If we could will ourselves to be happy, therapists would be out of a job. Willingness is not our belief in ourselves, or our desire to believe in ourselves, nor is willingness an act of effort, as we can physically pick up a pen, but trying to pick up a pen without action leaves us staring at it like an impotent telekinetic (Hayes and Smith, 2005).

Admittedly, we can control our behavior, yet our attempts to control emotion lead to distress, limited perspectives, unhealthy biases, and forms of self-judgment so critical that we may feel embarrassed, ashamed, or even terrified of our own feelings. For those forcing a smile, the effort to smile indicates the need to sigh. For those who feel at war with cisgender social norms, it does no good to charge headlong into an army.

Willingness can be found in our answer to one simple question: *Will I take me as I am?* (Hayes and Smith, 2005). We are not always ready to do this, as we must first identify what needs to be accepted in our lives. This needs-based self-examination can provide us agency in the therapeutic process, as it explores what is absent, what is present, what is tolerated, what is growing, and what has not yet grown. If we're willing to accept ourselves as we are, then our old measurements of distress no longer apply. Asking, *How anxious are you?* or *On a scale of one to ten how depressed are you?* implies a scoreboard and the false paradigm that somehow we're going to win or lose the game of life, just as the question *Did you have a good day?* compacts our complicated lives into a single judgment (Hayes and Smith, 2005). Willingness is our ability to accept *what is*, without measuring, comparing, or limiting ourselves by it.

## Presenting creative hopelessness

If we just want to be happy, we may feel like therapeutic mindfulness doesn't work—and from where we're sitting we're not wrong, because therapeutic mindfulness doesn't make our feelings go away, and it doesn't make us happy!

Creative hopelessness occurs when we realize our unworkable solutions are the real problem, and that all this mess came about from trying to control or avoid our feelings (Hayes, 2004). Even our pursuit of happiness has tripped us up, as happiness is not a goal but a byproduct of a value-congruent life. In fact, trying to be happy can be exhausting as it implies we *have to try* (Harris, 2008). Ironically, the effort exemplifies the absence. Trying to care only shows that we don't. In a similar vein, trying to lift self-esteem can often feel like a Pyrrhic victory. People are often surprised by this, as happiness and self-esteem are often associated with behavioral outcomes. Our hierarchical frame assumes:

"I'll be happy if I do____."

"If I do ____, I'll be proud of myself."

"Once I finish ____, then I'll be okay."

Letting go of our control tactics, and even the pursuit of happiness and the need for self-esteem, may seem downright mad! But a rich and meaningful life is the celebration of *what is*, not what should be. Embracing a whole emotional experience can provide a great deal of clarity, though allowing ourselves to accept our feelings after so many years of evasion can be hard. If we've spent our lives fighting to preserve hope, the term *creative hopelessness* can even sound threatening. When explaining this concept, note that creative hopelessness is neither defeat nor bleak despair. We're not giving up hope on life, love, community, acceptance, or the pursuit of social justice. There's a lot in this world worth advocating for, and many things we all have the power and personal agency to change. We are, however, giving up on the idea that we can somehow fight ourselves in the same way that we fight oppression. We're giving up on the idea that we can wave a magic wand and change who we are. We're giving up on the idea that *if I just do this, I won't feel that.* We're giving up on the idea that we can do something that will automatically fix our emotional experience or avoid something that begets all our troubles. There are many things in life that have solutions and answers, yet now we're giving up on any hope that emotions are curable.

Our positive, hopeful desire to help ourselves has become desperate, and in its own way problematic, exerting all our excess energy to be happy even when we're not! Many ACT metaphors illustrate this futility, from struggling in *quicksand*, to fighting a *tug-o-war*, to pulling on a *Chinese finger trap* only to get more stuck (Walser and Westrup, 2007; Sandoz *et al.*, 2010). In each, the more we fight against our emotions, the more futile it becomes. To demonstrate, try deleting a memory (Harris, 2009a). Remember how you got here, today. Visualize the commute, opening the door, and even sitting down in the chair. Now delete that memory. Try to erase it entirely from the mind. Really try, and see how it goes.

You can also try to numb a body part at will (Harris, 2009a). Without moving, try to numb an arm or a leg, to such extent we could amputate without anesthesia. Genuinely give it a shot. Most likely you'll get the point pretty quick, yet it's worth illustrating how emotions cannot be banished either.

Engaging our observational self allows us to transcend the internal conflict and our pressing desire to keep our emotions in check. Gender variant individuals often feel like we're up against something larger than ourselves, whether it's a body that doesn't fit, or a gender that has no place in society, or a family that doesn't understand, or a dichotomous and oppressive civilization. Every conditional statement, rule, and reason becomes an anchor weighing us down. Those just beginning to conceptualize gender can feel limited and incapable of dealing with all the surging external pressures and internal undertow. Great energy is expended to fight, shield, convince, advocate, camouflage, hide, distract, ignore, or recover from this great wave—which is perhaps the most suitable metaphor for those just starting to accept themselves. The *floating* metaphor, introduced by Emily Sandoz, Kelly Wilson and Troy Dufrene (Sandoz *et al.*, 2010), can easily be paraphrased as follows to benefit gender variant clients and reflect the immensity of our identity:

> *It sounds like you've been struggling with these feelings for a long time. I have this image in my mind; maybe you can picture it with me. Have you ever gone to the beach? If you haven't, can you imagine wading out into the water? There's a sweet spot where you can stand, and feel the water pushing gently back and forth. You might even enjoy it. Then you see a large wave ahead of you. Even if you're able to manage where you are now, that large wave is headed your way, and the water's starting to rise. If you look away, you'll be bowled over, or even swept out to sea. You definitely can't touch the bottom with your feet anymore, but there's a couple of things you can do, and it sounds like you've been doing them already! It sounds like you've been kicking your legs and trying to stay afloat, right? Doing everything you can to keep your head above water. And then the wave broke and you acknowledged your gender out loud, and it was scary! And now you're just starting to catch your breath—only to see another wave ahead. Sound about right? Maybe someone else you want to come out to. Maybe someone you're worried about finding out. But I wonder what would happen if you relaxed? Do you think you'd float? There are still going to be big waves, the ocean's pretty vast, but instead of trying to avoid the waves, or swimming as hard as you can through them, what would it be like to just float? Would you be willing to find out?*

Creative hopelessness is the point in the therapeutic process when we realize we need to give up on the agenda of emotional control, and it can come with a real emotional drop. All our attempts to change, alter, or avoid our problems have wound up costing too much, yet we may continue to question the worth of our emotional experience, leading to shame, anxiety, anger, depression, and regret. At this juncture, it's time to introduce several routes to emotional acceptance.

## Presenting emotional acceptance

We cannot control our emotions any more than we can control the weather, but we can change our relationship with both, just as someone can fight with an umbrella or laugh in the rain. Do we loathe the winter day, or appreciate the crispness of the air? Do we dread the summer, or lounge in the shade? Can we do both at the same time? In ACT, every emotion, thought, and sensation is seen as not only viable, but part of a complete life experience, and no matter how gigantic or dark our ever-changing clouds become, the sky always has room (Harris, 2009a; Strosahl and Robinson, 2017). When we perceive our observational self as expansive as the sky, the massive thunderheads and torrential rains hold no threat, as every blustering wind and scorching day is passing and impermanent (Harris, 2009a).

When we're fused, we feel like we're on the ground, being blown about, our umbrella now inside out. Running from the rain, we hide in a house, which gets blown over, so we hide in a bunker, which starts to flood! Validate these efforts to get out of the rain, even if they don't work or are admittedly avoidant, as gender variant individuals contend with typhoons. Every drop of rain is another transphobic microaggression, every gust a billowing trauma, and every crack of lightning another reminder that we're not in control (Stitt, 2014). Our emotional storms are certainly our own, but in this metaphor the high- and low-pressure fronts represent the social environments we react to. Defusion can be very difficult when we feel drenched and battered, and LGBTQ clients may protest that you don't understand the gravity of our situation, or that you're implying we accept our lot in life (Blackledge, 2015; Stitt, 2014). If this is the case, it's worth demonstrating how internal self-acceptance—the embrace of personal identity with all the emotions that go with it—is distinct yet interconnected with external self-acceptance, the interrelationship between self and community (Stitt, 2014). Not only does the line blur between internal and external self-acceptance, but individualistic and collectivistic cultures prioritize them quite differently, pitting nature against demeanor, and personal pride against social appraisal (Stitt, 2014). Instead of favoring one or the other, both will be addressed over the course of therapy as they're essentially inseparable. But in this moment, it's just us together again, client and clinician. Let's imagine if that same storm blew away every antagonist in our lives. Imagine if that hurricane swept the world clean of every cissexist, transphobic, homophobic, and racist person we have ever met. They're all gone, and yet the storm remains. Long after the argument, we brood over the insults. Long after the violence, we run our fingers over the scars. Long after the rejection, we feel weighed down by regret.

In this moment, we're addressing our internal self-acceptance. Having avoided it, we may need to recall that emotions do not dictate behavior. Anger is not hostility. Sadness is not wallowing. Fear is not flight. The entrenched belief that they're synonyms is the epitome of fusion. In ACT, the more fused we are, the more enslaved to emotional reactivity we feel.

"I always get into fights when I'm angry."

"I never leave my room when I'm down."

"I'm too scared to tell them how I feel."

Watch a butterfly and pay close attention to its flight. They don't fight the wind, they ride it. Using invisible eddies and currents, they let the wind carry them exactly where they need to go. Imagine what would happen if a butterfly tried to fight a gale. Fighting our emotions is like shaking our fist at the sky. It's expressive, but it doesn't accomplish much. Accepting the wind means changing our relationship with what we can't control, just as accepting emotions is to trust them as a natural, impermanent process. Uncomfortable feelings pose no real threat as they do not control action. The simplest and most difficult way to prove this is to weather the storm (Forsyth and Eifert, 2016).

As an exercise, *Weathering the storm* requires established rapport. If trust in the therapeutic relationship is absent, we may rationalize therapy as quackery and add ACT to our avoidance list. Additionally, this exercise is beneficial for levels of social and generalized anxiety, but may be too intense for high-risk clients with intense PTSD triggers or recent suicide attempts. Such cases represent intense levels of cognitive–emotional fusion, potentially too reactive for this exercise. Metaphors, including the *observational self as the sky*, *Joe the bum*, and the *passengers on the bus*, are gentler means of conveying ironic process and emotional acceptance (Harris, 2009a; Hayes *et al.*, 2012).

*Weathering the storm* asks the anxious, sad, angry, and guilty to do nothing but sit in contact with our emotions, to feel every drop of proverbial rain as it soaks into our clothes and makes us heavy (Forsyth and Eifert, 2016). Do not deliberately antagonize or upset the client but let us begin a mindful exploration of our own inner storm. What are the highs and lows in our life? What's frustrating or upsetting? For those with severe stress, adjust the exercise accordingly. Asking what angers or makes us anxious might open a Cat 5 hurricane, whereas asking what we find tedious or annoying may elicit a lighter shower. Unlike other modes of therapy which seek to manage the emotion or regulate the body with ten deep breaths, we're just going to wait, while noticing what we notice. First the barrage of judgment: "This sucks. I hate this." Then the battering reasons: "I only feel this way because..." Whenever possible, help us notice areas of our body which are tensing up, albeit our shoulders or hands or crinkled forehead, and inform us we're just going to wait. Wait for what? Nothing at all. How long will it last? Annoyances come and go, minor anxieties may last a few minutes, guilt sits around like a fog for hours, rage hammers down hail for a minute before dissipating, while a panic attack typically peaks at around ten minutes and tapers out into a prolonged sense of stress for a an hour or more, depending on the person. No doubt there are all sorts of things that might help us feel better, like breathing techniques, and positive mantras, and helpful distractions, but we're not going to use any of them right now. What we *are doing* is challenging the myth that we *have to do* anything.

We exert so much energy trying to alleviate, escape, or prevent distress that we begin to believe we can't handle it, that we'll crumble or explode or drop dead should we feel our feelings. *Weathering the storm*, as a short exercise, can challenge many of the myths and fears we have held for years. Our sympathetic and parasympathetic nervous system will find homeostasis, just not as quickly as we'd like, hence our frustration with our somatic experience. This exercise also demonstrates how accepting our emotions isn't a pursuit of comfort or happiness, or a stoic effort to survive and endure them (Forsyth and Eifert, 2016; Harris, 2008).

When we perceive a storm as something negative, we turn away from it. When a storm is perceived as natural, we can watch the thunderhead, feel the direction of the wind, and count our distance from the lightning by the seconds of the thunder. There's a lot to be learned from a storm, including if it's trailing off or driving in. In fact, our symbolic memory tells us clouds are white, but if we look at a storm, we'll see whole color spectrums in a cloud, from dark black to periwinkle blue, to hints of yellow, and suggestions of purple. Thunderheads rise, blizzards hurl snow at over 35 mph, and the flash of lightning we see actually sparks from the ground up. Culturally, however, the West was raised in a fairytale of dark and stormy nights, believing that the majority of emotions are *negative* (anger, sadness, fear, grief, guilt, regret, jealousy, boredom, despair) and that the minority of emotions are *positive* (happiness, appreciation, excitement, calm) (Harris, 2008). Maturing our relationship with emotion entails flexing our perspective, as there are numerous ways to see the world and its many storms, which is why gender affirmative ACT utilizes many of its early sessions building rapport. Rushing into techniques or jumping directly to what we're emotionally avoiding can short change the experience and the therapeutic relationship. Doing so may also indirectly imply that confronting avoidance by letting loose the floodgates is all that's needed to course correct, which is not the case (Hayes *et al.*, 2012).

To know and accept who and what we are includes accepting our emotions, yet this is by no means our therapeutic conclusion. Therapy in general is often perceived as a way to release pent-up feelings and get us in touch with our emotions; and while this can be a cathartic byproduct of ACT, it's not its primary goal (Hayes *et al.*, 2012). Challenging our avoidance to feel our feelings is only a step toward mental flexibility and value-congruent behavior (Hayes *et al.*, 2012). If clinicians focus solely on emotional processing, then therapy becomes a venting ground with little forward momentum. We might even sense this internally, having avoided our feelings for fear our tears would never end.

When it comes to our emotional wounds, some coagulate and begin to heal quite naturally, demonstrating the benefit of allowing emotions to run their course. Yet others can bleed out, demonstrating our need for value-congruent action. Imagine if we didn't know what physical pain was, having never experienced it directly. Imagine if we had never even heard about pain. Now imagine we trip and bash our knee. A sudden sensation rockets up our leg, and we don't like it, and we're further distressed because we don't understand it. Naturally, we try to get away from it but when we attempt to stand, the unnamed sensation only feels that much worse. Collapsing again, we accept something is happening, even if we don't know what it is, so we investigate. Looking down, we see something red, but we don't understand that either as we don't know what blood is or why it's necessary. Frustrated, we might try to ignore it again and walk home. We don't understand why we feel woozy or how our dizziness connects to the red on our leg. We might even try and do something about it, packing the cut with mud, thinking we can patch it like plaster. Having no experience with pain, we have no knowledge of medicine, and now our knee is infected. This metaphor is not a grim exaggeration, for even though a thought is just a thought and a feeling is just a feeling, the stressed and angry drop from cardiac arrest, just as the hurt and traumatized take their own lives. Accepting feelings alone is like accepting our wound without accepting our ability to do anything about it. Yet before we can accept our ability to do anything about it, we must first understand what's happening. Like physical pain, emotions are easier to accept when we understand their utility. When we are physically injured, our pain receptors tell us to pay attention to ourselves. Without them, there would be no self-care, no self-repair, and we would walk around with nails in our feet and splinters in our hands, without ever thinking to take them out. Our pain helps us to remove the source of injury, but it does not go away, as it reminds us to be patient with ourselves during the healing process.

In kind, our feelings are a phenomenal signaling system, broadcasting to others and to ourselves how our internal and external experiences are meshing. Emotions are not reasonable, yet they're also not without function, just as our physical pain marks the importance of our health, and our dashboard lights remind us to check the oil. They alert us that there's a crisis or that there might be a crisis. When we shift our therapeutic process from feeling for the sake of feeling, to understanding emotional utility, we proceed with mindful exploration.

Emotions we label *negative* indicate various unmet needs, which in turn flag the presence of our value constructs, even if our values have been neglected. Notably, we get phantom pains even when there's nothing wrong, and the check engine light can flash when the car's running perfectly fine. When the alert is the *crisis* we can feel paranoid even when we're perfectly safe, and lonely when surrounded by friends. In these situations we're accepting fear, but not reassurance, and accepting existential angst but not love. Value-congruent behavior may include defusing from the intrusive thoughts convincing us that we're hurt when we're healthy or broken when we're functional.

Research shows that when we try suppressing *negative* thoughts and emotions, we also decrease *positive* emotional expression (Gross, 2002). *Negative* and *positive* are italicized here as they're linguistic assessments of an emotional experience, loaning to the myth that sadness, anger, and fear are inherently bad, hostile forces, whereas joy, peace, and love are solely positive. Whenever possible, practice describing emotion without assessments like bad/negative/worse or good/positive/better, as this language can contribute to the rationale of experiential avoidance: "Why should I accept feeling bad?"

In the long run, suppression has little impact on preventing or altering our *negative* emotions, but we do feel less capable of expressing happiness, appreciation, or keeping a *positive* outlook. Part of this is due to how suppression is associated with a spike in the sympathetic nervous system, activating our cardiovascular system (Gross, 2002). To demonstrate this, let's hold a water bottle and squeeze it as hard as possible. Let's squeeze it so hard our hands begin to tremble! That's us. That's the tension that comes from trying to suppress everything. Holding everything in as hard as we can creates a reverberating pressure, and after a while our hands might even begin to feel numb. Squeezing this bottle certainly prevents us from doing anything else with our hands or our attention, just as suppressing thoughts has been shown to impair cognitive performance and verbal working memory (Morin and Hamper, 2012). Accepting a feeling for the sake of feeling isn't very convincing if we've spent years on the run from our emotions. Yet when we explore the utility of emotions, we can perceive them as a call to action, a starting gun for value-congruent behavior. Indeed, feelings are intrinsically tied to our value constructs. Just as every light casts a shadow, we can track every shadow back to the light.

Draw an outline of a hand on a piece of paper. Label the tips of our thumb *happiness*, then each finger in turn *sadness*, *anger*, *fear*, and *guilt* (see Figure 4.1). What would life be like without those other digits? If we got rid of sadness, anger, fear, and guilt? Some might say, "Pretty good, actually!" Giving a thumbs up is the universal sign of positivity, and for good reason! Our thumbs are anatomical marvels that let us build whole civilizations! We would not be where we are today without the thumb. But imagine going through life without any of our fingers. Just for fun, try opening a water bottle using only your thumbs. Using your knees as a clamp is cheating. Some are dexterous enough to get the lid off. If so, try drinking from the bottle, screwing the lid back on, and if that's all too easy, try tossing and catching the bottle *with just your thumbs.* Most of us can't get the lid off to start with.

So, our fingers are valuable, but what about our feelings? Each has something to teach us. Having labeled the fingertips, let's brainstorm what value each emotion connects to, and write them in the palm of our drawing. There is no singular set of values our emotions integrate with, yet the following demonstrate some examples you may come across in session.

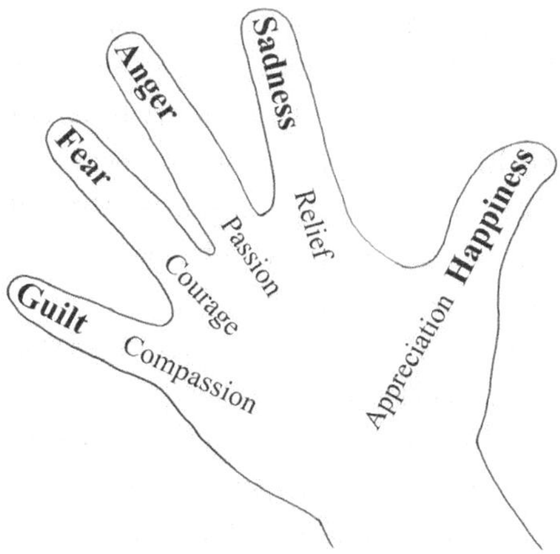


**Figure 4.1** *Hand diagram*

## *Happiness*

Happiness clearly connects to appreciation, for without appreciation, no matter how small, we could not be happy. Often, the apathetic and depressed interpret appreciation as an absent emotion, yet when appreciation is regarded as a value it becomes an active form of mindful behavior. This can be demonstrated by recalling how appreciative we are of our friend's ability to listen when we're having the worst day of our lives, and how appreciative we are to be out of the rain when it's pouring down.

## *Sadness*

What would be lost if we never felt sad in our life? Have you ever really *needed* to cry? Have you ever cried so much that afterwards, wiping your eyes, you proclaimed, "Man, I really needed that!" Have you cried and cried and cried just to get it off your chest? Those of us who have experienced this know for certain that without sadness we would lose catharsis or relief. Sadness can also indicate change or loss, marking a need to reinvest in familiar comfort. When we move to a new place, we may feel sad as we need to reinvest in connection, friendship, and community by reaching out to our far-off friends or making new ones.

### *Anger*

Anger so often ties to passion, so it's a great middle finger. By believing hostility and anger are synonymous, people often fear anger, but that's like assuming we're going to burn the house down because we own a lighter. Yet what would be lost if anger never existed? What would the world be like if no one ever got mad? There would be no war, true, but there would also be no passion, no conviction, and no drive to right what's wrong. Anger indicates when something important is under threat or has been damaged. We don't always know what it is, at first, but one of our boundaries has been crossed or one of our values has come under fire, whether it's safety, fairness, justice, dignity, peace, or love.

### *Fear*

Naturally, we run from fear, but when we sit with our fear what does it show us? Once upon a time our vigilance kept us safe in the wild, but now our vestigial instincts get the better of us. Fear grants us what no other emotion can: the opportunity for courage. Despite what the dictionary says, fearlessness is a poor synonym for courage as it implies we're only brave in the absence of fear. We are not afraid to eat a sandwich, as sandwiches are not too scary; therefore it is accurate to say that John is fearlessly eating his sandwich. Not many of us would call munching on a peanut butter and jelly sandwich all that brave, though. Yet were John testing for poison to save his family? Now, that would be courageous! Courage, when viewed as a value, is any willingly made action one is afraid to take.

### *Guilt*

Guilt is often deemed useless, like an emotional leech that makes us feel guilty about feeling sad, guilty about feeling happy, guilty about feeling angry, and then guilty about feeling guilt. It's one of the most hated emotions, primarily because it's the most nagging of all, and so we guard ourselves against it (Plutchik, 1991). Guilt makes us feel terrible about ourselves for wrongs we've committed; and when we avoid it, we often fuse to rationalizations, which we project onto others or the world at large (Plutchik, 1991). Some will even blame those they've hurt for making them feel bad or try and convince themselves that they don't care anyway. Yet, if we surgically amputated guilt, we would also sever our compassion, as we only feel guilty when we care about those we've harmed. Should we numb ourselves to guilt, we numb ourselves to compassion, responsibility, accountability, and redemption, ignoring guilt as our signal to make amends for the past, or adjust our behavior for the future.

Knowing that each client contends with a different set of feelings, tailor this exercise to include whatever emotions the client is primarily struggling to accept. Consider the possible connections in Table 4.1.

**Table 4.1 Emotions as value indicators**

| Emotion | Value indication |
|---|---|
| Happiness | Appreciation, meaning, purpose, self-worth |
| Sadness | Catharsis, relief, expression, creativity |
| Anger | Passion, determination, boundary, equality, justice |
| Fear | Courage, survival, comfort |
| Guilt | Redemption, compassion, responsibility, accountability |
| Grief | Relief, love, connection, family, honor, remembrance, nostalgia, sentimentalism |
| Shame | Pride, communication, vulnerability, belonging, acceptance |
| Worry | Trust, compassion, love |
| Envy | Aspiration, self-empowerment |
| Jealousy | Investment, assurance, connection |
| Loneliness | Connection, communication, trust, vulnerability, acceptance |
| Boredom | Spontaneity, imagination, exploration, innovation, curiosity |

## *Grief*

Grief is a heavy hitter, and one of the most enduring of all emotions. It emerges when we lose something most dear, and can linger for years and years. Yet without grief we never gain relief, since we never learn how to exhale the heaviness inside or honor that which is gone. Without grief, there would be no sentiment or nostalgia, and we would leave yesterday in the dust without another thought. We can also grieve what we never had, which is true for certain aspects of sex and gender we may not be able to actualize. Trans women may grieve not having a menstrual cycle like other women, while trans men can feel like they have a phantom limb for a penis, and even feel downhearted by not being able to impregnate their spouse (Bockting *et al.*, 2006). Grief is perhaps so long lasting because of how it connects to so many aspects of our lives, including love, connection, belonging, family, relief, honor, and remembrance.

### *Shame*

Shame is a fungus, a kind of mold that abhors the sun and thrives in the dark. Embarrassment crops up when we fail to live up to socially defined scripts, roles, or expectations (Keltner and Buswell, 1997). This evolves into shame when we feel such faults and failings make us unworthy of love (Brown, 2012). Outside of *fight* and *flight*, shame engages our *hide* response, manifesting as self-censorship, secrecy by omission, and a desire to conceal our face. Shame, therefore, points to our need for commonality and self-kindness (Skinta and D'Alton, 2016). Since shame is an inherently social emotion, social affirmation allows us to connect with a shared human experience, defined in LGBTQ circles as *pride* (Scheff, 2000; Skinta and D'Alton, 2016). When we're shut off, we can become stagnant and self-destructive; yet when we challenge this isolating mindset through active communication, the closer we feel to others, and in turn ourselves (Lynd, 1961; Scheff, 2000). Shame would have us believe that we are terrible, unworthy sinners, not because of anything we've done, but because of everything *we are*. Deconstructing the shame cycle can mean accepting what we are most ashamed of about ourselves, thereby disempowering our inclination to hide who we are. In this way, shame can point to our need to practice communication, vulnerability, connection, and above all self-acceptance.

### *Worry*

Worry exemplifies our need for trust, as worry is the sheer lack of it. We either worry because we do not trust our own powers to handle a situation, or we do not trust others to respect us, or we do not trust others to take care of themselves, or we do not trust the world to be anything but cruel. When we listen to our worry, we fuse with paranoid thoughts. Trust emerges when we begin to defuse from our worry, and collect experiences that empower our trust in ourselves, others, and the world.

### *Envy*

When we are envious of others it's because they have something we want; yet rather than make proactive steps, we fuse to a bitter, defeatist attitude. Losing a leg, we envy those who run, as we desire mobility. This points toward our need for self-empowerment, which is why the abled community removed the *dis*. Gender variant individuals may feel envious of masculinity, femininity, androgyny, acceptance, connection, and community if it's the very facet we desire to actualize in our life.

### *Jealousy*

Jealousy and envy are often treated synonymously, yet jealousy couples with passiveness, as we usually have something already and feel jealous when others encroach on it. We may have attention, connection, love, affection, success, and achievement, and feel jealous when the stability of these values is called into question. When we fuse to jealousy and possessiveness, we go on the offensive, causing us to grip tighter and puff out our chest. Defusing from the urgency, we can focus on reinvestment, reassurance, and reconnection.

### *Loneliness*

Loneliness occurs when our value for connection is strained or in need of commitment. By defusing from the rationale justifying our isolationism and solitude, and taking value-congruent action toward communication, trust, acceptance, and vulnerability, we learn to lower our shield, allowing for meaningful interactions daring to surpass superficiality.

### *Boredom*

Boredom is for the boring. In other words, boredom comes into play when we rely on external stimuli to entertain us and we cannot challenge or stimulate our own thoughts. We are accomplices to our boredom, feeding into humdrum routines, cynicism, and low expectation. External stimuli can only keep their novelty for so long, no matter what they are. Yet if we accept our monotonous complicity, we can defuse from our deflating beliefs, to identify our need for spontaneity, imagination, exploration, innovation, and curiosity.

Summarizing this, how can we hope to go through life without our fingers? How can we hope to be happy if we don't accept appreciation, catharsis, passion, courage, or redemption? *Carpe diem*! To seize the day, we must have a whole hand to seize it. In ACT our therapeutic goal is not to wallow in our feelings or chase after happiness like a rainbow, but to accept life's entire emotional experience. If we soldier on in spite of our feelings, even if we actualize our values, we're still pitting ourselves against our emotional process. Exploring the utility of our emotions demonstrates how each feeling indicates something important to us.

## Accepting dysphoria: Schrödinger's gender

Accepting that gender variance is not a mental disorder means re-conceptualizing the relationship between gender development and the clinical distress that is gender dysphoria (Richards *et al.*, 2016; Sennott, 2011; Schechter, 2016; WPATH, 2011). Gender variant people who are not preoccupied, distressed, or confused by our gender are not gender dysphoric as we are comfortable in accepting our gender identity, even if we endure minority stress (Bockting *et al.*, 2006). Clinically, gender dysphoria is described as the distress felt by individuals whose gender is discrepant with their birth sex, noting that not all gender variant people experience gender dysphoria, and that treatment to alleviate the symptoms are highly individual (American Psychiatric Association, 2013; Bockting *et al.*, 2004; WPATH, 2011). HRT and gender alignment surgery have been shown to be highly effective at treating gender dysphoria for gender variant clients, yet there's little research available for aiding nonbinary individuals with dysphoria (Gijs and Brewaeys, 2007; Gómez-Gil *et al.*, 2012; Gorin-Lazard *et al.*, 2013; Smith *et al.*, 2005).

To address the full range of people struggling with gender dysphoria, treatment options can also include defusing from intrusive transphobic or cissexist thoughts, mindfully exploring gender expression both privately and socially, ongoing individual, couple, and family therapy, and developing gender-positive peer support networks both online and off (Bockting *et al.*, 2006; WPATH, 2011). Community organizations, self-help groups, internet chat rooms, and one-on-one peer support can help make an abstract and potentially terrifying question mark into a feasible and far less terrifying exploration, regardless of what the client later identifies as (Bockting *et al.*, 2006). Unless you happen to have direct experience with the same gender constructs the client is turning over, gender variant peers can provide far more personal insight into feminizing or masculinizing appearances, social exchanges, and sexual experiences (Bockting *et al.*, 2006). As we address our gender dysphoria, we may also find a great deal of relief and catharsis through voice training, hair removal, padding, tucking, breast binding and penile prostheses should we, or should we not, desire hormone regimens or surgery (WPATH, 2011).

Gender affirmative ACT views gender variant people in the context of our minority stress, as internalized sexist and cissexist constructs exacerbate the already felt rift between sex and gender, adding cognitive dissonance to anatomical dissonance. Exceeding the very natural process of gender exploration, gender dysphoria feels like a ruminating confusion and/or a pervasive sense of distress with our sex and misgendered role. Being told we're a man or woman when we know we're not makes us feel disempowered and unhinged, as the majority cannot see or affirm the resonance we feel. Being told we're a man or a woman when we suspect we're not, but don't quite know what we are or what that means, is an equally alarming sense of disintegration.

Gender dysphoric clients may report a pervasive feeling of fraudulence, inadequacy, insecurity, and disorientation when trying to perform gender roles stereotyped to our sex. Anxiety, often presenting as worry and paranoia around being "discovered," is often coupled with a paradoxical depression stemming from an unmet need for acceptance and validation. In short, we feel confused yet again, as we want to be seen as we are but are terrified of condemnation. Adhering to the agenda of emotional control, we may desperately try not to think about it, refusing to acknowledge our sex phenotypes or even our whole bodies. Bypassing mirrors and reflective surfaces, gender dysphoric clients may depersonalize whenever we need to shave or apply makeup—as if taking care of someone else's face. Extremely dysphoric clients may avoid nudity, even when we're alone, leading us to shower without looking down, or halve our bathing time. Those with female bodies may feel incredibly uncomfortable, disgusted, anxious, angry, and sorrowful when they menstruate, while those with male bodies may feel distraught by erections and wet dreams (Bancroft, 2009; Beemyn and Rankin, 2011).

While online avatars can be a useful way to experiment and play with gender identity, some may spend countless hours developing a screen addiction to the internet. Gender dysphoric clients may try to ignore our voice, disliking how we sound. We may avoid social engagements that require gender-scripted behavior, or even any social situation on really bad days! As the bastard love child of anxiety and body dysmorphia, gender dysphoria can feel invasive and constant, or it can fluctuate with mood and emotional wellbeing.

Gender dysphoria drops us into depression when we repress our gender identity and even when we don't. It feels like there's no way to win. If we don't express ourselves, then we may feel like a fake for being closeted. If we do express ourselves, then we may feel like a fake for being something we're anatomically not. Even when we accept our gender variance, acceptance alone doesn't alleviate dysphoria. Self-actualization provides a path to gender stability, yet nonbinary people face an added level of dysphoria, as what we're trying to actualize is rarely recognized, let alone accepted by the status quo (Budge *et al.*, 2014; Richards *et al.*, 2016).

When no longer defined by dysphoria, it becomes apparent that many gender variant people do not experience this degree of personal dissonance or do so only momentarily during the first stages of development (Lev, 2004). It also becomes apparent that having gender dysphoria does not make one gender variant, since even people who identify as cisgender can question their gender and feel gender dysphoric (Drummond *et al.*, 2008; Joel *et al.*, 2014). Recall that *cisgender* and *transgender* are identity labels we resonate with given our gender schema. Prior to this stable identification, gender dysphoria is a queer Schrödinger's box in which a person *is* and *is not*, simultaneously. Trans women, long before HRT or SRS, have described feeling like a woman invisible even to themselves. Nonbinary people, before self-actualization, have described a pernicious doubt as they oscillate between binary and nonbinary. Trans men who once identified as women described how their manhood was always there, but was somehow locked away from their own awareness. This dysphoria is distinct from simple denial, as it shows the gestation of possibility within, that only they can bring into being by observing it. Some may emerge from Schrödinger's box as cisgender, free of gender dysphoria. Some may emerge as a gender variant identity, free of gender dysphoria. Some may develop a stable identity, yet feel ongoing traces of gender dysphoria, as they step in and out of that box of possibility throughout their lives. In any case, self-acceptance in the present moment may mean accepting that we're in a very confusing box, with a paradoxical cat that might be dead or sleeping—we're not sure.

From an RFT perspective, gender dysphoria sabotages our hierarchical and deictic frames. The *self*—that is to say our sentient psyche—begins to feel individuated from the body, which is perceived and treated as the *other*. Many gender variant people do not feel this way, and while we may feel incongruent with our body, we still connect with it. But a gender dysphoric mindset is a maddening one, as it can feel like a part of us is not us, or is even a traitor to us. This may range from aspects of our anatomy, social presentation, self-concept, or all of the above. Because we no longer fit the hierarchical frame, we begin to challenge our conceptual self to such a degree that we can feel a surreal sense of otherness deep inside.

> "When I look in the mirror, it's like I'm looking at a stranger. I mean, I know it's me, I'm in there somewhere, but I can't see myself."

> "When God was giving out bodies, I stepped in the wrong checkout line, that's all. I'd take it back, but I lost the receipt."

> "I feel like I'm insane. Like I'm trying to be practical. My body is real. I know it's real. So that means I have to be crazy. That's the only logical conclusion."

This dissonance, combined with and reinforced by internalized cissexism, can feel so crushing that people will go to great lengths to avoid thinking about it. Yet there comes a point where we have to accept our dissonance in order to work through it. Self-actualization is, therefore, an ongoing mind–body integration. This may include accepting the physical for what it is by relinquishing cisgender concepts of beauty or body image, and/or connecting and integrating with one's body through transition.

Being present doesn't mean being happy, or even happy with one's body, nor does it mean being clear about one's present situation. Sometimes, we have to accept that we're uncomfortable and uncertain. In Schrödinger's original thought experiment, we're presented with a radioactive isotope, a Geiger counter, a bewildered cat, and a flask of poison. Should the Geiger counter sense the isotope, it will shatter the poison, which may or may not kill the cat, and as long as the box is shut, the cat exists in a superimposed state with as much chance of being dead as alive. This is not a *happy* experiment. It is a truly unknown moment, impacted by our observation of it.

If we don't know our *true* gender, the box is shut tight, leaving us oscillating frantically between what could or could not be. If we do know our *true* gender yet still wake every morning plagued by dysphoria, the box is also shut, as we're leaning in favor of one direction while remaining restless and impatient that the wave function hasn't collapsed into its final outcome. In this case, accepting the present moment means admitting that right here, right now, we don't have the answer and are not yet actualized. Like all nine of the cat's lives, gender exists abstractly and intangibly as a liminal superposition, just waiting to exist the moment we open the box. Our *true* gender is, ultimately, whatever we make of it, the moment we observe it. The dilemma here is that we're afraid to open the box and fully connect with ourselves, so we're sliding the lid open an inch at a time. Observing a little here and a little there, we spy a paw, a tail, and another paw, slowly bringing ourselves to our own conclusion as to who and what we are.

There is often a great deal of pressure for us to know our gender, often forcing us into categories or labels before we're even certain. Social situations often force us into binary designations, like entering public bathrooms or clothing store changing rooms (Curtin, Ryu and Diamond, 2016). Defusing from our need to know, however, presents us with the mindful act of unknowing (Curtin *et al.*, 2016). Uncertainty, curiosity, doubt, and wonder are essential in our development, and accepting this allows us to come out as uncertain (Curtin *et al.*, 2016). If asked about our gender, it's perfectly acceptable to say, "I don't know" or "I'm still figuring it out," or "I'm gender squishy."

Keep in mind that we can struggle with gender dysphoria even when we know we're gender variant. Even if we're certain that we're a transsexual, agender, or genderfluid person, for example, we may still feel conflicted or incomplete within ourselves. More than a categorical label, gender is a living experience that takes time to embrace, accept, and integrate.

As the picture becomes clearer, the confusion of gender dysphoria evolves into a question of gender stability. This is progress, since we have identified a gender, even if it feels shaky and unstable in our presentation of it. If dissonance and resonance describe a level of identification with a certain gender construct, stability is our degree of congruence with it. This is noteworthy, should we feel incongruent with our resonant feelings, loving them while hating ourselves for loving them. When the conceptual self is in the midst of reforming, or when two or more conceptual selves compete, we begin to feel disingenuous, fake, confused, or foreign even to ourselves. Contemplate the daughter who knows he's a man but is afraid of coming out of the closet until he's old enough to live independently of his parents. He may state his gender very factually, but still feel unstable, being caught halfway between here and there. In contrast, a polygender/genderfluid person may have more than one stable gender identity, having learned to trust their fluid ability to move between gender states.

In cisgender development, gender stability often emerges by age seven (Cohen-Kettenis and Pfäfflin, 2003). For gender variant people, however, development is not age dependent. Arlene Istar Lev observed in their comprehensive guide *Transgender Emergence* (2004) how gender variant people progress through stages: self-awareness; information seeking and reaching out; disclosure to significant others; exploration and self-labeling; and finally acceptance and integration. In this emergence model, our stability—described as our comfort with our gender identity—tends to cultivate in the fourth stage of exploration and self-labeling. Stability is not, however, dependent on transparency, so we may be out and proud or entirely discreet. Consider an openly genderqueer client who doesn't feel socially obligated to "out" themselves to every stranger they meet. They may choose to tell people or permit others to assume what they like. Notably, genderfluid people with two or more gender identities have a unique relationship with stability, as stability resembles the ease of transition between gender constructs.

Wavering confidence, low esteem, or camouflaging gender do not impart or represent gender instability or gender dysphoria. Coming to terms with the socialization of gender and the empowerment of our personal voice takes time. By comparison, in cisgender development, a little boy becoming a man is stable in his gender but may still feel unsure of himself. That said, intelligibility also has no bearing on stability, as some can eloquently express their gender, while others may not have a label, or a word, or a coherent term for what they are—even if they've been what they are their whole lives (Valentine, 2007).

Gender instability is the degree of volatility we feel within ourselves in relation to our gender. When we feel unstable, direct explorations of gender can be highly emotional. Even simple lines of questioning may induce anxiety and somatic distress if we have a whole life invested in a gender construct that's now not only being called into question but beginning to feel vapid, incomplete, or farcical. There are those who would exploit this doubt by supplying answers to clients thirsty for them. Gender stability, as an area of exploration, maintains within it many controversial topics. It's here that people will explore "unwanted gender identity," perspectives of gender variance as a disorder, and options for conversion therapy. Definitively, the American Psychiatric Association does not endorse conversion therapy of any kind, yet clients may still ponder this controversial option, or feel pressured into it by friends and family even if they're not directly forced.

The subject of persistence and desistence is highly controversial, as rigid parents and reparative organizations often point to desistence as the possibility of their child "returning to normal." Even the language implies that there's some deliberate action *persisting* against cisnormative development. To challenge this framework, maintain a flexible conceptualization of gender, and provide us autonomy, we're going to call these shifts in gender identity exactly what they are: *identification* and *re-identification*.

Gender identity development is not always linear, and we may explore gender throughout our lives. Subsequently, *identification* and *re-identification* recognize that the gender explorative are still going to have a dynamic self-actualization process, complete with curiosity and uncertainty. Because of the biased research in this area, it's difficult to ascertain how many re-identify as cisgender in later life, but there are enough personal testimonies to show that cisgender re-identification does occur, including guitarist Naia Izumi who, after living seven years as a trans woman, went onto identify as a man and even win National Public Radio's 2018 Tiny Desk Contest for his song "Soft Spoken Woman." Historically, there are even a few post-op cases who struggled with regret and surgically reversed their procedure (Kuiper and Cohen-Kettenis, 1998). Amongst those interviewed, many stated that they had hidden their doubt and instability from their therapist. One even reported never actually identifying as a woman, undergoing SRS because they felt pressured by their partner to be a woman (Kuiper and Cohen-Kettenis, 1998). Such clients who re-identify as cisgender, or perhaps even nonbinary, may need emotional support should they go through a few liminal periods of instability and rediscovery. Having actualized a gender variant identity, they may find themselves moving through stages of dissonance and resonance yet again, with similar feelings of dysphoria, instability, and social anxiety. Some may hesitate to mention or express their gender variant past, feel disowned or unqualified to remain part of the LGBTQ community, or judge themselves critically for their gender exploration.

It's not the clinician's task to guide or direct a person's gender identity. Instead, help us direct our mindfulness to what is within our scope of awareness. What do we feel present within ourselves? What do we feel is true, acknowledging that life is impermanent and prone to change? For uncertain and precontemplative clients, now is not the time for action. Although we may not know why we feel unstable, we're aware something is off-balance, making now an opportunity to gently and mindfully explore our uncertainty, if we're willing to do so.

## Mindfulness exercise: **Instability or fluidity**

An iceberg, a blizzard, a storm cloud, an ocean, a river, and steam from a kettle all have one thing in common—they're all $H_2O$. Pure water is a powerful metaphor for stability, as it demonstrates how context dependent water is without ever compromising what it is. When we feel unstable, questions plague the mind: Who am I? What am I? Am I man? Am I woman? Am I something else? This uncertainty can be very disconcerting, yet before we can explore and accept who and what we are, it's pertinent to explore and accept our relationship with uncertainty itself. Hating uncertainty is like approving water but loathing steam, because we can't always see evaporation. When we hate uncertainty, we often struggle with impermanence and change, potentially compromising our own growth and adaptability. Yet even if we accept uncertainty, we may feel overcome by doubt, at which point we struggle to believe ice is water, because it looks and feels different. When we feel unstable or uncertain about our gender, or aspects thereof, our dysphoria may bounce between concrete concepts of *what is* and *what isn't*. Trying to resolve confusion or answer doubt, we'll hold on to inaccurate answers just because they provide us some structure. Gender variant people often recall a time in our life when we felt like we were experimenting with an identity that didn't turn out to be accurate, or living a lie even though we weren't deliberately lying. Clearly this ice-cube is made of stone because it's cold and hard, and we all know stones are cold and hard.

Before we can defuse from the concrete fallacies we use to avoid the unknown, we may need to expand awareness to areas of constancy and consistency. Even if our gender is up in the air—even if we don't know what label, identity, or body we even fit—there remain a few core qualities indicative of who we are at the very center of our being. If we have spent years identifying with a gender role or a gender identity, we may assume that the qualities of our character are intrinsically linked to masculinity or femininity. This is as true for cisgender people exploring the edge of their gender as it is for transgender people questioning their gender variance. Overwhelmed by this prospect, we may believe we'll lose ourselves should our gender fluctuate, as if the water will stop being water should the ice melt. Yes, our gender schemas maintain certain characteristics, just as steam is hot and ice is hard, yet what qualities of water can we rely on regardless of its form? To explore what's constant in our otherwise fluid experience, create a Venn diagram (see Figure 4.2) to list all the qualities we associate with men and women, and which we identify with in the middle.

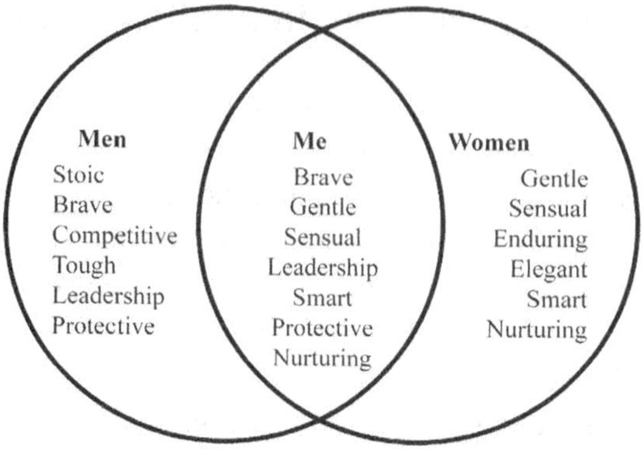


**Figure 4.2** *Gender Venn diagram*

If we're nonbinary, or simply expansive in our concept of gender, we can adjust the Venn diagram accordingly. For example, if we were born with a female body, we may share all the virtues women are "supposed to have" on one side, and all the virtues we feel nonbinary people can embody. If we don't adhere to labels, or we simply don't know what our variant gender is yet, we can simply write "something else," "something more," or "something other" on the Venn diagram (see Figure 4.3). Remember, we're exploring the profound qualities of our character, which are bigger and deeper than the words or labels we use for them.

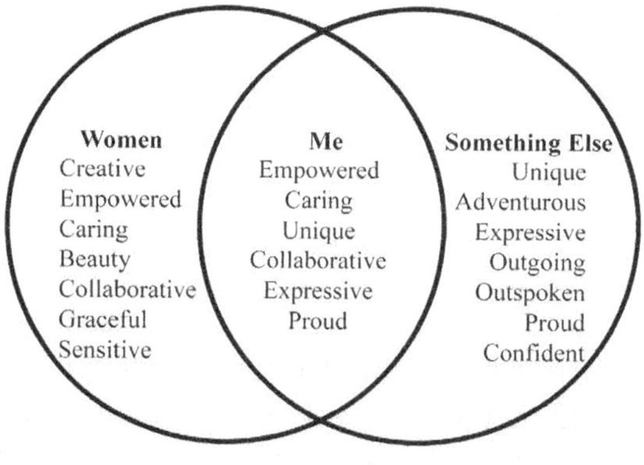


**Figure 4.3** *Gender expansive Venn diagram*

Likewise, if we question gender dichotomy as a whole, we can draw a Venn diagram with three overlapping triangles (see Figure 4.4). As an example, we may overlay the masculine and feminine with our third sense of otherness.

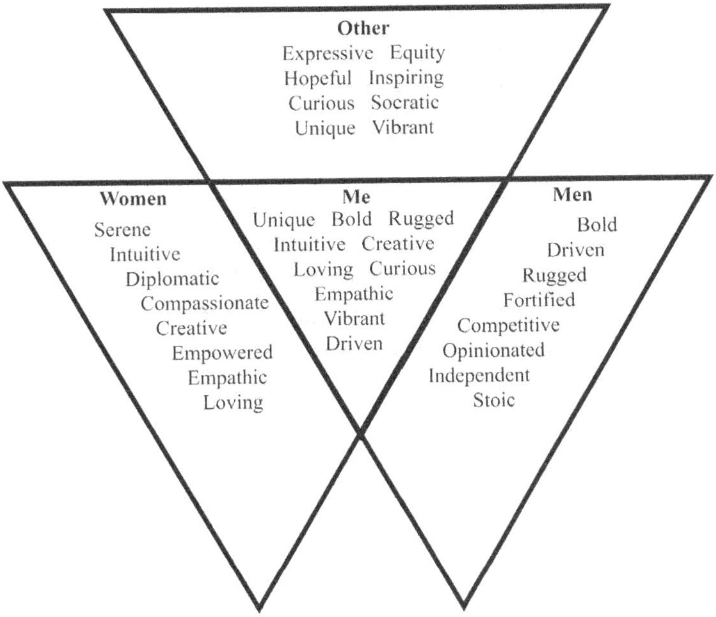


**Figure 4.4** *Nonbinary Venn diagram*

This exercise can help identify reliable qualities and value constructs that exist within us independent of gender, as well as those fused to a gender script. It is not necessary to defuse or uncouple values from a gender script unless the association has become so rigid as to be unworkable. Undoubtedly, we will have many judgments and negative associations we will need to practice defusing from, yet the defusion process can be exceptionally difficult when there appears to be no alternative. If we once presumed we were a man or a woman, our prior concept of self may begin to feel like an iceberg melting into the sea. We may feel loss, grief, and fatalistic hopelessness, until we realize that the water didn't actually go anywhere, it just changed form.

## Mindfulness exercise: **Where's your charge?**

Just as emotions are a somatic experience, so too is gender, which is why verbal language can never seem to do our feelings justice. A body scan is a classic mental health exercise, breathing in and out while progressively visualizing and connecting with each part of the body, from our head to our toes (Walser and Westrup, 2007). Dr. Emily Sandoz and Troy DuFrene, in their highly compassionate ACT text *Living with Your Body and Other Things You Hate* (2013), provide a few excellent ways we can notice our body from the inside out, from the outside in, and our response to both perspectives. There are also a number of phenomenal body scan techniques provided by the master of mindfulness, Dr. Jon Kabat-Zinn.

Before proceeding, be conscious of the client's risk of gender dysphoric stress. Some FtM clients may bind their chest to reduce the size of their breasts, which can be a potentially harmful long-term practice if done incorrectly. As a point of interest, medically safe chest-binders are available on the market from transgender apparel companies like gc2b, Underworks, FLVNT, and Trans-Vormer. However, FtM and transmasculine people still exploring their gender, alongside young people unable to purchase these products on their own, may have to use ACE™ bandages. This may be an irrelevant factor until you ask them to take a deep breath and find they literally can't. Some may feel anxious whenever guided meditations notice the breath, as it pulls awareness to the chest—an area of potential dysphoria and physical discomfort.

Body scans can be anxiety provoking if certain facets of the body hold emotional charge or feel like they're missing. People very quickly assume sexualized areas of the anatomy, including hips, breasts, and genitalia, hold the most emotional charge for gender variant people, yet our feelings and our judgment can fuse to any part of the body. Gender phenotypes in the face like our lips, eyes, eyebrows, forehead, and jawline can spark with self-critical electricity. Everything from the length of our hair to the length of our arms, from the size of our hands to the size of our Adam's apple, from the breadth of our shoulders to the width of our waist, can store dissonance and emotional pain. Yet so too can the absence of anatomy. Sometimes a body scan can generate distress when our awareness is inadvertently drawn to the lack of an Adam's apple, or breasts, or phallus, or muscle structure, like a gaping hole in our wholeness.

If we feel uncomfortable talking about anatomy we're disconnected with, normalize the discomfort, and move forward with our preferred language (Bockting *et al.*, 2006; Hill-Meyer and Scarborough, 2014). ACT provides many mindfulness activities that can easily be adapted to fit gender variant clients by de-gendering the use of language. The following exercise is left anatomically vague on purpose, as an example. While hands, head, heart, and legs can store within them points of dysphoria, the specific words carry little gender connotation. Yet terms like *chest* and *breast* can pop us out of the exercise, not necessarily because of a disconnection with our body, but because of a gendered charge associated with the label. A gender neutral substitution for *chest* or *breast* can include feeling *the lungs expand*, or *the sternum rise and fall.*

When working with gender dysphoric clients, a mindful body scan can reveal areas of dysphoric charge like buried emotional landmines. Though this exercise can be performed in any sitting or standing position, it may be most beneficial lying down. The following is a guided script you can use with gender variant clients who may be struggling with their anatomy.

*Before we begin, I'm going to ask you to take notice of a few things during this exercise. When I ask a question, feel free to answer out loud, or to keep the answers to yourself, whatever feels most comfortable. Alright, find a comfy spot.*

*Close your eyes and feel yourself settling into the chair, or the couch or the carpet. Feel the weight of your body sinking down. Let gravity settle everything into a comfortable position. Adjust if you need to. Let your breathing relax into its usual rhythm. Rest.*

*As you lie here, imagine yourself exactly as you are from a bird's eye view. Looking down from above, imagine your hands, feet, and head resting exactly as they are. Let your breathing relax into its usual rhythm. Rest.*

*As you gaze upon yourself, imagine the lights in the room begin to dim. Imagine your hands begin to glow like magic. The soft light begins to brighten. What color are they glowing? Are they dim or bright? Flashing light or constant glow? As you relax, look over the rest of your body. Are any other areas glowing the same color as your hands? Take notice. Are they dim or bright?*

*Follow them through your body, from your feet, to your knees, to your waist, to your shoulders, to your neck, to your head. Take notice of where they all are, and then slowly, gradually, let them fade back into the dark. Let your breathing relax into its usual rhythm. Rest.*

*Imagine yourself exactly as you are from a bird's eye view. As you gaze upon yourself, imagine your heart begins to glow like magic. The soft light begins to brighten. What color is it? As you relax, look over your body. Are any other areas glowing the same color as your heart? Take notice. Are they dim or bright? Flashing or constant glow?*

*Follow them through your body, from your feet, to your knees, to your waist, to your shoulders, to your neck, to your head. Take notice of where they all are, and then slowly, gradually, let them fade back into the dark. Let your breathing relax into its usual rhythm. Rest.*

*As you gaze upon yourself, imagine your legs begin to glow like magic. Their soft light begins to brighten. What color are they? Are they both the same color, or are they different? As you relax, as you rest, look over the rest of your body. Are any other areas glowing the same color as your legs? Take notice and let the light fade back into the dark. Let your breathing relax into its usual rhythm. Rest.*

*As you gaze upon yourself, imagine your head and your hair begin to glow like magic. Their soft light begins to brighten. What color are they? Are they both the same color, or are they different? As you relax, as you rest, look over the rest of your body. Are any other areas glowing the same color as your head and your hair? Take notice and let the light fade back into the dark. Let your breathing relax into its usual rhythm. Rest.*

*The lights in the room are starting to brighten. As they rise, float back down into yourself. Feel the gravity pulling you onto the chair, or the couch, or the floor.*

*Allow your breathing to relax into its usual rhythm, and when you're ready, open your eyes.*

Time can be spent unpacking each word, the visual associations with that area of the body, and any personal symbolism attributed to the colors. Perhaps red was warm and wonderful, perhaps red was pain and fire. Perhaps blue was cool and calm, perhaps blue was icy and void. We may not immediately understand our own inner color coding, yet a few exploratory questions can clarify a great deal:

*Did you like it? Did it resonate with you? Or did it feel strange, like you didn't like it? Did it glow like fire or electricity? Did it glow around the area or from within?*

Starting from an externalized astral projected viewpoint, allows us to spot areas of resonance and dissonance from an emotionally safe distance. Stepping into our bodies requires a great deal of trust in the therapeutic process, especially if we don't feel safe within ourselves. In order to accept and work through our emotional charge, we may begin to connect with our body through dance, yoga, sports, exercise, meditation, masturbation, sex, and even HRT and gender alignment surgery.

## Accepting gender: Defusing fear and denial

We sometimes delay accepting our gender identity, we sometimes delay, entering a contemplative holding period where we gather information, test our gender schema, and gauge our own tolerance about being a gender variant person (Devor, 2004). Notably, some clients will present a kind of resistance best described as a *gentle blockade*. Bricked together from cognitive dissonance, we may want to explore a difficult issue yet seem hesitant to do so. We may express a fear of judgment, including our own. Because of the sheer delicacy and discomfort, it's often advantageous to frame the session as a series of invitations, permitting the client to decide what we do or do not want to explore at this time. Walls are built for a reason. They're defensive, protective, safe, insulating, and able to suppress whole identities, concealing gender even from ourselves (Butler, 1990; Lev, 2004). The degrees of resistance vary from, *gentle blockades*, including shyness, awkwardness, and anxiety, to *hard blockades*, including denial to others, denial to self, and full repression.

In *Get Out of Your Mind and Into Your Life: The New Acceptance and Commitment Therapy* (2005), Steven Hayes and Spencer Smith astutely observe that willingness to feel emotions and experiences without judgment is not a matter of belief requiring some great exertion of effort. In session, Hayes would have his clients repeat to themselves, "I cannot touch my arm. I cannot feel my touch." Repeating this denial over and over again, he would instruct them to touch their left arm with their right hand. Were they psychically powerful enough to numb their arm? Hardly. They felt it. No matter how hard they tried to deny the existence of their limbs, they felt their hand touch their arm (Hayes and Smith, 2005).

Repression and denial are not problems to be knocked over with a wrecking ball. They are barriers created by repeating "I cannot acknowledge I'm different." Acceptance is not a task, or an action. It's not a mountain to climb or a war to be won, but a willingness to feel *what is*. Acceptance is feeling our right hand touching our left arm. Acceptance is feeling our heart rate speed up and slow down. Acceptance is recognizing how distinct our cat is from our dog, while seeing how similar they are as well. For this reason, any delay period is a prime time to increase contact with people who are dissonant and resonant with the gender we feel dysphoric with. Even if our gender is unlabeled, undefined, or even unspoken, encounters with people who are dissimilar provide us contrast, while those who are similar confirm our budding sense of self (Devor, 2004). If we're willing, there are many in the transgender and nonbinary community who do not fit simply, easily, or willingly into a single category, which provides us contact with people who are enthusiastically unlabeled. However, let's not get ahead of ourselves, as those struggling with repression and denial are a long way from willingness, let alone community contact! Even the word *acceptance*, if used in session at this stage, may be treated with disdain if it's perceived as a commentary on our identity.

"I'm very open minded, but..."

"What are you talking about? I completely accept myself. I just..."

To avoid, we may put all gender talk on hold, or only allude to it vaguely until the defusion practice creates enough mental space to approach the subject. We may spend our time talking about anxiety, stress, frustration—the source of which may be vague or questionable. Knowing the source of distress is not a prerequisite for the defusion process. If anything, defusion can sometimes provide the clarity to see what's really going on.

As we begin to trust our ability to feel emotions without fusing to them, and as we begin to trust the emotional safety contained within the therapeutic relationship, the more we'll start glancing at the blockade. Our willingness to address gender is on the rise, yet we may carefully orbit the issue without stating it directly. Intentional or not, our exacerbated sighs hint at something we can't say aloud. Responding to this bait is a gamble, as it gives us an opening to displace our discomfort onto you, our therapist. This can be sidestepped by recognizing your own awareness of our distress.

*I feel like there's something holding you back here. What do you feel it is?*

*I get the sense there's a lot of pressure building up. Where do you feel that in your body?*

When a gentle blockade is discovered, instead of analyzing it, invite us to explore it, as running a hand over a wall is far less threatening than hitting it with a sledgehammer. Intrusive advances typically increase anxiety, building the wall even higher, so simply observe the defense mechanism at work.

*You said you feel "locked up," where do you sense that in your body?*

*When you say you "can't talk about it," what do your thoughts tell you?*

Even if you suspect your client is hiding sexual or gender identity issues, telling us we're in denial is like spray-painting graffiti on a wall. It doesn't do anything but stain us with a label and justify our reason for building the wall in the first place. As accusatory, analytical clinicians with their sledgehammers and spray paint will be left in the cold with all the other graffiti provocateurs, ACT provides a gentler approach. If you suspect a client is truly in denial, or struggling with identity conflict, you're probably a few sessions in. At this juncture the agenda of emotional control has no doubt been introduced, though it may be worth refreshing. By normalizing how attempts to control emotions often lead to avoidance, the antithesis of self-acceptance, you can help us humanize our defense mechanisms, and even honor them for keeping us safe.

Perhaps the most common of all gentle blockades are the words "I don't know." Uttered quickly and even automatically, "I don't know" serves as an emotional eject button. It is to say, "Thinking about this is hard, so I'm not going to consider it." Clients are often surprised when therapists encourage agency:

*Of course you know, you're the only one who can. You may need to sit with this a while longer, but you'll figure it out. You're the only expert on yourself. Even if you don't know what's going on all the time, you've got all the keys to all the doors.*

If we have become so compartmentalized that we're legitimately oblivious about what we're hiding from ourselves, then you've encountered a hard blockade. In complete denial, we may resist vulnerability, as it risks our stability, connection, and even our own innocence. Hiding from ourselves, we may see gender deviance as a corrupting force in our life. To survive, we adopt the oblivious mantra "I don't know" to wall off what we feel looming within us.

Ironic process is the ultimate undermining of denial, as the more thoughts and feelings get walled up, the taller and more noticeable the wall becomes. This recognition is often enough for clients to get past a gentle blockade, but a hard blockade can have a hostile battlement. Blockades go up when we have little faith in our ability to handle what lies on the other side. Mindful breathing reminds us that not only are we very much alive, but how we will continue to breathe no matter how overwhelming our internal stress becomes. Likewise, emotional fusion and defusion practices will help build emotional resilience, reducing our perceived urgency. Let's try envisioning something external we find irritable. External problems are often easier to defuse from than internal ones, since we can mentally picture ourselves stepping back from the person, place, or subject in question.

*Imagine whatever it is being right in your face. Right there, inescapable. Now imagine taking two steps back. Feel any better? Now try ten steps back. It's still there, but you can probably breathe a little easier. Now imagine whatever bothers you being a hundred yards away. Can you still see it so far away? How about at 20 miles? Could you make it out a hundred miles away?*

With enough practice, we may become willing to acknowledge the blockade in front of us, at which point invite us to explore it.

*I feel there's a wall here. Do you sense that?*
"Yeah, I do."

*I'm wondering, would you like to explore it with me?*
"What do you mean?"

*Sometimes, when we feel some resistance, we can learn a lot by just being mindful of its presence. If you're feeling up for it, we can give it a try.*
"Okay. Do I have to stand up or anything?"

*Not at all. You can sit right where you are. Now, can you imagine that wall with me? Close your eyes. I want you to imagine a wall. Can you see it? What color is it? How big is it?*
"It's like red brick, but it's a hundred miles high."

*When you were talking before, I noticed you were hinting at something. Can you imagine a door in this wall? How big is it?*
"It's like a mouse-sized door."

*Like from Alice in Wonderland?*
"Yeah. It's real small."

*But it's there?*
"Yeah, I guess so."

*Is the door open or closed?*
"It's closed."

*Do you feel like it's locked, or is it unlocked? Or is it unlocked but kind of jammed so you have to push it a little?*

"It's...locked, I think."

*Do you know what's on the other side?*
"Yeah, I'm pretty sure."

*Is there a key?*
"Isn't there always a key?"

*Sometimes. What do you think you need to open that door? What do you think your key would be made of?*
"Oh, I know that. It's trust. I don't trust anybody. I don't even know if I trust you."

While some of us may be aware of our defense mechanisms, and even our denial, some may still be afraid of the unknown. Others may know the truth but speak with an anticipatory dread and deterministic doom.

*I feel there's a wall here. Can you imagine that wall with me? Close your eyes. I want you to imagine a wall. Can you see it? What color is it? How big is it?*
"It's blue. It kinda feels like my house."

*When you were talking before, I noticed you were hinting at something. Can you imagine a door in this wall? How big is it?*
"That's weird. When you said that, I saw my bedroom door."

*Is it open or closed?*
"It's open a little."

*Does it feel like it's easy to push open, or does it feel stuck a little?*
"It feels stuck."

*Do you know what's on the other side?*
"No. That's so weird. I don't know what I'm so scared of. The unknown, I guess."

We may still hold back, but we're beginning to realize that a house is more than bricks and mortar. It might need some doors, windows, maybe a nice skylight—all metaphors for context-appropriate transparency, vulnerability, and disclosure. By turning the wall into a house, we can enter and leave at leisure. Later, if we so desire, we may leave this house and walk the world without needing our defenses, but for now we value both privacy (the wall) and honesty (the window), safety (the wall) and trust (the door to be opened and closed), stability (the foundation) and adaptability (the decor), certainty (the roof) and mystery (the skylight).

The black/white, all/nothing mentality fears that coming out means coming out to everyone, or that disclosure means sharing everything. As our awareness is slowly building, invite us to establish a few people we can process out loud with. If we have a gentle blockade, a series of successful experiences can ease toward the benefit of approaching emotional discomfort. In session, processing aloud can include chatting about anything. As an icebreaker, try a few hypothetical questions, like what names we like, what fashion we admire, daydreaming about what life could be like if we could do anything. If we're bashful about this kind of talk, we may be more receptive to complaining. Sometimes, as a therapist, the most powerful thing you can do is to complain right along with us. That's right, kvetch, sigh, moan. Yes, this indulges our fusion, but it also allows us to explore judgment without judgment.

I really hate it when men treat me like _______________
I really hate it when people assume I'm _______________
I want to scream when my parents _______________
Sometimes I think society is so _______________

All these complaints provide a sneak peek into ideas to defuse from later, but for now complaining is actually practicing honesty. Take note of our focus, listen closely, be patient, and you might even hear our complaints turn into wishes, just as *I hate* this precedes *if only* that.

Any "I wish____" or "If only____" statement is the cutout for a doorway or a window. They're the first tentative evidence of our self-actualization values. "I wish I could open up." "I wish I could let people know." Even the heartbreaking, "I wish I knew what was wrong with me," illustrates a desire for awareness weighed down by low self-esteem.

With these wishes, we've begun adjusting the blueprint of our house. Keep in mind we're not yet committing to action, as we have yet to reveal what's behind the wall, yet we can still identify how to align with our values. We can, for example, explore our thoughts and feelings around secrecy, or what we need to feel safe in life. We'll address the wall in due time, when we're ready to open up—or not! This is perhaps where a therapist most needs to practice detachment from the outcome. We are more than our secrets, and more than our gender. As rapport builds, and we begin to trust you and, most importantly, ourselves, we begin to establish a door in that once impenetrable wall—and that alone is an amazing feat. Yet that door may not open.

Occasionally, we may return to the topic of gender, either anxiously or as a *seemingly* superficial topic, like we're knocking to see what's on the other side. Some therapists may feel saddened that their therapeutic relationship with a client may end before the door ever opens, or that their clients may retreat even once they come out. Male-bodied individuals often recur a purge-and-delay pattern, becoming so overwhelmed by their own femininity or androgyny that they jettison their gender variance over and over again before finally feeling ready to claim who they are (Beemyn and Rankin, 2011; Devor, 2004; Israel and Tarver II, 1997; Lewins, 1995; Stitt, 2013). The truth is, we may not be ready to address these issues, even if we're perfectly comfortable with you, because we are not yet ready to look that far within ourselves. And that's okay. Some clients may never repress their gender, or even go through a denial stage. Others may endure suppression and repression for years, fighting with ironic process. Take heart in the knowledge that all locks have a key, and that we will determine when it's time.

## Accepting kids: Mindful parenthood

> "There's lipstick on the mirror again. We laughed. He always stood apart from the other boys. We shrugged. He came home crying, 'My friends won't call me Natalie.' We paused."

> "I remember how she always tracked mud over the carpet, and when she hit a home-run when she was seven. It was a tomboy thing. Then last year her teacher asked what she wanted to be when she grew up, she said, 'A man.' Do you think it's a phase?"

Fortunately, there is a wealth of recent publications specializing in how to work with gender variant youth, yet there are many facets to bear in mind. Parents may range in attitude and acceptance, though many focus on whether or not to believe or affirm their child's gender expression, and whether or not to allow gonadotropin-releasing hormone (GnRH) analogs to suppress puberty, or to permit their teenager to undergo HRT or even gender alignment surgery (Amato, 2018; Bancroft, 2009). Understand that there is no blanket answer as every case will be unique, meaning there's often a steep learning curve for parents as the family system relearns how to adapt, flex, reinvest in itself, and find homeostasis.

There are multiple family system models to draw from, including Bowenian family therapy, Satir transformational systemic therapy, contextual family therapy, feminist family therapy, and the Olson circumplex model, to name a few. Each provides a distinct perspective on how gender roles, communication styles, power dynamics, family loyalties, and sociocultural differences influence the parent–child relationship. In particular, the Olson circumplex model approaches the family system with similar considerations as ACT, taking into account the level of cohesion, flexibility, and communication skills present in the family (Olson, 2000). Too little flexibility, in this model, leads to rigidity and the inability for roles to adapt or evolve. Too much flexibility and the family lacks structure, resulting in chaos and a lack of boundaries (Olson, 2000).

ACT does not endorse a specific family systems model, nor does it need to, as each present the importance of mental flexibility, and of stepping back to see the family as a whole. To this end, ACT's expansion of awareness, defusion from judgment, and commitment to value-congruent behavior fit neatly into a family therapist's toolkit. ACT can help parents see past their struggle to accept their child's gender exploration, to recognize their attempts to control discomfort, and the sacrifices this has cost both their family and their child. In turn, ACT can help children become aware of what Murray Bowen (2004) called *unresolved attachment*, evident in the guilt children may feel in their parents' company, or the defeated way some children relinquish all decision making to their parents, or the embitterment or rage they may hold for parents who don't accept or understand them.

Family systems work can be a difficult process, as parents may want to hold up their children's gender exploration as if it's an obstacle, a problem, or a disease to be cured. Some are looking to be reassured that their child will be okay; yet others may feel their own value constructs are being violated by their child's gender expansion. Pointing at myths and misinformation, these frustrated parents are unlikely to receive psychoeducation well, as their distress doesn't necessarily stem from misunderstanding per se. Chances are, they've had little contact with the LGBTQ community, as a rigid perspective of gender variance usually demonstrates. Yet on an intellectual level, the parent may actually be versed in gender variance but still not "agree" with it, marking their child as a threat to the norm. To navigate through this, clinicians need to practice calm, patient, inclusive language, normalizing all sides of the family. By highlighting metacommunication, you expand the focus from a singular person or specific conflict to explore how the family operates in the context of the world it operates in. That said, most sessions will be initiated by parents focusing all their love, worry, anger, and fear on their child, so let's begin there.

In one study, 110 transgender adults, looking back on their childhood, reminisced about the need for educated authority figures when they were kids, an open atmosphere to discuss their gender, and how pivotal it was to find freedom, validation, and recognition of their gender expression (Riley *et al.*, 2013). Granting that parents can't fulfill every need in their child's gender development, participants in this same study noted how parents could help a great deal by providing or permitting access to information, peer support, and gender specialists, and how much of a difference it would have made if their parents had gone on this educational journey with them (Riley *et al.*, 2013).

First, let's clear the air. Small children often play with gender expression, playing dress-up with their parents' clothes, or making a mess of their mother's makeup or their father's shaving cream. This doesn't mean they're transgender or even gender variant, but gender curious and perhaps even gender expansive (Brill and Kenney, 2016; Olson *et al.*, 2016; Tando, 2016; WPATH, 2011). As fewer than 30 percent of gender experimental children actually go on to adopt a gender variant identity—or fewer than 15 percent in some studies—parents are advised to view this curiosity as an exploration of self rather than an irreversible situation (Drummond *et al.*, 2008; Wallien and Cohen-Kettenis, 2008; WPATH, 2011). So how do parents know if their child is transgender, or genderqueer, or nonbinary? Short answer? They don't, but their kid will.

As there are many gender identities, so too are there various ages of onset. We can ponder and puzzle as to why this is, looking for some fork in the road or missed milestone or developmental detour, or hormonal brain lateralization, or response to trauma, or epigenetic starting point—and we may never deliberate an answer. The question is deep and powerful, but the reality remains unanswered. Right now, they're here, they're potentially queer, and they're looking up at their parents for help. Some kids will know themselves quite young and be very insistent about their gender (Olson *et al.*, 2016). Others may experiment, explore, and fluctuate as they grow older (Drummond *et al.*, 2008; Lev, 2004). This means that teens may continue to explore and re-explore their resonance with gender and sexual orientation constructs, much to their parents' chagrin.

> "She said she was a lesbian and now she's trans-masculine and likes people to call her boi!"
>
> "He said he was genderqueer, but now he says he's gay, and now he says he's gay and genderqueer. I don't get it."
>
> "She said she was transsexual and used to be really adamant about female pronouns, but now she's stopped taking hormones and is growing stubble again. What does it all mean?"

Simple. It means that they're figuring it out. All of us, as children and teens, contended with self-discovery and self-definition, a developmental phase Erik Erikson described in his 1950 publication *Childhood and Society* as *fidelity*, in which identity comes up against role confusion. Did we accept the cultural script, or find ourselves standing apart from the stereotype? If our relationship with our bodies is not cisgender, then our felt dissonance subverts or rejects the social norm. This can generate a great deal of distress and confusion for young people, whose personal identities conflict with what Erikson called clannish behavior preoccupied with in-group–out-group status. Fused to such frames of comparison, kids know their dissonance and resonance, even when there are no cultural scripts to account for it, just as they know they're different long before they have the words to describe it. The dizzying number of labels in the world today points to a generation of youth cobbling together a language to account for their differences. Wagging fingers, parents point to the personal fable, and how all kids think they're special. There is a truth to this, as being different can be a source of both uniqueness and insecurity, yet such myths are a product of our felt dissonance and resonance as children, not the cause of it. We don't say, "I'm different, so I'm transgender," we say, "I'm transgender, so I'm different."

You must therefore consider if the parent is projecting their own, unresolved adolescent issues. Bowenian family therapy addresses this in the three steps of family projection (Bowen, 2004; Brown, 2008). First, a parent may fear something is wrong, abnormal, or problematic with their child. Second, confirmation bias will kick in, and the parent will see what they fear in their child's anxious response to being treated as a problem. Third, the parent will change their behavior, treating the child as though there is actually something wrong with them. Bewildered, with fears of spreading contagion, parents may ask if their kids are somehow being influenced by their peers, or the internet, or those queer movies that keep getting Academy Awards. Perhaps, in their use of language or labels, yes, but their dissonance and resonance are entirely personal. Constructs like *gender bender*, *femme*, *butch*, *queer*, *trans-masculine*, *trans-feminine*, *genderfluid*, and *neutrois* are nuanced concepts historically arising from different geographical, generational, or LGBTQ cohorts, but underneath all the lingo is a personal identity well aware that it's different from the norm. Children who keep changing their name or pronoun are still in the midst of gender exploration and are trying on labels to see how they fit. The larger, and perhaps more influential, question in the long run is can their parents accept that this process is already happening?

Retrospectively, we can see certain patterns. Gender dysphoric children who re-identify as cisgender frequently identify as gay, bisexual, or lesbian (Drummond *et al.*, 2008; Green, 1987; Wallien and Cohen-Kettenis, 2008). Perhaps they challenged and redefined masculinity and femininity, or perhaps their parents mistook their sexuality for cross-sexed behavior, or perhaps their gender identity process was entirely independent of their sexual identity process, or perhaps they were completely intertwined. Perhaps it depends on the child! Once more, the causal question isn't as important as the child's development, as they will have to adjust either way. Also keep in mind that this process goes both ways, as a child who declares they're gay may realize they're gender variant later in life, or may have always been so, but placed their gender on the back burner out of shame, doubt, or because they simply prioritized their sexual identity development first.

So, what of children who identify as gender variant? The more extreme their gender dysphoria is as a child, the more likely they'll maintain their gender through adolescence into adulthood (Drummond *et al.*, 2008; Green, 1987; Wallien and Cohen-Kettenis, 2008). If connection to other gender explorative or gender variant children is rare, kids may split their conceptual self in two, hiding their private persona inside the protective shell of their public persona (Ettner, 1999). Developmentally, children begin to understand the basic premise of socially desirable behavior by age two, which is when we first begin to label the "good me" and the "bad me."

As children grow up, parents, teachers, peers, and media act as gender-socializing agents, behaving differently around children, toddlers, and even babies, based on their assumed sex (Cohen-Kettenis and Pfäfflin, 2003). Mothers tend to talk more to their daughters than to their sons; fathers use sex-typed behaviors to socially advertise a baby's sex; teachers criticize boys more often than girls but also give them added attention and feedback; boys are praised for winning and for being right, whereas girls are praised for obedience and compliance; and girls who choose boys' toys between the ages of two and five are largely ignored by children of the same age, whereas boys who choose girls' toys are ridiculed and bullied (Cohen-Kettenis and Pfäfflin, 2003). Feminist family therapy (Carter and McGoldrick, 2005; Hare-Mustin, 1978; Luepnitz, 2002), contextual family therapy (Boszormenyi-Nagy, 1987), and human ecology theory (Bronfenbrenner, 2005) expand on these observations by noting how sociocultural variables influence not only childhood development, but the formation of the family system and the interaction of performative roles therein.

When a child's gender falls prey to such hierarchical frames—dictating that a female baby is a girl, and girls need to be treated as sensitive—their cognitions fuse to a deep emotional response. Shrinking under admonishment, their whole face will turn bright red as their source of joy is attenuated, but not extinguished, by shame (Ettner, 1999). Like ironic forbidden fruit, the more their desire is pushed down, the more attractive it becomes, and the more shame they feel pushing it down, and so on until they rebel against the shame or drown in it (Green, 2012). Instead of forcing a child to suppress their feelings, parents can develop ways to support their child as they "try on" gender to see what fits, including gender expressive vacations, gender explorative playdates, and letting their child know they're not only supported moving forward, but that there's always a way back, too (Green, 2012; WPATH, 2011).

As children get older, there are three big steps in adolescent gender exploration, including: fully reversible interventions, like playing with gender expression, experimenting with names and pronouns, and even puberty suppressing hormones; partially reversible interventions, including HRT, as certain results like fat distribution can revert while other changes, like testosterone deepening of the voice, do not; and irreversible procedures like facial feminization surgery (FFS), SRS, and other gender alignment surgeries (WPATH, 2011). Whatever potential options the parent may explore, holding out for a phase to end isn't acceptance—it's tolerance at best. This brings parents to a few hard questions: *Are you willing to accept your child as they are? Are you willing to accept your child's gender exploration, knowing that you can't stop it? And are you aware of what values you believe, as a parent, are being violated by your child's process?*

ACT, as a therapeutic modality, concerns itself far more with the embodiment of our values in the present moment than with the outcomes of our goals. Identity development, therefore, is not a scheduled program to be controlled or measured, but a recognition of *what is* in its *state of becoming*. Growth, by its very definition, is active. This notion is often difficult for parents who diligently organize, orchestrate, and educate their children, trying as best they can to mark the calendar, pack lunches for tomorrow, pick them up from school, get them to practice, help them with their homework, and plan the whole year with possibly one free night for themselves in September if they can manage to fit it in. Parents are so often goal-focused planners, and for good reason. In ACT we learn to accept and decentralize our expectations for a final outcome or product by noticing what's experientially more potent and embracing the process. We all want to win the game, but did we have fun and put in effort while we played it? We all want to get the grade, but did we actually learn anything meaningful from the class? We can't deny what we want, but sacrificing our experiential lives to get it is a precarious path to regret, pessimistic defeatism, or Pyrrhic victory. This is as true for a child questioning their gender identity as it is for the parent reacting to it.

Whenever possible, it's best to strengthen the child's original family system through psychoeducation and mindfulness practices reinforcing empathy for the child. This may mean debunking a great deal of myths about LGBTQ people living promiscuous, unhappy lives, abusing drugs and alcohol before contracting HIV, being murdered, or dying all alone (Mitchell, 2012). In the long run, parental support greatly increases a kid's quality of life, as knowing their family supports them will increase their emotional resilience (McCann *et al.*, 2017; Simons *et al.*, 2013). However, this is not always possible, as some families implode into abuse. In violent incidents, the ethical protocol to protect the child's health and wellbeing and inform child protective services takes precedence.

In family therapy, before even addressing gender, assess the level of functionality within the family structure, as dysfunction often exacerbates gender dysphoria (Vanderburgh, 2008). When parents desire to have a boy instead of a girl, or vice versa, the child can pick up on this desire even if it's never verbally stated (Vanderburgh, 2008). Recognizing how gender roles and gender stereotypes can be used as defensive psychological armor, sexually abused children may actualize a different gender identity in order to distance themselves from what their aggressor desires, to adopt characteristics that may defend them, or as a way of desperately trying to be someone else (Vanderburgh, 2008).

Rather than rush to causal statements, monitor for maladaptive and formerly effective coping mechanisms that are no longer functional within the family. Openly gender variant children—through no fault of their own—are often centralized within family conflict, increasing the risk of child abuse (Vanderburgh, 2007, 2008). The distressing correlation here is that the more gender variant a child is, the more likely they'll be physically and verbally abused by their primary caregivers (McCann *et al.*, 2017). Bowenian family therapy interprets volatility as the parent's attempt to resolve their own family of origin issues (Bowen, 2004);

contextual family therapy echoes this as the parents holding on to their own filial loyalties in conjunction with social pressures (Boszormenyi-Nagy, 1987); meanwhile, feminist family therapy observes how partriachal systems maintain gender rules via threat of consequence and punishment (Stark and Flitcraft, 1988; Luepnitz, 2002). Complementing each perspective, ACT observes how acts of abuse and neglect are often attempts to control situations in order to avoid an unpleasant emotional state (Zarling and Berta, 2017). As the verbal language that shapes cognition is heavily influenced by parents and social mores, parents may fuse to ideas like "I can't let this happen," or "My dad would be so ashamed if they saw my son like this," or "I can't let the neighbors see my daughter like that," or simply "That's just wrong." When these beliefs are inflexible, people may try to exert control over their partners or their children, resulting in passive-aggressive commentary, corporal punishment, or domestic violence (Zarling and Berta, 2017).

Looking back on their childhood, trans women commonly recall their parents and playmates noticing their atypical gender expression around eight and nine years old (Grossman, D'Augelli and Salter, 2006). This is usually when the "sissy-boy" name-calling began, along with their parent's desperate attempt to physically discipline them (Grossman *et al.*, 2006). In a teen focus group, 66 percent said that their parents and siblings knew about their gender identity (Grossman and D'Augelli, 2006). Teenage self-reports have found that 54 percent of moms, and 63 percent of dads reacted negatively when their children first came out, and although there is a shift in attitude, 50 percent of moms and 44 percent of dads kept a negative view of their child's gender three years later (Grossman *et al.*, 2005; McCann *et al.*, 2017).

When listening to parental narratives, the subject of a child's gender is not so easily parsed between tolerance vs. intolerance, or even acceptance vs. rejection. Embrace or banishment might be the final outcome, but it's often a winding road to get there, marked by years of questions, arguments, misunderstandings, and rifts in the family system. Some parents notice their child's development early, even if their child hasn't pieced together the puzzle, which leads the parent to question, "What do I do?"

Wanting to understand, parents often seek out therapists, mental health literature, and various websites, all of which can present very conflicting information. Trying to discern how to help their child, each parent is caught in the agenda of emotional control. There has to be some action, some option, some way that they, as the parent, can fix this—a belief potentially stemming from a sociocultural narrative pressuring parents to embody independence, authority, and certainty. When a parent loses hope, they're most likely to abandon their child, kicking them onto the street. Such parents are unlikely to enter therapy with their child. As for those who do maintain the relationship, their hope may deliberately or inadvertently engineer obstacles for their child's psychological wellbeing. This leads to very different mindsets that parents may fuse with, exclusively or in combination.

### *The goal-focused parent*

A lot of trans-positive literature places gender autonomy with the child, which is empowering for the kid and terrifying for many parents who can't trust their child to feed the dog, let alone decide if they're ready for hormone therapy. Goal-focused parents, in their uncertainty, often want to "fix the problem." They may even overestimate the role of transition as a therapeutic tool to decrease a child's distress level. They may focus solely on the child's wellbeing, fearing that a transgender life equates to one of hardship and persecution (Brill and Kenney, 2016). Even the most open-minded parents may feel genuinely afraid of all the implications being gender variant may have for their child. They may question if the world will accept their children, or if their child will ever find love (Brill and Kenney, 2016). Goal-focused parents can strive so hard to be open, progressive, and accepting that their child's gender may, for a time, become overly central. They may try to do "all the right things," yet feel vexed when emotions come up in the family dynamic, as emotions are process-oriented experiences they can't "fix." For the goal-focused parent, hope is found in controlling the external, which may or may not be possible.

### *The restrictive parent*

Minimizing the child's reported gender, the restrictive parent takes the reins as an attempt to direct their child toward cisgender norms. Down this road, blogs, websites, and forums hyperfocus on gender dissidents, observing how gender experimentation can be just an experiential phase. Even rapid-onset gender dysphoria, a faux diagnosis attempting to account for why contemporary youth question gender norms, presents parents with the hope that if they can keep their child's gender variance from being affirmed, they'll grow out of it. Such parents resist believing their child's gender variance, especially if they overlooked or were oblivious to cues indicating that their child was gender atypical. Parents may fuse to denial, rejection, or even anger. Parents may try and train their child to "act like a boy" or "act like a girl" as if their gender nonconformity were a rebellious behavior to be disciplined (Green, 2012). They may restrict their child's access to social influences they feel are undermining or "confusing" their child's gender identity. When gender variance is viewed as an infectious social phenomenon, parents believe it's an idea reinforced by talking about it. Their seemingly sensible solution, therefore, is to not talk about it! Of course, people aren't magically being summoned into being, nor are they spell cast by an idea, nor does ignoring the issue make it go away. Shocked, parents may wonder if their child is just acting out to get attention, if somehow they parented them wrongly, or if they caused their child's gender dysphoria (Brill and Kenney, 2016). For the desperate parent trying to spare their child confusion and distress, the prospect of helping their kid grow out of these feelings presents a kind of hope.

### *The aggressive parent*

Embarrassed and ashamed of their children's behavior, aggressive parents fuse with rigid, intolerant mindsets, often stating what the world will or will not accept. They may guise their aggression and violence behind compassion, stating, "It's what's good for him" or "I just don't want her to have a hard life." Parents may ask impossible things of their child without realizing how futile they are. They may shout, "Can you just be normal?" Likewise, children often ask their parents the impossible, sighing exhaustedly, "Please don't worry about me." Both are desperate pleas to reduce a sense of distress that only the individual can manage on their own. Nothing the child can do will ease the parents' concern, while nothing the parents can do will change their child's identity. The more unique and gender-nonconforming their child is, the more hostile and direct an aggressive parent feels they have to be, increasing verbal and physical abuse (Grossman *et al.*, 2005). Preserving control and influence over their child's development becomes their primary goal.

### *The passive parent*

Unsure of the correct path to take, the passive parent advocates patience with a *wait and see* attitude. They may be biding time, if they hope their child is just going through a phase, or they may genuinely feel that the smartest move is to postpone the gender question until later (Brill and Kenney, 2016). From their vantage, doing nothing is perceived as neutral, which is why they may not realize potential areas of neglect. Silence is loud, and putting a pin in a child's development can have a serious impact on their esteem, especially if the child feels they're in limbo or put on hold from actualizing their authentic self (Brill and Kenney, 2016). Specifically, the passive parent leans back from the conversation, hoping that their child will be wise enough when they're older to figure it out.

### *The mindful parent*

To begin a very complex and emotionally charged conversation, first recognize the need for acceptance. Neither parent nor child can actively persuade each other, as acceptance cannot be achieved through argument. Aware of their feelings, the mindful parent is as curious of their own process as they are of their child's, since they are intertwined. Being attentive to their child's feelings and developing identity, the mindful parent also gauges their own thoughts and emotional reactions. Through an ongoing practice of self-monitoring, patience, and perspective taking, the mindful parent can expand awareness beyond immediate discomfort. Focusing on what's most important for their health and wellbeing, the mindful parent can also notice that their child has respective needs for their own. Much in the same way that a father realizes his daughter has a unique gender experience different from his own, and much in the same way that a mother realizes her son has a unique gender experience different from her own, mindful parents explore both the familiar and foreign needs of their gender variant child.

When it comes to being a parent, ACT asks primary caregivers to accept their emotional response to their child's development, personality, and identity, as well as their own role (Hayes *et al.*, 2008). By softly challenging the idea that they have to obey their own thoughts to be an instructional parent, or remove their intrusive thoughts to be an effective parent, ACT encourages caregivers to take their thoughts less literally in order to be genuinely present with their child (Hayes *et al.*, 2008).

In the beginning, clarify that acceptance is not concession or agreement. Parents may not believe that their child is truly transgender. They may say they're going through a phase or that they're just confused or experimental. Both clinician and client may adamantly disagree. Just remember the parent's point may be rooted in loss, shame, and even love. Certainly, some parents will be hostile, yet others are simply worried and ill-informed (Brill and Kenney, 2016). So, we start with acceptance. If they genuinely believe their child is going through a phase, then it does no good to fight it.

Rejecting it, shoving it down, and refusing to talk about it just means the conversation will happen without them. The question of gender is difficult on many levels, often because it questions and subverts the power differential between parent and child. The parent's authority is no longer absolute, as something is occurring within the child that the parent cannot discern for them. Intrinsically, parents understand how they play a huge role in their child's development, providing many templates for their child's gender schemas. However, their child's interpretation and relationship with these schemas remains largely their own. No matter how many lawn mowers they push, how many footballs they catch, or how many cars they fix, they're probably not going to "man up." Sorry, dad, but bicep strength, hand–eye coordination, and knowing how to fix a carburetor does not a man make. Telling a girl she's pretty and will make a beautiful bride one day does not entice tomboys out of their climbing tree. Sorry, mom, there is no recipe for sugar and spice and everything nice.

Fears of safety, preoccupation with sin, anger, disappointment, and even guilt and self-blame are rooted in the parent's love for their child, as their expectations for the child's future are rattled (Mitchell, 2012). The parent's distress may also be hitched to any unresolved, unspoken, or unmet needs they may have, including any value violation, incongruence, or dissonance they may be feeling within themselves. As clinicians identify the love in the family system, they can also introduce the potentials of coming out, as well as the profound benefits that honesty, authenticity, and genuine acceptance can have for the child and the family as a whole (Mitchell, 2012).

Frontload the parents that as the sessions unfold you're going to ask them periodically to step back and reflect on how they're feeling, and what their child is saying, rather than act aggressively with sarcasm, accusations, or over-talking (Tando, 2016). Though the shock and surprise are all too real, research demonstrates how positive family support can guard children from the risk of depression and anxiety (Grossman and D'Augelli, 2006; Grossman *et al.*, 2006; McCann *et al.*, 2017; Simons *et al.*, 2013). Starting with this, establish what the family can all agree on. Practice affirming the collective. What's important to *us* as a whole? What do *we*, as a family, desire? Often, a family can collectively agree that we care. We love. We want what's best, even if we don't agree or don't know what that is.

Returning to the fundamentals of mindfulness, we need to expand awareness beyond the desire to control. A useful technique is to rewind the clock, recalling moments when the parent had to trust their child's agency.

> *Do you remember when your child was learning how to tie their shoes? It took some time, didn't it? Remember those days when you had to get out the door—so instead of letting them fumble, you quickly tied their shoes for them? It would have only taken a minute if we'd let them figure it out, but we were in a rush. What we're doing now is challenging a false sense of urgency. I hear this strong need to do something to help your child, but they have to tie their own shoes.*

Gently explain the difference between anger as a valid emotion and hostility as a violent behavior. They may feel angry, sad, or distraught, but these emotions don't control their actions (Tando, 2016). Chronic rescuers and authoritarian parents often feel compelled to do something, to fix the problem, to find a solution, to resolve the issue, but their child's identity isn't fixable, as it isn't intrinsically a problem (Tando, 2016).

> *When you look back on those days, when they were so small with their lives ahead of them, did you think, "My child can't tie their shoes?" Or did you think, "My child*

*is learning to tie their shoes?" Do you remember how you felt when they couldn't do it? Do you remember how you felt when they finally did?*

*When they were tying their shoes, what would have happened if you had yelled at them? They would have broken down crying, and they wouldn't have learned how to do it. You've taught them a lot, more than even they may realize now. But tying shoe laces, in this metaphor, isn't gender. That's the shoe itself, which they tried on in the store and found comfortable. Tying the laces represents all those unique, nuanced twists and turns and folds and knots that only you could teach them as their parent. Those qualities that make them like you. What characteristics did they pick up from you?*

Progressively, through multiple strength-based sessions, members of a family can begin to see what makes their family dynamic, noting both the struggles and respective virtues. As a family system begins to trust the strengths of each member of the family, the false urgency to take charge, make the call, and do something is slowly released. This can be exceptionally difficult when a child is either quite young, rejects authority, or has made mistakes of their own. Actively engaging the family to identify and validate value congruence over outcome may help cultivate acceptance for all parties involved. Continuously validating expressions of love, respect, and acceptance can further decrease the idea that the immediate discomfort is insurmountable. Parents will need multiple resources, including emotional support systems of their own, independent counselors, connections to TransYouth Family Allies (TYFA), and Parents, Families and Friends of Lesbians and Gays (PFLAG), alongside medical consultation should HRT be assessed as a viable option.

## Accepting teens: Relational frame theory meets relational-cultural theory

Long before children settle on a label or begin actualizing their identity, their gender nonconformity becomes targeted (Brill and Kenney, 2016; Grossman and D'Augelli, 2006; Wyss, 2004). Perhaps they're genderqueer, or a butch lesbian, or an effeminate gay boy, or a transsexual person years away from transition—the sheer fact that they're different catches the ire of classmates and teachers alike (Wyss, 2004). Though sexual orientation gets rejected and ridiculed, it's our gender expression that usually serves as a target, as feminine boys and masculine girls are easy to spot. And even if an LGB teen doesn't present as overtly feminine, or masculine, or androgynous, or butch, sexual orientation is still mocked as if it sabotages or compromises one's status as a man or woman. Because of small behavioral cues that catch other people's attention, LGBTQ youth are often made aware of their differences before they realize what these differences even mean, or how they connect with their sexual or gender identity, though hindsight is 20/20.

Age of realization does not intrinsically correspond to age of disclosure as many kids keep their sexuality and gender private for years, doubting these impulses within themselves, or fearing rejection should they come out. One interview with 55 trans millennials found that disclosure to parents was not equal, with 43 of the kids being out to their mothers, but only 26 being out to their fathers (Grossman *et al.*, 2005). Comparably, the Trevor Project's 2019 survey found that only 51 percent of gender variant youth between the ages of 13 and 24 were out to their parents about their gender identity. There is a lot of emotional energy built up around disclosing to a parent, as the moment a kid says, "I'm transgender," or "I think I'm a boy," or "Mom, Dad, I've always been a girl," a wave of doubt and fear can run through the family. Some parents dread the social repercussions, for both their child and their family. Some are simply taken aback. Observably, a few bold teens successfully transition in high school, with or without parental consent, yet others may feel crushed by restriction, waiting to graduate and move out before they can begin living their life as their resonant self (Green, 2012).

When transgender kids with binary identities are socially supported in their transition process, research suggests anxiety and depression are significantly reduced (Greytak, Kosciw, and Boesen, 2013; Olson *et al.*, 2016; Simons *et al.*, 2013). These socially transitioned kids, whose gender was accepted and actualized by their family systems, still reported higher levels of anxiety than cisgender kids their age due to peer victimization, microaggressions, and atypical life experiences (Olson *et al.*, 2016; Wilson, Griffin, and Wren, 2005). Even when parents are wholly supportive, and the school is a safe place, and a child is allowed to use bathrooms and locker rooms, and join team games and sports with the other boys and girls, respectively, they may still experience a heightened awareness of self and body (Olson *et al.*, 2016). They may worry that they'll look like a boy with breasts or a girl with an Adam's apple, making puberty—which is a self-conscious time—even more frightful (Bancroft, 2009). Not only is their body developing, they may fear it's growing in all the wrong directions and in all the wrong ways.

Nonbinary genderqueer, genderfluid, and agender children can thrive when permitted full gender expression (Richards *et al.*, 2016; Vanderburgh, 2008). Unfortunately, an overtly binary world doesn't make this possible, meaning most social arenas, including schools and clubs, are unlikely to validate gender variance. By being their witness, you can validate their hardships, and increase emotional resilience by spotlighting people in their lives who do understand, or at the very least have the capacity to understand (Vanderburgh, 2008). These supportive people are not always the child's immediate family, making them all the more indispensable in their development. Teachers, coaches, friends, and neighbors are all potential sources for connection and support, as are *families of choice*. The LGBTQ community is very familiar with the concept of *found family*, *chosen family*, *family of choice*, *kith and kin*, or *hānai family*, all terms denoting the supportive family we adopt outside of our biological family. Children and teens are most at risk when they feel isolated and alienated, hence the need to connect them with peers, role models, and community resources who actively celebrate them (McCann *et al*., 2017).

As children and adolescents often have causal and emotional reasoning, promote age-appropriate explorations (Luthar and Cichetti, 2000).

Sean, for example, is only in therapy because they got caught at school with a knife in their pocket. They were charged and had a few days of house arrest but the charges were dropped after Sean's English teacher—perhaps the only person in the whole school who knew Sean was genderqueer—came forward in their defense. Knowing all too well that Sean was getting bullied, their teacher was able to plead their case to their parents, their high school, and the judge. It was the nicest thing anyone had ever done for Sean, but it also outed them in the process. Sean's angry about it all but they don't want to show it, and the first time the word *defusion* was mentioned they started picking at their fingernails.

Ramp up the ACT metaphors as allegories are easier to remember than psychobabble, but be cautious with teens who feel like they've heard it all before. Empower their agency by presenting them with an ACT concept and have them come up with their own metaphors. If they need more of a prompt, work with metaphors that fit their world in fun and interesting ways.

> *Ever feel trapped in a public place?*
> "Yeah, I took the subway this morning."
>
> *You ever notice, on the subway, how there are so many people actively trying to ignore each other? Like they're plugged into their headphones, or they're trying to read a book, or they're just avoiding eye contact. You ever do that?*
> "All the time. I usually have my hood up."
>
> *Can you imagine what would happen if the doors never opened, and the train just kept on riding?*
> "That would freak me out!"
>
> *Probably, at first, but after a while you'd probably start talking with people, right?*
> "We'd probably resort to cannibalism."
>
> *That was quick.*
> "Only takes a few days."
>
> *What if, during those few days of exploring for a way to stop the train, you found a caboose filled with enough supplies to last you for decades? But there's just no way to stop the train. Can't open the doors, or windows. There's no way out.*

"So we're stuck?"

*Essentially.*
"That sucks."

*Sure does, and you go through all the stages of grief. Denial, anger, bargaining, depression, everything. You try and find another way off, but every time you do, there's just no way to stop the train. At some point, you'd probably have to accept it, yeah?*
"Not me. I'd make trying to get off the train my hobby. What else have I got to do?"

*How long would you keep that up?*
"How long is the train going for?

*Eternity. A small civilization's already started. People are starting to raise kids.*
"I think I saw this movie. Huh... Knowing me, I'd probably get bored eventually."

*Exactly. What if that's what's going on here? What if your mind is the train, and all the people on board are your emotions, with no way on or off? At what point do you start getting to know them?*

The need for educated authority figures and safe-space stewards is clear, yet these safe spaces cannot be relocated to isolated pockets for teens to scurry between, as is literally the case in many settings, like schools with friendly classrooms and dangerous corridors (Riley *et al.*, 2013). Trans-positive clinicians are visible torch bearers lighting the way to community resources. By all means become an ally, but more so become an ally trainer. Teach others how to hold a safe space, in every academic, medical, and corporate sphere, and provide information to parents and adults trying to figure all this out (Riley *et al.*, 2013).

The big issues facing trans youth, from the mouths of the teens themselves, are the lack of safe spaces—from hangout spots, to bathrooms, to gender neutral locker-rooms—putting them at risk of violence, their inability to access health services including competent mental healthcare, and the emotional rollercoaster of gaining support from their family and their community (Grossman and D'Augelli, 2006; McCann *et al.*, 2017; Reisner *et al.*, 2015). The Trevor Project (2019) found that 78 percent of transgender and nonbinary youth had endured through verbal and physical discrimination in multiple social environments, and that 58 percent had been deterred, discouraged, or simply bullied out of using a bathroom that aligns with their gender identity. Another survey found that 83 percent wanted HRT, but 60 percent were struggling to find access to health services (Corliss *et al.*, 2007). This is problematic, as without proper consultation teens can find almost anything they want online, with medically dangerous repercussions. Feeling marginalized and invisible, trans teenagers often turn to peer social support and emotional avoidance strategies to get by (Grossman and D'Augelli, 2006).

When kids feel unsafe and unsupported in their lives, their grades tank. School becomes less of an education and more of an arduous gauntlet (Grossman and D'Augelli, 2006; Reisner *et al.*, 2015; Riley *et al.*, 2013; Wyss, 2004). Avoiding the source of fear, 47 percent of trans teens report skipping class at least once a month, if not taking off the whole day (Greytak, Kosciw, and Diaz, 2009). The more they're harassed, the more likely they are to shrug off college (Greytak *et al.*, 2009; McCann *et al.*, 2017). Likewise, the more they're bullied and traumatized, the more gender variant youth are likely to abuse drugs and alcohol as a means of avoiding their internal experience (Batten and Hayes, 2005; Garofalo *et al.*, 2006; Hayes *et al.*, 2008; McCann *et al.*, 2017; Reisner *et al.*, 2015; Rowe *et al.*, 2015; Russell *et al.*, 2011). According to the social stress model, we lean on substances as a maladaptive coping mechanism, yet gender variant youth may also use drugs and alcohol to socially underscore their difference from the norm, or to align with gender expansive subcultures and socially permissive countercultures (Reisner *et al.*, 2015). Their dreams dashed, their patience spent, or their faith in academia burnt to a crisp, they may pull away from higher education. Some may focus on transition, feeling unable to afford both a degree and the exorbitant cost of reconstructive surgery, electrolysis, HRT, and gender alignment surgery.

Kids are caught in a catch-22, and they know it. If they come out, they face hostility, which will take a huge chunk out of their self-esteem; but if they hide who they are, they risk disintegrating on the inside (Grossman and D'Augelli, 2006). As protecting a child from life's danger is impossible, especially for gender minorities, emotional resilience becomes one of the greatest predictors of lifelong success (Luthar and Cichetti, 2000; Masten, 1994, 2001). This ability to bounce back from trauma, violence, and oppression is not a magic power, but a series of ordinary, everyday reinforcements of personal empowerment (Masten, 2001; Strosahl and Robinson, 2017).

In real terms, resilience is learning how to cope with discrimination, process feelings in the aftermath, rise above, and still secure personal self-worth, self-acceptance, and accountability (Corliss *et al.*, 2007; McCann *et al.*, 2017; Reicherzer and Spillman, 2012). Resilience is not a hardened perseverance, but the development of a few key internal assets, including social competence, problem solving, autonomy and identity, and a sense of purpose and future (Benard and Slade, 2009). On their own, many kids push forward, gritting their teeth, suffering through the slings and arrows while trying their best to toughen up. This is an admirable kind of endurance, a survivalist's strength fortifying the self against the world, but it's not enough. Even if they tough it out into adulthood, the scars become callous, and they may fuse with rigid cynicism, continuously doubting the positive while pre-emptively defending themselves against the negative.

As teens are developing their social awareness, they tend to realize their resilience when it's witnessed and continuously validated by meaningful figures in their lives. This is where relational frame theory (RFT) neatly weds relational-cultural theory (RCT). A feminist, multicultural model branching from Jean Baker Miller's *Towards a New Psychology of Women* (1976), RCT places meaningful relationships at the forefront of our personal development and ongoing mental health. When we feel a reciprocal sense of resonance, growth is fostered on both sides. Marrying this to RFT, our relationships are living testaments to how we matter to each other, as our frame of self is reflected in our frame of other. By recognizing our similarities, celebrating our differences, and honoring our collaboration, we begin to feel that we not only matter, but belong to family, culture, or community larger than ourselves. When we're a part of a meaningful relationship, we not only feel like we know more about each other and ourselves respectively, we may also feel an increased sense of energy and self-worth alongside a desire to take action, build on the experience and cultivate more relationships (Miller, 1986).

According to RCT, the more a child encounters others who value their uniqueness, the more they will value their uniqueness within themselves (Hartling, 2008). Research professor Brené Brown (2012) conveyed this succinctly when her data found that people only feel a deep sense of love and belonging when they believe they are worthy of love and belonging. This self-worth is often impeded by what RCT calls the Central Relational Paradox, a conundrum whereby our natural drive to connect and find acceptance is interrupted by an underlying belief that we are unlovable, unacceptable, or unworthy of connection (Miller *et al.*, 2004). Hiding the very qualities that make us special or unique, we may get stuck in a social feedback loop whereby we feel stifled in our stifled relationships because we feel stifled by our stifled relationships. Having fused to a belief, ACT encourages us to loosen our hold on such rigid frames of thought, but this can be incredibly difficult for young people who, quite naturally, prioritize social integration. While ACT can help shift our relationship with our thoughts, young people need more than just mental exercises. They need evidence that they matter. All people wrestle with the unknown at times in their life, but gender variant youth often have to contend with the harsh realities of bullying, family conflict, and even homelessness. The rigid belief that they are unlovable may be backed up by all kinds of terrible experiences. Their cynicism, in this case, is backed up not merely by the past, but by their anticipation of a harsh future. Holding up their maladaptive defense mechanisms as battle-worn shields, gender variant youth sometimes attest that the whole defusion process is just fanciful. Some may acknowledge it as "a neat idea" but place no faith in the therapeutic process. They may have questionable faith in themselves or questionable faith in the world. And what a big thing the world is. How vast and uncompromising it can feel to the powerless. This is where rapport building means everything, as that felt sense of connection at the beginning of a therapeutic relationship—that initial spark of resonance—is the felt evidence we're looking for.

Many ACT therapists just starting out may focus too intensely on cognitive defusion exercises, as it's not uncommon for clients and therapists alike to believe that therapy is a wholly mental journey. Returning to our mind–body connection, remember that we tend to feel before we think, organizing our senses before interpreting their meaning. RCT applies this same concept to our social sphere, since we don't usually think "Oh, this is a great conversation" in the middle of the session. Not to say this doesn't happen! Appreciative clients may remark, "I'm glad to say this out loud," but more often this thought pops up after the fact, when what's said is said and we reflect back on what we felt. Investing genuine curiosity into a teenager's life and validating their emotional experience is a great way to nurture that felt spark, yet RCT expands on this in a few key ways. When a therapist shows they can be authentically moved by their client's process, the client in turn is moved, having seen firsthand how their very existence can reach another (Miller *et al.*, 2004). RCT also demonstrates, in a very similar fashion to ACT, how the nature of the conversation shapes the nature of the relationship, and in turn our respective sense of self. Resilience begins to thrive when the emphasis on self-esteem, control, and mastery is shifted to a more adaptable sense of self-worth, mutual empowerment, and competency (Hartling, 2008). By expanding on themes of interconnection, it becomes easier to be mindful of healthy experiences, initiate new relationships, and keep that feeling of mutual validation alight.

### *Self-esteem to self-worth*

When aiding gender variant clients, too many counselors focus on self-esteem without comprehending the conundrum of doing so. Although self-esteem is wonderful, it often carries a competitive edge, which is problematic for kids who do not or cannot compete with the academic prowess, beauty standards, or athletic expectations warranting esteem boosts (Hartling, 2008). Shifting focus from performance achievements to relational value, kids can begin to conceptualize self-worth by recognizing how they matter to people (Hartling, 2008; Singh *et al.*, 2011). This also includes incorporating the intrinsic worth of their racial/ethnic identity by recognizing the valuable insight, cultural knowledge, and personal perspective they have (Singh, 2013). Children and teens can easily expand awareness in this area by either recalling or learning to be mindful of who gives them a high five when they've done a good job, who asks about them when they're not around, who cheers them on and always wants their best, who listens when they have something to say, and who pays attention to them when they talk (Benard and Slade, 2009).

### *Internal control to mutual empowerment*

Attempting to persuade a gender variant teen to internalize their locus of control is a fool's errand, as so much of their life isn't in control, and if they do have an internal locus of control, they may attribute their difficulties to some personal deficiency rather than question the cisnormative game rigged against them (Hartling, 2008). This hyperfocus on control is not only exhausting, but feeds into the self-deprecation spiral. As an alternative, mutual empowerment presents the idea that both self and other can sway the experience of the relationship (Hartling, 2008). For gender variant teens of color, resilience builds with self-advocacy in the education system, especially when teachers and community members listen and collaborate with the student (Reicherzer and Spillman, 2012; Singh, 2013). Unfortunately, when adults are condescending to youth, this is not always an option, making it difficult to find an LGBTQ community or venue in which to affirm and express identity. For many, the internet becomes the bastion of connection, especially for gender variant people searching for others who also relate to their racial and cultural heritage and experience (Devor, 2004; Lev, 2007; Singh, 2013). Moving away from the isolating concept that they have to solve their problems alone, mutual empowerment can be as healing as it is strength building. Perhaps the best example of this is the mutual empathy built in a therapeutic relationship. Curious questions engaging how they help decide things in a class, how they help people when they're in trouble, how they get people to cooperate, how they help out at home, and how people in their world rely on them, all foster mutual empowerment (Hartling, 2008).

### *Social support to authentic connection*

Given the overall lack of supportive services for gender variant people, there remains a need for therapeutic, medical, academic, occupational, housing, and socioeconomic aid, yet above all there remains a need for social outreach. Community connection is an essential developmental step for gender variant people because, unlike other unidirectional aid, being able to meet someone who truly understands and who takes the time to develop an authentic connection, can emotionally uplift a kid in long-lasting ways (Devor, 2004; Hartling, 2008; Lev 2004). A hot meal is appreciated and a scholarship can build a sense of personal achievement, but tomorrow they'll be hungry again and unsure of whether or not they can stay in school. Having a two-way relationship allows for emotional attunement—that irreplaceable, empathic resonance between two people (Hartling, 2008). You can explore this by asking them who they have a heartfelt connection with, who they strive to make proud, and who they feel they can be real with. Authentic connection can also be fostered in the therapeutic relationship by providing a judgment-free atmosphere, and by lowering the guise of professionalism enough to demonstrate emotional sincerity. Teenagers in particular need to know you care about their interests, so be real with them on every level. See the movie they recommend and explore why it's meaningful, then give them a copy of your own favorite movie, knowing you'll never get it back. Listen to their favorite song in session and go online and laugh at funny videos together. Be frank, informative, and above all relational in conversations about sex and drugs, as any therapist who turns into a healthy public service announcement will be quickly ignored. As always, it's wise to review and adhere to any ethical codes associated with your profession, organization, or licensure. While being relational does not require personal disclosure on the clinician's part, there are moments in the therapeutic relationship when your personal experience may help to convey an idea or role model a situation. There are, of course, many boundaries to consider, including how your disclosure could adversely impact the client, the therapeutic relationship, or your professional reputation. The line between what is or is not appropriate to share in session is always contextual. If you do elect to role model vulnerability or personal authenticity, illicit details are generally gratuitous and unnecessary. Likewise, subjects that you're still processing in your personal life may be too raw and emotionally charged to bring into the session. A safe way to demonstrate authenticity in session is to only share retrospective anecdotes with a clear beginning, middle, and end. Just as ACT works with metaphors, ACT therapists can draw on their anecdotal experiences to serve as a comparative story, provided it fits the theme or content of the session. There is, perhaps, a subtle difference between relating—which can turn into commiserating or even stealing the client's thunder—and encapsulating an idea, emotion, or life lesson.

### *Mastery to competency through connection*

Hyperfocused on grades, careers, and what they want to be when they grow up, young people may feel they have to "master" something to be successful. Be perfect. Be the best. Be better. Conquer. Conquest. Win. A+. These ideas undermine a lot of kids, as it's never enough. Even the word *master* implies subjugation of another (Hartling, 2008; Jordan, 1991). Competency, by comparison, is socially collaborative, evolving through connection and mentorship with peers, role models, teachers, family members, and even therapists (Hartling, 2008; Jordan, 1991). This can be cultivated in session by exploring their likes, interests, favorite subjects in school, and games they not only like to play but like to teach others to play. You can also explore their role models, heroes, teachers, and friends they want to emulate, along with anyone who believes in their success and helps them figure life out.

As part of the mindfulness process, this interview aids in expanding perspective. Overgeneralizing, or catastrophizing their situations, teenagers often feel overwhelmed when they believe they have to exist within a strict set of parameters with little to no room for social, occupational, or academic shortcomings. Yet the more memories, examples, and individuals a teenager can connect with as examples of self-worth, mutual empowerment, and growing competency, the easier it is for them to defuse from intrusive thoughts and cognitions.

When a teen is able to define gender and is allowed to proactively access the trans-affirmative social, health, and academic resources they need, their level of stress drops and their personal pride and resilience increases (Corliss *et al.*, 2007; McCann *et al.*, 2017; Olson *et al.*, 2016; Singh *et al.*, 2011). As a form of mental flexibility, resilience transforms any insult or injury into a passing moment, and not a factual reality. The wind blowing through a forest. But a forest is made more stable with intertwined roots, so the more positive reinforcers a kid has, the more memories they can call on, and the more evidence they have of being accepted, understood, validated, and supported, making it easier to accept, understand, validate, and support themselves.

As ACT deals with value constructs, note that resilience isn't a static virtue, but an active process describing healthy adaptation to challenging situations (Benard and Slade, 2009; Luthar and Cichetti, 2000; Masten, 1994, 2001). Wherever possible, help reduce the number of obstacles in their life, knowing that emotions cannot be removed and need not be an obstacle. Emotional resilience, therefore, is an increase in mental flexibility in response to emotionally triggering and hurtful encounters (Luthar and Cichetti, 2000). This is where connection really comes into play, as resilience increases as teenagers actively build on community strengths, and connect with people who invest in their health and wellbeing (Hartling, 2008; Luthar and Cichetti, 2000; Pflum *et al.*, 2015). The more interactions and engagements they have across a diverse range of social scenarios, the more they can challenge the all-or-nothing, black and white thinking so commonly indicative of internalized cissexism.

## Accepting adults: Defusing cissexism and inadequacy

*What color is your bedroom wall? Purple! What kind of purple? A lovely shade of indigo. Can you picture your purple bedroom? This room, this is your color, this is your sanctuary. Is there a window in your room? Can you imagine the sun setting outside? Picture a sky of pink and orange shining through. Notice the tone of your purple wall as it starts to change—becoming warmer and brighter than it was before. Then the sun sets and the moon rises, and the room goes dim and dark until you see a faint white glow of the moon outside. Imagine your purple room looking paler and cooler in the moonlight, until that too starts to fade. Imagine fireworks exploding joyously in the night, and as you lie in bed, you see the light of each firework sparking red and green and blue across your purple wall. Watch the colors in the dark dancing with each far-off rocket, but now there's a lot of noise outside. Whatever party was going on is turning riotous out there, while you're safe in bed. There's shouting out there, and someone set a car on fire. The room fills with an orange light, as the belching flames outside cast shadows over your bedroom wall. You hear a siren. The fire department comes around, and the police, too. For a moment your whole room lights up with flashing red and blue. The fire's put out. The sirens are quiet, and the light goes away until there's nothing but pitch-black darkness.*

*So, here's the question. What color are your walls? Are they sunset-red? Moonlit-white? The color of firework flashes? Car-fire orange? Fire-truck red? Police-car blue? Or pitch-black nothingness? It's tempting to say they're a little of everything, as all those colors were projected onto your bedroom wall, but when the sun rises again we can see clearly what color your room really is.*

Defusing from internalized cissexism is like remembering the color of our bedroom even when the world outside projects so much through our window. Celebratory fireworks, like when we're praised for a gender role we don't adhere to, can be as much of an illusion as the chaotic car fires of our trauma. Sometimes glorious sunsets may even complement our indigo wall, like when we're accepted for our gender, but still internalize expectations for what that should look like. And when darkness fills the room, and we have no gender role or social script to see by, we may forget that we're surrounded by our own indigo.

Internalized transphobia and cissexism may present as a highly anxious, depressed state with very little self-tolerance or self-empathy. In session, we may call ourselves failures, freaks, faggots, and fuck-ups, echoing every expletive someone yelled at us from afar and every implicit insult we ever yelled at ourselves. Returning to RFT, those hierarchical pink and blue boxes of our childhood contain both real and perceived consequences for failure. To challenge the power of these expected punishments, we may first have to unlearn our prior understanding of gender, privilege, and oppression, before being able to feel whole in ourselves. In this way, self-acceptance and self-actualization often require the unbecoming act of unbecoming—a play on words alluding to the awkward dismantling of all we're "supposed to be" (Halberstam, 2011).

Help the self-deprecating step back from any and all internalized sexist, cissexist, heteronormative, or homonormative ideologies we're fused with. These may include rules we adhere to without realizing it. Even outspoken feminists and proud queer activists can inadvertently slip into patriarchal paradigms shaping how we perceive and value body types, gender phenotypes, and even proxemic and kinesic communication. Everything—from beauty standards, to how much food we're allowed to eat, to how much leg room we take up—becomes subject to this bias and bogus assessment. And we may not even realize it! Or if we do, we may judge ourselves, feeling like we failed a test we didn't even want to take.

Cissexism is prevalent in every social and institutional sphere, from blatant employment, housing, and bathroom discrimination, to sidelong glances, ignorant language, or general neglect of trans health and human rights issues. Be conscious that 63 percent of transgender people surveyed experience volatile discrimination detrimental to their quality of life (Grant *et al.*, 2011). Internalizing this, we not only insult ourselves, but begin to believe that our subclass status is somehow deserved—that disdain and abuse are just a part of our queer life we have to tolerate! It may begin to feel so prevalent and unrelievable that we begin to hate ourselves, and drift toward suicidal ideation, self-harm, and fantasies of self-destruction. We may feel resigned to our fate, stating, "It's just the way things are" or "I would love to live in a queer utopia, but that's just not gonna happen." Fatigued, our ability to fight is all but spent. Fortunately for us, creative hopelessness can turn our sense of failure on its head.

Embracing failure doesn't suggest accepting failure without growth or change but acknowledging that reflexive failure is one of our primary learning mechanisms for both adaptation and individuation (McIntosh and Hobson, 2013). In LGBTQ studies, the term *queer failure* presents a unique opportunity to artfully reclaim our failures as daily, unintentional acts of defiance (Halberstam, 2011; LeMaster, 2018; Muñoz, 2009; Nestle *et al.*, 2002). In this way, queer failure can take on two meanings, the first being that we have failed to live up to society's mundane social performances or, the second, as we're coming to find, that society has failed to affirm us (LeMaster, 2018).

As normative behavior is saturated with moral judgment, it's easy to believe gender norms are compulsory, as those who explicitly defy them or inadvertently fail them often lose social standing, respect, and even safety (LeMaster, 2018; Miller and Grollman, 2015). Yet this speaks more of the culture's intolerance than it does of us as deviations from the rule. Queer failure, as a therapeutic practice, is the mindful recognition and rejection of sexist and cissexist expectations that would otherwise undermine who we are. Having failed the social gender norms, we initially blame ourselves, believing there's something wrong with us; but when we embrace how hopeless it is to live up to something we're not, we get to be creative with who we really are. Also, the more we witness society's intolerance, the more we begin to realize that the issue does not intrinsically lie with the self but with the other. In that moment of realization, queer failure ceases to be a failure of the queer but a failure of society in response to the queer (Miller and Grollman, 2015; Muñoz, 2009).

Utilizing social mindfulness, let's focus on society like curious anthropologists studying a foreign culture. To begin, let's identify three situations or cissexist encounters we've experienced in the last week/month. Once we have them in mind, rank the experience from 1 (implicit microaggressions) to 10 (explicit macroaggressions). Clients who have experienced extreme hostility may potentially hyperfocus or avoid talking about such trauma. For our purposes here, it may be more constructive to redirect awareness to transgressions at the lower end of the scale if we're not yet ready to unpack deep scars. Know that we all rank our encounters differently. Those who regularly experience prejudice may rank verbal or sexual assault quite low, either minimizing their experiences or compairing them to more severe traumas in their life. Others may rank microaggressions quite high, especially if gender dysphoria or closeted living has made them hypersensitive to other people's criticism and social cues.

Expanding awareness from self to other allows us to observe the unhealthy relationship as it is. We may realize how we fuse with self-blame as a way of disempowering our transgressors by maintaining the illusion of control. Statements like "If I was only ____, then this wouldn't have happened" or "If only I had done____, they wouldn't have yelled at me" take the burden of responsibility in part to avoid our emotional process by hiding in a goal-focused train of thought, and in part to piece together some locus of control. Empowerment is important, but this retrospective critique of ourselves isn't empowering—it's desperate. Our control agenda wants to believe we can somehow change the outcome. We hold onto the false premise that maybe if we stood a certain way, or looked more passable, or had a friend with us, the transgression wouldn't have happened. Even therapists can fuse to frames of causation, turning the session into a preparatory conversation about "what we could do differently, next time." The positive intent is clear, but this protective focus heaps the responsibility of managing prejudice onto us, as if somehow we failed the situation, and that things will work out if we perform better next time. To safeguard against unintentional victim blaming, monitor your own judgment-based language, as exploring how to be *more* cautious or *less* impulsive implies performance assessment.

Few communities truly embrace gender variance, and even those that do may be unaware of their transgressions due to cisgender privilege. Yes, we can focus on advocacy, but first we must challenge the assumption that there is something wrong with us, or that we have failed society in some way. This can be difficult if the people we care about are being passive-aggressive or directly hostile toward us.

As we practice defusing these "if only" statements, enough mental space is generated to permit all the emotions we had kept at bay. We may break into tears, feeling neglected, abandoned, or unseen by those we once called kin, or we may feel angry, spiteful, hateful, or even furious at others for how they treated us. Fear, guilt, and shame are often deep-seated emotions, as so much of our process pivots around themes of rejection and acceptance (Zandvliet, 2000). Validate and spend time with these feelings, especially if we have never permitted ourselves to let go of our emotional control efforts. Validate the pain of disappointment, abuse, and societal abandonment at whatever level or intensity it's felt, as these emotions will point to what we both need and value most.

Hold out both hands and close all but one digit. This is the humbling reminder that for every lesson we learn in life we missed out on nine others. At first this can feel a little disappointing, but we're not omniscient, we can't know all, and realistically we probably missed out on a lot more than nine! But this one pointing finger is articulate, active, and our own. Sure, spending all our time learning *this* meant missing out on learning *that*, but let's not discount what *this* is. What do we know? What did we learn as a gender variant person that cisgender people cannot grasp? What did we learn from all those years in the closet? What can we teach that no one else can? Even if our teachers were ruthless, dolling out lessons in pain and oppression, from this we learned our fortitude, resilience, and even our sensitivity and the importance of compassion. Name what worthwhile and hard-won lessons we learned from gender, and then count up to ten. Name what we learned from our unique family. Name what we learned from our unique culture, from our neighborhood, from our nationality, from our religion, from our race, and our ability. Finding worth in both who we are and what we've been through, we can return to queer failure, observing our uniqueness as fundamentally powerful in and of itself.

When you, as a clinician, align with the client by highlighting our pain and insight, you help ground the session in a very real way, as you're not denying we missed out, or that we want to catch up. You're not denying how hard it was to be left out, or to be different. Futhermore, by helping dismantle unnecessary expectations and social standards, you're recognizing how no singular human being can live up to them all.

Internalized cissexism sticks with us when we feel a delay in our development. Even when we accept, appreciate, and celebrate our gender identity and sexual orientation, we can still feel like we're late to the pride parade. Having accepted ourselves as a gender variant person, we've begun to disidentify with our prior sex or gender identity, even if we present no external or visual difference (Devor, 2004). Not all undergo physical transition, yet as we accept our gender schema we begin to align with those we resonate with, leading once again to comparison (Devor, 2004). If we compare ourselves to cisgender men and women we may want to accomplish gender normative milestones or feel inadequate if we don't. If we're in transition we may use this feeling of delay as a motivational drive pushing us toward certain life goals. Comparably, if we just came out we may look to transparent members of the LGBTQ community with as much admiration and aspiration as we have jealousy and personal regret. And if we don't compare ourselves to others, then we may compare ourselves to where we believe we "should be," as if wistfully imagining some other universe where things worked out differently.

Having spent years trying to navigate or conceal gender, we may feel like we missed out on the kinds of social, affectional, and personal lessons cisgender heterosexuals experience through puberty, adolescence, and young adulthood. Or we may feel like we had to unlearn all our prior conceptualizations of self and start over—which takes time otherwise spent on careers or social connections. While internalized cissexism can pollute our thoughts with role expectations we won't or don't measure up to, the guilt, regret, inadequacy, and shame of identity delay persists because it stems from an unmet need we may actually desire. Feeling stunted or underdeveloped, our *should* statements reflect our longing to be fully actualized.

> "I should be good at this by now."
> "I should know better."
> "I shouldn't have been surprised."
> "I shouldn't have expected so much."

Seeing the milestones ahead of us, we become impatient with ourselves. This feeling of identity delay comes and goes for liminal gender constructs. For genderqueer, agender, and other nonbinary identities, it resurfaces with all our doubts and inadequacies as we compare ourselves to cisnormative or even transnormative gender identity development. Yet excitement and uncertainty go hand in hand, especially for those who come out later in life or postpone transition. Seemingly simple actions may feel wholly new, rebooted, and perhaps even virginal, which can be delightful at times and anxiety provoking at others.

> "I had my first kiss when I was 12, but I've never been kissed as a woman. Look at me, I'm blushing! I have a date tomorrow! A real date, but I'm nervous. Will he kiss me like a man or a woman? Is there a difference? How will I know if there is?"

> "So, I'm 34. Been working at the firm for three years. I've walked into that conference room a hundred times. But yesterday I got a knot in my gut because I introduced myself to a new client with gender neutral pronouns…in front of my boss. What if HR writes it down in a file somewhere? What are they going to do? Fire me? Can they fire me?"

We may explore this phase nervously, having to rediscover intimacy, sexuality, and self-empowerment. Or we may explode like a bull at the gate, from taking the opportunity to "catch up" on our postponed life, to varying levels of risk and experimentation. We may indulge in new wardrobes, diets, social scenes, sexual experimentation, and—in particular for young people—more celebratory and risk-taking behavior. Process this exciting and anxiety-provoking time, as our perspective of our experience will fortify either our resilience and ability to feel fulfilled, or our doubt and dissatisfaction, depending on our fusion to judgment. Just checking off goals on a bucket list can feel hollow and unsatisfying if we're still fused to old comparisons and expectations. For clients who feel delayed, we're shifting from "making up for lost time," which implies a constant comparison to others, to the present-based act of "moving forward."

Innocence is a seed before growth, which is why innocence can be observed in others now, but is reserved for ourselves in retrospect—"I was so young then. So bright eyed and gullible." Very few, burdened with guilt and shame, still believe we're innocent. Some may even devalue innocence, equating it with ignorance, obliviousness, or helplessness, none of which are synonyms. Innocence, in this context, is to explore the new, unknown, and uncertain without judging ourselves. To this end, we need to reclaim *queer innocence*, just as we reclaimed queer failure.

For LGBTQ individuals, queer innocence is the therapeutic act of mindfully exploring awe, wonder, nervousness, bashfulness, hopefulness, giddiness, and even awkward naiveté. These emotions are not deficiencies, but part of a developmental experience that may have been missed along the way, either because we were preoccupied with our dissonance, were coping with trauma, or because our inner girl never got a chance to play with dolls, or our inner boy never got to be rowdy with the other boys, or our inner androgyne was never asked on a date. When we challenge the assumption that inexperience is bad, those awkward feelings we've tried to control and those uncomfortable situations we've tried to avoid can actually become a launching point. Yet unlike cisnormative and heteronormative individuals who stumble through these learning curves as literal children, we may be all grown up—and yet still find ourselves growing! For some of us, life follows a linear trajectory; for others it can feel like it's out of order, as if we're aging backwards—having started so seriously we feel like we're getting sillier and more innocent with time. We may even feel like parts of our identity are progressing at different paces, like we're an adult in every way except our newly expressed gender.

If a child fell down trying to walk, would you berate them for not being "good enough?" Of course not, because we grant children patience to make mistakes and learn from them. Extending this same patience to ourselves is humbling, as we progressively accept what we don't know, and stop compensating for what we don't have. At whatever age we are when we begin to actualize, we are quite literally learning how to walk and talk again. How do we stride into a room with our head held high? How do we run in high-heels? How do we enunciate with a higher pitch? How do we make vocal fry sound natural? How do we laugh with a deeper cadence? How do we swagger like a man? Becoming conscious of our growth, we begin to accept how we are all innocently engaging in this bashful act of becoming, and all the awkward, delightful, embarrassing, and empowering experimentation that goes with it.

# 5

# Actualization

In trans-positive literature, the process of developing gender identity is often referred to as gender identity *acquisition*. Gender affirmative ACT makes a subtle distinction here, referring to this process as gender identity *actualization*. It may seem inconsequential, but small shifts in language can alter the whole story. The journey of acquisition, by its very definition, is a journey to acquire something we do not have. This concept reinforces a narrative of emptiness by focusing on an absence/obtain dichotomy. After all, what happens if we don't acquire it, whatever *it* is? Then do we have no gender identity? Or do we have the wrong gender identity?

Fascinated and puzzled, the West has scrutinized transsexual women, trying to make sense of whether they're *failed men* or *women all along* (Halberstam, 2005). Unable to allow the gender-ambiguous to be exactly that, *ambiguous*, psychiatrists, physicians, biographers, documentary filmmakers, journalists, and college students scribbling away at their bold new thesis, have all tried to shoehorn nonbinary identities into cisnormative research (Halberstam, 2005; Siebler, 2012). So far, scholars have been at it for a century and it doesn't look like they're stopping any time soon.

Listening to both personal and cultural testimony, the gender affirmative approach validates the distinct and unique ways individuals reconcile gender and body (Halberstam, 1998; Nagoshi and Brzuzy, 2010; Nestle *et al.*, 2002; Sennott, 2011). There are far too many intersecting variables of sex and culture to account for a single *right* experience or correct definition of gender identity (Nestle *et al.*, 2002). For example, some resonate with the phrase "a woman trapped in a man's body," yet this narrative does not apply to all transgender, transsexual, or nonbinary women (Sennott, 2011). It's a tidy little quote that ties up the loose ends of gender transition with a nice bow without ever questioning the binary (Sennott, 2011). Actualization, therefore, is the act of taking that which is most abstract within us and giving it tangible form. This is a central theme in

ACT as we begin to take steps toward value-congruent action. To actualize, by its definition, implies we already have something to act upon. If you tell us to go find ourselves then we will spend years looking and questioning. If you tell us to be what we already are, then the whole process of self-discovery becomes a form of self-admission and self-embodiment.

Our gender persists as much as our values, and when we are untrue to them we feel a weight on our chest or a twist in our gut. We typically know when we betray our core, yet we often fuse so tightly to excuses and judgments that we prevent ourselves from creating, generating, or manifesting what's most important to us. We may value our family, but if we never hug them, this notion fades into an idea. We may value honesty, but when we hide in shame, truth and illusion muddy together. When the literal shape and form of our body comes into question, we may lose sight of what is real.

When we're in sync with our intrinsic values, we accept who we are, embody what we stand for, and garner self-worth—of which happiness is a byproduct. As an *ongoing* process, we may align with certain values and simultaneously neglect or remain oblivious to others. Having focused on self-esteem, love, safety, and acceptance for so long, what other untapped areas are there? Passion, nurturance, skill, intellect, strength, experience, adventure, service, trust—what needs our attention currently?

For gender variant people, self-actualization is multidimensional. It is not a singular leap, but a progressive series of value-congruent actions bringing us ever closer to both personal self-acceptance and life satisfaction. Challenging avoidance by approaching the source of discomfort is typical of many cognitive behavioral approaches, yet in ACT we are the epicenter, and it's so hard to approach ourselves and our desires with naked honesty. Self-actualization is rarely a linear process, and we may fluctuate in our identity, gender, and willingness to express either. For this reason, self-actualization needs to be self-defined and self-determined. Much of the literature focuses on transition, and while self-actualization may include HRT and gender alignment surgery, transition is neither a prerequisite nor a synonym for this process. Self-actualization is a deliberate investment in our holistic growth, emotional homeostasis, personal resilience, and self-worth through value-congruent action, which may include HRT, gender alignment surgery, personal disclosure, family therapy, social activism, or not.

## Identifying values and defusing gender roles

Like gender and emotion, we know our values by a somatic sense of resonance. Even when we lose the game, we feel a warmth of pride for having tried so hard. Even though we're frightened of the stranger, we help them, as something in us feels like it's the right thing to do. Values can also carry a somatic sense of dissonance, as our gut knots when we betray them. When we cheat, we might walk away feeling "off," and when we avoid tests of our mettle we feel "rattled" or "on edge," our hands opening and closing as our legs pace back and forth. Yet identifying values may not be a simple task, as the lines blur between the personal values intrinsic to our character, the morals taught by our social group, and the ideals we strive to embody. As they all engage our emotional response system, they are all felt in the body, so how do we tell them apart, and why is it necessary to do so?

As children we're often asked, "What's the moral of the story?" Which is to say, "What's the lesson?" A moral, in this context, is a societal norm taught within our family, culture, theology, or nation. Morals can be internalized and integrated into our personal value construct, but it's useful to recognize their external sources, as going against our personal values can make us feel bad but going against our morals can have larger social implications. When a moral becomes inflexible, it solidifies into a rule. These rigid moral rules can become dissonant with our personal values, which are often influenced and accrued through our personal life experience.

Some common examples of dissonance that gender minorities may wrestle with are listed in Table 5.1.

**Table 5.1 Conflicting morals and personal values**

| Moral rule | | Personal value |
|---|---|---|
| Don't shame your family | May conflict with | Honesty |
| Be independent | | Community |
| Never show weakness | | Self-compassion |
| Don't make a scene | | Free expression |
| Be polite | | Holding boundaries |
| Fit in | | Diversity |

Because values, morals, and ideals all intersect, just asking us to state our core values can be problematic as many will respond with what we feel is socially appropriate (moral) or what we aspire to be (ideal). When all three align, we feel like we fit in our society, exemplifying the perspective, philosophy, and goals of our culture. Should all three fall out of sync, then we feel conflict within ourselves as that which we resonate with argues with the social messages we've internalized. Pressured by conditional statements, transactional relationships, and negative self-assessments we may try to swallow our values and conform to the moral rule, or rebel against it, forcing us to face any and all social repercussions. To explore this, take a list of virtues and categorize them into three circles: *What I am* (values), *what society wants me to be* (morals), *and what I aspire to be* (ideals) (see Figure 5.1).

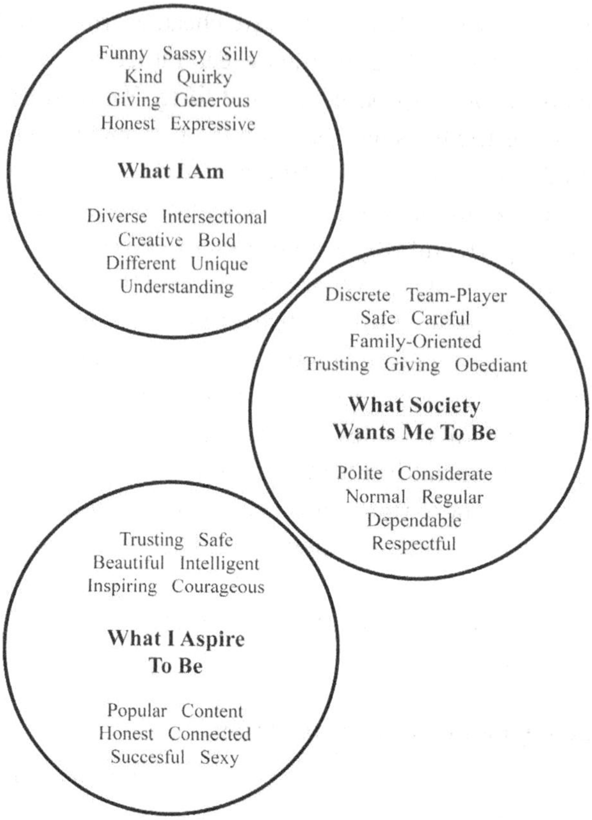


**Figure 5.1** *Circle diagram*

Not only does this pinpoint areas of tension or alignment, it also notices how much emphasis we put on our moral rules or personal values. Ideals are useful in that they give us something to work toward, yet they are problematic by virtue of being an idyllic potential, largely unattainable. The philosopher, Alan Watts (2015) once noted in his Zen dismissal of the higher-self and lower-self paradigm that chasing our potential is like chasing a thief up a staircase— they're always one floor above us! As we rise, so too does our potential, and so this higher self remains forever above us, having stolen our sense of wholeness and self-satisfaction. Idealism is such that when we finally get to the roof, our potential self may even grow angelic wings and fly away to some perfectionist heaven.

When our ideals resemble our morals but not our values, we bombard ourselves with guilt for being something we're not. As an exercise, try caring about something you find totally boring and profess how much you adore it. Or try hating something you absolutely love. Really try. Every effort will feel fake, because it is. Exercises in futility demonstrate how, when we give up on trying to be something we're not, and process our creative hopelessness, we begin to acknowledge what we actually are.

Cultural morals are frequently encoded into gender, creating *gender rules*. Boys and girls are supposed to dress, behave, and interact with each other and the world around them according to this code. When these gender rules are assimilated into a person's identity construct, they become gender roles, which are quite distinct from our gender identity. Transactionally, gender roles earn social worth through gender stereotypic virtue signaling. Though gender rules differ from culture to culture, and even generation to generation, Western society has globalized its gender rules, broadcasting masculinity as strength, competitiveness, assertiveness, independence, and protectiveness, with a rational yet paradoxically libidinous mind focused on action. These traits are embodied in athletic, economic, and leadership roles. Comparatively, Western gender rules idealize women as gentle, collaborative, interdependent, compassionate, and nurturing, with an intuitive yet emotionally oriented mind focused on image. These stereotypic feminine traits ascribe women to supportive, socially oriented, caregiver gender roles. Infiltrating so many facets of life, from the playground, to the classroom, to the workplace, to the bar scene—gender rules and gender roles show up in every social arena right up to the Oval Office.

Yet should we not align with these muscular heroes or sexy empaths because we do not fit or because we reject these social mores, then we find ourselves at odds with the mainstream script. If our core values do not align with these gender rules, life may take on all manner of complications and frustrations. Some classic examples are listed in Table 5.2. Some of us may easily reject gender rules in celebratory feminist rebellion. Others may do so only to find levels of internalized cissexism so deep we only realize them on reaching particular milestones of adulthood—like when we become the parents, role models, leaders, and social teachers passing on a torch we never realized was soaked in the same old oil.

**Table 5.2 Conflicting gender rules and personal values**

| Gender rules | | Personal value |
|---|---|---|
| Boys don't cry | May conflict with | Emotional honesty |
| Boys are rough | | Kindness |
| Girls should be nice | | Assertiveness |
| Girls don't give out | | Sexuality |
| Men should be strong | | Intimacy |
| Men should be stoic | | Passion |
| Women should be quiet | | Empowerment |
| Women should be interdependent | | Independence |

As cultures interact and integrate, cross-cultural gender rules can conflict. Collectivistic clients may even feel torn between their personal values, their culture's gender rules, and the individualistic gender rules that dominate the West. Even within a single culture, traditional gender rules may conflict with contemporary ones. Women are told to be docile and chaste, yet assertive and sexually empowered. Men are told to be stoic and aggressive, yet intellectual and socially conscious. In any case, collectivistic or individualistic, local or colonized, traditional or contemporary, we're getting restricted by someone else's rule of what a man or woman should be, and that's just the start.

When a society lacks nonbinary gender roles, many gender variant people get forcefully plugged into social power positions we don't fit, causing us to be misgendered or stereotyped. Defying this, Western queer culture actively defuses from *cisnormative* values, yet in so doing may also fuse with their new, *queer-normative* value constructs. Consider a butch lesbian, tough enough to handle high visibility, who may feel like she has to be their friend's aggressive defender. Dismantling the assumption that strength, fortitude, endurance, perseverance, ingenuity, and dominance are solely constructs of cisnormative patriarchy, butch individuals may embody all these characteristics and just as easily feel stuck in them.

The trouble is, prizing power, social status, belonging, and even romance, we can even come to like and aspire to these gender rules, even if we don't fit them. Our language of deficiency may even claim that we're somehow spineless, gutless, heartless, brainless, or creatively soulless, as if we actually lost a physical prerequisite for our values. Making the attempt, we may feel like an outright imposter, discounting our effort. Using courage as an example, we often idealize bravery as the absence of fear, thereby discounting potentially brave acts because we also felt nervous. To add impermanence into the mix, some ideals are only momentarily attainable, and may come with an added price. Beauty standards are a clear example of this, as we can idealize sex appeal and spend a great deal of time, energy, effort, money, and emotional labor to "look good." And even if we discount our natural beauty to fit a cultural standard, we can only do so during that idyllic window of youth.

If the ideals in our circle exercise resemble our values, then we may be more accepting of ourselves, yet remain fused to an outcome or unit of measurement, acknowledging we're good but not quite "good enough." Our natural drive to *better* ourselves can impede our ability to *accept* ourselves, should we avoid today in favor of some better tomorrow. Defusing from our judgmental standards of assessment helps us recognize and affirm our personal value construct, accepting that we are already that which we aspire to be. Values are not tangible items we gain or lose, nor do they magically manifest where they did not previously exist. We can prioritize and re-prioritize values, moving them around over the course of our lives, but we don't suddenly gain courage, thoughtfulness, or determination where there was none before. Perhaps we avoided these qualities, suppressed them, or were never given the chance to let them shine, but they were always there. For more on this, watch *The Wizard of Oz*.

Differentiating between our ideals and our values is tricky business as they use the same virtuous language. Temporally, values exist in the here and now, as they're neither obtained in concrete ways nor constrained by time (Hoare *et al.*, 2012). Even when we don't align with our values, our emotional reactions, in particular guilt and regret, are evidence of their presence. When we conceptualize values as a goal or outcome, we place them at a distance, or treat them as an impermanent behavior. This comes through loud and clear when we say, "I want to be honest" or "I'm trying to be kind." Though our intention is to put in our best effort, our desire "to be" inadvertently implies "we are not." Snatching that loose thread, our cynical mind can unravel our desire to be "good" by reminding us that we're "bad." Yet when values are treated as an experience, as a form of resonance felt in our body via our emotional response system, we begin to recognize what matters to us in the present moment. In this way, our values become a direction, allowing us to generate goals, shift behavior, and define the obstacles ahead of us (Hoare *et al.*, 2012; Hayes *et al.*, 2012). When beauty is a value, we resonate with life's beauty, actively appreciating ourselves both with and without makeup. We see beauty in what is. If a virtue is workable, which is to say it contributes to our benefit and can be actualized in the present, then it's in the scope of our values.

Ideals, by contrast, exist in the future. They are not something we are but a potential that can only be attained in strict parameters by following strict rules. They're often future-based goals, upcoming outcomes, or unattainable dreams of perfection. Success, as an example, can be a present-based value embodied in our work ethic, or it can be an idealistic ladder, always climbing from promotion to promotion. When beauty is an ideal, it fuses to judgment in order to assess how well we style our hair or fit our clothes, and it's lost the moment we become disheveled, or out of shape, or too old for youth culture. This is a particular issue for those in transition still discerning—not whether they are a man or woman—but what it socially, experientially, and existentially means to be a man or woman. ACT approaches this by exploring the qualities and characteristics we have in the present, as self-actualization is an affirmative process based in the here and now.

If we idealize honesty, then we *try to be* honest, the effort of which ironically implies that we're not honest because we have to try. If we idealize gender and all the rules associated with it, when we *try to be* a man or woman, our effort ironically contributes to our sense of dysphoria and fraudulence. By resituating focus to the present, we can affirm that we are, already, our gender, and that the effort to appease someone else's standard, or even our own, is optional.

Gender variant individuals who have already figured this out sometimes dismiss, or take umbrage with transformational, metamorphic, or transitional gender narratives. We may attest, instead, that gender is constant and possibly neurological. While this perspective certainly testifies to a great deal of self-knowledge, gender schemas and gender expression can continue to change with personal growth, even if a labeled gender identity remains constant. Others, however, may not have this constancy, being uncertain of our gender, or even our definitions of it.

If we express feeling stuck in a gender role, try identifying people who challenge or redefine gender roles in our life, including celebrities and fictional characters. Gender identity is as personal as our value construct, which is why we have such diversity. Some men are sensitive empaths, or curious explorers, or decisive engineers. Some women are creative artists, or courageous athletes, or nurturing mothers. Some are all of the above. Yet when we don't obey gender rules, what happens to our gender roles? What, then, does it mean to be a father, brother, son, husband, or boyfriend? What does it mean to be a mother, sister, daughter, wife, or girlfriend? Do we like the gender roles as they exist in our community or do we want to change them? What associations do we connect with them? Are we offended if we're asked to be the bridesmaid and not the best man? What rules, reasons, and judgments do we use to shape these archetypes? And how do we feel when we break from them, or don't fit them, or find ourselves lacking role models for a gender outside this dichotomy? How do we react to the dominant bread-winning feminine or the nurturing child-raising masculine?

A unique complication can occur if we focus solely on actualizing our values without first defusing from scripted morals and perfectionist ideals that are no longer functional. If we can't defuse from these unworkable roles, we begin to limit what we believe possible for ourselves. We state, "I'm not the kind of person to ____" or "I could never do that." These self-stereotyping cognitions can become so rigid that they impede our self-actualizing and value-congruent behavior. The honest may lie because they're not the sort of person to rock the boat. The hardworking may limit progress because they're an independent person who never asks for help. Soon, we're protesting what we can or can't do, even in situations where we're quite capable. Words like "I can't," or "I'd never," or "I only," or "I can't imagine" enter our vocabulary as we perpetuate lives we don't enjoy or patterns we know are unhealthy. Should our feminine script favor compliance, accommodation, and empathy, we may find ourselves agreeing to things we don't want to do. Should our masculine script demand tough stoicism, we may push people away, when all along we just needed a hug.

*Zooming out*, we can practice observing: "This is me, having the thought that fathers have to be stern," or "This is me, having the thought that a stone butch can't cry," or "This is me, having the thought that girls have to be polite," or, for emphasis, "This is me, having the *fucking* thought that girls have to be *fucking* polite." As we continue our defusion process, we may progressively move away from morals and ideals that no longer serve us, disempowering the associated judgments of who we're "supposed to be" in favor of our personal values and our self-determined gender roles.

## Value exercise: **I should, if only...**

When values, morals, and ideals differ, it's like me, myself, and I can't agree. Part of us knows what's important to us, yet social expectation demands what we *should* do, while our wishful thinking laments "If only I could" (Harris, 2008). *Should* statements are often carried on tones of guilt or obligation, and persist by tying behavior to our desire for success and positive appraisal.

"I should get my work done."
"I should really call my mom."
"I should tell my friends I'm transgender."
"I should speak up more."

While *should* statements can certainly contain our personal value, *I should* linguistically concedes that *I haven't*. Minimizing our process, we may state that we don't know why we haven't acted on our values, morals, or ideals, or why we shrug them off for "no good reason." Yet exploring our patterns of behavior often reveals how our desire to be safe, to "save face," and to stay calm engages emotional control tactics.

"If only" is a powerful phrase reflecting longing and aspiration, uttered by many in transition, many building courage, and many excluded by society. Reflecting awe, "If only" hints at how pressing the underlying emotion is.

"If only I were braver."
"If only I were prettier."
"If only I were bolder."
"If only I was sassier."

Inside each *I should* and every *If only* statement is an important value needing to be actualized. Open the box. Look inside. "I should ____" begs the question, "What will happen if I don't?" The concern therein hides the value. A statement like "I'm afraid people won't like me" reveals the need for connection, friendship, belonging, family, love, and loyalty. A statement like "If I don't dress like a guy, people might beat me up" prioritizes safety, security, and courage. Borrowing and adapting the miracle question from solution-focused brief therapy (Shazer *et al.*, 2012), try asking: *If there was no problem, and everything was how you wanted it to be, how would life be different? How would life change for you, and what values would be present?* Our "if only" fantasies tend to ride on assessment-based thinking. We want to be smarter, better, prettier, more popular, more courageous, less anxious, and so on. Our frames of comparison and distinction have become so fused that we may feel that we're lacking some vital quality. We may even rule that we're simply "not enough." This cognitive pattern is fundamentally transactional, and for whatever reason we feel there's a deficit. Sometimes, our "if only" fantasies address our hope for something bigger than ourselves. Externalizing locus of control and responsibility, we may feel the world would accept us "if only people were more open-minded" (Stitt, 2014).

Because of this deficit-based mindset, we tend to think about our problems in a transactional way. When framed as a conditional statement ("if this, then that") we focus on doing, giving, and trying *more* as a means of obtaining what we want. This treats abstract concepts based on perspective and judgment (beauty, courage, love, intelligence) as if they're tangible resources to be gained and lost, or as action-based behaviors upheld by effort and motivation, or undermined by the lack thereof. The statement "I'd exercise if only I had more energy" conceptualizes energy as an absent object, when every fitness trainer knows exercise can actually up-regulate the body, providing a felt sense of energy. The statement "I'd exercise if only I wasn't so lazy" uses labeling to justify the believed deficit. It's another way of saying "I'd have energy if I were an energetic person."

When asked to imagine how life would be if we positively assessed ourselves, we typically picture a positive outcome (see Table 5.3). Maybe we'd come out, or make lots of friends or build up the courage to ask someone out. Yet to get there we often believe we have to attain something we simultaneously believe we don't have. If we're not careful, even our values will be treated to this transactional, goal-oriented mindset. "I'd tell them the truth if only I were more honest" is just another way of saying "I'd be honest if I were honest." "I'd be able to cope if only I were more patient" is just another way of saying "I'd be calm if I were calmer." When values are treated as goals, they can become problematically cyclical. After all, if the end is the beginning, we can't start because the beginning is the end. So if values are not the same as goals, how can we change our thinking about them?

**Table 5.3 Wishing on present values**

| If only | How would life change? | Present values |
|---|---|---|
| If only I were braver | I'd come out | Honesty, transparency, authenticity |
| If only I were prettier | I'd be popular | Attention, validation, social esteem |
| If only I were bolder | I'd ask that guy out | Romance, connection, love |
| If only I were sassier | I'd stand up for myself | Boundaries, confidence, humor |

When we drive a car, how we drive (our values) doesn't change our destination (our goals) (Hayes *et al.*, 2012). We could drive recklessly, swerving all over the road, or cruise along a nice scenic route. Certainly, our met goals are great mile markers for a value-congruent life, but achievements alone don't alleviate regret, provide satisfaction, or heal pain; and when they do, our relaxation, joy, or relief lasts about as long as the interim between our achievement and the next goal down the road.

In session, recall how many times we got what we wanted only to have our moment of pride deflated by a new problem. Now compare this to any time we didn't get what we were after, but felt proud of ourselves for trying. Was there ever a time we didn't get what we wanted but were easily able to let it go? If we're able to identify the values in our wishful thinking, we can certainly generate therapeutic goals, yet the goal alone isn't our focal point. If, for example, we desire to be honest, our transparency doesn't have to be an all-or-nothing situation. Just sharing that we're going through something difficult in our lives without filling in all the details still exemplifies honesty, even if we're not completely forthcoming. If we value beauty, taking steps to join or create a body-positive culture can be a huge step. Even if we don't necessarily *feel* pretty, or believe we fit a stereotypical beauty form, we can still affirm, appreciate, and encourage ourselves and others. If we want to be bolder, sassier, and more outspoken in our lives, that doesn't mean we have to be an onstage comedian 24/7. By actively speaking our truth when it's pertinent to do so, high-fiving our quips when they're funny, and validating our courage when we share, we're actively embodying our values in the moment.

Setting value-congruent goals is a core part of ACT, yet we're shifting our awareness from effort to embodiment, from *trying* to be honest to *being aware* of our honesty, from trying to connect to *being aware* of our connection, and from trying to be pretty to *accepting* body appreciation. In so doing, our conditional statements begin to loosen their grip.

## Value exercise: **Colorful circles**

Struggling to identify our values is perfectly natural. Some of us are nonverbal learners, or may have an undeveloped value vocabulary, or may be new to thinking about this sort of thing. For all these reasons, and more, it's useful to have a value sheet and a handful of colored pencils in every therapist's office. In this exercise, we're going to explore values we feel society prioritizes, values we personally want, and values we know we actively practice.

Sifting through the colored pencils, the first step is to find a color we associate with society. Depending on the context of the session we may be exploring our circle of friends, our family of choice, our family of origin, or even the values of the social majority. Let's say we don't like our community very much, so we pick the worst color of brown we can find. With our society pencil, let's circle ten values we feel we're told to follow (see Table 5.4), These often include the morals and social expectations we believe we're supposed to live up to.

**Table 5.4 Value list**

| | | | |
|---|---|---|---|
| Acceptance | Devotion | Honesty | Responsibility |
| Achievement | Dignity | Humor | Resourcefulness |
| Adventurousness | Diligence | Independence | Romance |
| Assertiveness | Directness | Industriousness | Safety |
| Audacity | Diversity | Influence | Security |
| Authenticity | Dominance | Justice | Self-Love |
| Authority | Duty | Keenness | Self-Respect |
| Autonomy | Egalitarianism | Kindness | Sensuality |
| Awareness | Elegance | Knowledge | Service |
| Balance | Eloquence | Kookiness | Simplicity |
| Beauty | Empathy | Leadership | Spirituality |
| Belonging | Endurance | Learning | Stability |
| Benevolence | Equality | Love | Status |
| Boldness | Equanimity | Loyalty | Success |
| Candor | Ethics | Openness | Thoughtfulness |
| Compassion | Fabulousness | Optimism | Tidiness |
| Challenge | Fairness | Originality | Tolerance |
| Charm | Faith | Patriotism | Traditionalism |
| Citizenship | Fame | Peace | Trustworthiness |
| Commitment | Ferocity | Perseverance | Understanding |
| Community | Freedom | Pleasure | Uniqueness |
| Competency | Friendliness | Poise | Usefulness |
| Conscientiousness | Glamor | Popularity | Wealth |
| Contribution | Gratitude | Queerness | Wisdom |
| Courage | Growth | Reason | Wit |
| Creativity | Gregariousness | Recognition | Wonder |
| Curiosity | Harmony | Reputation | Work Ethic |
| Depth | | Respect | |
| Determination | | | |

In a similar fashion, let's select a second color—our favorite color! Take a moment to appreciate what we like about it or what it reminds us of. Then, with our favorite color in hand, let's circle three values we personally want to embody more of in our lives. We usually like these values, and some of us may proudly walk the walk and talk the talk in our daily lives. But sometimes we may feel a sense of distance from our favorite values, especially if they're more akin to our ideals and aspirations. If this is the case, our desire to embody our favorite values actually implies that we're currently removed from them, or not embodying them enough. Sometimes, they may be the same as the social values we circled before, or else they may be completely different, originating from our own perfectionism or desire to control.

Bringing our awareness to the present, our third colored pencil represents how we feel today. Maybe we're a sad blue or a jubilant orange or an enigmatic purple. Whatever the case, take a moment to explore this feeling, then circle three values we are currently embodying, today. Looking over our three favorite values and our three present values, do any overlap with society's ten? If they do, explore what went into prioritizing them that way. Maybe we feel in sync with our community or family expectations, or maybe a part of our multifaceted identity agrees while another aspect of us doesn't. How easy or difficult was it to identify what values we embody? What thoughts and feelings linger around our circled answers?

This exercise can be useful to expand both our awareness and our vocabulary around the vital question: "What's important to us?" It's also a useful primer should we feel at odds with ourselves but don't necessarily know why.

## Value-congruent action and the ACT matrix

Value-congruent action allows us to take progressive steps toward actualizing our self-identity, while recognizing that identity is not static. Even if our gender is stable, its nuanced layers change over time as we grow, heal, and adapt. We may have dreams and goals we're actively working toward, but there is no telling who we will become in our future iterations, or if our values may shift accordingly. Reconnecting our awareness to the present moment, we can, at the very least, account for who we are now and permit ourselves to act according to what we hold most dear.

The ACT matrix is a useful instrument to help sort our awareness into a mindfully developed action plan, since it reveals how we contribute to, and detract from our desired goals (see Figure 5.2). For the gender explorative, the ACT matrix can help grapple the complexity of self-actualization, along with any circumstances related to social, familial, occupational, and personal wellbeing. Since this is only an abbreviated introduction demonstrating how to apply the matrix to gender dynamic issues, you're encouraged to study *The Essential Guide to the ACT Matrix* (Polk *et al.*, 2016) and *Mindfulness and Acceptance for Gender and Sexual Minorities* (Skinta and Curtin, 2016) to utilize the full ACT matrix effectively in session.

After years of studying RFT and functional contextualism, Kevin Polk introduced the ACT matrix by asking five core questions (see Figure 5.3).

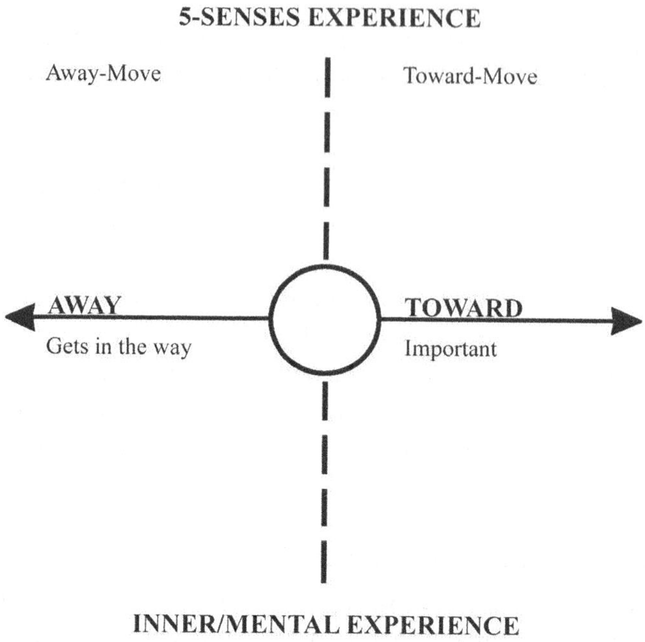


**Figure 5.2** *Matrix template*

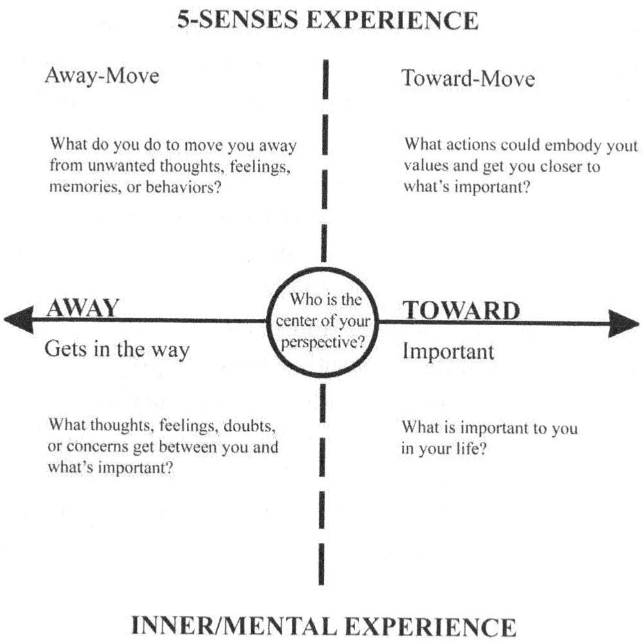


**Figure 5.3** *Matrix questions*

Answering these questions, we begin to see how our sense of self stands at an axis between our external experience (five senses) and our inner experiences (internal mind) (Polk *et al.*, 2016). Recognizing this, our behavior can be divided between actions, activities, and expressions that move us *away* from distress, and actions, activities, and expressions that move us *toward* what's important to us.

Tim agrees to draw an ACT matrix in session, since he doesn't know what to do about his family. Having come out in college, Tim's been taking testosterone with the help of his university health center. His parents are supportive, too, and though Tim's proud, he's starting to feel nervous about returning to his hometown. Judging his own fears as "irrational," Tim's worried about slipping into "old behaviors," "playing the part," and "acting like a girl," which he defines as "dressing down" in his old, less masculine outfits and speaking in a soft voice. He knows his parents love him, but they haven't spent a lot of time together in the past few years, and he doesn't want them to feel like they've lost a daughter. Tim feels like his dad doesn't actually understand and is begrudgingly tolerating his transition. Tim also feels that his mom will eventually accept him, but secretly feels "disappointed again," since an emotional rift occurred when Tim started dating girls back in high school. In session, Tim often repeats, "I don't get to see my family often, I just want them all to be happy."

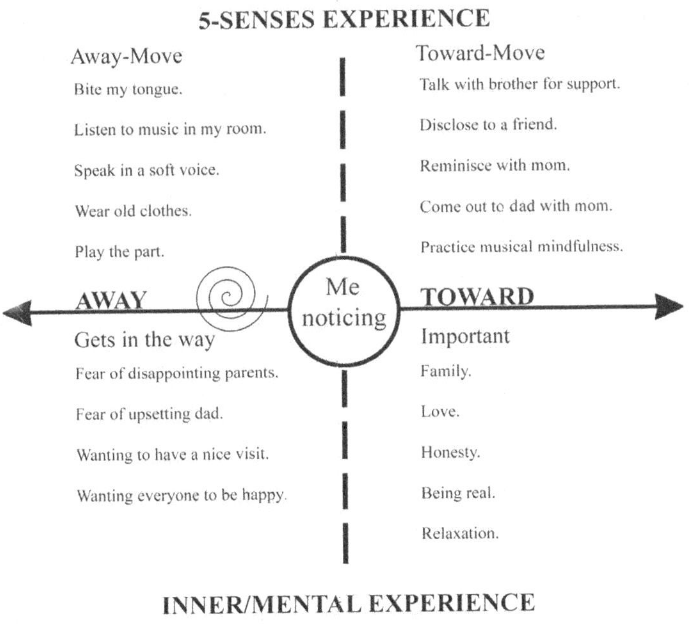


**Figure 5.4** *Tim's matrix*

When asking each of the five questions, point to each quadrant with gentle cues rather than over-explaining or trying to map Tim's answers for him, as the matrix is also an exploratory mindfulness exercise. It's effective to begin in the lower right quadrant, starting with who and what is important to Tim as a way of priming his answers as he moves clockwise to the top right quadrant (Polk *et al.*, 2016). Let Tim direct his answers, even if you don't necessarily agree with him (Polk *et al.*, 2016). For example, he may place an unhealthy behavior in the top right quadrant if he believes it moves him toward a desired goal (Polk *et al.*, 2016). This is often the case for people who struggle with addiction and emotional avoidance, especially if they believe their unhealthy behavior helps them relax or escape discomfort. Fortunately, Tim is very self-aware, and he astutely recognizes how his love for his family and fear of hurting them is impeding his ability to be honest. Even though his family have already stated their support, he worries that his parents are secretly disapproving. If anything, Tim's away-moves have actually been a passive if somewhat painful way to preserve his family connection, but they ironically create emotional distance. Draw a spiral between *what gets in the way* and Tim's *away-moves* to illustrate the stuck loop (see Figure 5.4). If he continues to be afraid, he continues to bite his tongue, and if he bites his tongue, he continues to be afraid. This is unworkable.

While brainstorming how to embody his values during his visit home, Tim remarks how in the past he has used music as an escape or a way to spiral into despair. By contrast, Tim shares that he has recently made an empowering tracklist of self-affirming songs. Tim calls this "musical mindfulness," as it helps him embody his feelings rather than run from them. Building his courage a song at a time, Tim shares that he's finally willing to be open about who he is; he's just concerned about the familial strain of doing so. Talking with his brother would be a great first step, as his brother is already supportive. So would identifying old friends from high school he wants to reconnect with. Opening up to people we know are already supportive is called a *soft disclosure*. Even though soft disclosures can be potentially nerve racking, there's a high probability of the conversation turning out well. With allies in his hometown to provide support, Tim can work his way to a *hard disclosure*, in this case building a deeper relationship with his dad. This is confusing for Tim because his dad already knows he's transgender, even though Tim has never really shared much about his experience. Asking Tim if he would prefer talking to his family all together or talking to his parents individually, Tim leans toward the latter. He feels that reminiscing with his mom about dating girls back in high school would be an awkward but potentially useful opportunity to reconnect. With his mom at his side, Tim feels he could build up enough courage to talk with his dad about his experiences as a man (see Figure 5.4).

Clinicians are warned against pushing options on their clients, as a therapist's values may explicitly or implicitly influence a client's decision-making process. At the end of the day, it is the client who is committing to their values, so they need to be aware of the possible situations and consequences of their actions (Hayes *et al.*, 2012). In this case, Tim is painfully aware of the possible pitfalls, as being honest and real about who he is may cause strain in his relationships. To provide a client the opportunity to individuate their values from that of the therapist, it may be worth asking: *If we stopped working together, and tomorrow you had a new counselor, how committed to these actions would you be?* (Hayes *et al.*, 2012). If the client feels uncertain about their toward-moves, return to what's important and take a good long look at those values. There are distinct nuances, after all, between honesty, transparency, vulnerability, and communication. In this case, Tim is well aware of his values, as he's been wanting to establish a deeper connection with his family for most of his life.

To understand why we fall back into old patterns, we can explore the short-term (ST) and long-term (LT) effectiveness of his away-moves (see Figure 5.5).

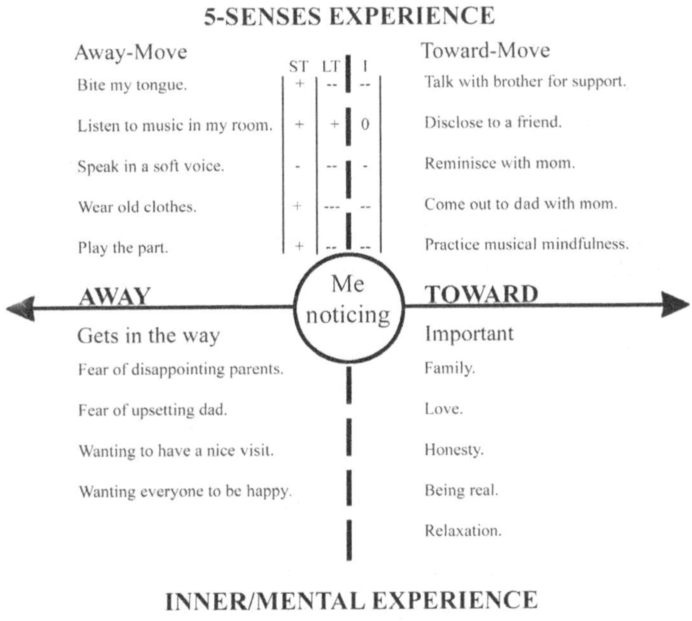


**Figure 5.5** *Rating moves*

Rating each with a plus or minus sign (see Table 5.5) it becomes apparent how alleviating internal distress that gets in our way doesn't actually get us closer to what's important. For Tim, dressing down is an obvious away-move, as it moves him away from his stated desire to be honest, be real, and relax as himself. Tim gives dressing down in his old clothes one plus in the short-term column, as it's moderately effective at relieving his anxiety at home. Unfortunately, this relief is fleeting, and fitting in with his parents' image of him doesn't help overall. For this reason, Tim also gives wearing his old clothes three minus signs, as it makes things drastically worse in the long term (see Figure 5.5).

**Table 5.5 Rating scale**

| | |
|---|---|
| +++ | Highly effective |
| ++ | Effective |
| + | Moderately effective |
| 0 | No effect |
| - | Makes things worse |
| -- | Makes things significantly worse |
| --- | Makes things drastically worse |

Focus more on rating than explaining each move, and let Tim assign as he sees fit, as there's no need to coerce him to a preconceived idea of what is or is not healthy (Polk *et al.*, 2016). As Tim ranks his behavior, he'll naturally begin to observe how control tactics tend to benefit the short term, if at all.

Sketching visual metaphors on the ACT matrix, Kevin Polk (2016) draws a shovel by our away-moves since they make the hole we're in deeper, and a ladder connecting what gets in our way in the bottom left quadrant to our toward-moves in the top right. If Tim can accept his internal obstacles, like his fear of disappointing or upsetting his parents, he can recognize the situation he's in and climb the ladder toward value-congruent action. On occasion, however, an attempt to alleviate distress can actually move us toward what's important. Exercise, socializing, and the creative arts can sometimes fall into this area, as each can be used as an avoidance tactic while simultaneously embodying personal value. To tell if the corresponding away-move actually advances Tim, draw a third column in the top right quadrant of the matrix for what's important (I). Adjusting the rating scale, which had previously been used to measure the away-move's effectiveness over time, the plus and minus signs can now indicate how effective the away-move is at moving us toward what's important. In Tim's case, none of his away-moves get him any closer to what's important to him, though he ranks listening to music in his room as a 0, stating that it neither adds nor detracts from his situation (see Figure 5.5). Keep in mind that using music as an away-move is an old pattern of behavior, not to be confused with the musical mindfulness of Tim's self-affirming tracklist.

Since this is an adaptable plan, there is no such thing as failure in this process. Moving away from or toward a desired outcome can feel like a cha-cha of setbacks and victories, but Tim is actively shifting away from self-degrading language to accept both his identity and his emotional process.

When preparing for a hard disclosure to friends, partners, or family members, it's beneficial to practice mindfulness exercises integrating self-compassion. For Tim, this includes a square breathing routine he's used every session for a month, with the option of listening to one of his empowering songs while doing so. Before the end of the session, time is taken to frontload Tim that, no matter the outcome, there will most likely be a lot of felt tension, and with it the temptation to fall back into old avoidance strategies—hence the need for mindful practice. Tim is hopeful as he likes having plans, but he remains nervous. As extra support, Tim agrees to a phone session if needed, which he not only appreciates but adds to his quadrant of toward-moves.

Realistically, shifting from short-term emotional-control tactics to value-congruent action is easier said than done, so let's explore a bump in the road. A fortnight passes, and Tim arrives early to his next session. He sits hurriedly on the couch and holds his breath. When asked about his trip, he says it was a complete disaster. His brother wasn't any help, and though he had an okay conversation with one of his old friends, when it came to talking with his mom he "chickened out" only to get into an argument with his dad. In the heat of the moment Tim blurted out, "I'm a gay man," which thoroughly confused both his parents—in particular his mom, who was convinced Tim was a lesbian back in high-school. After that, Tim said he hid in his room for most of the visit, just like he did when he was a kid.

As Tim is very agitated, casually draw awareness to his feelings, noting the frustration, anger, and fear currently at play. Tim is angry at his dad for yelling at him, but he's mostly angry at himself for even trying to connect. Catching the intonation, it's worth noting the possibility that Tim might be angry at his therapist, too. When asked if some of that anger is present in the therapeutic relationship, Tim explains that he's just mad about the whole situation, and that the experience reinforced his fears of estrangement. As Tim tends to hide his tears, encourage him to take a breath and release. Abstain from judgment-oriented language like *It's good to cry or Don't you feel better now*? as he may not agree with either statement. While exploring emotional utility and how even these difficult emotions are an extension of his values can be beneficial, now is not the time. Emotional acceptance isn't about liking our feelings, or intellectually interpreting their worth. Instead, we need to take a moment with Tim's sadness, love, hope, and despair, and simply acknowledge his heartache for what it is. If the session leaps directly back to the matrix, Tim may feel his therapist is trying to defend a model, or imply that Tim didn't do it right. Disappointed in himself and the situation, Tim is looking for fault, being stuck in a goal-based mindset of success and failure. Practicing mindfulness can aid in emotional acceptance, while also reinvigorating Tim's value-congruent actions. As Tim has yet to use his musical mindfulness exercise, bring it into play during the session. Have him select a song from his self-empowerment tracklist and practice mindful breathing.

It's worth mentioning how family, love, honesty, being real, and relaxation are continuous experiences that don't have intrinsic finish lines. Since there are often many pitfalls, setbacks, and relapses along the way, frontload how value-congruent actions are beneficial experiences that do not depend on outcome. The *Two Kids in the Car* metaphor (Harris, 2009a) is a great way to exemplify this: the goal-focused child impatiently wants to get to the beach, demanding, "Are we there yet? Are we there yet?" whereas the value-focused child explores their experience by listening to music, staring out the window, and playing games. Then the car breaks down, and they have to go home. Both children are disappointed, but the goal-focused child feels their day is ruined because they didn't get to the beach—they didn't accomplish the goal. To distract from this, they switch the goal for a new one, impatiently demanding, "Are we home, yet? Are we home yet?" The value-focused child is just as disappointed, because they too wanted to get to the beach; but now that they have to go home, they spend their time listening to music, staring out the window, and playing games, having never lost sight of fun, family, connection, and curiosity.

From the vantage of Tim's observational-self, it becomes possible to recognize how the situation is ongoing, allowing the dialogue to shift from outcome to experience. His relationship to his friends and family still exists, even in this awkward form. When it's emotionally appropriate, revisit the events of his trip, highlighting Tim's values where they're present. Keep in mind there is no rigid plan, and that the matrix is never set in stone.

> *Even though you didn't use some of the techniques we talked about, you still took a huge step toward honesty and being real with your family.*
>
> *I hear a lot of regret and uncertainty right now, but I also hear a lot of courage. It may not seem like it, because we're only brave when we're also really scared, right?*
>
> *The ACT matrix is kind of a map to follow, but a map is not the terrain. It sounds like you used some of your short-term techniques, but you also tried some long-term ones! You talked to your brother. He wasn't any help, but you did it. And you came out to your friends, which may not have been as impactful as you wanted, but you did that... What else was there? Oh! You did talk with your parents, even if it was an argument! That was always going to be difficult, but let's just acknowledge that you did it!*

It's possible to draw up a whole new matrix to figure out the next steps, but returning to his original matrix provides the opportunity to practice defusion, emotional acceptance, and commitment to his values. Tim can still reach out to his brother, follow up with his mom, or talk to his dad, modifying his expectations accordingly. Originally, he had hoped his brother would implicitly jump in to help, but Tim now realizes he needs to explicitly ask his brother for support. Likewise, Tim is starting to recognize how committing to family, honesty, and being real means walking his parents through unfamiliar concepts, like how a self-identified lesbian in high school can transition into a gay man in college. This is going to require more patience and emotional labor than he was prepared for, yet he's already started thinking of books and movies he could share with his mom to help her understand, without him having to explain directly. Tim wishes he could, and feels like he'll be able to share openly, but he's learning to accept his own emotional vulnerability. His transition is still new to him, and his connection to his parents is a powerful force in his life—so much so, the role of parental educator is too much to carry on his own. Tim observes how, much like the original plan, he wants to progressively build up to speaking with his father again, and how this will probably be easier to accomplish over the phone. Taking another step toward being real with his family, Tim decides to call his brother today, as a precursor to calling his mom tomorrow. Observing the stress and the need for a support network, he's invited to have the call with his brother in session, if needed.

Recalling the *Two Kids in the Car* metaphor, each jolt and bump in the road presents a real-world opportunity to practice experiential living through emotional acceptance and value-congruent action. When we feel like we've "missed the chance" or somehow "failed the test," we tend to fall into self-judgment, yet life is not a test or a race to be won. There is no finish line, no final conclusion to our personal growth, though we sometimes wish there was. Observably, our satisfaction is derived from witnessing the sincerity of our effort and our alignment to our values.

In Tim's follow-up session, less time was spent on direct technique. Some clients may need to be reminded of defusion and be led in an exercise. Be conscious, however, of being too heavy-handed with techniques. Having attempted ACT, Tim was momentarily in doubt about its effectiveness, and even his desire to proceed with what could be a very distressing experience. Humanizing the process requires spending time being human. ACT clinicians are cautioned against their own desire to fix, solve, or be outcome-oriented. As Tim has just made a valiant attempt, take time to experience all the hope, fear, embarrassment, regret, and even shame that goes along with it. The more Tim observes his values in his actions, and even in his emotions, the more capable he will feel in handling this very difficult family dynamic.

## Value integration

Experiences with cissexism can complicate the defusion process, as our control strategies can reflect a kind of value-congruent survivalism. The agenda of emotional control often appears on the ACT matrix in our short-term away-moves, providing temporary relief while moving us away from what's actually important to us. A classic example is avoiding our parents because we feel guilty when all along we want to make them proud. Fused to internal judgments, we fight our guilt, shame, embarrassment, love, and worry, by either beating ourselves up for not being "good enough," or projecting blame onto our family. By ignoring their phone calls, we save ourselves from discomfort in the short term, only to build pressure around our awkward holiday get-togethers. By contrast, avoiding a violently abusive ex-lover is not an emotional control tactic per se, as we are all too aware of our fear, and are accepting our emotional process in order to evade a very real and physical danger (Hayes and Smith, 2005). If we did not accept our fear in this abusive case, we would tolerate their company and pretend everything was fine even when they knock us to the floor.

Knowing when avoidance is an act of emotional suppression, or a necessary survival tactic, is rarely clear. The sociocultural prevalence of cissexism and transphobia blurs this line, leaving us wrestling with both real danger and ex-consequentia thinking, until we don't always know if we're being precautious or paranoid. Some of us resolve this dissonance by fusing to anecdotal reasoning, making us very adamant and steadfast in our perception of the world. Mettled self-assurance can be as rigid as fearful uncertainty. Optimism can be as inflexible as pessimism. We may view the world as a terrible place and rise to the occasion to fight it or flee into isolation. Either way, we have crystalized a judgment about the whole planet in order to explain or justify our reactive behavior.

Violence and hostility are terrible, but the potential for violence and hostility present in minority stress is so pervasive we may develop a kind of Stockholm syndrome for our own hypervigilance. To protect our vulnerability, and reconcile the critical thoughts fused to our caution, we may develop a set of values geared toward survival. This can challenge the typical ACT process for gender variant people should our investment in security, protection, privacy, endurance, fortitude, and willpower no longer be workable. Important and powerful, these values keep us safe, yet they can get muddled with the piety of our thinking self, leaving us tending to our most basic needs and no more.

ACT presents core values as the virtues as an internal compass guiding us to our healthiest and most self-congruent behavior. Having explored how internal values can conflict with social morals, and how present-based values can conflict with future-based ideals, what happens when there are two or more value systems vying for different outcomes? A common example includes the behavioral contradictions between safety and adventure, as the pursuit of safety favors structured containment, whereas adventure flies with the risk of freefall. Another example pits love against self-expression, locking us in the closet for fear of compromising or hurting our family. Neither our love of family nor our need for self-expression is a socially constructed moral or a lofty ideal; or if they were, they have since been adopted and internalized as value constructs deeply tied to our personal health and wellbeing.

By reflecting on how value constructs are not mutually exclusive, explore how to integrate both values. Consider the hours of preparation and safety checks the sky diver has to master before the jump, exemplifying both safety and adventure. Consider coming out to an accepting friend or wearing that risqué outfit out on the town with a group of supportive allies to embody love and self-expression. Many times, we can integrate values so that safety and adventure, love and self-expression, or honesty and vulnerability can be embodied simultaneously and without contradiction. Yet some situations appear to demand a choice.

Richard's been fretting for over two years now since he knows his Catholic family will be unsettled when he comes out as Raina. For two years he's hidden feminine clothes in a lock-box in the trunk of his car, and for two years he's gone on long road trips to queer-friendly conferences where Raina can be herself, only to pack it up and drive home. Richard's tried to balance his values before, but compromises don't always feel fulfilling. The middle ground can feel like half of each and the whole of nothing. Having postponed coming out, ironic process is taking its toll on Richard, and even the family is commenting on how he's spending more and more time away.

It would be inaccurate to say one value schema is false or superficial, and counterintuitive to the whole ACT process to judge values as *negative* or *bad*. It would also be counterintuitive to place these two value sets in a temporal paradigm. Terms like *old values* and *new values* may be inaccurate if Richard has felt this dissonance for as long as he can remember. Brené Brown accounts for this dissonance in her bestseller, *Daring Greatly* (2012), by demonstrating how our *aspirational values* are often misaligned with our *practiced values*. For example, if we aspire toward honesty and integrity, we may still dismiss opportunities to speak our truth if we practice values associated with rationalization and letting things go (Brown, 2012). In Brown's model, and indeed much of the ACT literature as well, the ultimate goal is to bring ourselves into alignment so that we practice the values most important to us. However, the language of aspiration and practice resides in a temporal frame, situating what we want to be and do in an aspirational future incongruent with our present-based practice. On top of this, the subject of priority isn't always so clear, especially for people who belong to more than one cultural community or find dissonance between two aspirational values. We can aspire to be proud and humble, bold and cautious, prepared and spontaneous, and we may alternate accordingly. This becomes quite evident when working with at-risk populations, as we aspire to survive just as much as we aspire to self-actualize, and may switch our practice contextually. To explore this nuance means addressing how our *survival values* may differ from, but are no less important than, our *self-actualization values*.

Presented with an option, Richard can find his primal drive to "get through," "fight on," or "hide away" pitted against his social resiliency and natural inclination to grow. His ability to thrive is not a lofty, heavenly, angelic ideal beyond reach. In fact, any internal conflict is evidence that his self-actualization values are at least equal in power and importance to his survival values.

Maslow's (1954) pyramid introduced the idea that self-actualization occurs when basic physiological safety, belonging, and esteem needs are met. Housing First models of intervention have demonstrated this in action (Tsemberis, 2010). However, this model is also privileged, as most pyramids tend to be, as it potentially places oppressed people unable to meet their own needs out of reach of self-actualization. Indeed, Maslow suggested that a state of self-actualization, which he defined as a growth-motivated rather than deficiency-motivated being state, was actually quite rare in society, as people's deficiencies distract them to meet their needs (Maslow, 1954). Maslow later adapted his pyramid again, noting how many of the qualities he attributed to self-actualization were indicative of an even higher level of self-transcendence—marked by a state of being-cognition that sets aside ego needs to serve a greater meaning or purpose (Koltko-Rivera, 2006). In this definition, self-actualization risks becoming a form of idyllic enlightenment, rather than a present-moment expression of personal authenticity.

Gender affirmative ACT adjusts *self-actualization* as a growth-motivated state to a growth-motivated process distracted, but not blockaded, by a needs-based process. The more our basic needs stack up, the less likely we are to feel a sense of personal growth. Nonetheless, some of the greatest artistic and musical revolutions came about during the darkest points of human history, demonstrating how sometimes we need to grow and self-actualize in order to meet our basic needs. This latter point is lit up in neon when working with gender variant clients. While some have the safety we need in order to self-actualize, others may not feel safe until we come out.

Notably, survival values and self-actualization values are not mutually exclusive (see Table 5.6). Safety, for example, is both a survival need and, for those recovering from trauma, a huge point of growth. When self-actualization is taken off the perch of enlightened ideals and placed in the realistic scope of value congruence, it becomes possible to find peace in chaos, growth in hardship, and epiphany in poverty. This sentiment is core to many Vedic faiths of India, in many of the mindful practices of Buddhism, and even in Viktor Frankl's logotherapy (1946), as his experience in a concentration camp led him to observe how we are intrinsically capable of discerning meaning, and therefore value and choice of attitude, even in the direst of circumstances.

In Richard's case, he's progressively undermining himself on both fronts. He can't attain a sense of esteem, trust, safety, acceptance, and awareness, yet his need for privacy, safety, integrity, stability, and innocence are also compromised by his short-term behaviors (see Table 5.6).

**Table 5.6 Survival and self-actualization values**

| Cognition | Emotion | Behavior | Survival value | Self-actualization value |
|---|---|---|---|---|
| I can't say it | Shyness | Avoid topic | Privacy | Esteem |
| I'm scared to say | Anxiety | Avoid feelings | Safety | Trust |
| I don't want to say | Hostility | Offensive/ defensive | Integrity | Safety |
| I'm not____ | Resistance | Denial to others | Stability | Acceptance |
| I don't know | Confusion | Denial to self | Innocence | Awareness |

For Richard, the longer he hides from his family, the more aware his family is that he's hiding, and the more suspicious of him they become. Although there's a chance they may never find out, Richard's need to be honest is reaching a critical point, evident in his increased secrecy. Yet even Richard knows nothing tempts a person to invade someone's privacy more than a proverbial keep-out sign. Even his kids are starting to think he's having an affair, and in a way he is; he just so happens *to be* the other woman. A choice is building in Richard. Rather than encourage one way or the other, validate his survival values while exploring the practical workability of his options.

Accepting fear is difficult when the stakes are high and the risk of losing his family is real, yet by trying to avoid his discomfort Richard now lives in a perpetual state of discomfort. Defusion exercises like *Zooming out* or *Yes, and...* may be useful to expand beyond his reactive survival instinct. Likewise, mindfulness techniques can help Richard center on the present moment, allowing him to draw out a matrix. For Richard, however, the matrix can be a window to his competing values.

On a matrix, survival values tend to be the operating drive behind many away-moves, whereas self-actualization values tend to contribute to many toward-moves, though not always. Exploring what's important to Richard and what gets in his way shows how Richard avoids fear and worry the most, which is ironic as fear and worry motivate much of his behavior (see Figure 5.6). Identify what values his away-moves embody to glimpse the positive intent in his behavior. Then, as you begin collaborating on his toward-moves, help Richard develop a value-congruent action plan integrating his survival and self-actualization values, where possible. This may require expanding what the expression of these values may look like, as it will most certainly require accepting discomfort. Richard definitely values privacy, yet he never meant to be so private with his spouse. Couples counseling, as an example, integrates both privacy and trust, as it provides a safe, confidential, and controlled environment for Richard and his spouse to stabilize their relationship. Entering into couples counseling does not automatically jump Richard to disclosing his gender identity during their first session together. Indeed, Richard can take all the time he needs. However, it does expand Richard's value for integrity beyond himself, to include consideration of his spouse's integrity. Likewise, couples counseling would also challenge Richard to expand his awareness, and indeed his preoccupation with being accepted, beyond himself to include his awareness of his wife's process, and how to accept her emotional response. While Richard insists he prioritizes his family's wellbeing—and while this is most certainly true—Richard's control tactics presume the worst of the very people he loves.

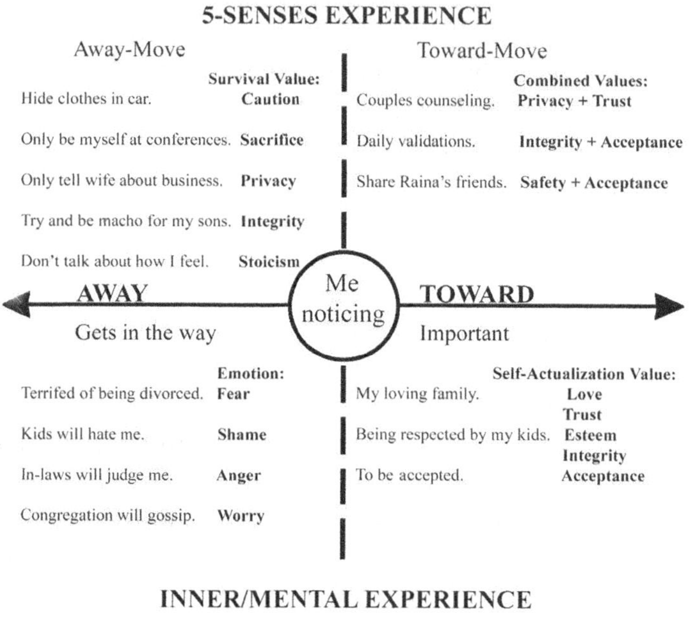


**Figure 5.6** *Survival and self-actualization matrix*

Other examples of value integration include daily validations of courage, for though Richard has found ways to express Raina, Raina's ego strength will remain fragile until her expression is defused from shame. Accepting Raina also means accepting her integrity as an identity, so she is no longer a threat to Richard's integrity as a father and a husband. Instead of validating the *good dad* archetype, Raina can validate her ability to be a healthy, fair, educational, compassionate, nurturing, and loving parent.

Another potential option is to introduce Richard's family to Raina's friends. Currently, Richard is straddling two worlds, and has been terrified that they might cross-contaminate each other. However, selecting mature, tactful individuals who understand that Raina is not yet out to her family presents a low-risk, if uncomfortable, opportunity to integrate safety with emotional acceptance. This is a potentially challenging exercise to work up to, as Raina may be as self-conscious of showing people Richard as Richard is of letting these two worlds interact. By observing safety amidst discomfort, Raina can build emotional resilience, while reducing some of the potential *drop* of disclosure, as it's one thing to learn one's spouse is a woman, and another to learn about her second life. Such friends can also provide a safety net for the whole family, giving the family a compassionate resource the day Raina does speak up.

Perhaps Richard's right, and his family will be thrown into turmoil, or perhaps they will move through turmoil to understanding after a long and bumpy road. All we know for certain is that Richard holds himself and his family in a shadowed state of doubt, at odds with what Raina values most. Any action will, therefore, be fraught with anxiety, so slow down, and explore Richard's emotional acceptance of Raina, and her acceptance of her growth edge.

## Value-congruent disclosure

Let's visualize a family gathering, with everyone in our life who does and doesn't know about our gender (Curtin, Ryu, and Diamond, 2016). As we picture ourselves walking into the crowd, what do we notice? Where are we tense in our body? Where are we relaxed? What emotions come up as we look from person to person? In the second part of this exercise, picture the same gathering of people, but let's imagine we've already come out (Curtin *et al.*, 2016). As we visualize everyone, what do we feel? What do we notice? What physical sensations are we aware of?

Sometimes, when we picture everyone knowing, we may feel relieved, but it's not uncommon to feel quite the opposite. Ironic process is known intimately by anyone who's ever been in the closet. Striving to conceal our sexuality or gender identity only brings it to the forefront of our mind. The closeted don't just sit in a classroom, boardroom, or restaurant—we sit in a classroom, boardroom, or a restaurant monitoring and censoring our thoughts and behavior while simultaneously attempting to mind-read what everyone else is thinking. Do they know? What if they know? What if we tell them? What if we don't? Hiding embodies fear and fragility. We hide when we're afraid or feel unable to cope. Clamping down on our whole body, we hold our tongue, hold our breath, stay as quiet as we can, keep our heads down, wait, and wait, and wait with the hope that maybe, just maybe, either the fear or the danger will go away... And when it doesn't? Stress, and all the maladaptive coping mechanisms that follow.

The coming out process is not a singular formative experience, nor is it uniform. Transgender stage models often overlook how age of realization and gender development milestones intersect with cultural perspectives of sexual and gender identity. Around the world, disclosure takes on not only different levels of social imperative and, in some countries, even legal consequence, but the very act takes on a different meaning. Even *coming out* as an American colloquialism has changed in definition. Before the 1950s, gay men had used the term in a celebratory initiation akin to a young lady being *brought out* at a debutantes ball, yet as the Stonewall riots raged against oppression, the term came to imply shirking off shame by revealing the *skeletons in the closet* (Chauncey, 1994; Hooker, 1965). At the height of the AIDs crisis, in an era of civil rights champions, punks, and radical feminists, some LGBTQ youth outed themselves as a controversial, courageous, and dangerous rite of passage. Others were violently outed, their discovery resulting in disownment, or worse.

Comparatively, the French only recently adopted the term, emulating the American, homonormative narrative as a kind of mechanical ritual, a practice of public proclamation so often shown on TV. The French term *s'assumer* means "to assume" one's identity, to live comfortably with oneself, a concept that focuses far less on social disclosure and far more on a person's intimate integration of identity (Provencher, 2007). In Japan, the LGBTQ community contends with familial homophobia (*uchi*), and quiet homophobia (*otonashii*), defined as the expectation to suppress one's feelings to the most socially accepted norm, thereby amplifying disclosure to a form of political advocacy (Tamagawa, 2016). Colloquially, coming out (*kaminguauto*) is used as a term of confession for any hushed secret (Tamagawa, 2017).

With so many cultural contexts and personal imperatives, some gender variant people may come out at the start of our actualization process, or after a period of personal experimentation. Others may only come out after a medical procedure, refraining from disclosure until completing top surgery or facial reconstruction, or until starting HRT. Shaking off shame, some wait to begin anew after severing from old familial ties or oppressive communities. There is no set, linear path to disclosure, as there are so many social settings in which we naturally explore and present our multifaceted identity. Additionally, those who have already transitioned may face a second layer of disclosure, questioning whether or not to let people assume they're cisgender, or to be open about their birth sex and trans experience. Downplaying one's anatomic past is not a new phenomenon by any means, as history is dotted with post-mortem surprises, including the famous jazz pianist Billy Tipton who was only outed by his coroner.

By contrast, some trans people may highlight being gender variant. They may take pride in their *experience* as a transgender individual, or their *identity* within the LGBTQ community. Some may come out only in safe contexts. Some may take pride in disclosure, others may feel fatigued by it, and many have felt all of the above. We may even feel we have little choice, appearing "noticeably different" or "unable to pass" in our gender nonconformity. Conversely, we may feel like we're under a cloak of social invisibility, as if our identity is overlooked as "vaguely androgynous" unless we actively label ourselves. Nonbinary people may even hold back from telling anyone. Of those nonbinary people who refrain from disclosure, 86 percent said they didn't share because most wouldn't understand, while 82 percent confessed it was simply easier to stay quiet (James *et al.*, 2016). This is quite understandable when 63 percent of the same group felt like their gender identity was dismissed as unreal, inauthentic, or *just a phase*, with a further 43 percent fearing a violent reaction should they be honest (James *et al.*, 2016).

Certainly, there are many locks on the closet door, yet there are also a few unhealthy reinforcers to get wrapped up in, like warm coats hung up inside. Two, in particular, involve using the closet as a tool to create connections. Transactional analysis observes what's known as the *drama triangle*, in which individuals fuse with interchangeable persecutor, rescuer, and victim roles (Karpman, 1968). Faced with discrimination over the lifespan, some may develop a victim mindset, and in turn look to a lover, friend, or confidant to be the rescuer. Elevated by an unhealthy level of attachment, the rescuer becomes the keeper of secrets and an excuse not to disclose to anyone else. "As long as I have my best friend, I'll be okay. They're the only one I need."

In turn, the rescuer may not realize how they're enabling. They may even feel exasperated by how long it's taking them to come out. If this exhaustion is noticed, the closeted may accuse the rescuer of not being patient or understanding enough. The closeted may even seek out another rescuer. Though this may seem manipulative on a cursory level, the co-dependent mindset isn't always aware of its own neediness. Instead of investing in a larger social support network—which is admittedly difficult—the co-dependent mindset seeks safety from one manageable source. This behavior is more evident when working with secretive teenagers, yet also comes up in the course of marriage counseling, when the spouse is "the only one who knows."

Clinicians must also be conscientious of not falling into the rescuer role of Karpman's triangle (1968) as clients "who have never told this to anyone" may become overly attached to the therapeutic relationship. Treating your office as an oasis in the desert, we may express a genuinely powerful appreciation, saying, "I feel like this is the only place I can be myself," or "This is the only place I can be honest," or "You're the only one who gets it." If we're new to actualizing gender, this is quite natural and no cause for alarm. As the keepers of the oasis, you hold a safe space for vulnerability, but when we begin to build a home at the oasis we are no longer progressing. Without compromising trust or vulnerability, clinicians can help expand a client's support network so that we're not sequestered to a single safe space, locked hand-in-hand with our one and only ally. After all, there's no point in bottling water if we're going to stay at the oasis, and there's no point in putting on a warm coat if we're just going to stay inside.

The second warm coat in the closet is the fetishization of the closet itself. This taboo coat makes the closet exciting by associating danger with the secret frontier of self-exploration. Just as getting drunk can be more exciting when we're under 21, and having sex can be more titillating in public places, so too can the closet become exhilarating. Keeping secrets can be exciting. The danger of being caught lends a sense of adventure to an otherwise stressful experience. Though we may hate being in the closet and swear up and down about the risks of transparency, we may simultaneously lean into it, engaging in risk-taking behavior as if tempting fate. This behavior is not representative of the majority of people struggling to be open, as most find nothing sexy about shame, yet for a select few, gender secrecy becomes a kind of scintillating self-sabotage.

Feeling unable to come out, we may want to be caught in the act, or else find excitement right on the edge of social consequence. Borrowing or stealing clothes from spouses, friends, or stores, we may then go to extreme lengths to hide our wardrobe. Secretly going out at night in cross-gender clothing, or hiding cross-gender clothes under work uniforms, this taboo mindset may edge toward more blatant modes of expression. Transgender paraphernalia, including books, movies, and undergarments may be left out in the open, just to see if it sparks conversation with someone in the house—even if we go on to lie about it! Cheating on cisnormative partners with trans-positive lovers, we may even lead a double life, only to have our worlds overlap and collide into each other. Burdened with cognitive dissonance and even tragic romanticism, the taboo mindset conceals the truth to prolong the excitement in an almost addictive fashion.

Do not assume all who engage in such behavior secretly desire to be caught. Many are absolutely terrified, impulsively risking our marriages, families, and—in nations inhospitable to gender variance—potentially our lives. When shame attenuates pleasure, we don the taboo coat, becoming addicted to the cycle of thrill and self-admonishment. Wearing the taboo coat, clients will describe feeling "compelled" to sneak out, lie, or withhold, attempting so frequently to stop ourselves from engaging what we desire most, only to "fail," judge ourselves as "sinners" or "perverts," and decry, "It's like I couldn't stop myself." This coat may not seem all that warm when we beat ourselves up in wrecked embarrassment, but then we describe our escapade with a wry smile, and the cycle repeats. Gender variance is not a debauched form of hedonism, but it can be if we fuse judgment to it, for the more we label our resonant pleasure as wrong, bad, naughty, sinful, and forbidden, the more exciting it is to break the rules.

Our emotional process can reveal much about our conceptualization of self and the coming-out experience. Phrases like "I'm not ready" or "Now's not the time" may need to be taken into deep consideration, as we may have an unmet emotional prerequisite to coming out, which we may or may not get. Flat out asking what we need in order to feel "ready" often elicits a blank stare if we have no idea what our needs are. We may think we have to tough it out and just tell everyone, or feel like we'll never be ready to tell anyone. Emotions, however, provide evidence of our unmet needs. Anger often exemplifies a crossed boundary, fear illustrates our need for safety, and worry requests a sense of certainty it may not get.

Realistically, we may not be able to establish boundary, safety, or certainty in every situational disclosure, yet it's possible to build a broader foundation considering these needs. Outside of the whole subject of gender identity, help us practice assertive communication as needed, or develop a social support network where we feel genuinely safe, or work toward accomplishable goals within our immediate locus of control. Outside of gender, we disclose aspects of our lives all the time! We communicate what we do or do not like, what we do or do not feel comfortable with, and what we are or are not certain about. Practicing emotional transparency in multiple areas of our life grants us opportunities to practice our acceptance of discomfort, and our commitment to value-congruent action.

Desiring to help, too many clinicians overly focus on gender disclosure when there are plenty of other areas in which to practice communication, courage, and self-worth (Mizock and Lundquist, 2016). What other social situations are annoying or frustrating? Where else do we feel stuck or feel like we can't speak our mind? Who do we feel nervous or awkward around? Gender aside, what do we want people to know or support about who we are? Sometimes, as we practice opening up, we may naturally disclose facets of our gender to others as we feel more comfortable. If this occurs, unpack the experience, yet never assign disclosure as therapeutic homework, as doing so can create a false success/fail paradigm, adds unnecessary pressure to the process, and creates a power differential stemming from the clinician's expectation (Ali, 2014; Rachlin and Lev, 2013). Should we "fail" such an assignment, we may feel guilty and avoid our next session. Instead, value-congruent actions encourage clients to embody honesty in diverse contexts should we value honesty, and lean into our nervousness should we value courage.

It may even be worth exploring the short-term benefits of being in the closet (Ali, 2014; Mitchell, 2012; Rachlin and Lev, 2013). Experiential avoidance does, after all, insulate us from danger, albeit for an added cost and hidden fee. Even though we feel worried and anxious, and even though we don't actually feel safe, secrecy is a control tactic that promises safety, at least in the short term. Immediately, right here, right now, we feel fine because no one knows. This track of thought, of course, leads us to feeling fraudulent and even criminal, like we're getting away with something, or that everyone would blow up if the truth was known.

Sandoz and Dufrene, in *Living with Your Body and Other Things You Hate*, ask the self-concious to look ahead and imagine our upcoming week. Do we have plans? Where will we go? Who are we going to see or meet up with? Of all the plans, places, and people, how might avoiding our gender identity or gender expression shape our week? What activities might we not participate in because we're restricting our gender? And in each scenario what values do we feel are present? Will we have any opportunity to express our authentic self in the upcoming week, either in private or public?

Originally designed to improve body image, this exercise asks us to then make a small commitment toward acceptance, the more specific the better (Sandoz and Dufrene, 2013). In this context, acceptance isn't synonymous with a soft or hard disclosure, as we're not committing to tell anyone. We are, however, committing to a gender affirmative act of our choice on the edge of our comfort zone. Leaning into the discomfort can build emotional resilience while validating the queer innocence so often buried by shame.

Let's write down three commitments, following the formula:

> "When I think/feel____and I think/feel____I'll practice acceptance by ____."

> "When I feel alone, and I feel like no one understands me, I'll practice acceptance by calling Alex. They're genderfluid, so they get it."

> "When I think I'm going to get stared at when I buy makeup, and I feel ashamed, I'll practice acceptance by purchasing at least one new lipstick."

> "When I feel scared that people will judge how I look, and I feel like I want to dress down, then I'll practice acceptance by wearing my earrings, even if I don't wear my whole ensemble."

Taking small steps toward self-expression, even in private, helps us normalize the physical reality of being a gender variant person. Even tiny experiments like wearing high heels around the house, or going out one evening wearing eyeliner, or going for a drive around town wearing a packer, allow us to validate resonance. Such moments also provide opportunities to continue our defusion practice, as judgmental thoughts are sure to flash through our mind. Likewise, community connection creates opportunities to receive positive validation from others and practice emotional resilience when no current validation exists. Even if the whole wide world fails to notice what we did with our hair this morning, our one good friend will smile and take note. Even if the whole wide world has no idea we're a gender variant person, our queer support group will wink and smile at the little changes and tiny efforts on our part.

Applying this same technique to internal dissonance can further challenge our emotional avoidance tactics.

> "When I think I'm alone, and I think no one understands me, I'll practice acceptance by taking a deep breath and counting five people I had positive interactions with this week."

"When I think mean thoughts about myself, and I think I'm ugly or pathetic or whatever, I'll practice acceptance by giving the judgment in my head a silly voice and reminding myself I'm not my thoughts."

"When I feel scared that people will judge how I look, and I feel like I want to dress down, then I'll practice acceptance by validating that I'm being brave because I'm scared."

Any possible alternatives that don't involve avoiding, suppressing, or controlling our felt discomfort exemplify acceptance by acknowledging the source of distress, disempowering the rigid thought constructs associated with it, and committing to follow through (Sandoz and Dufrene, 2013). Far more difficult than it sounds, we may make a number of dry runs on our commitments, like going shopping only to ditch the cart before reaching the checkout counter, or intending to introduce ourselves with our preferred pronoun only to pull back at the last second. The judgments that follow create another opportunity to practice defusion, as well as a chance to once more address success and failure as an unworkable paradigm.

"When I think I've failed, and I think I've ruined everything, I'll practice acceptance by validating what I was able to do and deciding to try again."

"When I feel embarrassed, and I think people are going to judge me, I'll practice acceptance by imagining my anxiety as an innocent child and talking to myself gently."

"When I think I'm stupid for even trying, and I think I should just give up, I'll practice acceptance by playing a song my queer side resonates with."

Exasperated, we may ask, "Why does value-congruent behavior matter if I'm still stuck? I can try to be open but it doesn't matter if I'm still hiding in the closet." Though frustrated, we're observing how important it is to express gender authentically, highlighting our own strength in the struggle and value in the dissonance. Agree how important it is for us, yet note how we're also fused to an expectation. Our rational mind is aware that just buying the lipstick or introducing the pronoun isn't a final outcome, yet there's an inbuilt hope that "If I can do this, then I can do that" or "If I can do this, then it'll be easier when I do it again." This may very well be true, yet there's also no guarantee that the outcome of our present situation will influence future events.

When emotional resilience is treated like a goal, it's framed as something we're trying to attain, which reinforces the idea that it's something we lack. So too with courage, capability, happiness, and so on. When emotional resilience is treated as our response to current stress in this moment of discomfort, we reinforce the message that we are already emotionally resilient, not in spite of our fear, stress, or worry but because of their presence. Like any stress test, we only know what's durable by how much it endures. Few clients will believe this if a clinician explains it, as discussing stress—although stressful—is not a stress test. Clients will often point this out by saying, "I can talk about it here, but there's no way in hell I can talk about it out there."

Fused to "I can't" mantras, we may return to closeted behavior quite addictively, especially if we're approaching actual disclosure. If we're pragmatic, or avoidant, or both, we may gravitate toward focusing on our thoughts or behavior in order to escape our emotional experience. We may talk at length about what we did or didn't do, overlooking how we felt about the action. Subsequently, we may continuously try to "lay-up the shot," engineering moments to disclose only to "miss." Just like our prior dry runs, these can be quite valuable moments to identify rules, reasons, judgments, and roles weighing down our conceptual self. However, if we continue to avoid our feelings on the matter, these dry runs may actually reinforce our negative self-talk, and along with it our fusion to absolute thinking.

"I always chicken-out. I can never open up."

"I try, but I just can't bring myself to say it."

"They'll never understand, so why even bother?"

Disliking emotions, we can become wary of self-awareness, expecting introspection to hold some kind of danger. If we feel stuck in the disclosure process, draw awareness to our willingness to look within. Maybe we've wrestled these feelings for a long time, or maybe we've only recently connected the dots. In either case, willingness can be found within our identified values, should we express themes of transparency, authenticity, and openness. If, however, we value privacy, then we may be looking to our therapist to support our choice to remain in the closet, as coming out may add unnecessary pressure to our lives (Ali, 2014; Rachlin and Lev, 2013). When it comes to revealing our authentic self, value-congruent action is as contextually dynamic as our identity, requiring us to examine both what we're disclosing, and to whom. For every tier of identity is a layer of emotional charge, a history of personal development, and a swathe of judgments both internal and external. We may, for example, have no qualms about sharing one aspect of ourselves, like our gender, sex, sexuality, or personal uniqueness, but feel quite nervous about sharing another.

- *Disclosing my gender*: Disclosure depends on how comfortable we feel about sharing who we truly are. Accepting oneself wholly is not synonymous with expressing oneself transparently. Some may opt for radical honesty in all situations; others may require levels of safety, trust, and community support before disclosure.

- *Disclosing my sex*: Cissexism unnecessarily hyperfocuses on anatomic sex as a means of discounting transgender identity. In response, gender affirmative therapy prioritizes physical and mental health over physical form and appearance, as our gender identity and how we live in our own lives takes precedent over our perceived gender and how we look to others. Anatomic sex is not irrelevant, however, as disclosing physical differences to potential romantic and sexual partners unfamiliar or inexperienced with gender variant bodies can be a delicate issue, or a sticking point for anxiety, or a lot of fun, depending on the emotional context (Hill-Meyer and Scarborough, 2014). Furthermore, our relationship with our body may be an area of great sensitivity depending on our transition goals, body image, and level of self-worth.
- *Disclosing my sexuality*: Some of us may feel like we have to come out of multiple closets. Just as gender identity is loaded with social tiers and nuanced forms of initiation, so too is sexuality. Testing the boundaries of social convention, it is not uncommon for gender variant people to be sexually experimental with orientation, monogamy, polyamory, and Bondage/Discipline, Dominance/Submission, Sadism/Masochism (BDSM).
- *Disclosing my uniqueness*: While open about gender and sexual orientation, we may or may not voice our experience as unique individuals, especially if our perspective or experience goes against the hetero, homo, transnormative or even queer-normative script.

Disclosure questions focusing on *when* and *where* are often a subtle disguise for *whom* we should be open with. When we mention "coming out at work" or "coming out at school" there's a relational context teetering between rejection and connection. There is no right or wrong to determining who "needs to know," so pay attention to the level of casualness or urgency present in our language. Likewise, if we express that our family "deserves to know," we may be grappling with an underlying guilt. Presenting a different vernacular, we may fearfully share who we "have to hide from." The more volatile our environment, the more pressure we may feel to hide. Problematically, if we ignore the fire, we still choke on the smoke, as ignoring or hiding our gender to sustain safety may increase the stress levels contributing to self-harm and suicide.

Tired of the closet, we may state, "I don't want to hide anymore," or "I want to be open with everyone," or "I hate having to constantly ask if it's okay to be me around people." Each thought illustrates not only our willingness to be transparent, but also our conscientiousness and willingness to take on social risks.

Many times, when people think of disclosure, they focus on the individual readying themselves to open up. However, it takes two to tango. LGBTQ ally training often focuses on basic active listening skills, teaching allies to hold space for the individual. Yet people's skillsets vary, and with each social circle we may find ourselves coping with different hopes, fears, expectations, and disappointments. After all, it's very different to open up casually than it is to be "outed" without permission. It is also very different to respectively disclose to friends, family, academic peers, or co-workers, since different social groups have varying degrees of amiability, compassion, and understanding. Indeed, each social circle brings with it an array of different questions.

- *Strangers*: How much do we care/worry/notice strangers knowing we're gender variant? How vulnerable do we feel being self-expressive in public? Do we believe people are compassionate, despondent, or cruel?
- *Acquaintances*: How much do we care/worry/notice acquaintances knowing? How do we feel about co-workers and peers accidentally/deliberately getting our pronouns wrong? Do we fear any social/emotional/physical repercussions from being out to these acquaintances?
- *Friends*: How much do we trust our friends to understand who we are and how we feel? Is there a chance of harming a relationship by being transparent? How do we feel about remaining friends with someone who is "trying to accept" us?
- *Family*: How much do we trust our family to understand who we are and how we feel? Is there a chance of harming a relationship by being transparent? How will our family process our gender identity?
- *Employers*: Is it relevant for our employer to know? Do we believe gender is relevant in the workplace? Could disclosure endanger our job or future job prospects? Do we trust our employer?
- *Authority figures*: Do we trust people with influence over our physical/emotional/legal wellbeing? Is there risk of harm or power abuse?

Observing all these tiers to disclosure, draw a bullseye with three concentric rings (see Figure 5.7). Label the largest circle the *risk zone*, the middle circle the *unsure zone*, and label the center the *safe zone*. This exercise can help determine willingness, as well as how many options for disclosure are available. First, let's make a list of 20 people we have social interactions with in a typical week. If we isolate a lot, let's see if we can identify 20 people, even if it's the clerk behind the cash register or that one barista who smiled at us that one time, or even our landlord who stops by once a month.

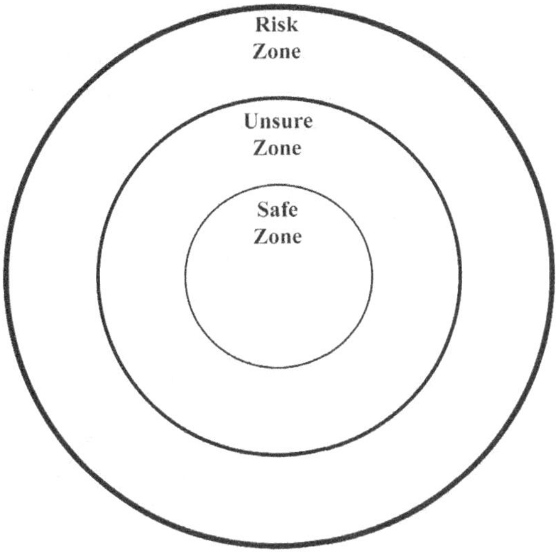


**Figure 5.7** *Disclosure bullseye template*

Regardless of whether or not they know our gender identity, arrange all 20 people into the safe zone, unsure zone, and risk zone, respectively. It may seem like preaching to the choir, but the more people we decide to come out to in the safe zone, the better. Even if we know there's no chance of rejection, we may still feel tense, nervous, awkward, silly, anxious, and afraid to do so.

Safe zone disclosures are an excellent opportunity to practice emotional mindfulness, defusion, and value-congruent action as we may still feel awkward or anxious about disclosing. To illustrate this in session, try asking—if we've already come out to you—to come out again, right now. It may sound silly, since you already know, and some clients may have no problem saying it again, but others may still be fused to judgments—not necessarily about gender, but about disclosure, or being the center of attention. Inquire how it felt the first time gender came up in session, and how it feels now. Was there hesitance then? Is there hesitance now? Did we have certain reservations or concerns in the back of our mind, and what values helped develop the therapeutic relationship as it stands?

But what if no one's in the safe or uncertain zone, cramming all 20 people into the risk zone? If this happens, regardless of whether it's a skewed perspective or a legitimate danger, inquire where you, the therapist, sit in the bullseye. If the client feels they're able to be honest with you in session, this can be a unique and very frank opportunity to re-examine rapport. If there's uncertainty in the therapeutic relationship, a therapist may be set in the unsure zone. It may help to specify areas of disclosure. For example, they may be open to exploring family issues in session, but still feel uncertain about openly discussing sex and sexuality. If the therapeutic relationship is solid and trust is established, the client may place you in the safe zone. Either way, no matter where you're placed, the therapeutic relationship provides a comparison point to revisit a possible spectrum. Emotions are often relative to context. Even if all 20 individuals are still in the risk zone, ask the client to identify if any of them are riskier than the others? Are any of them marginally safer? Are any of them closer to where you're placed on the bullseye? Do any of them demonstrate empathy, even if they lack understanding? Having a point of comparison can sometimes wiggle loose a rigid viewpoint, as it asks the client to distinguish, differentiate, and humanize.

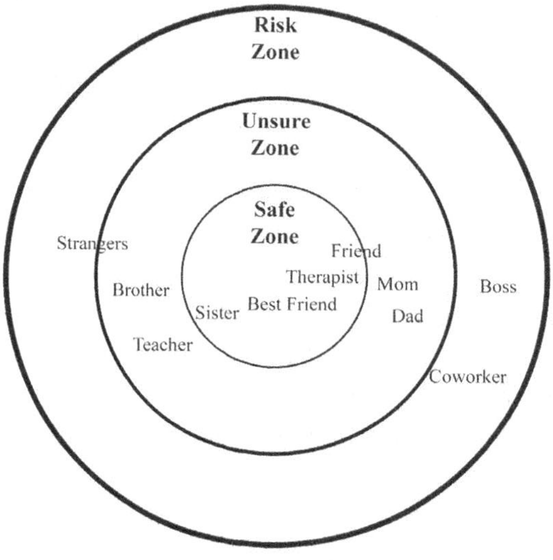


**Figure 5.8** *Disclosure bullseye example*

Disclosure isn't just about declaring gender. If it were, therapy would consist of handing over a megaphone and sending us outside. Instead, disclosure is our degree of personal authenticity with others. This doesn't equate to being vulnerable with every member of humanity, but part of authenticity does rely on our ability to be personally genuine in our expression (Budge, Tebbe, and Howard, 2010). Not only is this difficult, it can be quite rare in public settings where even commonplace expressions of personality or mood are eclipsed by social nicety. Even cisgender heterosexuals hide mundane skeletons in their closet, their emotional remains hung up on polite statements like "I'm fine" or "I'm doing good" even when their bones are rattling. So why do gender variant people have to be personally authentic if so many others aren't? The answer: we don't. No one has to do anything, but the risks we face are substantially higher because of how minority stress pervasively impacts our global functioning.

As we begin to feel stable within ourselves, revisit this bullseye from time to time to see if anyone moves between zones. Did we ever open up to someone we're uncertain about? People in the uncertain zone can be tricky, not only because we can't tell which way they'll go, but also because they might not even care. Ambivalence can feel invalidating. In turn, explore if we've opened up to anyone in the risk zone, and if we're preoccupied with doing so. Sometimes, we'll steam toward the risk zone, counting on a reaction, not because we're self-destructive per se, but because we believe that doing so is the only way to stop thinking about it. Hard disclosures of this kind may include coming out to parents, children, pastors, and even police officers. On the flip side, some of us may avoid the risk zone at all cost, leading us to run away from our communities to start anew, or even contemplate suicide (Grant *et al.*, 2011; James *et al.*, 2016).

Expanding our number of confidants, increasing exposure to gender variant individuals, and increasing our frequency with safe-space interactions can progressively demystify gender and the process of disclosure (Yep, 2003). This may take some time, but as physical and emotional risks decrease, we will be more inclined to defuse from our conditional statements and hang up our warm coats. By accruing more trans-positive relationships, and more opportunities to be open, we build up a successive series of positive social interactions we can resource as examples of psychosocial health.

## Value-congruent expression

Gender expression can be a fun, creative art form. When we accept and validate who we are, our gender expression can become an extension of our joy. Funnily enough, when we're secure in our gender, we're often irreverent about it, demonstrating a mental flexibility in our humor. Our expression does not determine our identity, though we can find comfort when our expression conveys a little of who we are as people. When gender expression is flexible, it becomes playful, having defused from the judgmental rules stating what men or women can or cannot wear, share, or express. However, when we become rigid, gender expression becomes a very stiff, serious subject. Perhaps we feel uncomfortable with "abnormal" dress or behavior, or perhaps we feel compelled to look or behave a certain way to combat the hardships of being an invisible minority. In consequence, contemporary Western society has developed cisnormative, transnormative, and queer-normative rules of expression gender variant people may or may not fuse with, presenting all kinds of dissonance and fashion faux pas.

Gender expression can take on more importance than we'd sometimes like to give it, especially in societies that do not visually recognize nonbinary or gender nonconforming people. In the absence of nonbinary gender frames, gender variant people are often misgendered, even by well-meaning friends and family who just "forget" or "space" on our pronouns. Trying to prevent this, the androgynous and gender neutral may develop gender expressive rules as well, avoiding the feminine hour-glass figure, or the upside-down triangle of masculine fashion. This effort to articulate, demonstrate, or present ourselves may take up a disproportionate amount of time, energy, focus, and concern. Like a single person trying to fight a whole army, tension, fatigue, and emotionality can run high if we're focused on an external solution to a societal problem. Exhausted, resilience can drop, leaving us feeling highly sensitive and fused to judgment, either of ourselves for having failed the norm, or of others for trying to reinforce it. Traditional gender expressions, roles, and archetypes, even if they're enjoyed and appreciated by others, may be seen as offensive or threatening, eliciting anxiety or disdain.

> "God help them if they expect me to wear a dress!"
>
> "I saw a picture of myself as a little kid in overalls and Wellington boots and it was cute, I guess, but I just... I tore it in half. I just couldn't look at it."
>
> "I am so fucking tired of having to correct people all the goddamn time. Can't one person, just one person, see me for what I am?"

For some, gender expression is personified creativity, a way to communicate a little about ourselves and our resonance, yet it can also be a means of gaining social worth, donning emotional armor, or using social camouflage. If left unchecked, gender expression can become a sticking point of contention between our conceptual self and our social expression. As fashion so often ties to body uneasiness and gender dysphoria, it's not something we can simply discard. Noticeably, gender expression is the most daily and visibly recognizable form of cisgender privilege. Gender variant people often go to great lengths to find clothes that fit our dimensions or express our gender accurately, overcoming judgmental cashiers and snarky window-shoppers just to buy a new dress. Curious and quizzical children react to genders they're not familiar with, or thin their eyes at gender diversity as their parents panic to move them away, avert their gaze, or politely change the subject. Job sites may overlook, rule out, or "misplace" our résumés, stating that we wouldn't be a "good fit." And should we get the job, employers may later skip over our promotion, not knowing how to "market" gender variant employees, or believing that their clientele would be averse to us. Even friends may not invite us to certain public events to "protect" us from controversy, when all along they were protecting themselves from embarrassment or discomfort. And just as people stereotype the preferences, skills, and capabilities of men and women, gender variant people may be ruled out of certain activities because "they don't look like they would like that sort of thing." And let's not even get into the bathroom debacle!

Gender expression can carry a lot of emotional charge and real-world consequence should we deviate from social norms. As our hierarchical frames struggle with pluriformity, each new cultural and generational cohort either knowingly or unknowingly develops restrictive rules and normative expectations (Zandvliet, 2000). The only question left is whose norms we're trying to adhere to or break from, as gender variant people have to simultaneously sift through *cisnormative*, *transnormative*, and *queer-normative* rule sets.

## *Cisnormative expression*

Seeking recognition and belonging, we often fuse with cisnormative gender expression. Men are deemed handsome, their expression is idealized as a chiseled, muscular form and a proud swagger. Great emphasis is placed on upper body strength, shoulder breadth, and body hair. Body language is expansive, claiming space while restricting hand articulation. Cisnormative men may point or raise a fist, but excessive hand movements are deemed effeminate. In this hierarchical binary, women are deemed beautiful, their expression is idealized as a curvaceous form and elegant grace. Emphasis is placed on youthful image, sex appeal, fashion, and accentuating makeup. Body language is restrictive, drawn inwards, taking less space while articulating more with their hands.

Anyone rolling their eyes at this point isn't alone, as even cisgender people deal with the unnecessary pressure of conforming to these stereotypes. Traditional gender roles, marketed body types, and perfectionist beauty standards can feel imprisoning for men and women as well as anyone between or outside of those categories. For many, cisnormative gender expressions can be an obstacle, an ideal or both, as perfectionist standards are impossible to attain.

## *Transnormative expression*

Those in transition may use cisnormative gender roles and their associated modes of expression as a means of affirming identity and gaining recognition. The assumption that this is a mandatory rule for transitioning men or women, trans people, or any gender variant person, is what's known as being *transnormative*. As the medical model placed so much emphasis on transition, the transnormative narrative stresses the importance of HRT and SRS. Though both can reduce dysphoria, especially for people who identify as transsexual (Gijs and Brewaeys, 2007; Smith *et al.*, 2005; WPATH, 2011), clinicians can inadvertently reinforce this transnormative narrative when they believe transition is the only treatment for gender variant people (Zandvliet, 2000). Additionally, transnormative gender expression has traditionally emphasized not only the same image standards as cisnormative gender expression, but also gender variant invisibility. Passability becomes a transnormative goal and in turn an idealized pressure (Pusch, 2005; Spade, 2006; Zandvliet, 2000). As a set of rules, transnormativity inaccurately assumes that all trans people adhere to stereotypic gender expressions, and in turn that all gender variant people seek a binary transition. When this perspective is carried by gender variant people, we may feel a social pressure to transition, or else reject the very idea of transition, thinking it's a form of selling out to a mainstream narrative (Bockting *et al.*, 2006; Serano, 2016).

## *Queer-normative expression*

On the whole, gender variant individuals in the West often, but not always, lean toward social constructionist views, permitting a more fluid view of sex and gender (Nagoshi *et al.*, 2012). Yet even with such a relativistic construct, black and white thinking can still come into play, leading us to typify the atypical and make even gender variant schemas rigid and inflexible. Adhering to cultural memes of a certain generational or geographic point in LGBTQ history, we may feel like we have to look a certain way to be "read" as gay, lesbian, nonbinary, or transgender. Much like ethnocultural differences in gender expression, there are uniquely queer masculinities and femininities generated from the Western LGBTQ movement over the past century (Halberstam, 2005). For gender variant individuals, both hetero-and homonormative gender expression can be a source of inspiration, complication, or strife, depending on our self-actualization process. Bears, butches, bois, leather daddies, femmes, twinks, and fairies all intersect sexuality and gender, creating queer-normative body images and performance scripts we may align, misalign, or desire to align with, if not reject or redefine. As queer communities often blur or outright challenge binary scripts, some may also clash with transsexual identities that adhere to binary gender roles, while others may totally accept them as part of a perceived continuum (Serano, 2016).

Admittedly, in the early stages of the coming out process, some may experiment with hierarchical gender constructs, overcompensating in dress or body language to gain recognition. To put this growing point in perspective, cisgender teenagers stereotype gender expression all the time, playing with *athletic boy* and *sassy girl* cliques. It's quite typical for people to focus on or accentuate a single facet of their identity or self-image as it develops. Fashion, form, expression, and popularity may take on incredible importance during this trial period of self-discovery.

Following both queer and transgender theory, socially constructed aspects of identity, including gender roles and their corresponding value associations, intersect and integrate with our self-schema and relationship with our body (Nagoshi and Brzuzy, 2010). Yet should rules, reasons, judgments and roles fuse with our gender expression, how we look and act become a mandatory uniform. Even if we genuinely and authentically align with these mannerisms, fashions, and social behavior, we may begin to feel constrained as we get older and find our aging bodies and nuanced gender constructs no longer fit our conceptual self. When we believe we "have to play along" with a social norm because "that's just the scene," or "that's just the way it is," or because "that's what other people like," then our expression no longer serves us. If anything, we're captive to a norm, and have limited our actual expression.

These stereotypic rules are distinct from our gender role, as it's quite possible to fulfill a gender role without them (Table 5.7). However, when they combine, they impact all of the associations comprising our gender schema. The more concrete rules we have, the more rigid our gender roles become, and the more judgmental we are toward those who don't fit the mold, including ourselves.

**Table 5.7 Gender rules, roles, and stereotypes**

| Gender expressive rule | Gender role | Stereotype |
|---|---|---|
| Modern women should speak their mind | Mother | Modern mothers speak their mind |
| Women should be meek | Wife | Wives are meek |
| Women should be beautiful | Daughter | Daughters are beautiful |
| Modern men should be sensitive | Father | Fathers are sensitive |
| Men should be loud | Husband | Husbands are loud |
| Men should have short hair | Son | Sons have short hair |

Outside of these familial gender roles, the LGBTQ community has a number of sexual and body image scenes that, while not gender roles per se, link gender expression to socially appraised performances (See Table 5.8). These stereotypes are just as bogus and inaccurate as the sexist and cissexist stereotypes above, yet the stress of queer gender roles may be compounded by the pressure to be visible, accepted, and respected as a sexual and gender minority.

**Table 5.8 Queer gender rules, roles, and stereotypes**

| Gender expressive rule | Queer gender role | Stereotype |
|---|---|---|
| Men should be funny | Bear | Bears are funny |
| Men should be stubborn | Drag king | Drag kings are stubborn |
| Women should be thin | Drag queen | Drag queens should be thin |
| Lesbians should have short hair | Butch | Butch lesbians have short hair |
| Agender people should be visible | Androgyne | Agender people look androgynous |

As symbolic archetypes, stereotypes may work within a very specific context, outside of which such broad generalities don't apply, even when we believe them. Insidiously, even when we don't believe these thoughts, and disprove them to ourselves, they can still haunt us from time to time, leading us to compare ourselves to standards we don't agree with. We may feel like we have to act or look a certain way in order to fit in, stand out, or play the part as we understand it, or we may find ourselves at odds with the normative image of the scene as it's presented, adding to our experience of exclusion.

> "I'm gay but I don't like gay culture, and I feel like nobody knows unless I act femme."

> "Look—in this world, you're not a woman unless you look like a woman!"

> "Of course, I was the one that got decked. Being butch means I run defense."

Much like working through denial, we must start with our willingness to open up, as defusing from gender performative behavior means revealing our multifaceted self. When we use gender expression to fit in or flag others of a similar disposition, sexual orientation, or social scene, we may feel we have to be a model, leading us to hit the gym, buy the clothes, get the haircut, and clone the look of our times.

### *Self-expression*

As a trans woman, Hannah feels proud of her self-actualization process, having started HRT when she was 16, and undergone genital reconstructive surgery when she was 24. She feels comfortable with her body most of the time, but recently she's expressed a fear of cutting her hair. Although she's accepted by her friend group, she's looking for a visible way to show people she's gay, as she's been looking for a girlfriend for a few years now and is starting to think people overlook her. For the first time in many years, however, she's worried that people will mistake her for a man if she cuts her hair short. Despite introducing the subject in session as "no big deal," Hannah's reasoning becomes quite dramatic, as she desires facial reconstructive surgery to ensure no one will mistake her for a man, so she can get a haircut, so people will think she's a lesbian. Laying her thoughts out in order, Hannah cringes at herself, feeling embarrassed for even bringing it up. Practicing her ongoing defusion exercise (*Yes, and…*) Hannah acknowledges that she's embarrassed, and safe to talk about it, and feeling neurotic, and lonely, and hopeful, and determined to find someone. Hannah goes on to explain that she does wear rainbows, but most just assume it's because she's part of the transgender community.

Hannah's unmet needs are twofold, as she desires love and validation for her sexual orientation. As you explore Hannah's process, it's clear that looking a certain way is just a means to an end, as asking if she would cut her hair if she had a girlfriend causes her to shrug. This doesn't minimize the issue by any means. For invisible minorities, *flagging* includes both intentional and unintentional modes of expression that convey our sexual or gender identity. This can include anything from fashion, to body language, types of eye contact, and communication style. Types of flagging differ between geographical and generational cultures, meaning some people naturally align with the homonormative cues, while others do not. To make things more complex, unless one is connected to the LGBTQ community, no amount of flagging can guarantee connection. Turning on a dating app doesn't mean much if we're the only gay person for a hundred miles. Hannah is connected to the LGBTQ community as a whole, but she has not yet been able to engage, create, or even encounter a lesbian community. There are few social spots specifically catering to women, let alone lesbians, but a little online resourcing identifies an annual camp-out where Hannah is hoping to make at least a few queer, female friends.

If our gender expression is used as camouflage, we may still be wrestling with points of disclosure. It's still possible to practice value-congruent gender expression in private by experimenting with clothes, body language, and cadence that resonates with authenticity and comfort. As a clinician, you're not seeking to strip our camouflage, or pressure us to be our "true self," as such messages only reinforce a black/white, true self/false self dichotomy. When we no longer fight our temptation to hide, we can practice accepting our fear and "letting things be." For example, long before building the nerve to come out, some may have to expand past denial and overcompensation.

When the lads asked Terry, who hates football, if he's going to the match, Terry jumps in and says yes because he doesn't want the lads to think he's less of a guy. Next thing he knows, he's in a screaming stadium having a miserable time, wearing a scarf for a team he doesn't even care about. Instead of Terry playing the part to protect his manliness, help him observe his feelings of inadequacy without reacting to them. By just letting things be, Terry can check in with what he really wants—which is to go home and watch *RuPaul's Drag Race* with his friend Sarah. Before we get to honesty, we sometimes have to move away from our impulse to lie, and give permission to ourselves for giving ambivalent, if vague, answers for a time. Five years later, Terry has tits and goes by the name Catharine, and all the girls want Catharine to come out dancing and she says yes because she feels it's expected of her. Next thing she knows, she's in a noisy club with an overpriced cocktail, being hit on by the old lads who don't even recognize her, when all she really wants is to go home and watch *RuPaul's Drag Race* with her wife Sarah. Once again, Catharine's learning how letting things be is perhaps far less stressful than lying, even if she's not yet ready to be honest or transparent.

Tired from camouflage, a gender vacation may be in order. Gender vacations visit a safe space where we can play, explore, experiment, and actualize our presentation far away from our cisnormative community or place of work. This can be a weekend retreat alone, though community support is definitely encouraged, as a visit to gender supportive friends can be very empowering. Yet even on these vacations, we can hear echoes in our head, having internalized all the old playground accusations and street-side heckles.

"That's a girl's shirt. You can't wear a girl's shirt!"

"Seriously, never wear that. You look like a bearded lady."

"You can't get away with that! It's too femme."

Can fabric have a gender? Only that which a culture imposes on it, which is why we rarely see men in lace outside of the 1800s period-piece dramas. Flannel is another unique example, so let's unbutton an old stereotype. In the 1940s the lesbian community adhered to certain gender norms, often pairing the butch with the femme, which was later scrutinized by the feminists of the 1960s, who accused them of perpetuating a patriarchal stereotype in the same way transsexual men and women are often accused of perpetuating cisnormative roles today (Bockting *et al.*, 2006; Halberstam, 1998; Inness, 1997). Flower power lesbians and young gay radicals began favoring androgyny, slowly giving rise to the *boi* image, sporting boyish haircuts, hiking boots, and the tell-tale flannel shirt (Inness, 1997). A masculine garment associated with bearded lumberjacks and mountain men, the flannel shirt was a way of conveying rugged independence. A fun way to subvert cisgender norms, it soon became a great way of flagging sexuality to others. For some actualized men, now looking back, it was also the early stages of gender questioning, gender testing, and gender experimentation.

Fabric, fashion, and form have as much power as we give it, and it changes in a very quick amount of time. The *Flannel shirt* exercise can be visualized with any stereotypic fashion statement indicative of our pressure to conform: v-neck shirts, tight pants, leather jackets, combat boots, flowy garments, pink ribbons, blue jeans, baseball caps, anything symbolic of the gender expression we feel stuck with. Perhaps it's that dress we bought but never looked right in, or maybe it's that vintage smoking jacket our dad used to wear that we associate with toxic masculinity. For this version, we'll use the aforementioned flannel shirt.

Imagine wearing that affronting flannel shirt. With eyes closed, really picture it. What color is it? Is it short sleeve, long sleeve, torn sleeve, or rolled up? Is it buttoned or completely open? Is it old and musty or brand new from the store? Is it itchy? What face do we make when we envision wearing it? What emotions come up? It's okay to laugh and cringe since we're playing with stereotypes, which are the equivalent of mental toys.

Note that there's something wrong with the shirt. It doesn't fit right at all! Does it feel like it's too big or too small? Does it feel really baggy or really tight across the shoulders? Does this even feel like our shirt? Did we pick it out or did someone give it to us? What stereotypes do we associate with it? Imagine finding a tag still attached. It reads: "I'm not allowed to be____." Weird. What are we not allowed to be? Flipping the tag over, the other side reads: "I'm not allowed to show____." What are we not allowed to show?

As we explore our gender expressive rules, let's take a moment to check in with ourselves. Do we want to modify the shirt or get rid of it? If we want to modify it, how can we make it our own. Rip the sleeves off? Shred it? Sew on patches? Tie it in a knot? With these adjustments, do we want to take it off or keep wearing it? If we want to keep wearing it, what do we appreciate about this flannel shirt image? If we decide to take it off, how do we imagine doing so? Do we unbutton it gently or rip off the buttons? Do we throw it on the ground or hang it in the closet for another day?

If we visualize ripping, throwing, hanging, or dropping the shirt, explore how it feels to be without it. What emotions come up? Some may express a kind of relief and appreciation. Others may feel frustrated and defiant, or naked and exposed. Acknowledge these emotions, but let's keep our eyes closed and envision walking to our wardrobe again. Granted the ability to wear whatever we want, with money being no object, what would we wear? How would we like to present ourselves? Let's describe our ensemble and spare no detail. Imagine all the places we could wear this outfit to, and how much fun we could have. Affirming our style, take a moment to reflect on how diverse our expression can be. Think of all the looks, images, and fashions as they pertain to different places and social groups we either belong to or wish to belong to.

Statements like "I have to be____" or "People won't like/accept me if I don't____" focus on a performative rule or expectation—the essentialist flannel shirt. When this is viewed as optional, we may very quickly identify a natural mode of expression, even if we're still hesitant to express it. Saying, "I have to act/dress/look/behave like____" is actually saying, "I'm not allowed to act/dress/look/behave how I want to." This is easily understood when combating hetero-and cisnormative expectations to come out of the closet, yet now we may also have to combat homonormative and transnormative expectations, as well. The *Flannel shirt* exercise is a lead-up. It has far less to do with the shirt now tossed on the floor or hung back up in the closet, and far more to do with that final question: *What do you want to show?* After all, gender expression was never about the clothes, as fashion, form, and behavior are symbolic acts demonstrating how we see ourselves and how we want to be accepted.

If we use gender expression as a form of emotional armor, whether that's a tough-guy, rebellious-queer, or stone butch demeanor, or if we're wearing an emotional mask, trying to hide our tears behind a smile and reapplied mascara, cultivating awareness requires a gentle acceptance of the behavior. For whatever reason we're shielding or masking ourselves, it does no good to judge ourselves for it. As people wear armor to defend against someone else, and people wear masks to please someone else, take extra time to reflect on how we view interrelationships. We may know exactly why we're fronting, or we may be so externally focused that we rarely look within. Try exploring all the situations in which defensiveness comes into play. When do we feel we have to toughen up, or rebel, or turn cold? When do we have to put on a show, or swallow our tears, or put on a smile? The more aware we are of this performance, the more aware we are of being stuck in it, at which point we can begin to assess which needs are being met and which are not, which survival values are in play, and which self-actualization values are on the sideline.

Named Jinghua at birth, Steve was disowned by his family when he cut off his hair in defiance of his father and proclaimed himself a man. As a second generation Chinese-American, Steve laughingly jokes that he named himself after the most masculine patriotic superhero he could think of, yet as the sessions progress it's clear there's a hollowness in his laughter. Steve expresses that he feels not only disowned by his family, but also by his culture, yet not by choice. He flippantly disregards this, changing the subject to poker and humorously musing that he has a gambling problem. Yet over six months of treatment, he retells the story of Jingua's rebellious haircut on four separate occasions, each time forgetting, if not feigning to forget, that he'd told the story before. The story marks the moment Steve became Steve, and though his pride and anger are evident in his voice, his untapped sadness is palpable. When asked if he's ever grieved Jinghua, Steve answers indirectly, telling a story about his grandfather's funeral, and how neither his father nor his mother shed a tear, treating the whole occasion with solemnity and no more.

It takes little prompting to return Steve to that point of fusion where Jinghua brandished the scissors, and for Steve to launch into his anger at his dad; but this time ask Steve to close his eyes and visualize the whole scene like it's a stage. See his father shouting, and his mother biting her thumb, and Jinghua stampeding to the bathroom, and then imagine everyone frozen in place like a photograph. Where is everyone? Mom is in the living room, dad is on the stairs, Jinghua's staring angrily in the bathroom mirror. Dim the house lights, make everything black and quiet except for a single spotlight on Jinghua. Ask Steve to picture their face and ask what Jinghua needed in the moment. As Steve rattles out his need for acceptance and respect and how his family will never give it to him, ask Steve what he can give Jinghua in this moment, if they were standing in front of him like a separate person. Stammering, Steve says forgiveness, as their rebellion had cost them more than they'd expected, and connection, as they've felt lost ever since. With these two points you can begin to help Steve work toward self-forgiveness while fostering his connection to self and culture.

When we conceal, hold back, or shield an aspect of ourselves from judgment, it may be worth reviewing our company and the quality of our support network. Should they seem trustworthy, then we're probably fused to our own fear of rejection. Yet if they really don't provide us with opportunities for emotional honesty, we may need to expand our social group.

Once more, you're not attempting to disengage gender expressive social armor. At no point encourage us to be "more sensitive" or "less tough," as our demeanor is tasked with protecting our nature. Yet bodyguards are not the same as prison guards, and when our demeanor neglects our nature, it backfires against us. By expanding our awareness to our neglected emotional process, we can incorporate and express multiple sides of ourselves without compromising or jettisoning the others. Old punks are still rebellious at heart, long after the last mosh pit, and Goths can still appreciate tortured existentialism while driving their two kids to basketball practice. Correspondingly, we can value and express our gentleness without compromising our masculinity, we can wear a dress without compromising our genderqueerness, and we can still be a woman in torn blue jeans. Later, as we begin to experience ourselves as a multifaceted whole, the felt pressure around passability, self-image, and fitting in may begin to lift, allowing us to inhale self-appreciation and exhale relief (Zandvliet, 2000).

## Value-congruent self-actualization

Courage, self-compassion, authenticity, and commitment bring us progressively toward physical self-actualization. This can be an empowering experience, and a grieving process of severance in every emotional and literal sense. In no uncertain terms, the body is changed, altered, and adjusted to align with our resonating self. Yet how do we know if we're ready, and is it the clinician's place to assess our readiness or vouchsafe us for HRT or gender alignment surgery?

When clinicians indiscriminately plug gender variant people into a transsexual narrative, making body management through HRT, surgery, clothing, hair, and so on a primary focal point, they neglect what is otherwise a very personal and very individual growth process (Finn and Dell, 1999). Transition is central to many transsexual men and women, yet it's only one of many gender narratives. More to the point, cissexism rejects gender variant people's bodies, albeit nonbinary or in transition. Public discourse whispers about beauty in one ear and shouts cissexism in the other, impacting, influencing, and even regulating our private relationship with our bodies (Finn and Dell, 1999). Should clinicians become gatekeepers to medical treatment, the power differential may actually prevent us from being genuine and honest in session (Bess and Staab, 2009; Poteat *et al.*, 2013; Rachlin, 2002; Singh and Burnes, 2010). As a survival mechanism, many clients learn how to "read a room," adjusting disclosure to meet the clinician's standards for recommendation (Reicherzer *et al.*, 2011). If we believe you won't help, we'll probably ditch you and find a clinician who will, or even fly to a surgeon in Bangkok without any therapeutic assistance at all.

WPATH's (2011) *Standards of Care for the Health of Transsexual, Transgender, and Gender Nonconforming People*, Volume 7 (SOC) permits far more room for clients and clinicians to develop a therapeutic goal on a timeline reasonable to our transition. For many years the Harry Benjamin International Gender Dysphoria Association (HBIGDA) presented guidelines for the real-life experience (RLE). As a therapeutic process, the RLE asked clients to live as our preferred gender role for a minimum of three months before therapists should consider HRT, and a minimum of one year for surgeons to consider performing phalloplasty, metoidioplasty, or vaginoplasty (HBIGDA, 2001). The RLE, however, presented a number of unique problems, especially for clients in hostile, transphobic environments, and for those who don't fit gender role stereotypes. It also required therapy, which left many feeling pathologized (Ekins and King, 1998; Rachlin, 2002; Raj 2002). Working around this for reasons of autonomy, dignity, or necessity, gender variant people would seek surgical procedures abroad, or even fake letters of recommendation to receive HRT or SRS. Additionally, some researchers found that clients who didn't bother with the RLE did not report higher rates of regret (less than 1%) or suicide amongst post-op clients (Lawrence, 2001).

Now, WPATH's SOC focuses less on time constraints, allowing clinicians to recommend HRT and gender alignment surgery provided we're living in an identity congruent to the gender we're transitioning to, have the capacity to understand the risks of treatment, can make a fully informed decision, and have any present mental health concerns reasonably managed (Rachlin and Lev, 2013; Selvaggi *et al.* 2012; WPATH, 2011). A recommendation for gender alignment surgery involves: a complete history of our gender actualization; a clinical rationale to support our request for surgery; the history of our therapeutic relationship, including how long we've worked together and what therapeutic modality was employed in session; a diagnostic and psychosocial assessment (some clinicians submit the Gender Identity Questionnaire, or the Transgender Identity Survey); a statement of informed consent signed by the client; and a statement that the clinician is available to coordinate care as needed (Bockting *et al.*, 2004; WPATH, 2011). The World Professional Association for Transgender Health has a template example for this letter in their SOC.

This letter of recommendation for genital reconstructive surgery can be written according to the clinician's best judgment (Bess and Staab, 2009). And therein lies the crux, as judgment can be swayed by cisgender bias or transnormative expectations. As always, you must challenge your own biased expectations, as even well-trained, trans-positive therapists—who may even be gender variant themselves—may give pause with certain eager or urgent clients. Hyperfocusing on transition is not uncommon for gender variant individuals, as it demands great deliberation, conviction, emotional labor, and monetary expense. Yet you may feel concerned if your client seems to avoid the intrapersonal process. Remarks like "Things will be better when..." or "Once I transition, I'll be able to..." or "I'll be more confident after my surgery" demonstrate a form of conditional thinking, placing transition on a pedestal. Yes, transition is correlational with increased esteem and reduced dysphoria, yet self-actualization is a holistic process building life satisfaction through value-congruent action in every personal, social, occupational, and even spiritual circle.

Areas of concern for gender specialists writing recommendations for HRT or gender alignment surgery include: psychological instability and severe psychiatric issues, in particular personality disorders; isolation from or lack of contact with gender variant people; introversion leading to a lack of social and survival skills; an unwillingness to be open with family; disinterest in self-education; a pressing desire to rush to transition; and ongoing substance abuse (Rachlin and Lev, 2013). Note that most clients, by the time we elect HRT or gender alignment surgery, are highly capable of making an informed decision (Bockting *et al.*, 2006; Rachlin and Lev, 2013). Instead of demanding psychological health, which will prompt us to put our best foot forward or flat out lie to meet the gatekeeper's standards, you can help psychologically distressed clients develop a workable approach to transition by drawing out a matrix (Leonard and Grousd, 2016; Reicherzer *et al.*, 2011). When the inherent physical, emotional, and monetary strain of surgery is normalized, it becomes easier to see how short term away-moves like substance abuse or social isolationism distance us from what's most important.

Value congruence can help gauge stability, emotional resilience, and ability to adjust post-procedure. When it comes to self-actualization, we may have experimented with gender expression both privately and publicly, and may have a lot to unpack in this area. In these narratives we encode a range of value constructs, evident in how we cope with stress and interact with the world around us. The presence of stress and struggle should not be a deterrent to recommendation, as it's unreasonable to expect us to be free of anxiety or depression when we feel at odds with our own body or in conflict with society. However, future-focused, solution-oriented clients are often the most determined, the shadow of which being impatience and expectation. The goal-focused individual may overestimate personal readiness, or underestimate the emotional toll, pressing you to hurry things along. Rather than call this out, or try to deflate the importance of transition, you can help expand awareness to check in on a holistic level. Unlike RLE, which emphasized gender expression as a test of emotional resilience, value congruence explores the deep, underlying motivators we engage to live a fulfilling life. Undoubtedly, this includes how our values relate to gender expression, yet also how we meet our emotional, social, monetary, and physical needs.

In essence, using gender presentation as a measure of readiness pressures us to perform, whereas exploring our alignment to our most salient values observes our adaptability, mental flexibility, emotional resilience, and willing commitment.

Picture two highly feminine trans women going through gender alignment surgery, yet one self-actualizes to commit to their sense of authenticity, while the other does so hoping to escape their insecurity. Now picture one highly feminine trans woman, with both thoughts wrestling in her head. She wants to eradicate her fear in order to be authentic. This is where defusion can be of great benefit; as both her emotional process and her personal values are valid, she just needs to practice defusing from one in order to align with the other.

As a mindful way to approach self-actualization, which can seem too large or abstract to grasp, a matrix lets us highlight how we want to proceed by recognizing what holds us back (see Figure 5.9). Mapping our intrusive thoughts about anatomy, body image and fear of persecution, it becomes easier to understand our stuck cycles of behavior (Leonard and Grousd, 2016). To mindfully explore our options, try asking what life would be like if we we expressed our most authentic self? What would our relationships look like? How would we present ourselves? What would our sex life be like? How would we feel in our bodies? (Leornard and Grousd, 2016). By envisioning this future, we can trace back our steps to what's important.

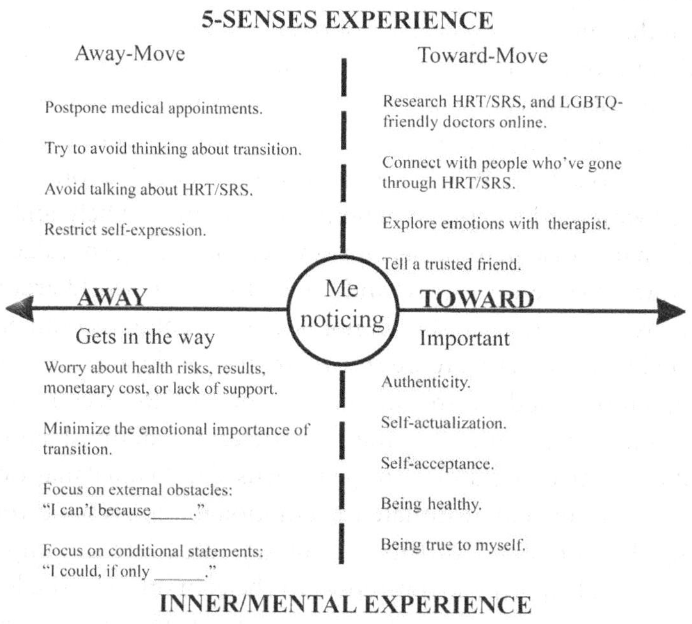


**Figure 5.9** *Gender actualization matrix*

Transition can be exceptionally difficult when we lack support. Defiant, some may rationalize that no one can understand, or that transition has to be done alone. Hopeful, we may fuse to the idea that transition will solve our problems. The *I'm having the thought* and the *Antonym and alternative* exercise can create enough mental space to permit understanding, support, and acceptance, so that self-actualization doesn't teeter on the fulcrum of surgery. Certainly, HRT, SRS, and other forms of surgery get a lot of focus, yet charged points of cognitive-emotional fusion can be found in many aspects of self-presentation, especially for those just beginning to transition. During this stage of development, don't be surprised if whole sessions explore the finer points, and surprising emotional hurdles, of personal grooming habits. To shave or not to shave? To grow our hair or cut it short? How does makeup impact self-worth? Clothes, shoes, and jewelry can all hold charge, and therefore the opportunity to defuse from judgment, accept our resonance, and practice value-congruent self-expression.

Steps toward self-actualization can sometimes resemble models of exposure therapy. You may even invite clients to express openly in session, using your office as a safe place to experiment with presentation. Opportunities for exploration can include everything from how we wear our clothes and groom our hair, to voice training, HRT, facial reconstructive surgery, as well as top and bottom surgery.

## *Clothes*

Experimenting with gender expression, both privately and publicly, may induce distress, anxiety, and even panic. If we restrict our gender expression, we may spend countless hours perusing shops or browsing the internet before finally purchasing the outfit we've had our eye on for weeks. We may immediately revel in it, or try it on, take it off, try it on, hide it, try it on again, look in the mirror, question, doubt, and then deliberate if it's the kind of thing we'll wear only in private or if we're brave enough to wear it in public. Leaning away from our judgments with mantras like "I am not my thoughts" allows us to notice how one outfit can walk down two competing runways. Perceptibly, the dress is still the same dress, but how we conceptualize ourselves determines whether or not we're *cross-dressing* or *just-dressing*.

To cross-dress is to don the outfits and ensembles of the opposite sex. This can be a lot of fun if it's a carefree action playing with drag or attending a gender-bender ball. For some transvestites it can even be quite erotic, especially in staunch cultures that deem cross-dressing taboo. If, however, cross-dressing is fused to toxic masculinity, those who dress as women are spat on for trying to emulate the "weaker sex," while those who dress as men are shunned as frauds. Donning such clothes for the very first time, we may call ourselves fake, or pathetic, questioning: "What am I doing?" or "Why am I such a freak?"

As long as we feel like we're cross-dressing, then we're cognitively admitting that we're a stranger in a strange land. Statements like "I try and dress *like* a man" or "I *dress up* in women's clothes" further demonstrate this felt notion of appropriation. Saying "I dress *like* a woman" acknowledges that we do not count ourselves as a woman, or we don't pass the criteria for what we believe a woman is. With this mindset, our clothes clad both self and other, like an identity shrouded in an emulation. For drag kings and queens, this relationship with authenticity and compartmentalization is a natural part of the show. Society disdains liars yet praises actors, as we naturally recognize how every performed character is a genuine facet of the self. But if we're in transition we're seeking to integrate, not compartmentalize our identity, and should we feel unstable in our gender we may question if we're a "real" man or woman, or if we're "just a cross-dresser."

Just-dressing occurs when our relationship with gender expression transitions from mimicry to authenticity. We no longer *dress like* a man or woman, because we feel stable *as* a man or woman. We no longer *dress up*, because we feel congruent in our gender. Funnily enough, our clothes may stay the same. Nothing may visually change about our presentation except, perhaps, that we've relaxed into our expression. The term *just-dressing* intones that one is both *just* (fair) and *justified* (correct) in accepting the mundane act of *just* (simply) putting on clothes. Our language begins to shift accordingly as we focus less on what "we want to be" or "wish we were," to "liking the color of these new boots or loving the cut of this new top."

Building a self-expressive wardrobe takes both time, defusion from judgment, and a measure of self-acceptance. We may buy a skirt or a shirt, get it home, try it on, and realize we didn't have the hips or the shoulders to really pull it off. This is not solely a transgender phenomenon, but for gender variant people there's an added pressure. Do we send the outfit back and find something more workable; shrug our shoulders and wear it anyway; adjust our bodies through shapewear, padding, exercise, or surgery to fit the image in our mind; or let go of that image, altogether? There is a distinction between accepting our gender and accepting our body type, after all. Sure, we can wear platform shoes every day in order to keep those trousers that are three inches too long, or we can accept that we're not that leggy and buy equally sexy trousers that also happen to fit. Decisions of this kind are not always simple or clear, especially if we're in transition, as our current existence may be discrepant from what we're trying to be. To lessen this divide, we have to be honest about our current motivator for self-expression. Are we compensating, or working overtime from a place of fear, idealism, or perfectionism? It may be time to reassess our fashion choices. It may be time to graduate from those chaffing bandages to a professionally made binder, or from that stuffed bra to feminine contouring shapewear. Nonbinary people may feel the need to go outside cultural convention to stand out or, if we're tired of our own frames of distinction, we may need to relax and not try so hard. In each case, we can benefit a lot from defusing judgment. For those who adhere to fashion, we're all permitted fashion faux pas. For those who claim their own identity first and foremost, there are no fashion faux pas.

## *Hair*

Hair? What's the big deal about hair? Absolutely nothing, until it means absolutely everything. Having brushed, combed, and kept a certain look for years, there can often be a lot of cognitive–emotional fusion tied into our hair. When people try to touch our hair, we may bat their hand away, worried someone will mess it up. A strand amiss, a hair askew, a curl frayed, too much frizz, not enough volume, too flat, too long, too short, too bald—so many judgments are stuck into our hair like bubblegum! We'll even judge how good or bad our day will be by how our hair looks when we wake up in the morning. There's certainly a lot to defuse from here, so let's talk about *passing* and *presumptuous gender*.

Human beings are phenomenally presumptuous. We don't need complete information to operate. An old Oxford experiment once illustrated how poelpe can raed jmulbed wrods poridved the frsit and lsat lteters are the smae (Rawlinson, 1976; Rayner *et al.*, 2006). We look for context over content to such a degree that most of our assessments are made from periphery scans and silhouettes of form. In many Western cultures, boys have short hair, girls have long hair, men have facial hair and body hair, and women shave it all. There's a long history to the patriarchal subjugation of body hair. Even Ovid, the ancient Roman poet, added a make-up tutorial for women in his how-to-guide *Ars Amatoria* (*The Art of Love*) recommending they shave their legs and armpits so as not to bristle like a goat (1979). And if you want a ludicrous romp through beauty's byproducts, look up a brief history of the merkin. Gender expression and sex identification are braided into hair, and have been for thousands of years, often for many seemingly silly reasons. Today, much like the jumbled letters we scanned to read a sentence, people will scan through a crowd, making instantaneous presumptions about gender based on clothes, body language, and most commonly, hair.

In the 21st century, women wear clothes once deemed traditionally male. In fact, a woman can wear culturally male uniform, swagger in a culturally masculine way, and still be read as a woman if she has a pony tail. Yet should she grow a moustache? It's as if Clark Kent took off his glasses and became Superman. Radical, but true. Sure, some people may focus in and say, "Hey, the letters in this word aren't spelled right" or "Hey, is this some kind of psych test from Oxford?" But for the barely attentive masses moving through the world, the impression has changed the presumptive gender.

"Would you like some coffee, *sir*?"

"Excuse me, *Mister*, I think you dropped this."

"Hey *fella*, nice moustache."

Presumptive gender isn't our actual gender, it's just what the masses think we are. If their presumption aligns with our actual gender, then we feel as though we "passed." But if our goal isn't "passing," which is often the case for the nonbinary person, then we feel projected on, yet again.

Even without transitioning genders—a quick shave or a new haircut garners attention. Even wearing our hair a little differently because it's wet from a shower will elicit comments from friends and co-workers not used to our hair being down. Just as we have our own gender schemas and body maps, we also maintain body maps for other people. Physical frames of distinction allow us to spot our friends and family even from a distance, just by their stance or silhouette. More than this, we begin to fuse judgments to hairstyles, creating stereotypic inferences like, "I'd never date a guy with a man bun," or "The guy with the goatee's always the villain," or "The guy with the goatee, man bun combo is clearly a hipster villain."

Hair can carry an emotional and therefore ceremonial symbolism. We may chop our hair when we grieve, go to war, or make a lifelong change. We tie memories and identities into our hair like ribbons and beads. When emotions are fused with self-image, a haircut can be a tearful way of letting go of our childhood, or old beauty standards, or familial gender rules. Defusing from rules is one thing, but emotions linger. The sense of severance can shift progressively to a sense of gain, as we move from exploring what we're letting go of to what we're stepping into. Hair magic is ancient. Cultures around the world have tied, weaved, and braided prayers, spells, and intentions into their hair. Hair is the most personally stylized way to show we're rugged, tough, sleek, clean, vivacious, sexy, natural, or authentic. These driving values are important as many gender variant people go above and beyond when it comes to hair care, from testosterone cream to grow moustaches, to thousands of dollars on electrolysis to remove body hair, to hair implants and extensions to cover bald spots. Then there's the emotional cost. The looks, the comments, and the judgments, from friends and family, to absolute strangers, to children wondering if we're boys or girls. Do we answer, do we educate, do we simplify, do we clarify, or do we smile and walk away?

Yes, hair means nothing until it means absolutely everything.

## *Voice training*

The easiest and perhaps most cringeworthy way to illustrate fusion to critical self-judgment is to play back a recording of your own voice. Ever listen to yourself in a video or on an answering machine? Ever hit the off-button as fast as you can? Phenomenologically, bone conduction makes our voices sound differently inside the chamber of our skull, so when we hear a recording it seems odd, foreign, and weird (Mills and Stoneham, 2017). Now imagine that same dissonance coming to the forefront of your attention every time you hear your own voice, whether it's recorded or not.

Not all gender variant people feel voice-discrepant, yet it can be a self-alienating experience if we do. Speaking sparingly or softly mumbling, we may avoid our own voice, or try not to think about it. If so, speech therapy can become an emotionally therapeutic intervention as well as a powerful step toward self-actualization (Carew, Dacakis, and Oates, 2007; Dacakis, Oates, and Douglas, 2012; Hancock and Garabedian, 2013; Martin, 2007; Van Borsel *et al.*, 2000). HRT can help to lighten or lower register, more so for trans men attaining a deeper resonance, but the rise or drop in pitch from HRT is not dependable (Adler, Hirsch, and Mordaunt, 2012; Martin, 2007; Van Borsel *et al.*, 2000; Van Borsel, De Cuypere, and Van den Berghe, 2001). Some MtF clients may undergo a tracheal shave in order to sound more feminine; yet surgery comes with both monetary and emotional costs, and even if we undergo treatment, we will still need to relearn our register. Some medical professionals even warn against surgery to adjust voice modulation, as cricothyroid approximation is rarely satisfactory as it decreases vocal range and can negatively impact voice quality and volume (Asscheman and Gooren, 1992; Martin, 2007).

This means it's time to exercise our voices! Encourage clients seeking voice modulation to find a professional vocal coach or speech–language pathologist (Clark, 2016; Davies and Goldberg, 2006). However, many of us can't afford one, live in rural areas where there is no vocal coach, or find that speech trainers in our area don't specialize in feminizing, masculinizing, or gender neutralizing voice inflection. Ever resourceful, some practice with the help of videos on the internet, or practice vocal range while driving the car, or privately emulate the speech patterns of actors, actresses, friends, and family (Davies and Goldberg, 2006). As a mindfulness exercise, help us note points of emotional resonance in our literal resonance. Who are our vocal templates? Who do we want to sound like?

Don't worry if voice training isn't in your therapeutic skillset, as you can still help us explore our relationship with progress. A therapeutically confidential office can be an amazing soundproof room to both practice training and process doubt. In the beginning, warm-up and cool-down exercises are needed to prevent vocal fatigue, meaning you can help the impatient build awareness around physical self-care (Adler *et al.*, 2012). Even in session, have us practice the tension-releasing exercises most speech pathologists introduce to relax our jaw, tongue, neck, shoulder and larynx (Adler *et al.*, 2012). Feminizing a voice calls for vocal flexibility, expanding range while maintaining voice quality when talking, laughing, singing, and even coughing and clearing one's throat (Davies and Goldberg, 2006). On the other hand, diaphragmatic breathing in a stable speaking posture can help masculinize a voice by amplifying sound and supporting a deeper chest voice (Adler *et al.*, 2012).

Clients keen to practice can find this exciting, as there are so few willing to sit down and listen to the literal highs and lows of our voice! Yet others may need to defuse from a lot of judgment to proceed. How people talk carries a lot of social pressure. Accents are subjected to classism. Speed of communication is incorrectly associated with intelligence. Pronunciation and enunciation are subjected to racial discrimination. Huskiness of voice is subjected to generational criticism and slut shaming. There's a lot of harsh fodder for cognitive–emotional fusion, even without gender! As the desire to sound a certain way often ties into an associated gender schema, we may judge ourselves for sounding too masculine or feminine, or for not sounding masculine or feminine enough.

Voice training is far less about sounding like a man or woman, and far more about harmonizing with ourselves and finding our optimal pitch and comfortable bandwidth (Adler *et al.*, 2012; Mills and Stoneham, 2017). Yes, there are vocal stereotypes like stiff masculine mouth movements, articulate feminine mouth movements, uptalk intonation, lisps and vocal fry, yet these are more indicative of a person's personality and character. Gender is usually distinguished by frequency and resonance, with men falling between 65 and 260 hertz with a chest voice, and women between 100 and 525 hertz, using a broader range than men, often with a higher head voice (Adler *et al.*, 2012; Clark, 2016; Hancock and Garabedian, 2013). That said, notice the huge overlap in pitch. The distinctions between masculine, feminine, and gender neutral voices are often very subtle. Spotting this, the *genderedness* of a voice is emphasized by our word choice, articulation, nonverbal facial expressions, hand gestures, body language, and culturally gendered conversational style (Clark, 2016; Van Borsel *et al.*, 2000).

Voice training, as a practice in patience, is easily undermined by critical self-doubt. Matthew Mills and Gillie Stoneham present the inherent mindfulness in voice training in their guide *The Voice Book for Trans and Non-Binary People* (2017). Focusing in, we often get caught trying to balance what we want to sound like with our worry about other people's judgments (Mills and Stoneham, 2017). Defusing from these critical thoughts, we can focus in on our breath and the memory of our target pitch, acknowledge the vulnerability and the requisite courage, and then connect with what we want to convey (Mills and Stoneham, 2017). In this exercise, it's important to *focus out*, expanding awareness from our own critical self-judgment to the listener we're engaged with. Rather than fret about what they may or may not be thinking, focusing out allows us to connect as verbal, nonverbal, and paralinguistic cues all align us with the person we're talking to (Mills and Stoneham, 2017). Voice tuning is inherently vulnerable, as it's a mindful interaction between two or more people; as such it's worth identifying people we can actively practice with.

## *Hormone replacement therapy*

Gender variant people often feel relief when we begin HRT, in part because we're empowering self-actualization, and in part because hormones can influence both mood and temperament. Those taking testosterone sublingually, or through injections, or through patches, sometimes report an increased boost in confidence, competitiveness, and aggression, which can also lead to "brooding" or "moodiness," when a client feels stifled (Archer, 1991; Van de Poll and van Goozen, 1992; WPATH, 2011). Those who take anti-androgens in order to feminize often report a reduction in these same emotional areas, which can feel relieving. The introduction of estrogen, like estradiol, can increase emotive responses, and clients may report feeling more tearful or emotionally expressive (Slabbekoorn *et al.*, 2001; WPATH, 2011). Evidently, the benefits of HRT are many, as HRT has empirically been proven to reduce stress, body uneasiness, anxiety, and dissociation, while increasing quality of life (Bouman *et al.*, 2016; Colizzi *et al.*, 2013; Colizzi, Costa, and Todarello, 2014, 2015; Costa and Colizzi, 2016; Gómez-Gil *et al.*, 2012; Gorin-Lazard *et al.*, 2013; Newfield *et al.*, 2006).

Yet for all of these emotional turns, the journey to love, embrace, and accept oneself is ongoing, and HRT is no cure for stress. Even if we understand this on an intellectual level, the gravity may only hit us later. Role models are a phenomenal resource for anyone going through HRT, as only those who have gone through this experience can truly speak to it.

Clients on testosterone often find their voice deepens, facial hair grows and becomes coarser, and their libido increases. Biological females may note their clitoris enlarges (up to 4 cm in some cases), a cessation of menses, atrophy of breast tissue, and hirsutism (Feldman and Safer, 2009; Green, 2012; WPATH, 2011). Clients taking feminizing hormones often find that hair thins and grows at a slower pace, their redistributed body fat increases breast hemisphere circumference (up to 12 cm), the nipples and areole enlarge, and their libido reduces with both frequency of erections and a reduction in testicular size (Feldman and Safer, 2009; WPATH, 2011).

There are medical concerns and side effects we will need to consult with our endocrinologist or primary physician about, as hormone regimens influence body fat distribution and therefore cardiovascular disease, and are also filtered through the liver, presenting a number of potential risks (Feldman and Safer 2009; WPATH 2011). Acknowledging this, our readiness to begin HRT need not be subject to severe scrutiny, as we can opt out at any time. It is arguably more dangerous to deny a client HRT, as this pressures us to obtain and self-medicate illegally (Spade, 2006). Fortunately, more and more naturopathic doctors and obstetrician–gynecologists have also begun providing HRT, and branches of Planned Parenthood, operating on an informed consent model, now supply hormones to clients, provided we pass a physical screening (Planned Parenthood, 2018).

De-pathologizing gender variant identities has begun to move the role of gatekeeper from mental health clinicians to medical practitioners (Hale, 2007; Lev, 2009; Singh and Burnes, 2010). Individuals with a stable gender identity should receive prompt consideration for HRT if this is requested; yet should an individual present or express elements of confusion, distress, self-harm or substance abuse, recommendation to a therapeutic gender specialist is best (Lev, 2009; Rachlin and Lev, 2013). More often than not, distress around HRT tends to relate to heightened expectations, or the overall anxiety of beginning transition.

By collaborating with clients, we can assess our hopes, fears, and expectations together. How much do we know about HRT and the outcomes thereof? Are we pursuing physical change, or are we hoping for a less measurable, psychological transformation? A collaborative assessment is especially advantageous for nonbinary clients, whose use of HRT differs greatly from transsexual treatment. Nonbinary clients may be seeking a means of actualizing androgyny or gender neutrality, which HRT can help with, provided all parties involved are able to be transparent about this goal. There are some phenomenal time lapse videos on the internet showing FtM, MtF, and nonbinary people taking hormones for the course of a year. There are also some very honest testimonials on websites like Susan's Place (Susans.org) and Trans Pulse (TransgenderPulse.com), sharing the highs and lows of success and disillusionment, as HRT has its limits.

## *Facial reconstructive surgery*

Of all the medical procedures there are, facial feminization surgery (FFS) and facial masculinization surgery (FMS) present a delicately fragile area of cognitive-emotional fusion. ACT helps us step back from judgment to accept what cannot be changed, but what happens when we *can* change what we judge so harshly? When we're stuck in a gender dysphoric mindset, we may feel an array of shock, surprise, and disgust when accidentally catching ourselves in a reflection. Being so central, physically and psychosocially, the face conveys so much of our verbal and nonverbal content. There is no part of human anatomy as personal as the face, and therefore no area more emotionally potent when dissonance occurs. We'll even fuse arbitrary rules with our face, like "Girls don't have big noses" or "Men don't have weak chins." Yet even if we don't critique ourselves aesthetically, our reflection may take on a surreal sense of otherness.

"It's not my face."

"It feels like I'm hiding in there, somewhere."

"When I look in the mirror, I don't see me."

There are many reconstructive procedures to both masculinize and feminize, from rhinoplasty to jaw and chin contouring, cheek, and forehead augmentations, even thyroid cartilage enhancements to create Adam's apples, and tracheal shaves to remove them. Both surgery and recovery time can present even further dysphoria as the bandaged areas will swell temporarily. Note that a mental health assessment is not required to seek facial reconstructive surgery (Bowman and Goldberg, 2006; WPATH, 2011). Yet if we have brought the subject to a session, then we're already exploring our emotional charge, and may be looking for reassurance.

In complex cases it can be difficult to assess mental preparedness for such procedures, yet a lot can be gauged—not in our relationship with our face—but in our fusion to expectation. Before surgery, daydreams are to be expected, but we may play too much with gender-swapping apps spitting out unrealistic selfies, or else we may spend hours on photo image software, contouring our profile pics to disproportionate dimensions. Differently, we may struggle to imagine what we would look like post-surgery.

It can be incredibly grounding, especially for nonbinary people, to explore the natural androgyny of the human face. As an experiment, try blending, highlighting, or downplaying phenotypes through makeup, facial hair, piercings, clothing, and so on. If the desire for facial reconstructive surgery continues, we may decide to consult a surgeon. This can create another emotionally charged moment, as a specialist will run our photograph through a simulation to demonstrate the outcomes of facial reconstruction, bringing us face to face with anticipatory excitement or stark disillusionment. If we hope to attain an unreasonable beauty standard, or end dysphoria, we may feel dissatisfied or struggle with post-operative adjustment. In any case, emotional charge is to be expected.

## *Body shaping and top surgery*

Body shaping includes a number of surgeries, including hip and buttock augmentation, abdominoplasty, and calf implants, yet perhaps the most common and most emphasized is top surgery. For masculinizing bodies, this looks like a mastectomy whereby the breast tissue is removed. For feminizing bodies, this looks like a breast augmentation, usually involving silicone or saline implants. Though further research is needed to measure pattern of behavior amongst gender variant people's prioritization of medical care, some opt for top surgery before facial or genital reconstruction, especially if they're FtM. This may be because they view the procedure as a less invasive change than facial or genital reconstruction, with less risk of complication, or because of its affordability, or because of a sense of building authenticity.

Top surgery can be an emotionally powerful procedure. Some FtM clients will have spent years chest binding, enduring physical suffering in order to feel authentic. In one of the largest chest binding surveys, involving 1800 respondents from 38 countries, 97 percent reported having at least one or more negative health risks as a result of consistently using compression binding, elastic bandages, duct tape or plastic wrap (Peitzmeier *et al.*, 2017). These included everything from itching to rib fractures, spine changes, shoulder popping, muscle wasting, numbness, headache, fatigue, weakness, lightheadedness, coughs, respiratory infections, heartburn, abdominal pain, digestive issues, breast changes, tenderness, scarring, swelling, acne, skin changes, and infection (Peitzmeier *et al.*, 2017). In all, 53 percent reported back pain, 53.3 percent dealt with overheating, 48.8. percent felt chest pain, 46.6 percent for obvious reasons had shortness of breath, 44.9 percent felt consistent itching, 40.3 percent felt that binding gave them bad posture, and 38.9 percent had correlational shoulder pain (Peitzmeier *et al.*, 2017). Remember this when a young trans man seems to adjust themselves in session, or requests to turn up the air conditioner.

For feminizing bodies, HRT can increase breast size to a limited degree, yet breast implants may provide a level of confidence by potentially, but not necessarily, reducing dysphoria. Such augmentation can shift the emphasis of dimension, as increased breast size can make the waist appear smaller, and shoulders appear less broad. Depending on the body in question, this can be a big step toward making peace with the mirror.

### *Sex reassignment surgery and bottom surgery*

Bottom surgery includes a number of gender alignment procedures altering the genitals, including SRS. The permanence of these procedures can make bottom surgery a powerful and emotionally charged step. Perhaps we've dreamed of this for years, or put it off because we were trepidatious, or worried that the procedures weren't advanced enough, or simply didn't have the cash or the courage. But now the hour is here. We may have even squirreled money away, or we may be flat broke and wondering if our insurance covers it, or how to crowdfund, or ask our parents for money, or take out a loan, or find a professional who has a medical installation plan, or fly to another country where the surgery is cheaper. At $20,000 for just bottom surgery, not including follow-up costs for potential complications or any other transitional procedures, many gender variant people have to weigh transition against other life goals, like investing in a house, being able to afford college, or simply paying the rent.

MtF clients before SRS may elect to have an orchiectomy, removing the gonads to reduce testosterone production, after which estrogen doses can be reduced from anywhere between a third to a half (Martin, 2007). Therapeutically, this can also serve as a mindful precursor to further transition efforts, as such experience can bring to light any potential discomfort with surgery and medical environments. Even if we feel ready to transition, we may not feel comfortable with hospital settings, hesitating to trust even the most professional doctors.

A vaginoplasty constructs female genitalia, and there are a number of differing procedures, from split or full thickness skin grafts, to inverted penile skin flaps, to rectosigmoid vaginoplasty (Kim *et al.*, 2003; Schechter, 2016). Much of this is determined, quite simply, by what the patient has to work with, as size of pre-existing genitalia, age, and even body mass all play a factor. However, an educated decision about the choice of procedure needs to be made, alongside who to elect the procedure from. This latter point often means doing background research on surgeons, reviewing not just their websites but searching through online forums with the hope of connecting with prior patients and their honest testimonials. This can be difficult if we have a language barrier or are naturally introverted.

FtM clients and nonbinary clients with female anatomy may elect to have a hysterectomy, alongside a bilateral salpingo-oophorectomy, removing the ovaries and fallopian tubes. This procedure can greatly reduce dysphoria associated with the menstrual cycle. Elective hysterectomies can also have a unique social impact on a family of origin, as even supportive family members may not grasp the true significance of our gender expression until we're put under the knife. When discussed openly, the emotional ripple around medical procedures can bring families to deeper levels of acceptance, or grieving, or reignite old polarizing arguments.

Phalloplasty is the construction of male genitalia, a long sought-after goal for many trans men. When asked, 81 percent of FtM clients hoped for an aesthetically appealing result when naked, 96 percent of whom wanted a scrotum, 92 percent wanted a distinguishable glans, and 86 percent desired an erection (Hage *et al.*, 1993). However, the surgical procedures required have lagged behind vaginoplasty techniques for decades, and have only recently begun to advance, making it more difficult to find a competent surgeon. One of the most applied techniques is the forearm free flap phalloplasty, which grafts tissue from the forearm to create a shaft, which may require electrolysis to remove hair. Variations of this include the musculocutaneous latissimus dorsi free transfer flap, which uses tissue from the side of the chest and is therefore hairless, and the suprapubic phalloplasty, which uses tissue from around the pubic bone, though it tends to have a less natural appearance. Each technique has pros and cons, including aesthetic results, scar tissue, and differences in sensitivity depending on the nerve concentrations, on top of which each technique often calls for multiple procedures as the phallus needs to heal before being fitted with an erectile prosthesis. This healing process can span over 9 to 12 months—and that's without complications from infections or necrosis. During this time, FtM clients may feel emotionally fatigued and request extra support, or else opt out of therapy for a time only to reemerge months later. In either case, try offering phone or online sessions, spending time reinforcing self-care and emotional backing, especially if they have little to no support.

Knowing the full details of these procedures is worth the added homework, as clients will also be stumbling through medical jargon to make sense of it all. Fortunately, they will be consulting with a trained medical professional about all this, so you need not be an expert on evolving medical procedures. Your therapeutic role is to be mindful of the client's process, and potential to over-process. We may, for example, take it upon ourselves to research at home. While there are many wonderful success stories posted online, there are also sad horror stories complete with pictures. Doubt, fear, and worry, are pretty natural for anyone about to undergo surgery, let alone actualize identity. After years of waiting, we may be very calm and collected, or we may worry about some very legitimate concerns.

> "Will it affect my sex drive? Will I have sensitivity? Will I be able to orgasm? This is one of the biggest decisions in my life and I don't mean to prioritize my sex life over my body, but I am, okay? I'm a woman, I've always been a woman, and I'm scared that if I do this I won't be able to orgasm."

> "I can't believe I'm asking this. This is so embarrassing, but I wonder if my vagina will be deep enough for my lover? He says he'll accept me as I am, but we've never talked about this."

> "Maybe I'm vain, but is it too much to ask for a good-looking cock? Most people don't like the way they look, and there's some ugly ones, but I pay attention. I just don't want an ugly dick. I just want it to look real... I just want it to be attractive. Do other guys think about their own cocks that way?"

As the outcome of every procedure is unique to the person's anatomy, which is in turn influenced by age, body weight, and even the size of pre-existing genitals, such questions have no immediate answer. In many ways this is the precipice of self-actualization and the unknown. Such concerns are intimately personal and very legitimate, so ignoring or trying to *move past* this pre-emptive anxiety is unrealistic. Expansion, however, can help us connect to the excitement in the nervousness, the love in the worry, and the hope in the uncertainty, making room for all. Defusing from comparative frames can also help us own the process, as our concerns are both significant and unique while simultaneously common and normal. Everyone, regardless of gender, scrutinizes their bodies at some point, yet there's an element of genesis and a spark of gamble in gender alignment surgery that cis people do not have or experience. There's a creative imperative tied to an unknown variable, as we're not in complete control of the outcome. Processing this often reveals another spectrum of very practical and equally valid concerns.

> "What if the surgery doesn't go as planned? Will I heal in time to get back to work so I don't lose my job?"

"Do I need to budget for a second surgery? I pulled enough money together to make this work, but I've heard stories. If the doctors tell me I do, I'll just have to go into debt."

"So, I'm really not vain, I swear, but...do you think people will see me differently? Will I see myself differently? Will I regret it?"

These questions often need more case management, so help clients develop a financial calendar with contingency plans. Do we have a family of origin or a family of choice to fall back on? Do we have a safety net in our bank account, or an emergency credit card? How honest are we with our employment? Are we just pretending to have a cold for a week, thereby increasing the risk if something goes wrong? Can we take a temporary leave, and if we can't, are there potential job opportunities in the wings? Throughout all this, we will no doubt have a slew of "I can't" statements, pointing out very real limits of our power alongside internal blocks to defuse from. The most looming thought, of course, is "Will I regret it?"

Post-operative regret is actually quite rare—ranging between less than 1 or 2 percent—and when it does emerge, it tends to reflect a client's disappointment with the outcome, rather than a client's desire to de-transition (Bowman and Goldberg, 2006; De Cuypere *et al.*, 2005; Dhejne *et al.*, 2014; Lawrence, 2001; Smith *et al.*, 2005; van de Grift *et al.*, 2018). A longitudinal study spanning 50 years of transition in Sweden found that only 2.2 percent regretted transition (Dhejne *et al.*, 2014). Echoing this small percent, risk of regret seems to stem from lack of family support, late life transition, and historically poor surgical outcomes, though this regret often alleviates over time (Cohen-Kettenis and Pfäfflin, 2003; Kuiper and Cohen-Kettenis 1988; Landén *et al.*, 1998; Lawrence, 2003). Not to overlook such minorities within the minority, some clients may shift gender many times, attempt de-transition, or harbor regret about coming out, or HRT, or gender alignment surgery.

To pre-emptively address and safeguard against transition regret, clinicians must cultivate an emotionally transparent atmosphere where we can explore, question, and express our own personal narratives through open dialogue. You may also need to provide access to information, and clarity between sex identity and gender identity. The more mental flexibility we can practice, the more adaptable we will be moving forward. Having concerns about regret is a natural part of committing to—what must be treated as—a nonreversible procedure. Once more, ACT can help defuse from judgmental thoughts we harbor against ourselves for having such concerns. If we're still fused with an incongruent gender role or adhering to incongruent gender rules, surgery may not be advisable, as the pendulum is still swinging between two competing conceptualizations of self.

Transition, for something so immense, is a delicate subject swaddled in emotion. Many clients will be adamant about our self-actualization process from beginning, to middle, to end. Yet some may bluff, believing we have to hide our natural uncertainy in order to convince a gatekeeping therapist. Dissonance and resonance go hand in hand. Clarity and confusion are queer bedfellows, and not everyone who begins to self-actualize fully transitions, and not everyone who begins to self-actualize knows this at the start. Our relationship with gender can change, just as we reevaluate our perception of ourselves. This is all part of the journey.

A highly applicable mantra meditation for self-actualizing clients can be found in John Forsyth and Georg Eifert's *The Mindfulness and Acceptance Workbook for Anxiety* (2016). Unlike positive affirmation mantras attempting to reinforce a positive being state through repetition, Forsyth and Eifert's "I am" mantra focuses on *what is* as it exists in the present moment. Unlike positive affirmation mantras attempting to focus on the here and now by uncoupling from the past and future, *what is* includes all the evidence of yesterday and all the potential for tomorrow. This expansion of perspective acknowledges both our inertia and momentum.

Forsyth and Eifert's (2016) mantra begins by asking us to breathe naturally for 20 seconds before thinking the words "I am". Without straining or pushing the thought, or focusing on tempo, rhythm, or internal volume, we repeat "I am" silently to ourselves. Our mantra may drift in the distance, or speed up, or slow down as other thoughts and feelings come into mind. When we notice these thoughts, softly return to the mantra "I am... I am..." Every time a new thought or feeling comes up, gently return to the mantra, repeating this process for ten minutes or so. Take some time with the stillness that follows, sitting quietly with our eyes closed for the next two to three minutes as we settle into our bodies, making contact with our present reality.

As an ancient practice, mantras reinforce and strengthen neural pathways through repetition. Often, positive self-statements that focus on a singular aspect, quality, or value can be susceptible to ironic process (Wood, Perunovic, and Lee, 2009). By contrast, repeating "I am" can be incredibly validating as it includes all that is, was, and could be. "I am" is expansive, inclusive, and open-ended without a conclusive, singular answer. When we practice this "I am" mantra twice a day, we're engaging the constancy of our observational self in the context of any evolving moment (Forsyth and Eifert, 2016). No matter what path to self-actualization we take, no matter what transition options we deliberate, we are and continue to be. This concept can be silly and serious, as engaging an "I am" mantra while looking at breast reduction options online, or thinking "I am" while finally perusing the women's shoe section may seem odd, yet it can also feel quite reassuring. We change, we grow, we transition, we self-actualize, and we permit ourselves to be that which we are every day, making "I am" the most affirmative declaration we could ever speak.

# 6

# Adaptation

When validated and accepted on an individual and communal level, stress, anxiety, and depression amongst gender variant populations remain at developmentally comparable levels to the cisgender majority (Budge, Adelson, and Howard, 2013; Olson *et al.*, 2016). An adequate treatment plan, therefore, includes a holistic comprehension of a client's global functioning as it's influenced by minority stress (ALGBTIC, 2009; Burdge, 2007; Hendricks and Testa, 2012; Reisner *et al.*, 2015; Richards *et al.*, 2016). Depathologizing gender variance, however, doesn't mean our demographic is free of mental health issues, but that our issues may not be intrinsically tied to our gender identity. When we challenge the idea that gender variant individuals inherently suffer esteem or mood disorders, we begin to see a population subjected to an unhealthy medical narrative. Mental health issues can, and often do, arise independently of gender identity, and clients seek therapy for a whole score of intrapersonal and interpersonal reasons (Leonard and Grousd, 2016; Lev, 2004; Rachlin, 2002; Richmond *et al.*, 2012).

Acknowledging this, gender exploration and gender actualization can certainly intersect with our mental health. The complex interplay of stress, depression, anxiety, and even misdiagnosis can certainly factor into our journey toward self-acceptance, personal resilience, and psychological adaptability (Glavinic, 2010; Lev, 2004; Richmond *et al.*, 2012; Shipherd *et al.*, 2010; Singh *et al.*, 2011). A truly holistic, integrative approach to gender affirmative therapy means addressing both ecological and psychosocial concerns, as well as any present and pre-existing mental health issues. Some clients working toward transition may feel this is a distraction or a postponement of our gender alignment, so it's best to frame mental health in the context of gender development, as addressing these issues now will help increase our emotional resilience and life satisfaction (Bockting *et al.*, 2006).

When gender is no longer perceived as a threat to mental health, it becomes possible to explore the complexity of risk-taking behaviors, body dysphoria, depersonalization, derealization, depression, anxiety, trauma, and suicidal ideation without cisgender bias. The following entries are not a comprehensive treatment plan for such mental health issues, but an introduction to how gender identity intersects with mental health, and how to adapt and apply pre-existing ACT techniques for gender variant people with these diagnoses, respectively.

## Old stories and new resources: ACT for risk-taking behavior

Risk-taking behaviors come in many forms, from unsafe sex, to substance abuse, to self-harm, extreme dieting and disordered eating, to dangerous thrill-seeking. Finding the positive intent in risky behavior reframes even the unhealthiest of actions as an attempt to reduce tension in order to cope with or evade stress and trauma (Batten and Hayes, 2005; Briere, 2006; Richmond *et al.*, 2012; Rowe *et al.*, 2015). Mundane, daily acts of discrimination increase self-harm and risk-taking behaviors amongst gender variant populations (Miller and Grollman, 2015; Clements-Nolle, Marx, and Katz, 2006). To challenge the longstanding assumption that transgender people are psychologically fragile (neurotic, hysteric, narcissistic, sissy, pansy, confused, etc.), observe how openly gender nonconforming and visibly transgender people are targeted, ridiculed, and antagonized. Sadly, gender variant people are often torn down through direct trauma, or emotionally worn down over time, increasing the likelihood of such desperate measures (Miller and Grollman, 2015). Bombarded by prejudice, the agenda of emotional control engages risk-taking behavior to either distract from or control our feelings. This is not always a conscious process, as avoidant behaviors are often impulsive and reactionary.

This risk-taking behavior is correlational with depression, anxiety, and the cissexist psychosocial stressors impacting self-esteem (Mizock and Lewis, 2008; Nemoto *et al.*, 2004; Richmond *et al.*, 2012; Xavier, 2000). Yet the impact of minority stress can be hard to see at a rave, amidst all the sweat, and MDMA and vibrating bass boosters. It can be hard to spot at the Folsom Street Fair, with all the leather and chains and riding crops. It may not seem obvious on that new motorcycle, pushing 90 mph with no helmet. It may seem irrelevant in the bedroom, swiping right on this week's third one-night stand. When we're having fun, we minimize risk, and avoid the origin of our impulse. Knowing this, risky behavior can also be indicative of identity delay, especially if we actualized later in life. Feeling like we have to catch up for lost time, we may rely on the agenda of emotional control to compensate for regret.

It is not the therapist's place to judge or condone behavior. If we're struggling, the dissonance will be evident in our presentation of each matter. Whether or not these experiences are *unhealthy* or *maladaptive* depends on us, our distress, and our level of global functioning. Like a teenager unable to prioritize, this experimentation phase is necessary, yet psychoeducation may be required to reduce the risk of harm to self or others.

## *Sexual risks*

Sex can be an incredibly empowering validation of gender. It can also become a point of fixation when it's relied on extensively to validate gender in lieu of self-affirmation and meaningful relationships (Bockting *et al.*, 2004). Like the taboo coat in the closet, the more shame and social invalidation builds up, the more addictive sexual relief can become. Yet like all addictions, tolerance builds up, satisfaction goes down, and instead of meeting the actual emotional need, we may pursue riskier forms of sexual behavior. Having multiple sex partners or engaging in BDSM, even in its most extreme forms, does not constitute sexual risk provided there is consensual communication and safe sex practices involved. Sexual self-harm risks range from sexually compulsive behavior lacking impulse control, lack of safe sex negotiation and safe sex practices, the inability to hold physical and sexual boundaries, deliberate self-endangerment, or reckless intoxication for the purpose of sex. Sexual self-harm risks also include any sexual or relational acts that knowingly or neglectfully damage our health and wellbeing or that of our partners. These include, but aren't limited to: compromising physical health by passing on a sexually transmitted disease via neglect or irresponsibility; maintaining or remaining in nonconsensual and abusive relationships; or compromising psychological health by lying about sexual interaction, and emotional infidelity.

Safeguarding against these risks is critical for gender minorities on the whole, but more so for gender variant sex workers. Being underpaid and underemployed in an overly sexualized society leads many gender variant people to capitalize on our novelty via the sex industry (Clements-Nolle *et al.*, 2001; Garofalo *et al.*, 2006; Mcllelan, 2017; Nemoto *et al.*, 2004; Richmond *et al.*, 2012; Xavier, 2000). The amount of trans pornography is staggering, given how small the population is, and that's not including off-screen prostitution, stripping, and professional BDSM. The 2015 US Transgender Survey found that 12 percent of respondents had engaged in sex work (James *et al.*, 2016). Some may feel trapped in this line of work and may need your active help to find healthy work alternatives. Others may be proud of our sex work, feeling that we're exploiting the exploiter, getting a cut, or even changing the narratives of sexual normativity. Others may have fused to a pride narrative in order to safeguard vulnerability.

Sex work can lead to unsettling and even traumatizing encounters with the law, as institutionalized cisgenderism results in police targeting and even assaulting trans women around the globe (Garofalo *et al.*, 2006; Mogul, Ritchie, and Whitlock, 2011; Nadal, Davidoff, and Fujii-Doe, 2014; Nichols, 2010; Reck,

2009; Stotzer, 2014). More accurately, sex work can be used as an excuse by police to harass LGBTQ pedestrians, as 11 percent of gender variant people, in one year, were stopped by officers assuming they were sex workers (James *et al.*, 2016). Trained to profile, the police unnecessarily target visibly transgender individuals. Yet even that doesn't explain police cruelty, as 6 percent of gender variant encounters with police end in verbal, physical, and even sexual assault—demanding sex under threat of arrest (James *et al.*, 2016). Even progressive institutions profile LGBTQ community as a high-risk demographic, meaning that the same police who used to arrest us for being a "pervert," and potentially assaulted us in the process, now feel justified to "protect" us from ourselves.

Check your value judgments here. Sex work is many things: an over-glorified industry; the last choice for the desperate; the enslavement of the invisible; and the objectification of the powerless. It can also be: an empowering celebration of the body; an accepting sex-positive community; a cornerstone of queer history; and for some, a way of affording surgery and college at the same time. Sex work can be traumatizing or enlivening, depending entirely on the person's options, locus of choice, type of sex work, and conscientiousness of the community they work with. Discovering that a client is a sex worker, or has engaged in sex work, is not indicative of distress, as many professional dominatrixes will point out. Only recently have healthy, sex-positive, trans-positive, and feminist-friendly representations of gender variant sex and sexuality entered the scene, with the aid of such notable icons as Buck Angel, Billy Castro, and Jiz Lee, to name a few. As such, there are healthy examples of a trans-positive sex industry, though they are admittedly few.

The increased risk of sexual exploitation, substance abuse, and low self-esteem contribute to why the rate of HIV amongst transgender populations (1.4%) is five times higher than the cisgender average (0.3%) (Clements-Nolle *et al.*, 2001; James *et al.*, 2016; Lombardi, 2001; Richmond *et al.*, 2012; Xavier, 2000). Trans youth are at a significantly higher risk of contracting HIV, especially when correlated with lack of parental support, homelessness, unemployment and the subsequent depression that follows, which in turn decreases the likelihood of using a condom, getting healthcare, or adhering to antiretroviral treatment (Garofalo *et al.*, 2006; McCann *et al.*, 2017).

Exploring safe sex practices in session may include how to use condoms and dental dams, and exploring how discrimination and victimization lead to safe sex fatigue (Garofalo *et al.*, 2006; Lombardi, 2001; McCann *et al.* 2017). Worn down by stress, it becomes easier to dismiss health concerns, marking safe sex as a hassle (Garofalo *et al.*, 2006). Gender variant youth are particularly susceptible to partner pressure, as they don't want to make their partner mad, nor do they want to be rejected (Garofalo *et al.*, 2006). Psychoeducation may also include how to navigate consensual sex and practice sex-positive communication; how to identify risks and dangers of substance abuse; what to do if someone is overdosing on a depressant, stimulant, or hallucinogen; how to develop back-up plans and sex-positive support networks; and, if relevant, how to delineate between healthy and unhealthy BDSM communities.

Moving past sexual stigma, value congruence can certainly apply to healthy, consensual forms of sex work, as we learn how to bring communication, trust, patience, safety, social support and self-respect into practice in order to minimize physical, emotional, and even legal risk.

## *Transition risks*

For those in transition, risk-taking behavior can also include procuring hormones from nonmedical sources (Garofalo *et al.*, 2006). When there's little to no access to appropriate healthcare, scouring the internet for ways to import estrogen, anti-androgens, or testosterone may seem like the only alternative. The consequences of self-medication can be dire, as an unbalanced regimen can result in mood swings, and thromboembolic and hepatic disease (Garofalo *et al.*, 2006; Israel and Tarver II, 1997).

In many places where MtF and trans women live in poverty, whether in New York and Chicago in the USA, or Bangkok, Thailand, and Lima, Peru, some may also dabble with *pumping* (Guadamuz *et al.*, 2011; Silva-Santisteban *et al.*, 2012; Wallace, 2010). As an underground profession *pumpers* are unlicensed medical practitioners who inject loose silicone into a person's lips, cheeks, jawline, hips, calves, buttocks, and breasts (Wallace, 2010). Unlike silicone implants, loose adulterated silicone is injected directly into the body, risking HIV infection, hypercalcemia, renal failure, and death (Visnyei *et al.*, 2014; Wallace, 2010).

Likewise, FtM and trans men lacking support, especially if they're underage, may covertly find illegal ways to procure testosterone (Spade, 2006). Black market testosterone cypionate and testosterone enanthate are used by body-builders to bulk up, and their quality is unreliable and unsafe. Yet even when they are clean, both present risks of increased blood pressure, bad cholesterol (LDL), weight gain, and a decreased sensitivity to insulin, and can affect mood, potentially impacting any pre-existing mood disorder (Asscheman and Gooren, 1992; Feldman and Safer, 2009; Slabbekoorn *et al.*, 2001; WPATH, 2011).

Agender individuals reducing the role of gender expression may also elect to go to more extreme lengths, as it's often difficult to find medical practitioners willing to engage in gender nullification surgery (Vale *et al.*, 2010). Through legal medical practices, some female-bodied clients achieve elements of this through hysterectomies, labiaplasty, and breast reduction, while some male-bodied clients are able to obtain orchiectomies. Outside of this, agender individuals may seek out body-modification artists nicknamed *cutters*, or perform body-modification alone (Vale *et al.*, 2010). This can include the removal of nipples and even full castration. Of post-castrated males, over two-thirds deemed themselves as a gender other than man or woman. The remainder deemed themselves male, with a handful identifying as female, having utilized castration as a step to becoming MtF or MtE (male to eunuch), often after many years of premeditation (Johnson and Irwig, 2014; Johnson *et al.*, 2007; Roberts *et al.*, 2017). Notably, interest in castration does not have an inherent bearing on a person's gender, and can be indicative of a sexual paraphilia, extreme religious devotion, or as some researchers debate, body integrity identity disorder and/or body-dysmorphic disorder (Agoramoothy and Hsu, 2014; Johnson *et al.*, 2007; Lawrence, 2010; Roberts *et al.*, 2017).

Alliance with trans-positive clinicians is imperative to sidestep some of the more extreme risks of taking HRT and gender alignment surgery quite literally into one's own hands. By exploring options, and navigating the complexities of the medical system, you can help massively decrease the risks involved. For clients facing the expenditure of surgery, this may include developing crowd funding campaigns, working through budgets, helping clients obtain insurance that provides transgender healthcare, and even assessing all the pros and cons—from cost, to safety, to procedural outcome. Even for agender and other nonbinary clients, you can help by coordinating with a licensed endocrinologist to provide anti-androgens so clients can experience the psychological and emotional shift a full orchiectomy would provide (Vale *et al.*, 2010). Collaboratively, we may need to think outside of the box by assessing the quality, hygiene, and professionalism of licensed body-modification practitioners. Once again, risk correlates with desperation. The more options there are, the easier it is to defuse from intrusive thoughts to make a healthy, informed, value-congruent choice.

## *Self-harm risks*

Unlike transition risks attempting to align sex and gender, non-suicidal self-harm attempts to alleviate distress by spiking cortisol. Adhering to the agenda of emotional control, cutting and self-injurious behavior is often used as a brake system attempting to end, relieve, or distract from unwanted emotional experience, to such a degree they may even instigate episodes of depersonalization (Chapman, Gratz, and Brown, 2006; Suyemoto, 1994). Furthermore, depressive clients may express a lack of energy, which, when combined with depersonalization, increases the risk of suicidal ideation and self-injurious behavior (Michal *et al.*, 2010; Zikić, Cirić, and Mitković, 2009).

Gender variant youth may struggle with self-harm, such as cutting and burning, when they lack healthier coping skills, or are excluded from healthier coping skills, such as sport (Arcelus *et al.*, 2016). Gender variant youth with strict religious backgrounds or communities with rigid gender roles also present an increased risk of self-harm, as deviance from the norm leaves kids fighting an internal battle with shame and feelings of untrustworthiness (Grossman and D'Augelli, 2006). Of 189 adolescents and young adults in Australia, 70 percent said they self-harmed (Smith *et al.*, 2014). In the UK, the risk of self-harm doubled for trans youth in contrast to cisgender kids of the same age (Arcelus *et al.*, 2016). A Scottish study including 68 trans and 29 gender questioning children found that 96 percent of transgender adolescents between age 11 and 19 had self-harmed (Bridger *et al.*, 2017). The larger, British equivalent of this study, including 594 trans and 297 gender questioning children in the same age bracket, found that 84 percent of trans-identified youth had self-harmed (Bradlow *et al.*, 2017). An American study including 97 respondents found that 42 percent of transgender adolescents had self-harmed, with 30 percent attempting suicide (Peterson *et al.*, 2016).

## *Drug risks*

There is little research focusing on the role of substance abuse specifically for gender variant populations, or the effectiveness of substance abuse treatment programs for this population (Flentje, Heck, and Sorensen, 2014). Certain patterns are observable but may be localized geographically or within generational cohorts. In a study from Washington State, bisexual, lesbian, and transgender women were more likely to use heroin, whereas bisexual, gay, and transgender men had a higher prevalence of stimulant abuse (Cochran and Cauce, 2006). In a San Francisco study, FtM clients in substance abuse treatment were more likely to have family conflicts, and to live with a substance abuser, but were more likely to have a job than cis men struggling with the same addictions (Flentje *et al.*, 2014). MtF clients in this same study had a higher use of needles, methamphetamine use, and increased rates of HIV than cis women in treatment, but were less likely to have children (Flentje *et al.*, 2014).

The relationship between harassment for gender nonconformity and alcohol abuse is as easy to grasp as the bottle, as visibly gender variant clients face an increased risk of violence, abuse, bullying, and social rejection, especially for gender variant people of color (Hendricks and Testa, 2012; Keuroghlian *et al.*, 2015; Nemoto *et al.*, 2004; Reck, 2009; Reisner *et al.*, 2014, 2015; Rowe *et al.*, 2015). This same relationship exists between gender-related trauma, depression, and abuse of both prescription and illegal drugs (Benotsch *et al.*, 2013; Clements-Nolle *et al.*, 2001; Flentje *et al.*, 2014; Keuroghlian *et al.*, 2015). Highlighting the impact of environment, gender variant minorities are most at risk of substance abuse when we have unstable housing, are impacted by public discrimination, and engage in sex work, illustrating the need for a Housing First model prioritizing safe spaces as the foundation of recovery (Tsemberis, 2010; Keuroghlian *et al.*, 2015).

When medical, social, and familial systems neglect a person, desperation ensues. With few options available, and the risk of persecution stacked against us, tiring ideas loom in the mind. Flippant to health, dismissive of safety, we may ask:

"Why not? What have I got to lose? It's not like I can do anything else..."

"It's not like anyone cares, so I may as well, right?"

"Yeah, it's dangerous, but so what? I was never going to live long, anyway."

ACT uses mindfulness to exist in the present, yet a risk-taking mindset may believe all we have is the moment. Displaced by a depressing past, with little hope for a healthy future, the here and now may be all we afford ourselves. This can feel like an exhaustive *memento mori* as much as a celebratory *carpe diem*. Struggling from paycheck to paycheck presumes there *is* a paycheck, or any kind of reliable income. When we're in the narrows taking it day by day, mindfulness is quickly eclipsed by urgency.

Pursuing the instant gratification of substance abuse, orgasm, or thrill to soothe or distract from the imminent threats of life can often leave us running in place. Immediacy is reactionary, responding as needed to all manner of stress. When we fuse with this mindset, we'll roll the dice, drink the bottle, or make the money, since we don't know when we'll get another chance. Addiction, as the ultimate form of fusion, can become so complete that it circumvents the prefrontal cortex—bypassing conscious thought. When this happens, we act on impulse, reaching for another cigarette, dialing that number one more time, or opening up the razor kit before we even realize what we're doing. Becoming emotional escape artists, we take risks so as not to feel, or to try and selectively pick and choose our sensory experience, only to have our control tactics backfire when they trade all our dopamine for an immediate, ecstatic burst of delirium.

Removing judgmental language like *good* or *bad* or *better* or *worse*, ask if we feel like we're running toward something, away from something, or both. This often aids in clarifying our intent, as our pursuit of risky behavior may be trying to gain an unmet internal need (love, connection, excitement, empowerment, pride, experience), meet a role expectation, attain real-world stability, or escape dangerous or volatile living situations. Conversely, it may identify something we don't want to address, including heartache, loneliness, abandonment, attachment issues, or trauma. We may be reluctant to address areas we're actively avoiding. To contrast, not all risk-takers are emotional escape artists. Many are very willing to get help, but just assumed no one cared, or that the help offered wouldn't work. Faced with a new possibility, we may melt into guilt, regret, and shame, or we may fortify an iron will, stating that we did what we had to do, or we may get wrapped up in a confusing mix of both.

Exploring our short-term goals and survival values on a matrix can aid precontemplative awareness. When we begin to realize our actions are not necessarily contradictions of our values, but misguided applications thereof, it becomes easier to accept our whole self and all its contexts. By recognizing the underlying, ever-present value constructs, it becomes easier to identify necessary changes in behavior. This is a meaningful step, particularly if we feel there's something intrinsically "wrong" or "broken" in us that we can't shake.

ACT introduces value-congruent behavior as the path to right action, yet we can warp this to point out values even in unhealthy dynamics. The bully points to their integrity. The addict points to their freedom. Rather than argue against this, or try to prove otherwise, work with it. Humanizing our impulsivity, have us list our emotional motivators. This is a simple way to demonstrate that we're not *bad* or *evil*, but scared, anxious, worried, lost, confused, angry, or desperate. Take time to explore the full extent of our feelings. Anger blazes on. Fear can't believe it's safe to try anything else. Even delight can endanger us, as the risk-taking mindset views stability as mediocrity, and mediocrity as a living death.

When we fuse to an impulsive, immediate mindset, it becomes difficult to believe we can change. The alcoholic may want to be sober but can't imagine a life without temptation. The sex addict may see there's a problem but over-identify with thrill-seeking or emotional dependency. When locked into survival values, defusion seems farfetched. Maybe we're riding that motorcycle at top speed again because we're a thrill seeker. Maybe we're hitting that club again because we're a party animal. Maybe we're hitting ourselves again because we're a freak. Maybe we believe we were always this way and that it's a lost cause; or maybe life molded us into what we are, so even if we're not to blame, our locus of control is equivalent to wishing on a star (Stitt, 2014). Whatever the case may be, there's always a story.

Sob stories, sappy stories, surreal stories, even stories of redemption, rebellion, and revenge—all reinforce why we are the way we are. Our stories not only extrapolate why we're fused to all our reason-giving thoughts, but also justify them, often by typifying certain themes and reducing all the characters involved to base archetypes (Strosahl and Robinson, 2017). By examining emotionally distressing thoughts and memories, ACT challenges the idea that we're a reliable narrator (Forsyth and Eifert, 2016; Strosahl and Robinson, 2017). Like film producers leaving edits on the cutting room floor, we play up drama and downplay context, turn up the theme song, and omit the dialogue, not because we're liars but because we don't have eidetic memories, and because we're limited to our perspective. The camera was only capable of capturing the scene from one angle, and we didn't record everyone's lines, and we lost some of what we had on tape, so we fix it in editing.

As a perspective-taking exercise, observe how we're all protagonists in our own story. Some may argue this, especially if we don't feel like the protagonist or even the central character in our own lives. Some may feel more like anti-heroes, deserving victims, or even sinful monsters.

> "No, I deserve this. I'm not a man, so I can't be a father, and that's what my son needed."

> "You can't cheer me up, Doc. I know I'm a sadomasochistic, transvestic freak, and on some days I'll wave that flag with the rest of 'em, but freaks don't get to have love, Doc. It's just not a thing."

> "I drink, my dad drinks, my grandad used to own a pub in Ireland. Liver cirrhosis is a rite of passage."

Adapting Kirk Strosahl and Patricia Robinson's (2017) autobiography exercise in their *Mindfulness and Acceptance Workbook for Depression* can help us deconstruct our old narratives. First, we're instructed to write a short autobiography, including the formative experiences in our life, including our highest highs and lowest lows, the passions and traumas, our relationships with friends, family, and intimate partners, and how each has affected us as a person (Strosahl and Robinson, 2017). Once it's written, we can look for certain themes within the story, then draw two columns on a piece of paper (See Table 6.1). In the first column, we list any recurring themes, or specific situations we ruminate about. In the second column, we list the impact it made in our life (Strosahl and Robinson, 2017).

**Table 6.1 Story and impact**

| Story | Impact |
|---|---|
| I was beaten up as a kid for being femme | I stopped trusting people |
| I never had many friends in high school | I learned that life is generally lonely, but that I could deal with being by myself |
| My dad disowned me when I came out | He showed me how shitty he is, and how unforgiving family can be |
| I was raped by my first boyfriend | I still get really anxious around men and I stopped enjoying sex for a long time |
| There's not a competent doctor in my state | I learned that there's really no place for me here |

Because our stories rely on our relational frames, often making causal inferences, they can seem like the truth (Hayes *et al.*, 2012; Strosahl and Robinson, 2017). As truth is subjective, it's often self-serving. If we say, "I'd literally die of shame if I told someone," don't launch into a medical debate trying to negate death by shame or attempt to convince us that we're speaking figuratively and not literally.

ACT explores the workability of the thought, not its accuracy. In this case, telling ourselves we'd die of shame grinds us to a halt.

Subjected to passive microaggressions and volatile macroaggressions, we may sometimes feel like our life is a scoreboard of cruelty. We may wind up thinking that people either don't understand or don't care about the unique challenges we contend with. We can spend years trying to accept ourselves, only to be invalidated by an ignorant school board or a paranoid political body. We can spend years developing a community, only to have a friend commit suicide or get murdered. And because these stories are so often ignored, we fight all the more to have them seen, which is a powerful form of advocacy and vulnerable form of courage with one psychological drawback: We can get stuck in the story. It doesn't matter how justified, righteous, well-reasoned or urgent a story is if it blocks us from meeting our needs (Strosahl and Robinson, 2017). When our narratives detract from our ability to function, we start feeling like we're in an emotionally painful loop, leading us to take more and more risks to either distract ourselves or drown out our feelings. Life-affirming adventures are great, provided they affirm our lives and don't hide us from them. Yet people the world over will compromise functionality, preferring to be right rather than explore feelings, expand awareness, or adjust behavior (Zettle, 2004, 2007). In the same way that an overbearing film producer can ruin a good movie by trying to micromanage the director's creative vision, our thinking self has made a mess of things yet again. Only later, however, do we get the director's cut.

As a thought exercise, draw two columns again. Fill the first column with the exact same story as before. Yet this time, let's expand our awareness to include equally true life lessons and life changes (Strosahl and Robinson, 2017). This doesn't mean forcing ourselves to look on the sunny side, or reinterpreting our original answer, though we may need to talk through different ways we can look at our life. When it comes to sharing our life story, the tale itself remains the same, but how we tell it naturally changes over time. We add layers of depth and clarity, nuance and perspective. Likewise, trauma victims can be frustrated by the notion that somehow pain taught us something, or that there was anything *to learn* from bigotry, assault, or sexual trauma. The sentiment that "all things happen for a reason" can often feel invalidating, even if it may be true, as it favors intellectualization over emotional experience. To expand perspective, inquire what each story made us pay attention to, identifying the importance therein alongside what we want to embody in ourselves (see Table 6.2).

**Table 6.2 Story and impact values**

| Story | Impact |
|---|---|
| I was beaten up as a kid for being femme | *What do you pay attention to?*<br>I pay attention to other femme kids 'cause I know what they're going through.<br>*What's important?*<br>Respect. Respect is important, and dignity.<br>*What do you embody?*<br>Respect. Kindness. Compassion. |
| I never had many friends in high school | *What do you pay attention to?*<br>Social relationships. I feel jealousy.<br>*What's important?*<br>Friendship, connection, love.<br>*What do you embody?*<br>I'm polite, and generally nice. I try to be. |
| My dad disowned me when I came out | *What do you pay attention to?*<br>Now that I'm a dad I pay close attention to being as fair and understanding as I can be.<br>*What's important?*<br>Being a good role model.<br>*What do you embody?*<br>Love and loyalty. |
| I was raped by my first boyfriend | *What do you pay attention to?*<br>I pay attention to what men do, not what they say.<br>*What's important?*<br>Safety, trust, respect.<br>*What do you embody?*<br>Feminism and human compassion. |
| There's not a competent doctor in my state | *What do you pay attention to?*<br>A doctor's reputation.<br>*What's important?*<br>Knowledge, experience, the willingness to learn.<br>*What do you embody?*<br>Patience. Persistence. |

Even the most dangerous, maladaptive coping mechanism is brought into play to meet a social, emotional, or appetitive need, yet the subsequent cost often outweighs the benefit. While our stories do not always justify our substance abuse, self-harm, personal neglect, or reckless behavior, they can reinforce these behaviors. When our options are limited, we may adamantly believe there's only one available choice, yet even with community support and resources available, the old story can keep us trapped in old, unhealthy behaviors. As we learn to expand on our narratives, you can help us validate and accept our survival values by identifying our self-actualization values as they appear in new layers of the story. Observably, self-actualization values may appear dissonant to, or even the opposite of, risk-taking behavior, just as those who are compassionate for others may also self-harm, and those who are empathic can neglect personal needs. The more self-actualization values can be identified in the story as it exists, the easier it is to expand our perspective of self and therefore behavior. Following up on our stories, explore other occasions where we demonstrated respect, kindness, compassion, courtesy, love, loyalty, knowledgeability, curiosity, patience, and persistence, instead of risk-taking control tactics. Take time with these value-congruent narratives, as the willingness to try alternative ways to meet our needs greatly depends on defusing from our old story.

When therapists build a truly safe, compassionate, and understanding container, clients slowly capitalize on therapy as a risk-free relationship. It is, in this moment that your reliability as a clinician may take on a whole new dimension of case management. Working with gender variant people may entail taking on a more active role, as discerning healthy, long-term goals are all lovely hypotheticals, but we need all the help we can get to make them happen. The risk-taking mindset reacts to its environment, resolving tension expediently through the resources available. It is not enough, however, to simply make a healthier resource available. Place a slice of cheesecake next to a salad and see where your eyes go.

Fused to frames of distinction, we may believe it's not worth it to try, or that we're not worthy of help. We may think that we may never be sober, or that self-love is a storybook fairytale written by people who have never known pain. Community connection works because it naturally challenges our frames of distinction. When we see people similar to ourselves develop healthy coping mechanisms, we begin to recognize that we are not as isolated in our issues as we once thought. If we don't relate with them, however, we may grip tighter to our frames of distinction. For gender variant risk-takers, it can be incredibly hard to defuse from frames of distinction because of our very real and very distinct issues, obstacles, and crisis. We can only begin to see our similarity in others if we can develop trust, and we can only develop trust if we believe someone—no matter how different we may first believe they are—genuinely invests in us.

There is a sad question, asked with intonations of doubt and awe: "Why do you want to help me?" As a clinician, consider your answer. Helping someone because it's the right thing to do demonstrates a moral imperative. Helping someone because you are a compassionate, empathic person role models your value congruence. But helping us, because you're invested in who we are, doesn't just speak to your compassion and empathy, it shows it. At the core of therapy is a relational experience that both client and clinician may shy away from, and so we talk about values without ever embodying them. To take a step toward recovery, we need to know you're invested, and that you're willing to get up out of your chair and help.

The Housing First model repeatedly demonstrates the positive impact of having a stable living situation (Tsemberis, 2010; Keuroghlian *et al.*, 2015). Originally developed for substance recovery, the Housing First model integrates with a trans-positive ecological perspective and ACT's holistic approach—so know every spare bed in town! It's one thing to refer a client to domestic violence shelters, halfway houses and charity organizations, but some communities may not have these available, and some organizations may even turn transgender people away (Mottet and Ohle, 2003; Reck, 2009). Besides which, though many nonprofits try their best, stability and emotional safety are not always apt descriptions for these so-called sanctuaries, as 70 percent of trans people experience violence, harassment, and hostility at homeless shelters (James *et al.*, 2016). It may be necessary to get creative by coordinating with established members of the local LGBTQ community to physically build safe spaces if there are none. When funds are not available, this may even resemble a vetted couch-surfing network maintained by community organizers who want to give back. Why vetted? Two noteworthy reasons: Hopping from one random living situation to the next increases the risk of further victimization, making a vetted safe space a deep comfort (Mottet and Ohle, 2003). Additionally, if we struggle with sexual impulsivity, substance abuse, or have a history of sex work, we may use dating apps and couch-surfing websites as a means of procuring hook-ups and clientele. Anticipating this, a vetted network of platonic, sober living spaces can help us follow-through on our long-term, value-congruent actions (Maguen *et al.*, 2005).

Familiarize yourself with the sociopolitical climate in your area, and the law as it pertains to the rights of gender minorities (White and Goldberg, 2006). As housing discrimination against gender minorities is an ongoing problem, develop a comprehensive list of *accessible* resources in your area. These include everything from transgender groups, activities, and social networks to trans-friendly recovery programs, shelters, and foodbanks (Sheerin, 2009; Singh *et al.*, 2011). For those struggling with substance abuse, self-harm, and sex addiction, check out the local support groups and 12-step programs like Alcoholics Anonymous (AA), Narcotics Anonymous (NA), and Sex and Love Addicts Anonymous (SLAA). And when we say "check out," we mean sacrificing a few weekends to attend them personally. Support groups are community oriented, which means the atmosphere changes depending on the demographics of those who attend.

Though typically run in the same way, some chapters are more progressive, religious, or homogenous than others. Know which chapters in your community are LGBTQ-run or are, at the very least, LGBTQ-friendly. Recommending a support program you're not personally familiar with is a bit like playing roulette. A poor fit, in the best scenario, means we simply won't attend. A poor fit in the worst scenario may expose us to further risk.

There's a lot of work to be done, so create time to locate career opportunities, draft résumés, and work toward an occupation elevating our health and wellbeing. This doesn't mean just talking about it. This means present-based value-committed action, filling out applications and even calling up potential job locations in session. Stepping up not only gets us closer to our life goals, but reaffirms the therapeutic relationship, and with it our belief in ourselves. Should we return empty handed, feeling dejected and rejected for the one-hundred-thousandth time in our life, we may need your energy. Help us try again, and again, and again, role modeling not just persistence, but flexible resilience. Help us apply for jobs we know we're good at, and jobs we're not certain about, and shoot a résumé at the long shot, too, just in case they might say yes.

Feeling downtrodden, we may fuse to the idea that we could never afford a higher education, or that classism, racism, and cisgenderism have locked academia's gates. If higher education shows up as a dream, see if we're willing to turn it into a plan. This may involve helping us write essays, as many progressive colleges and universities actively seek to provide scholarships and grants to LGBTQ individuals. Follow-up on CampusPride.org, as an ever-expanding list of campuses in the USA cover the cost of HRT, surgery, and transition-related expenses.

Even if you're not a social worker, it's imperative to build a network of resources broader than the universities, mental health agencies, and nonprofits in your area. A network includes: the gay-owned coffee shop down the road; the old grocer on the corner whose daughter had SRS three years ago; the construction worker who's ostensibly straight but always volunteered for pride; the nightclub owner who hosts that big drag show once a year; the agender manager at the computer store who's always very polite; and the college professor who always directs *The Vagina Monologues*. Provided it doesn't present a direct conflict of interest to your practice, connect clients to safe zone places of work, and if possible, reach out to make introductions personally.

Realistically, these business owners may owe you no favors. They may even be hesitant to hire us, not because we're gender variant but because we may be overcoming substance abuse, have a very limited résumé, don't own a car, and may have an unstable living situation or even questionable citizenship. It may take some time to find someone who will even give us a chance, which is all the more reason to network beforehand as you will need to know how to access resources

(Chavez-Korell and Lorah, 2007). To be truly effective in this area, you need to be an active member of the LGBTQ community, as there's no way to know who would be receptive to a gender variant employee on hard times unless you ask them directly. Whenever possible, befriend business owners, especially those run by LGBTQ persons. Talk story. Keep their contact info. Perhaps you'll never need to call on their help, at which point you'll have made a few friendly acquaintances, and it's always wise to know the chef personally. Yet should you need their help, a well-timed business card can be a ticket to a better life.

Many clinicians may be cautious about becoming over-involved in a client's life, and there is indeed a boundary. Consider yourself a guide to the sanctuary, but not the sanctuary itself. This can be difficult to hold on to as you witness our highs and lows, peaks and perils. When our lives are at risk, we take risks with our lives. We may search out life-affirming thrills, or run from our feelings for fear they might crush us. To flex our rigid, risk-taking mindset and all its maladaptive coping mechanisms, we need evidence of an alternative, resonance with our role models, and opportunity to grow. You cannot give us this first-hand, but you can help us expand awareness, broaden horizons, and create connections. The broader our community, the more role models there are, and the more resources we have to rely on. The risk is worth the cost only when there seems so little to lose. To break this cycle, we have to find something to live for, and a healthy means to do it, which you can aid by introducing us to a supportive, productive community, and by showing that you really are invested in our personal growth.

## Befriending bodies: ACT for body dysmorphia

Gender dysphoria is psychologically distinct from the body dysmorphia borne of unhealthy beauty standards and unrealistic body image (Maguen *et al.*, 2005). The *DSM-5* presents body-dysmorphic disorder as a preoccupation with perceived defects or flaws in one's physical appearance, resulting in habitual mirror checks, excessive grooming, skin picking or continually seeking reassurance from others (American Psychiatric Association, 2013). The wrench in our proverbial gears, body dysmorphia can throw off gender actualization and undermine self-acceptance. Unsatisfied with transition results, the body-dysmorphic mindset may become addicted to the scalpel, going in for procedure after procedure, or it may never feel satisfied with self-actualization as it's an ongoing process and not a result. Excessively comparing appearance to others, we may begin to feel like it's not enough to transition if we can't achieve a certain beauty standard. In essence, our aspirational body image has become narrowed and inflexible, so we begin to excessively measure our appearance, whether it's our weight, height, or even our face (Sandoz and Dufrene, 2013). Note that body dysmorphia isn't symptomatic of gender dysphoria or gender variance, as many of us live at peace with our bodies. Yet when gender dysphoria and body dysmorphia overlap, they present a unique therapeutic obstacle. The distinction is that gender dysphoria can find therapeutic relief in the physical transition process (Gijs and Brewaeys, 2007; Gómez-Gil *et al.*, 2012; Gorin-Lazard *et al.*, 2013; Smith *et al.*, 2005; WPATH, 2011), whereas body dysmorphia will simply find another flaw to focus on.

As gender is inextricably linked to cultural beauty and body image standards, gender self-actualization is often punctuated by body shaming like an inspirational coming-of-age movie interrupted every ten minutes by beauty product commercials. Body dysmorphia divides our self-concept, framing our body as a deictic other to separate from, if not over-identify with. When we say, "I hate my thighs," our language is possessive and compartmentalized. Our thighs are a *thing* we own, like an inanimate object to be judged or appraised. When we operate from this mindset, we experience ourselves like a jockey whipping a horse, or like a driver steering a car without ever checking the gas tank (Watts, 2015). So divided, our thinking self emancipates from our somatic self, calling it "disgusting" or "gross." When body dysmorphia presents as such, our critical self-statements triangulate between our aspirational self-image and a somatic sensation we actively avoid.

> "I wish I was beautiful, but I sweat all the time and I'm fucking gross."
>
> "Cheese? I feel fat just by looking at it. I hate eating. Is that physically possible? I used to be thin when I was younger, but now I'm just unmotivated."
>
> "*You disgust me.* I say it every time I look in the mirror. I won't even be thinking about anything; then when I see myself, it just comes right out. *You disgust me.*"

The body-dysmorphic mindset uses control tactics to avoid the physically natural processes of our somatic self. Paranoid that we sweat "too much" or that we "smell bad," we may, for example, duck out of exertive behavior, carry spare clothes, or shower religiously in an attempt to conserve the short-term feeling of being "fresh." If we're self-conscious of our body-mass index (BMI) we may regulate what we can or can't wear, as if hiding our body from our own eyes. Disordered eating patterns and obsessional tendencies demonstrate these control tactics in the extreme; yet even if we don't meet the diagnostic criteria, we may still adhere to unnecessary diets. Though many are familiar with anorexia, binging, and bulimia, body-dysmorphia does not require an eating disorder, which is one reason why it's so overlooked or minimized. A desire to be "healthy" or "beautiful" can be a thinly veiled excuse to constantly pick at ourselves, just as our investment in beauty products, skin cleansers, and hair care treatments may be our unsatisfactory solution to self-loathing.

Interestingly, when we say, "I'm fat," or "I'm ugly," we overidentify with a single aspect of our self-concept, which may or may not have any bearing in reality. We may be stick thin and believe "I'm fat," having fused so totally that our eyes lie to us in the mirror; or, should we have a larger body type, "I'm fat" encodes all manner of implications, from "I'm rejected," to "I'm unappreciated," to "I'm ridiculed." Over identifying with a critical self-judgment is not an integration of our divided internal self-schema, but a layering of constructs, eclipsing one over the other. Demonstrating this is pretty straightforward. If we're too critical to appreciate ourselves, let's write down all the positive qualities of a person we admire, whether it's a friend, family member, or celebrity. On a second piece of paper, write down one physical *defect* or *flaw* that person has. Let's really use that judgmental mind of ours. If we don't want to be so critical of others, ask how society might judge that person's body? Would they say the person we admire has a big nose? Are they overweight? Are they old? Whatever *flaw* it is, let's write it on the second piece of paper in big, thick letters. Now, place the second paper over the first, eclipsing all our admiration for them behind a single *flaw*. Without peeking, let's try to remember what admirations we originally wrote down, and when we say them out loud, your task as the therapist is to repeat only what's on the eclipsing piece of paper.

> "They're funny, and well known for being generous."
> *So, they have a big nose?*
>
> "Yes, but they're also nice, and they won an Academy Award once."
> *Because they have a big nose?*
>
> "No, because they did this really dark but powerful movie about the Brazilian rainforest."
> *Sounds to me like they have a big nose.*

After a few tongue-in-cheek rounds, the demonstration becomes clear, as no matter what positive observation is made, we're routed back to our one, obsessional criticism. Observing the frequency of personal dissatisfaction felt by young cis women, and the muscular idealism of young cis men, we may even normalize distress by fusing with odd justifications:

> "I hate the way I look, but what girl doesn't? Isn't everyone self-conscious? I mean, it's not like I have an eating disorder or something."
>
> "I'm totally against the absurd beauty standards, but it still hits me. I've always been a woman, but... I don't know... am I shallow to think I'll always be ugly?"
>
> "Even growing up, my mom made us check the mirror by the door before going out. She always said that people will judge you as soon as look at you."

Unhealthy body fixation presents differently across a range of genders, yet consistently leads to maladaptive efforts trying to avoid or alleviate this distress (Sandoz and Dufrene, 2013). Trans people anxiously striving to pass may inadvertently develop unhealthy, self-conscious thoughts and behaviors that stick around long after transition. Others may struggle through the whole transition process, unable to actualize an unrealistic body image. Trans women often have to come to terms with having a larger frame, while trans men may attempt to size themselves up, wishing to be broader or taller than they are (Maguen *et al.*, 2005; Schilt, 2010). Inarguably, this distress exemplifies gender dysphoria, but self-actualization alone may not alleviate the conceptual self's inflexible body map.

To explore the overlap of gender and body-dysmorphia, let's hit the gym with Mike. As a self-actualized gay man, Mike naturally explored ways to increase muscle tone and upper body strength to appear masculine. Over the past few years, however, Mike's hyperfocus on muscle mass has become his new religion, as he spends excessive time working out—to such magnitude he'll ignore personal injury. His mantra? "Gain over pain." This excessive attempt to control his form certainly connects to Mike's gender identity, yet the hypermasculine idealism striving to be attractive to other men has become more indicative of a body image issue (Bockting *et al.*, 2006). Many gender dysphoric clients go through a period of distress pertaining to nudity, yet Mike is far more preoccupied about being seen as small or weak. Keep in mind, he's jacked. He hits the gym every day, and he still bulks up his clothes to accentuate his masculine shape. Likewise, height is archetypally associated with power and hegemonic masculinity, creating a source of contention for some trans men who not only wish they were taller, but berate themselves for being short (Schilt, 2010). To compare, gender dysphoric FtM clients often want to be taller, or feel odd because they're not as tall as they feel they should be, while body-dysmorphic Mike thinks he's diminutive, even at 5 feet 8 inches. Leaping to conclusions, he'll make bizarre inferences, presuming people judge him as much as he judges himself.

> "They don't like me at work. They don't respect me, and I know why. It's 'cause I'm short! Hah! You thought that I was gonna say because I'm trans, but they can't even fucking tell! They have no idea, but men are so shallow. If they can look over your head, they won't look you in the eye!"
>
> "I've been skipping work a lot to go to the gym. Told my boss I was sick but the truth is I haven't hit my goal yet. At least that's what I tell myself. I don't even enjoy it anymore, I just have to go. It's like the goal posts keep moving."
>
> "Listen, I joke with my friends that I only ever have sex with my boots on, but it's true, I literally only ever have sex with my boots on. That's not a fetish is it? 'Cause it's not about the boots. I just don't want people to know I'm short. And I feel more grounded in my boots anyway. And I hate my small feet."

For Mike, the hierarchical frame is that "I am Mike," "Mike is a man," and "men are big." Having aligned the first two points of the triangle, Mike has resolved the gender dysphoria from his youth. He totally accepts himself as a man, yet this latter belief that "Men are big" threatens the stability of this, leading not only to his control attempts, but a distorted self-concept. While certainly gendered, it would be inaccurate to attribute this to gender dysphoria, as the phenomenon occurs across the board. Transgender and cisgender people alike can reduce contact with the somatic self in favor of a conceptual self fused to gendered rules, ideals, and beauty standards. Keep in mind, gender dysphoria pits us against our sex phenotypes, leading us to worry about being more or less masculine or feminine. Yet body dysmorphia piles on extra worries about being too fat or too thin or too ugly.

Genderqueer and agender people may experience a unique form of body dysmorphia, including picking at our skin, anxiously monitoring how BMI genders our bodies, or fixating on youthfully androgynous or idyllically lithe physiques. Scoffing at cisnormative beauty standards, and often lacking peers to compare with, the nonbinary person may not always see our own perfectionist ideals or queer-normative image standards turning against us. If we actively rebel against society's *should* statements, our own *should* statements may take the form of wishes or conditional statements. We may sigh, "I wish I were thinner." We may even determine, "I only like myself when I'm 140 lbs."

Positive self-affirmations can be helpful for those with a semblance of esteem, yet they can also be quite harmful, since stating, "I am a lovable person" or "I'm beautiful" ironically engages our internal critic, creating an unhealthy paired association (Hayes *et al.*, 2012; Wood *et al.*, 2009). Preoccupied with looks and continuously unsatisfied with our body, regardless of transition or stage of self-actualization, we may start to avoid even kind people. In the same way we smirk and scroll past inspirational pride memes on a really bad day, positive affirmations can come across as an invalidating form of rescuing. Compliments are stripped apart as well-intentioned but naïve, as you cannot debate us into liking ourselves or our body. Indeed, when we feel at odds with our body, rescuing behavior can reinforce dysmorphia by keeping focus on appearance.

"You were always the heart-breaker, even as a kid."

"You're beautiful."

"I wish you could see yourself how I see you."

"You always put yourself down, but I wish I was as sexy as you."

The positive intent in these statements creates a puzzling scenario. If we dare to believe the compliment, we feel crazy since a dissonant part of us refutes it outright. If we reject the compliment, we may feel angry or disappointed in others who don't grasp what we're going through, and/or guilty because we recognize the positive intent but can't accept it. Supportive parents, friends, and lovers attempting to raise our esteem through positive reinforcement, flattery, and image-based compliments can expect to hear, "You just don't understand!" As every compliment ironically engages a criticism, we may avoid those we love to escape the whole ironic process, only to feel an added tier of guilt, frustration, and loss without our support network.

As we judge ourselves the most when we're in a bad mood, we can use judgment itself like a starting gun to signal our awareness and do a quick body scan. Are we frustrated, tired, hungry, or under pressure? We can focus on hating our body, but is hating our body the impetus for our mood, or just the product of it? If it's not the impetus for our mood, then let's check what unmet needs have to be addressed.

Harassment, discrimination, and social rejection negatively impact our ability to appreciate our body, especially when such harassment is directed at our gender (Israel and Tarver, 1997; Riley *et al.*, 2011; Tabaac, Perrin and Benotsch, 2017). Negative interactions with medical professionals can also contribute to poor body image, especially if we're seeking assistance for the bodies we feel are being rejected (Grant *et al.*, 2011; Kenagy, 2005; Riley *et al.*, 2011; Whittle *et al.*, 2007). When a trans woman enters a hospital with a broken leg and finds herself interrogated for her gender, or when a genderqueer person requests HRT and the endocrinologist presumes they're not *ready* based on how they look, they're respectively made to feel self-conscious about their image. For gender variant people, our ability to accept our body is also balanced with our satisfaction with life, self-esteem, and ability to manage both anxiety and depression (Tabaac *et al.*, 2017). As with gender dysphoria, the gender affirmative ACT approach to body dysmorphia is an ecological one, working with both our internal self-talk and cognitive framework, while helping to build or acquire a healthy social environment.

Recall that acceptance isn't merely gritting our teeth. It's not just having a body and learning how to *deal* with it. Acceptance embraces *what is*, presenting us with two arduous points. The first is that acceptance doesn't occur all at once. In body-dysmorphic cases, take time to explore frustration, angst, and discomfort, as these feelings may actually underline our willingness to grow. How much of our energy has been invested in trying to change, fix, or ignore our body? How much time have we spent hating it? Observing the futility of our control tactics turns our perception of the problem on its head, as our body isn't the actual obstacle. We may hate how short we are, or loathe our skeletal structure, or despise our genetics, but the actual problem is our judgmental attitude.

As for the second point? Body acceptance is not antithetical to gender self-actualization, though it can feel like cherry picking. In this case, body acceptance engages our mindfulness to accept our somatic self, the part of our living experience that is tangible, sensory, and potentially at odds with our conceptual self. Asking a gender variant person to accept our body for what it is may not be apropos if we're in the midst of transition, or if our gender identity isn't congruent with our phenotypes. However, asking us to defuse from judgment while being mindful of our changing physicality allows us to build a relationship that isn't solely built on criticism.

We are all physically growing and changing with time, with or without hormone regimens, breast augmentations, or facial surgery. Some gender dysphoric body discomfort—like backache from breasts, menstrual cramps, facial hair or lack thereof, and even morning wood—can all be remedied. Yet parts of our physicality are pretty universal. Perspiration, tummy rumbles, flatulence, jiggly cellulite, ingrown hairs, acne, and belly pooch are all non-gendered examples of this. Body acceptance, therefore, is about releasing our ideals to accept ourselves as an organism.

When we define our body in concrete terms, we try to ignore all the versions that came before and after, like stating the make of a car but ignoring the year or the model (Forsyth and Eifert, 2016). So, when we say, "I hate my body," we're not only judging our entire, global experience and generalizing it as *bad*, we're also believing it's consistently, constantly, and continuously bad. We believe our body will be like this, all the time, forever. This can prompt the body-dysmorphic mindset to frown at acceptance. Should we believe our body is not only *bad* but *eternally bad*, acceptance sounds like a prison sentence. Twisting this, the body-dysmorphic mindset may also assume we *have to accept* being too fat or too thin, or too masculine or too feminine, or too ugly or too plain, and mock us if we can't (Blackledge, 2015). At this point, acceptance begins to feel like a lofty enlightened goal, leaving us in the guilty shadow of vanity and superficiality.

Acceptance, in this case, is not about agreeing with our criticism, but accepting that our bodies change over time, and that they're never consistent. Having gone through puberty and explored our gender presentation, we can understand this intellectually, but time is a physical comedy, and we may not yet get all its in-jokes about building sandcastles by the sea. Fortunately, our relationship with our body doesn't have to be an eroding one. Indeed, our relationship with our body can be a potential friendship—not necessarily a drama-free friendship, but one reliant on curiosity and compassion. Language is the subtle key here, as many compassionate people spare no kindness for themselves, choosing to feed a proverbial dog even as they starve. As such, we may initially reject certain values—not because they're absent, but because we can't accept them for ourselves.

"Oh, sure, I'm really compassionate, but I wouldn't say I have self-compassion."

"It's a cliché, but I am my own worst enemy. My friends say I'm the kindest person they know, but I'm not forgiving."

> "I don't appreciate myself. Never have. I'm grateful. I'm glad I exist, but I don't appreciate myself."

In self-help body-image books, there's a lot of talk about *self-love*. Yet self-love is a tall order, and for many gender variant people, loving our bodies can at first seem counterintuitive (Hill-Meyer and Scarborough, 2014). Unless we're an infatuated Romeo, we don't typically fall head over heels the moment we meet someone. A person may catch our eye, and so kindle affection. If this is true for our relationship with others, then it's also true for our relationship with ourselves, which means that long before *self-love* we progress through *self-like* and *self-acquaintance*.

Mindful exercises like the *Sensory awareness* activity resituate the mind-body relationship from body as appearance to body as experience. When we can't appreciate our form, we can still appreciate our function. We may not like our lips, but we appreciate eating. We may not like the size of our hands, but running our fingers over velvet is delightful. We may not like our profile, but the feel of a breeze on our face is still relaxing. With help, we can work to find pleasant sensations: perhaps the smoothness of a pebble, or the coolness of the air, or the smell of lavender. Although naturally regulating, the goal isn't to calm or necessarily soothe distress, but to observe how we can appreciate the very part of us we reject.

Some of us may state that *we do appreciate* our body's function, we just hate how it looks. Tread lightly here, as the gender variant demographic—perhaps more than any other population—has been subjected to the *surgery as solution* medical model. Even healthy mindsets based on values of self-alignment and self-actualization may admittedly dislike certain sex traits and phenotypes we were born with, hence our desire to change them! Yet when this judgment is the loudest thought in our mind, transition becomes less about self-actualization and more about escaping internal judgment. Similarly, body-dysmorphic, gender variant clients may desire aesthetic surgery in part because we want to self-actualize, and in part as an emotional control tactic.

Instead of trying to stop or ignore our judgment, the ACT approach is to acknowledge it. We wince at the mirror, frown at the reflection, try to fix our hair, or flick imaginary dust off our shoulders. We all doubt and question and criticize what we look like since we tend to grow, age, and transform faster than our conceptual self can adjust. This is why we say a new outfit is "growing on us," or why we might need a day or two to adjust to a new haircut. We may recognize how normal self-criticism is, yet for some of us the frequency and intensity of these thoughts are turned way up. How mean are we to ourselves? How often does our inner fashionista tear apart our ensemble and poke apart our body? Defusion exercises like *I'm having the thought* or *Personify the distress* can help identify shame and self-disgust as intrusive thoughts we've over-identified with. Yet we may not struggle with *who* we are, per se, just *what* we are in physical form. While mindful sensory awareness can help increase our mind–body connection, increasing contact with a body we despise or feel disgusted by may actually generate discomfort and distress.

It's often said that compassion, kindness, loyalty, family, and love are easier to give to others than to ourselves. This seems especially true when it comes to appreciating our bodies. Yet let's not take this outward generosity at face value, since we tend to give varying degrees of compassion and kindness depending on the context and the person. We may be more generous, vulnerable, intimate, or trusting with a lover than a friend, and more so with a friend than a stranger. How do we demonstrate our values with new people in our lives? How do we show kindness to a passerby on the street? Do we share a smile or a wave? If we value any of the aforementioned qualities but hurry down the sidewalk with averted eyes, can we commit to waving at five people a day? This may sound unrelated to body dysmorphia, but humanizing others practices the same defusion tactics needed to humanize ourselves.

Often, when we meet someone new, we may give them the critical once over, but we soon find aspects we *also* appreciate about them. As we commit to patience, trust, or courtesy, we will literally give new acquaintances "the benefit of the doubt," noticing our doubt and deliberately setting it aside to let them finish their story. Practicing this value commitment for the benefit of others is, of course, a dress rehearsal for extending that same value commitment to ourselves. Are we only generous to beautiful people? Do we only show kindness to those with idyllic proportions? Hopefully not, but fusing so totally to frames of comparison and distinction leads to superficiality. Of course, it's easier to be compassionate with people we like, but can we practice the same compassion in stressful relationships? Can we appreciate a quality or characteristic in someone even if we don't know them or necessarily like them? The more experiential examples of value commitment we have to draw on, the more we're faced with our own double standard.

When we engage our bodies like a tenuous stranger or a loathsome ally, we only tolerate it because we have to. Reinvesting in a physically mindful relationship is to quintessentially give our body the same "benefit of the doubt" we would give a friend, or even a stranger. We're not "faking it 'til we make it," since we're not pretending to be doubtless any more than we're pretending to be judgment free. Yet nor are we allowing our doubt and judgment to stop the proverbial conversation, shut us down, or ruin our friendship with ourselves.

Acquainting ourselves with our body is to discern our thoughts from our behaviors and defuse from our all-or-nothing mindset. Just as we like our friends with all their flaws and foibles intact, so too can we be gracious with ourselves.

As we acquaint ourselves with physical awareness, it becomes easier to observe what we do appreciate. However, like any budding relationship, we need to take our time. We rarely leap from self-acquaintance to self-like in one session; and when we do, we may be trying too hard, wanting so desperately to believe our own words. Learning to defuse from judgmental thoughts takes time, as does mindful expansion. Befriending our body, even if we don't admire or praise it, is a pivotal step, especially if we have a history of disordered eating and self-harm.

In session, ask what thoughts are present. Can we differentiate our dislike of this from our desire to like that? Practice creating room for each thought to exist. It's okay to wish our hands were smaller, or our legs were longer, or our breasts were larger or even nonexistent. As some of these aspects of our physical form are potentially adaptable, gender variant clients sometimes need extra time to reflect on the role of cisnormative beauty standards in our decision-making process. Moving toward self-like isn't sitting around giving ourselves compliments, but an active process taking back the time and energy otherwise spent on self-criticism. How frequently do our judgmental thoughts pop in, and how loud are they? Learning to like ourselves is exemplified in our willing defusion practice, as we can opt to engage and amplify these thoughts or expand past them when they emerge.

The body-dysmorphic mindset often lists various forms of distraction as self-care, including watching TV, videogames, reading, listening to music, hanging out with friends, and so on. On an ACT matrix, most of these techniques are short-term away-moves that neglect the body. What are some physical activities we can use to practice defusion and mindful awareness? Everything and anything will work, from hugs, to cooking, to sitting on a couch. Let's make a list and rank them in degrees of potential stress. Bubble baths, stretching in the morning, and going for a walk are, hypothetically, low-stress examples. Comparatively, dancing (even alone), masturbation, sex, or simply looking in the mirror can be areas of high stress. Never assume what is high or low stress for body-dysmorphic or gender dysphoric clients, as it's possible to increase mental rigidity and therefore distress around any aspect of the somatic self. Chart out low-stress physical activities and encourage us to practice our *Sensory awareness* exercise in each one. Should a judgmental thought enter the mind, we can practice the *Yes, and...* or *Personify the distress* exercises to expand beyond the thought and draw our awareness back to our physical senses. Over the next few weeks, we can work up the list accordingly, learning how to recognize intrusive thoughts about our body, and expand beyond them to keep contact with our present-based experience. Each encounter provides an opportunity to befriend our body by committing to willingness, persistence, and resilience in the face of judgment. Though searching for happiness and comfort is not the intended goal of these experiential somatic exercises, joyful experiences naturally reinforce our willingness to try again.

As we're not looking to extinguish our judgments, we may still oscillate from time to time, recognizing what we both like and dislike about our bodies, just as we can like and dislike certain qualities in our friends. We're not yet at a point of total self-love, but we are moving away from assessing our somatic and bodily experience on false paradigms of beauty. For those who are wondering if self-love is even possible, or if that too is a perfectionist ideal, the answer is only as believable as one's experience with love itself. After all, we can't force ourselves to love someone, as love is an emotion and not a controllable action. We can express love, but when the emotion is absent, we're presenting flowers we stole from a graveyard. Love, and to that point self-love, is perhaps the ultimate mindfulness exercise. The more we look within, expand beyond our limits, accept our authentic self, and appreciate our authentic form, the more we'll notice what we appreciate and perhaps even adore.

## Driving dazed: ACT for dissociation

Road hypnosis is scary. Driving our daily commute, our consciousness dissipates, leaving our body to drive the car without us. We were awake the whole time, possibly thinking about this or that, and in a blink we're home! This is an example of common dissociation, as we checked out of the present moment, and completely lost our awareness (Neziroglu and Donnelly, 2013). We don't remember putting on our blinker, or the right turn, or putting on the parking brake, or anything—and we're a little alarmed by that! Hold on. Is there someone in the back seat? Imagine blinking out of road hypnosis and realizing we not only had a passenger the whole time, but that they'd been trying to tell us they're in the wrong car! Returning to ACT's *passengers on the bus* metaphor (Hayes *et al.*, 2012), our bus driver just realized their entire bus is full of noisy people all vying for their attention. They were always there, but only now are they aware of them!

Waking up in a body that isn't *right* is a surreal experience. Every primal, human instinct is called into question, and nothing feels natural. Add trauma and minority stress, and some clients may disconnect from both emotional and somatic awareness. Pushing the eject button, we may detach into states of depersonalization, or compartmentalize, which includes a range of psychoform symptoms, such as amnesia, flashbacks, sensory loss, and alterations to identity (Brown, 2013). Such compartmentalized, hypnotic-like states present great risk to clients, if we engage in activities we may not be able to recall later (Brown, 2013; Rothschild, 2000). Yet being numb doesn't negate the existence of emotion; if anything, it's an indicator of its very existence.

Have you ever sat on your hand until it went numb? The peculiar sensation of not feeling your hand is so bizarre because it brings attention *to* your hand. Similarly, the numb are often very aware of our numbness, provided that is, we haven't checked out. A quick conversation with the dissociative mindset often reveals unhealthy perspectives of ourselves or the world, framing emotional ejection as a subconscious means of escape. It doesn't just hold back our tears and control our affect. If anything, it feels like the well has run dry, or that we forgot where the well even is! This may not be deliberate, yet statements like "It's better to feel nothing than be angry" or "I don't cry when I'm sad" indicate mental rigidity. We may become incredibly stubborn, gripping tightly to a rationale to explain why our emotions are untrustworthy. In this case, emotions and their somatic expression are judged as *bad* or even *dangerous*.

Dissociative episodes are most well known for their amnesia and fugue states, though it remains possible to dissociate from thoughts, attention, and even physical experiences—blanking out for a moment, or selectively forgetting parts of an interaction without omitting the whole thing (Rothschild, 2000; Williams and Poijula, 2002). The dissociative mindset may struggle with conventional ACT techniques, including mindfulness exercises engaging the observational self, since we may already feel like a perpetual observer, existing outside of our sensory experience. We may even fear that defusion will set off a dissociative episode. Depending on the extent of these symptoms, the typical definition of *experiential avoidance* may not be appropriate if we are not conscious of the stimuli we're presumed to be avoiding. This unique subcategory of the agenda of emotional control is described here as the *agenda of emotional distance*.

While emotional control strategies employ experiential avoidance like running away or ignoring overwhelming stimuli, emotional distance employs a form of perceptual ejection, removing the individual—not from specific stimuli—but from cognitive/emotional processing as an experiential unit. Essentially, the agenda of emotional distance doubles-down on the agenda of emotional control, subconsciously striving to disconnect from the body via dysphoric desomatization (Medford *et al.*, 2005). We're still fused to a cognition, yet the associated emotion is so threatening that our awareness of it is blocked. Seeming calm, we don't realize we're clenching our fist. Telling cold stories, we may describe horrendous events in our life without a tremble in our voice. When asked how we feel, we may say "I don't know," or "I don't feel anything," or shut down, or launch into a cerebral explanation.

Striving to "keep together" and "stay composed" as a rule can make facing the full spectrum of our hopes and fears a somatically overwhelming experience, especially if we're already incongruent with our body. If we adamantly claim we can "turn off" our emotions, we may be noticing a manipulation of the sympathetic nervous system. Suppressing our emotional response, in many cases, actually increases our heart rate, like trying to put out a fire by fanning it (Gross, 2002; Sloan, 2004). Yet this doesn't hold true for everyone. Just as we can learn to regulate and control a physiological response, we can also, to our detriment, suppress our feelings so as not to suffer from increased arousal (Sloan, 2004). This felt detachment often leads to a surreal feeling of disconnection, since our emotional process remains even if our heart rate doesn't spike.

We may state, "I should be scared right now, but I'm not" or "I think I'm supposed to cry, but I don't feel anything." Dissociated, we may lose our defensive reasoning and enter a state of melancholy or, in extreme cases, flashbacks, hallucinations, catatonia, and amnesia (Brown, 2013; Rothschild, 2000; Shiloh *et al.*, 1995; Williams and Poijula, 2002). We may begin to talk slowly, become entirely mute, or be unable to identify our own emotions (Fink and Taylor, 2003; Ramirez *et al.*, 2001). Shut down, our mannerisms may take on an exhausted, defeated, or vacant quality, reporting feelings of "mind emptiness" (Sierra and Berrios, 1998), or symptoms of desomatization, including disembodiment or an overall indifference to pain (Medford *et al.*, 2005). The cyclical relationship between dissociation and self-harm cannot be overstated. Should we feel overwhelmed by feelings, we may attempt to re-engage a dissociative state through substance abuse or self-harm (Asmundson, Stapleton, and Taylor, 2005; Feeny *et al.*, 2005; Prigerson *et al.*, 1997; Simeon and Abugel, 2006).

It's here we need to mark a distinction, as peritraumatic dissociation during a traumatic event is not deemed pathological, unlike the symptoms of chronic dissociation that follow severely traumatic encounters (Neziroglu and Donnelly, 2013). Peritraumatic dissociation is that strange calm in the eye of a storm, where everything seems to slow down in the middle of a fight, or a car wreck, or a volatile situation, and we no longer feel stressed. Gender variant people subjected to one hardship after the next may unintentionally engage this response on a frequent basis. This alone does not warrant a dissociative diagnosis, yet should this felt detachment continue, it can lead to a number of emotional, social, and occupational lulls. Experiences of dissociation vary, though they can be split between symptoms of *detachment* and *compartmentalization* (Brown, 2013).

## *Detachment*

As an altered state of consciousness-spanning disorders, detachment is often reported by those with depression, anxiety, and PTSD, yet it rarely presents as a primary complaint despite its prevalence (Ackner, 1954; Brown, 2013; Feeny *et al.*, 2005; Shimizu and Sakamoto, 1986; Steinberg, 1991). Detachment is often experienced as an emotionally numb state of depersonalization and derealization, which are both odd yet common experiences (Brown, 2013).

Depersonalization feels like there's a distance or a buffer between us and our senses, even though our reality testing remains intact (Steinberg, 1991). In 2015, 29.6 percent of transgender participants surveyed reported depersonalization, in contrast to 12.2 percent of the cisgender populace (Colizzi *et al.*, 2015). Forced gender roles, coupled with a dysphoric relationship with sex phenotypes, may contribute to *a false sense of self*. Likewise, we may attempt to distance ourselves from somatic emotional experiences associated with masculinity (brooding, anger, pride) or femininity (sadness, fear, disgust).

We may report feeling like a ghost—conveying a sense of complete self-removal—or of sitting somewhere behind the eyes, operating the body like a puppet or a robot (Medford *et al.*, 2005; Simeon and Abugel, 2006; Spiegel and Cardena, 1996). We may feel detached or unreal, as if wearing a mask or living one step behind ourselves (Ackner, 1954; Fewtrell, 1986; Jacobson, 1959; Simeon *et al.*, 2003; Spiegel and Cardena, 1996; Steinberg, 1991). Because of this hypo-emotional detachment, the depersonalized mindset may be less likely to avoid triggering situations, meaning we'll walk into a nightmare because we're numb to our own fear (Sierra and Berrios, 1998). Relationally, after accounting for depression and dissociation, these numb depersonalized states can be predictive of PTSD (Feeny *et al.*, 2005).

Be aware that depersonalized high-self monitors are often *too good* at defusion techniques, insisting that we're always objective even when our rationale proves to be slippery, vague, or bereft of emotional awareness. Mistaking honesty for vulnerability, we may assume that talking about emotions is the same as feeling them. Though there are many nuanced differences between the emotionally accepting state of defusion and the emotionally rejecting state of depersonalization, they can be difficult to differentiate. After all, both the International Space Station and the moon are in the Earth's orbit, but one is habitable, close, and capable of seeing the Earth in detail with the naked eye, whereas the other is cold and distant. The moon does provide perspective, it's true, yet living there would only give us a macro impression of our planet's oceans, clouds, and continents without seeing any of the life they hold.

If depersonalization questions our frame of self, then derealization questions our frame of other, leaving us feeling like we're watching a movie. We may struggle to verbalize the strange feeling that the world is somehow unreal, or describe feeling emotions but discount their importance, impact, or relevance in the same way we care about characters until we turn off the TV (Fewtrell, 1986; Shimizu and Sakamoto, 1986; Steinberg, 1991). Like depersonalization, this surreal feeling may result from activation in the right prefrontal cortex, spiking attention, coupled with an inhibition in the anterior cingulate, dampening awareness (Medford *et al.*, 2005; Phillips *et al.*, 2001; Sierra and Berrios, 1998). This could neurologically account for the immediate sense of hypervigilance matched with the dreamy, unreal quality of being over-stimulated (Sierra and Berrios, 1998).

If we're isolated, alienated, and disconnected from an LGBTQ community, we may feel like we've landed on a different planet. Off-hand, this is not indicative of derealization, as navigating a cisnormative, heteronormative planet as a gender variant person can be a lonely and unusual experience. Yet isolationism, invalidation, and a closeted experience may contribute to the erosion between self and other, decreasing trust in reality. As a form of emotional distance, derealization assumes we can't get hurt if nothing matters, and that any physical or emotional pain is irrelevant.

When we're depersonalized and distanced from our own body image, we're less likely to reflect hostility when made aware of our social identity. However, if we're suffering from derealization regarding the unreality of others, we may report physically aggressive attitudes when we begin to be mindful (Bovasso, 1997). When the irrelevant becomes relevant, and the intangible becomes solid, we may feel strife, guilt, and confusion as it dawns on us that our actions and our environment actually matter.

Egocentric, the derealized perspective prioritizes *self* as more salient than *other*. Even if we have low self-esteem, or count ourselves as figments in the dream, we still maintain that everything's an illusion because we see it as an illusion. As abstract notions, these aren't debatable. Indeed, whole spiritual beliefs are based on this idea, and the derealized mindset loves to cite metaphysical manifestos as its citations. The ACT response to ontology is simple: *Does this work for you? Is it functional?* (Hayes *et al.*, 2012). Answers may be split, as derealization may keep us emotionally insulated, but also impact our relationships with others and our own personal satisfaction with life.

## *Compartmentalization*

Compartmentalization includes all the incidents of amnesia, hallucination, flashback, somatoform disorders, and altered identity that relinquish mental control, only to have our disrupted functions continue without us (Brown, 2013). An example of this is the loss of time experienced by people with dissociative identity disorder (DID) or dissociative fugue, as they continued walking and talking without mental consent (Neziroglu and Donnelly, 2013). If we overidentify with a dissociative diagnosis, we may find it harder to engage awareness, as our mental rigidity keeps our emotional eject button viable (Neziroglu and Donnelly, 2013).

From an ACT perspective, DID may exemplify the most extreme case of schema incongruence, as DID reflects a failed integration of identity, memory, and consciousness (Brown, 2001; Spiegel and Cardena, 1996). Infrequent cases of trans individuals struggling with DID exist in the literature, which are distinct from DID clients with opposite sex alter egos, warranting vigilance from mental health practitioners (Brown, 2001; Colizzi *et al.*, 2015; Saks, 1998; Schwartz, 1988). Furthermore, DID is not in any way, shape, or form an appropriate diagnosis for polygender individuals alternating between two or more gender schemas, as those who alternate between genders report the experience as stress relieving and self-fulfilling, whereas DID is marked by increased levels of disorientation and insecurity (Bockting *et al.*, 2004; Israel and Tarver II, 1997). The presence of DID is not a contraindication for SRS, as a client who accepts and adequately manages their DID may be considered eligible for gender alignment surgery depending on their stability (Brown, 2001; Bockting *et al.*, 2006).

Cases of DID are best handled by specialists in this complex area, as DID requires an in-depth level of case management. Specifically, DID cases are not viewed as a collection of individual identities, but as a contextual whole (ISSD, 2011). Over many sessions, trained clinicians help whichever identity is present in session to become aware of the others, building toward assimilating points of fusion where two or more identities merge, progressively building to one unified identity (ISSD, 2011). Mindful acceptance could prove beneficial for clients learning to accept both DID and their emotional response to this diagnosis. In complex cases, ACT techniques may also help to explore and engage any shared values between identity constructs, taking one small step toward whole integration.

Research using the Dissociative Experience Scale (DES) found that the prevalence of dissociative symptoms is consistently higher amongst trans populations than cisgender control groups. One study found that trans people scored a mean of 18.33 on the DES, in contrast to the cisgender 2.8 (Kersting *et al.*, 2003). Comparably, a longitudinal Italian study found that the mean DES score began at 19.05, but subsequently dropped to 9.31 following HRT (Colizzi *et al.*, 2015). Repeatedly, findings illustrate that, as transgender individuals begin to take steps toward self-actualization, whether through HRT or gender alignment surgery, our dissociative experience is greatly reduced (Colizzi *et al.*, 2015; Kersting *et al.*, 2003; Walling, Goodwin, and Cole, 1998; Wolfradt and Neumann, 2001). A conundrum occurs, of course, when dissociation becomes an obstacle to our ability to help ourselves.

If we drift off in session, or become absorbed in our own internal world, agree on a way to "bring us back," possibly by tapping our leg, snapping your fingers, waving your hand in front of us, calling our name, or in extreme cases using smelling salts (Harris, 2016). Whenever possible, normalize dissociation as an emotional defense mechanism that's helped us survive (Harris, 2016). Should we explain how emotional distance has helped us, ACT therapists will accept this answer without debate as the unfolding sessions will reveal whether or not it's true (Harris, 2016). To explore this sentiment, use the same Socratic questioning used to challenge the agenda of control to inquire what emotional distance has cost us (Forsyth and Eifert, 2016; Harris, 2009a, 2016; Orsillo *et al.*, 2004). This may include less passionate relationships, fewer meaningful connections, loss of motivation, lower vitality, and disconnection with self. Validating our willingness to maintain connection, begin by exploring the observational self, and the operations leading up to detachment and compartmentalization.

If we eject in response to an unwanted cognition, help us build resilience through increased contact with the thought before attempting defusion. The *Soldiers on parade* meditation has been used effectively by ACT practitioners working with dissociative clients and, depending on the population, the imagery can be adapted to *Protestors on the march* (Neziroglu and Donnelly, 2013). In this exercise, we're learning to notice when our mind's eye shifts from looking *at our thoughts* to looking *from our thoughts* (Neziroglu and Donnelly, 2013).

> *Imagine a line of tiny protestors marching out of your left ear. Waving tiny little signs, they march down your shoulder and down your arm. Each of their banners and signs has a thought on it, maybe a written phrase, an opinion, a critical thought, or maybe just a picture of a frowny face or a happy face. Imagine them walking all the way down your arm, hopping onto your lap, down your leg, and marching right out the door. Now, keep watching them, but try not to jump down to their perspective. Stay up here looking down at those tiny people for as long as you can. If you find yourself imagining things from their perspective, or feel like the parade has stopped, or start questioning the point of the exercise, see if you can notice what happened before the hiatus, then go back to observing what was on their tiny signs.*

In this exercise we're not trying to prevent our mind from wandering away or getting sidetracked, nor are we trying to change what's on the tiny signs; instead we're trying to observe our pattern of disengagement (Neziroglu and Donnelly, 2013). What thoughts lead us away from observation? Doubt? Boredom? Frustration? As potential precursors to experiential avoidance, noticing these feelings in our body can help initiate sensory mindfulness to ground us in our body. Slowly, we can build awareness around mundane, daily emotional expressions and distressing thoughts, even if we don't feel connected to them. At first we may be unfamiliar or unprepared for the physicality of emotion (shaky hands, shortness of breath, racing heartbeat), and in session in vivo exposure is advisable to experience and normalize emotion (Eifert and Forsyth, 2005). Ironically, the depersonalized mindset may deem emotional regulating exercises unnecessary if "we don't feel anything," or unsatisfactory if they don't rid us of painful emotions. ACT can be quite valuable here, as breathing and mindfulness exercises are not introduced as a form of emotional regulation, but as a means of expanding awareness (Blackledge and Hayes, 2001). Any calm felt through defusion practice is a beneficial byproduct, but not its initial function.

As dissociation stems from our experiential avoidance of our internal world, drawing mindfulness to our external world is incremental (Harris, 2016; Neziroglu and Donnelly, 2013). As children, we interact with the world tangibly, touching and interacting with everything. As adults, we'll see the bark of a tree and know it's rough without ever having to touch it. We have enough distinguishing frames logged into our memory to tell that marble is smooth and a cactus is spikey. Retreating into our own heads, adults move through the world, thinking about this and worrying about that, while barely interacting with it. Early in session, try introducing physical mindfulness via our passive senses (sight, sound, touch, taste, smell), and then by having us actively interact with our environment by pressing our hands against a chair, or pushing our feet down and noticing the pressure (Harris, 2016). You can also call our awareness to the surface of our body, including the temperature we feel, the tears on our cheek, and the sweat on our skin (Harris, 2016). Sifting our hands through sand, rubbing our face with a velvet cloth, and holding ice cubes can also help ground us in the present moment. As rapport builds, humorous sensory exercises are also an excellent way to center, as chewing on a mouth full of peanut butter is very preoccupying.

As a takeaway exercise, ask us to track everything we touch with our hands in a day: the coffee mug, the car keys, the steering wheel, the door to the office, the button on the elevator, the chair, the keyboard. Rinse and repeat. After following this, ask us to break from the routine by touching something new every day. Maybe run our hand over a tree on our daily walk, or stick our hand directly in a bowl of ice cream and squish it with our fingers. Trying foods we've never eaten, going places we've never gone, talking to new people about old ideas, talking to old friends about new topics, standing on our head, swimming in the ocean, painting our face, even getting stung by a bee, can all help us connect with ourselves in the present moment.

As we're gradually exposed to sensory stimulation, we're gradually exposed to our emotional response system. The concept of accepting emotions without necessarily liking them may be daunting for some, so begin with that observation (Harris, 2009a; Hayes and Smith, 2005; Hayes *et al.*, 2012). Highlight any initial anxiety we may have about emotional exploration as an emotional exploration! If we're nervous, where do we feel our tension? Should we begin to feel numb again, ask us to notice it, and compassionately accept the experience as a passing moment no matter how long it lasts (Harris, 2016). This is a two-steps forward, one-step back process, progressively leaning into our discomfort rather than away from it.

Challenging the agenda of emotional distance reveals the illusion of emotional immunization by proving how emotions remain present even if we don't feel proximal to them. Observing our emotional responses in everyday stimuli eases us into self-awareness. Since the agenda of emotional distance does not always permit emotional awareness, it may be crucial to examine how we express anger without realizing we're angry, or paranoia without realizing we're afraid. If we're consciously, or perhaps unconsciously, rejecting emotion, we'll sidestep emotional vocabulary. Ask us if we're sad, angry, or happy and we'll probably shrug, or say, "I don't know." You can troubleshoot this by homing in on our body without using emotion-based language.

*Did anything make you clench your fists today?*

*Did anything make you take a heavy sigh this morning?*

*Have you smirked at anything—not laughed, but just smirked at something silly or stupid?*

*Did anything make you hang your head today, like your head was really heavy or you had to just stare at the ground?*

*Did anything make you rub your face or your eyes today?*

Note that we're not interpreting or labeling these emotions, yet. We're just observing the natural processes that exist independently of our consciousness. In the same way that we do not command our heart to beat or our liver to filter blood, the body naturally generates emotion. Our throat will close, our feet will tap, our eyes will roll, our armpits will sweat, our stomach will knot, and yes, our heart will beat faster, even when we don't consciously know why. During this interim stage of treatment, we may experience cognitions/emotions as irrational, requiring you to validate our experience while differentiating sensation from behavior, that is, anger from violence, depression from self-mutilation, etc. (Eifert and Forsyth, 2005; Hayes *et al.*, 2012). A social support network is advisable, including a phone contact to aid us with emotional immediacy and social role modeling. If our catchphrase is "I'm fine," we may need support outside of session as we're often unaware of our somatic emotional needs. It may never cross our mind, for example, to ask for a hug or listen to the soothing voice of a friend.

Should an emotion present itself in session, let's practice feeling it in the body. In the case of anger, notice any smirk, sarcasm, or snarky comment, and appreciate it for its emotional honesty, even if it's passive-aggressive. In the case of alexithymia, the inability to name emotions, provide an emotional vocabulary chart, but emphasize that we're not too concerned with exactitude, as emotions are squishy anyway (Harris, 2016). As we begin to familiarize ourselves with our physical responses, it's worth exploring the context of each situation. Are we aware of our twitching eye, exhausted body language, drop in our voice, or our sassy sneer? Whatever we notice in our body, you can let us attribute a feeling to it by pondering the specific behavior aloud: *I wonder which feeling causes your eyes to thin like that.*

Direct observations made by the clinician can be challenging if we're emotionally distant, and a critical part of us may split hairs over what does or doesn't constitute a *smile* or a *frown*. The more anatomic the observation, the less threatening it becomes.

*The corners of your mouth just turned up. What feeling do you connect with that? Your forehead just crinkled and your eyebrows came together. Can you feel it?*

If we're uncertain of our answer, replicate the expression with us. Ask us to do it again as you join in, allowing us to collaborate on observations of each other's body language.

*I'm noticing that when my eyebrows come together, like this, I feel a lot of tension, right at the bridge above my nose. Do you feel that? Where else do you feel tension?*

*When you first started talking, you clamped your hands between your legs. Can you try that again? What words come to mind when you see me in this position?*

Some will take this exercise very seriously, others will laugh as we're effectively making faces at each other, and some will feel passively indifferent. Whatever the case, incorporate that emotion into the exercise as well.

*I noticed, as we're doing this, we're both leaning forward in our chairs with our feet planted on the floor. Let's take that position again. We're kind of leaning in, aren't we?*

*You did something just now. Would you call it a chuckle or a laugh? Ever notice the feelings in your torso when we do that?*

*Sometimes the feeling of not feeling is actually a feeling in disguise. Sounds weird, I know, but I want you to try something. I'm going to sit like you are now, leaning back in my chair. If you were to see me sitting like this, what do you suppose I'd be feeling?*

Helping us become aware of our emotional process when we are detached or compartmentalized takes time and patience, and is often a crucial step in both trauma recovery and gender actualization. Likewise, helping us identify disengagement patterns helps us observe behaviors leading up to a dissociative episode. Be slow and incremental in this process, however, as we are literally exploring triggers that we're unaware of. Before addressing the emotional distress of our internal world—which may be too overwhelming at this time—broader, impersonal subjects are useful to practice fusing and defusing from. Sociopolitical issues that impact our life are a great example, as are reactions to movies we disliked, or annoyances we may have with peers and co-workers. Even something as small as our dissatisfaction with lunch can serve as a launching point for somatic awareness and emotional acceptance. Keeping a daily diary is also an excellent way to track cognitions, mood, and dissociative episodes, and process how thoughts and feelings interact as we progress from session to session (Harris, 2009a; Walser and Westrup, 2007; Zettle, 2007).

## Hedgehogs and butterflies: ACT for anxiety and trauma

Even without meeting the criteria for generalized anxiety disorder, social anxiety disorder, or PTSD, gender variant clients often report symptoms of anxiety and hypervigilance. Cisgenderism and transphobia take their toll. Aspiring professionals stepping into the office may swallow their beating heart. Even standing in line at a grocery store can fray the nerves. Even after coming out, developing friendships and intimate relationships may take on an added difficulty, not because there is any inherent danger or risk of judgment, but for fear that there might be.

If we're subjected to passive microaggressions, hostile macroaggressions, and the potential threat of cisgenderism and transphobia, it is perhaps more effective to conceptualize anxiety and PTSD as overlapping symptom sets on a continuum of hypervigilant, stress-induced behavior. In the year leading up to the National Center for Transgender Equality (NCTE) US Transgender Survey, 46 percent of gender variant individuals were harassed, 9 percent were physically assaulted, and 10 percent were sexually assaulted (James *et al.*, 2016). Of 27,715 respondents from all 50 states, Guam, Puerto Rico, American Samoa, and the District of Columbia, 47 percent reported being sexually assaulted at some point in their life (James *et al.*, 2016). These numbers are higher amongst racial minorities, with 53 percent of African American, 58 percent of Middle Eastern, and 65 percent of Native American gender variant people surviving sexual assault (James *et al.*, 2016). This includes 61 percent of gender variant people who are differently abled (James *et al.*, 2016). And if we thought we were safe at home, 54 percent of transgender respondents were subjected to intimate partner violence (James *et al.*, 2016). Quite arguably, there's a lot to worry about.

To structure these alarming numbers, violence toward gender minorities falls into three general categories (Richmond *et al.*, 2012): *Interpersonal violence* includes every one-on-one interaction with a single antagonist; *collective violence* exceeds the horror of group hostility to include the subtle, pervasive intolerance within social institutions, making us afraid to call for legal protection and medical help even when we need it; and *self-directed violence* makes us afraid to be alone with our own thoughts (Richmond *et al.*, 2012). Even if we haven't experienced any direct physical or sexual trauma, the lingering threat and perceived expectation of harm in a variety of social, academic, and occupational settings may lead to persistent, nonspecific anxiety we may not be able to attribute to any singular cause (Nadal *et al.*, 2015). This may sound strange to cisgender clinicians, but many times gender variant people will walk into the room hoping for nothing—hoping for a non-reaction. No grimaces, no winces, no frowns, no smirks, no insults, no glares, no notice. Truth be told, everyone likes a little attention now and then, but gender variant people are recurrently subjected to the worst kind of attention. Anxiety flares in social settings when we're continuously forced to be conscious of our environment. It's hard to gauge all the sidelong looks, quick glances, and long stares. It's exhausting to have all these hopeful *maybe* statements dangling like carrots from possibility's *what if* stick.

> "Maybe they'll like me. Maybe I'll get an A on the test. Maybe the girls will hang out with me. Maybe my parents will like my boyfriend."

Then, right when we lift our heads, anxiety beats us with the same stick. As we hate not knowing, anxiety solves this problem by becoming a pessimistic wannabe telepath, reading minds and predicting the future to near absolute determinism.

> "They hate me. My teacher's a bigot. The girls think I'm a queer freak. My parents will never accept my boyfriend because they don't accept I'm a man."

Fusing to faulty ex-consequentia thinking patterns, we assume that the symptoms of anxiety indicate danger, even if we can't immediately identify a trigger (Engelhard and Arntz, 2005). As our thinking self-hates a mystery, we frantically fill in the blanks with our own justifications, fusing all our fret and fear into an explanation. Our answers may be accurate, or not, but we'll never know as we're too scared to find out. After all, when we're anxious, asking someone their opinion of us can be absolutely terrifying!

Piling worry on worry, anxiety contributes to internalized cissexism by playing the blame game, and the blame game demands a loser, whether it's us or them. If it's us, we'll scurry along with downcast eyes, swaddling ourselves in the cloak of invisibility to avoid embarrassment or shame. If it's them, then we'll label all others as enemies or obstacles.

> "They're nice people, really—I mean I've got nothing against them—I just can't be around them right now. I'm just going back to my place. I'll call you later, but I won't, but I'm going to say I will as I back slowly toward the door."

In the USA, 3.5 percent of the overall population meet the criteria for generalized anxiety disorder. By contrast, a survey of 351 transgender participants found that 40.4 percent of trans women and 47.5 percent of trans men have anxiety (Budge *et al.*, 2013). To drive the point home, this same study found that avoidance strategies increased distress, whereas social support decreased distress (Budge *et al.*, 2013). So, avoiding our problems not only leads to them piling up, but it also undermines us further by shrinking our stress tolerance. The more often we tell ourselves "I can't," the more cemented that belief becomes. To avoid stress and fear, we may develop rituals and compulsive attitudes, reinforcing "I can't" beliefs with an "I have to" attitude, which may or may not be tolerable.

"I can't be honest, I have to keep my job."

"I can't go to school today, I have to skip."

"I can't say no to him, I have to be considerate."

Alarmed by our somatic fear response, anxiety hyperfocuses on control tactics. This can be a huge obstacle for many cognitive behavioral strategies encouraging us to approach the source of our fear (Orsillo *et al.*, 2004). Fortunately, approaching value congruence is a more accessible rationale for exposure, as is approaching emotional acceptance as a whole (Orsillo *et al.*, 2004). Doing so can still require some troubleshooting, as worry can arrest value-congruent action, especially when the future-focused catastrophes being anticipated eclipse our present awareness (Orsillo *et al.*, 2004). Additionally, an anxious mindset may pursue a value to avoid some other unwanted experience. A sexual trauma survivor may, for example, be very committed to avoiding thoughts, feelings, and memories tied to the abuse in order to live a rich and meaningful life, only to have aversion undermine intimacy (Wilson and Murrell, 2004). Our self-protective measures are not to be dismissed, as avoidance goals can still reflect survival-based values.

Experientially, anxiety is the fear of fear. It is the participant observer. It's our thinking self-adding extra commentary to our already quickened heart. Interestingly, for those with generalized anxiety disorder, worry actually reduces distress for a short while. While decreasing social resilience in the long run, worry preoccupies the mind and grants a short-lived illusion of control (Budge *et al.*, 2013; Hayes and Smith, 2005; Orsillo *et al.*, 2004; Sloan, 2004). To return our somatic awareness, try asking what happens when we're afraid. Do our palms get clammy? Do our hands shake? Do we feel tension in our legs? Does our mind go blank or do we feel it whirring like a turbine? Does our heart beat like a bongo? Do we hold our breath? We probably don't like these feelings at all, and that's the problem. These feelings aren't likeable, so we avoid them. When our sympathetic nervous system kicks into fight or flight mode, terror reminds us of our physical limitations, social standings, and visceral mortality. Fear is a fundamental human feeling. If we accept it, we can process, regulate, and move on. If we don't accept fear, we may unintentionally fuse with the very feeling we despise. By attempting to avoid provoking places, people, or situations, we ironically become stressed about monitoring our own stress.

"When I'm at work, I always go to the bathroom at the same time, about an hour before lunch break, because I know no one will be around. It's just easier that way. And I'm not disabled, but I always use the disabled stall because it's the only one with a lock on it. You know they say you're most likely to get assaulted in a bathroom?"

> "So, I'm 40 years old, and I feel like I'm on a school playground. Like, there's this guy who works at the market at the end of my street. I think he's the manager's son or something. He's always there. He's like 20 or something. Last year, he gave me this look. He probably doesn't remember, but I do. It was complete disgust. I didn't go back for a few days, but then I said to myself—I'm going to do it. I mean it's the closest market to my house, I could avoid it but I don't want to. So I went back, and there he was at the checkout, and I got my things, and I stood in line, and my heart was racing, and I'm 40 years old feeling like I'm about to get my lunch money stolen, and he smiles and tells me to have a nice day and I walk out shaken, feeling like I'm crazy! Now I don't go back there at all."

> "So, I'm on my phone, swiping left, swiping right, trying to find a date or something. And I'm out on my profile. Little rainbow emoji and everything, so no one can accuse me of catfishing anyone! Anyway, this guy started chatting me up, and it's got his name and location, so I look him up online. I probably spent an hour checking out all his posts and pictures. Looking for what? I don't know. I just got this thought in my head... Guys don't message me often, so I'm always like: Did someone put him up to this? Is he just trying to get the trans-hook-up notch on his belt? I didn't message him back. Did I find anything? No. Seemed sweet, but I just get all paranoid and I don't need that kind of stress. I should just delete my profile."

Unwilling to give up our avoidance strategies, our anxious mindset prefers the terrible known over an unfamiliar alternative. If we have endured trauma, we may even grip our trauma narrative out of a strange kind of obligation. We may believe that, should we move on, or manage to live happy and healthy lives, those who hurt us are somehow let off the hook. The Latin phrase *corpus delicti*, "the body of the crime," is often used in law to demand evidence, for if there's no corpse there's no crime (Hayes, Strosahl and Wilson, 1999; Walser and Westrup, 2007). Even if we want to forget what happened, or heal from it, we may fixate on our fear as the lasting evidence of our trauma. In this light, emotional distress, substance abuse, or social conflict, can be a way of holding on to the pain, not for the sake of pain itself, but to not pardon the crime, or the criminal, whether it's society or self.

Our survival mentality, in trying to keep us safe, begins to see danger everywhere, including in the mirror. Our inner survivalist equivocates about safety in order to maintain vigilance, even when we're at home with friends and family. Even the word *acceptance* can provoke anxiety, especially if we believe it equates to conceding to our fears or existing in a constant state of suffering (Walser and Westrup, 2007). Implying that we should tolerate anxiety-provoking situations or personal traumas is akin to saying we should yield to sexism, cissexism, or racism as inevitable endurance tests. Instead of accepting the distressing situation, therefore, we're learning how to accept the reality of pain as an emotional experience. We have been hurt in the past, will encounter scary situations in the future, and deal with the reality of each in the present.

For the highly anxious, especially those prone to PTSD flashback, mindfulness exercises can help foster dual awareness for both the intrusive memory and the present moment (Williams and Poijula, 2002). Defusion tactics viewing our memory like a video recording can allow us to practice rewinding, playing, pausing, and fast-forwarding (Williams and Poijula, 2002). Visualizing memories in this manner, we can begin to differentiate by verbally describing what we are doing in present time (sitting in a chair, practicing breathing exercises, holding a comfort object) before verbally describing an anxious or traumatic memory (Williams and Poijula, 2002).

Journaling, collaging, or creating visual representations of a chronological life story have also been shown to reduce stress and improve overall health in trauma cases, especially when shared in session (Bockting *et al.*, 2006). Trauma narratives often illustrate the broken bones of our conceptual self, yet rather than challenge the content of these stories, ACT contacts the contextual self, distinct from the story (Luoma and Villatte, 2012). As the reader reading the story, we're free to close the journal or fold up our collage at any time. Mindfully holding them in our hand, mindfully explore what they feel like to touch. Are they heavy or light? Do they feel well made or fragile? What colors stand out? What do we notice about the handwriting? Or the way the collage is stuck together? To demonstrate how to reduce our attachment to the conceptual self, place the journal or collage out of sight, somewhere in the room, before engaging in another sensory mindfulness activity. It's still ours, even if it's sitting behind the table, and it still exists, even when we're not actively looking at it, but it doesn't have to be our all-consuming focus.

To gain perspective, we can also take an inventory of what our subsequent control behaviors have cost us in the past year (Forsyth and Eifert, 2016). By recalling all the events, conflicts, and missed opportunities that have played out, we begin to notice how it's not our fear that messes us up, but our attempts to evade it.

*What were your interpersonal costs? Did you avoid your friends? Did you stay in when you wanted to go out? Did you never call them back? Did you conceal your identity? How often do you bite your tongue? Have you put off calling your parents?*

*What were your career costs? How does anxiety show up at work? How's your confidence level at work? How does anxiety impact your work performance?*

*What are the emotional costs? How often do you feel sad? Scared? Mad? How many days a week do you feel the urge to cry? How many days a week do you feel emotionally numb?*

> *What are the mental costs? Can you quantify how much time you spend judging yourself? How many anxious thoughts do you have a day?*
>
> *What are the health costs? How much time do you spend shut inside? How has anxiety impacted your ability to exercise? How has anxiety impacted your diet? Do you eat more or less, healthier or unhealthier, when you're anxious? Do you use drugs or alcohol when you're anxious?*
>
> *What are the financial costs of your anxiety? How much money do you spend on drugs or junk food? How much do you spend on extra gas, driving in circles to avoid your destination? How much did you spend in tuition on the classes you were afraid to attend? How much did you spend on the outfit you were too nervous to wear?*
>
> *What are the costs to your freedom? How many times a week do you feel trapped, or stuck in a situation? How many different tasks and chores do you have to do before you can feel okay, and how much time do you spend doing them? (Forsyth and Eifert, 2016)*

Catastrophizing, the anxious mindset may explain, quite matter-of-factly, how the world will collapse if we "give in to fear" (Orsillo *et al.*, 2004). Indeed, the exhaustion associated with anxiety is a kind of adrenal fatigue, as we're always fighting it. Experiential avoidance is actually very effective at taking action, whether it's running away, slamming the door, or hanging up the phone. These actions may backfire, but anxiety always demands that we *do* something to fix it. Some may even ritualize actions, fusing to behavioral rules as an attempt to manage emotions or cope with a situation. As long as fear is an insufferable experience, we'll feel compelled to relieve ourselves through control tactics, even if they don't make sense (Forsyth and Eifert, 2016). Obsessional, we may run back inside to check the stove, even though we know it's already off, or get out of bed to check the front door, even though we know it's already locked. Yet *knowing* we were worrying about nothing doesn't actually provide any relief, as we have yet to accept the futility of our efforts.

To demonstrate creative hopelessness, let's write a *get lost list* to cover everything we have ever wished to reduce, distract ourselves from, or completely eliminate (Walser and Westrup, 2007). Everything we want to just get lost! This may include feelings, thoughts, places, people, and—if we're self-loathing—even our gender.

> "What's on my get lost list? My feelings—anger, fear, anxiety, worry, sadness, crying, depression, pain, powerlessness, feeling lonely. Being heartbroken. Feeling abandoned. Judging myself. Thinking I'm ugly. Feeling like I'm crazy. Worrying about other people's judgments. Homophobic men. My stepdad. Low self-esteem. My hatred of my body."

Encourage specificity whenever answers become as vague as "my feelings" or "my school" (Walser and Westrup, 2007). Which specific emotions? What specific aspects about school? Are we talking about the people or the classes? In the *get lost list*, draw two columns for everything healthy, and everything unhealthy we've tried to make go away (see Table 6.3). Take time to brainstorm since there are usually a few memories we might be hesitant to address, having already tried to "push them down" or "get past them" or "make the most of it." Recall every change effort, regardless of how effective the outcome was (Walser and Westrup, 2007). It's perfectly acceptable if we put a change effort in both columns, or perceive lethargic activities as healthy, as this is all relative to our lifestyle.

**Table 6.3 Healthy and unhealthy control**

| Healthy | Unhealthy |
|---|---|
| Running | Drinking |
| Going to the gym | Watching TV/playing videogames |
| Talking to friends | Ditching school |
| Getting out of town | Avoiding the phone/pushing people away |
| Never talking to my stepdad | Throwing out my clothes |
| Getting high | Getting high |
| Going to therapy | Agreeing to things to get people to like me |
| Going to a naturopath | Staying quiet in class |
| Buying new clothes | One-night stand |
| Having a makeover | Trying to talk with stepdad (bad idea!) |
| Choosing a new name | Pizza |
| Insisting on pronouns | Controlling what people know about me |
| Focusing on my work | Focusing too much on work |

Out of everything in our *healthy* and *unhealthy* list, did any of it make the *get lost list* go away? Some may point out how a few efforts did provide relief, or made certain things go away for a little while, but a little absolutist humor quickly illuminates the ineffectiveness.

In the course of this session, revisit how the goal of eliminating emotions was hopeless, not us (Walser and Westrup, 2007). Some may argue that control tactics actually do work, and that we want to figure out how to control more. Treat this with curiosity, explore how these areas have worked, and be careful not to debate, as doing so will only reinforce this perspective. Perhaps this insistence stems from avoidance, perhaps our methods are actually working! Only we will know for certain. If we've voluntarily entered therapy, however, we have most likely encountered an aspect of life where we feel stuck. Rather than phrase this exploration as what does/does not work, it may be more apt to phrase this exploration as when this does/when this does not work. Doing so illustrates how, inevitably, we all reach a point where everything that can be done has been done, and that some aspects of life are not fixable.

To explore this, let's list five to ten scenarios where we felt nervous, and identify our goal in each situation. In that moment, how did our anxious, avoidant mindset try to solve or fix the problem? To expand on alternatives, how might our cautious, curious mindset proceed instead? In turn, how could we courageously approach the situation (see Table 6.4)?

**Table 6.4 Anxious, cautious, and courageous mindset**

| Context | Goal | Anxious | Cautious | Courageous |
|---|---|---|---|---|
| Riding the bus | Get to work | Spend too much on cabs | Ride the bus without making eye contact | Ride the bus with friends |
| Sitting in class | Learn | Leave | Stay and fidget | Focus on the teacher |
| Talking to men | Make friends | Don't | Introduce myself | Ask them to hang out |
| Walking home | Get home safe | Always take shortcut | Walk in daytime | Walk whenever I like |
| Speaking up | Be valued | Don't | Raise my hand | Speak up |

This differentiation between anxious action, cautious action, and courageous action is a practical safety measure. It may be sad, but value-congruent action takes great bravery for LGBTQ individuals in inhospitable and physically dangerous environments. By observing how willingness is not a courageous feeling we have to muster but a choice of action, we can emphasize the power in making a decision *because* we are afraid (Forsyth and Eifert, 2016). In this way, the flag of fear is not a signal to retreat, but a signal to advance one step past our comfort zone.

Gloria, for example, just wants to walk home without being afraid. She's not planning to run a gauntlet, here, but she does need to assess her safety given her neighborhood. Gloria's coping mechanisms for her anxiety currently include wearing shades to avoid eye contact and listening to soothing music as she walks, but she always feels like she's hiding. Today, however, she's decided to practice some mindfulness techniques, grounding her awareness in her breath, her pace, her stride, and even her environment. Her plan is to literally stop and smell the roses whenever she notices herself hurrying. Today, she takes time to window-shop, admire the surrounding gardens, and notice the sunset; and she even saw a cool car driving by.

About halfway through her walk, Gloria becomes aware that she's starting to mind-read. She's starting to assume people are judging her. Expanding her awareness beyond their facial expressions, she makes room for another thought. She wonders about the birds perched up on the eaves, and she keeps walking. Gloria's well aware of her judgments, and of ironic process, so she tries letting her thoughts expand further. Her shoes pinch a little. They're cute, but she's thinking of giving them away to her friend Cyndi. Cyndi's birthday is coming up in a month, and she never treats herself. It might be worth taking Cyndi on a girls' night out. But seriously though, what kind of birds are those? Gloria's thoughts will come and go, along with her awareness of being stared at. Maybe her onlookers are transphobic. Maybe they just hated her shoes. Who knows? Gloria's chest feels tight, and her pace picked up, so she takes a moment to slow down. She still needs to defrost that chicken. She could invite some friends over. What's wrong with her shoes, anyway? They're awesome, but they're definitely not a size 10. That bird is definitely a cardinal. They say cardinals are the spirits of the dead coming to visit. Gloria's been thinking about visiting her grandpa ever since her grandma passed six months ago. Cooking chicken takes too long. It's easier to order out. Hey look, Gloria's outside her front door. She made it.

Expansion differs from distraction, in that we fully expect concerning thoughts to come back. By permitting our internal and external awareness to flow unobstructed, we add our anxiety to a myriad of other thoughts or feelings without hyperfocusing on it. By no longer trying to get rid of our anxiety, or ignore its existence, we can accept both our fear and our ability to experience it. Over time, our anxiety may even reduce and dissipate as our trust in personal resilience increases. This, however, may seem difficult when we feel eroded by hostile encounters.

After a few months of mindful meandering, Gloria feels pretty confident about her commute home, until one day some random guy calls her out for being transgender. He literally follows her for half a block, shouting obscenities. Recounting this in session, Gloria shares how "it could have been worse" in tones of foredoomance, as if expecting it to get worse. She doesn't know who the guy was, or where they're from, or if she will see them again. After weeks of excellent work, her anxiety is through the roof! She may need to wear shades and headphones for a bit, but that's not a setback. Neither is taking a cab, or getting a ride, or asking a friend to walk her home. In each case, Gloria is challenging her paralysis and flight response by finding a way to work through a potentially hostile problem.

Should Gloria judge herself, practice expanding accountability to the aggressor. More than shifting blame or attempting to change the client's self-critical cognitions, expanding accountability looks at the larger context of events. Expanding the focus of anger can actually help the defusion process as it challenges automatic self-deprecation. Yes, Gloria is angry at herself, and she can also be angry at the day, and at the society that made the world what it is, and at the abuser in question, and at the abuser's mom for giving birth to them. Her critical self-judgment doesn't dissipate, nor are we trying to counter or ignore these judgments, yet Gloria's upset about more than just this one day. Validate any catharsis found in anger yet be aware that there's a difference between motivated confidence and embitterment preparing for war. The attitude "I'm not going to let them push me around" is useful as it helps Gloria take action, yet such a mantra can keep Gloria on edge, as it expects an attack that may never arrive. Even bold clients may walk on edge, half-prepared to fight or flee. Finding the utility in fear may be necessary for a time if she needs to guard herself, yet she may need to engage her observational self to assess how often she's truly at risk and how much time she spends anticipating the worst.

Pretending she's fine, trying to ignore her fear, or tough her way through it, may have far more adverse physical and psychological health risks in the long run, especially when all this stress is coupled with discrimination. Anxious clients struggle with both willingness and acceptance, hoping against hope that the feelings will just go away. At the end of the day, however, Gloria's faced with an ongoing process, and a single question: *Would you rather be afraid, or afraid of being afraid?*

The anxious encounter ACT with great trepidation since the very idea of accepting fear may, in itself, be anxiety provoking. There it is! That electrical twitch of fear clad in resentment! That anxious distress armored in sarcastic dissent!

"You've got to be kidding me! You don't know how hard that is!"

"Screw anxiety. I don't want to accept that."

But what if anxiety wasn't the villain of the story? What if we met anxiety with gentle kindness? What if anxiety was less a monster and more of an adorable hedgehog, spiny but cute? What if we were to treat anxiety with patience and humor? (Forsyth and Eifert, 2016).

When we catch ourselves fidgeting, fretting, or worrying, we hit anxiety with judgment. In ACT, it's not our fear that's the problem, but our mind's reaction against it. Treating anxiety with compassion is easier said than done, yet it's worth introducing this idea to a client. Whenever we notice that impulse to insult ourselves or curse our anxiousness, encourage us to give our thoughts compassionate warmth.

"Alright, alright, I'm just scared, that's all. I'm just scared."

"I know I'm nervous, but I'll get through this."

Acceptance means handling our anxiety with openness, even when we want to close ourselves off. Self-compassion is to extend kindness and humor to ourselves even when we feel most cynical and dire. We can achieve this by cultivating awareness around anxiety and permitting it to exist.

*Did you notice that's the third time you've applied your lipstick in the past hour? Laugh and call yourself a diva. Yes, you know you're nervous, and that's okay. Yes, you know you keep fixing your makeup, and that's okay, too.*

*Did you notice you keep gripping your knees when you sit? Lean in to it, grip your knees tight, and make it an unshakeable power-pose. Yeah, people might notice you're taking a really solid stance, and that's okay, we're just showing how we feel right now.*

Catching our behavior is intrinsically self-conscious. The judgments in the back of our head are all pretty predictable, and totally acceptable, like a little hedgehog curling up on itself. Let's visualize that anxiety as a prickly little ball in the palm of our hand. *What's important right now?* Maybe we want to share how we feel, or go to work as our genuine self, or ask that person out on a date—not knowing how we'll be perceived! Let's give it a shot, hedgehog in hand. The prickles in our palm can steal our attention, but it can't stop us.

Functionally, emotions are a highly sensitive signaling system letting us know what personal needs require tending to, and fear is no exception. Where do we feel fear in our body? Our jaw may clench, our hands may shake, our legs may tighten, and butterflies may flutter in our chest and our stomach. These areas sensitize when we're outside our comfort zone, because our sympathetic nervous system spikes, redirecting blood from our digestive tract to our limbs. The highly anxious can suffer irritable bowels as this response is constantly engaged and re-engaged, changing intestinal permeability, gastrointestinal secretion, and throwing off the whole microbiome (Konturek, Brzozowski, and Konturek, 2011). When we become anxious, we begin to fear this feeling, so we treat it as a threat, like an enemy within our body. Increasing avoidance, we also increase our sensitivity to this response, becoming even more susceptible to it (Budge *et al.*, 2013).

Imagine, for a moment, literal butterflies gliding so gracefully and effortlessly through life. When we feel that gentle nervousness fluttering in our stomach, we can treat it as a call to action, the signal to step forward rather than step away. What situations cause us butterflies in our stomach, and how can we lean into discomfort rather than avoid it? What value-congruent action can we commit to, even in a swarm of butterflies? Sometimes, when we've gone too far, our adrenalin can generate nausea like a knot in our stomach, or perhaps an angry hedgehog. What situations cause us to feel in over our head, overwhelmed, or nauseous? Acknowledge how the more we fight these feelings, the pricklier they get. Yet even these intense feelings can be a call to action, reminding us to regulate and initiate self-care.

## The velvet cage: ACT for depression

*What would life be like if you weren't depressed?* When asked this question we can spot our need for acceptance, belonging, connection, pride, self-worth, self-esteem, honesty, transparency, harmony, balance, stability, and love, in the same way we can tell what's missing by the shape of its absence. Yet having been unable to feel these nurturing values and personal needs for so long, the depressed may minimize them, fusing to the mantra, "It doesn't matter, nothing matters, what's the point?"

As a clinical diagnosis, major depression is marked by: a diminished pleasure in activities; a feeling of fatigue or of being slowed down; a diminished ability to think, decide, or concentrate; significant weight loss or weight gain; insomnia or hypersomnia; or recurrent thoughts of death (American Psychiatric Association, 2013). Comparatively, persistent depressive disorder carries many of the same hopeless feelings, with the distinction of being far more continuous (American Psychiatric Association, 2013). Major depression is far more episodic, whereas clients with persistent depressive disorder may not remember a time when they didn't feel depressed. In either case, both generate a cyclical fusion to experiential avoidance, as low self-esteem blocks our motivation to try, which blocks our ability to build esteem (Kanter, Baruch, and Gaynor, 2006; Strosahl and Robinson, 2017).

When a demographic struggles with internal conflict and external oppression, be conscious of the environmental factors that contribute to depression. Surveys and clinical interviews have found that 51.4 percent of trans women, 48.3 percent of trans men, and 53 percent of genderqueer individuals experience depression (Budge *et al.*, 2013, 2014). Yet to survey the real-world obstacles facing gender minorities, we need to conceptualize depression as it relates to gender dysphoria, minority stress, poverty, personal and social grief, and PTSD. The diagnostic distinctions are incredibly relevant when developing a client's treatment plan, as defusing from intrusive beliefs in one area may be undermined by unaddressed beliefs in another. Diagnosticians unaware of, or unskilled with, gender variant issues can misdiagnose in both directions, telling a client they have depression, without accounting for either gender dysphoria or trauma (Glavinic, 2010; Lev,

2004). Contrariwise, diagnosticians can also bundle everything into gender dysphoria, encouraging transition without ever fully addressing a client's underlying mood disorder. ACT takes a *Yes, and...* approach, recognizing that gender variant people can experience comorbid issues to various degrees of intensity, just like anyone. Even if a client doesn't meet the criteria for a certain diagnosis like PTSD or gender dysphoria, they can still fuse to unhealthy cognitions pertaining to trauma or gender-related issues. For clients subject to such multidimensional stress, depression is best described as a wrought iron cage, with each rusty bar separate yet connected to the rest.

If we have lost friends, family, or community in the wake of disclosure, we may state we're depressed—and we're not wrong—yet our described loss, emptiness, and heartache may be more aligned with grief. Not only this, but social censorship in gender oppressive communities can disenfranchise bereavement, stifling and arresting the grieving process (Doka, 2002). Imagine being barred from attending a friend's funeral because of what we represent to our transphobic family, or feeling unable to acknowledge a deceased lover's pronoun for fear of being judged at work. We may also harbor loss around our family or our prior gender roles, especially if we've been disowned or if our transition was markedly dramatic. We may also consider how gender dysphoria, traumatic violence, minority stress, unemployment, and lack of access to healthcare can moderate or mediate depression (Burdge, 2007; Chang and Chung, 2015; Nadal *et al.*, 2012, 2015).

Noting that internalized cissexism is a huge contributor to depression but not its defining feature, we may also fuse with depressed thoughts completely independent of gender identity. We may feel inadequate, insecure, or incapable in ourselves as a person. As a mental shortcut, depression is addicted to causation. Leaping to blame, depression wants to know the reason for its woes, even if it means martyring our self-worth. Be careful, therefore, not to infer that we're depressed *because* of our experience with gender, as the depressed mind will run with that for years.

Mood disorders pit our thinking self and our somatic self into a cage fight. Rejecting our emotional discomfort in our bodies, our thinking self will identify any possible reason to explain why we feel terrible—our physical pain, our oppressed social power, the way we look, the obstacles in our path, our experiences with failure or rejection, our IQ, our economic background—whatever causal or comparative frame can account for why we're stuck *down here* in this caged oubliette, when they're all *up there* in their life-affirming palace. We rarely pick arbitrary reasons, as the thinking self is the most critical of itself, wielding frames of comparison and frames of distinction like weapons. It will construct well-thought-out arguments to justify our somatic experience, if not mentally twist the narrative to fit its reasoning. Soon we're depressed about having depression, so we start looking for a way to escape both thought and feeling. Bogged down by self-criticism, fatigue, and a lack of motivation, we may attempt to suppress our mood by trying not to think about it. Believing distraction is our only salvation, we push down our memories and the bodily emotional experience that is our mood; yet the more we push them down, the more we fester and ruminate on them, so we push them down more, only to fester and ruminate more (Dagleish and Yiend, 2006). Mood is the language of the somatic self. It speaks to us through bodily emotionality. Yet when our somatic self is exhausted, deflated, defeated, when our arms feel heavy, and our legs feel tired, and our voice closes in our throat, and a dark, dull sensation in our chest pulls us down to the ground, the thinking self turns on it. Frustrated by our mood, and blaming us for feeling the way we do, the thinking self begins to build a cage around us, as protective as it is punishing.

We can see this cage in Talia's vacant, insomniac stare as she ambles late one night in the freezer section of her local grocery. Her glassy far-away eyes fix on the space between here and nowhere as she eats spoonfuls of ice cream she hasn't even bought yet. She lost her cool at work, blew up, got fired, and is now cradling rocky-road at 11:30 pm on a Tuesday. Although Talia has dealt with depression for much of her adult life, this particular episode overlaps with minority stress, though no gender dysphoria is present. Talia has no question, confusion, or distress about being a woman; but every time she went to work, a particular co-worker deliberately abused her pronouns until she just couldn't take it, and now she's blaming herself because she "knew better" and thought she was "more composed than that."

Empirically proven as a beneficial treatment for depression, ACT doesn't seek to dispute mood or restructure cognitions, focusing instead on how to accept intrusive mindsets and decentralize their mental position, thereby disempowering depression's convincing rhetoric (Hayes *et al.*, 2008; Zettle, 2004, 2007). By focusing on defusion, acceptance, and in the moment value commitment, ACT may be particularly useful at deterring the onset of a depressive episode in response to life's stressors (Hayes *et al.*, 2008). ACT doesn't accept our miserable plight as it is, but it does challenge us to look at what truly is within our power to change. To explore this, let's make a list of ten events or situations Talia's struggled with in the past week (Strosahl and Robinson, 2017). When the list is complete, verbally explore each encounter, obstacle, or situation, observing circumstances that—by their very experiential nature—cannot be controlled or changed from those which can (see Table 6.5). Do not, however, engage this exercise unless you, as the therapist, have first addressed your own bias, as cisnormativity is pervasive but not infallible.

**Table 6.5 Accept or control**

| Event | Accept or control? |
|---|---|
| I keep snapping at people for getting my pronoun wrong | Control |
| I was fired from my job for yelling at a guy who kept calling me "sir" | Accept |
| I keep thinking people won't hire me 'cause I'm trans | Accept |
| I get nervous every time I go in for an interview | Accept |
| I stopped sending in applications | Control |
| I get angry at myself for feeling so defeated | Accept |
| I eat a lot of ice cream to feel better | Control |
| Then I feel pathetic for eating so much ice cream | Accept |
| I don't even pay for it, I just put it back in the freezer | Control |
| I can't sleep well, anyway. That's how I know I'm depressed | Control |

Walking through this example, there are actually quite a few aspects of Talia's life she has control of, but a few hardships she will be unable to change. Being angry at someone deliberately misgendering her is totally acceptable, as Talia's anger indicates how others have trespassed against the dignity of her gender and personhood. Yet the phrase "I keep snapping" implies that somehow Talia can't stop herself, which isn't the case. Talia already accepts that she's lost her job, and she already accepts her anger, but believes she will blow up every time she gets angry. This rigid expectation can be loosened with the *Internal volume and proximity* exercise, or the *I'm having the thought* exercise, segueing into emotional mindfulness activities to reduce the perceived urgency around her anger.

Talia's expectation and nervousness around being judged, and even her self-directed criticism, may also need to be accepted, as her control attempts have stopped her dead in her tracks. Avoiding the situation, she's stopped applying for jobs, distracting herself instead with shoplifted chocolate-chip mint. Talia is going to be nervous in her next job interview, and given her last interaction, it's unrealistic for her to pretend people aren't judgmental. Yet, she can also expand beyond these thoughts, raising awareness around her full emotional experience while reaffirming her competence as a professional. The *Yes, and...* exercise can help expand Talia's awareness beyond her depressed tunnel vision, as mindfulness can increase metacognitive awareness, which in turn can reduce the risk of relapse in depressed patients (Teasdale *et al.*, 2002). Metacognition alone may not be enough to defuse from depression, since the depressed mindset can still hold various perspectives, and mood is a physical sensation (Teasdale *et al.*, 2002). Introducing mindfulness exercises to explore and describe multiple thoughts, memories, and experiences in nonjudgmental language can help Talia to take in more than just her initial assessment or appraisal of them (Teasdale *et al.*, 2002). Talia can also adapt her behavior by identifying and actively practicing other self-soothing practices. Her increased sugar intake late at night is contributing to her sleeplessness, as is going out and milling around grocery stores. Talia testifies that she only does this because she can't sleep, but while ice cream doesn't cause insomnia, late-night sugar intake certainly abets her sleeplessness.

To get out of the cage, the bars of minority stress, oppression, trauma, and even gender dysphoria are best approached holistically and ecologically, working with our psychological reaction while simultaneously addressing our physical, psychosocial, and socioeconomic reality. This may include helping us obtain antidepressants as needed, helping us out of potentially dangerous and volatile environments, helping us access social, medical, or occupational resources, and reaffirming our self-actualization process through presentation, HRT, or surgery, as desired (Sheerin, 2009; Singh *et al.*, 2011; WPATH, 2011).

As the depressed narrative unfolds, listen for rigid rule following, emotional reasoning, judgment in the form of negative self-talk, and inflexible identity constructs. Also monitor for the typical line-up of control tactics, from avoidance, to isolation, substance abuse, and TV as a distraction (Batten and Hayes, 2005; Hayes *et al.*, 2008). Imprisoned in a complex system of self-deprecation and emotional avoidance, the depressed often engage in increasingly desperate measures to self-soothe, only to find little comfort in these actions (Strosahl and Robinson, 2017). Comfort may even be the underlying short-term survival value at work, as if lining the bars of our cage in soft, black velvet. There's an odd comfort in a depressive, self-fulfilling prophecy, as there's nothing quite as certain as self-deprecation, amotivation, and despair. When the unknown is frightening and the known is nerve racking, lying down in defeat gives us the small, bitter satisfaction that our pessimism was right all along. "It wasn't worth it. There was no point. I should have just stayed in bed." To defuse from this cynical perspective means letting go of being right.

So habituated, we appraise any situation instantly, assessing whether or not it's pleasant or unpleasant (Strosahl and Robinson, 2017). Discomfort and distress engage our fight or flight response, so we sidestep situations, or pessimistically monitor our lives for faults. Experiential avoidance is governed by our tendency to create and obey self-maintained rules (Kanter *et al.*, 2006). Our despairing proclamations attempt to evade the source or symptom of our discomfort by focusing on action, or the lack thereof, over our emotional experience (Harris, 2008; Kanter *et al.*, 2006). When this fails, we persecute ourselves mercilessly, especially when our attempts to suppress our feelings prompt them to increase in intensity and frequency, proverbially and literally, like an alcoholic with a hangover (Blackledge and Hayes, 2001; Wenzlaff and Wegner, 2000).

"I just want to be happy," therefore "I'm not."

"I can't stand this," therefore "I'm weak."

"I can't handle this," therefore "I don't know what I'm doing."

"I shouldn't feel like this," therefore "There's something wrong with me."

In distress, we often blame our conceptual self, wondering why we're so messed up or if there's something wrong with us, and we're very quick to answer our own question. Judgments ensue, and soon we convince ourselves that we're weak, pathetic, unlovable, or even monstrous, shameful, and deserving of hate. When first introduced to self-acceptance, the depressive mindset may think we have to accept how "terrible" we are, or that we *have to* mandatorily concede to our feelings, or that we're a failure if we don't (Blackledge, 2015). We may perceive acceptance as a hard and arduous journey we simply don't have the energy for, prompting us to automatically give up hope before we've begun. Therein lies motivation's ultimate lie. We assume that one day we'll find the motivational key to open the cage, but all along there was never a lock. The depressed mindset creates conditional statements, demanding reasonable and unreasonable prerequisites that will never align without effort. Like trying to drive to the gas station because the car's empty, we'll sit by the side of the road, hoping someone else will rescue us, or lamenting that no one cares, when all along we could get out and walk. Setting motivation aside, ACT stresses that our willingness to help ourselves is not a feeling but a choice (Forsyth and Eifert, 2016; Hayes and Smith, 2005). Yet even when we're willing to put in effort, it can often feel like our berating thoughts want to tear us down for even trying.

It may feel as if our desire to better ourselves just makes us all too aware of our flaws (Wood *et al.*, 2009). Attempts to build self-esteem and self-worth with positive self-talk may actually cement our depression further, as all our effort reminds us of how much we have to try (Blackledge and Hayes, 2001; Wood *et al.*, 2009). This can lead to the hopeful mantra "Fake it 'til you make it." This idea tells us that if we keep repeating a statement it will somehow come true. This fundamental tenet of CBT can actually work should an ambition imperative feature in our self-actualization values; yet if we're deeply entrenched in depression, "Fake it 'til you make it" simply reinforces our felt sense of fraudulence (Nielsen, 2015; Wood *et al.*, 2009). Putting on a show, we may don a smiling mask, feeling like we have to meet expectations, or that lowering the mask would be tantamount to giving up. Then the mask drops. We get tired. Our ability to focus gets derailed. So, our survival values kick in, and we curl up on ourselves in a state of restless hibernation and minimal exertion.

The depressed mindset comes very close to creative hopelessness, insomuch as it feels hopeless. Giving up on our control tactics, we stop fighting our internal critic, give up on our fake smiles, and stop forcing ourselves to do anything. In session, try collaboratively charting our behavior patterns, as giving up on life isn't the same as giving up on depression. Ask what a really depressing day looks like. What do we do? Stay in bed late? Drag ourselves to the couch? Forget to eat during the day? Eat way too much at night? The pattern points to a set of rules, such as "I don't have the energy to____" or "I can't be bothered to____" Reintroducing creative hopelessness, demonstrate *Internal volume and proximity* and how to *personify distress*, as even if we're feeling hopeless, we're still being formulaic—far from anything creative!

When elephants are born into captivity they're often tied to a big heavy stake with a big heavy rope. Pulling against it, they find they can't go anywhere, so they pace slowly back and forth in their cramped pen. As they get older, the big heavy stake is progressively replaced with smaller and smaller pegs, as the big heavy rope is replaced with lighter and lighter lines until one day, all grown up, this powerful pachyderm paces back and forth, its ankle tied to a string it could easily snap and a peg it could simply rip out of the ground. Even outside of their cramped pen they will pace back and forth, believing they can't go anywhere. We condition ourselves the same way. Like our habituated elephant, we convince ourselves that we *can't*, because we *couldn't*, or we *can't* because we *haven't*.

When we're depressed, many sessions may be spent practicing how to be a witness to our thoughts and feelings, rather than a victim of them. The observational self sees the peg and rope for what it is, a pattern of reinforced conditioning. Trauma, cultural pressure, familial abandonment, social humiliation, romantic conflict, heartbreak, loss, and even self-harm and previous suicide attempts can all be cited as very real and heavy ropes tied to very real and heavy stakes. As previously stated, should our current predicament include active abuse and neglect, then, like our baby elephant, we may need external help and social support in a very real way. Yet many times these events are haunting memories of cissexism and homophobia, harking back to when we felt truly helpless. So, here's the question: *Who's in charge here?*

Is the peg in charge? Is the string in charge? Is the man who tied it to the elephant's ankle in charge? Or is the elephant in charge? By bringing us into our present state of awareness, we can recognize our memories of the past and our willingness to try something new, thereby creating an empowering opportunity. Indignation and anger can be a jump start for motivation. *Who's in charge here?* When our depressive thoughts bully their way into our mind, we can thank them for their input and dismiss them like tiny people trying to tie tiny bits of string to our feet (Hayes and Smith, 2005). Have us stomp our foot and proclaim who's in charge! Now let's prove it. Stand up and walk around the room saying, "I can't walk and talk at the same time" (Hayes and Smith, 2005). After a few laps it's clear we can walk and talk at the same time, despite what our mind says. Taking this further, what's something mundane we believe we can't do which is actually quite within our power? Do we tell ourselves we can't ____ because it's too embarrassing or too hard? If we say we can't call our sister, point us to the nearest phone. If we say we can't apply for a job, spend the session crafting an email to a prospective employer. We may take up the challenge or, if we're weighed down by depression, we may reach for the phone and pull back our hand. We may type the email, send it, and click undo immediately.

A shut-down is a last-ditch effort to avoid our somatic mood. We stammer, "I can't, I can't." So close yet so far, the cage suddenly feels very solid. Let's take a breath. Let's take more than one. As we exhale, remind us that we're making the call *while* feeling discomfort, or filling in the résumé even if we don't believe it will work. We're nervous, awkward, embarrassed, tired, sad, stressed, and our mind has all sorts of things to complain about! But who's in charge here?

Dialectical behavior therapy (DBT) often uses opposite action to counter thought. Defying the mind by doing the exact opposite proves how thoughts are just lengths of string with no actual power. As the ACT equivalent of this, the *Who's in charge?* exercise doesn't fight the peg or the stake. Instead, *Who's in charge?* as a form of *pattern-smashing* has us act in accordance with our personal empowerment (Hayes and Smith, 2005). Despite its name, *pattern-smashing* is a gentler approach than opposite action, but relies on a similar principle. The difference is that instead of opposing our intrusive thought, we're broadening our attention to remember how powerful we really are. An elephant, after all, doesn't need to scrutinize string to remember it's an elephant. It doesn't even have to fight it. It just needs to start walking, and the string will snap effortlessly. With our values in charge, we can select an alternative to the pattern, not necessarily its opposite. For example, if we habitually state "I can't be myself at work," we can smash the pattern by being ourselves in the company of co-workers outside of work. By contacting our self-as-context, it become easier to see that it's not work which is most important in this context, but being ourselves. This is exceptionally difficult when we're depressed, as we believe that "being ourselves" intrinsically means being depressed in the company of others. We may say, "I never join in because I always bring people down." Smashing this pattern may look like inviting people over to our house, which puts the ball in their court to join in, or joining in with the goal of complimenting five people. Over time, this can possibly generate eudaemonic pleasure, defined as the joy gained from bringing others joy, but for now that's not even our goal (Strosahl and Robinson, 2017). This may sound odd, but we're not trying to stop ourselves from feeling depressed, or even trying to enjoy the event; we're simply smashing the pattern.

As an exercise, we can practice *thanking our mind*. Observing a depressive thought, *thanking our mind* allows us to politely acknowledge the thought before expanding our awareness (Harris, 2008; Strosahl and Robinson, 2017). In this case, let's pick up a physical object, turn it over, then write down what we notice about it (Strosahl and Robinson, 2017). As we write, encourage us to favor descriptive terms like *rough*, *smooth*, *light*, *heavy*, *colorful*, and so on over judgment-based language like *beautiful*, *ugly*, *nice*, or *boring* (Hayes and Smith, 2005). When we've written a paragraph or so, ask us to write any intrusive thoughts that may have crept into our mind during this exercise, whether it's "This is pointless" or "This is stupid," or even our original, depressive cognition. Once again, ask us to thank our mind for these thoughts, and expand. This time, let's visualize a person and practice describing them without judgment. What do they look like? What qualities, characteristics, and personal attributes do they have? After a paragraph, we can check back in with our mind to see if any judgments were lurking in the background about this person, such as a criticism or a compliment (Strosahl and Robinson, 2017). Instruct us to thank our mind again for each of these judgments before refocusing our thoughts to a difficult situation or event in our life that pulls at our emotions. Ask us to visualize this moment, and then write down the event in descriptive terms, including the time and place, the people involved, and so on. When we're finished with our account, ask us to write down any judgmental thoughts we had about this occasion, including points of blame, accusation, self-deprecation, and any evaluations we have about the people involved (Strosahl and Robinson, 2017). Again, have us thank our mind one last time before reviewing what we noticed about this exercise. How did it feel to engage this observational perspective? What was it like to experience a judgment, and to thank it rather than fight it?

Without motivation, focus, passion, or pleasure, some particularly depressive days are nonverbal. We may express a sense of alogia, as if we're too tired to think. By fostering emotional resilience and engaging our willingness to try, ACT reinforces the power of choice—even when we feel drained and fatigued—by helping us notice more than what's missing in our present-based experience. The mindful *Sensory awareness* exercise can be useful, as we need not think in order to feel. Taste is perhaps the best example of this, as even words like *sweet*, *salty*, *bitter*, *sour*, can describe our meaning without ever conveying the essence of the flavor. We are, however, so quick to judge what foods we do or don't like. In mindfulness eating exercises, we're encouraged to smell, touch, and examine something edible like a grape, taking our time to explore it fully in our mouth before biting. If we notice a judgmental thought, ask us to acknowledge the thought, thank the mind for thinking, and return to the tactile and sensory exploration. Biting down on the grape, we taste the sweetness of the juice and the change in texture, practicing description over assessment, accepting our experience over our judgment of the experience.

Accepting depression may mean accepting antidepressants. It may also mean being aware of and accepting our sleep cycles as they exist in the present, capitalizing on points of energy where they appear, or reducing the number of set goals in a day where possible. Yet it also means accepting thoughts as just thoughts and learning how to observe them without judgment. We're not seeking to make our depression go away, yet we're also not going to concede to our depression's apathetic dismissal of life.

As our cynical side is autocannibalistic, we turn on ourselves, judging ourselves for judging ourselves. To challenge this pattern, ACT encourages us to thank our critical mind for providing us with cynical, pessimistic, or depressive thoughts, in the same way that our pet cat is trying to be nice by bringing us a headless mouse (Hayes and Smith, 2005; Strosahl and Robinson, 2017). It doesn't know we don't eat mice, it just wants to share or show off its trophy. Reacting with disgust doesn't actually do anything, and unlike dogs, cats don't care if you point your finger at them. By thanking the cat, we change our reaction to the situation, even if there's still a mess to clean up.

We've all practiced this at some point, or else seen the value in it. Remember that one birthday as a kid when you got that really stupid gift? What did you do? You might have thrown a hissy-fit. Alternatively, you may have thanked the giver politely, entertained it for a second, set it aside, and gone to play with the better toys. Learning how to thank our mind for noticing how tired we are or noticing how our procrastination has gotten the better of us changes the game. Our typical self-deprecation patterns aren't particularly functional, as we berate ourselves for mistakes already made or for feeling sad, tired, or numb. Politely noticing the thought, and disengaging our tendency to argue with ourselves, allows us to move toward what's more important.

## Building bridges: ACT for suicidal ideation

When we're at odds with our body, and feel condemned by others, and all our attempts to control our thoughts and feelings have come to naught, the agenda of emotional control presents suicide as a seductively reasonable solution (Barnes *et al.*, 2017; Baumeister, 1990; Hayes *et al.*, 2012). It promises a permanent end, a way out, a penultimate exit. More to the point, imagine growing up with the staggering knowledge that in the USA 46 percent of trans men, 42 percent of trans women, and 48 percent of trans youth attempt suicide at some point in their life, in contrast to 4.6 percent of the cisgender population (Haas *et al.*, 2014; James *et al.*, 2016; Kessler, Borges, and Walters, 1999; Nock *et al.*, 2008; Nodin *et al.*, 2015). Internationally, of the 50 percent of gender variant people who attempted suicide in India, most were younger than 20, of which 31 percent actually ended their lives (Virupaksha *et al.*, 2016). A Japanese survey of 1138 gender variant people found that 10.8 percent had engaged in suicidal behavior, mostly in junior high, but that 62 percent struggled with suicidal ideation (Harima and Ishimaru, 2010).

Victimization and self-annihilation can almost seem like part of a social script, making programs like the Trevor Project (2019) and Trans Lifeline (2019) needed now more than ever. As a non-profit focused on preventing suicide amongst LGBT youth, the Trevor Project (2019) found that 54 percent of transgender and nonbinary young people between the age of 13 and 24 had considered suicide while a startling 29 percent had actually made an attempt. As a point of fact, Trans Lifeline, a suicide prevention hotline run by and for transgender people, has taken over 70,000 calls since it went live in 2014.

To make life even harder, we can feel caught in disgrace, unable to share our suicidality due to social stigma, so let's take the mystery out of suicide. From a lifespan perspective, the 2015 US Transgender Survey found that 82 percent of gender variant people contemplated, thought, or ruminated about suicide at some point on this long journey (James *et al.*, 2016). Whenever working with potentially suicidal clients, heightened awareness is required to maintain physical safety, and all clients must be informed in the first session of a clinician's duty to protect should we risk harming ourselves or others. We may censor ourselves, however, should we believe admitting an intrusive daydream will cause you to call the cops, or the psych ward, or even our mum. Feeling like we have to appear stable and confident can undermine our desire for honesty and transparency in session, thereby increasing our felt sense of shame, fraudulence, and self-deprecation (Zettle, 2007).

Without condoning or validating suicidal behavior, you can begin by normalizing suicidal thought. As embracing life also means accepting death, present your openness to this mortal subject. As gender variant people can feel alienated twice over when we feel suicidal, a therapist brave enough to role model existential defusion can go a long way. The point is not to commiserate by any means, but to demonstrate how we're not defective for thinking about death or even killing ourselves. Cultures all over the world acknowledge the ubiquity of human suffering, and if we compound racial, sexual, and gender oppression with familial altercations, blocked access to healthcare, increased risk of both sexual trauma and HIV, financial hardship, and even heartbreak, suicidal thoughts become a sadly typical and oddly solution-focused stress response (Barnes *et al.*, 2017; Clements-Nolle *et al.*, 2006; Hayes *et al.*, 2012; Hendricks and Testa, 2012; Miller and Grollman, 2015; Virupaksha, Muralidhar, and Ramakshrina, 2016; Zettle, 2007).

If treated as an abnormality, those who openly discuss the death option are deemed macabre, morbid, and mad, further perpetuating the shame cycle. From such a cold perspective, the high prevalence of suicidality amongst LGBTQ populations is misinterpreted as fragile instability, or as a side effect of sexual and gender deviance from the norm. So let's look at the norm! Across the globe, 2.7 percent of cisgender people attempt suicide, while 9.2 percent will experience suicidal ideation during their tumultuous teens, stressful adulthood, existential midlife crisis, and final choices of their winter years (Nock *et al.*, 2008). As suicidality is far too common to be considered *abnormal*, we begin to see the mundane man behind the curtain is none other than our agenda of emotional control pushing experiential avoidance to its very limit (Chiles and Strosahl, 2005; Hayes *et al.*, 2012; Luoma and Villatte, 2012). In a retrospective study of suicide notes the majority of writers described death as a way to escape emotional pain (Baumeister, 1990). Taking this point alone, mindfulness practices that expand awareness beyond the immediacy of emotional pain, thereby lessening urgency and preoccupation with distress, can aid in recovery (Chiles and Strosahl, 2005; Luoma and Villatte, 2012).

Though all experiences are unique, normalize the impact minority stress has on a person and how natural it is to feel worn down, excluded, and alienated (Hendricks and Testa, 2012; Pega and Veale, 2015). Faith in our future is determined by our ability to conceptualize ourselves in this future. This isn't just imagining ourselves on a tropical beach, as the suicidal mindset can do that. Yet believing we'll ever get there, or that it'll be worth it if we do, is unlikely if we're fixated on the futility of life. Mental flexibility is not only difficult but feels exhausting in the face of such intrusive thoughts. Furthermore, while there are many complex reasons why people contemplate suicide, our ideation of it stems from our desire to avoid an unwanted emotional or physical pain we cannot control (Barnes *et al.*, 2017). The prospect of approaching this pain, let alone accepting it, may seem horrendous or pointless when we're on edge. It is imperative to explore this subject with great tact and attention to safety. Even if we don't express our suicidality outright, ruminating about the past, worrying about the future, and degrading our self-concept can increase our reactive and impulsive behavior (Barnes *et al.*, 2017). A potentially useful instrument in this area is Wegner and Zanakos' (1994) White Bear Suppression Inventory as it's adapted for suicidal ideation (WBSI-SI), as it measures the failure of suppression tactics as they appear in the form of intrusive thought (Barnes *et al.*, 2017; Rassin, 2003; Williams *et al.*, 2011).

The depressed and suicidal often report being unable to recall specific memories or details from life (Dagleish and Yiend, 2006; Luoma and Villatte, 2012). This overgeneralized memory can impair problem-solving abilities, returning us again and again to the same dire conclusion (Luoma and Villatte, 2012). Neurologically, the brain is a complex web of axons and dendrites. Repetition strengthens the connection between neurological pathways by increasing the density of white matter (Strosahl and Robinson, 2017), which is why we mutter someone's name a few times under our breath before shaking their hand—just to get it right! Repetition, repetition, repetition. If we say "I suck" a thousand times, our days get longer and our arms feel heavier. Soon, "I suck" becomes an automatic thought.

Repeated so often, our cognitive pathways access that self-deprecating thought faster than any other idea in our head. And if society insults us, too, repetition brings these thoughts to mind even if we don't believe them. "You're a sinner." "You're disgusting." "You're a freak." "You're not a real man." "You're a pervert." "You should kill yourself." Repetition, repetition, repetition. Even when we try and fortify ourselves against these statements, sheer frequency and intensity strengthen even the nastiest neural pathways.

> *Imagine a rope bridge. Now imagine that every time we cross this bridge it gets stronger. The rope bridge becomes a chain bridge. The chain bridge becomes a wood bridge. The wood bridge becomes an iron bridge. After years of bullying and name-calling, after growing up in transphobic places, with sexist and cissexist families, this bridge has gotten stronger and stronger. Now it's fortified with wrought iron, with thick metal cables and fortified trusses.*

Determining what specific thoughts and feelings we're trying to escape from helps us progressively approach these internal experiences and hold them in mind (Barnes *et al.*, 2017). As some lose contact with emotions or struggle to say them aloud, an emotion wheel or emotional vocabulary list can be instrumental (Barnes *et al.*, 2017). Ask us to write ten intrusive thoughts we have about ourselves, even if we don't believe them totally. These may include beliefs about our gender if it's a dimension of our internal dissonance, but don't assume it is. When asked to share intrusive thoughts, we often second guess ourselves, since verbalizing them can feel like we're conceding to them in some way. We'll preface "I know this isn't true, but..." or "Don't get me wrong, but sometimes I feel..." We may even seek to blame the external, stating, "Well, I don't believe this, but society says..." Gently sidestep such guarded delivery by acknowledging that a belief bridge takes parts from all over. Sometimes we build the pylons from what other people have told us. Sometimes we build the arches from what we've told ourselves.

Looking at our ten negative beliefs, let's circle any absolute statements or overgeneralizations. How many beliefs include words like *all*, *always*, *I often*, or *I usually*? How many make sweeping declarations like "Men are____" or "Women have to be____?" Did we write any identifying statements like "I am a loser," or "I am weak," or "I am pathetic"?

Fused to a judgmental mindset, loathing ourselves, our life, our gender, our body, our family, and even our world, we reinforce each plank on our bridge to nowhere. Suicidal thinking is rigidly dichotomous, swinging between evaluations of good/bad, right/wrong, happiness/sadness, and hope/hopelessness, only to come up short every time, making introspection a painful examination of presumed failure (Baumeister, 1990; Luoma and Villatte, 2012). Instead of challenging the product of dichotomy "I am bad, wrong, sad, and hopeless," ACT disrupts the infallibility of thought itself by observing the active process of thinking in the present moment (Luoma and Villatte, 2012). Doing so allows us to recognize that suicidal thoughts are not the nightmarish monsters we fear we're too weak to vanquish, but a perspective we've indulged for too long (Luoma and Villatte, 2012). Though suicidal ideation can be hard to defuse from, boredom can actually help.

Morbidity is creatively dark and beautifully grim, yet suicidality saps even our twisted fantasies of imagination. At this point our suicidal thoughts render a basic, albeit intrusive, triangle: stimulus plus death equals death by stimulus. See a knife? Imagine being stabbed. See a cliff? Imagine jumping off it. See a moving car? Imagine stepping in front of it. Such thoughts may be shocking when they're unexpected, or alarming if we've never had them before, but experience them on a daily, weekly, or monthly basis and they become repetitive and clichéd.

As *Personifying the distress* can be an effective way to describe unwanted thoughts and feelings while also maintaining distance from them, let's give our bridge to nowhere a toll booth (Barnes *et al.*, 2017). Now, let's imagine that a really boring person with a really boring voice keeps beckoning us over. Let's give them the most boring name we can think of: *Bob*. When Bob calls us over, we know exactly what he wants. It never changes. He wants us to pay to use his bridge to nowhere. *What's that, Bob? You want us to feel bad because we thought about jumping off a cliff? You say that every day, Bob. Got anything new?* In this exercise we're not dismissing sadness, or even hardship. We're flippantly dismissing Bob, that part of us that only ever has one idea to every solution. He'll be back tomorrow, and we may have to wave him off again, but for now we have to turn toward something difficult, something Bob doesn't think we can deal with.

Defusing from suicidal cognitions may simultaneously turn us toward life's challenges and the emotions we've tried so hard to avoid. Points of internalized cissexism and transphobia may emerge, alongside points of trauma, neglect, and emotional abuse. By refocusing on any experienced social injustice or internalized binary, we can start to explore our emotional process in context of our environment. This is a huge step, as it brings us close to the creative hopelessness within both queer failure and queer innocence. Since suicidal ideation is a repetitious internal monologue, we may either shut down in an attempt to silence our internal noise, or else hijack the session with ruminating thoughts and fears. Both present opportunities for emotional and value exploration, as the control attempt illustrates that some part of us still wants to live. By exploring the self in context, observe how life's obstacles challenge and shape the values they paradoxically oppose. Experiences with rejection can stoke fear alongside the warm desire for acceptance. Excommunication can also seed values of belonging and connection. Even suicidal guilt indicates conscientiousness or compassion for friends, family, and possibly even ourselves. From this we can build a new bridge, not to replace the last, as Bob won't be decommissioned for a while, but to provide us with more than one option when we encounter emotional turmoil.

As the clinician, specifically target conditional rules, especially those associated with the primary source of distress, whether it's alienation, loneliness, trauma, or gender dysphoria (Barnes *et al.*, 2017). You can also help clients decentralize and disidentify from language with classic ACT responses like *So your mind is saying...* and *Is that your everything-is-hopeless thought again*? and *Is that Bob talking*? (Barnes *et al.*, 2017). Despairing, we may state that we genuinely do hate ourselves, or claim there is no dissonance. If so, ask if we're tired of being tired, or tired of hating ourselves, or exhausted by our suicidal thoughts, or angry at ourselves for having them. Any frustration with our depression demonstrates motivation and drive, in the same way the shipwrecked will exhaustedly tread water when stranded out at sea. We have an in-built drive to stay alive. This can, however, compete with our in-built drive to meet our needs, should we believe our needs can be met by dying. This may sound odd, but it is sometimes possible to glean our unmet needs in our suicidal fantasies. The exhausted, in need of rest and peace, so often daydream about closing their eyes and falling asleep forever, just as those in need of self-acceptance and self-forgiveness cut and mutilate the bodies they hate. Those who feel trapped often fantasize about the freedom of free-fall, and those desiring respect, recognition, and even revenge imagine being found with a noose and a note. Yet ask if life would be worth living if we felt rested, at peace, and were free to accept and forgive ourselves while being respected and recognized, and we usually pause. Much like the tropical beach, we can imagine such a life, but stranded out at sea it seems impossible to get there—at least currently.

Intrusive thoughts are intrusive because we don't want to believe them, and our weak survival instinct points to a second bridge. It may be a flimsy rope bridge by comparison to Bob's reinforced toll-bridge, but the fact that we're still alive, and still struggling to get our needs met, observes its presence. The more we express ourselves in healthy, reinforcing ways, and the more opportunities we have to demonstrate our resilience through value-congruent action, the stronger our second bridge becomes. An ACT matrix can actually flex imagination. Checking off goals is a great way to collect evidence of our effort and success, yet it will all feel hollow if our mental rigidity can't derive personal meaning from it. Our imagination, in conjunction with our relational frames, allows us to both allocate and observe meaning in life. When we allocate meaning, we are all too aware of our projections, which is why our allocations may not feel meaningful, as is the case with forced metaphors and poetry that tries too hard in its visual imagery.

Mindfully observing meaning, by contrast, can take two routes of its own. The first mindfully observes being. This can be practiced by observing a subject for what it is, simply as it is. The ants on the floor walk in a line to help carry food back to their nest. That is the meaning, yet though it's meaningful to the ant, we—as egocentric beings—don't deem it very meaningful because it doesn't involve us directly. Monks can live in this manner, having released their ego, but it's a bit much to expect from most people, especially when they are suicidal.

More often, when we search for meaning, we're actually searching for "meaning as it pertains to me." As the vast majority of the universe has very little direct relevance to the self, we can feel disappointed, even insignificant, as our sense of self feels minimized. The second route, therefore, is to mindfully observe resonance. This can be practiced by observing the interconnections between us and everything we experience. Let's identify someone we care about and describe them in detail. Really fuse with the memory. Now, let's name something in the room that reminds us of that person. A moment ago the room was just a box of objects, barren of meaning. Now, the lamp is our best friend, Janice, the pattern on the carpet is our grandmother, and the tree outside reminds us of our old dog, Falkor. The ability to connect meaning allows us to integrate and establish connection between our internal and external experience.

Our imagination allows us to allocate meaning to anything, a power many therapists use to their advantage. Pointing at a chair, a therapist may tell a client to imagine their mom sitting there; or giving them a pillow, they may ask them to hold it like a child, or even their inner child. Our imaginations are powerful, but when the exercise is over the chair returns to being furniture and the pillow loses its infancy. This may be because the object we projected on was random, or the exposure to it was too short, or not repeated enough to elicit an ongoing response. Sentimentalism exemplifies how repeated associations can give inanimate objects powerful meaning—just ask any divorcee who's ever thrown away their wedding ring, or any widow still polishing their husband's shoes. The inherent difference is that when we allocate meaning, we consciously decide what it symbolizes, whereas when we resonate meaning, our subconscious processes make the connection for us. When a selected object becomes associated symbolically with a person, place, or time, it connects because it *feels right*, which is to say there is enough subconscious background information linked together that our body responds before our conscious mental awareness.

When asked to point at something nostalgic about mom, some might shoot out an arm, knowing exactly what it is! Others may take more time, looking around and "trying" different things. "Maybe that bookcase, no…not the bookcase. She kinda likes the color of the chair but…" For this exercise, let's literally get up and walk around, as we need to feel objects with all our senses. Statements like "No, there's nothing in here" may not indicate a mental block as much as an absence of cultural, familial, or personal symbolic encoding. An office can only contain so much, after all. If this is the case, ask us to bring in something from home that does connect to our mom in some way. Examine not only the object, but how it relates. Perhaps it's the color, shape, or texture. Perhaps there's a memory associated with it, or a shared emotional reaction, or any number of conscious or subconscious archetypes. This ability to make a connection is the operating principle behind sand tray therapy, in which clients select miniatures from a collection representative of their inner world. It's also the operating principle behind gift giving. We'll walk around shops for hours looking for "the right gift" and though there's a lot of good ideas, nothing seems to fit, or seem worthy, or feel meaningful until... "A plushy sloth wearing a panda onesie? He loves sloths, pandas, and onesies! This is totally him."

In metaphorical terms, allocating meaning is imagining a rainbow; resonating meaning is seeing a rainbow. "But everyone can see a rainbow," Bob shouts from the back. Not so. To see a rainbow, three things must align: the sun, the rain, and you. Since light refracts at a certain angle, you can only see a rainbow when you're in the direct position to see it. Nature photographers know this well, and so rainbows do not elude them.

Developing attainable, realistic, and renewing goals provides us more opportunities to expand awareness beyond Bob's boring bridge, provided these goals connect us with our environment in a meaningful way. Relapse is not only common, but part of the process. Sometimes we get down on ourselves, beat ourselves up, or read something heavy in the news and let out a long, drawn-out sigh. Sometimes we fall back into regret. Sometimes we regress to an old schema, going back to Bob's bridge to pay his stupid toll with self-deprecation and self-harm. But now there's a choice in behavior. ACT asks us to commit—not once, but every day, as the more we build our bridge, the less money Bob has to maintain his. This isn't just a metaphor. Our medial prefrontal cortex is where we build our personal self-narrative, integrating self-referential information, personal history, and social encounters into an identity schema (Strosahl and Robinson, 2017). Like Bob's bridge to nowhere, negative self-stories decrease activation in the neural pathways connecting our prefrontal cortex to our pleasure center, whereas positive self-stories are correlated to increased activation (Strosahl and Robinson, 2017).

If we shut down or express that there's nothing in life worth living for, we may need to explore our context of self. Gender variant people who are closeted, refraining from self-actualization, or are currently in pre-transition, may actually be observing that there's nothing in our life worth living for *as we are now*.

The *Seven-year change* exercise relies on the common knowledge that we'll never notice our hair growing if we look in a mirror every day, but an old photo will tell all. By visualizing our development, we detect both the constancy of the observational self and the malleability of the conceptual self. Also, by circling the growth of our values on a list of virtues, the *Seven-year change* exercise observes times we generated meaning in our life. This may be difficult for those who have undergone radical transition, or for those who have experienced childhood trauma, so encourage patience and gentleness at each step. For some, this exercise may take 15 minutes, for others the whole session.

> *First, we're going to close our eyes and take three deep, audible breaths, just for practice. One...two...three. Now, slowly, cup your hands together like you're lifting water. Can you imagine, once upon a time, that you were this small? Can you imagine that you were once small enough to be carried in two hands? Have you ever seen a photograph of yourself as a newborn? Describe the picture to me in detail. Were you lying down or being held? Did you have a stuffed animal? What color was it? Did it have a name? It's hard to imagine ourselves as newborns, as we don't remember coming into this world, but I want to hold that innocence in your mind. Everything was new, and simple. Can you circle three values on this sheet of what was most important to you as a newborn?*

Explore each value, and why we feel the value is important, even if we didn't receive it. This is an excellent opportunity to observe the development of secure, insecure, anxious, or disorganized attachment as a potential theme to return to in later sessions, but try not to get sidetracked. If we struggle with breathing exercises, any brief sensory exercise will help us create contact with our present-based awareness.

> *Now, something amazing happens. We're growing. Beginning to walk and talk and think and express. Children grow so quickly. By the time we're seven years old, we have likes and dislikes, hopes and dreams. Can you remember being seven or eight years old? It's okay if you don't remember the specific age. Our earliest memories are usually snapshots, like photographs, but there comes a point when all the mental pictures start rolling together like a movie in our mind's eye. When did that movie start for you? What toys do you play with? What games?*

Keep a soft focus during this exercise. Specificity can block memory, as we're exerting too much energy looking for "the right answer," which can be a stifling experience. Unless we have a very exact memory, childhood nostalgia tends to blur together, so grant us wide open doors, inexact and open to however we interpret the prompt.

> *Allow yourself to be a child for a moment. Do you remember your bedroom? How was it decorated? Embody that inner seven-year-old. Do you have friends? Siblings? Are you an only child? Do you play outdoors or indoors? What do you think's cool? What sucks? What are you scared of? What makes you laugh? Now, those values you circled as a baby no doubt remain true, but try circling three new things your seven-year-old self found super important.*

If we had a difficult childhood, it may be difficult to pinpoint our values, and we may need help identifying them in our experience. Take time to explore, for example, how important curiosity is to the rascal, or safety is for the scared, or resilience is for the fragile. Then return to our breathing or mindful, sensory exercise to make contact with the present moment.

> *Now, another huge jump is about to happen. We're going to leap from our seven-year-old selves, to our 14-year-old selves. Oh god! It's puberty. Middle school. Entering high school. Everything's changed. We're not little kids anymore. Things are getting serious. What grade are you in? What music are you listening to? What's your fashion like? Who are your friends and do you guys hang out? What's going on at home? What are you aware of now that you weren't aware of when you were seven? What don't you believe anymore? What do you believe? What's important? What do you want people to see about you? What are you trying to hide? Really hold on to that transforming teenager. Do you remember? Circle three new values that your 14-year-old self knew were important.*

As puberty is often an arduous milestone, exploring this age range may summon painful memories. It is never useful to *shut a client down* or practice thought-stopping techniques, as this undermines the very practice of emotional acceptance. However, you may guide us by linking painful memories to the development of healthy value constructs. Just as those who have undergone trauma may value safety and trust, those who were alienated or cast out may value understanding and friendship. Again, have us exhale and practice our breathing or sensory exercise.

> *Now we're going to make another huge jump, from 14 to 21. A lot happened. A lot changed. How are you different from your 14-year-old self? Where are you living? Are you working now? Do you have a car? Who are you hanging out with? Has your fashion changed? What music are you into now? What obstacles are you dealing with? What's important to you? Circle three new values you gained.*

If we're not yet 21, ask us to jump to whatever age we're at. The level of growth that occurs for teenagers is such that there is often a large difference between the 14-year-old and the 16-year-old experience. The point is to illustrate how identity and social role shift. Having entered the age of adulthood, the weight of responsibility balances with our desire for freedom. Passions emerge, evolve, or die as we grow and sever from old interests. Explore these changes, then have us practice our breathing or sensory exercise again.

> *A lot of young adults believe adulthood is a finish line, but as we get older we realize that this isn't the case. The difference between a seven-year-old and a 14-year-old is vast. The difference between a 14-year-old and a 21-year-old is just as wide. So too*

*is the difference between a 21-year-old and a 28-year-old. Careers. Homes. Families. Travel. Even more self-discovery. Circle three values you gained through your 20s.*

If we're not yet 28, you can round out the exercise by exploring which three values we're moving toward and are aspiring to manifest in our lives. It's also worth illustrating how this process is continual. The change in lifestyle, self-image, social role, and personal identity between a 28-year-old and a 35-year-old, a 35-year-old and a 42-year-old, a 42-year-old and a 49-year-old, a 49-year-old and a 56-year-old, a 56-year-old and a 63-year-old, a 63-year-old and a 70-year-old are all strikingly different. This exercise can continue all the way to our current age, remembering to end with the same breathing or sensory exercise implemented at the beginning, and between, each phase.

As sessions reinforce that "I am" is not a static prison, we engage a broader sense of self. Our evolving value constructs contribute, reflect, and compliment our core identity as we continue to grow. Though the life of an acorn is quite different from the life of an oak, we can't deny the potential tree within. Exploring this to its monumental depth is both a central privilege and hardship for gender variant people, as we often have to let go of old concepts in order to grow. When we are able to connect with a gender variant community, levels of comfort and resilience rapidly increase, greatly reducing suicidal ideation (Budge *et al.*, 2014; Frost and Meyer, 2012; Hendricks and Testa, 2012; Pflum *et al.*, 2015; Testa, Jimenez, and Rankin, 2014; Walch *et al.*, 2012). Affirmation of this kind works so effectively because it not only validates who we are, but increases resonant connection, thereby expanding what we believe is possible and allowing us to see suicidal ideation as the mental shortcut it is. Yet rather than push back against suicidal ideation or attempt to chop it out of our lives, we can use it as a signal to accept our distress, expand our awareness, connect with others, change our environment, and imagine less permanent solutions to our temporary problems.

# 7

# Affirmation

With awareness, acceptance, and value-congruent action on our side, ACT actively affirms who we are as gender variant people. Taking an ecological perspective, we impact our environment just as deeply as our environment impacts us (Lev, 2004; Mallon, 2009; Riley *et al.*, 2011). Our existence is illuminating, as our distinct bodies, unconventional life experience, and very presence elicits questioning, curiosity and inspiration in some, and unsettled discomfort in others. The onus of social clarity or transphobic chaos is not ours, however, unless we blame darkness on candlelight. We are only breathtaking to those who have never met the likes of us, as we are only shocking to those who are easily shocked. This tense relationship between self and other can generate a great deal of self-consciousness, yet there's an undeniable power here which, should we accept it, can be affirmed for all its worth.

LGBTQ affirmative therapy entered the scene in the late 1970s in response to the gay rights movement (Sheerin, 2009; Zandvliet, 2000). Challenging homosexuality as pathology, affirmative therapy pointed out how neither sexuality nor gender destabilized psychological health, and that any noted instability derived from traumatic encounters with, and internalization of, homophobia and transphobia (Lev and Sennott, 2012; Sheerin, 2009). At this point, decades of research demonstrate how sexual and gender minorities thrive when affirmative therapists help us decrease shame and guilt, validate emotional process, and help us develop a deep and meaningful identity (Sheerin, 2009).

Gender affirmative therapy celebrates all aspects of our multifaceted self as it intersects with gender. Unlike positive affirmations which often praise and compliment, ACT affirms the strength in the struggle and the struggle in the strength by recognizing the deep connection between our emotions and our value constructs. While not defined solely by our minority status, our unique power does intertwine with our unique paucity. Affirmation celebrates what we bring to the tribe, to the family, to the village, to the community, and affirms what only we can know. Affirmation spotlights the gain made when we enter the room, and the loss of our absence. This kind of self-observation comes up again and again over the lifespan as our relationship with both ourselves and the world we inhabit encounters social role, romantic relationships, family and community, and academic and occupational careers. Self-affirmation plays a vital role in maintaining our physical health and wellbeing, as self-actualization is an ongoing process that continues through old age to our final questions of legacy.

## Rolling dice: Defusing social roles

Multifaceted people naturally adjust demeanor in different situations, presenting one persona or role to co-workers while revealing another to friends or family. But sometimes we feel stuck in certain roles, hoping for approval or fearing reprisal. In-group vs. out-group status takes its toll whether we belong or whether we don't, yet transgender exclusionism can have a huge impact on mood, psychological and physical health, as well as our attitude toward ourselves and others (Reicherzer *et al.*, 2011; Valentine, 2007; Wight, 2011). When we do not feel like we belong, not only does our self-worth take a hit, but so too does our personal empowerment. Some gender variant people can develop a locus of internal control and responsibility, yet so too an internal locus of acceptance, which is to say our personal appraisal of self is prioritized over social validation (Stitt, 2014). Some gender variant people can develop an external locus of control, responsibility, and acceptance, in which case social validation is a must (Stitt, 2014). Of course, there are multiple permutations. Someone with internal control, external responsibility, and external acceptance may feel inclined to be rebellious, as they have an internal drive but blame society for not letting them in. Someone with external control, internal responsibility, and internal acceptance may feel helpless in the great scheme of things, but still take it on themselves to cope without others. These are not aspects to defuse from, as they're often reflective of a person's culture of origin or personal value construct (Stitt, 2014). Having an internal or external locus of acceptance is neither preferred nor inherently problematic, yet as routes to personal self-acceptance they do represent different paths to value-congruent behavior. Individualistic cultures may, for example, find self-acceptance in acts of individuation, whereas collectivistic cultures may find self-acceptance in acts centered on family inclusion (Stitt, 2014). Be mindful of this when we express feeling stuck in a social role, as the solution isn't always to abandon the role nor even redefine it, though such options are available.

If a gender role is a societal set of rules and behavioral norms fused to our gender, and an expressive stereotype is a preformed expectation for what our gender or sexual orientation "should look like," then a social role is a rule-set based on our social status and function within a community. When our social position is highly valued, the experience can seem positive, as the high school quarterback is praised for being an athlete, a student, and a popular classmate. When social roles intersect with historical racism, ethnic groups are often reduced and dehumanized to a single trait valued within the society, generating false assumptions like "Chinese people are good at math" or "African-Americans are great at basketball." When social roles intersect with historical sexism, males and females are unnecessarily divided into gender roles. Social roles are powerful and often have rigid hierarchical frames, and can be found on every side of every social justice debate. We can adopt social roles in order to fight or break the sexist and racist status quo, potentially getting stuck in new power dynamics while trying to subvert the old power dynamics. We can also adopt social roles in order to compete within our social status bracket, attempting to become the best version of our role should we believe doing so will help us climb the social ladder.

But does Western society have any social roles specific to gender nonconforming people? With such heart-wrenching stories of banishment and excommunication, at first glance it feels like there's no place for anyone outside the gender norm. At first glance it appears that gender minorities have to either hide our uniqueness in order to blend in or perform social roles with our gender tacked on as a caveat.

> "He was such a great teacher; I had no idea he was born a woman!"
>
> "I was talking to Diane the other day—you know, the trans lady who works in the office across town."
>
> "Listen, I have nothing against transgender people, but this is a daycare facility and I have to consider what the parents will think."

Defying this notion, gender variance has been around from time immemorial, and even Western society has social scripts to permit our liminal existence, yet they too come with a price. When these scripts are incorporated into our schema, we step from socially dominant gender rules and gender roles into the tokenized sector of gender variant social roles. One could argue that a gender variant social role is inherently a gender role. There is, however, a transactional nuance to be observed, as a gender role uses a person's gender for gain, whereas a gender variant social role uses a person's liminality for gain. Unlike gender roles that categorize men and women into oppositional and hierarchical frames of comparison and distinction, gender variant social roles are applied to anyone who is not cisgender, and do not consider our actual gender. There is, indeed, an oppositional and hierarchical frame at work, yet cissexism divides us between cisgender and non-cisgender, lumping all transgender, transsexual, nonbinary, and third gender people into one category. If our gender is not actually recognized, then it becomes apparent that the social roles we're culturally assigned have less to do with our identity, and more to do with our otherness, and how this otherness can be employed or exploited.

Sit with the homeless queer kids on a street corner, chat with the stripper saving up for her SRS, mull over essays with the nonbinary academic, and sip champagne with the self-made-man on the eve of his retirement, and notice how gender variant people not only exist in every social class, but commonly intersect worlds. We're too dynamic for a single label, too diverse to fit a single stereotype. Multifaceted multiculturalism makes social roles a tight fit, yet hierarchical thinking so loves to categorize, so we get boxed into archetypes based on how our gender uniqueness interacts with society. It is inaccurate to say contemporary Western culture has no gender variant social scripts, or that cisnormative culture fails to place gender variant social status. If this were true, there would be no transsexual or genderqueer stereotypes. Yet unlike stereotypes which are solely reductionist frames of distinction, social scripts generate a social transaction, whether we like it or not. This makes them far more difficult to defuse from, as social roles can provide us direction and guidance in lieu of value-congruent behavior. In short, when it comes to sharing who we are with others, it's easier to play the part that gets the most applause than it is to share the vulnerable work in progress that is our multidimensional whole. This is not to say that who we are in a social role is inauthentic, though at times it can feel that way. The limited identity we maintain within a social role is best described as a persona, as it reflects only a few facets of who we are.

While there are many archetypes and personas to fuse to and defuse from, there are four gender variant social roles frequently observed in contemporary Western culture: *the activist*, *the outsider*, *the star*, and *the beacon*.

## *The activist*

> "No one seems to care! But I can't stop, 'cause clearly no one else is going to do anything."

> "Yeah, I feel sad and angry, but it's not like I can do anything about it. I don't want anyone to pity me."

> "Sometimes I feel like everything I say counts half as much as everyone else. Like I have to fight for anyone to see me."

The activist is exactly that, a social activist rallying people together in times of crisis. Recall the cross-dressing drag kings of Le Monocle in pre-war Paris, and Marsha P. Johnson and Sylvia Rivera adorned in drag, waving their stilettos at Stonewall before founding the Street Transvestite Action Revolutionaries, or

STAR for short (Nestle *et al.*, 2002; Ziegler and Rasul, 2014). Gender-bending individuals are often at the forefront of visibility and therefore danger, giving them a unique place in society. As they boldly draw attention to sociopolitical issues, they also draw attention to themselves, which is why cissexist memes are often generated around their performance as feminists and social justice warriors.

Many approach self-empowerment by taking on identity politics, attending advocacy groups, candlelight vigils, starting petitions, or bringing neglected issues to the dinner table whenever possible (Chavez-Korell and Johnson, 2010). Empowered rallies and political marches bring people together, and are phenomenal for bolstering pride, yet they're also loose pretenses for building a sense of belonging, connection, family, or home (Lev, 2007). Those fused to the activist social role may feel internal pressure to be on the front line, applying their visibility to constant social and political use. Like a soldier in peace time, they don't always know how to relax or step down. Small talk is difficult when the activist is painfully aware of so many power discrepancies. Loneliness emerges, if they feel like people don't take the issues at hand seriously, or as seriously as they do. Internalizing this role, some may relate to the savior, martyr, dissenter, or rebel archetype.

Fused activists are often very vocal about values, and may try to "cut to the chase" in session, shortcutting mindfulness to get right to the value-congruent action. Subsequently, they may not be aware of their own shadow, unaware of how values can become overly rigid as well. Persistence can become a "never say die" attitude, pride can forgo, stoicism can omit vulnerability, and sensitivity may be eclipsed by wit, humor, sarcasm, and sass. In the end, it's not their passion to see the world become a loving and accepting place that's undermining their livelihood, but the anger, resentment, and trauma being utilized as their driving force to do it. The role, however, demands they fight on, fusing the activist to statements like:

"I don't have time to rest."

"If I don't, no one else will."

"I can quit when I'm dead."

The activist role favors alloplastic, goal-focused thinking as a form of emotional avoidance. Those stuck in this role may take a great pause when first introduced to creative hopelessness, having spent their lives believing in, or trying to believe in, their ability to change the world in the face of adversity. The prospect of not having to fight may be worrisome, until they see how driving on through willpower and sheer determination isn't sustainable.

## *The outsider*

"Sure I'm lonely, but I can't make people like me, and I wouldn't want to. People have a right to their opinions. I'm just used to it by now."

"No, you don't have to worry about me, I'll be okay. I'm fine."

"I went to the LGBT resource center once, but people didn't really seem to like me."

Different from everyone else, the outsider has been alienated by their social group, leading them to defiantly endorse themselves, or assume that, since there's no one like them, their gender resonance must be wrong, bad, or abnormal (Green, 2012). Stuck at arm's length, the outsider fuses to rigid frames of distinction, maximizing their differences and minimizing their similarities. Holding in their feelings, those who suppress their thoughts tend to weaken their social supports or wind up having fewer friends, in part because they can't reach out and in part because people may be less inclined to like them (Gross, 2002). To understand the outsider as a social role, observe the unrivaled difference between accepted belonging and tolerated harboring. Certain cisnormative communities tolerate gender variant people as the "aliens among us," their microaggressions giving away the disdain beneath their courtesy. People maintain in-group/out-group status *within* every social microcosm, casting the outsider as the social outlier, the community deviant, and the familial black sheep. Doing so provides the social group a subject to galvanize against, blame, or compare themselves to.

When a community rejects gender minorities, the outsider may begin to value independence and self-reliance. In social interactions, the outsider's voice is met with confusion or disdain, which means the more they communicate, the more they feel alone. They may even feel it's best to bite their tongue and shrink back. Relationships, if any, may be developed through sympathetic comradery with other outsiders, or through support systems. These support systems, however, may feel unsatisfactory if the outsider is so fused to the role that they feel "beyond help."

Outsider archetypes include the pariah, the hermit, or the loner self-image, which may be used to justify, rationalize, or provide reasons as to why they're on the outside. Others, who deeply desire connection, may align with orphan archetypes, expressing a deep sense of abandonment. For some family dynamics this may be quite literal; yet others may feel abandoned in the broader context of their community, yearning for a connection they may have never experienced. Fusing to the outsider social role often generates a feedback loop of alienation or isolation. As a social transaction, the outsider is permitted uniqueness at the cost of acceptance, as everyone agrees they're different, and spits at their feet for it.

People feel alienated when identity is reduced to a singular construct deemed critically different. Fused to such a rigid frame of distinction, the outsider may be overwhelmingly like someone else and still believe they're alien because of some essential dissimilarity. If this defining quality is inflated to eclipse all other facets of their character, it may even begin to take on a life-or-death urgency. For many, gender was not intentionally inflated. Usually, the increased pressure derives from the overplayed message, "You're different and should die" or "You're different and should be celebrated." In either case, the frame of distinction is reinforced.

Isolationism is distinct from alienation, as aliens may strive to be social, whereas isolates convince themselves that others are no longer necessary. Furthermore, isolates differ from introverts in that they wallow in their solitude, whereas introverts thrive in their solitude. Isolationism, as a maladaptive defense mechanism, is a fused system of beliefs associating social engagement with distress. The solution? Remove all interaction with humanity. The side effect? Loneliness. In ACT this can be understood as a value of self-preservation, safety, and security conflicting with connection, belonging, and love.

## *The star*

> "I'm fabulous, that's undeniable, but heavy is the head that wears the crown."

> "When the kids at school used to tease me, I just turned around and let them have it. I don't take shit from anyone."

> "Sometimes I feel like I'm wearing a smiley mask or something. The show must go on, you know."

Those who actively fight alienation and isolationism to carve out a sense of belonging tend to discover one of two outcomes. Either they actualize a full, multifaceted identity, or they fuse to the qualities the social majority actively celebrate, becoming a tokenized star (Catalano, 2014; Pusch, 2005).

It becomes apparent how little the well-intentioned majority understand about the star's actual identity or culture by how they treat them with novelty and intrigue. However, positive affirmation is addictive, especially for people who are rarely celebrated, so the star "plays the part," overemphasizing the importance of fashion, image, or social scene. They may even enjoy this social role immensely, until they feel stuck in the stereotype, or exhausted from having to keep the show going. They may even fuse with over-the-top expression or behavior in order to uphold their novelty as the rock-star, badass, or diva.

Like the outsider, the star experiences a great deal of alienation, yet they are less likely to isolate, feeling that if they take time for themselves they may lose their social status or community purchase. They may avoid being alone with the daunting prospect of introspection. Accepting their emotional experience, they may come to realize a deep detachment akin to loneliness in a crowded room, and performance fatigue. They are accepted, provided they stay in the spotlight, forever on stage, celebrated but still separate from the audience. This can be understood as a value dissonance between uniqueness, individuality, and personal identity, clashing with relatability, connection, and social identity.

Mistaking pride as a substitution for self-worth, some may be puzzled as to why pride and bravery aren't enough to attain happiness, harmony, or balance. Those raised in transactional societies expect success to equate with happiness, only to find hollow victories, Pyrrhic victories, or dissatisfaction. Having come out of the closet, burnt it down to the ground, and danced around its ashes, stars may feel confused by the fading of the afterglow, and the return of uncertainty.

## *The beacon*

> "A lot of people love me, but I don't usually get invited to parties. That's okay, parties aren't really my thing."

> "I love helping people, but I don't expect them to help me. I don't think they could, anyhow."

> "I do lot of rites of passage work, because I feel the need to provide what I never had."

The beacon refers to one of the oldest transgender social roles, still maintained in various counterculture scenes. One-part sage, one-part bohemian, and one-part queer diplomat, the beacon provides refuge to every curious and questioning waif estranged from conventional society. Historically, gender minorities have been the most visible of the LGBTQ invisible minority, making us both targets and lighthouses for those outside of the norm (Devor, 2002; Nestle *et al.*, 2002). When a community values transgender liminality, gender variant people take on a shamanistic light, as a bridge between genders, or as gatekeepers to la vie bohème. Identifying with the dissenter, educator, artist, bohemian, and healer self-image, the beacon is exactly that: a shining light. In cultures that value third gender identities, these individuals may become literal healers and shamans (Sell, 2001).

As altruism and insight are highly valued, those fused with the beacon role may not realize when these qualities contribute to their distress, as they're often well loved and well respected within their community. If the star is celebrated for their novelty, the beacon is celebrated for their wisdom, experience, acumen, and emotional labor. As such, a beacon may feel like they've finally found their place, and this may very well be true! Yet much like a village elder, the beacon may be consulted more often than they're befriended, visited by those seeking aid more often than they're invited out to play.

The beacon is a very particular social role as it's one of the few that elevates gender variant individuals. Yet like many historical mystics, seers, healers, and professors revered for their knowledge, their personhood is lost, since acknowledging them as people would reduce their revered mystery. Though able to help many, they may feel that others are unable to help them. Likewise, as their interactions are often so meaningful, they may not notice the one-way interaction, or else accept the power dynamic as the fee for community appreciation.

When we fuse with roles, we can become fatigued by them, or develop issues with intimacy and vulnerable disclosure. Yet even though we're taxed by our social survival mechanism, we may negate the cost. Having found a way to navigate the world, we concede to our binding rules of engagement as if there's no alternative.

Ironically, the very act of striving to "fit in" or "find a niche" or "maintain a place," becomes further evidence of distinction, contributing to a lonesomeness we may or may not willingly admit to. As we accept our emotional experience, a deep loneliness may come over us, veiled behind our frustrated opinions about ourselves and society. By increasing mental flexibility, and challenging the parameters of social role, we can be encouraged to share our multifaceted self with others. Just like soft disclosures in the coming out process, it's best to select friends and social networks which have a high probability of acceptance and social growth. Our fused activists may need to experiment with letting their guard down. Our fused outsiders may need to experiment with trust and letting people in. Our fused stars may need to experiment with authenticity and whole presentation. And our fused beacons may need to experiment with being playful, or letting others heal them.

It doesn't help that the LGBTQ community is not always as warm as it may first appear. The working assumption that there's a universal, uniform LGBTQ community we're initiated into the moment we come out sadly isn't true. The disillusioning truth is that the rainbow is far more of a coalition than a community (Lev, 2007). Age differences, cultural differences, spiritual and political differences, even class differences, all contribute to the amazing diversity within the rainbow. Rather than conceptualize the LGBTQ community as a home where we can belong, it may be more accurate to conceptualize the LGBTQ community as a rainbow city, within which we can make a home. It's a lovely neighborhood, but sometimes it can feel like trying to fight for a rent-controlled apartment. It's all about who you know, which is exactly why intergroup contact can help reduce stigma, increasing our ability to transcend any social role or self-stereotype we may feel trapped in (Walch *et al.*, 2012). Yet even in the transgender block of the rainbow city, we're not always accepted uncritically on the basis of our gender variance (Bockting *et al.*, 2006).

Exposure to diversity can be a phenomenal way of broadening our understanding of self and others, yet finding intergroup cohorts of similar age range, with connections to similar ethnic, cultural, and spiritual backgrounds can help ease us into expressing our multifaceted self. Shielding our nature behind our social demeanor, we often simplify ourselves for others who do not intrinsically understand our background. Yet finding someone who understands how, for example, one's sexuality as a trans-masculine person deeply influences their Hindu family, or how one's nonbinary gender is layered with their African American identity, can be comforting and self-empowering. Since finding these cohorts may not be possible in some geographic locations, we must simultaneously explore how to maintain our multifaceted identity while surrounded by people who are dissimilar from ourselves on almost every level. In other words, we must learn how to compare without getting stuck in our comparisons, and to validate distinction without getting stuck in our distinctions. If we only disclose certain facets of our identity to those whom we personally relate to, then we'll inevitably close ourselves off in a majority of situations. Closed off, we may forgo our voice, our uniqueness, and so be assimilated by culturally hegemonic cisgender norms or tokenized because of the aforementioned roles thrust upon us. To help us defuse from this, you can affirm the multifaceted self by exploring our complexity. Acknowledging that others may not understand us is difficult if we have an external locus of acceptance, but we can still learn to delineate when we're being accepted for who we are versus how we're perceived (Stitt, 2014).

To expand on our conceptual self, imagine rolling a six-sided die. We can roll a 1, 2, 3, 4, 5, or 6. As multifaceted people, we act differently around our parents than we do our personal friends, passionate lovers, and professional co-workers. Let's spend some time defining at least six different sides we show in six different social circles. How do we show up at work? How do we behave on our sports team? How do we act around our siblings? What role do we play with friends? What role do we play with lovers? How do we behave when we meet someone for the first time? Then ask how many sides we show to people. Most likely, our close friends have seen a few of our dimensions, but our co-workers may have only gleaned one or two sides of us. Recognizing that we show different sides to different people also begs the question of how many sides we show, and in what combination. How many times do we roll that die in a social situation? After all, we can roll a 1. We can roll a 1 and a 2. We can roll a 2 and a 5. We can roll a 1, 2, 3, 4, and a 5, but the only person who gets to see all six sides simultaneously is our self. That's the unique wonder of being who we are, and the privilege we get for being inside our own head. Our multifaceted privacy is also what contributes to feeling like an imposter or worrying that other people can't or won't understand us.

Taking an inventory of our personas can help conceptualize how we interact with our social environment, and how we cultivate trust. Those who have not fully self-actualized commonly compartmentalize gender identity, adjusting presentation in different social groups. Some may be out to friends but not family; others may be out to family, but not at work. Some may be a son to their parents and a girlfriend to their lover. Some may be an outsider at school but a star at work, and so on. And gender roles are only one aspect of our dynamic personal identity. No doubt we have more than six sides, just as there's yet another side to this metaphor. Certainly, we can be deliberate about our social presentation, yet a lot of us stumble into friendships and even relationships by sheer chance, much like the roll of a die.

The difference, of course, is that a die is random, whereas we are responding to needs we may or may not be aware of.

*What brings out side 1? What do you need present to bring out this side of you?*

*What brings out side 2? What do you need present to bring out this side of you?*

*When can you show more than one side of you to someone?*

*What do you need to show more than one side of you to someone?*

The avoidant may shrug off active engagement, saying that all we need is time to cultivate trust. This, however, is a cunning way to dodge an answer, as we've all known people for years that we never got closer to. On the flip side, we can meet a brand new person and have a new friend by the end of a weekend camping trip. Time alone is not the arbiter of trust, nor is trust all or nothing. We may trust someone with our feelings, but not our money if they have a gambling problem. We may trust someone to take care of our cat, but not our children if they're not good with kids. We may trust someone to take care of our children, but worry when they spend too much time with our life partner if they're really flirtatious. We may trust someone with our life but not a bottle of booze. Just as we have multifaceted parts of our identity, so too do we have multifaceted requirements for our trust. Those closest to us know our complexity, and have also proved their trustworthiness on multiple levels—hence our belief in time, as time contains within it multiple opportunities to exemplify trust. However, we can also create opportunities for people to exemplify trust by going out on a limb to trust them, or by watching how they interact with others. But what are we looking for? That depends on our persona's personal needs.

*What does your side 1 need to trust someone?*

*What does your side 5 need to trust someone?*

For example, we may only go to the movies with someone once we trust their sense of humor; or we may eat lunch with someone every week, but only go to that nice restaurant for dinner once we're sure of their intention. We may state that we're very trusting, and yet struggle with transparency. We may state that we don't trust very easily, and yet struggle with boundaries. When we fuse to a singular facet of ourselves, we glaze over our own complexity and our dynamic tier of personal needs to create living contradictions and all-or-nothing paradigms.

As we engage an array of diverse context, with a myriad of people who are equally as multifaceted, the thinking self will pop in to make sweeping generalizations and broad social judgments. By practicing a defusion exercise like *Internal volume and proximity*, we can relax the piety of these thoughts enough to expand our awareness to our social context. In doing so, it becomes possible to access our multidimensional whole, and feel less like a tokenized, one-dimensional character.

Building resilience and self-worth, we may eventually attempt a hard disclosure, expressing ourselves in ways atypical of the social role we feel stuck in. This may include extending relationships to turn co-workers into friends, or introducing already established friends to a deeper tier of personal truth, or publicly sharing a passion, hobby, activity, or cultural practice. In the end, our personas are not falsehoods unless we say we have only one social role, at which point we're forced to hide or deny any part of us that doesn't fit this characterization. By holding our social roles lightly, we understand ourselves in the context of what works (Leonard and Grousd, 2016). Furthermore, by holding our social roles lightly, we actively express who we are by deciding how to express ourselves in the moment.

## Spiral in and spiral out: Lovers, partners, and abusers

There's certainly a great deal of complexity in any relationship, yet before we dive into interpreting ourselves and our beliefs about love and sex, let's take a moment to appreciate our lovers and all their forms, foibles, fixations, fascinations, fantasies, and even faults. Understandably, those who date gender variant individuals often feel their own sexual scripts growing and changing too, often within the same relationship (Belawski and Sojka, 2014; Mellman, 2017).

Out one night, we see two guys intimately chatting in a restaurant. Michael's an FtM self-identified jock on a date with his cis boyfriend, Tom. Validating Michael's identity as a sporty gay man, and their own androphilic attraction to physiological males, Tom identifies them as a gay couple, though he had to think about this. Over wine and breadsticks, they're discussing what it means to be pansexual, and if that estranges them from the gay community. Any conversation about sexuality is a mishmash amalgam of physical attraction, affectional attraction, and how social classifiers impact their lives. Binary hetero and homonormative scripts do not always capture the lived experiences of attraction and relationship, leading many to suss through what it means to be gay, straight, bisexual, or pansexual (Belawski and Sojka, 2014; Mellman, 2017). What do they resonate with, how do they see themselves as a couple, what community do they connect to, and in turn which communities accept Michael and Tom as they are?

Lovers, partners, and spouses of gender variant people are diverse in attitude and perception. Some have a specific attraction for cross-sexed and queer gender dynamics, some may have been unaware of their partner's gender identity until later in the relationship, and some may have even played an integral role in their partner's transition process (Malpas, 2006; Meier *et al.*, 2013; Mellman, 2017). That said, there are some unique considerations for *cisgender partners*, *trans-amorous cisgender partners*, and gender variant individuals with *gender variant partners*.

## *Cis partners*

In broad strokes, cisgender partners include those who either knowingly or unknowingly enter into a relationship with a gender variant person before, during, or after their actualization process. Cisgender individuals whose lovers, partners, or spouses "come out" after years of being together are often hit by shock and grief (Boyd, 2003; Malpas, 2006, 2012; Raj, 2008; Witten, 2003). When asked, cis people whose partners actualized their gender often expressed sadness and anxiety around the transition experience, often worrying about physical health and safety, and what their future would look like should their identity, levels of intimacy, and sexual connection change (Joslin-Roher and Wheeler, 2009). They may love their self-actualizing partners but feel disheartened if they also loved and relied on that person's presumed gender role. There's no shame in this, though it's often confusing, and cis partners can be surprised by their own feelings of revulsion or arousal (Lev and Sennott, 2012). Heterosexual women, for example, can have a hard time if they're not attracted to their partner's cross-gender behavior, or if they're not interested in lesbian sex (Lev and Sennott, 2012). Their acceptance, tolerance, or disgust are not constant either, as their patience and ability to accept their partner's cross-gender behavior may depend largely on the moment (Boyd, 2003). Comparatively, as trans men often present a masculine aesthetic even before coming out, cis partners are often less shocked and more inclined to remain in a relationship (Lev and Sennott, 2012). When working with relationships in transition, maintain a both/and position, rooting for the cis partner's best interest, their partner's gender actualization, and the healthiest expression of the relationship (Malpas, 2012).

Cis partners who reinvest in the relationship, or knowingly enter into a relationship with a gender variant person, may become introspective about their own gender identities. Reflecting on themselves, cis partners can begin to question their own relationships with their bodies, body image, and gender roles, becoming increasingly more self-conscious (Malpas, 2012; Pfeffer, 2008). Should their gender variant partner have body-hiding habits (concealing phenotypes or body-fat) cis partners may even begin to adopt these same behaviors (Pfeffer, 2008).

Back in our romantic restaurant we see another couple trying to reconcile some recent disclosure with a date night, but nothing's quite the same anymore. Clara fell in love with Terry, adoring the masculine qualities he presented, only to find out Terry is Sherry. Fidgeting with her fork, Clara keeps breaking eye contact. She still loves Sherry, but a foundational part of the relationship dynamic has changed. Even partners who are supportive of their lover's transition may question what their own emotional and physical needs are, and if it's feasible to have these needs met within the evolving relationship. For inventive and flexible partners, this can actually work with a little creativity, but for those with very rigid parameters and gender roles? Perhaps not. It's certainly possible to defuse from gender roles and limiting cognitions about spousal expectations, but sexual orientation is what it is, which is why Clara keeps playing with her fork. She doesn't know how to say it. She knows herself well enough to say she's straight, and now she's married to a trans woman, presenting a very difficult question: "Am I intolerant if I'm not happy with this? Am I close-minded if I am unsatisfied with this change in my life?" This is a very personal question with no clear answer. Sherry is still the same person, after all, but Sherry doesn't want to go by *husband* anymore, and Clara's not attracted to having a wife. Humorously, Sherry jokes that Clara can call her *was-band*. Clara smirks.

Clara's sadness and sense of loss are every bit as valid as Sherry's growth, yet while Sherry has support, Clara isn't certain how to gain clarity or emotional validation. She may find they can stay together, as some partners relearn sexual intimacy in a new dynamic, especially when transition positively affects their partner's connection to their body (Brown, 2010; De Cuypere *et al.*, 2005). Or, if Clara doesn't walk away, she may find their relationship evolving into a nonconventional partnership far more intimate than friendship, yet far more dynamic than what she once conceptualized as marriage (Hines, 2006).

A similar process occurs when cis people start dating an already actualized person without knowing they're gender variant. Surprise, curiosity, frustration of perceived secrecy, questions of betrayal, and even the relief of honesty can arise at different levels of intensity should disclosure occur on the first date, a month into the relationship, or after a year or even longer.

For Naveah, sitting alone by the window, being transsexual is a small part of her identity. Naveah thinks of her gender experientially, as more of a delayed puberty irrelevant to most conversation. Tonight, however, she's meeting Caleb for the second time, and she feels it's something she has to talk about. To compare, cisgender people don't typically go around sharing their awkward puberty stories, of how they went from being boys to men or girls to women. Cisgender privilege allows them to exist as is, and that natural acceptance is what many gender variant people desire. For Naveah, the last step in her transition process was for gender and all its pressure to take a backseat in her life. Yet despite being a non-issue for her, it may be quite an issue for her date. The last guy she went out with threw water in her face and stormed out the door, but Caleb seems understanding. He's late to the restaurant, but excited to be there. The conversation dances around the topic until finally Naveah asks if he's ever been to a pride parade. This is her little test to determine Caleb's exposure to the LGBTQ community. Caleb happily shares a story about the first time he waved a rainbow flag, and how he used to volunteer as an ally when he was still in school. Finally, Naveah opens up, more so to end her awkwardness than to demonstrate her courage. Caleb swallows, takes another drink, and smiles—all actions Naveah is painfully aware of. He says he's fine, but he also says he's never dated a trans person before. In the back of his mind, Caleb is struggling with a few thoughts.

> "Did you keep it a secret on the whole, or did you keep it a secret because you couldn't trust me, specifically?"

> "If you kept this hidden, what else are you hiding?"

> "Why are you telling me now?"

As there's no simple, all-encompassing answer, Caleb's ruminating on the interaction. Naveah was able to build up trust to share, which is a net positive for their second date, and he's also aware of his attraction to Naveah as a person. In situations like this, however, cisgender privilege becomes quite evident in Caleb's thinking, and a bit of psychoeducation may be needed to humanize how difficult it can be to open up about gender. Likewise, Naveah is practicing defusion from her fears, and the intrusive thoughts engaging her defensive reflex every time Caleb reaches for his glass.

So they stick with it. Having never dated a gender variant person before, Caleb finds himself shocked by, of all things, his own thoughts and emotional reactions. Wanting to educate himself so as not to be accidentally offensive, Caleb goes home that night and takes a deep dive into trans politics, increasing his sensitivity around the hardships Naveah has lived with all her life. As their relationship progresses, this can be problematic when Caleb "takes offense" on behalf of Naveah, or "speaks up for her." Impatiently, Naveah explains to him how it's like showing up late for the battle and thinking he has to defend those who've been on the front line for years.

Cis partners who have never dated a gender variant person before may find their world opening up to a whole range of issues and social circumstances they were never familiar with. This can sometimes be difficult for even the most patient gender variant person. Moments of surprise and awe—like taking a new partner to a gender-bender ball, introducing them to queer music, movies, and art, or even introducing them to new ways of having sex and showing affection—can be delightful. On the flipside, new partners may go through all the stages of frustration and anger should they encounter cissexism, or awaken to the cissexism around them.

"A part of me really appreciated how he wanted to stand up and defend me, but when we got home he was still so mad. I've dealt with this my whole life, so I know how to deal with it, but he doesn't. He's never had someone reject him like that."

"I love her, but she always makes this big production—always slipping gender into the conversation. Like, she used to be straight, but now she's in a queer relationship she thinks she gets to be an advocate or something. I know it's her way of processing, but I'm kind of tired of it."

Other cis partners may become increasingly conscious of cisgender or heterosexual privilege they were previously unaware of, having never encountered gender discrimination of this kind before (Lev and Sennott, 2012). For those who identify as straight this can be startling, as they vicariously, and in some cases directly, experience minority oppression for the very first time. For some it can even be a deeper exploration and understanding of their own sexuality (Joslin-Roher and Wheeler, 2009; Malpas, 2006). Preconceptions of masculinity, femininity, and gender roles may be called into question, which they may or may not feel able to discuss openly with their partner. Some may use secrecy and privacy to avoid seeming naïve or unprogressive, or to avoid "burdening" their gender variant partner. Others may share their experiences openly, exploring stressful issues together.

## *Transamorous cis partners*

Transphobia often leaves cis people who are specifically attracted to gender variance trapped in a unique closet with two locks. One padlock is the overall stigma around transgender and nonbinary people, as the general populace barely understands gender variance, let alone cisgender people who prefer their company. The felt isolation around this can lead to distress, hostility, depression, and patterns of casual/noncommital relationships with trans lovers (Mcllelan, 2017; Mellman, 2017). Both cis men and women can feel unable to share or disclose their attraction, lest they be accused of being a "tranny-chaser" (Boyd, 2003; Mcllelan, 2017; Tompkins, 2014). This accusation points at cisgender privilege, the second padlock on the transamorous closet.

As gender variance is often eroticized, the trans-amorous have to determine within themselves whether their attractions are based on this fetishization, on a vicarious pleasure they have within themselves, or on a genuine attraction to the individual. Many also look to discern the social power differentials that exist in their relationship, and if they're attracted to this privileged role. Pansexual narratives occasionally minimize this by stating, "I'm attracted to anyone *regardless* of gender," yet transamorous people, who can identify as gay, straight, bisexual, pansexual, or asexual, are *specifically* attracted to gender variant people. Though unfair to scrutinize the basis of this attraction more than any other, the unique differential in power and privilege prompts many transamorous partners to question and scrutinize themselves, sending them rising and falling through phases of doubt and personal insecurity.

To illustrate a sexual facet of this power dynamic, one study found that men sexually engage trans women differently, based on their own sexual orientation (Weinberg and Williams, 2010). In other words, men who identified as straight glossed over the trans woman's penis and male phenotypes, whereas men who identified as bisexual did not (Weinberg and Williams, 2010). While this behavior is certainly an expression of each man's sexual orientation, it is also indicative of how gender variant bodies are treated, depending on the perception of those they interact with.

From the gender variant side, encounters with transamorous people range from healthy romance to unwanted fetishization (Tompkins, 2014). When a transamorous person is genuinely attracted to a person's unique gender identity, then it can be an incredibly validating relationship for both individuals. This is especially true for nonbinary genderqueer, genderfluid, and agender individuals whose affectional and sexual activities may differ from cisnormative intimacy. However, objectification of gender variant bodies can be very counterintuitive and invalidating, especially for FtM and MtF people in transition who may not want someone to be aroused by their transition status.

## *Gender variant partners*

Transgender people date transgender people, nonbinary people date nonbinary people, the butch date the butch, the femmes date the femmes, and all combinations thereof date each other and more! In a world where so few seem to grasp gender variance, having a partner in crime who implicitly understands can be a great relief (Belawski and Sojka, 2014; Inness, 1997). It is not unheard of for trans men to crush on other trans men, for trans women to adore other trans women, for trans men to propose to trans women, or for genderqueer people to find their healthiest connections are with other genderqueer people. This presents a few unique complications in a relationship. The first is being an actual partner in crime depending on how protective or discriminatory our state or country is when it comes to LGBTQ relationships.

It's hard enough being a social outsider or camouflaging with the masses whilst knowing one's private truth may take some aback. Now multiply that feeling by two. Bubbling out of love and social defense, some partners may isolate together, fostering interdependence. This is only problematic when partners begin to feel like all they have is each other.

Simultaneously, partners may struggle with interrelationship comparison, especially if they have different definitions of gender. Consider a trans woman who appreciates the feminine archetypes, dating a trans woman who's more of a tomboy in their presentation. Each may question what it means to be a woman, what it means to transition, and if they need to be more like their partner's concept of femininity in order to make the relationship work. Consider a trans man who is dating a genderqueer person. Each may question the validity of their gender constructs and compare themselves to each other out of a desire to "fit in" with the relationship. Partners may also compare if they're at different stages in their actualization process, creating odd power differentials between the experienced and the inexperienced. Those who are just beginning may desire a mentor yet be frustrated if they don't align with their lover's exact path to self-actualization. Those who are further along may feel an obligation to be the mentor they never had, creating a power imbalance they may not in the long term enjoy. Or, those who are further along may feel the pressure to be a mentor, even though they're feeling just as vulnerable and lost in their own transition.

Differentials also exist should one partner be more "passable" than the other. Twinges of jealousy may crop up alongside moments of caution, as we're naturally more vigilant of danger when we're in the company of those we love. Partners may feel like they have to be on guard when they're together in public spaces more often than when they're alone in public spaces. Without ever having an open conversation about it, partners may only make public appearances in safe, controllable environments, and come up with odd little reasons about why they shouldn't go to new venues—"Oh, I'm just not feeling like going out. I'd probably get bored anyway." Partners can feel tired, irritable, and worn down, their minority stress compounded. In trying to avoid this distress, relationships may collapse under the weight of it, yet breaking up need not be the solution.

Relationships naturally evolve as each person explores deeper facets of their identity over time, yet through it all we can still hold onto old ideas about our partners and our relationships to them. Moving through the old narrative, let's make a belief inventory about the relationship.

On a date it's important for me to be________________
On a date I often act________________
On a date I should act________________
In a relationship I rarely________________
In a relationship I usually________________
In a relationship I always________________

We can hold onto a lot of negative self-assessments about our performance in a relationship. We may state, "I'm no good at this sort of thing," or excuse a behavior, believing "It's my pattern, I always do this in relationships," or that "It always ends the same way." We fault ourselves for not being able to begin, maintain, or even end a relationship as needed. Such beliefs may lead us to avoid relationships altogether or feel like we have to try extra hard just to impress someone, or conceal our most vulnerable feelings.

Those who have never been in a relationship aren't immune to this kind of fusion, either, as we can hold on to untested scripts assuming "how things are." Believing the rumor mill, they may state their fears as facts, claiming, "That's just the way it is because guys are like that," or "Every girl I know says the same thing," or "I've never met someone different."

Disillusioning myths, we learn the hard way how different relationships really are from what we believe them to be. Such myths include: the idea of the perfect partner; that a partner will somehow complete us; that relationships should be fun and easy; that true love is everlasting; that love is all we need; that we should never bring up the past; that seeking therapy means the relationship is already doomed; or that any conflict in a relationship can be resolved (Gottman, 2011; Gottman and Silver, 2015; Harris, 2009b). Take time to inventory what myths we might harbor about relationships. How do we define a healthy relationship? How do we define an unhealthy relationship?

Working with gender variant people and our partners can sadly take a dark turn. Our frames of distinction, comparison, opposition, and hierarchy can lead to great insecurities, and insecure lovers so often attempt to control their partner's emotional process. This can quickly lead to lies, secrecy, manipulation, coercion, and submissive docility. Worse yet, attempts to control a lover's thoughts and feelings can escalate into verbal and even physical assault. Intimate partner violence can take on added cruelty in gender variant partnerships, as physical abuse can belittle gendered anatomy, mutilating or molesting the chest and genitals as a means of shaming a person into submission (Goodmark, 2013; White and Goldberg, 2006). Sexual coercion also manipulates gendered power discrepancies to convince us that only the abuser can love us *because of our bodies*, or that rough sex is how "real men" or "real women" do it (Cook-Daniels, 2008; Goodmark, 2013). Psychological abuse includes: dictating what we can or cannot wear to the point of stealing and hiding gender affirmative accoutrements like chest binders and wigs; deliberately using the wrong pronoun as a power play; or threatening to out our sex or gender (Cook-Daniels, 2008; Goodmark, 2013).

Do not, however, presume the underlying cause of cruelty. Unlike other aggression models, which focus on angry thoughts and power dynamics, ACT examines violence in context (Zarling and Berta, 2017). This approach allows ACT to aid aggressors in violent relationships as much as the victims of it. By tracing the antecedents to their outbursts—like stress, childhood trauma, and their own experiential avoidance—aggressors can outline the rigid thoughts and learn to observe them without obeying them (Zarling and Berta, 2017). Unlike other therapeutic modalities that attempt to control intensity or frequency of outburst, ACT focuses on the aggressor's internal relationship with their cognitions to alleviate the false urgency to act out (Zarling and Berta, 2017).

Victims of partner violence also have internal conflict to unpack. As victims of abuse may minimize violent incidence, be sensitive to how the relationship is described, as there are often rules of self-preservation encoded therein. "I have to____" statements or phrases like "He expects me to____" silently nod toward unspoken consequence. Those in abusive relationships may need added support to hold boundaries, relocate, and even file a restraining order. Gender variant populations face a disproportionally higher risk of being stalked—16 percent in contrast to the 6 percent reported by cisgender populations—which, coupled with negative interactions with the police, leave many without a safety net (James *et al.*, 2016). It may be worth developing a check-in system during escalated periods when we're attempting to leave an abusive ex. If we have limited friendships, which is often the case if our ex has restricted communication or kept us socially isolated, you may consider being a part of that check-in system by encouraging us to text when we get home after a session, or to phone you directly if we're unable to call the police on our own.

Experience of this kind can leave a huge dent in our ability to trust others or believe in ourselves. In the aftermath, we may revert to gender camouflage or pretend to be cisgender, just to reduce the incidence of conflict and hostility, or to even hide from our ex. Facilitating room for us to feel the full extent of our pain, fear, and betrayal is vital, as suppressing our feelings can rapidly drop us into depression. So as not to lose sight of what's most important, drawing up an ACT matrix can provide agency and forward motion. Learning to defuse from all-or-nothing or catastrophic thinking, it's possible to move through the fear, yet restoring faith in self and the prospect of a healthy loving partner takes both time and experience. Value-congruent steps connecting us to friendship and community are often a healing interim before trying a new relationship. There are healthy partners in the world, and a veritable army of people to love, yet when we're fused to self-deprecation, trauma, or fear, we may be unable to believe they exist.

For both gender variant people and our prospective partners it can, at times, be difficult to determine when to look within or when to express emotional honesty. Since fusion occurs as forms of both internalization and externalization, we begin to fear situations that might cause us to implode or explode. To figure this out, let's draw a spiral on a piece of paper, or better yet on the palm of our hand (see Figure 7.1). The spiral is one of the most sacred shapes in the cosmos, representing the galactic immensity of the Milky Way. It's also the whole therapeutic process summed up in one squiggly line. Funneling in and out, the spiral connects the external world to the world behind our eyes, as each is intrinsically linked to the other.

When we internalize cissexism, we spiral in, like we're being sucked into our thoughts. In the center of the spiral, smack-dab in the center of our palm, let's draw an implosive black hole. Internalization, self-blame, self-hatred, and suicidal ideation are common for those sucked into this extreme end of the vortex (Clements-Nolle *et al.*, 2006). Often, the agenda of emotional control manifests in this black hole as social avoidance, withdrawal, isolation, and depersonalization. This can make it difficult to connect with others, allow for vulnerability, or communicate our feelings. For the introspective and introverted, deep existential thought is often a personal blessing and a curse. If anything, when we find ourselves stuck in the black hole, the act of expressing outwardly or asking for help can feel like risky behavior. In the black hole, we fear that others will judge us as harshly as we judge ourselves. We may feel crazy because of how bizarrely complex, dissonant, and even contradictory our cognitions have become, and how distraught, apathetic, or empty we feel.

Those who respond to transphobia by turning in on themselves often express disdain for displays of emotionality and aggression. As toxic masculinity uses testosterone like a solar flare, we may try and distance ourselves from emotive expression—to such an extent that we may fear or judge ourselves for having aggressive thoughts. The line between assertive anger and aggressive hostility has become both blurred and gendered. MtF and transfeminine people may try and shrink their voice and their bubble of personal space should they associate aggression and extroversion with masculinity, or should they not want to call attention to themselves. This social role embodies the sexist construct of the meek, docile, and self-doubting "little woman." Comparatively, FtM and transmasculine people may feel like they have to inflate themselves, or else question their manliness should they distance themselves from masculine sparring.

On the other extreme, internalized trauma and cissexism can also lead us to spiral out, so let's mark the outermost tip of the spiral with a jagged explosion—a miniature, palm-sized supernova hurling emotions around. This classic form of fusion includes yelling, shouting, arguments, and even violence. Fusing to cissexist gender constructs, we may feel explosive, or even project these cissexist expectations and attitudes onto others. Striving in vain to contain our stress, anger, and outrage, we may become demanding, hostile, and bullying in a desperate attempt to control or avoid whatever external stimuli we blame for our feelings, including our partners.

As we look at this spiral, note how fusing to inadequate, critical, self-deprecating, and self-destructive thoughts can polarize us in either direction. Defusing from black holes and supernovas is the same therapeutic process, beginning the moment we realize we're too close to either of these gravity giants. So, let's mark where we start to get drawn into intrusive thoughts at both ends of the spiral. Try asking: *Do you notice the thoughts trying to pull you in? When was the last time you felt pulled in like this? What thoughts went through your mind in that moment?*

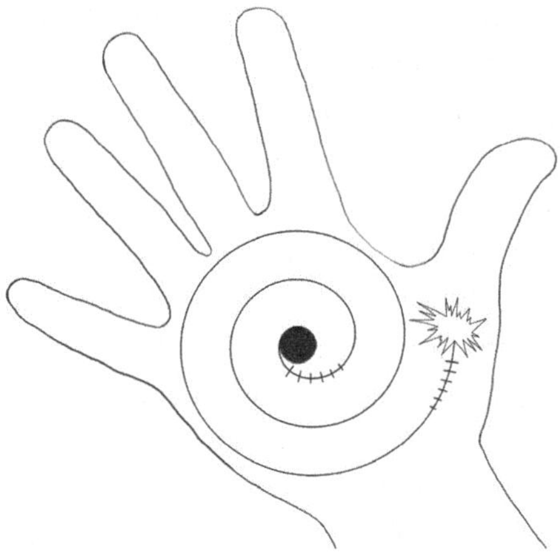

**Figure 7.1** *Hand spiral diagram*

Control attempts strive to prevent us from slipping into the black hole of despair, yet they also keep us stuck in place, insulated from emotional expression. In kind, the outwardly emotive may avoid the internal process, believing introspection will unravel everything. Presuming there are only two options, we usually favor the galactic devil we know.

In this metaphor, the longest stretch of the spiral represents our healthy emotional experience and psychological homeostasis. Note that mental health isn't synonymous with happiness, but emotional resilience, mental flexibility, and contextual adaptability. We may feel sad, but it doesn't wreck us. We may feel angry, but we express it without obliterating the house. Naturally, we drift back and forth along this broad length of the spiral. On some days we're more emotive and expressive, on others we're more introspective and thoughtful.

Check in to see where on the spiral we are today. If we're closer to the center, our process may include learning to express some of our innermost thoughts, even if they're scary at times. This is a perfect opportunity to present your therapeutic office as a confidential safe space. Vulnerability, after all, requires practice, and before we can communicate our thoughts and feelings effectively to our romantic partners, we may first need to practice verbalizing what has remained silent for so long. If we place ourselves closer to the outside of the spiral, our process may include learning to look within ourselves, even if we don't know what we'll find yet. As this is the opposite of our typical avoidance strategies, this exercise cuts right to the chase. Externalizing, we may want to talk about our partner's problems and issues, or our lack of partners and the difficulty with the dating scene, or why society will never accept gender variant lovers, all to avoid observing our own hand in it.

Defusion techniques that reduce the gravity of thought, like giving the cissexist insults in our head a cartoonish voice, or personifying our negative self-talk as a ghost unable to touch or do anything, create enough inertia to break orbit from these black holes and supernovas (Blackledge, 2015; Hayes and Smith, 2005). Living day to day in a cisnormative world with cisnormative rules and cisnormative expectations can make cognitions quite rigid, while increasing our fear of consequences. We may worry that expressing how we really feel will sabotage or undermine everything we've worked so hard to build, keep, and maintain. We may fear our feelings will shake us to the ground or shake others to the ground! We are, in essence, trying to save ourselves from ourselves. Worse yet—should we view ourselves as the deviants society would make us out to be—we may even protect those we love from our very existence. When this is the case, we would rather implode on ourselves than bring anyone else down, or explode outwards rather than have people think we're weak.

All this and more can whirl behind our eyes as we sit staring at a spiral in our palm. Fortunately, coupling defusion with awareness practices focused on queer failure and queer innocence can give us enough rocket fuel to jet away from these cissexist gravity giants (LeMaster, 2018; Miller and Grollman, 2015; Muñoz, 2009). When out of the danger zone of emotional impulsivity, we begin to see how the gravity of gender is not actually the problem. On some planets the low gravity makes us light and bouncy, on others we feel seriously heavy. Supernovas and black holes, by contrast, are gravity giants— areas of fusion so excessively absolute that gender becomes destructive. ACT is a form of imaginal exposure therapy, as we visualize many distressing situations through metaphor, yet it's also a form of in vivo exposure to our bodily experience of emotion. The more affirmative, everyday experiences we have with gender expression, value congruence, and emotional acceptance, the easier it becomes to enter the safe orbit of our observational self. In this habitable zone, we can engage prospective partners in a thoughtful, compassionate, and communicative way, being true to our own values while recognizing that between all those supernovas and black holes is a gravitationally balanced galaxy of stars.

## The affection effect: Relationship norms

Romantic and affectionate relationships can be incredibly validating during our self-actualization process and over the course of our whole lives (Roland and Burlew, 2017). The effect of human affection on psychological wellbeing is powerful and profound, for when an intimate partner witnesses the rejection of our old identity and is capable of embracing our actualized gender, it becomes far easier for us to be affirmative of who we are (Devor, 2004; Meier *et al.*, 2013). As our greatest allies, our lovers and life partners can help us find courage when we're most lost, and safety when we're most wounded. A certain element of chemistry is encouraging, as trans men are more likely to feel validated when an intimate partner is attracted to men and masculinity, trans women are more likely to feel validated when an intimate partner is attracted to women and femininity, and nonbinary people are more likely to feel adored by partners attracted to personal authenticity (Devor, 2004). If such chemistry is absent, gender variant people are more likely to engage in superficial flirtation and anonymous sexual encounters in order to feel the physical and emotional confirmation intimacy provides (Devor, 2004).

Meaningful relationships, as any long-term lover knows, are a continuous process balancing and rebalancing passion, trust, and commitment (Gottman, 2015; Sternberg, 2007). Communication is quintessential as *love* is understood very differently between people. Love may even carry dissonant connotations within our own conceptualizations. Our beliefs pertaining to trust, passion, and commitment range in context, and can therefore be contradictory. We maintain schemas about what love is, even if we're uncertain if we've ever been in love! We sometimes hold onto preformed ideas about potential partners we've only ever dreamed of. We may fight our own self-esteem, questioning whether or not we'd even make a good partner, or wondering how we measure up to other cisgender vixens or transgender Casanovas. We may even carry cultural notions of love, courtship, monogamy, friendship, or sexuality that we're not even sure *we* agree with.

Like everyone, gender variant people differ greatly in our range of relationship experience, so before we dive into the complexities of relationship let's normalize some hopes and fears. The prospect of connection and acceptance is exciting, yet the fear of rejection is substantial (Hines, 2006). If we transitioned early in life, we may ponder how to disclose our history if we're not directly open about it. We may worry about the physical and emotional risks in the disclosure process. Or, if we stayed in the chrysalis of actualization for some time, we may feel a kind of identity delay, especially if we missed out on the opportunity to form romantic relationships in adolescence and young adulthood. In particular, the Transgender Aging Network (TAN) cautions how negotiating safe sex practices can be difficult for trans women who transitioned later in life, should they have spent decades in heteronormative marriages that downplay the use of prophylactics and STD testing (Cook-Daniels, 2008). You must therefore be savvy in how you address relationships with a client, at any age.

Watch Marco as he preps himself for a date. He's got his best sneakers on. Twitterpated, he spent the whole session tapping his foot, which is adorable for a 42-year-old. He says he's really hopeful, but then something slips through—a phrase of the bluest kind: "I just don't want to get my hopes up." Having been hurt before, Marco never lets himself get excited, having sutured his broken heart back together with newly established rules of emotional engagement, which he consistently carries over into new relationships where they don't apply. Even in session, his heartache has shown up in the therapeutic relationship, with side comments like:

> "I'm sorry I snapped, it's just that my last boyfriend used to gaslight me..."
>
> "I don't know why I said that, you're the most patient person I know."
>
> "No, I trust you, really! I just don't trust easily, that's all..."

For self-actualizing clients like Marco, who only came out three years ago, their first foray into relationships is experimental on many levels. Years have been spent fantasizing about date night, and now that Marco's finally here he's both overwhelmed by judgments and underwhelmed by normalcy, which he shows in his next session.

> "Remember last year when I told you I wanted to take a girl out? Well I finally did. It wasn't as nerve racking as I thought it would be. I always thought I'd play Prince Charming, and I did. Opened the door for her, that kinda thing. But I was just myself. At the same time, though, it was kinda blasé. I wouldn't say it was a letdown, but I couldn't tell if she was that into me. I guess that's a male milestone too, right? *Rejected by a woman.*"

New relationships usually progress through three stages, from our excited limerence, to establishing trust, to building commitment (Gottman, 2015). Wounded by the past, it can be difficult to trust limerence, as our attraction to someone doesn't always match their ability to date a gender variant person. In response to this, people can generate a number of defensive and potentially maladaptive tactics and work-arounds, each with their own obstacles, complications, and potential for experiential avoidance.

The first is to dismantle the romantic stages of progression altogether, remaining in the libidinous rush of limerence for as long as possible. To prolong our excitement, we may come up with passionate ways to spike dopamine, the pleasure hormone, phenylethylamine, the love hormone, and oxytocin, the cuddle hormone (Gottman, 2015). Romancing the very concept of romance, we'll talk about the importance of passion, Eros, and chemistry, yet compartmentalize ourselves, feeling unable to build trust. Acts of mistrust may include concealing aspects of our sexual anatomy, gender identity, or emotional process. Even if we're out about our gender, we may not be open to talking about our history, deeming it "uncomfortable," "awkward," "emotionally painful," or a "complete turn-off." So clammed up, the relationship can stifle, the novelty of passion wears off, and the absence of trust can lead to maladaptive behaviors to keep the relationship going, like break-up-make-up sex, cheating, substance abuse, or simply letting the relationship disintegrate over time.

> "Listen, I love Paul, but he doesn't get it! I want to be present. Right here, right now! Isn't that what all those self-help books talk about? He always says he wants to get to know me better, but I'm right here! And it took a long time for me to get here and I don't want to talk about all that old shit."

> "I laughed at myself the other day because I think I'm a chronic cheater. I don't mean to be. I just fall in love with people, and then I keep falling in love with other people. I'm not polyamorous, though. I just get kind of…bored. I hope that doesn't make me sound shallow."

A second defensive tactic is to remove romance from limerence altogether, minimizing the need for emotional connection to focus solely on adrenaline and pheromones. Prioritizing sex over love has the benefit of bravado, allowing us to assertively ask someone out, or to hook-up with people without ever approaching vulnerability. Gender variant individuals, whose bodies can fall outside typical sex and romantic narratives, can find this approach quite empowering, as it proudly acknowledges our anatomic difference and asserts our sexual atypicality. The toll, however, is emotional absence, as our sexual novelty is celebrated in lieu of our personal identity.

> "Daddy don't play that way. When I'm out with my crew they know I'm the strap-on king, but *I do not* kiss. That's my one rule! No kissing. Kiss someone, and *bam*, they're crushing on ya hard. I don't need that."

> "To be honest…I can't believe I'm saying this, but I like being the mistress. I like being the other woman. I've had a couple of threesomes with married couples, and they really appreciate me, and I like that, and then I get to leave before things get complicated. But recently I've started wondering why I like it, and there's this sad part of me that thinks that if I can't have a happy relationship like that maybe I can have it vicariously."

A third defensive tactic is to withhold limerence for the trust-building stage, turning the dating scene into an interview process assessing for open mindedness. Trust often builds organically over a period of time, yet for gender variant individuals so often rejected by social norms, we may feel we have to test someone's safety level first. Developing a crush on someone, we may hold back for ages, watching to see if our crush is open to the idea of dating a gender variant person. We may feel like we don't *fall* in love, but *descend into it slowly*, befriending people first in order to cultivate trust before permitting ourselves to "have feelings." Similarly, *demisexuals* describe being unable to have sexual attraction for people unless that emotional connection is established first. Some resolve this through online dating sites, which can provide a physically safe arena to disclose gender identity before meeting a potential lover in person. Some resolve this by entering the dating scene with a rigid set of rules, presenting hoops for their date to jump through before disclosing further.

> "If he also loves Queen and David Bowie, then I let him know my obsession with RuPaul; and if he's into RuPaul, I ask if he's ever been to a drag show; and if he's into drag shows, then I tell him my stage name."

> "I stopped going on *dates* a long time ago. Instead I go on *days*. Like, I'll invite someone to go camping with me and some friends so there's no distractions, just hours of hiking and talking. I get a really good impression that way, and if we have a good time, then I ask if they want to come back to my place for a shower—because camping's dirty, you know?"

A fourth tactic is to rush limerence and trust-building simultaneously through over-disclosure. Intimate secrets and personal truths are quickly brought to the forefront as a way of building the excitement of disclosure or testing a person's ability to handle vulnerability, sexuality, or gender uniqueness. When this is reciprocated, prospective new partners can talk long into the night, cultivating passion and trust simultaneously, yet this may risk burnout. In short, we may run out of things to share! Over-disclosure, however, can be problematic if we're unaware of, or struggle with social boundaries. For example, there are many people wholly capable of accepting all of our personal and intimate truths, yet they may be overwhelmed by receiving all of them in one go. Some may sense our urgency to test them—and most people don't like to be tested!

> "I tell everyone everything and it works out for me. Like, I was seeing this one girl, and on the first night we started talking about last year when that cop put me in handcuffs just to frisk me, and that led to talking about handcuffs, and I told her I'm a leather-dom and how I started at Folsom, and she was totally into it."

> "I'm fucked up. I know I am, so I feel like I have to throw all my crazy cards on the table. I just have to get it out there. And if they can't handle it, then they can't handle me."

A fifth tactic is to minimize limerence and trust and focus on commitment, which often entails imposing rules and regulations onto the relationship or onto each person in the relationship. Rooted in the insecurity of absent trust, the relationship becomes pragmatic (Sternberg, 2007). If this is workable to all parties, then the transactional relationship continues; if not, the control tactics will drive partners to rebel against the rules and therefore each other.

> "I'm not allowed to so much look at another person unless I want to get an earful, so I make sure to kiss her on the cheek as much as possible whenever we have company over."

> "The deal is, he can sleep with whoever he wants, as long as he shows up for me. I just don't ever want to hear about it, I don't want to know, and I sure as hell never want to see their face."

These vulnerable work-arounds are only effective if they're capable of meeting our sexual and affectional needs. Each approach may work well in some contexts, yet each relies on emotional control tactics, either closing off trust and vulnerability, or curtailing limerence for the sake of safety and self-preservation or, in the case of over-disclosure, by using transparency as a defense mechanism. This fusion to romantic rules is often developed to protect us from any risks we associate with physical or emotional intimacy. Some may have even been so traumatized by prior encounters that the sheer prospect of dating elicits an array of fears and negative belief constructs.

> "So...this guy asked me out the other day. I'm not going to call him back though. I've been burned before. Yeah, he might be nice, or he could freak out on me."

> "I know we've been over this, and I know how hypocritical this sounds, but any girl who would want to go out with me probably has something wrong with her."

Balance teeters on how we emphasize our identity. Since community affirmation increases esteem and psychological wellbeing, partners may follow a heteronormative interpersonal script to feel validated by a straight community, or a homonormative interpersonal script to feel validated by a gay community, yet still potentially feel a loss without a trans community (Budge *et al.*, 2013; Mellman, 2017). Though divided by sexual orientation and assumptions of gendered performance, homonormativity and heteronormativity are far from opposites, as both perpetuate binary gender norms (Fabbre, 2014; Mellman, 2017). Those with ethnocultural differences in gender expression, or who exist outside of this binary, are often seen as deviant, odd, and therefore queer. Yet even queer people can band together and create new interpersonal scripts to sift through.

### *Heteronormative relationships*

FtM and MtF clients following heteronormative scripts are often very conscious of sociocultural gender roles. Embracing the man as provider/protector and the woman as nurturer/emotional laborer can be a gender affirming force in a relationship, or a role to get completely stuck in (Mellman, 2017; Nagoshi *et al.*, 2012). Trans men dating cis women often report a felt empowerment as they step into this guardian role, yet fusion to male gender roles can also blockade communication, especially in unhealthy heteronormative dynamics where men fail to accept influence from women, emotionally disengage, or escalate hostility (Gottman, 2011; Gottman and Silver, 2015; Mellman, 2017; Yep, 2003). Trans men can also feel pressure around heteronormative gender roles, especially when it comes to being the decisive financial provider (Mellman, 2017).

Similarly, after navigating far too many transphobic encounters accusing them of deception, trans woman dating cis men can feel genuinely recognized as a woman. Unfortunately, they may also struggle with permeable boundaries should they obey the unhealthy heteronormative script demanding women to be constantly receptive to their partner's physical, emotional, or sexual advances (Schilt and Westbrook, 2009).

For those in transition, heteronormative scripts are laced with gender performance—hence the pressure to pass and the violence aimed at us if we don't (White and Goldberg, 2006; Wyss, 2004; Yep, 2003). Yet some partners don't want to be perceived as cisgender or heteronormative. Lesbian, gay, bisexual, and pansexual partners whose lovers are in transition can feel a surreal sense of erasure and social invisibility should the external world view them as a straight couple (Joslin-Roher and Wheeler, 2009; Pfeffer, 2008). In either case, the experience and precedence of violence against trans men and women can increase stress, internalized transphobia, and therefore mental rigidity (Iantaffi and Bockting, 2011; Siebler, 2012; Yep, 2003).

## *Homonormative relationships*

FtM clients who identify as gay men often desire a deep recognition of their sexuality. As the homonormative script underscores the importance of community integration, some trans men even report validation of their sexuality as having more importance than validation of their gender (Mellman, 2017). Yet navigating the gay community as a trans man can be fraught with frustration and anxiety, as acceptance is not always given, let alone sexual and romantic intimacy (Bauer *et al.*, 2013; Bockting *et al.*, 2009; Mellman, 2017; Schleifer, 2006; Sevelius, 2009; Zandvliet, 2000). Dating sites are filled with superficial profiles stating "No fats, no femmes, no queens," which is depressing for many gay men, but especially so for FtM trans men trying to find something meaningful in gay hook-up culture. Likewise, FtM gay men may also feel pressured to be sexually dominant to distance themselves from stereotypic feminine constructs of submission, or to prove their libido as a man (Mellman, 2017). Loneliness valuing connection may be at odds with self-worth, valuing confidence, or self-protection valuing safety. Dating apps, online forums, and gay clubs provide social access points for invisible minorities, yet they so often feel like a game with strict social rules and expectations.

Inexperience with the scene, combined with a desire to prove their legitimacy and masculinity as gay men, can make it difficult to negotiate safe sex or say no to risky behavior (Reisner, Perkovich, and Mimiaga, 2010). Fortunately, not everyone in the scene is looking for a one-night stand, as there is a broad diversity of androphilic trans men. A study in Ontario, Canada found that out of 227 trans men surveyed, 173 (63.3%) were MSM (men who have sex with men), many of whom identified as gay or bi (Bauer *et al.*, 2013). Yet homonormative pressure doesn't let up even after settling down, as being seen as a mainstream, monogamous gay couple can add unnecessary social and political pressure to both marriage and child-rearing (Mellman, 2017).

MtF lesbians also encounter homonormativity perpetuated by exclusionist lesbian groups for womyn-born-womyn (Mcdonald, 2006; Pattatucci-Aragon, 2006; Rubin, 1992). The desire for recognition and the need for legitimacy is very real, yet quickly undermined when rejected—not only by the heteronormative majority—but by another marginalized group (Mcdonald, 2006; Nash, 2011; Nataf, 2006; Pattatucci-Aragon, 2006; Rubin, 1992). In some circles, sisterhood is evident, yet in others, groups quantify their victimization, comparing and competing to discount and exclude each other unnecessarily (Pattatucci-Aragon, 2006; Zandvliet, 2000). It may also seem easier to find a girlfriend if one adopts a stereotypically lesbian presentation—an added pressure to an already stressful situation. Sadly, this means trends in homonormative fashion and behavior can at times feel as oppressive as those of the heteronormative majority.

## *Queer-normative relationships*

Queer scripts write a new narrative, either by rejecting the hetero- or homonormative concept of gender within our relationships, or by subverting those that already exist (Mellman, 2017). Nonbinary relationships, polyamorous and polysexual relationships, and BDSM power dynamics, are just a few of the complex dimensions queer couples may navigate and balance (Belawski and Sojka, 2014; Mellman, 2017). Those *living the lifestyle* can feel like we're trapped in the dom, sub, master, or slave role without a safe word to get us out. Some may feel alleviated when we no longer have to measure up to a sex or gender role, or define ourselves by specific labels (Mellman, 2017). Yet the desire to compare can still nag at the back of our minds, and though queer dynamics are diverse, surveys and interviews of queer relationships observe a few queer norms. These include an egalitarian distribution of power that utilizes and celebrates each person's unique skillset while equally prioritizing the needs of all partners within the relationship, flexible and evolving relationship boundaries, and sexual exploration (Mellman, 2017; Weitzman, Davidson, and Phillips, 2012). These all sound great, until we feel like we don't fit these either.

In life, whatever gets us out of the box becomes the next box, and queer relationship dynamics are no different. Those who felt torn between the prevailing hetero- and homonormative scripts, may also compare themselves to other queer scripts, or fuse to ideas of what queerness is *supposed to be*—ironically defeating the liberty of nonconformity. Compersion is a great example of this. As the antithesis of jealousy, compersion is the joy felt witnessing someone else's joy (Pines and Aronson, 1981; Weitzman *et al.*, 2012). Some queer relationships are monogamous (married/committed couple), some agree to polyfidelity (married/committed group), some are polysexual (open sexually), and others are polyamorous (open romantically). In each relationship, jealousy is counterbalanced by compersion. Meditating on our perception of our relationships can be valuable, yet feelings aren't controlled by willpower, meaning we can't make compersion appear any more than we can make jealousy disappear. Just as the polyamorous often feel pressured to be monogamous, the monogamous may feel pressured into polyamory—as if the openness of a relationship is somehow indicative of how progressive they are as a person. Of course, this isn't true, but fusion makes it seem very real.

Fusing to differing interpersonal scripts, poly partners may get stuck in power discrepancies because of primacy, differences in affection, sexual attraction, or responsibility. They may also stick to a relationship formation which may not necessarily work for all parties involved. Keep in mind that polyamorous relationship formations are diverse, and can include triads, multiple primaries, group marriage, primary-plus (primaries with an additional lover), and polysexual friend groups (Weitzman *et al.*, 2012).

Each normative interpersonal script is a series of "I should" statements tied to an emotional process, whether it's fear of repercussion, or pride of fitting in. Whatever the case may be, the relationship has been subjected to a transactional standard of performance. A lot of energy can go into keeping or repairing our standards and boundaries, as transactional relationships can be incredibly taxing. At the best of times we meet the spoken or unspoken transaction with flying colors, proving we're worthy of the relationship. Yet no one can run a race forever. Should we not accept ourselves for being human, inadequacy and insecurity build up, internalizing anxiety and depression, or externalizing resentment and anger—or both!

Even relationships that never cross into abuse or neglect can still wield overbearing control tactics trying to restrict or contain emotional affect on all sides. We may wonder how much of our behavior is based on pleasing, impressing, or keeping others in our lives because we're afraid of being alone. How often do we try and control the relationship, or dominate the conversation? How often do we try and ignore aspects of the relationship we don't like? Identifying fusion within ourselves is difficult, yet it can take twice the daring and intimate honesty to identify fusion in a relationship. Does our internalized cissexism obey certain rules in certain places and in certain company? Do we have to be on "good behavior" around the family? Do we have to be low key or stop holding hands in public? Should we not bring up the past when we're around friends? What are the relationship rules bogging everything down, and can we practice being aware of them when they come up?

Learning to recognize the impact of minority stress in a relationship can be a humbling experience, and a sure test of vulnerability. Russ Harris, in his text *ACT with Love*, guides us to remember the acronym L.O.V.E.: *letting go*, *opening up*, *valuing*, and *engaging* (2009b). This can be a complex undertaking in gender dynamic relationships, as minority stress is not something we can simply let go of, and years of caution and vigilance can make it difficult to open up. So, let's take this a step at time.

Take a break from the stories. Lean back from all those amusing anecdotes about how we met or how we work so well together, even those angry moments we've held onto with quiet resentment. *Letting go* returns us to our defusion practice, as our relationships are not our memories of them (Harris, 2009b). Any relationship we have is inevitably with two people: the real person physically standing in front of us and our conceptualization of them that exists in our head. This cognitive copy of our partner is an emotionally charged story reinforced by romantic memories, future fears, harsh comparisons, expectations, and disappointments. When the story eclipses the person in front of us, we may anticipate their reaction, rejection, or reprisal, or we may feel unable to relinquish our criticism. *Letting go* asks us to step back from every narrative that begins with "He always says" or "She always does," and to relinquish our attempts to control our partner's thoughts, feelings, or actions (Harris, 2009b).

*Opening up* is a practice of mutual mindfulness and vulnerable transparency, including our fears of repercussion. Not only are we afraid, we're afraid of admitting our fear. Not only are we angry, we're angry that our anger might make our lovers angry. Not only are we sad, we're worried about bringing our loved ones down. When so much is kept inside for so long, it folds in on itself. How does each partner feel when they're alone? How do we feel in each other's company? What respective emotional truths do we hold onto? Are we open to each other's emotional experiences, and are we open to our own? Are we willing to explore pain, or tempted to close ourselves off?

Insecurity is valid. Fear is valid. Pain is valid. Innocence is valid. Even inexperience is valid, should we not know what to do or say. *Opening up* can be practiced in candid conversation, or by collecting our thoughts by writing down ten emotions we have, or even ten questions about ten things we do not understand. First and foremost, we're not here to answer these questions, and neither party in the relationship is tasked with the job of providing an answer. The mystery of a lingering question mark can drive us up the wall when we cannot accept the unknown; and even if there is an answer, it doesn't always feel satisfactory. Yet giving voice to the uncertainty allows us to witness each other's commitment to the process. This alone is not enough to heal a relationship, yet for many it's a large step as we're agreeing to sit with discomfort and show it. From here, we can take an honest look at what's most important to each of us respectively, and decidedly choose to invest in the relationship.

As in any relationship, there are *your values*, *my values*, and *our values*. The collective values of a relationship are most often those that are mutually shared, yet some partners come together to form something larger than themselves. Couples sometimes attest to a bravery, outspokenness, or generosity they value when they're together, but prioritize less when they're apart. So, explore each person's values independently, and together. Indeed, gender dynamic relationships can engage and approach disclosure, closeted behavior, and social camouflage as respective individuals or as a unit. Some partners may even know this about each other, and use this defense mechanism as a patsy to call sincerity into question.

"You're only saying that because you think that's what we're supposed to say."

"I know you believe that, but I know that's not the whole truth, and I know you're not sharing everything because you don't want to hurt me."

Even when privately asked to jot down values, partners may write in the "right answer," listing love, family, honesty, connection, and belonging, without actually identifying what's needed most. Exploring deeper, ask what it would take to be totally honest. What do we need to feel like we're truly loved? What has to be in place for us to know we truly belong? What need is the most difficult to ask for? What fear is holding us back? It's here in this value exploration that partners in transition discover a crossroad between commitment or dissolution. Down either path, our values can aid us a great deal, yet let's explore dissolution for a moment.

If we fuse to our judgment and abandon our values, we may progress down the path of *separation-destruction*, leading us to retroactively condemn our own memories in order to distance ourselves (Malpas, 2012). Bitter and venomous, we may say, "I never loved you, anyway." Yet if we're able to defuse heartache from our cynical cognitions, we can commit to *separation-construction*, ending the relationship with integrity and compassion (Malpas, 2012).

Recognizing each other's respective values, partners can find common ground, which brings us to *engaging*. People tend to assume that a relationship is dysfunctional when there is more negativity than positivity; and though there's certainly a cost–benefit analysis, how many of us have looked to pack our bags at the first sign of negativity? Criticism, defensiveness, contempt, and stonewalling can be challenging, yet avoiding argument is perhaps the biggest danger (Gottman, 2011). Partners naturally bid for emotional connection, pitching statements, conversation starters, questions, eye contact, and body posturing to flag their need to connect—and this includes arguments. Though certainly not enjoyable, turning away from these bids for attention by disengaging or withdrawing predictably leads to a relationship disintegrating over time (Gottman, 2011).

In the beginning, partners had each other's full attention, yet that can lapse over time, especially if couples employ experiential avoidance. Painful feelings are difficult, yet our ability to engage each other in the most arduous, sorrowful moments while remembering those integral values can guide us to mindful communication (Harris, 2009b). When angry, our negative sentiment overrides our perspective, so we hear even neutral statements as having a dark slant (Gottman, 2011; Weiss, 1980). Rather than avoid conflict or confrontation, successful repair attempts occur when we talk fully and openly about our stress, building on both trust and emotional attunement (Gottman, 2011). Learning to accept our partner's emotional affect, as well as our own, allows us to view our issues as joint problems we need not avoid (Gottman, 2011).

Value-congruent relationships work when our value constructs are similar or complementary to each other, the relationship does not shy away from emotional distress, and each person is capable of having their needs met either in the relationship or independently of it. No singular person can meet everyone's needs, and it can be a great strain to place such an absolute expectation on one person. Additionally, if one of us values long-term commitment and the other values immediate gratification, the relationship gets jammed. There are many unique aspects to a relationship, but in common parlance there is a big difference between a relationship going forward and a relationship going sideways. Going forward, partners invest in each other's growth. They respond to bids for attention but, in turn, do not demand every waking second of attention. In order to go forward, we actually encourage those we love to take the time and space they need to pursue their passion, creativity, and education. And yes, we can step in every now and then to bring a kiss, or a coffee, or food, or a sexy distraction, before straightening their proverbial tie and sending them back to building their dream. And yes, every once in a while, relationships going forward have to have *the talk*.

One turns to the other: "Are we getting what we need?"
The other turns to the one: "Do you love who I've become?"

When relationships go forward, we don't fall in love once, we continuously reinvest because we're not the same as when we started. Relationships are an active process of falling and re-falling in love, again and again, as we grow and self-actualize over time.

Going sideways, relationships emphasize spending as much time as possible together, before work, after work, and texting throughout the day. The emphasis is on attention as the value isn't growth, it's attachment. This can feel wonderful and exciting. Trips are planned, and we adventure off together, or find ourselves in a comfortable routine, or find ourselves just trying to survive. We're still growing, but not intentionally, as our goal was to keep things the same, invest in fun, or keep our heads above water. Eventually, partners feel stifled or trapped, not because we've necessarily fallen out of love, but because we're growing and we didn't plan on it.

One turns to the other: "You're not giving me what I need."
The other turns to the one: "You've changed, you're not the man I married."

For relationships going sideways, love is fun and comfortable, until it isn't. Partners are typecast into roles. When we don't meet them, the relationship ends. Many relationships are a bit more diagonal. They have elements of both, teetering one way or the other, not because of how our partners treat us, but by how we treat ourselves. If we do not invest in ourselves, our partner never has the opportunity to invest in us, and the whole thing will go sideways.

## Family fusion: Family of origin and choice

Never has a word been spoken with such mutual love and dread as *family*. Families can be beautiful, frightful, uplifting, or down-putting. Some families are accepting of our gender self-actualization, others are lovingly tolerant, or impatiently tolerant, or completely intolerant, or violently hostile, or utterly estranged. And some families may be working their way up or down this ladder.

Culture plays a huge role in family therapy, as family systems, depending on race, ethnicity, nationality, and religion, favor differing value sets. Some maintain allegiance and loyalty above all, no matter how much they argue. Others maintain a culture of silence, prioritizing familial honor above shameful individuals. Others may process familial discord by quarrelling their way to resolution, yet others may be truly inconsolable, arguing only for the sake of venting. How to work with gender variant family systems warrants its own book, as well as its own curriculum in every multicultural counseling course. As there's so much to cover, this section is an introductory primer to commonly held issues in gender variant family systems.

Expanding the concept of family means also recognizing the obstacles and intricacies when working with a *family of origin*, defined as the family system the child was born or raised in, and our later *family of choice*, defined as the intimate

LGBTQ support system we gather over the lifespan (ALGBTIC, 2012; Bowen, 2004; Roland and Burlew, 2017).

## *Family of origin*

Families of origin, in contrast to families of choice, may be less inclined to seek therapy when in distress, especially if they sustain a culture of shame or silence. Collectivistic cultures emphasizing the family system over the individual may see therapy as potentially threatening, focusing instead on suppression. Yet individualistic cultures emphasizing social status can also abide codes of silence, fearing to "air dirty laundry" in case the neighbors find out. Staunch British dignity, Southern sensibility, Japanese honor, Italian family loyalty, and Russian self-sacrifice are all examples of powerful moral constructs designed to keep the family together. Ironically, and perhaps unfortunately, when these cultural morals become inflexible, they can drive the family apart. When working with family systems, especially those with deep roots, do not attempt to supplant the cultural morals. Instead, aid the family system by helping them view the client's gender as nonthreatening to this culture. When possible, the cultural moral construct, or even the more localized family value construct, may actually provide a path to acceptance.

When gender variant people come out, there is a multidirectional impact on the family. One survey found that, of those who transitioned between the age of 25 and 44, 38 percent had children (Grant *et al.*, 2011). Simultaneously, a client may also process this disclosure with their own parents, siblings, and spouses. With so many directions, family systems are not always uniform, leading to divisions, sides, allegiances, and triangulations. Different dimensions of stress and conflict in a family can exist at different levels of stress at different times. In other words, our parents may accept us, but our kids may be embarrassed by us, or vice versa. Our spouse may be supportive, but our siblings are pointing fingers, or vice versa. For families of origin, these dimensions of stress include parts of a family in *crisis*, in *conflict*, in *exodus*, or in *absence*. As family dynamics are so often fluid and complex genograms webbing differentials of power and acceptance, such dimensions of stress are not a linear stage model. A family in crisis may or may not enter into conflict. A family in exodus may not remain in exodus but spend years apart before reconnecting. In ACT terms, these dimensions of stress are best conceptualized as examples of rigidity in a family system resulting in short-term and often maladaptive control tactics.

### Family in crisis

A family in crisis is in a state of shock. For families of gender variant individuals this can come about in a number of ways. The first, and most commonly discussed, is when we come out to our family. This can be a startling moment, especially if we're a parental figure. Some trans and nonbinary parents may enter into a phase of gender dysphoria, being surprised by our own gender resonance if it had been repressed. Others may have been trying to keep these feelings at bay for years. Having grown up in oppressive and possibly abusive environments, we may have tried everything in our power to suppress gender resonance, taking on every cisnormative ideal possible (Green, 2012). Hoping to fake it 'til we make it, we followed the script, got the job, settled down, and had kids—our avoidance of our gender dysphoria having gone so far as to start a family (Green, 2012). Some make it work, playing the parental role provided there are small concessions for gender variance, like sneaking out to the LGBTQ scene or cross-dressing when the family's not around (Green, 2012).

Crisis is resolvable provided the family system can accept a foundation of love and positive regard, and provided gender roles are flexible, allowing dad to become another mom, or mom to become the family's second dad (Witten, 2003). Humor is an invaluable way to practice mental flexibility, and playful nicknames can be useful for children uncomfortable with switching parental labels (Hines, 2006). Likewise, some kids may need a period of distance to adjust to the concept, before reconnecting and refamiliarizing themselves with their transitioned parent at a later date (Hines, 2006).

This is not, however, the only sort of crisis that gender dynamic families have to contend with. *Vicarious minority stress* and *vicarious trauma* frequently occur, yet are hard to acknowledge, resulting in frustration, anger, fatigue, sadness, and anxiety. Vicarious minority stress includes all those horrible "guilty by association" moments when a family member is mocked, ridiculed, rejected, or dismissed because another member of the family is LGBTQ. Bullies shout, "Your dad's a tranny!" The church parishioner cautions you about the rumors regarding your husband. The nurse argues with you about your spouse's legal name when admitting them to the hospital. The money's tight and the frustration is high because your trans fiancé never seems to get called back after the interview. You find yourself fielding a police officer so they don't corner your trans daughter alone. Feeling isolated, you attend the local PFLAG meeting hoping to connect with parents of trans youth, only to find you're the only one in the group with a genderqueer kid. All this stress builds up, even when you're not the LGBTQ minority in question.

For children whose parents or siblings come out, vicarious minority stress can twist into frustration, anxiety, and resentment, displacing blame to their trans family member. Organizations like Children of Lesbians and Gays Everywhere (COLAGE) can be useful as they provide resources for people whose parents are LGBTQ. Yet these new encounters with cissexism can be highly alarming, even for adults. Shocked by micro-, meso- and macroaggression, people with cisgender privilege may have never dealt with minority ridicule, and so lack the resilience or skills to cope.

Similarly, *vicarious* or *secondary trauma* occurs when family members witness the level of stress impacting someone they love. Though not experiencing the trauma first hand, witnessing the aftermath is emotionally impacting. Watching a child, parent, or sibling break down in tears, or come home ridiculed, or tell stories of trauma and fear, weighs heavy on the heart. When family systems implement control tactics or survival strategies, they may begin to set rules, or hold back emotional honesty as a means of "protecting" each other. Clinicians are also susceptible to secondary trauma, as listening to a client's trauma narratives can generate intrusive thoughts and images, which can erode a clinician's empathy and lead to compassion fatigue and burnout (Walser and Westrup, 2007). ACT can be useful for both family members and clinicians by framing the self-as-context, so that the intrusive thought or image can be released as a passing mental experience (Walser and Westrup, 2007).

Again, provided the foundation of love remains, the family can survive crisis, but the injustice and fear for their loved one's safety can indirectly emerge as angst, frustration, anxiety, and depression. Surviving crisis, however, is distinct from repairing or saving the family, which implies doing, fixing, rescuing or defeating something for the family to be saved. This particular thought can undermine a family's therapeutic process, as trying to "go back to the way things were" or "make it up to everyone" insinuates that our present gender is intrinsically subversive or toxic to the family system. In turn, trying to "keep the family together" implies that the family is divided, and while this can be physically true, if it were emotionally true there would be no therapeutic intervention. Even if we cut someone out of our heart, the scar tissue recalls their presence. In essence, the family is already together, and it's the behavior of their togetherness which is problematic. There will certainly be value-congruent goals for all parties involved, yet these may be put on hiatus until there's a group consensus about what's most important within the family *regardless of the outcome*. If parents decide to divorce each other, for example, deciding to role model respect, warmth, and amicability can significantly improve their child's wellbeing and ability to cope (Hines, 2006). By reinvesting in both our individual values, and our shared values as a family, we can actively move beyond our judgments of each other to hold onto what's important, no matter what shape the family grows into.

## Family in conflict

A family in conflict has taken the shock of crisis and fused it with argument and blame. It's here that family members, on all sides, will ask:

"Why are you doing this to me/us?"
"What's wrong with you?"
"Did you even consider____?"

"Why can't you just____?"

Families in conflict are far from acceptance, having come to an impasse of rigid thinking. Labels, judgment, and rationale will get thrown from one side of the room to the other. The drama triangle will be in full swing. In this situation, family members are often preoccupied with "what to do," being unable to find a resolution since—like our emotions—gender is not something to be *resolved* or *fixed*. If members of the family believe that gender variance is equatable to mental illness, then they may argue that supporting gender variance will compromise the mental health of someone they love (Green, 2012). Underlying this, partners, parents, and children may fear that the gender variant person may stop loving them, should they perceive their self-actualization as taking precedence over the relationship, or that the period of self-actualization will never end, or that the person they love will transform into someone so different that the relationship will evaporate (Green, 2012). Provided family members can defuse from their irrationality and commit to humanizing value constructs, a family can pull out of this nose dive. Otherwise, the friction between rigid mindsets can lead to the family's erosion.

## Family in exodus

Anticipating that 57 percent of gender variant individuals have experienced rejection from their families, it may be time to accept that some family units will break up (Grant *et al.*, 2011). Just as parents can disown trans kids, children may cut ties with trans parents or restrict visitation to trans grandparents (Witten, 2003). It may no longer be healthy for all parties involved to try and tolerate an abusive or emotionally distressing family system. After years trying false compromises or maintaining a happy façade, we may need to face the stark reality that our children aren't going to call us anymore, that our ex scowls at the sight of us, or that our parents prefer to tell people that we died rather than admit we transitioned.

Gender variant adults facing the latter half of life without familial support are at increased risk of depression, anxiety, and substance abuse (Fredriksen-Goldsen *et al.*, 2013). Building a new support network, and even establishing a family of choice, will help reinstate self-worth, yet there may still be a very discouraging grief. Bereavement of this kind can be quite torturous, for unlike the grief of widows, the subject of loss may very well be alive. This can spur curiosity, desire to reach out, shame in doing so, self-directed anger, and anger at the situation.

Bargaining with ourselves, we may desperately want to reach out and be terrified of doing so. Should we force the issue, family members might get a restraining order, leaving us feeling even more villainized. If we have a family in exodus, we may fuse to parental scripts that can no longer apply. Sure, there may be hope of reconnecting with our children in the future, or of rekindling a relationship, yet rejection has boiled into stress and despair, right here in the present. If this is the case, don't ask us to defuse from our role as a parent, sibling, or child, but to review the rules of behavior that no longer serve us.

## Family in absence

Time has passed, and either certain members of the family, or perhaps the family as a whole unit, have become estranged. We may fuse to hope, holding on to some small possibility that one day, just maybe, our family will call. In some cases, however, parents and grandparents may die before we can come to terms with how everything unfolded, leaving us chiseling regret on their tombstones (Witten, 2003). Fused with despondency, we may continue arguments with ghosts, venting all the things we "should have said" or lamenting that we never got the chance.

Losing a family, as a grief process, may cut so deep we turn to substance abuse, or hyperfocus on work or romantic relationship to fill the void and preoccupy the mind. Should anger turn toxic, we may reciprocate rejection, villainizing those who turned us away. Many gender variant people experience abuse from family members, yet animosity can amplify anger into hatred so that, even decades later, just the thought of family becomes triggering. So embittered, we may reason that it's better to feel hatred than it is to feel hurt. ACT clinicians may rightly ask, *Who does this hatred serve?* As a survival tactic, this fusion to hate may have been necessary to escape an unhealthy relationship, but even if it helped us emotionally emancipate ourselves, who does it serve now?

It's very difficult to accept the pain of familial absence, as there seems to be nothing we can do about it. There's no fix, no solution; and even if we reach out, we may just be opening ourselves up for a second round of rejection. Should we make the attempt, the family system may be able to reconcile, or just fall back into conflict and exodus all over again. In any case, it may be worth it, just to know that we tried! If regret is antithetical to peace of mind, then we may find closure in that bizarre space of creative hopelessness. Accepting that the relationship is over means accepting the pain of severance, allowing the ghostly patterns of our old, vestigial roles to finally dissipate like smoke.

> "My father disowned me on his deathbed, and I'm here still trying to make him proud."

> "My son hasn't called in ten years. I called him once, and he told me his mom is dead. I was angry, and I ended up shouting something so stupid. I shouted, 'you know, 'I'm a man but I'm still your mom!' He hung up."

Even though family members may be very much alive, working with a client whose family of origin is absent closely resembles grief therapy. By exploring the emotional content we may have been trying to distract ourselves from, or have otherwise been ruminating on, we can begin to authentically express our pain and find meaning within our emotional process (Speedlin *et al.*, 2016). Defusion, in this context, is not defusion from memory, as memories may be all we have left of our family of origin. We can, however, defuse from self-blame and the emotional labor of familial obligation. Even if we were excommunicated, or banished from the family dynamic, a part of us may still feel like we have to do things a certain way or live to a certain standard imposed by relatives who'll no longer look us in the eye.

Living in the past, or avoiding it entirely, we may ritualize seemingly mundane things. Small examples include feeling like we have to buy or cook certain foods because that's how the family always did it, or refuse to eat certain foods, launching into a tirade about why we hate that dish because that's how, once again, the family always cooked it. We may follow old rules, or fuse to new ones to rebel against the authorities of the past. We may enjoy large parts of our life, and then recall old family criticisms cutting through the years, like echoes still bouncing around from childhood. We may engage brand-new relationships with brand-new family dynamics, and still hold onto unspoken expectations of passive-aggressive communication, hostility, trauma, and abandonment. We may perceive threats where there are none, or mistrust allies who are actually trustworthy. When learning to defuse from these thoughts, it's very natural to regress into guilt and regret. Over time, our ability to observe these intrusive thoughts can succor our awareness of self-worth. We are most at risk when we fuse to the illusion of control, as we'll blame ourselves for past conflicts which, if left unchecked, can progress into self-punishing thoughts and behaviors. Practicing acceptance is to take a step back from blame to see that—even if we were argumentative or angry at the worst of times—our pain is still valid.

Gender affirmative family therapy begins by noting that the gender variant person is here to stay, and that they're never going to fit the traditional cisgender model (Mitchell, 2012). As therapy progresses, each member of the family works through frustration, loss, and grief. As the family identifies and defuses from their defense mechanisms, you can provide psychoeducation to debunk the myths clouding gender variance (Mitchell, 2012). Accepting the gender variant person in question means accepting an expanded definition of family. This leads to many sessions helping the family interact with the social world, as each family member navigates shame and social uncertainty (Mitchell, 2012). Knowing this, you must engage the family, making the first session one of the most difficult.

Applying gender affirmative ACT to a family system may require working out of order from the typical ACT progression by identifying and committing to values first. Often, time is spent working with awareness and mindfulness, permitting emotional acceptance, core values, and committed action. However, in the midst of crisis, when tensions are high, you may, as a clinician, get only one shot at helping a family open up. Let's be real, the pressure's on. If the family thinks you're a quack, they'll march out of the session and never come back, which in turn can aggravate the client's situation. Be aware that some cultures and religious communities view mental health therapists as subversive. Propaganda and false information on the internet portray trans-positive therapists as enablers playing into "transsexual neuroticism." Family members may believe the gender variant person is unstable, going through a phase, or invalidate gender variance as if it's "not a real thing." Yet if a family member believes all this and *still* comes to family therapy, then there's hope yet!

First, ask each member of the family to privately write down any judgments they may be harboring about themselves, the situation, and anyone else in the room. Judgments aren't inherently direct insults, they're also our hopes for other people and their perceived potential, alongside what we wish they did or didn't do or say. Ask everyone to also write down something good about the family, something bad, something right, something wrong, something they love, and something they hate. Even though we make judgments all the time, few like to record them or be seen as judgmental. Normalizing that we all have private assessments of each other can be helpful, as can letting them know that no one is going to read what they write, so they can be as honest as they like.

Once everyone's written down their judgments, good and bad, have them fold the paper and hold it in their hand for the remainder of the session. Tell them you're not keeping score, you're not keeping count, nor are you going to pretend this is a judgment-free atmosphere, but you are going to ask each member of the family to be mindful of their judgments. If they think of any more judgments about themselves or the family as the session unfolds, ask them to write it down privately, and keep the paper folded in their hand.

From the get-go, you're not looking to convince anyone of anything. No one is going to have their mind changed by the end of this session, a point potentially worth making. Those who are goal focused are characteristically frustrated by this, so begin by noticing how everyone's presence is indicative of a shared value, and that we just need to find out what it is. This approach works well for clients who have invited their families into session, as those who answered the call still desire a connection. However, some clients—in particular children—may be dragged to therapy by their family. Even though they don't say it aloud for fear of conflict, they may believe they have no shared values with their parents. Such clients may be biding time until they're old enough or capable enough to leave the family. During periods of individuation and self-actualization, it's very natural to reevaluate or discard family morals, ideologies, politics, religion, and traditional gender roles.

Families may need help detailing their values, as they may not see similarities. Take, for example, a parent who values religion and a child who values friendship. Opening up these values, we find that religion can be a combination of valuing tradition, structure, respect, obedience, piety, humility, and belonging. In contrast, a child who just wants to hang out with their queer friends may get yelled at by their parents, who rile about blood being thicker than water. Yet the child's expansion of friendship shows how much they value connection, kindness, relatability, respect, emotional support, fun, adventure, belonging, and validation. The overlap of respect and belonging demonstrates the family's common ground, as they're paramount in both religion and friendship. If there are no overlapping values, explore the comparisons and distinctions. How are respect and obedience different yet connected? How is humility and kindness linked? It may also be telling to ask how each person interprets and expresses these values, as communication styles differ in how people display respect, honor, and love.

Pausing the dialogue, return to the paper in everyone's hands. They're not going to open the judgments or read them. Instead, ask them to keep it folded, but to hold it out at arm's length, and keep their arm extended. Ask them to hold their arms up for as long as they can. Whatever they do, don't let the paper drop. With a room of uncertain people with their arms outstretched, briefly review what meaningful similarities came up in their value constructs. For families in crisis or families in conflict, take time to affirm the values of each individual, and how each contributes to the family culture's shared values. Highlight common ground, along with any observable willingness displayed in session. By the time you're done, some family members may still be holding out their arms; others may have let them drop. Ask what they physically notice about the experience. Maybe their biceps are heavy, or their shoulders are tight. Note how it was first easy to hold a piece of paper, but over time it became a real chore. Have each member of the family describe the experience. Clearly, they don't know what each person wrote, but we can all observe everyone struggling with their respective judgments. We naturally want to focus on what we wrote down, and a part of us may still want to, but it's exhaustive.

Permit everyone to lower their arms and ask what they physically feel with their arms at rest. Note how the judgments are still present, all folded up, but we don't have to exhaust ourselves with them. In so doing, we can explore what's really important to the family. If this interests them, then ask if they are willing to commit to another session, to learn how to lower the stress they have with themselves and each other.

We will introduce more of the ACT terminology like fusion and defusion in the next session, but as some families may have negative assumptions about mindfulness, awareness, and therapeutic acceptance, it's best to end a family's first session by solidifying goals in their familial language. Decreasing stress, for example, is an easily understood and universally desirable goal in therapy. Should someone ask what to do with the piece of paper, inquire if they feel like they want to recycle it or share. Some may very much want to share, perhaps to get something off their chest or to re-engage conflict. If this is the case, ask them if it would be okay to store the piece of paper in your desk until the next session. When the next session rolls around, ask the client if they can remember what they even wrote on their judgment list. Those who can't remember quickly spot the impermanence of their critical thoughts, while those who do may have a lot of stored-up emotionality, providing a great segue for introducing cognitive–emotional fusion and defusion.

Over the course of several sessions, everyone learns to flex the *conceptual family*. Like the conceptual self, our conceptual family is an idyllic mental genogram of roles, rules, and behaviors we associate with the family system. Learning how to flex the conceptual family creates room for everyone to grow. Even when families commit to acceptance, one person's gender self-actualization may alert old, unexplored areas of fusion, including vestigial hopes within the family it may be time to adapt or let go of—for example, swapping out Mom's desire to bequeath her bridal veil in favor of dad sharing his cufflinks, or reconceptualizing the prospect of grandkids. Family traditions may need to be reinvented and visions of the future may need to be reimagined, validating that the loving relationship is prioritized over what the loving relationship looks like, or how the loving relationship was supposed to play out. Denial can have a resurgence in a family, as parents who accepted names and pronouns at one time can return to preformed mental templates of their now grown and fully transitioned child, as if trying to reclaim their daughter in the man, or their son in the woman (Green, 2012).

As this isn't a linear stage model, family systems that were once utterly estranged can reconnect, just as families can oscillate back and forth between crisis and conflict, or enter a period of exodus only to renew their marriage vows. As we cannot control the future, all outcomes are possible, though probability depends on value congruence, and the family's ability to hold space for each other. Working with families of origin can be both incredibly rewarding and incredibly heartbreaking, especially when families enter into exodus. As your client's therapeutic advocate, it's quite natural to feel protective of them, yet this transference from clinician to client can impede the process if it creates an adversarial or defensive atmosphere in session. You must therefore be mindful of your own fusion process and defuse your bias accordingly.

### *Family of choice*

The nuclear family archetype seems to have the staying power of uranium's radioactive half-life, yet it's only one of countless familial patterns. LGBTQ family systems are often quite dynamic, operating within the social spheres of our family of origin *and* our family of choice (Roland and Burlew, 2017). Always honor a client's family system and know that when it comes to family of choice it's okay to ask about our relationships, as there's often a powerful story of connection, adoption, and kinship, filled with examples of love and compassion. Naturally, asking *Who do you define as being in your family?* and *How do you characterize these relationships?* opens the subject for the client to lead (Bockting *et al.*, 2006). It's even worth sketching out a family of choice genogram, identifying the value constructs each person role models.

Like any family, tension and conflict spark with shifting power dynamics, evolving relationships, changing life goals, and developing communication skills. Families of choice can also experience periods of crisis, conflict, exodus, and absence, though the subject of tension may change. Families may enter crisis or conflict in response to abusive behavioral patterns, addictions, loss of employment, distress around illness, and how to navigate familial roles. On top of this, families of choice have some issues specific to being LGBTQ, including *social recognition of legitimacy*, *surrogate grief*, *direct and vicarious trauma*, *sexual tension*, and *gender variant parenthood*.

## Social legitimacy

Externally, families of choice can lack social recognition as they're rarely legitimized in heteronormative society. Families of choice are incredibly diverse. They can closely resemble traditional family models, with parental and even grandparent figures, yet they can also deviate from this pattern, subverting or throwing off familial norms entirely. Lesbian partners may call upon dear friends to be a sperm donor without integrating that person into the father role. The patriarch may be female. The matriarch may be male. Those concepts may get tossed in the trash. Families of choice may resemble tight-knit friend groups of a similar age range, or communal living situations integrating multiple LGBTQ generations. Families of choice may be incredibly vanilla and include even heteronormative families who genuinely accept gender variant people. Or they can be very queer BDSM leather families with structured power dynamics, loyalties, mentors, and protectors. Families of choice can be sexual or nonsexual, or blur the line between the two. They are, for all intents and purposes, whom we live with, love, rely on, and consider home, and should be respected as such.

As they are rarely legitimized, families of choice may have to go to extra lengths to legally safeguard members of the family. This can be exceptionally difficult in parts of the world that do not honor LGBTQ marriage, civil union, or adoption. This can lead to some very precarious situations requiring members of the family to lie on behalf of those they love, in order to authorize, sign for, represent, claim, defend, or visit the most meaningful people in their lives in the most disastrous of situations. This is made all the more complicated when gender variant individuals are prevented from obtaining IDs and legal documents that include their actualized name and gender. While 70 percent of people surveyed internationally agree that gender minorities should be able to obtain IDs that match their expressed gender, 24.3 percent of South Africans, 23.8 percent of Americans, 24.3 percent of Koreans, 20.7 percent of Russians, and 20.3 percent of Peruvians remain against gender variant ID changes (Flores *et al.*, 2016b). Yet even outside of court, families of choice are cast puzzling looks, as parent–teacher associations, hospitals, police officers, military organizations, penitentiaries, and wedding planners all scratch their heads trying to understand who is related to whom and how. This confusion blows up further in polyamorous family systems, or when using queer or sex-positive identifiers. Tongue in cheek, never take the word "daddy" for granted.

## Surrogate grief

Families of choice can also struggle internally. Perhaps the most common element is surrogate grief from the family of origin. Step-parents encounter this often, especially when joining a widowed family. Even though love and respect are present, family members—especially the new parental figures—may discover themselves standing in the shadow of old trauma or loss. Wounds left over from the family of origin, or even a person's old life, may begin to impact the family of choice in unhealthy ways. Displaced anger, emotional transference, expectations of failure, disappointment or abandonment, substance abuse, or simply unprocessed sorrow, can affect these new relationships. We may be afraid to express grief in our family of choice, feeling that our gloom might chase them away, or that we'll trigger other people's abandonment issues, or that we'll disappoint our new family, or compare them unnecessarily to a family of origin they may never be able to replace. Identifying this grief response can help us defuse from our projections, old narratives, and unhealthy thought patterns. Unable to fix, heal, or solve the problem, all sides can become tired, frustrated, and irritable without meaning to. ACT can be incredibly useful in this bereavement process, as loss of this kind isn't a "fixable" problem. Inviting the family of choice into the bereavement process to accept the presence of grief can actually bring a family of choice together. Instead of being left in the dark, or pushed away, the family can come together to honor loss, memorialize the deceased, celebrate growth, bid good riddance, or affirm severance, depending on what's needed most.

## Direct and vicarious trauma

Reciprocal respect and unconditional love can form a powerful bond amongst many families of choice, which is further cemented when cohorts band together in the face of adversity. Facing trauma together and alone, families of choice often help each other process anger, fear, jealousy, victimization, hatred, and pain, because they intimately understand, or can hold space for those in need. This can present families of choice with a kind of emotional fatigue, as one hammer drops after the next. While any family is impacted when a family member goes through distress or is the target of emotional or physical violence, families of choice often comprise LGBTQ members who have experienced similar incidents of their own. Though rallying around the person in need, triggers can still domino through the family system, calling up old maladaptive coping mechanisms, nightmares, and paranoia.

Vicarious trauma can also loom over a family after such terrible events, like when a cloud comes over the house after the kids come home from another day of bullying and harassment. Though not the direct victims, other members of the family can experience a similar stress response, feeling waves of anxiety, worry, and lapses of depression as they watch someone they love endure trauma. Not wanting to detract, burden, or steal the spotlight from the person most in need, we may hold our feelings in, leaving our vicarious traumas unaddressed. Taking care of others at the expense of taking care of ourselves, we may feel compassion fatigue and grow progressively more impatient and resentful toward the victim for being victimized. It is hard to accept, but sometimes even the allies need allies, and even the healers need healing.

## Sexual tension

Sexual tension in a family of choice is a delicate subject. Many families of choice are solely, strictly, and quite naturally platonic. Others? Not so much. This is observable within the BDSM, sex-positive, and poly community, yet also within more vanilla social circles than some would care to admit. This is neither taboo nor surprising, especially between adults feeling belonging, validation, acceptance, and unconditional love for the first time in their lives from individuals who have no biological relationship. Sexual tension can, however, be confusing for all parties involved if the relationship didn't start with a sexual or romantic intent. Developing a crush on an old friend we had previously deemed a "brother" or "sister" is a common demonstration of this. Yet in families of choice there can be an elevated level of seriousness and risk felt by LGBTQ individuals not wanting to endanger their only support network. This tension may be further complicated by age differences, and the role of each person within the family of choice.

Some families of choice have clearly defined, concrete roles with set power dynamics. Other families are far more fluid and nebulous, sharing roles contextually. Over time, people begin to rely on these dynamics just like any family does, yet crushes and heartaches can make matters very complicated. When you are not familiar or versed with our family dynamic, we may minimize or glaze over these issues even when we most need to talk about them. Camouflaging ourselves in session we may, for example, talk about having a crush on a "friend" without revealing that our "friend" is also the only father figure we've ever had. This isn't Freudian, and the last thing we want is to be accused of having an Electra complex. Going the other way, we may speak about our family of choice in strictly familial terms, without mentioning when we fell into bed together, or the evolving iterations of our layered relationships. Old lovers can become new "brothers" and "sisters" just as easily as old friends can become new spouses.

## Gender variant parenthood

One of the most amazing transitions of all is when a family of choice becomes a family of origin for the next generation. Though many parents come out as gender variant in later years, some openly gender variant families decide to become trans parents or gender nonconforming parents. Some decide to do so biologically by bringing a child to term—an already emotional experience now loaded with minority stress and the possible reemergence of gender dysphoria. Others may do so through the rigmarole of adoption. After all the research validating and defending LGBTQ adoption, gender variance—in particular—is still used nefariously to subvert the adoption process, disqualify foster care rights, deny parental custody, and even have biological children removed from trans parents (Roland and Burlew, 2017). Public support for transgender people having the right to adopt is highest in Spain (74.5%), Canada (74.0%), and India (73.3%) and lowest in Peru (31.7%), Russia (24.1%), and Poland (26.5%), with the USA (62.7%) and Britain (66.9%) ranking as mostly in favor (Flores *et al.*, 2016b).

With a baby in their arms, gender variant parents face community backlash, interrogation from other parents, and a barrage of questions from every pediatrician, preschool teacher, and babysitter who has to throw in their two cents. "How will the baby be affected?" "Won't having a transsexual mom confuse the child?" "What happens if they get teased at school?" And those are the supposedly compassionate questions, as parents also have to face random sneers, confused grimaces, fanatical finger pointing, and accusers saying they're unfit to be a parent. Such encounters come in waves over the years. With any luck they're few and far between, resembling the awkward encounters with cisnormative people they've dealt with for most of their life. Yet children grow, and the subject of their parent's gender identity is handled differently by children, adolescents, and teenagers. A subject once openly discussed and embraced may be ushered aside in shame by preteens just wanting to *fit in*, or become a source of pride for progressive teenagers wanting to *stand out*. Disclosure, as a family, can be revisited many times over 18 years, reevaluating the child's comfort and even questioning the parent's integrity. To normalize this, every parent of every gender winds up reevaluating their child's comfort and questioning their own integrity as a parent. This dynamic just happens to be a gendered one, with the maximized weight of social norms behind it.

ACT can help gender variant parents, most of all, with how rigidly they hold their conceptual self. As gender roles, *mother* and *father* are chock-a-block with cisnormative constructs and idealized behaviors parents may feel pressured to identify with, only to feel like they're not good enough. Insecurity in this area can then lead to overcompensation, controlling behavior, experiential avoidance, or a felt lack of self-worth. Uncovering what conceptual and cognitive rules they feel trapped in can lead parents to defuse from what they think they "should be for their child" in order to be present in meeting the family's whole needs. Nonbinary and gender-nonconforming people may also look for ways they can decouple gender from parenthood. Value explorations are a powerful tool in this process, as parents can identify what is most important to them, and develop ways to exemplify nurturance, patience, and playful education as an emotionally resilient caregiver.

For both families of origin and families of choice, conflicts emerge when family members fuse to rigid, inflexible rules, perceptions, and expectations of each other. Tokenized, members of the family system often get reduced to a transactional relationship. When this happens, we begin to believe that we *have to* live up to certain expectations, that we *can't share* what we truly feel, or that some terrible repercussion will befall us if we're actually honest. In some cases, the terrible repercussion we fear may not actually be paranoia, making cognitive defusion a short-term solution without familial intervention.

Learning how to hold space for each other is no easy task, especially when family members turn to each other for needs they're not equipped to provide. If this ends the relationship, then it was a very transactional, one-dimensional relationship! And that might even be the problem. Many times, when family members are distressed by gender transitions or by shifts in family role, new questions come to the forefront: Do we actually love them for who they are, or are we in a relationship with a role? How much do we truly know about them? How much do we want to know?

Resistance to a parent's emotional process, or neglect of a child's feelings, or disinterest in anything that breaks character, indicates fusion to a set of family roles. Acceptance may demand actually seeing family members for who they really are. People can live together for years, cohabitating in the same house, without actually knowing the first thing about their hopes, dreams, aspirations, concerns, transitions, or transformations—especially in cultures of silence. Reactionary family members may state, "I don't want to know." Defensive family members may state, "I don't want *them* to know." Nervous family members may state, "I don't feel comfortable sharing." Yet underneath each avoidant answer is an emotional process pitting discomfort with the issue against the desire to be a family. Again, if the family agreed to therapy, even just one session, then there's a sliver of evidence that a part of them wants to reconnect. Voicing fear, stress, and confusion is difficult, yet when communication is shut down, so too is connection, leaving only roles that no longer fit.

Family roles, and their respective boundaries, naturally grow with the children, age with the parents, and expand through wedlock and each new generation. In this way, flexible families take turns being there for each other over time. Comparatively, rigid families fight for control, struggle to ask for help, or worry that their vulnerability will somehow compromise their character—even when vulnerability is needed most of all! Recognizing rigidity and cognitive-emotional fusion within the whole family system can help normalize familial conflict, and the therapeutic process, before even introducing the subject of gender.

Family members uncomfortable with gender transitions are trying to freeze a moment in time, without realizing the quandary of control. A son frustrated that his father has transitioned into a woman is angry that he's losing his masculine role model—which presumes his parent has magically lost those characteristics of strength and bravery (which they haven't), or that his masculine role model has been undermined, calling his own identity into question. Even in queer families of choice, we can get stuck in concrete, formulaic thinking. We may presume one of us has to be the protective backbone in the family, and one of us has to be the money-making sugar daddy, and one of us has to be the emotional laborer. Asking someone to stop playing these roles may be near impossible, as it's like asking a parent not to provide for their child. Yet listing the rules we prescribe each role, and challenging the rigidity thereof, can potentially create enough space for emotional transparency, and the chance to connect as real people.

## Occupational chess: Gender, academia, and the workplace

Much of our social conditioning, and therefore mental rigidity and cognitive-emotional fusion, is developed in school and at work. Even someone with motivation and high self-esteem can loop into the vicious cycle of work and fatigue and work and fatigue—their esteem hinged on their productivity (Harris, 2008). Fusing to our academic standing or occupational role, we wind up adhering to unsustainable lifestyles in order to make the grade or the paycheck. This is made all the more complicated when our ego or professional identity is hinged on gender.

Patriarchies pressure masculine identities to bring home the bacon and be the breadwinner in order to make some kind of socially dominant BLT, while never learning the nurturance required to grow lettuce or tomatoes. Feminine identities feel this same pressure twice over, as contemporary working women are pressured to be professional—as the patriarchy defines it— without compromising stereotyped femininity. Too much one way and they're deemed a bitch or a battle-ax; too much the other way and they're deemed inferior and *too gentle for the job*. In cisnormative workspaces, women of equal training and skill are all too aware of how light their paychecks are, how white-collar cis men are promoted faster, and how manual, blue-collar trades frequently deny women the training needed to advance (Schilt, 2010). Additionally, if the #MeToo movement demonstrated anything, it was how pervasive and prevalent harassment and sexual assault are at every socioeconomic tier, profession, and job site. Fortunately, the outpouring of empowerment also demonstrated how cultures of silence can be broken when we fight for what's most important to us.

Gender socialization theory suggests that the occupational disparity between the sexes begins when our social systems and cultural media dictate gender-appropriate behavior (Schilt, 2010). If this is true, not only do our typecast gender roles influence which jobs and occupations are deemed viable for men and women, we fall prey to the same stereotypic thinking (Schilt, 2010). We begin to believe that certain occupations are above us, or below us, or that we could never adapt to a work environment or change the work environment to adapt to us. This model presents the idea that women dominate helping professions as they're socialized to be caring, as men vie for higher-paying positions since they're socialized to compete (Schilt, 2010). This theory does not, however, account for the full extent of gender segregation and institutionalized sexism, as even occupations stereotypically favorable to women, like nursing and childcare, still bypass women in favor of men (Schilt, 2010). Academic and occupational power imbalances are a multidimensional intersection of institutionalized sexism, cissexism, racism, and ethnocentrism, experienced firsthand by various generational and socioeconomic cohorts. That's a lot to take in, for sure.

Backdropped against this complicated sexist disparity, gender minorities may encounter experientially dynamic moments of oppression and, in some cases, even privilege. Trans men, by virtue of being men, not only transition their bodies but so too their social standing in patriarchal cultures. Sexologist Aaron Devor explores this in *FtM: Female-to-Male Transsexuals in Society* (1997), as does transgender rights icon Jamison Green, whose deeply personal book *Becoming a Visible Man* (2012) details the pleasure and pain of transitioning into a male-dominated world. Yet to really feel it, just listen to Quinn Christopherson's powerful song "Erase Me." Winner of National Public Radio's 2019 Tiny Desk Contest, Christopherson's beautifully visceral voice captures how strangling social erasure and newfound male privilege can be. Conversely, trans women, by virtue of being women, may relinquish their male privilege (Dugen, Kusel, and Simounet, 2012; Schilt, 2010). It is not uncommon to hear "I present as ____ at work, because it's easier," or "I'll transition fully once I retire." As the living embodiment of gender dissonance and gender empowerment, gender variant people are often very aware of the disparity between the sexes, and potentially are all the more sensitive to it. Trans men, appreciative of their masculinity, can find disdain and frustration with males born into a privileged social standing, while simultaneously remaining sensitive to the sexism restricting, limiting, and objectifying women (Schilt, 2010). Trans women entering into the workplace often do so with a feminist perspective, understanding and empathizing with this same issue only to feel discredited should co-workers and employers discount their authenticity as women. Nonbinary people are largely ignored or written off as eccentric, leading some of us to compartmentalize our public and private life to extreme degrees of separation. In fact, nonbinary individuals are twice as likely to tiptoe around pronouns than trans men and trans women, reflecting how difficult it is to correct pronouns as a liminal identity (James *et al.*, 2016). Visibly gender variant people who are actively open about their gender identity or are in the midst of transition, can also find it exceptionally difficult to get hired. With little to no alternatives, many work under the table where they are not legally protected, if not completely underground, with one in five gender variant people making money through sex work or drug sales (James *et al.*, 2016).

The only reason we can see this glass ceiling is because of the amount of red tape strapped over it. Adding to micro- and macroaggressions, mesoaggressions are largely bureaucratic, taking form as codes of conduct in the employee handbook or standard protocols of behavior for the rank and file. Like the glass ceiling, some mesoaggressions go unseen, like when proactive organizations attempt to go gender blind, ignoring people's personal identity to plug them into a job, which is all well and good unless other co-workers can't stop staring. Treating gender as a non-issue, school campus and work settings often have no protocols or regulations in place to address even the simplest of situations, as nothing can be simpler than going to the bathroom. Of all gender topics, toilets became a bizarre battleground exemplifying how even basic human needs get caught up in other people's mental rigidity. Like the red tape, some mesoaggressions attempt to control behavior and expression through sexist and cissexist code words pertaining to what is or is not "appropriate." Furthermore, such red tape doesn't conceptualize the needs of gender variant individuals. In the USA, employees who qualify under the Family Medical Leave Act are allowed to take off 12 weeks for parental, family, or medical care, but since they are 12 unpaid weeks, many gender variant people living in poverty can't afford our own time off (HRC, 2018). Living paycheck to paycheck does not afford slip-ups, especially if we're trying to support a family, or know from firsthand experience how hard it is to find work. As many organizations do not perceive gender alignment surgery as a "legitimate" reason to take time off, we may have to plan whole aspects of our life on a financial gamble. We may be hesitant to mention our need for medical leave, anticipating potential backlash or hostility in the work environment even if we do have paid time off (HRC, 2018). This leaves us having to strategically plan, not just our budget, but potentially our employment options around our transition procedures.

Applying gender affirmative ACT vocationally requires practical research on your part, as helping us gain upward mobility and/or financial security means having a full scope of available resources. What opportunities are available to us? Take some time to look into General Education Development (GED) tests, trade schools, and how to apply for associate degrees, and bachelor's, master's, or PhD programs, as we will need a healthy balance of emotional support and practical knowledge. Make a list of available grants and scholarships for LGBTQ students, like the Point Foundation Scholarship, the Pride Foundation Scholarship, or the Out to Protect Scholarship for LGBTQ individuals pursuing a career in law enforcement. Like a lot of funding, grants and scholarships are often localized—like the Live Out Loud Educational Scholarship for the tri-state area of New York, New Jersey, and Connecticut—and competition for the national scholarship programs is high.

The application process can actually become an exercise in both self-affirmation and emotional acceptance, as financial aid programs and university applications often require a personal essay. Favoring diversity, distinction, and work ethic, review boards are quite supportive of underdogs who've overcome obstacles to exemplify strength. Yet essay writing is a skill in itself, and when coupled with the sensitivity of disclosure, and the fear of judgment, it can be a nail-biting experience. Aspiring to higher education we may minimize our experience and so dull our uniqueness, or maximize our gender and overshadow our complexity, or eclipse our ingenuity and perseverance by focusing too much on our obstacles.

Accepting the intertwining threads of hope and fear, anticipation and dread, excitement and nervousness, defusion exercises can help applicants observe our own expectation and doubt over the weeks and months it takes the review board to respond. These same feelings, however, become far more immediate on the hot-seat of an academic or job interview. In the wake of rejection, the *Yes, and...* exercise can be useful to expand beyond blame-centered thinking, as there are many reasons why we may or may not make the cut. To defuse from critical self-judgments and assessment-based language, the *Pizza words* exercise may also be useful to step back from the "not good enough" mantra.

As rejection letters rarely give feedback, and job interviewers simply don't call back, applicants may fuse to frames of comparison without enough information to compare, causing us to fill in the blank with our most pessimistic thoughts. Instead of arguing with this pessimism, or proving it otherwise, ACT sidesteps the debate. Maybe the interviewer was transphobic, maybe they weren't. Maybe they didn't think our outfit was professional enough, maybe they did. We'll never know for sure. Keeping an eye on the prize, applicants can identify how success, self-fulfillment, and occupational stability remain important, encouraging us to try, and try, and try again.

Putting ourselves out there as a gender variant person is a daily practice in emotional resilience. Yet eventually the letter arrives or the phone rings, which is not only when the real work begins, but when we come face to face with our coping mechanisms or lack thereof. Entering college and the workforce, we can fuse to rules, reasons, judgments, and roles in reaction to performance stress. "I should" statements, conditional "If this____, then that____" beliefs, and the wistful "If only" hopes can mire us in a rigid pattern of thinking backed up by real-world risks.

## *In the classroom*

So, we ran the gauntlet, either graduating high school, or dropping out and muddling along before getting our general equivalency and applying to college. According to the 2015 US Transgender Survey, 2 percent of gender variant people do not complete high school, 11 percent only have a high school diploma, 40 percent attend college only to drop out, 9 percent obtain an associate degree, 25 percent earn a bachelor's, and 13 percent go on to obtain a master's or PhD (James *et al.*, 2016). For gender variant people, college can be a unique series of very difficult choices. For young people living independently for the first time, college provides an opportunity for growth, education, and experimentation. It's often a container for us to come out for the first time, or encounter an actual LGBTQ community, or experience our first non-heteronormative relationships. Though rare, some colleges have even begun to cover transition services on their student health plan, and many more have on campus LGBTQ resource centers and LGBTQ-ally student unions. Yet college can also be difficult, as that 40 percent attrition rate demonstrates. The financial strain alone would be enough, especially when combined with the financial costs of gender alignment surgery. We may drop out of school in order to afford surgery, or find we have to drop out of school because we have no family support, or can't afford the tuition costs, or find we can't get a school loan because of prior criminal charges. Yet even if we can find the money, it's not always worth the emotional cost.

The connection between school bullying and academic downfall is evident amongst gender variant teenagers. As harassment goes up, so too does absenteeism, as the kids skip school to avoid stress, dropping not only their grades but their very aspirations to get an education (Greytak *et al.*, 2009; Grossman and D'Augelli, 2006; Reisner *et al.*, 2015). But what about our college demographic? When surveyed, gender variant college students report problematic hostile campuses rife with discriminatory institutional policies and peer harassment, causing many to hide their gender (Beemyn and Rankin, 2011; Dugen *et al.*,

2012). While only 2 percent of gender variant people who attend college drop out because of harassment, that 2 percent represents 16 percent of visibly transgender students (James *et al.*, 2016). With so much emotional weight stacked on top of all those overpriced textbooks, why do some make it through? There are certainly points of racial and socioeconomic privilege to consider, and even environmental factors like how safe a university is—which can be looked up in the USA through the Campus Pride Index. Yet one of the universally predictive factors for psychological distress, health issues, and academic attrition is the level of experiential avoidance applied to cope with stress (Hayes *et al.*, 2008). Just ask the guy who ditched class because he was too nervous to walk in late, or the girl wearing shades in the back row to hide her hangover. For gender variant students tackling typical college tribulations as well as minority stress, the need for support is clear, but sometimes it's our alleged supporters who are the problem.

Teachers and school counselors are well meaning but tend to be uninformed about gender issues, and few schools provide services for gender variant healthcare issues (Dugen *et al.*, 2012). In both the classroom and campus society, MtF students have been less likely to step into leadership roles, potentially because they don't want to call attention to themselves, or because they're consciously or subconsciously conforming to the stereotype of female passivity (Dugen *et al.*, 2012). MtF and intersex students also report less mentoring than FtM students, potentially due to the faculties' discomfort around MtF and trans-feminine presentation (Dugen *et al.*, 2012). FtM students report stepping into personal pride and allyship while navigating the toxic masculinity sometimes found in college fraternities (Catalano, 2014). Differing from visible MtF students, FtM students expressed how they continuously have to come out, making their gender identity public knowledge in order to be recognized (Catalano, 2014). Levels of comfort varied for FtM students when it came to working with faculty administration, since many school representatives pretended to be inclusive in order to be politically correct, but invested very little thought or energy into gender-inclusive school policies (Catalano, 2014).

In a culture where many young people are studying culture, history, feminism and women's studies, psychology, sociology, and even biology and anatomy, gender variant college students often become a living specimen for the subject of other students' study. In the midst of self-actualization, many gender variant students try to gain distance from their old presentation, only to be reminded of it by the curiosity of aspiring academic scholars (Pusch, 2005). Gender identity is clearly important, but gender variant students desire to be seen as more than just a sociopolitical issue (Catalano, 2014; Pusch, 2005). The desire for a gender variant community is frequently voiced by students, especially if they feel that this community is either nonexistent or exists only as an adjunct to a larger LGBTQ scene (Catalano, 2014).

College- and university-based clinicians are encouraged to actively develop campus-wide trans-affirming language, LGBTQ ally training with specific emphasis on gender variant issues, anti-bullying and harassment programs, gender variant support groups, and petitioning the schoolboard to include gender-based healthcare (Greytak *et al.*, 2013; McCann *et al.*, 2017). In session, defusing from intrusive thoughts, expanding awareness, and introducing both queer innocence and queer failure can help cultivate the emotional resilience needed to graduate or enter an equally cisnormative workforce.

## *On the job*

Work can already be stressful, especially when employers demand an air of professionalism. Respect, courtesy, and conscientiousness are just good manners, but some occupations demand more. Often, service jobs and those that require interaction with the public, provide uniforms and behavioral scripts. Needing the money, and perhaps even liking our job, we all play along. But what happens when others won't let us? A waitress is a waitress until the customer doesn't want to be served by *that* waitress. A doctor is a doctor until the client files a formal complaint at the hospital, stating they felt *uncomfortable*. A teacher is a teacher until a parent at the PTA meeting protests that they had no idea their kids were learning math from a trans person.

Though many employers may be oblivious to this, our workplace is a natural arena for gender actualization as it's where we spend the majority of our time. Socialization, disclosure, and expression all intertwine with our desire to be professionals, or at the very least our desire to survive until Friday. Small moments of gender affirmation in the workplace can be truly empowering, just as pronoun neglect or gender abuse can be disempowering, even when they're not intended. For example, although entering into the workforce as a man can have privileges of rank, respect, and financial reward, not all trans men feel like they receive these benefits. Those just beginning to transition, or those who opted out of HRT, often find their gender is discounted if they're still seen as women (Schilt, 2010). Trans men of short stature or who have thin or absent facial hair may also be discredited for appearing youthful, like when a customer or co-worker assumes a 30-year-old professional is a teenage intern (Schilt, 2010). Over time, HRT can help trans men "age into" their masculinity, yet such encounters in the workplace may prompt trans-masculine clients to feel self-conscious about their presentation of authority, especially when on the job (Schilt, 2010).

Through no fault of our own, visibly gender variant people provoke the status quo, and even progressive companies can struggle to navigate gender-based issues with their employees, just as employees can hesitate to bring it up.

Minding her own business, Maria stands outside during her cigarette break when a random passerby shouts from their car like a drive-by shooting. Those repelled by gender variance will frown, point, or shout, before writing an angry letter to the company, taking it up with the manager, or bemoaning the business online. On the other side of the same coin, those who are intrigued by gender variance will applaud the company, thinking they're so progressive for hiring diverse employees—which is actually a very low bar with little indication of the company's policy.

Shrugging it off, Maria stubs her cigarette and goes back inside, only to find her co-workers equally divided. There are a few cool people to chat with, but the boss has an eye out for her, his sensitivity heightened now that he has a queer employee. When employees are transparent about their transition, they often have to deal with the confusion of their co-workers, especially in occupations dominated by men (Budge *et al.*, 2010; Chavez-Korell and Lorah, 2007; Maguen *et al.*, 2005). Heteronormative, cisgender people talk about their personal lives all the time, but since Maria doesn't fit the script, even an innocent weekend partying with her friends can sound taboo. Called over, the boss warns in a hushed, almost conspiratorial tone, how "that kind of talk is indecent," and how he'd hate to write Maria up.

Let's be honest. Humans are organic, messy; and even when we're professional, our humanity shines through. Yet gender variant people are rarely given a pass, especially in the workplace, as others find our very existence *indecent*. Complaining about bras on hot days, women will adjust badly constructed underwires, and most co-workers won't bat an eye. But when Maria does this, people are reminded that she's a trans woman, warranting a finger wag from the manager. Despite being against the handbook's policy on sexually suggestive language, men continue to huddle around watercoolers trading sexual innuendos like illegal stock tips. For those boxed in cubicles, this can even become a rite of passage into the toxic masculinity of office politics, but one double entendre from Maria and all of a sudden HR is "very concerned."

Certainly, not all work atmospheres are so prejudiced, but in retail and the service industry—where laborers are expendable and LGBTQ ally training is pretty non-existent—petty co-workers hunt for ways to fire those who don't fit, or in HR terms "just don't seem to be a team player." Certainly, we all make mistakes, but it becomes evident how in-group vs. out-group status dominates the workplace when even those on their best behavior are ushered out the door.

Résumé in hand, Maria debates with herself about how transparent she should be at her next interview, figuring she should either dress down as a "man" to get the job, or be transparent so as not to be outed later at the worst possible moment (Israel and Tarver II, 1997). Deciding to be open, Maria goes through interview after interview. If gender variant people are not passable or do not fit the binary box, landing that new job can be exceptionally hard, especially for trans people of color (Budge *et al.*, 2010; James *et al.*, 2016; Maguen *et al.*, 2005).

Finally, Maria lands a legitimate job combining her personal skills and talents with decent pay, and even good healthcare, which is actually the first time Maria's ever had insurance! She's out, making friends, and on the first day her manager gave her this weirdly awkward, if endearing, monologue about their bathroom policy and how she can use whatever restroom she likes. It's all going pretty great, but there's this one guy... His comments started small, but they're building, and now someone keyed Maria's car, and now someone smashed her coffee mug—which meant they had to physically take it from her desk—and now someone's starting rumors, and now someone's keyed Maria's car for a *second* time. And Maria knows who it is, and she wants to confront them, but she also doesn't want to risk this amazing job!

When gender variant people seek out career counseling, there's a high likelihood we're struggling with workplace intolerance. We may be looking for support in the professional-coming-out process, or need help exploring better job opportunities, or, in some cases, options for legal action (Chavez-Korell and Lorah, 2007). In the workplace, gender minorities endure physical intimidation, verbal harassment and pronoun abuse, and ridicule for using the restroom from our co-workers and, more troublingly, our employers (Budge *et al.*, 2010; Chung, 2003; Dispenza *et al.*, 2012; Whittle *et al.*, 2007). In all, 41 percent of gender variant employees were either denied a promotion, fired, forced to quit, or skipped over in the hiring process because of our gender, *in one year* (James *et al.*, 2016). It becomes very clear, very quickly, why 53 percent hide gender identity at work (James *et al.*, 2016). Even those of us who came out years ago to our friends and family, may feel like we have to dress down, put off transition for years, or hide our transition on the job site (Israel and Tarver II, 1997). Most employees figure out how to balance personal nature with professional demeanor, yet not all of us feel safe enough to present our gender in the workplace. When there is a perceived risk to self or occupation, the division between personal nature and professional demeanor becomes a literal double-life, split by anxiety and stress.

Avoidance is often the first action for survival, so we duck our heads for eight hours a day. Terrified to correct her employer's use of pronouns, Maria's tactic is to abstain from scrutiny. She never asks for a raise or time off, evading every possible source of conflict that could be used against her later, which is why—even though her boss seems super friendly—Maria doesn't want to bring up the harassment issue. If the guy denies it, Maria assumes everyone will think she's "just a paranoid drama queen," or that the issue might escalate, forcing her to leave. While Maria currently likes her new job (harassment aside), many gender variant people cling to jobs we're overqualified for, underselling ourselves to stay in positions we may even hate for fear that no one else will hire us. All kinds of rationale crop up at this point, combining the hard facts of being a transgender person in an intolerant world with a self-defeating prophecy. This can lead to real stagnation, especially when 30 percent of individuals who are differently abled, 40 percent of American Indians, 31 percent of African Americans, and 28 percent of Latinos feel stuck in a job they want to leave because of onsite discrimination (James *et al.*, 2016). Those in poverty are most likely to hide, conceal, or avoid the subject of gender at work because the stakes feel so high, which is sad considering that 29 percent of gender variant people in the USA live in poverty—double that of the cisgender population (James *et al.*, 2016).

Our values deeply influence our career choices, yet our need for physical and social survival deeply influence our values (Brown, 2007). Although value exploration can exemplify our personal strengths, we may struggle to view our occupational dreams as realistic because of the discrimination we face. Even if we feel self-empowered, opportunity isn't knocking on our door. If anything, we're knocking on opportunity's door, hoping fortune will open up and give us a chance—and that's if we've fought tooth and nail to get there. Some of us feel like we're watching opportunity's door at the edge of opportunity's garden, barred from opportunity's gate by opportunity's intolerant guard dog. We're not here to accept that life is unfair, but to accept our feelings about this obstacle if we're ever going to do anything about it.

Preoccupied with very real occupational risks, we may need help to access our observational self. As we're trying to be as careful in our occupation as we can, it can often feel like we're pawns in a giant game of chess. All the knights and rooks and bishops lord power and privilege, though we can only take one step at a time. So why do we march forward, knowing the risk? What's the incentive? We're told that, when a pawn reaches the far side of the board, it gets to become a queen. This old rule is literally called *promotion*, as the pawn can also become a knight, rook, or bishop, transforming as the player sees fit. But when we're in the middle of the board, surrounded on all sides, we begin to feel stressed out. We don't like being the pawn, so we try to become a queen, only to find the game doesn't end! Frustrated by this, we try to imagine ourselves as above it all, like the chess player, winning out against a shadowy opponent, yet somehow—even then—we only end up defeating ourselves. Metaphorically, ACT addresses this conundrum as an endless board game (Hayes, Strosahl and Wilson, 2012) paraphrased in the following:

*Imagine standing on a giant chessboard that stretches from here to infinity. Thousands of black pieces seem to work at odds against thousands of white pieces, each bishop, rook, pawn, and queen being a thought or belief. Some, like depression, blame, hatred, and fear belong to the white team. Others, like confidence, comfort, and a sense of control belong to the black team. For endless hours one side fights the other for control of the board, with no end in sight. As we stand on this board, all the pieces seem larger than we are, but we're giving it our all. Logically, we believe if we knock enough pieces off the board we'll somehow win, but the board goes on forever and there's always another pawn. Defusing from our thoughts and stepping into our observational self allows us to be bigger than the kings and their errant knights. So, what does that make us? The chess player? Who are we playing against? If we're the chess player, we're still invested in winning a game that will never be won or lost. In this metaphor, we are the board itself, vast enough to hold all the pieces, capable of containing all the moves and countermoves, while being independent of them all. The chessboard remains a chessboard, regardless of any leaping knights, promotions, or checkmates.*

Ask us to notice our language, the emotions therein, and the absolute statements. We may dip into fusion again, so ask us once more to notice the noticer. Reality is reality. Our boss may be a tyrant, our co-workers may be intolerant—that may all very well be true—but a shift in perspective can help a great deal.

Language constructs not only our narrative, but our relationship to those narratives. This does not change the reality of our situation, the oppression experienced, the prejudice encountered, or the fear felt, but it can shift our relationship with these experiences. Fundamentally, how our conceptual self is connected to our occupational growth, and how our occupations interweave with our personal lives, is at the core of career counseling (Chung, 2003; Hoare *et al.*, 2012;). It's usually our place of work that demands our most formidable defense mechanisms, from the smiling mask of courtesy, to cold endurance, to binge working, to emotional avoidance, to even a stiff drink. Anything to get through the day. Some jobs are wonderful, imparting powerful life lessons as we employ our passion to our growth edge, but gender variant people have to work triple time to get there, and even then run across a professional world beyond our control. Does that social helplessness spur a sigh? Exhaustion? Anger? Frustration? Worry? Notice it. Ask us to notice what we felt when we used words like "have to" and "never?" It's not worth debating the factuality of these statements. Just help us notice the emotion around those absolute rules. Then help us notice the noticer. Who's on the inside feeling trapped?

Revisiting our value inventory returns us, once again, to the conflict between our survival values and our self-actualization values, as every value-congruent action seems to have a price tag. We're often told to trust our gut, but when we're anxious, and our livelihood rides on keeping our job, our gut voices our drive to survive. Acceptance comes with the risk of rejection. Transparency in the workplace may lead to conflict in the workplace. Our survival values seek stability and safety, so we tell ourselves:

"Whatever happens, don't get suspended."

"Stay safe, you need this job."

"Just don't call attention to yourself. They don't need to know."

Often our self-actualization values are hidden inside of our safety instinct, on a deeper level. Unpack the urgency and we'll probably find a litany of personal needs close to home, as we need to earn an income, pay rent, support our family, and so on. Therein we will also find the essence of what we need to thrive, including our draw to freedom, sovereignty, autonomy, and love. Unfortunately, when we fuse to the "don't get fired" mantra, we mentally reduce ourselves to pawns only capable of taking one step forward. Asking how we can balance our desire to be transparent with our desire to be autonomous allows us to see more pieces on the board and thereby expand our options.

As a clinician, be cautious of approaching occupational therapy from a point of cisgender privilege. Motivating us to ask for a raise, or time off, or to speak up about harassment, without first assessing the risk involved, can land us in hot water. To test for risk, we can assess our co-workers, employer, or work setting. Like at the beginning of a chess game, we first sort out whose pieces are whose. Even if we don't have any allies at work, can we make some, and what unhelpful thoughts prevent us from doing so? Who would be receptive to gender diversity? Who would be neutral? And who is a potential risk? Often, there's a sense of uncertainty, as we're not 100 percent sure a co-worker will be understanding.

If we're in a genuinely hostile environment, then let's review our self-actualization values and how they correspond to our available options so that we don't get stuck in misery just for the paycheck. In the case of harassment or unfair treatment, it may be worth going higher up the chain of command. Is there a human resource department, a field manager, or union representative to contact? Realize that many gender variant people cannot afford legal representation, and that protection varies from place to place. For example, city ordinances can protect employees against gender discrimination on a local level, even when the broader state or county has no anti-discrimination laws. Verse yourself in gender variant legal rights in case civic action is needed, yet the drive to file any complaint or petition must originate from the client. We may want to build courage in order to take on these issues, but it's not our obligation to do so. We may just want to have a life without our job, or our very existence, targeted at the center of a political debate.

Playing the field, it may be necessary to discreetly pursue alternative job opportunities, actively interviewing for a new position as our authentic gender. The old saying, "It's all about who you know" remains true, and even though there may not be LGBTQ-owned businesses in rural areas of low representation, there are still LGBTQ-friendly opportunities. By letting people know that we're not just looking for a job, but a job where we can be open, honest, and transparent, we are accepting our need for advocates and allies. This, of course, quickly leads to another area of fusion—lack of experience.

How often do we say, "I'd never apply for that" or "I would, but I'm not qualified"? How often do we only stick to what we know, getting the same kind of job over and over again, as if there's some rule that says, "once retail, always retail" or "service industry for life." Yes, our résumé builds on our qualifications, but our qualifications also build on our résumé. When we fuse to a single-minded concept of our skillsets, assuming we're just a pawn, we believe we can only move in a linear fashion. Stepping back into our observational self, we can view all our skills. We can start whole new tracks, starting again at square one, or we can augment the résumé we have, rewriting it to reflect our other skillsets, emphasizing our creativity, perhaps, or maybe our people skills, or maybe our leadership qualities. In this way we can move diagonally into new positions, like a bishop, or hop over the usual progression like a knight. Ever thought about working in the tourist industry? Health and human services? In the arts? As an educator? In politics? In the environment? There's a whole world out there in need of help from anyone with the gumption and willing enough to lend a hand.

"But I can't, because I'm transgender."

"I've tried, but no one wants to hire me."

"There's no way I can afford that."

The obstacles are real, yet these thoughts stop us from trying or trying again. Notice them. Do they keep us where we're at or progress us to where we want to be? Those doubts aren't going anywhere; but if we listen to them, neither is that résumé. For visibly gender variant people, finding a meaningful job or career can be a daunting process with numerous social risks. Likewise, academically or professionally investing in ourselves asks us to transcend our survival agenda—and surviving can be hard enough to do as it is! Just getting a job was difficult, but then finding a form of work where we feel able to be our true selves, and progress in skill and personal self-worth, may be hard to imagine. At this intersection, our willingness to commit to values is far more pertinent than goal setting. If the goal is to get out of the cave, or get to the other side of the chess board, or cross the finish line, or get the diploma, or get the dream job—but we don't believe this is feasible—we end up wanting to want. We may literally say, "I want to want to try." This tricky thought is like a double negative, as wanting to want only indicates that we don't, or that we could desire it if we believed it was a desirable thing to want. Committing to personal values, by contrast, returns us to what is most important right now, where we are. If we're exhausted from being overworked or underpaid, let's start with how to bring rest and respect into our lived experience. This may look like addressing the job site, expanding social networks outside of the work environment, fishing for new occupational opportunities, and establishing a self-care routine. As evident by our engagement in underground economies, gender variant people often have to think outside of the box in order to survive, yet it's also possible to think outside of the box in order to thrive.

Ask us about our dream job and have us detail why it's appealing. Add exploratory questions about how we would ideally interact with employers and co-workers, as therein we'll find a variety of personal values (Hoare *et al.*, 2012). Finding value-congruent work can be difficult in a suburban sprawl of retail and service jobs, yet there are also the tourist and hospitality industries, construction and carpentry, data administration, computer support specialists, various nonprofits, as well as many independently owned small businesses that do not require a college degree. There are also some well-paid jobs that only require an associate degree, like computer programming, IT security, service delivery analysis, and med-technicians specialities including sonography and radiology. When the job market is already competitive, we may need to apply far and wide, consider moving for a position, return to school, or attend a skills training course. We can also explore how to collaborate with allies to set up a small business or become self-employed.

Frequently, it's those around us who focus on gender and make it an obstacle—like a caveat filled with subtext. She's not just a dentist, she's a "transsexual dentist." He's not just a chef, he's "that one cook in the kitchen that looks like a dude." Notice of this kind is often an act of depreciation. It is to say that we're a professional *but we're also* transgender, as if our gender is a deficit. It's not always intended that way. Many people are actually trying to cheer us on, being truly glad to see us doing well. Such novelty, however, only indicates the sparsity of success for gender variant people, or the rarity of encounter for the cisgender person making the observation. The comment isn't gender affirmative, which would be odd to hear even if it was meant to be! Imagine saying, "I only go to FtM dentists" or "Everyone knows trans men are the best at root canals." As this rarely happens, except for a few oddly sexist people with equally odd preferences, gender variant people often find that communities who love, embrace, and value our personality, intelligence, competence, skill, work ethic, and even friendship, still do not have the framework to appraise worth in our gender. For those who seek to make gender a non-issue, this is preferable. "I'd rather people see me over my gender, anyway." Yet for others—even if gender is not central to our identity— it's still vital to who we are, and in some cases how we approach our work. This dilemma is similar, but not equivalent, to the cis women who entered the workforce in broad-shouldered power suits in the 1970s and 1980s. There was not, at that time, a feminist appraisal of women's strengths in the workforce. To "play the game," cis women had to adopt the competitive, pragmatic, and emotionally detached values stereotypically associated with masculinity. Although this remains the case in many professions, more and more career paths are redefining—not the task or the job at hand—but how the task or job can be accomplished. Doing so allows for a greater diversity of value-oriented behavior, providing competitiveness for the competitive and collaboration for the collaborative, but also a greater degree of communication and leadership styles. As these value constructs can be encoded into gender, either on an individual or cultural level, expansive work environments allow for greater degrees of inclusion.

The relevance of one's gender in the workplace is best determined by the person, not the profession. That said, gender blindness is not indicative of gender inclusion, as we cannot pretend that people who have the same skillset have the same experience or application of that skillset. Every gender, as it is felt, embodied and expressed by the individual, carries with it many potential strengths complementary to our work, if the individual elects to apply them and if there is an accepting academic or work environment to do so. You can actively help the community by providing gender awareness and sensitivity training to academic, private, and nonprofit settings; aiding schoolboards, programs, and agencies about gender affirmative enrollment and employment outreach; and providing advocacy and therapeutic mediation services for college campuses, employees, employers, and unions.

## Health, stealth, and hospitals: Gender affirmative medicine

While sitting in a waiting room, flipping through photoshopped magazines sans queer representation, so many questions run through Jordan's head. "Do they need to know my gender? Is it relevant? Do they need to know I'm taking hormones? What happens if they find out?" He doesn't know, as the last time he went to the doctor he was treated rather coldly by the physician at the clinic, and the time before that he was treated like a living specimen by a highly excitable nurse intern. He tried to come in a few days ago but panicked in his car and left before even getting to the waiting room.

Numbers vary, but around 14 percent of gender variant patients are not out to our doctors, biting our tongues in the company of white coats (Grant *et al.*, 2011). A further 75 percent of LGBTQ adults—and these are adults, mind you—are not even transparent about sexuality, letting doctors assume we're straight, or downplaying our sexual activity so as not to get slut shamed by an MD (Grant *et al.*, 2011). In the USA and many parts of the world, anti-discrimination laws vary, meaning healthcare is not a guarantee, even when we most need it (Pega and Veale, 2015). Jordan, for example, has been putting this off for weeks, even though he's worried about his liver after dosing himself with testosterone he bought off the cryptomarket. Orally taken methyltestosterone is no longer made available in most countries because of its tendency to cause hepatic dysfunction (WPATH,

2011). But Jordan doesn't know that. All he knows is that the whites of his eyes are turning yellow.

Taking the big picture, health is sociological, with those at the top of the hierarchy living longer than those at the bottom, presenting gender variant individuals, particularly transgender people of color, with sizeable risks and obstacles pertaining to physical health and wellbeing (Pega and Veale, 2015; Witten, 2003). Barriers to accessing healthcare include: being flat broke and therefore unable to pay for it; completely lacking insurance or else lacking insurance that covers transitional care; and cissexist encounters with hospitals and healthcare providers (Hanssmann *et al.*, 2008; Kenagy, 2005; Lombardi, 2001; Pega and Veale, 2015; Sperber, Landers, and Lawrence, 2005).

## *Medical discrimination*

There's no reason to ever deny emergency medical care, yet hospitals have historically been the battleground for many legal, ethical, and medical complications pertaining to gender. Lambda Legal, an American nonprofit fighting for LGBTQ civil rights, found that 70 percent, out of a sample including 397 transgender, 220 gender nonconforming, and 83 two-spirit patients, had been discriminated against by healthcare providers (2010). These incidents ranged from derogatory statements and clearly biased assumptions to 20 percent of gender variant patients being blamed for our problems, and 27 percent being blatantly denied care (Lambda Legal, 2010). A survey of 182 transgender patients in Philadelphia revealed that more than 26 percent had been denied medical care, 52 percent struggled to access healthcare that year, and over a third had no primary care doctor whatsoever (Kenagy, 2005). This same finding was echoed in Chicago, when a sample of 111 trans patients found that 12 percent were refused healthcare, 14 percent couldn't even get emergency healthcare, and 3 percent were refused mental health treatment (Kenagy and Bostwick, 2005). In the UK, 17 percent of 872 online survey respondents reported being refused service by disapproving doctors in the National Health Service (Whittle *et al.*, 2007). Prejudice is an emotionally taxing obstacle, but institutionalized rejection can reignite every fear of stigmatization. Knocked down by keepers of the Hippocratic Oath, we doubt not only our self-worth, but also our self-image. This can contribute to unhealthy relationships with our bodies, including self-neglect and total ambivalence to health, disordered eating, self-harm, and substance abuse (Batten and Hayes, 2005; Chavez-Korell and Lorah, 2007; Israel and Tarver II, 1997; Kenagy, 2005; Maguen *et al.*, 2005; Riley *et al.*, 2011; Whittle *et al.*, 2007).

Rather than deal with cruel or incompetent doctors, some gender variant people may avoid routine medical care, putting off check-ups, postponing appointments, or looking up what we need to know online (Lombardi, 2001;

Maguen *et al.*, 2005). Avoidance can't work forever, as we all get injured and worn down, especially when subjected to so much stress! Yet even if we do concede to help, we're up against a wall. Discriminatory employment practices that do not honor LGBTQ families often prevent gender variant individuals from being able to carry loved ones on an insurance policy, or vice versa (Wheeler and Dodd, 2011). For transgender people of color, access to healthcare can even be shut down, resulting in 17 percent of gender variant African Americans and 8 percent of Latinos relying on ERs as the sole or primary source of medical care (Grant *et al.*, 2011). Then, if we do manage to get signed in to a hospital, whole sections of the building are sex segregated, creating emotionally tumultuous, personally invalidating and legally questionable experiences (Feinberg, 2001; Richmond *et al.*, 2012). Doctors will hyperfocus on a person's gender even when it's irrelevant to the appointment, which means literally going in for a sprained ankle only to be asked about our genitals (Sperber *et al.*, 2005). And god help us if, for medical reasons, we actually do need to talk about our genitals!

### *Fertility and pregnancy*

Exploring fertility options as a gender variant person opens up a whole new test-tube of gametes, and we may even weigh our priorities between transition and parenthood (Hoffkling, Obedin-Maliver, and Sevelius, 2017). It shouldn't be surprising to medical professionals to learn that gender variant people can also want kids, yet there's often an awkward pause (Daar *et al.*, 2015). First of all, HRT alone isn't enough to make one entirely infertile, so it's possible for pre-op trans men to become pregnant, and pre-op trans women to impregnate. This may sound obvious, but there's still an amazing amount of misinformation out there when it comes to safe sex.

HRT and gender alignment surgery can certainly impact a person's options and ability to have children, but there are options. Provided the testes or ovaries haven't been removed by a gonadectomy, discontinuing HRT for a period of time (estimated between three and six months) can increase the chance of fertility (Daar *et al.*, 2015). As extended use of estrogen can damage sperm production, clomiphene citrate has been used to stimulate spermatogenesis, but studies as to its effectiveness are few (Daar *et al.*, 2015; Wu, Forbes, and Jarvi, 2017). If we intend to undergo gonadectomy, hysterectomy, phalloplasty, or vaginoplasty, help us plan for the future, as we may decide to cryopreserve sperm, oocytes, or embryos (T'Sjoen, Van Caenegem, and Wierckx, 2013). This is a luxurious expense, of course, which many can't afford. Preserving gametes may be more complicated for those who transition at a young age. While stopping puberty blockers like GnRH typically resumes gonadal developmental, most proceed with HRT, which may have long-term effects (Amato, 2018; Bancroft, 2009).

Specifically, pregnant trans men psychosocially adapt in several ways, and may need added support in therapy. To do so we must first challenge the assumption that all trans men abhor their female bodies and would never permit themselves to be impregnated, as this is a vestigial, essentialist concept (Green, 2012). Some certainly do not identify with their female anatomy, while others feel comfortable individuating their motherhood and manhood, or integrating their identity as the pregnant father (Green, 2012). Depending on the flexibility of their conceptual self, trans men navigate the first nine months, and the following years of child-rearing, in several ways, depending on their comfort, safety, support, and personal values.

Camouflaging as a cisgender woman for nine months allows them to get the services they need without interrogation, yet doing so can cause them to question themselves and their esteem (Hoffkling *et al.*, 2017). Going stealth about their pregnancy allows them to maintain their masculine identity, albeit as a man getting progressively fatter before going on a miraculous weight loss plan at the end of nine months (Hoffkling *et al.*, 2017). As cisnormative society cannot equate pregnancy and masculinity, this technique can work almost too successfully, leading to a surreal experience as those around them are completely unaware that they're pregnant (Hoffkling *et al.*, 2017). It can also make it difficult to reach out and connect with prenatal and social support services for expecting mothers, including Lamaze. Some may find it easier to socially withdraw, avoiding interaction with others, which, if left unchecked, can turn into an isolating pattern extending from nine months into the first few years of parenthood. The third option is to be out and proud, which can be a powerful, reaffirming experience if they have an active support network, yet also a potentially nerve-racking exposure to transphobia (Hoffkling *et al.*, 2017).

Gender dysphoria can certainly reemerge before, during, and after pregnancy as an individual grapples with the implications of reproduction and parenthood, the psychosocial stress of cissexism, and the physiological and emotional rollercoasters that naturally occur during pregnancy. The typical affirmations equating pregnancy to a beautiful process may have little to no bearing, so it's worth validating that struggling with—or even flat-out hating—the pregnancy process does not make one a bad parent by any means (Hoffkling *et al.*, 2017). Some may abstain from breastfeeding, or may have already had a mastectomy, once again prompting doubt. Identifying these questions and self-criticism, ACT can help acknowledge and defuse many of these critical forms of self-judgment, helping the client to bond with their child and reaffirm their parental role.

## *Exercise and personal health*

Empower us to be actively involved in our own health, as gendered institutions—including everything from gyms and their binary locker rooms, to swimming pools and swim-suit dysphoria—can obstruct our pursuit of personal wellbeing.

Physical and mental health practices, such as sports, tai chi, jogging, yoga, meditation, and therapy, can be incredibly vitalizing for gender variant individuals integrating mind and body. The androgynous may dislike gendered exercise routines that focus on masculinizing or feminizing muscle gain. Strength training often builds muscle, bulking and masculinizing the body, whereas muscle isolation routines for women often focus on hour-glass stereotypes. Realistically, it's possible to develop an exercise routine that corresponds to our body type and desired result, meaning nonbinary individuals who don't desire hypermasculine biceps or hyperfeminine glutes can develop a personalized workout, combining various kinds of cardio, swim training, and push–pull training.

Unfortunately, there may be more pressing health concerns than our cardio, as gender variant people can have some unique medical concerns. When it comes to surgery, implants can rupture, fat grafting for body contouring is not without its problems, and genital reconstructive surgery has a host of complications, from necrosis to vaginal collapse.

When it comes to HRT, masculinizing hormones can lead to an increased risk of hypertension, weight gain with increase in visceral fat, polycythemia, and potentially hyperlipidemia, and a higher risk of blood clots and cardiovascular disease (Feldman and Safer, 2009; WPATH, 2011). Feminizing hormones also increase the risk of cardiovascular disease, as well as elevated liver enzymes, gallstones, venous thromboembolic disease, hypertriglyceridemia and possible Type 2 diabetes (Feldman and Safer, 2009; WPATH, 2011). With all these risks, gender variant people are often advised to make executive life choices committing to a healthy diet, weekly exercise routine, and reducing if not completely quitting alcohol and tobacco use (Feldman and Safer, 2009; Richards *et al.*, 2016). As part of our ongoing health checks, we may also need to regularly monitor the lipids, glucose, and ratio of red blood cells in our bloodstream, as well as our bone mineral density (Richards *et al.*, 2016). Presuming, of course, we can afford healthcare.

Poverty has a detrimental impact on health, which is evident when treating communities hard hit by HIV and AIDs. In a 2001 study, HIV was found in 2 percent of FtM patients, and in 35 percent of MtF patients (Clements-Nolle *et al.*, 2001). Rallying around these numbers, a 2008 meta-analysis found that 27.7 percent of MtF individuals in the USA tested positive for HIV (Herbst *et al.*, 2008). Internationally, a 2013 meta-analysis found that 19 percent of over 11,000 transgender women worldwide tested positive for HIV (Baral *et al.*, 2013). Accounting for these discrepancies means recognizing the ruthless face of institutional racism. Clearly, trans women are at a higher risk of contracting HIV, but that number leaps from 3.4 percent to 19 percent for MtF African Americans (James *et al.*, 2016). The direct correlation between risk and destitution is evident amongst many racial and ethnic minorities stripped of resources, work opportunities, and adequate healthcare (Clements-Nolle *et al.*, 2001; Nadal *et al.*, 2014; Nemoto *et al.*, 2004).

ACT has been used effectively with sexual and gender minorities with HIV and AIDs by helping reduce the stigma and associated worthlessness that come with the diagnosis (O'Hayer, Bennett, and Jacobson, 2016). To demonstrate defusion, repeat "AIDS, AIDS, AIDS" over and over until the word loses all meaning (O'Hayer *et al.*, 2016). To experience self-as-context, *Pattern-smashing* is introduced by identifying a rigid rule, such as "I never talk about having HIV" and intentionally breaking it (Hayes, 2005; O'Hayer *et al.*, 2016).

Slowly but surely, through training programs that challenge the gate keeping medical model, health professionals are beginning to incorporate a gender variant person's self-determination (Bockting *et al.*, 2004; Hanssmann *et al.*, 2008; Lev, 2004; Pega and Veale, 2015; Singh and Burnes, 2010). As a mental health practitioner adjunct to this system, you can help us develop work-arounds, find resources, and advocate on our behalf, while also helping us process our potentially stressful encounters with doctors, insurance agencies, and debt collectors. In session, role playing can be a useful way to practice how to advocate for ourselves when confronted with a doctor (Maguen *et al.*, 2005). This activity usually highlights areas of fusion, including deep-seated beliefs about not being taken seriously, having our health issues or gender identity minimized by others, or predicting a pessimistic outcome that undermines our ability to try (Maguen *et al.*, 2005).

Laying our behaviors out on an ACT matrix can help us observe avoidance tactics habitually neglecting or compromising our physical health. Value-congruent action, however, is tricky when squaring up against institutions that blockade adequate healthcare. For those who have no insurance, or whose insurance doesn't cover transitional costs, taking the time in session to research possible health options exemplifies active self-care. If there are no nonprofits or alternative healthcare options available, explore the costs of each respective procedure to determine what can be covered by a credit card, healthcare credit card, or personal loan. Unfortunately, all come with interest, late fees, and red tape, so it's equally important to set goals to raise money, assess our budget, and crowdfund accordingly, while simultaneously developing self-care skills for emotional fatigue. The hustle is hard, and it's made even harder through illness, injury, or for those who are differently abled. For those with access to insurance, it's worth exploring all of the policies in the certificate of coverage, as some exclude services related to transition.

Value-congruent action can also include looking for gender-competent physicians or finding a nurse practitioner willing to develop their skills. Ideally, it's best to work with an endocrinologist with expertise in this area, yet they are few and far between, leaving many gender variant individuals having to cobble together a health and wellness team from well-intentioned physicians willing to learn. As a clinician, have a few doctors, nurse practitioners, and clinics in your contact list that you know, as a fact, work with gender variant patients—especially if they're low cost or operate sliding scale fees.

Coming to terms with flesh, and bone, and sinew can be a unique, powerful, and periodically saddening relationship between who and what we are. When we begin to employ the agenda of emotional control, we may try and avoid thinking about the body, avoid attending to its needs, avoid somatic stimulation, or focus on sensory pleasure over physical pain. We may try and transcend the physical, and so neglect our needs if we believe mindfulness is solely about the mind, or else white-knuckle our way through our aches and pains. Jordan, having noticed the whites of his eyes starting to yellow, waited for a few weeks hoping it would go away, just so he didn't have to go to the doctor. It wasn't until his girlfriend pressured him, rather threateningly, to go to the doctor that he even made an appointment. Jordan's best friend, Mike, has a very different problem. As Mike's ID matches his gender, he always has insurance and billing complications when he needs a pap smear, but Jordan has a different issue to deal with.

He's naturally nervous about his health, but he's feeling preoccupied with the setting. The lights, the coughing people in the waiting room, the sign-in sheet. He already knows what's going to happen next. After about an hour of sitting in the world's most uncomfortable chair, a door's going to open across the hall and a woman with a clipboard is going to say the wrong name. They're going to say *Amanda*, and he's going to stand up and walk toward her, and she's going to be very confused, because Jordan doesn't look like an Amanda and they never really did. Then they'll have a hushed conversation by the door with the security guard watching over them. And all the while Jordan will think to himself, "I don't need this. This is fucking stupid. I should just go." And the security guard will stand up, and Jordan will bolt like the last time he tried to get help, and he'll try and console himself that at least this time he got further than the parking lot, but what does it matter if he has jaundice?

But it hasn't happened yet. Jordan's predicting the future, yet he notices his hand gripping that unusually uncomfortable chair, and he realizes his anger is masking his anxiety. A memory catches him, something his old therapist taught him during a rough patch in high school. He hasn't been in therapy for years, but this silly counselor taught him a silly thing about perspective, so he starts to think to himself, "I don't need this. This is me, thinking I don't need this. This is me, sitting in a really uncomfortable chair, thinking I don't need this. This is me in a badly lit waiting room, sitting in a really uncomfortable chair, thinking I don't need this. This is me, in a stupid clinic, in a badly lit waiting room, sitting in a…" The door opens. On cue, the nurse calls "Amanda." Launching himself to his feet, Jordan approaches, and feels his hands are clammy, which might be a liver issue, or nervousness, he doesn't know which! He wants to run, because the nurse blinked just like he knew she would, and he realizes he hasn't stopped walking. He introduces himself, and corrects his name, and the nurse smiles a curious smile that makes Jordan think he might get a phone number out of this. And she makes a note on the corner of her clipboard: "Preferred name: Jordan."

## Legacy and life: ACT for gender variant seniors

We all reevaluate our relationship with our bodies as we age, since our bodies morph whether we like it or not, yet for gender variant people time presents some unique questions. Youth often provides a natural androgyny, either through baby fat or lean composition; yet as our body mass index changes, gender dysphoric and body dysmorphic feelings can sometimes rekindle. Nonbinary genderqueer and agender individuals may struggle with the onset of later life secondary sex characteristics, like male pattern baldness, fat redistribution, and skin sag, should such changes bring unwanted attention to sex phenotypes. Parts of our body we had "resolved not to think about" may even be demanding our attention with health concerns, such as menopause or erectile dysfunction; or in more extreme instances, breast, ovarian, testicular, or colon cancer. Such health concerns are naturally troubling, yet they are made all the more complex when we do not connect with, feel dysphoric about, or maintain critical judgment of this anatomy. Likewise, polygender individuals who could once shift fluidly between genders in our androgynous youth may feel like we're at a crossroad, as if our ability to flow is being inhibited by a body that insists on masculinizing or feminizing itself with each decade. Considering all this, nonbinary and gender nonconforming individuals may reconsider HRT, FFS, FMS, mastectomies or other forms of surgery as we age in order to actualize or preserve our identity.

If we have experienced persecution in the past, the physical disempowerment of aging and the social invisibility of ageism can feel unsettling. Also, if we wrestled with suicide, HIV, or extreme violence, we may not have expected to live so long, which leaves us holding a mixed bag of relief, sadness, and unpreparedness (Fabbre, 2014; Halberstam, 2005). Older clients may hesitate to explore this issue, assuming many won't understand the gravity around gender and aging. Not only are there few gender roles and gender variant role models, there are even fewer for gender variant senior citizens. Defusing from the unhealthy hetero- and cisnormative model of aging returns us, once again, to queer failure and the act of unbecoming (Halberstam, 2011). Dismantling old notions of what it means to enter our autumn and winter years, we may need to redefine connection with age and identity, building on values like grace, integrity, resilience, wisdom, empowerment, and seniority (Fabbre, 2014, 2015).

Older clients may struggle to reconcile the generational survival skills of youth with the changing sociopolitical climate. Without discounting the dangers trans youth face, we must acknowledge that two generations ago this conversation wasn't even being had. A book of this nature would have never been published. Public attitudes change with public attention; and as society evolves, so too do our communication styles, value constructs, and defense mechanisms in response to it.

Gender variant support groups can actually clash when age demographics can't find common ground, as being trans is no more cohesive or bonding than any other gender. That's like saying all women should get along *because* they're women, or all men are brothers *because* they're men. Certainly, role models are a phenomenal resource in any LGBTQ community, but when conceptualization of gender identity, outness, queerness, feminism, progressivism, and activism vastly differ between generational cultures, respective members of the trans community can inadvertently alienate each other. As much of the literature and social services are very youth-centric, transgender senior citizens are not always considered or accommodated. Gender variant seniors have distinct personal, social, and health issues, as discrimination against gender is further coupled with ageism.

Of transgender baby boomers, one study found that only 28 percent were open to anyone about their identities (Metlife, 2010). To place this secrecy in context means recognizing several dynamics, including cultural attitudes toward *disclosure and late life transition*, increased fear of *discrimination*, as well as thoughts on *legacy*, *bereavement*, and *end of life concerns*.

### *Disclosure and late-life transition*

Generational cohorts hold different perspectives of gender, gender expression, and even gender disclosure. Timing is a prime example of this. With the historical dangers facing gender minorities in the workplace, many of the *silent generation* chose to remain silent, while many baby boomers only opted to come out after retirement (Roland and Burlew, 2017; Siverskog, 2014). MtF individuals are more likely to come out later in life than FtM individuals, and may negotiate with themselves about the timing of doing so, carefully planning to transition once they have "served" a certain amount of time in male gender roles, as the worker, the father, or the husband (Cook-Daniels, 2006; Fabbre, 2014, 2015). As a survival strategy, endurance and discretion may indicate value constructs elevating career to such a degree it may even eclipse personhood. Notably, 70 percent of transgender individuals 65 and older reported postponing transition for fear of discrimination in the workplace (Grant *et al.*, 2011).

Increased fear of loss, alongside an increased level of risk, may also contribute to us biting our tongue. Of those who transitioned after 55, around 82 percent are parents, demonstrating an investment to a gender role (Grant *et al.*, 2011). With years to weigh the pros and cons, to ponder, postpone, and ponder again, we can fuse with our rationale. We may fear that transition might jeopardize our marriage, and that our gender may be used against us in court as a sign of instability. We may fear that transition might emotionally impact our child in some way, that our child will be bullied, or that our child may feel alienated from us. We may hope that our family will be able to "handle" our transition once the children are mature adults. And these are, sadly, valid concerns, as 57 percent of gender variant individuals who came out in their autumn years experienced family rejection, leaving them to piece together a new social support network (Fredriksen-Goldsen *et al.*, 2013; Grant *et al.*, 2011; Roland and Burlew, 2017). Some transgender seniors also reported physical and verbal abuse from family members (Witten, 2003). Psychologically, this can be quite challenging, as our gripping fears provide no alternative but to hide and wait. Honesty could risk the family, causing strain with children, grandchildren, and even parents if they're still alive. Ruminating for so long, we may postpone transition so as not to disappoint or upset our own parents and may quietly be waiting for them to die of old age in order to avoid conflict or distress. With appropriate intervention, family dynamics can shift toward acceptance, but some only manage to come out once relationships fade, albeit through divorce, children leaving home, or death (Roland and Burlew, 2017).

At the core of this disclosure process, however, are some fundamental value constructs worth recognizing, including acceptance, safety, and personal honesty. Gender variant seniors are more inclined to come out when the benefits of disclosure begin to outweigh the stress of concealment, including the psychological strain of marginalization, but for some even the physical impact of such stress on our autoimmune and cardiovascular system can be risky (Roland and Burlew, 2017). Such steps may also be expedited by the existential recognition of time, as there's only so much sand in the hour glass, and only so many chances left to be authentic (Roland and Burlew, 2017).

## *Discrimination*

Risks of discrimination against gender variant seniors may also heighten as cisgenderism and transphobia intersect with ageism. Senior citizens frequently feel relocated to a second-class social status, yet many gender variant individuals—especially those who are also racial and ethnic minorities—have spent decades feeling marginalized (Finkenauer *et al.*, 2012). For some, ageism is just another drop in the bucket—yet another prejudice to overcome! Yet for others it may strike a blow to the ego, multiplying fears of powerlessness. Gender-based discriminatory encounters increase depression, and the adverse effects on both mental and physical health can be massively detrimental, leading to lethargy, weight gain, increased cardiovascular stress, and suicidality (Auldridge *et al.*, 2012; Fredriksen-Goldsen *et al.*, 2013; Hughto and Reisner, 2016; Witten, 2003).

Risks of discrimination are especially high for those who transition later in life, should our sex phenotypes appear incongruent with our gender identity (Auldridge *et al.*, 2012). The stigmatization of coming out compounds stress, especially when health complications limit options for gender affirming surgery (Roland and Burlew, 2017; Siverskog, 2014). Both medical practitioners and direct-care living centers without sensitivity training can be alarming and potentially harmful should staff ignore preferred names or pronouns, or go so far as to neglect or physically abuse us (Ansara, 2015; Auldridge *et al.*, 2012; Cook-Daniels, 2008; Finkenauer *et al.*, 2012; Hughto and Reisner, 2016).

In the USA, if a nursing home operating under Medicaid and Medicare funding refuses a patient's hormone treatment, does not assist us with our desired clothes, isolates or neglects transgender patients, or subjects us to harassment or abuse, then they're in direct violation of the Nursing Home Reform Act (NHRA) (Auldridge *et al.*, 2012). This protection of a senior citizen's privacy, dignity, autonomy, and personal freedom is rare in many parts of the world, with Tonic Housing (2018) only just establishing the UK'S first LGBTQ-friendly care village. Of course, this presumes we can even afford healthcare of this kind in our old age. In all, around 50 percent of older trans individuals face financial strains impeding the ability to meet basic needs, from food to medicine (Witten, 2016).

As is the case when marginalized communities are hit with one financial and emotional obstacle after the next, the risk of alcohol and drug abuse increases (Roland and Burlew, 2017). It's here that we become incredibly reliant on our family of origin—should they accept us—or our family of choice. Families of choice are powerful support networks, especially when they're intergenerational, as they provide opportunities for elders to role model and pass on knowledge and experience (Hughto and Reisner, 2016). However, when a family of choice comprises a single generational cohort, the mortal exodus leaves those behind without support.

### *Legacy*

Nostalgia and regret often lead us to ask what our life amounted to. In the end, was it all worth it? Legacy questions are, at their essence, value explorations. Are we satisfied with all we have stood for? Are we at peace with both our accomplishments and the driving forces that led us to them? When speaking about legacy, explore our appraisal of monetary, academic, or occupational success or achievement. We may view our successful accolades quite differently, or find regret undermining our self-worth. Value-incongruent success is a haunting ghost, whereas value-congruent legacy doesn't require a gold medal or a retirement gift in order to feel successful.

Our legacy is what we're remembered for, but more than that it's what we remember ourselves for. As the author of our story and its primary audience, we know the characters and the crimes as intimately as we know the plot and the plot holes. It becomes hard to conceptualize legacy when we reserve the term for the penultimate result of our life, but these value explorations regularly pop up when we come to the end of a chapter. Graduation, promotion, moving across country, starting a family, speaking at a wake, changing careers, retirement, and even gender alignment surgery bring us to both an end and a beginning. In such moments we ask ourselves: Did we climb the mountain for us, or for the fame of it, or to flee the danger behind us? Were we running toward something? Were we ever truly present? Or were all our accomplishments just different incarnations of escapism? Did we talk the talk *and* walk the walk? In the moment, it can be hard to tell, but regret reminds us when we didn't and fond nostalgia reminds us when we did.

Liminal identities often regret lost time. How many years disappeared while we were hiding, or surviving, or trying to recover? Being so focused on getting through the day, we may not have stopped to gauge our intention or our alignment with what's most important to us. Sometimes it may even feel like our values were sacrificed just to get by. Though this need not be the case, some value-congruent steps can have real-world repercussions. When we come out later in life, we often worry that we'll sacrifice all we've built so far, and in some cases we do! After decades of investment we might lose our job, or community respect, or even be disowned by our family. Feeling too old, too tired, or too burnt to try again, let alone be remembered for anything, we may amble on with the jaded knowledge that all our work will be torn apart by the rumor mill.

If we've been out all our lives, especially if we're nonbinary, the focus on survival and connection may have been so all-encompassing that there never seemed time for retrospect or the luxury of legacy! Yet legacy is neither a luxury nor a privilege—it only seems that way when we fuse it to dreams of grandeur. Our legacy is not a statue built in the middle of town, or a social media account with a million followers, though it can be. In life there are many different kinds of legacies—of fortune and empire, of innovation and creation, of healing and charity, of experience and wisdom, or of nurturance and family. There are legacies of knowledge and genius, nature and balance, truth and justice, laughter and love, glory and fame, righteousness and change, and even legacies of community and safety. Remember Marsha P. Johnson and Sylvia Rivera, who made their legacy in motion with the throw of a brick and a beer bottle. Remember Reed Erickson, the philanthropist whose Erickson Educational Foundation (EEF) donated hundreds of thousands of dollars to trans-positive organizations like the Harry Benjamin Foundation, and the John Hopkins Gender Identity Clinic (Matte and Devor, 2007). Then remember the trans person walking down the street, whose very existence encouraged a smile though we didn't even know their name. Our legacy can be modest or grand in scale, yet the question is whether or not we're proud of it and undeniably of ourselves.

Returning to relational frame theory, our legacy can be viewed as the retrospective analysis of our relationship between self and other. All our lives *the other* has impacted *the self*. Society, family, rules, regulations, and expectations have hit us and cradled us, shaped us, and formed us. When we think of legacy, however, we want to know how *the self* impacted *the other*. Did we leave a dent or a scratch? Did one seed sprout? Did one person appreciate us? Did we appreciate ourselves? All valid questions, made all the more desperate by memories of disengagement, social rejection, isolation, disownment, marginalization, and oppression. Fusing to a transactional perspective, we can mistake values for valuables, and legacy for commodity, at which point our reputation can either be earned or bankrupted. When we think of our life in such transactional terms, our good name can even be stolen or defaced by character assassins and emotional saboteurs.

Observing how we overidentify with our accomplishments and deficits, you can help us notice our transactional, goal-focused language. This is no easy task when we're trying to assess the merit of our whole lives! Like pleading with St. Peter at the gate, or watching Anubis weigh our heart against a feather, or playing chess with the Grim Reaper, neither bargaining nor bemoaning will help us now. "If only I hadn't got such a raw deal, I could have got into the afterlife! Just give me some time and I'll do better!" The atheist equivalent of this is having our biography assessed by a pretentious 19-year-old college student a century after we're put in the ground.

So, if our legacy is not our transactions, accomplishments, deficits, or regrets what are we talking about, here? The essence of a conversation can't be found in the words said. Put this book down, walk away, and try to remember the specific sentence opening the second paragraph, three pages before this one. Unless we have an eidetic memory or decided to memorize the whole book line by line, we're not going to remember. What sticks with us are the core ideas, themes, and feelings contained within. We'll remember our reaction, resonance, and even our dissonance, too! We'll remember a feeling of the content that lingers long after the specifics of the idea are gone, which is why we'll misquote books and attribute ideas to the wrong author. And that's okay. Even the Greek proverb "A society grows great when old men plant trees in whose shade they know they shall never sit" has been misattributed and rephrased from its debated Roman originator, Caecilius Statius, who wrote in 166 BCE: "He plants trees to serve another age." In much the same way, our legacy is not a singular action, or epitome of heroism, or glorious second, or well-crafted speech—or how any of it will be remembered, portrayed, or conveyed, as we won't be around to correct anyone. Historians, after all, may be good bookkeepers, but time is a janitor who mistakes the in-box for the waste-paper basket.

Our legacy is the feeling in it, and through it, and behind it that stems from our alignment with our core values. When we're out of sync, we regret our life, as even the most wonderful of memories become tainted by all the *could have beens* and *should have gones*. Our power of analysis is so great that we can imagine, visualize, regret, desire, and fear untold possibilities about our future. This imagination only gets stronger in retrospect, for looking back we can see all we could have said or accomplished measured alongside all the missed opportunities. There's no undoing life, yet creating mental space from our retrospective judgment can help us expand our attention to how we exemplify our legacy right now. Ceasing to be a transaction, legacy no longer calls for past investment, as an overdrawn account in the bank of emotionality need not jeopardize our present self-worth.

When we're in sync with our values in present time, even our most arduous memories can exemplify our self-worth if we're able to view past hardships from a place of current acceptance. When helping gender variant seniors explore legacy and self-satisfaction, try recalling examples of perseverance, resilience, and empowerment. If there is no singular memory, the very fact that we're still standing is evidence of something powerful that kept us going through it all. Certainly, people will remember us unfairly, and maybe we even played the villain in a story or two, yet we were always growing, and always influencing our social environment. And if we want to impact the world more, help us explore how we can. Even if we can't build a great empire, we can still contribute to organizations, programs, and nonprofits that align with what's most important to us. Art, music, and literature are also a way of creating, remembering, and giving back when we lack money or energy. Socially, we can gather who's most important to us, and if they are with us no longer, we can memorialize them in some way. And if we want to be remembered, we can teach what we've learned to a new generation, and even to our therapist. Ultimately, a legacy is our last chance to pay something forward. After all, as a misquoted poet once said, "Civilizations thrive when we plant trees we will not live long enough to see."

## *Bereavement*

Bereavement is a natural heartache for the loss of those we love, yet when our greatest love is devalued by society, the depth of loneliness can be unbearable.

*Disenfranchised grief* occurs when our relationship is not sanctioned, received, or respected by our community, causing our mourning process to be stifled or even hidden (Doka, 2002). As not even death is immune to stigma, the pervasiveness of disenfranchised grief goes way past the religious zealots protesting at LGBTQ funerals, to include every small comment, as widows are presumed heterosexual and we continue to correct pronouns post-mortem.

Imagine, for a moment, not being able to speak our partner's name without being shot down by intolerant family members. Imagine not being able to share our loss with co-workers who know nothing about our personal life. Or imagine crying openly and being called disgusting because of whom we cry for. Imagine showing a person a photograph and having to correct every misgendered assumption: "No, they were *my husband*."

Depending on our level of openness, we may even retract to the closet in times of mourning, withholding our identity from even medical professionals (Grant *et al.*, 2011; Roland and Burlew, 2017). It is not uncommon for one partner in a relationship to carry the candle of courage or compassion, or for two of us to hold the same candle together, to embolden each other in our love. And without them? We may even want the candle to die out, as we already feel left in the dark. Socially we may feel uncertain about who knows what about our relationship, or what it even means to go on alone (Roland and Burlew, 2017). Sometimes they completed us, but more often they were just the brave one, or the clever one, or the kind one, or the social one, leaving us fused to rules that no longer apply without them:

> "I never had to do this on my own. She always introduced us."
>
> "You know, he wouldn't like me talking about that..."
>
> "Ever since they died it's like...I just stopped being a part of that community. I haven't had a conversation with a queer person in years."

When we're grieving, our thoughts feel real, as if we truly can't get out of bed (Speedlin *et al.*, 2016). Honoring the loss and validating the pain, ACT has demonstrated its usefulness throughout the bereavement process, as it illustrates how our language stifles our ability to recover (Speedlin *et al.*, 2016). Absolute statements and fatalistic doubt underscore our distress by fusing our sadness to our judgment. Feeling helpless and powerless by a memorial stone, we try to "pull" ourselves together, "pull" ourselves up by our bootstraps, and "pull" through, knowing all too well we're dragging a weight behind us. Each "pull" is a control tactic trying to keep our pain inside. Learning how to talk about our grief is a huge step, as so many try so hard not to acknowledge it, but language is limited, and sometimes the loss in our life feels truly indescribable (Speedlin *et al.*, 2016). Grief is a unique emotion as it doesn't rely on our inner monologue, and we can spend weeks feeling thoughtless, and empty, and numb (Speedlin *et al.*, 2016). To be present with this feeling, truly present, requires noticing despair without judging it, and feeling sad without forcing extraneous meaning on it (Hayes *et al.*, 1999; Speedlin *et al.*, 2016).

Visualizing our mind as a stage, with the spotlight focused on our grief, provides us an opportunity to turn up the houselights, and explore all of a relationship, and not just the end. During this dire time you can help us develop unique ways to honor our loss, including engaging in the deceased's favorite activities, writing them a letter, or seeing the world through their eyes. For LGBTQ individuals who may have had to compartmentalize our lives, one particularly cathartic exercise includes recalling all the funny, awkward, silly, sexy, romantic, and above-all queer things that only we experienced together. Going further than nostalgia, isolated sexual and gender minorities in our senior years can greatly benefit from not only expressing our genuine emotions, but also our uncensored memories.

### *End-of-life concerns*

There is very little research regarding end-of-life care for gender minorities, yet it's clear that many senior facilities and hospice programs are neither familiar nor comfortable with transgender clients (Arthur, 2015; Stincombe *et al.*, 2017; Witten, 2014a). End-of-life concerns include health challenges, how to navigate disability and illness, and how to prepare for death. A comprehensive survey of 1963 international participants found that transgender people felt deeply concerned about becoming helpless or chronically ill—a worry increased by an unpreparedness for this final stage of life (Witten, 2014b; Witten and Eyler, 2012; Stincombe *et al.*, 2017). Of gender variant respondents over 61 years old, only 8.1 percent had completed a will, only 9.1 percent had an advanced care directive, and only 7.4 percent had a durable power of attorney (Witten and Eyler, 2012). Actively having these discussions can actually increase personal integrity and even the quality of death experience by validating the power of choice (Larson and Tobin, 2000; Witten and Eyler, 2012). Sadly, when asked who would take care of them should they befall a major illness or injury, 30 percent of the total respondents had no idea (Witten and Eyler, 2012).

Having a deep connection with a religious leader is often a positive predictor of psychological wellbeing in our final years, yet this may be no simple task for gender variant seniors who have experienced spiritual persecution in the past, or even in the present (Blank, 2011; Porter *et al.*, 2013; Witten and Eyler, 2012). We may have very real concerns that our church, mosque, or synagogue will not honor our funeral rites, or that even our tombstone will be chiseled with the wrong name or pronoun by family members wishing to erase our gender (Koon Teh, 2001; Witten, 2014a, 2015; Witten and Eyler, 2012). To cope with some of these concerns, some contemplate de-transitioning or reverting to a cisgender status just to find social connection, or else commit suicide (Koon Teh, 2001; Witten, 2014a, 2015).

Faced with the very real concerns of discrimination, reduced autonomy, isolation, loneliness, and the fear of senility, it's clear why gender variant seniors struggle with control-oriented therapy techniques (Witten, 2016; Witten and Eyler, 2012). Having lived a lifetime striving to empower ourselves, the final years can be difficult to accept because of how much control is relinquished. Even though age, and all the issues thereof, are inevitable, cognitive behavioral techniques often challenge our thoughts about loss by having us focus on what we've gained in life, which is only effective if the merits of old age align with our values (Roberts and Sedley, 2016). The reality of our fading independence and health can feel eroding; as such ACT presents elders with a means of shifting our relationship with loss itself (Petkus and Wetherell, 2013). The distinction here is that you're not attempting to convince us that getting old is *good*. In fact, we're placing no value judgment on it. We are, however, accepting the reality of what is.

Attempting to avoid emotional distress by suppressing thoughts may actually dwindle our sense of meaning in our final years (Krause, 2007). In the general population, senior citizens with chronic illness fall deeper into depression and anxiety when they strive not to think about their situation (Andrew and Dulin, 2007; Ayers *et al.*, 2010; Petkus, Gum, and Wetherell, 2012; Petkus and Wetherell, 2013). Time will tell if it's a generational observation or an aspect of getting older, but it seems that seniors struggle to identify their emotional process, or even symptoms of anxiety and depression (Petkus and Wetherell, 2013; Wetherell *et al.*, 2009). More often, seniors express worry, disinterest or fatigue as somatic complaints, like a loss of appetite or energy (Wetherell *et al.*, 2009; Petkus and Wetherell, 2013). This is where emotional awareness exercises can help reconnect us with our whole process, which may certainly include worry, fatigue, fear, wonder, awe, grief, denial, anger, appreciation, and joy.

Actively deciding not to talk about our process, spending excessive time sleeping, or reducing emotional awareness to focus solely on fatigue and physical pain, are clear examples of avoidance at work, yet so too is overengagement. When we do not accept our health concerns, we may push ourselves to keep going in old age, in part because we want to live life to the fullest, but also to avoid anxiety (Petkus and Wetherell, 2013).

When working with gender variant seniors, begin with a strength-based approach of our values. In comparison to sessions with younger clients, more time may be spent establishing these value constructs via our personal narrative (Petkus and Wetherell, 2013; Roberts and Sedley, 2016). No doubt, we have a lifetime to resource examples of resilience, endurance, and adaptability, alongside many coping strategies we've developed over the years (Roland and Burlew,

2017). Be tactful and gracious when presenting defusion, as seniors often have an established personal narrative with many elements of fusion therein. At this age, we witness how literal cognitive fusion is, as decades of repetition can strengthen our neural pathways to incredible degrees. We may recount stories from years before in vivid detail or express our perspectives with an unquestionable level of certainty, trusting in our years of experience.

It's very natural to crystalize our conceptual self, which accounts for why we feel older than we are in youth, and younger than we are in old age. Having fused to this conceptual self, it may be difficult to incorporate new aspects into an identity we have spent years valiantly defining and defending. One of the hardest examples of this is the realization that we don't lose our identity just because we need help. When we fuse to independence, and define our quality of life through autonomy, time itself becomes an eroding threat. For those of us who have spent decades discreetly concealing our gender, or for those of us who blazed trails when help and allyship were rare, accepting help in the here and now can be very difficult.

When presenting defusion tactics, clarify how we're not diminishing the narrative, but expanding into it. Classic colloquialisms like "We're more than the sum of our parts" and "We're the author, not the story" are useful not only to illustrate the therapeutic intention, but progress us to defusion exercises like *I'm having the thought* (Roberts and Sedley, 2016). Having seen the world change, and having transformed so many aspects of our identity, profession, and social role over the years, it can be powerful to explore and validate examples of resilience, flexibility, contribution, adaptation, and even self-sacrifice in our life story (Roland and Burlew, 2017). A lot of personal meaning can be mined from the past in order to observe our current strengths and sense of purpose (Hughto and Reisner, 2016; Roland and Burlew, 2017).

It is quite natural to explore values as they pertain to religion and spirituality, as faith is at once a value and a value guide. Faith differs from morality, insomuch as morality tells us what society expects, whereas faith can only exist from a central locus of identity. History has shown us time and again that a religion can force people to obey, but not believe. In this way faith relies on our hierarchical frames, as we place our self-schema in the context of the infinite. Paradoxically, even faith in nothing is still faith, as nihilism is a powerful belief. Even atheists can derive great strength from the motto: *Carpe diem, quam minimum credula postero*, "Seize the day, put very little trust in tomorrow." An ACT-based approach is to ask us to imagine (unless this has already happened!) that a physician has given us two years left—two years left of good health to get our affairs in order (Petkus and Wetherell, 2013). What is most important? How will we spend our time? For those with health issues, this may actually be a reality, at which point clinicians become sounding boards and allies to help us prioritize and actualize our final, value-congruent goals.

For gender variant seniors, especially those estranged from our biological family, loneliness can be a deciding motivator to continue living. We may express a desire to reconnect with our family, knowing all too well this may be our last chance, and that our family may not be receptive to rekindling any kind of relationship. Should we desire to reach out, we may need help locating old friends and family as we explore the core of our message. Defusing from old stories, resentments, and old wounds, help us sit with our narrative while increasing contact with the present moment. Through all the years of pain there remains a powerful intention. This may be a desire to connect, yet resentment is also powerful, so don't be surprised if we still harbor anger toward our family, as we may be looking for one last chance to slam the door. In either case, the value is clouded by fear of rejection, angry argument, or spiteful comeuppance. You may do well to ask, *What is most important, here? What would you want them to know about you*?

We may want to express our love and forgiveness, or to let those in our past know we made it—that we survived—and that we're proud of ourselves. We may be filled with curiosity, desiring to reach out just to learn what happened to everyone we used to know. As immediate family members may not be receptive, we may ponder reaching out to others in our past who can provide us reassurance of character. Though there is no substitute for an estranged spouse, or child, or grandchildren, old family friends can sometimes provide us with a secondary process, having indirectly witnessed the conflict while remaining sympathetic. It's always worth asking, *Who was in your corner*? *Who do you think might be understanding, now*?

Family therapy may be possible, yet the overarching goal is to help us live our remaining years in congruence with our values, without exerting unnecessary physical, emotional, and mental strain trying to avoid our feelings. Accepting estrangement does not mean rejecting the love or compassion that clearly remains, despite the pain and relational distance. Just as creating art and writing memoirs are a form of self-exploration, so too are our last affairs. Do-not-send letters, as a therapeutic exercise, allow us to express our fondness, frustration, or forgiveness, for our own benefit without actually mailing them (Zettle, 2007). In this case, it may be pertinent to write or record a final message, allowing us to express everything we wished our family members would know, understand, or accept. Having us read our letter aloud brings us face to face with regret, pain, love, loss, hope, and perhaps even forgiveness. The therapeutic intention is simple, but potentially profound, as we have the opportunity to express what's most important to us without having to convince anyone of anything. Owning our life means claiming the final word on the matter, whatever that may genuinely be. While this can help prepare for the end, this exercise can actually help us live more freely. Instead of ruminating on all the things we should have said in the past, we focus on all the things we have to say in the present, for in the end the present was all we ever had.

# Epilogue:

# Of Moths and Meaning

In January of 1862 a wizened man carried a small box to his greenhouse. Stowed inside was a gift from Madagascar with a letter signed by his esteemed horticultural colleague, James Bateman. Carefully prying the lid open, the man found a star-like African orchid nestled inside. Its long green spur measured 13.8 inches, too long for any known insect to drink nectar from. Whatever pollinated this unusual flower needed an equally long proboscis, though there was no evidence that such a creature existed on Earth. This hypothesis was later corroborated by Alfred Russel Wallace, who suggested that an African hawk moth could potentially accomplish such a feat. The flower, *Angraecum sesquipedale*, was later nicknamed after the wizened man holding its soft petals to the light—*Darwin's orchid*.

Twenty years later, in April of 1882, Darwin died, his funeral at Westminster Abbey attended by thousands, including philosophers, scientists, and lords. Twenty-one years after his burial, in the lush jungles of Madagascar, a hawk moth was witnessed landing on a flower, *Xanthopan morganii*, the Morgan's sphinx. A marvel in its own right, its proboscis was long enough to drink from Darwin's namesake orchid.

No doubt, to predict the moth we must first observe the orchid. In literal terms, to prepare to work with an invisible and under-represented minority we must first observe the intersection of current biological and sociocultural phenomena, knowing that sometimes we have to anticipate their existence even if we have not encountered them directly. The Morgan's sphinx conundrum is most problematic for researchers, whose task it is to disprove their hypothesis, which is like trying to disprove the hawk moth before it's even been discovered.

In order to work effectively with gender variant populations, you must be mentally flexible. Unlike other populations that therapists prepare to work with, the range of sexual and gender identities in the world are too numerous and complex to prepare for ahead of time, and attempts to do so result in essentialist and reductionist taxonomies. Exposure is the best education and therefore the best way to maintain mental flexibility, as the more diverse interactions you have, the more likely you are to let go of preconceived ideas about gender minorities. Indeed, every observation made in this book, including every study, statistic, and psychological perspective, is limited to its time and place.

When gender minorities are studied by gender-privileged people, we are pinned like specimens under glass. Yet when we are included, it becomes evident how faulty frames of opposition are in social contexts. The opposite of cisgender is not transgender, any more than the opposite of a moth is a butterfly. If anything, they are far more similar. All genders have unique distinctions in their development, and though gender variant people go through far more dynamic periods of self-actualization, every gender schema goes through perfectly natural stages of chrysalis, reformation, and emergence. After all, what it meant for Suzy to be a six-year-old girl turned out to be quite different from what Suzy feels as a 67-year-old woman, just as what it meant for Paul to be a six-year-old boy turned out to be quite different from what Pauline feels as a 67-year-old woman.

Conceptually, ACT presents many techniques applicable to those actualizing their gender, including transgender, nonbinary, and even cisgender people coming to terms with who they are. By defusing dichotomous thinking, albeit positive/negative, good/bad, man/woman, gay/straight, we begin to form a larger, contextual picture inclusive of our strengths and struggles as they exist and interconnect. A caterpillar is methodical and subsequently slow. A butterfly is elegant and subsequently fragile. Over-thinkers are phenomenal intellectuals, the socially nervous are very conscientious, and the stubborn have great willpower. When we defuse from our judgment, we progressively begin to accept ourselves, as our dilemmas are not a parsing of good and bad, but the degree to which we mentally limit ourselves. By examining our personal schemas, incongruities may be observed between our values and our behavior, requiring a shift toward mindful self-awareness. Additionally, ACT metaphors can provide a creative, non-restrictive mode for both adults and youth to discuss the complex interrelationship between sexual orientation, gender identity, gender expression, and social role.

ACT has proven to be efficacious with a range of mental health issues, as it directly addresses our tendency to avoid emotional distress, and how to accept our experiential process (Hayes and Smith, 2005; Hayes *et al.*, 2012). As the gender explorative, gender expressive, and gender dynamic are often far afield of our comfort zones, ACT can provide us with healthy and mindful alternatives to emotional escapism. Comparative research and continued case studies are still needed to gauge ACT's effectiveness throughout the multicultural array of gender minorities. Quite arguably, because of this phenomenal diversity, there can be no rigidly manualized treatment plan applicable to all gender variant people.

The emotional resilience and mental flexibility that ACT provides make it a powerful tool for gender specialists, as the techniques presented are adaptable in application.

By aligning with the client, you no longer stand before us as gatekeepers, but beside us as guides looking toward the same exciting, scary, and inspiring horizon. As collaborators on a journey, with genuine understanding of each other's intentions, it becomes easier to shoot sidelong looks of caution when we begin to take unnecessary risks or fall back into old habits. The felt urgency around self-actualization, especially for young people, can be undeniable, yet herein lies the benefit of defusion. You're not here to doubt our goal or desire, but to draw awareness to the emotional impetus and rigid cognitions influencing our focus and behavior. By taking mental space and embodying our values, a distinct shift occurs. The goal to self-actualize remains the same, but our fear-based motivation gives way to self-affirmation. Mindful acceptance, hand in hand with value commitment, can aid in both physical and mental adjustment over the lifespan by highlighting resilience and self-worth. In turn, this may even decrease the potential for regret by openly exploring areas of avoidance. Social, emotional, and situational control tactics can show up in a number of ways at each step of the journey, and from time to time we'll need to revisit the ACT matrix in order to comprehend our excited stories and painful pitfalls.

We often resist a particular emotion, having experienced only the painful facets of it, yet it is our somatic affect, our feelings of dissonant discomfort and resonant elation that show us what truly matters. We know within ourselves what feels genuine, sincere, and comfortable in our relationship with our body and indeed with our relationship to our cultural parameters (Sennott, 2011). Gender actualization, as it appears throughout our lives, is not just the question of how we manifest within our body, but how that manifestation reflects our innermost being. Gender identity is an identity foremost. This simple notion gets easily lost in all our talk of sex phenotypes and socially scripted performance, as our interactions with others are often our first, formative memory of comparison and distinction. We remember not being like *them* or feeling an affinity for something outside of our allocated box, and so we became aware of social expectations and gendered power dynamics. We forget that our relationship with our body existed long before the linguistic labels and cognitive categories.

At the heart of acceptance is the deep-felt understanding of impermanence, as relationships, emotions, cognitions, and the very body itself naturally transform over time. This is difficult for many, as we so often freeze our conceptual self in place, like moths and butterflies who still believe they're caterpillars. If gender is the color and intricacy of our wings, then some caterpillars may be surprised at their own nature, emerging as the emerald swallowtail butterfly, the monarch, the blue morpho, the Luna moth, the giant owl butterfly, or even the Madagascan sunset moth. Defusion is not easy, as it brings us into personal contact with our feelings. In kind, the classic image of the chrysalis is not a fanciful one, as it can be terrifying to let go of our old incarnations, liquidate, reform, and rediscover who we are. For those of us who always knew we were gender variant, this can mean letting go of emotional guarding, or the rigid rules of self-preservation, or even literal parts of our body. For those of us who discovered only later that we were gender variant, this can mean letting go of everything we once thought we were. For those of us who are growing up, this can mean letting go of our childhood. For those of us struggling with who we are, this can mean letting go of the old narratives that hold us back.

We will not always be understood, and we will not always understand ourselves, as the words cannot convey the depth and resonance of our feelings. Accepting fluidity, the only question that remains is how avoidantly passive or willingly active we are in this ongoing process. A tree never stops growing branches, but an arborist can help. The river doesn't stop flowing because it reached the ocean, but the brackish delta becomes a new ecosystem. And the hawk moth continues to exist whether there's anyone around to validate it or not. When gender identity is accepted in this way, not as a final product but as a lifelong experience, it becomes a source of joyous levity and powerful integrity.

Ever and always, proceed as you wish to go on, and remember:

To be *fierce* is to be proud of yourself in the face of adversity.

To be *fabulous* is to inspire others by being exactly who you are.

# References


Abbott, D. and Burns, J. (2007) What's love got to do with it? Experiences of lesbian, gay, and bisexual people with intellectual disabilities in the United Kingdom and views of the staff who support them. *Sexuality Research and Social Policy: A Journal of the NSRC*, 4(1): 27–39.

Ackner, B. (1954) Depersonalization: I. Aetiology and phenomenology. *Journal of Mental Science*, 100(421): 838–853.

Adler, R., Hirsch, S., and Mordaunt M. (2012) *Voice and Communication Therapy for the Transgender/ Transsexual Client: A Comprehensive Clinical Guide* (2nd edition). San Diego, CA: Plural Publishing.

Agoramoorthy, G. and Hsu, M. (2014) Living on the societal edge: India's transgender realities. *Journal of Religion and Health*, 54(4): 1451–1469.

Ali, R. (2014) A trans-positive approach to therapy with transgender clients: an exploration of therapists' subjective experiences. *Electronic Thesis and Dissertation Repository*, 1979. The University of Western Ontario.

Alipour, M. (2016) Islamic shari'a law, neotradtionalist Muslim scholars and transgender sex reassignment surgery: a case study of Ayatollah Khomeini's and Sheikh al-Tantawi's fatwas. *International Journal of Transgenderism*, 17(1): 91–103.

Amato, P. (2018) *Fertility Options for Transgender Persons*. Center of Excellence for Transgender Health. Retrieved from: http://transhealth.ucsf.edu/trans?page=guidelines-fertility

American Psychiatric Association (2013) *Diagnostic and Statistical Manual of Mental Disorders* (5th ed.) Arlington, VA: American Psychiatric Publishing.

Andre, A.P. and Guitierrez, L. (2010) In Our Skin. In K. Bornstein and S.B. Bergman (eds) *Gender Outlaws: The Next Generation* (pp.157–162). Berkeley, CA: Seal Press.

Andrew, D.H. and Dulin, P.L. (2007) The relationship between self-reported health and mental health problems among older adults in New Zealand: experiential avoidance as a moderator. *Aging and Mental Health*, 11(5): 596–603.

Ansara, Y.G. (2010) Beyond Cisgenderism: Counselling People with Non-Assigned Gender Identities. In L. Moon (ed.) *Counselling Ideologies: Queer Challenges to Heteronormativity* (pp.167–200). Aldershot: Ashgate Publishing.

Ansara, Y.G. (2015) Challenging cisgenderism in the ageing and aged care sector: meeting the needs of older people of trans and/or non-binary experience. *Australasian Journal on Ageing*, 34(2): 14–18.

Arcelus, J., Claes, L., Witcomb, G.L., Marshall, E., and Bouman, W.P. (2016) Risk factors for non-suicidal self-injury among trans youth. *Journal of Sexual Medicine*, 13(3): 402–412.

Archer, J. (1991) The influence of testosterone on human aggression. *British Journal of Psychology*, 82(1):1–28.

Arthur, D.P. (2015) Social work practice with LGBT elders at end of life: developing practice evaluation and clinical skills through a cultural perspective. *Journal of Social Work at the End-of-Life and Palliative Care*, 11(2): 178–201.

Asmundson, G., Stapleton, J., and Taylor, S. (2005) Are avoidance and numbing distinct PTSD symptom clusters? *Journal of Traumatic Stress*, 17(6): 467–475.

Asscheman, J. and Gooren, L.J.G. (1992) Hormone treatment in transsexuals: interdisciplinary approaches in clinical management. *Journal of Psychology and Human Sexuality*, 5(4): 39–54.

Association for Lesbian, Gay, Bisexual, and Transgender Issues in Counseling (ALGBTIC) (2009) *ALGBTIC Competencies for Counseling Transgender Clients*. Alexandria, VA: Author.

Association for Lesbian, Gay, Bisexual, and Transgender Issues in Counseling (ALGBTIC) (2012) *ALGBTIC Competencies for Counseling LGBQIQA*. Alexandria, VA: Author.

Auldridge, A., Tamar-Mattis, A., Kennedy, S., Ames, E., and Tobin, H.J. (2012) *Improving the Lives of Transgender Older Adults: Recommendations for Policy and Practice*. Sage and NCTE. Retrieved from: https://transequality.org/sites/default/files/docs/resources/TransAgingPolicyReportFull.pdf

Aultman, B. (2014) Cisgender. *Transgender Studies Quarterly*, 1(102): 61–62.

Ayers, C., Petkus, A.J., Liu, L., Patterson, T.L., and Wetherell, J.L. (2010) Negative life events and avoidant coping are associated with poorer long-term outcome in older adults treated for generalized anxiety disorder. *Journal of Experimental Psychopathology*, 1:146–154.

Ballan, M.S., Romanelli, M., and Harper, J.N., IV (2011) The social model: a lens for counseling transgender individuals with disabilities. *Journal of Gay and Lesbian Mental Health*, 15(3): 260–280.

Bancroft, J. (2009) Transgender, Gender Non-Conformity and Transvestism. In *Human Sexuality and Its Problems* (3rd ed.). London: Churchhill Livingston, Elsevier.

Baral, S., Poteat, T., Strömdahl, S., Wirtz, A., Guadamuz, T., and Beyrer, C. (2013) Worldwide burden of HIV in transgender women: a systematic review and meta-analysis. *The Lancet: Infectious Diseases*, 13(3): 214–222.

Barford, V. (2008) Iran's "Diagnosed Transsexuals." British Broadcasting Corporation. Retrieved from: http://news.bbc.co.uk/2/hi/7259057.stm

Barnes, S.M., Smith, G.P., Monteith, L.L., Gerber, H.R., and Bahraini, N.H. (2017) ACT for Life: Using Acceptance and Commitment Therapy to Understand and Prevent Suicide. In U. Kumar (ed.) *Handbook of Suicidal Behaviour* (pp.485–504). Singapore: Springer.

Batten, S.V. and Hayes, S.C. (2005) Acceptance and Commitment Therapy in the treatment of comorbid substance abuse and post-traumatic stress disorder: a case study. *Clinical Case Studies*, 4(3): 246–262.

Bauer, G., Redman, N., Bradley, K., and Scheim, A. (2013) Sexual health of trans men who are gay, bisexual, or who have sex with men: results from Ontario, Canada. *International Journal of Transgenderism*, 14(2): 66–74.

Baumeister, R.F. (1990) Suicide as escape from self. *Psychological Review*, 97(1): 90–113.

Becatoros, E. (2008) Tradition of Sworn Virgins Dying out in Albania. *Die Welt*. Retrieved from: www.welt.de/english-news/article2536539/Tradition-of-sworn-virgins-dying-out-in-Albania.html

Beemyn, G. and Rankin, S. (2011) *The Lives of Transgender People*. New York, NY: Columbia University Press.

Belawski, S. and Sojka, C. (2014) Intimate Relationships. In L. Erickson-Schroth (ed.) *Trans Bodies, Trans Selves: A Resource for the Transgender Community* (pp.335–354). New York, NY: Oxford University Press.

Benard, B. and Slade, S. (2009) Listening to Students: Moving from Resilience Research to Youth Development Practice and School Connectedness. In R. Gilma, E.S. Huevner, and M.J. Furlong (eds) *Handbook of Positive Psychology in Schools* (pp.353–369). New York, NY: Routledge/Taylor and Francis.

Benotsch, E.G., Zimmerman, R., Cathers, L., McNulty, S., *et al.* (2013) Non-medical use of prescription drugs, polysubstance use, and mental health in transgender adults. *Drug and Alcohol Dependence*, 132(1–2): 391–394.

Benson, K. (2013) Seeking support: transgender client experiences with mental health services. *Journal of Feminist Family Therapy*, 25(1): 17–40.

Bettcher, T.M. (2007) Evil deceivers and make-believers: on transphobic violence and the politics of illusion. *Hypatia*, 22(3): 43–65.

Bess, J. and Staab, S. (2009) The experiences of transgendered persons in psychotherapy: voices and recommendations. *Journal of Mental Health Counseling*, 31(3): 264–282.

Bidell, M. (2012) Examining school counseling students' multicultural and sexual orientation competencies through a cross-specialization comparison. *Journal of Counseling and Development*, 90(2): 200–207.

Blackledge, J.T. (2015) *Cognitive Defusion in Practice: A Clinician's Guide to Assessing, Observing, and Supporting Change in Your Client*. Oakland, CA: Context Press.

Blackledge, J.T. and Hayes, S.C. (2001) Emotion regulation in Acceptance and Commitment Therapy. *JCLP/In Session: Psychotherapy in Practice*, 57(2): 243–255.

Blackless, M., Charuvastra, M., Derryck, A., Fausto-Sterling, A., Lauzanne, K., and Lee., E. (2000) How sexually dimorphic are we? Review and synthesis. *American Journal of Human Biology*, 12(2): 151–166.

Blanchard, R. and Collins P. (1993) Men with sexual interest in transvestites, transsexuals, and she males. *Journal of Nervous and Mental Disease*, 181(9): 570–575.

Blank, R. (2011) End-of-life decision making across cultures. *The Journal of Law, Medicine and Ethics*, 39(2): 201–214.

Bockting, W., Benner, A., and Coleman, E. (2009) Gay and bisexual identity development among female-to-male transsexuals in North America: emergence of a transgender sexuality. *Archives of Sexual Behavior*, 38(5): 688–701.

Bockting, W., Knudson, G., and Goldberg, J. (2006) Counseling and mental health care for transgender adults and loved ones. *International Journal of Transgenderism*, 9(3–4): 35–82.

Bockting, W., Robinson, B., Benner, A., and Scheltema, K. (2004) Patient satisfaction with transgender health services. *Journal of Sex and Marital Therapy*, 30: 277–294.

Bodarky, G. (2017) Cross-Dressing Academy Helps Put Men in Touch with "Femmeselves." National Public Radio, March 4, 2017. Retrieved from: www.npr.org/2017/03/04/516847731/cross-dressing-academy-helps-put-men-in-touch-with-femmeselves

Bogaert, A. (2015) Asexuality: what it is and why it matters. *The Journal of Sex Research*, 52(4): 362–379.

Bolich, D.G.G. (2007) *Conversing on Gender: A Primer for Entering Dialog* (Revised ed.). Raleigh, NC: Psyche's Press.

Bornstein, K. (2012) *A Queer and Pleasant Danger: A Memoir*. Boston, MA: Beacon Press.

Borschel-Dan, A. (2015) Why Jewish Communities Welcome 7-year-old Transgender Kids. *Times of Israel*, April 24. Retrieved from: www.timesofisrael.com/why-jewish-communities-welcome-7-year-old-transgender-kids

Boszormenyi-Nagy, I. (1987) *Foundations of Contextual Therapy: Collected Papers of Ivan Boszormenyi-Nagy, MD*. New York, NY: Brunner/Mazel.

Bouman, W.P., Claes, L., Marshall, E., Pinner, G., *et al.* (2016) Sociodemographic variables, clinical features, and the role of preassessment cross-sex hormones in older trans people. *The Journal of Sex Medicine*, 13(4): 711–719.

Bovasso, G. (1997) The interaction of depersonalization and deindividuation. *Journal of Social Distress and the Homeless*, 6(3): 213–228.

Bowen, M. (2004) *Family Therapy in Clinical Practice*. Oxford, UK: Rowman and Littlefield Publishers.

Bowman, C. and Goldberg, J. (2006) *Care of the Patient Undergoing Sex Reassignment Surgery (SRS)*. Vancouver Coastal Health, Transcend Transgender Support & Education Society, and the Canadian Rainbow Health Coalition. Retrieved from: www.amsa.org/wp-content/uploads/2015/04/CareOfThePatientUndergoingSRS.pdf

Boyd, H. (2003) *My Husband, Betty: Love, Sex and the Life of a Cross-Dresser*. New York, NY: Thunder's Mouth Press.

Bradlow, J., Bartram, F., Guasp, A., and Jadva, V. (2017) *School Report: The Experiences of Lesbian, Gay, Bi and Trans Young People in Britain's Schools in 2017*. Centre for Family Research, University of Cambridge and Stonewall. Retrieved from: www.stonewall.org.uk/sites/default/files/the_school_report_2017.pdf

Brett, M.A., Roberts L.F., and Johnson T.W. (2007) Eunuchs in contemporary society: expectations, consequences, and adjustments to castration (Part II). *Journal of Sexual Medicine*, 4(4): 946–955.

Bridger, S. Bradlow, J., Gusap, A., and Jadva, V. (2017) *School Report Scotland: The Experiences of Lesbian, Gay, Bi and Trans Young People in Scotland's Schools in 2017*. Centre for Family Research, University of Cambridge and Stonewall. Retrieved from: www.stonewallscotland.org.uk/system/files/school_report_scotland_2017.pdf

Briere, J. (2006) Dissociative symptoms and trauma exposure: specificity, affect dysregulation, and posttraumatic stress. *Journal of Nervous and Mental Disease*, 194(2): 78–82.

Brill, S. and Kenney, L. (2016) *The Transgender Teen: A Handbook for Parents and Professionals Supporting Transgender and Non-Binary Teens*. Jersey City, NJ: Cleis Press.

Bronfenbrenner, U. (2005) *Making Human Beings Human: Bioecological Perspectives on Human Development*. Thousand Oaks, CA: Sage Publications.

Brown, B. (2012) *Daring Greatly: How the Courage to Be Vulnerable Transforms the Way We Live, Love, Parent and Lead*. New York, NY: Avery.

Brown, D. (2007) Career Information, Career Counseling, and Career Development (9th ed.). Boston, MA: Pearson Allyn & Bacon.

Brown, G.R. (2001) Sex Reassignment Surgery in a Patient with Gender Identity Disorder and Dissociative Identity Disorders: Report of a Successful Case. Paper presented at 17th Biennial Symposium of the Harry Benjamin Gender Dysphoria Association, Galveston, TX.

Brown, J. (2008) We don't need your help, but will you please fix our children? *Australian and New Zealand Journal of Family Therapy*, 29(2): 61–69.

Brown, N. (2010) The sexual relationships of sexual-minority women partnered with trans men: a qualitative study. *Archives of Sexual Behavior*, 39(2): 561–572.

Brown, R.J. (2013) Dissociation and Somatoform Disorders. In F. Kennedy, H. Kennerley, and D. Pearson (eds) *Cognitive Behavioral Approaches to Understanding and Treatment of Dissociation* (pp.133–147). New York, NY: Routledge.

Budge, S., Adelson, J., and Howard, K. (2013) Anxiety and depression in transgender individuals: the roles of transition status, loss, social support, and coping. *Journal of Consulting and Clinical Psychology*, 81(3): 545–557.

Budge, S., Rossman, H., and Howard, K. (2014) Coping and psychological distress among genderqueer individuals: the moderating effect of social support. *Journal of LGBT Issues in Counseling*, 8(1): 95–117.

Budge, S.L., Tebbe, E.N., and Howard, K.A.S. (2010) The work experiences of transgender individuals: negotiating the transition and career decision-making processes. *Journal of Counseling Psychology*, 57(4): 377–393.

Bullough, B. and Bullough, V.L. (1997) Are transvestites necessarily heterosexual? *Archives of Sexual Behavior*, 26(1): 1–12.

Burdge, B. J. (2007) Bending gender, ending gender: Theoretical foundations for social work practice with the transgender community. *Social Work*, 52(3): 243–250.

Butler, J. (1990) *Gender Trouble: Feminism and the Subversion of Identity*. New York, NY: Routledge Press.

Butler, J. (1993) *Bodies That Matter: On the Discursive Limits of Sex*. New York: Routledge Press.

Carew, L., Dacakis, G., and Oates, J. (2007) The effectiveness of oral resonance therapy on the perception of femininity of voice in male-to-female transsexuals. *Journal of Voice*, 21(5): 591–603.

Carroll, L., Gilroy, P.J., and Ryan, J. (2002) Counseling trangendered, transsexual, and gender-variant clients. *Journal of Counseling and Development*, 80(2), 131–138.

Carter, B., McGoldrick, M. (2005) *The Expanded Family Life Cycle: Individual, Family, and Social Perspectives, Third Edition*. Boston, MA: Allyn & Bacon.

Case, L.K., Ramachandran, V.S. (2012) Alternating gender incongruity: A new neuropsychiatric syndrome providing insight into the dynamic plasticity of brain-sex. *Medical Hypotheses*, 78(5): 626–31.

Catalano, D.C.J. (2014) Welcome to Guyland: Experiences of Trans* Men in College. *Doctoral Dissertations*, 60. Retreived from:https://scholarworks.umass.edu/dissertations_2/60

Chang, T. and Chung, Y. (2015) Transgender Microaggressions: Complexity of the Heterogeneity of Transgender Identities. *Journal of LGBT Issues in Counseling*, 9(3): 217–234.

Chapman, A.L., Gratz, K.L., Brown, M.Z. (2006) Solving the puzzle of deliberate self harm: The Experiential Avoidance Model. *Behavior Research and Therapy*, 44(3): 371–394.

Chauncey G. (1994) *Gay New York: Gender, Urban Culture, and the Making of the Gay Male World, 1890–1940*. New York, NY: Basic Books.

Chavez-Korell, S. and Johnson, L. (2010) Informing counselor training and competent counseling services through transgender narratives and the transgender community. *Journal of LGBT Issues in Counseling*, 4(3–4): 202–213.

Chavez-Korell, S. and Lorah, P. (2007) An Overview of Affirmative Psychotherapy and Counseling with Transgender Clients. In K.J. Bieschke, R.M. Perez, and K.A. DeBord (eds) *Handbook of Counseling and Psychotherapy with Lesbian, Gay, Bisexual, and Transgender Clients* (2nd ed.) (pp.271–288). Washington, DC: American Psychological Association.

Chiles, J.A. and Strosahl, K.D. (2005) *Clinical Manual for Assessment and Treatment of Suicidal Patients*. Arlington, VA: American Psychiatric Publishing.

Chung, Y.B. (2003) Career counseling with lesbian, gay, bisexual and transgendered persons: the next decade. *Career Development Quarterly*, 52(1): 78–86.

Clark, C.J. (2016) *Voice and Communication Therapy for the Transgender or Transsexual Client: Service Delivery and Treatment Options*. Graduate Independent Studies - Communication Sciences and Disorders. 2. Illinois State University.

Clegg, C. (2014) Japan Slowly Begins to Openly Discuss Crossdressing Men in Heterosexual Relationships. *SoraNews24*. Retrieved from: https://soranews24.com/2014/06/08/japan-begins-to-more-openly-discuss-crossdressing-men-in-heterosexual-relationships

Clements-Nolle, K., Marx, R., Guzman, R., and Katz, M. (2001) HIV prevalence, risk behaviors, health care use, and mental health status of transgender persons: implications for public health intervention. *American Journal of Public Health*, 91(6): 915–921.

Clements-Nolle, K., Marx, R., and Katz, M. (2006) Attempted suicide among transgender persons: the influence of gender-based discrimination and victimization. *Journal of Homosexuality*, 51: 53–69.

Cochran, B. and Cauce, A. (2006) Characteristics of lesbian, gay, bisexual and transgender individuals entering substance abuse treatment. *Journal of Substance Abuse Treatment*, 30(2): 135–146.

Cohen-Kettenis, P. and Pfäfflin, F. (2003) *Transgenderism and Intersexuality in Childhood and Adolescence: Making Choices*. Thousand Oaks, CA: Sage Publications.

Coleman, E., Colgan, P., and Gooren, L. (1992) Male cross-gender behavior in Myanmar (Burma): a description of the acault. *Archives of Sexual Behavior*, 21(3): 313–321.

Colizzi, M., Costa, R., Pace, V., and Todarello O. (2013) Hormonal treatment reduces psychobiological distress in gender identity disorder, independently of the attachment style. *Journal of Sexual Medicine*, 10(12): 3049–3058.

Colizzi, M., Costa, R., and Todarello, O. (2014) Transsexual patients' psychiatric comorbidity and positive effect of cross-sex hormonal treatment on mental health: results from a longitudinal study. *Psychoneuroendocrinology*, 39: 65–73.

Colizzi, M., Costa, R., and Todarello, O. (2015) Dissociative symptoms in individuals with gender dysphoria: is the elevated prevalence real? *Psychiatry Research*, 226(1): 173–190.

Conron, K.J., Scott, G., Stowell, G.S., and Landers, S.J. (2012) Transgender health in Massachusetts: results from a household probability sample of adults. *American Journal of Public Health*, 102(1): 118–122.

Cook-Daniels, L. (2006) Trans Aging. In D. Kimmel, T. Rose and S. David (eds) *Lesbian, Gay, Bisexual, and Transgender Aging (20–35)*. New York, NY: Columbia University Press.

Cook-Daniels, L. (2008) *Sexual Violence, Elder Abuse, and Sexuality of Transgender Adults Age 50+: Results of Three Surveys. FORGE*. Retrieved from: http://forge-forward.org/2008/03/trans-aging-3-surveys

Corliss, H.L., Belzer, M., Forbes, C., and Wilson, E.C. (2007) An evaluation of service utilization among male to female transgender youth: qualitative study of a clinic-based sample. *Journal of LGBT Health Research*, 3(2): 49–61.

Corsini, R.J. (2002) *The Dictionary of Psychology*. Philadelphia: Brunner-Routledge.

Costa, R. and Colizzi, M. (2016) The effect of cross-sex hormonal treatment on gender dysphoria individuals' mental health: a systematic review. *Neuropsychiatric Disease and Treatment*, 12: 1953–1966.

Curtin, A., Ryu, D., and Diamond, L. (2016) Coming out with Compassion. In M. Skinta and A. Curtin (eds) *Mindfulness and Acceptance for Gender and Sexual Minorities* (pp.50– 68). Oakland, CA: Context Press.

Daar, J., Amato, P., Benward, J., Collins, L.R., *et al.* (2015) Access to fertility services by transgender persons: an Ethics Committee opinion. Ethics Committee of the American Society for Reproductive Medicine. *Fertility and Sterility*, 104(5): 1111–1115.

Dacakis, G., Oates, J., and Douglas, J.M. (2012) Beyond voice: perceptions of gender in male-to-female transsexuals. *Current Opinion in Otolaryngology and Head and Neck Surgery*, 20(3): 165–170.

Dagleish, T. and Yiend, J. (2006) The effects of suppressing a negative autobiographical memory on concurrent intrusions and subsequent autobiographical recall in dysphoria. *Journal of Abnormal Psychology*, 115: 467–473.

Dalton, A. (2010) A Drag Queen Born in a Female Body. In K. Bornstein and S.B. Bergman (eds) *Gender Outlaws: The Next Generation* (pp.93–97). Berkeley, CA: Seal Press.

Daskalos, C.T. (1998) Changes in sexual orientation of six heterosexual male-to-female transsexuals. *Archives of Sexual Behavior*, 27(6): 605–614.

Davies, S. and Goldberg, J. (2006) Clinical aspects of transgender speech feminization and masculinization. *International Journal of Transgenderism*, 9(3–4): 167–196.

Davies, S.G. (2007) *Challenging Gender Norms: Five Genders among the Bugis in Indonesia*. Belmont, CA: Wadsworth Cengage Learning.

De Cuypere, G., T'Sjoen, G., Beerten, R., Selvaggi, G., *et al.* (2005) Sexual and physical health after sex reassignment surgery. *Archives of Sexual Behavior*, 34(6): 679–690.

Denticel, D. and Dietert, M. (2015) Liminal spaces and the transgender experience. *Theory in Action*, 8(2): 69–96.

Devlin, J.T., Matthews, P.M., and Rushworth, M.F. (2003) Semantic processing in the left inferior prefrontal cortex: a combined functional magnetic resonance imaging and transcranial magnetic stimulation study. *Journal of Cognitive Neuroscience*, 15(1): 71–84.

Devor, A. (2004) Witnessing and mirroring: a fourteen stage model of transsexual identity formation. *Journal of Gay and Lesbian Psychotherapy*, 8(1–2): 41–67.

Devor, H. (1989) *Gender Blending: Confronting the Limits of Duality*. Bloomington, IN: Indiana University Press.

Devor, H. (1993) Sexual orientation identities, attractions, and practices of female-to-male transsexuals. *The Journal of Sex Research*, 30(4): 303–315.

Devor, H. (1997) *FTM: Female-to-Male Transsexuals in Society*. Bloomington, IN: Indian University Press.

Devor, H. (2002) Who are "we"? Where sexual orientation meets gender identity. *Journal of Gay and Lesbian Psychotherapy*, 6(2): 5–21.

Dhejne, C., Oberg, K., Arver, S., and Landén, M. (2014) An analysis of all applications for sex reassignment surgery in Sweden, 1960–2010: prevalence, incidence, and regrets. *Archives of Sexual Behavior*, 43(8): 1535–1545.

Diamond, L. (2005) A new view of lesbian subtypes: stable versus fluid identity trajectories over an 8-year period. *Psychology of Women Quarterly*, 29(2): 119–128.

Diamond, M. (2002) Sex and gender are different: sexual identity and gender identity are different. *Clinical Child Psychology and Psychiatry*, 7(3): 320–334.

Diamond, M. (2010) Sexual Orientation and Gender Identity. In I.B. Weiner and W.E. Craighead (eds) *The Corsini Encyclopedia of Psychology* (4th ed.) (pp.1578–1579). Hoboken, NJ: John Wiley and Sons.

Diamond, M. and Sigmundson, H.K. (1997) Management of intersexuality: guidelines for dealing with persons with ambiguous genitalia. *Archives of Pediatrics and Adolescent Medicine*, 151(10): 1046–1050.

Dispenza, F., Watson, L.B., Chung, Y.B., and Brack, G. (2012) Experience of career-related discrimination for female-to-male transgender persons: a qualitative study. *The Career Development Quarterly*, 60(1): 65–81.

Docter, R. and Fleming, J. (2001) Measures of transgender behavior. *Archives of Sexual Behavior*, 30(3): 255–271.

Docter, R. and Prince, V. (1997) Transvestism: a survey of 1032 cross-dressers. *Archives of Sexual Behavior*, 26(6): 589–605.

Doka, K.J. (ed.) (2002) *Disenfranchised Grief: New Directions, Challenges, and Strategies for Practice*. Champaign, IL: Research Press.

Dreger, A.D. (2000) *Hermaphrodites and the Medical Invention of Sex*. Cambridge, MA.: Harvard University Press.

Dronkers, N.F., Plaisant, O., Iba-Zizen, M.T., and Cabanis, E.A. (2007) Paul Broca's historic cases: high resolution MR imaging of the brains of Leborgne and Lelong. *Brain*, 130(5): 1432–1441.

Drummond, K.D., Bradley, S.J., Peterson-Badali, M., and Zucker, K.J. (2008) A follow-up study of girls with gender identity disorder. *Developmental Psychology*, 44(1): 34–45.

Dugen, J.P., Kusel, M.L., and Simounet, D.M. (2012) Transgender college students: an exploratory study of perceptions, engagement and educational outcomes. *Journal of Student Development*, 53(5): 719–736.

Eifert, G.H. and Forsyth, J.P. (2005) *Acceptance and Commitment Therapy for Anxiety Disorders: A Practitioner's Treatment Guide to Using Mindfulness, Acceptance and Values-Based Behavior Change Strategies*. Oakland, CA: New Harbinger Publications.

Ekins, R. and King, D. (1998) Blending Genders: Contributions to the Emerging Field of Transgender Studies. In D. Denny (ed.) *Current Concepts in Transgender Identity* (pp.97–115). New York, NY: Garland.

Ekins, R. and King, D. (1999) Towards a sociology of transgendered bodies. *Sociological Review*, 47(3): 580–602.

Eligon, J. (2017) Transgender African-Americans' Open Wound: "We're Considered a Joke." *New York Times*. Retrieved from: www.nytimes.com/2017/08/06/us/black-transgender-lil-duval.html

Engelhard, I. and Arntz, A. (2005) The fallacy of ex-consequentia reasoning and the persistence of PTSD. *Journal of Behavior Therapy and Experimental Psychiatry*, 36(1): 35–42.

Enke, A.F. (2013) The Education of Little Cis: Cisgender and the Discipline of Opposing Bodies. In S. Stryker and A.Z. Aizura (eds) *The Transgender Studies Reader* (pp.234–247). New York, NY: Routledge.

Erikson, E.H. (1950) *Childhood and Society*. New York, NY: W.W. Norton.

Ettner, R. (1999) *Gender Loving Care: A Guide to Counseling Gender-Variant Clients*. New York, NY: W.W. Norton.

Fabbre, V.D. (2014) Gender transitions in later life: the significance of time in queer aging. *Journal of Gerontological Social Work*, 57(2–4): 161–175.

Fabbre, V.D. (2015) Gender transitions in later life: a queer perspective on successful aging. *The Gerontologist*, 55(1): 144–153.

Fassinger, R. and Arseneau, J. (2007) "I'd Rather Get Wet Than Be under That Umbrella": Differentiating the Experiences and Identities of Lesbian, Gay, Bisexual, and Transgender People. In K.J. Bieschke, R.M. Perez, and K.A. DeBord (eds) *Handbook of Counseling and Psychotherapy with Lesbian, Gay, Bisexual, and Transgender Clients* (pp.19–49). Washington, DC: American Psychological Association.

Feeny, N., Zoellner, L., Fitzgibbons, L., and Foa, E. (2005) Exploring the roles of emotional numbing, depression, and dissociation in PTSD. *Journal of Traumatic Stress*, 13(3): 489–498.

Feinberg, L. (2001) Trans health crisis: for us it's life or death. *American Journal of Public Health*, 91(6): 897–900.

Feldman, J. and Safer, J. (2009) Hormone therapy in adults: suggested revisions to the sixth version of the Standards of Care. *International Journal of Transgenderism*, 11(3): 146–182.

Fewtrell, W.D. (1986) Depersonalisation: a description and suggested strategies. *British Journal of Guidance and Counselling*, 14: 263–269.

Fink, M. and Taylor, M. (2003) *Catatonia: A Clinician's Guide to Diagnosis and Treatment*. New York, NY: Cambridge University Press.

Finkenauer, S., Sherratt, J., Marlow, J., and Brodey, A. (2012) When injustice gets old: a systematic review of trans aging. *Journal of Gay and Lesbian Social Services*, 24(4): 311–330.

Finn, M. and Dell, P. (1999) Practices of body management: transgenderism and embodiment. *Journal of Community and Applied Social Psychology*, 9(6): 463–476.

Flentje, A., Heck, N., and Sorensen, J. (2014) Characteristics of transgender individuals entering substance abuse treatment. *Addictive Behavior*, 39(5): 969–975.

Flores, A.R., Brown, T.N.T., and Herman, J.L. (2016a) *Race and Ethnicity of Adults Who Identify as Transgender in the United States*. Los Angeles, CA: Williams Institute.

Flores, A.R., Brown, T.N.T., and Park, A.S. (2016b) *Public Support for Transgender Rights: A Twenty-Three Country Survey*. Los Angeles, CA: Williams Institute.

Flores, A.R., Herman, J.L., Gates, G.J., and Brown, T.N.T. (2016c) *How Many Adults Identify as Transgender in the United States?* Los Angeles, CA: Williams Institute.

Forsyth, J.P. and Eifert, G.H. (2016) *The Mindfulness and Acceptance Workbook for Anxiety* (2nd ed.) Oakland, CA: New Harbinger Publications.

Frank, D. and Cannon, E. (2010) Queer theory as pedagogy in counsellor education: a framework for diversity training. *Journal of LGBT Issues in Counseling*, 4(1): 18–31.

Frankl, V. (1946) *Man's Search for Meaning*. Boston, MA: Beacon Press.

Fredriksen-Goldsen, K.I., Cook-Daniels, L., Kim, H., Erosheva, E.A., *et al.* (2013) Physical and mental health of transgender older adults: an at-risk and underserved population. *The Gerontologist*, 54(3), 488–500.

Frost, D.M. and Meyer, I.H. (2012) Measuring community connectedness among diverse sexual minority populations. *The Journal of Sex Research* 49(1): 36–49.

Gainor, K.A. (2000) Including Transgender Issues in Lesbian, Gay, and Bisexual Psychology: Implications for Clinical Practice and Training. In B. Greene and G.L. Croom (eds), *Education, Research, and Practice in Lesbian, Gay, Bisexual and Transgendered Psychology: A Resource Manual* (pp.131–160). Thousand Oaks, CA: Sage.

Gallese, V., Eagle, M.N., and Migone, P. (2007) Intentional attunement: mirror neurons and the neural underpinning of interpersonal relations. *Journal of the American Psychoanalytic Association*, 55(1): 131–175.

Gamson, J. (2000) Sexualities, Queer Theory, and Qualitative Research. In N. Denzin and Y. Lincoln (eds) *Handbook of Qualitative Research* (2nd ed.) (pp.347–365). London: Sage.

Garofalo, R., Deleon, J., Osmer, E., Doll, M., and Harper, G. (2006) Overlooked, misunderstood, and at-risk: exploring the lives and HIV risk of ethnic minority male-to-female transgender youth. *Journal of Adolescent Health*, 38(3): 230–236.

Gendlin, E.T. (1962) *Experiencing and the Creation of Meaning*. London: Collier-Macmillan.

Giambra, L. (1980) A factor analysis of the items of the imaginal processes inventory. *Journal of Clinical Psychology*, 36(2): 383–409.

Giambra, L. (1989) Task-unrelated thought frequency as a function of age: a laboratory study. *Psychology and Aging*, 4(2) 136–143.

Giambra, L. (1995) A laboratory method for investigating influences on switching attention to task-unrelated imagery and thought. *Consciousness and Cognition*, 4(1): 1–21.

Gijs, L. and Brewaeys, A. (2007) Surgical treatment of gender dysphoria in adults and adolescents: recent developments, effectiveness, and challenges. *Annual Review of Sex Research*, 18(1): 178–224.

GLAAD (2012) *Victims or Villains: Examining Ten Years of Transgender Images on Television. GLAAD.* Retrieved from: www.glaad.org/publications/victims-or-villains-examining-ten-years-transgender-images-television

Glavinic, T. (2010) Student voices blog research shows lack of support for transgender and gender nonconforming youth in US school systems. *Inquiries Journal: Social Sciences, Arts, and Humanities*, 2(1): 1–2.

Goethals, S. and Schwiebert, V. (2005) Counseling as a critique of gender: on the ethics of counseling transgendered clients. *International Journal for the Advancement of Counselling*, 27(3): 457–469.

Gold, D.B. and Wegner, D.M. (1995) The origins of ruminative thought: trauma, incompleteness, nondisclosure, and suppression. *Journal of Applied Social Psychology*, 25(14): 1245–1261.

Gómez-Gil, E., Zubiaurre-Elorza, L., Esteva, I., Guillamon, A., *et al.* (2012) Hormone-treated transsexuals report less social distress, anxiety and depression. *Psychoneuroendocrinology*, 37(5): 662–670.

Goodmark, L. (2013) Transgender people, intimate partner abuse, and the legal system. *Harvard Civil Rights–Civil Liberties Law Review*, 48(1): 51–104.

Gorenberg, H. (2011) *Health and Medical Organization Statement on Sexual Orientation, Gender Identity/Expression and "Reparative Therapy."* LAMBDA Legal. Retrieved from: www.lambdalegal.org/publications/health-and-med-orgs-stmts-on-sex-orientation-and-gender-identity

Gorin-Lazard, A., Baumstarck, K., Boyer, L., Maquigneau, A., *et al.* (2013) Hormonal therapy is associated with better self-esteem, mood, and quality of life in transsexuals. *The Journal of Nervous and Mental Disease*, 201(11): 996–1000.

Gottman, J.M. (2011) *The Science of Trust: Emotional Attunement for Couples.* New York, NY: Norton.

Gottman, J.M. (2015) *Principia Amoris: The New Science of Love.* New York, NY: Routledge.

Gottman, J.M. and Silver, N. (2015) *The Seven Principles for Making Marriage Work* (Revised ed.). New York, NY: Harmony.

Grant, J.M., Mottet, L.A., Tanis, J., Harrison, J., Herman, J.L., and Keisling, M. (2011) *Injustice at Every Turn: A Report of the National Transgender Discrimination Survey.* Washington: National Center for Transgender Equality and National Gay and Lesbian Task Force.

Green, J. (2012) *Becoming a Visible Man.* Nashville, TN: Vanderbilt University Press.

Green, R. (1987) *The "Sissy Boy Syndrome" and the Development of Homosexuality.* New Haven, CT: Yale University Press.

Gressgård, R. (2013) Asexuality: from pathology to identity and beyond. *Psychology and Sexuality*, 4(2): 179–192.

Greytak, E.A., Kosciw, J., and Boesen, M. (2013) Putting the "T" in "resource": the benefits of LGBT related school resources for transgender youth. *Journal of LGBT Youth*, 10(1–2): 45–63.

Greytak, E.A., Kosciw, J., and Diaz, E.M. (2009) *Harsh Realities: The Experiences of Transgender Youth in our Nation's Schools.* New York, NY: GLSEN.

Gross, J.J. (2002) Emotion regulation: affective, cognitive, and social consequences. *Psychophysiology*, 39, 281–291.

Grossman, A. and D'Augelli, A. (2006) Transgender youth: invisible and vulnerable. *Journal of Homosexuality*, 51(1): 111–128.

Grossman, A., D'Augelli, A., Howell, J., and Hubbard, S. (2005) Parents' reactions to transgender youths' gender nonconforming expression and identity. *Journal of Gay and Lesbian Social Services*, 18(1): 3–16.

Grossman, A., D'Augelli, A., and Salter, N. (2006) Male-to-female transgender youth gender expression milestones, gender atypicality, victimization, and parents' response. *Journal of GLBT Family Studies*, 2(1): 71–92.

Guadamuz, T.E., Wimonsate, W., Varangrat, A., Phanuphak, P., *et al.* (2011) HIV prevalence, risk behavior, hormone use and surgical history among transgender persons in Thailand. *AIDS and Behavior*, 15(3): 650–658.

Haas, A.P., Rodgers, P.L., and Herman, J.L. (2014) *Suicide Attempts among Transgender and Gender Non-Conforming Adults: Findings of the National Transgender Discrimination Survey.* American Foundation for Suicide Prevention and The Williams Insitute. Retrieved from: https://williamsinstitute.law.ucla.edu/wp-content/uploads/AFSP-Williams-Suicide-Report-Final.pdf

Hage, J., Bout, C., Bloem, J., and Megens, J. (1993) Phalloplasty in female-to-male transsexuals: what do our patients ask for? *Annals of Plastic Surgery*, 30(4): 323–326.

Halberstam, J. (1998) Transgender butch: butch/FTM border wars and the masculine continuum. *GLQ: The Journal of Lesbian and Gay Studies*, 4(2): 287–310.

Halberstam, J. (2005) *In a Queer Time and Place: Transgender Bodies, Subcultural Lives.* New York, NY: New York University Press.

Halberstam, J. (2011) *The Queer Art of Failure.* Durham, NC: Duke University Press.

Hale, J. (2007) Ethical problems with the mental health evaluation standards of care for adult gender variant prospective patients. *Perspectives in Biology and Medicine*, 50(4): 491–505.

Hancock, A. and Garabedian, L. (2013) Transgender voice and communication treatment: a retrospective chart review of 25 cases. *International Journal of Language and Communication Disorders*, 48(1): 54–65.

Hanssmann, C., Morrison, D., and Russian, E. (2008) Talking, gawking, or getting it done: provider trainings to increase cultural and clinical competence for transgender and gender-nonconforming patients and clients. *Sexuality Research and Social Policy*, 5(1): 5–23.

Hare-Mustin, R.T. (1978) A feminist approach to family therapy. *Family Process*, 17(2): 181–194.

Harima, K. and Ishimaru, K. (2010) Gender identity disorder and suicide. *Journal of Psychiatric Treatment*, 25(2): 247–251.

Harmon, A. (2012) Eight Months in Solitary: Is a Government Turf War over Immigration Putting Transgender Lives at Risk? *Advocate*, May 7. Retrieved from: www.advocate.com/news/news-features/2012/05/07/transgender-detainees-face-challenges-broken-immigration-system

Harris, R. (2008) *The Happiness Trap: How to Stop Struggling and Start Living*. Boulder, CO: Trumpeter Books.

Harris, R. (2009a) *ACT Made Simple*. Oakland, CA: New Harbinger Publications.

Harris, R. (2009b) *ACT with Love*. Oakland, CA: New Harbinger Publications.

Harris, R. (2016) *Working with Dissociation*. Retrieved from: www.actmindfully.com.au/upimages/Working_With_Dissociation_-_Russ_Harris_-_www.ImLearningACT.com.pdf

Harrison, J., Grant, J., and Herman, J. (2012) A gender not listed here: genderqueers, gender rebels and otherwise in the National Transgender Discrimination Survey. *LGBTQ Policy Journal at the Harvard Kennedy School*, 2: 13–24.

Hartling, L. (2008) Strengthening resilience in a risky world: it's all about relationships. *Women in Therapy*, 3(2): 51–70.

Hayes, S.C. (2004) Acceptance and Commitment Therapy and the New Behavior Therapies: Mindfulness, Acceptance and Relationship. In S.C. Hayes, V.M., Follette and M.M. Linehan (eds) *Mindfulness and Acceptance: Expanding the Cognitive-Behavioral Tradition* (pp.1–29). New York, NY: Guilford Press.

Hayes, S.C., Luoma, J., Bond, F., Masuda, A., and Lillis, J. (2006) Acceptance and Commitment Therapy: model, processes and outcomes. *Behavior Research and Therapy*, 44(1): 1–25.

Hayes, S.C., Pistorello, J., and Biglan, A. (2008) Acceptance and commitment: implications for prevention science. *Prevention Science*, 9(3):139–152.

Hayes, S.C. and Smith, S. (2005) *Get Out of Your Mind and Into Your Life: The New Acceptance and Commitment Therapy*. Oakland, CA: New Harbinger Publications.

Hayes, S.C., Strosahl, K.D., and Wilson, K.G. (1999) *Acceptance and Commitment Therapy: An Experiential Approach to Behavior Change*. New York, NY: Guilford Press.

Hayes, S.C., Strosahl, K.D., and Wilson, K.G. (2012) *Acceptance and Commitment Therapy: The Process and Practice of Mindful Change* (2nd ed.). New York, NY: Guilford Press.

HBIGDA (2001) *The Harry Benjamin International Gender Dysphoria Association's (HBIGDA) Standards of Care for World Professional Association for Gender Identity Disorders* (6th version). Retrieved from: www.cpath.ca/wp-content/uploads/2009/12/WPATHsocv6.pdf

He, L. (2016) Latin America: The Most Deadly Region for Transgender Communities. *Equal Times*. Retrieved from: www.equaltimes.org/latin-america-the-most-deadly?lang=en#.W43MNehKiUk

Hendricks, M. and Testa, R. (2012) A conceptual framework for clinical work with transgender and gender nonconforming clients: an adaptation of the Minority Stress Model. *Professional Psychology Research and Practice*, 43(5): 460–467.

Herbst, J.H., Jacobs, E.D., Finlayson, T.J., McKleroy, V.S., Neumann, M.S., and Crepaz, N. (HIV/AIDS Prevention Research Synthesis Team) (2008) Estimating HIV prevalence and risk behaviors of transgender persons in the United States: A systematic review. *AIDS and Behavior* 12(1): 1–17.

Hill-Meyer, T. and Scarborough, D. (2014) Sexuality. In L. Erickson-Schroth (ed.) *Trans Bodies, Trans Selves: A Resource for the Transgender Community*, (pp.335–354). New York, NY: Oxford University Press.

Hines, S. (2006) Intimate transitions: Transgender practices of partnering and parenting. *Sociology*, 40(2): 353–371.

Hird, M.J. (2002) For a sociology of transsexualism. *Sociology*, 36(3): 577–595.

Hoare, P.N., McIlveen, P., and Hamilton, N. (2012) Acceptance and Commitment Therapy (ACT) as a Career Counseling Strategy. *International Journal for Educational and Vocational Guidance*, 12(3): 171–187.

Hoffkling, A., Obedin-Maliver, J., and Sevelius, J. (2017) From erasure to opportunity: a qualitative study of the experiences of transgender men around pregnancy and recommendations for providers. *BMC Pregnancy and Childbirth*, 17(2): 332.

Holdsworth, N. (2013) Boys don't dance, do they? *Research in Drama Education: The Journal of Applied Theatre and Performance*, 18(2): 168–178.

Hooker, E. (1965) Male Homosexuals and Their Worlds. In J. Marmor (ed.) *Sexual Inversion: The Multiple Roots of Homosexuality* (pp.83–107). New York, NY: Basic Books.

Huba, G., Aneshensel, C., and Singer, J. (1981) Development of scales for three second-order factors of inner experience. *Multivariate Behavioral Research*, 16(2): 181–206.

Huba, G. and Tanaka, J. (1983) Confirmatory evidence for three daydreaming factors in the Short Imaginal Processes Inventory. *Imagination, Cognition, and Personality*, 3(2): 139–147.

Hughto, J.M.W. and Reisner, S.L. (2016) Social context of depressive distress in aging transgender adults. *Journal of Applied Gerontology*, 37(12): 1517–1539.

Human Rights Campaign (HRC) (2018) *2018 US LGBTQ Paid Leave Survey: Report on the Experiences of Transgender and Non-Binary Respondents.* Retrieved from: www.hrc.org/resources/2018-us-lgbtq-paid-leave-survey-report-on-the-experiences-of-transgender

Iantaffi, A. and Bockting, W.O. (2011) Views from both sides of the bridge? Gender, sexual legitimacy and transgender people's experiences of relationships. *Culture, Health, and Sexuality*, 13(3): 355–370.

Inness, S.A. (1997) *The Lesbian Menace: Ideology, Identity, and the Representation of Lesbian Life.* Amherst, MA: University of Massachusetts Press.

International Society for the Study of Trauma and Dissociation (ISSD) (2011). Guidelines for treating dissociative identity disorder in adults (3rd revision). *Journal of Trauma and Dissociation*, 12: 115–187.

Israel, G. and Tarver II.D. (1997) *Transgender Care: Recommended Guidelines, Practical Information and Personal Accounts* (1st ed., pp.3–55) Philadelphia, PA: Temple University Press.

Jacobson, E. (1959) Depersonalization. *Journal of the American Psychoanalytic Association*, 7: 581–610.

James, S.E., Herman, J.L., Rankin, S., Keisling, M., Mottet, L., and Anafi, M. (2016) *The Report of the 2015 US Transgender Survey.* Washington, DC: National Center for Transgender Equality (NCTE).

Jampole E., Konopak B., Readance J., and Moser, J. (1991) Using mental imagery to enhance gifted elementary students' creative writing. *Reading Psychology*, 12(3): 183–197.

Jampole, E., Mathews, F., and Konopak, B. (1994) Academically gifted students' use of imagery for creative writing. *Journal of Creative Behavior*, 28(1): 1–15.

Joel, D., Tarrasch, R., Berman, Z., Mukamei, M., and Ziv, E. (2014) Queering gender: studying gender identity in "normative" individuals. *Psychology and Sexuality*, 5(4): 291–321.

Johnson, J. (2013) Cisgender privilege, intersectionality, and the criminalization of CeCeMcDonald: why intercultural communication needs transgender studies. *Journal of International and Intercultural Communication*, 6(2): 135–144.

Johnson, T. and Irwig, M., (2014) The hidden world of self-castration and testicular self-injury. *Nature Reviews Urology*, 11(5): 297–300.

Johnson, T.W., Brett, M.A., Roberts, L.F., and Wassersug, R.J. (2007) Eunuchs in contemporary society: characterizing men who are voluntarily castrated (Pt. I). *Journal of Sexual Medicine*, 4(4, Pt 1): 930–945.

Jordan, J. (1991) Empathy and Self Boundaries. In J. Jordan, A. Kaplan, J. Miller, I. Stiver, and J. Surrey (eds) *Women's Growth in Connection.* New York, NY: Guilford Press.

Jorgensen, C. (1968) *Christine Jorgensen: A Personal Autobiography.* Bantam: 1st Printing edition.

Joslin-Roher, E. and Wheeler, D.P. (2009) Partners in transition: the transition experience of lesbian, bisexual, and queer identified partners of transgender men. *Journal of Gay and Lesbian Social Services*, 21(1): 20–48.

JTA (2017) Reconstructionist Rabbis Affirm Full Inclusion of Transgender, Gender-Fluid Jews. *Jewish Telegraphic Agency.* Retrieved from: www.jta.org/2017/03/29/news-opinion/united-states/reconstructionist-rabbis-affirm-full-inclusion-of-transgender-gender-fluid-jews

Kaeble, D. and Glaze, L. (2016) *Correctional Populations in the United States, 2015.* Bureau of Justice Statistics. Retrieved from: www.bjs.gov/content/pub/pdf/cpus15.pdf

Kanter, J.W., Baruch, D.E., and Gaynor, S.T. (2006) Acceptance and Commitment Therapy and Behavioral Activation for the Treatment of Depression: Description and Comparison. *The Behavior Analyst*, 29(2): 161–185.

Karpman, S.B. (1968) Fairy Tales and Script Drama Analysis. *Transactional Analysis Bulletin*, 7(26): 39–43.

Keltner, D. and Buswell, B. (1997) Embarrassment: its distinct form and appeasement functions. *Psychological Bulletin*, 122(3): 250–270.

Kenagy, G.P. (2005) Transgender health: findings from two needs assessment studies in Philadelphia. *Health and Social Work*, 30(1): 19–26.

Kenagy, G.P. and Bostwick, W.B. (2005) Health and Social Service Needs of Transgender People in Chicago. In W.O. Bockting and E. Avery (eds) *Transgender Health and HIV Prevention: Needs Assessment Studies from Transgender Communities across the United States* (pp.57–66). Binghampton, NY: Haworth Medical Press.

Kersting, A., Reutemann, M., Gast, U., Ohrmann, P., *et al.* (2003) Dissociative disorders and traumatic childhood experiences in transsexuals. *The Journal of Nervous and Mental Disease*, 191(3): 182–189.

Kessler, R.C., Borges, G., and Walters, E.E. (1999) Prevalence of and risk factors for lifetime suicide attempts in the National Comorbidity Survey. *Archives of General Psychiatry*, 56(7): 617–626.

Keuroghlian, A., Reisner, S., White, J., and Weiss, R. (2015) Substance use and treatment of substance use disorders in a community sample of transgender adults. *Drug Alcohol Dependence*, 152: 139–146.

Kidd, J. and Witten, T.M. (2008) Understanding spirituality, religiosity and faith in the transgender community: implications for aging. *Journal of Religion, Spirituality and Aging*, 20(1–2): 29–62.

Killingsworth, M. and Gilbert, D. (2010) A wandering mind is an unhappy mind. *Science*, 330(6006): 932.

Kim, S.K. Park, H.J., Lee, C.K., Park, J.M., and Kim, C.M. (2003) Long-term results in patients after rectosigmoid vaginoplasty. *Plastic and Reconstructive Surgery*, 112(1): 143–151.

Kinnish, K., Strassberg, D., and Turner, C. (2005) Sex differences in the flexibility of sexual orientation: a multidimensional retrospective assessment. *Archives of Sexual Behavior*, 34(2): 173–183.

Koltko-Rivera, M.E. (2006) Rediscovering the later version of Maslow's hierarchy of needs: self-transcendence and opportunities for theory, research and unification. *Review of General Psychology*, 10(4): 302–317.

Konturek, P.C., Brzozowski, T., and Konturek, S.J. (2011) Stress and the gut: pathophysiology, clinical consequences, diagnostic approach and treatment options. *Journal of Physiology and Pharmacology*, 62(6): 591–599.

Koon Teh, Y. (2001) Mak nyahs (male transsexuals) in Malaysia: the influence of culture and religion on their identity. *International Journal of Transgenderism*, 5(3).

Kotula, D. (2002) *The Phallus Palace: Female-to-Male Transsexuals*. Los Angeles: Alyson Publications.

Kourbatova, K. and Redfield, E. (2014) Immigration. In L. Erickson-Schroth (ed.) Trans Bodies, Trans Selves: A Resource for the Transgender Community (pp.40–53). New York, NY: Oxford University Press.

Krause, N. (2007) Thought suppression and meaning in life: a longitudinal investigation. *International Journal of Aging and Human Development*, 64: 67–82.

Kuiper, A.J. and Cohen-Kettenis, P.T. (1998) Gender role reversal among postoperative transsexuals. *International Journal of Transgenderism*, 2(3).

Kuiper, B. and Cohen-Kettenis, P.T. (1988) Sex Reassignment Surgery: A study of 141 Dutch Transsexuals. Archives of Sexual Behavior, 17(5): 439–457.

Kusalik, T. (2010) Identity, Schmidentity. In K. Bornstein and S.B. Bergman (eds) *Gender Outlaws: The Next Generation* (pp.54–60). Berkeley, CA: Seal Press.

Lambda Legal (2010) *When Healthcare Isn't Caring: Lambda Legal's Survey on Discrimination against LGBT People and People Living with HIV*. New York, NY: Lambda Legal.

Landén, M., Wålinder, J., Hambert, G., and Lundström B (1998) Factors Predictive of Regret in Sex Reassignment. *Acta Psychiatra Scandinavica*, 97(4): 284–289.

Larson, D. and Tobin, D. (2000) End-of-life conversations. *JAMA: The Journal of the American Medical Association*, 284(12): 1573–1578.

Lawrence, A.A. (2001) SRS without a One Year RLE: Still No Regrets. XVII Harry Benjamin International Symposium on Gender Dysphoria, Galveston, TX.

Lawrence, A.A. (2003) Factors associated with satisfaction or regret following male-to-female sex reassignment surgery. *Archives of Sexual Behavior*, 32(4): 299–315.

Lawrence, A.A. (2010) Desire for castration is not a body integrity identity disorder: comment on Johnson *et al.* (2007), Brett *et al.* (2007), and Roberts *et al.* (2008). *Journal of Sexual Medicine*, 7(2, Pt 1): 852–853.

LeMaster, B. (2018) Pedagogies of Failure Queer Communication Pedagogy as Anti-Normative. In A. Atay and S. Toyosaki (eds) *Critical Intercultural Communication Pedagogy* (pp.81–96). Lanham, MD: Lexington Books

Leonard, T. and Grousd, L. (2016) Using ACT Interventions to Help Clients Explore the Possibilities of Gender Identity. In M. Skinta and A Curtin (eds) *Mindfulness and Acceptance for Gender and Sexual Minorities* (pp.30–48). Oakland, CA: Context Press.

Lev, A.I. (2004) *Transgender Emergence: Therapeutic Guidelines for Working with Gender-Variant People and Their Families*. Binghamton, NY: Haworth Clinical Practice Press.

Lev, A.I. (2007) Transgender Communities: Developing Identity through Connection. In K.J. Bieschke, R.M. Perez, and K.A. DeBord (eds) *Handbook of Counseling and Psychotherapy with Lesbian, Gay, Bisexual, and Transgender Clients* (2nd ed.) (pp.147–173). Washington, DC: American Psychological Association.

Lev, A.I. (2009) The ten tasks of the mental health provider: recommendations for revision of the World Professional Association for Transgender Health's Standards of Care. *International Journal of Transgenderism*, 11(2): 74–99.

Lev, A.I. and Sennott, S. (2012) Transsexual Desire in Differently Gendered Bodies. In J.J. Bigner and J.L. Wetchler (eds) *Handbook of LGBT-Affirmative Couple and Family Therapy* (pp.113–128). New York, NY: Routledge.

LeVay, S. (1993) *The Sexual Brain* (1st ed.) (pp.103–135). Cambridge, MA: Massachusettes Institute of Technology Press.

Levi, S. (2006) "Ableism." In G.L. Albrecht (ed.) *Encyclopedia of Disability*. Thousand Oaks, CA: Sage Publications.

Lewins, F. (1995) *Transsexualism in Society: A Sociology of Male-to-Female Transsexuals*. South Melbourne, Australia: Macmillan Publishers.

Livingstone, T. (2008) The relevance of a person-centered approach to therapy with transgendered or transsexual clients. *Person-Centered and Experiential Psychotherapies*, 7(2): 135–144.

Livingstone, T. (2010) Anti-sectarian, queer, client-centeredness: a re-iteration of respect in therapy. In L. Moon (ed.) *Counselling Ideologies: Queer Challenges to Heteronormativity*. Farnham, Surrey, UK: Ashgate Publishing.

Lombardi, E. (2001) Enhancing transgender health care. *American Journal of Public Health*, 91(6): 869–872.

Losty, M. and O'Connor, J. (2018) Falling outside of the "nice little binary box": a psychoanalytic exploration of the non-binary gender identity. *Psychoanalytic Psychotherapy*, 32(1): 40–60.

Lucal, B. (1999) What it means to be gendered me: life on the boundaries of a dichotomous gender system. *Gender and Society*, 13(6): 781–797.

Luengsuraswat, B. (2010) Proof. In K. Bornstein and S.B. Bergman (eds) *Gender Outlaws: The Next Generation* (pp.242–245). Berkeley, CA: Seal Press.

Luepnitz, D.A. (2002) *The Family Interpreted: Psychoanalysis, Feminism, and Family Therapy*. New York, NY: Basic Books.

Luoma, J.B. and Villatte, J.L. (2012) Mindfulness in the treatment of suicidal individuals. *Cognitive Behavioral Practice*, 19(2): 265–276.

Luthar, S.S. and Cicchetti, D. (2000) The construct of resilience: implications for interventions and social policies. *Development and Psychopathology*, 12(4): 857–885.

Lynd, H.M. (1961) *On Shame and the Search for Identity*. New York, NY: Science Editions.

Maguen, S., Shipherd, J., and Harris, H. (2005) Providing culturally sensitive care for transgender patients. *Cognitive and Behavioral Practice*, 12(14): 479–490.

Mallon, G.P. (2009) *Social Work Practice with Transgender and Gender Variant Youth*. New York, NY: Routledge Press.

Mallory, C., Brown, T., and Conron, K. (2018) *Conversion Therapy and LGBT Youth*. The Williams Institute School of Law. Retrieved from: https://williamsinstitute.law.ucla.edu/wp-content/uploads/Conversion-Therapy-LGBT-Youth-Jan-2018.pdf

Malpas, J. (2006) From otherness to alliance: transgender couples in therapy. *Journal of GLBT Family Studies*, 2(3/4): 183–206.

Malpas, J. (2012) Can Couples Change Gender? Couple Therapy with Transgender People and Their Partners. In J.J. Bigner and J.L. Wetchler (eds) *Handbook of LGBT Affirmative Couple and Family Therapy* (pp.69–85). New York, NY: Routledge.

Mark, K., Rosenkrantz, D., and Kerner, I. (2014) "Bi"ing into monogamy: attitudes toward monogamy in a sample of bisexual-identified adults. *Psychology of Sexual Orientation and Gender Diversity*, 1(3): 263–269.

Martin, K. (2007) Transsexualism: a clinical guide to gender identity disorder. *Current Psychiatry*, 6(2): 81–91.

Maslow, A.H. (1954) *Motivation and Personality*. New York, NY: Harper and Row Publishers.

Masten, A.S. (1994) Resilience in Individual Development: Successful Adaptation despite Risk and Adversity. In M. Wang and E. Gordon (eds) *Educational Resilience in Inner City America: Challenges and Prospects* (pp.3–25). Mahwah, NJ: Lawrence Erlbaum Associates.

Masten, A.S. (2001) Ordinary magic: resilience processes in development. *American Psychologist*, 56(3): 227–238.

Matsuno, E. and Budge, S. (2017) Non-binary/genderqueer identities: a critical review of the literature. *Current Sexual Health Reports*, 9(3): 116–120.

Matte, N. and Devor, A.H. (2007) Building a better world for transpeople: Reed Erickson and the Erickson Educational Foundation. *International Journal of Transgenderism*, 10(1), 47–68.

Matzner, A. (2001) *'O Au No Keia: Voices from Hawai'i's Mahu and Transgender Communities*. Xlibris.

McCann, E., Keogh, B., Doyle, L., and Coyne, I. (2017) The experiences of youth who identify as trans* in relation to health and social care needs: a scoping review. *Youth and Society*, 51(6): 840–864.

Mcdonald, M. (2006) An other space: between and beyond lesbian-normativity and trans-normativity. *Journal of Lesbian Studies*, 10(1–2): 201–214.

McIntosh, D.M.D. and Hobson, K. (2013) Reflexive engagement: a white (queer) women's performance of failures and alliance possibilities. *Liminalities: A Journal of Performance Studies*, 9(4): 1–23.

Mclleland, J. (2017) *Trans*Am: Cis Men and Trans Women in Love*. Berkeley, CA: Three L Media.

McMillan, R.L., Kaufman, S.B., and Singer, J.L. (2013) Ode to positive constructive daydreaming. *Frontiers in Psychology*, 23(4): 626.

McNeil, J., Bailey, L., Ellis, S., Morton, J., and Regan, M. (2012) *Trans Mental Health and Emotional Well Being Study, 2012*. Edinburgh: Scottish Transgender Alliance.

McQueen, P. (2011) A Life Less Liminal? Issues of Inclusion and Recognition for Trans-Identities. ECPR General Conference, University of Iceland, Reykavik, 25–27 August.

Medford, N., Sierra, M., Baker, D., and David, A. (2005) Understanding and treating depersonalization disorder. *Advances in Psychiatric Treatment*, 11(1): 92–100.

Meier, S.C., Sharp, C., Michonski, J., Babcock, J.C., and Fitzgerald, K. (2013) Romantic relationships of female-to-male trans men: a descriptive study. *International Journal of Transgenderism*, 14: 75–85.

Mellman, W. (2017) Beyond the Gender Binary in Sexual Scripts: Dating and Relationships among Transgender Men and Their Non-Transgender Partners. Columbia University Academic Commons.

MetLife (2010) *Still out, Still Aging: The MetLife Study of Lesbian, Gay, Bisexual, and Transgender Baby Boomers*. Westport, CT: MetLife Mature Market Institute.

Meyerowitz, J. (2002) *How Sex Changed: A History of Transsexuality*. Cambridge, MA: Harvard University Press.

Michal, M., Wiltnik, J., Till, Y., Wild, P., *et al.* (2010) Type D personality and depersonalization are associated with suicidal ideation in the German general population aged 35–74: results from the Gutenberg Heart Study. *Journal of Affective Disorders*, 125(1–3): 227–233.

Miller, J.B. (1976) *Towards a New Psychology of Women*. Oxford, England: Beacon Press.

Miller, J.B. (1986) What do we mean by relationships? *Work in Progress*, 22. Wellesley, MA: Stone Center Working Paper Series.

Miller, J. B., Jordan, J., Stiver, I., Walker, M., Surrey, J., and Eldrige, N. (2004) Therapist's Authenticity. In J. Jordan, J., M. Walker, M., and L Hartling, L. (eds.) *The Complexity of Connection* (pp.64–89). New York, NY: The Guilford Press

Miller, L.R. and Grollman, E.A. (2015) The social costs of gender nonconformity for transgender adults: implications for discrimination and health. *Sociological Forum*, 30(3): 809–831.

Mills, M. and Stoneham, G. (2017) *The Voice Book for Trans and Non-Binary People*. London: Jessica Kingsley Publishers.

Mitchell, V. (2012) Coming Out to Family: Adrift in a Sea of Potential Meaning. In J.J. Bigner and J.L. Wetchler (eds) *Handbook of LGBT-Affirmative Couple and Family Therapy* (pp.131–148). New York, NY: Routledge.

Mizock, L. and Lewis, T. (2008) Trauma in transgender populations: risk, resilience, and clinical care. *Journal of Emotional Abuse*, 8: 335–354.

Mizock, L. and Lundquist, C. (2016) Missteps in psychotherapy with transgender clients: promoting gender sensitivity in counseling and psychological practice. *Psychology of Sexual Orientation and Gender Diversity*, 3(2): 148–155.

Mock, S. and Eibach, R. (2012) Stability and change in sexual orientation identity over a 10-year period in adulthood. *Archives of Sexual Behavior*, 41(3): 641–646.

Mogul, J.L., Ritchie, A.J., and Whitlock, K. (2011) *Queer (In)Justice: The Criminalization of LGBT People in the United States*. Boston, MA: Beacon Press.

Monro, S. (2007) Transmuting gender binaries: the theoretical challenge. *Sociological Research Online*, 12(1).

Morin, A. and Hamper, B. (2012) Self-reflection and the inner voice: activation of the left inferior frontal gyrus during perceptual and conceptual self-referential thinking. *The Open Neuroimaging Journal*, 6: 78–89.

Mottet, L. and Ohle, J.M. (2003) *Transitioning Our Shelters: A Guide to Making Homeless Shelters Safe For Transgender People*. National Gay and Lesbian Task Force. Retrieved from: https://transequality.org/issues/resources/transitioning-our-shelters-guide-making-homeless-shelters-safe-transgender-people

Movement Advancement Project (MAP) (2016) *Unjust: How the Broken Criminal Justice System Fails LGBT People.* Center for American Progress and the Movement Advance Project. Retrieved from: www.lgbtmap.org/file/lgbt-criminal-justice.pdf

Muñoz, J. (2009) *Cruising Utopia: The Then and There of Queer Futurity.* New York, NY: New York University Press.

Murray, S.O. and Roscoe, W. (1998) *Boy-Wives and Female Husbands: Studies in African Homosexualities.* New York, NY: Palgrave Publishers Ltd.

Nadal, K., Davidoff, K., and Fujii-Doe, W. (2014) Transgender women and the sex work industry: roots in systemic, institutional, and interpersonal discrimination. *Journal of Trauma and Dissociation*, 15(2): 169–183.

Nadal, K., Skolnik, A., and Wong, Y. (2012) Interpersonal and systemic microagressions toward transgender people: implications for counseling. *Journal of LGBT Issues in Counselling*, 6(1): 55–82.

Nadal, K., Whitman, C., Davis, L., Erazo, T., and Davidoff, K. (2015) Microaggressions toward lesbian, gay, bisexual, transgender, queer, and genderqueer people: a review of the literature. *The Journal of Sex Research*, 53(4–5): 488–508.

Nagoshi, J. and Brzuzy, S. (2010) Transgender theory: embodying research and practice. *Affilia: Journal of Women and Social Work*, 25(4): 431–443.

Nagoshi, J.L., Brzuzy, S., and Terrell, H. (2012) Deconstructing the complex perceptions of gender roles, gender identity, and sexual orientation among transgender individuals. *Feminism and Psychology*, 22(4): 405–422.

Nakamura, K. and Matsuo, H. (2003) Female Masculinity and Fantasy Spaces: Transcending Genders in the Takaruzka Theater and Japanese Popular Culture. In J.E. Roberson and N. Suzuki (eds) *Men and Masculinities in Contemporary Japan: Dislocating the Salaryman Doxa* (pp.59–76). New York, NY: RoutledgeCurzon.

Nash, C. (2011) Trans experiences in lesbian and queer space. *Canadian Geographer/Le géographe canadien*, 56(1): 192–207.

Nataf, Z.I. (2006) Selections from "Lesbians Talk Transgender." In S. Stryker and S. Whittle (eds) *Transgender Studies Reader* (pp.439–448). New York, NY: Routledge.

National Public Radio (2018) *Meet Naia Izumi, the 2018 Tiny Desk Contest Winner.* Retrieved from: www.npr.org/sections/allsongs/2018/04/24/605005960/meet-naia-izumi-the-2018-tiny-desk-contest-winner

National Public Radio (2019) *Announcing the 2019 Tiny Desk Contest Winner.* Retrieved from: www.npr.org/sections/allsongs/2019/05/16/723269208/announcing-the-2019-tiny-desk-contest-winner

Nemoto, T., Operario, D., Keatley, J., and Villegas, D. (2004) Social context of HIV risk behaviors among male-to-female transgenders of colour. *AIDS Care*, 16(6) 724–735.

Nestle, J., Howell, C., and Wilchens, R. (eds) (2002) *Genderqueer: Voices from Beyond the Sexual Binary.* Los Angeles, CA: Alyson Publications.

Newfield, E., Hart, S., Dibble, S., and Kohler, L. (2006) Female-to-male transgender quality of life. *Quality of Life Research*, 15(9): 1447–1457.

Neziroglu, F. and Donnelly, K. (2013) Dissociation from an Acceptance-Oriented Standpoint. In F. Kennedy, H. Kennerley, and D. Pearson (eds) *Cognitive Behavioral Approaches to Understanding and Treatment of Dissociation* (pp.237–248). New York, NY: Routledge.

Nichols, A. (2010) Dance Ponnaya, dance! Police abuses against transgender sex workers in Sri Lanka. *Feminist Criminology*, 5(2): 195–222.

Nielsen, K. (2015) Fake it 'til you make it: why community college students' aspirations hold steady. *American Sociological Association*, 88(4): 265–283.

Nieuwsma, J., Walser, R., and Hayes, S. (2016) *ACT for Clergy and Pastoral Counselors: Using ACT to Bridge Psychological and Spiritual Care.* Oakland, CA: New Harbinger Publications.

Nock, M.K., Borges, G., Bromet, E.J., Cha, C.B., Kessler, R.C., and Lee, S. (2008) Suicide and suicidal behavior. *Epidemiologic Reviews*, 30(1): 133–154.

Nodin, N., Peel, E., Tyler, A., and Rivers, I. (2015) *The RaRE Research Report: LGB and T Mental Health – Risk and Resilience Explored.* London: PACE – Project for Advocacy Counselling and Education.

O'Hayer, C.V., Bennett, D.S., and Jacobson, J.M. (2016) The Lasting Impact of HIV/AIDS. In M. Skinta and A. Curtin (eds) *Mindfulness and Acceptance for Gender and Sexual Minorities* (pp.228–245). Oakland, CA: Context Press.

Olson, D.H. (2000) Circumplex model of marital and family systems. *Journal of Family Therapy*, 22(2): 144–167.

Olson, K., Durwood, L., DeMeules, M., and McLaughlin, K. (2016) Mental health of transgender children who are supported in their identities. *Pediatrics*, 137(3).

Ord, I. (2014) *ACT with Faith: Acceptance and Commitment Therapy with Christian Clients: A Practitioner's Guide.* Compass Publishing.

Orsillo, S.M., Roemer, L., Lerner, J.B, and Tull, M.T. (2004) Acceptance, Mindfulness, and Cognitive-Behavioral Therapy: Comparisons, Contrasts and Application to Anxiety. In S.C. Hayes, V.M., Follette, and M.M. Linehan (eds) *Mindfulness and Acceptance: Expanding the Cognitive-Behavioral Tradition* (pp.66–95). New York, NY: Guilford Press.

Otis, H. (2015) Genderqueer: what it means. *Ursidae: The Undergraduate Research Journal at the University of Northern Colorado*, 4(3).

Ovid (1979) *The Art of Love and Other Poems*. Translated by J.H. Mozley. Cambridge, MA: Harvard University Press.

Pargament, K. (2007) *Spiritually Integrated Psychotherapy: Understanding and Addressing the Sacred*. New York: Guilford.

Pattatucci-Aragon, A. (2006) Challenging lesbian norms: intersex, transgender, intersectional, and queer perspectives. *Journal of Lesbian Studies*, 10(1-2).

Pauly, I. (1998) Gender Identity and Sexual Orientation. In D. Denny (ed.) *Current Concepts in Transgender Identity* (pp.237–248). New York, NY: Routledge Press.

Pega, F. and Veale, J.F. (2015) The case for the World Health Organization's Commission on Social Determinants of Health to Address Gender Identity. *American Journal of Public Health*, 105(3): 56–62.

Peitzmeier, S., Gardner, I., Weinand, J. Corbert, A., and Acevedo, K. (2017) Health impact of chest binding among transgender adults: a community-engaged, cross-sectional study. *Culture, Health and Sexuality*, 19(1): 64–75.

Peterson, C.M., Matthews, A., Copps-Smith, M., and Conrad, L.A. (2016) Suicidality, self-harm, and body dissatisfaction in transgender adolescents and emerging adults with gender dysphoria. *Suicide and Life Threatening Behavior*, 47(4): 475–482.

Petkus, A.J., Gum, A., and Wetherell, J.L. (2012) Thought suppression is associated with psychological distress in homebound older adults. *Depression and Anxiety*, 29(3): 219–225.

Petkus, A.J. and Wetherell, J.L. (2013) Acceptance and Commitment Therapy with older adults: rationale and considerations. *Cognitive and Behavioral Practice*, 20(1): 47–56.

Pfeffer, C.A. (2008) Bodies in relation—bodies in transition: Lesbian partners of trans men and body image. *Journal of Lesbian Studies*, 12(4): 325–345.

Pflum, S.R., Testa, R.J., Balsam, K.F., Goldblum, P.B., and Bongar, B. (2015) Social support, trans community connectedness, and mental health symptoms among transgender and gender nonconforming adults. *Psychology of Sexual Orientation and Gender Diversity*, 2(3), 281–286.

Phillips, M., Medford, N., Senior, C., Bullmore, E., *et al.* (2001) Depersonalization disorder: thinking without feeling. *Psychiatry Research Neuroimaging*, 108(3): 145–160.

Pines, A. and Aronson, E. (1981) Polyfidelity: an alternative lifestyle without jealousy? *Alternative Lifestyles*, 4(3): 373–392.

Planned Parenthood (2018) *Hormone Treatment Services*. Retrieved from: www.plannedparenthood.org/planned-parenthood-great-northwest-hawaiian-islands/patient/services-transgender-patients

Plutchik, R. (1991) *The Emotions*. Lanham, MD: University Press of America.

Poerio, G., Totterdell, P., Emerson, L., and Miles, E. (2015) Love is the triumph of the imagination: daydreams about significant others are associated with increased happiness, love and connection. *Consciousness and Cognition*, 33: 135–144.

Polk, K., Schoendorff, B., Webster, M., and Olaz, F. (2016) *The Essential Guide to the ACT Matrix: A Step-by-Step Approach to Using the ACT Matrix Model in Clinical Practice*. Oakland, CA: Context Press.

Porter, K.E., Ronneberg, C.R., and Witten, T.M. (2013) Religious affiliation and successful aging: findings from the Trans MetLife Survey. *Journal of Religion, Spirituality and Aging*, 25(2): 112–138.

Poteat, T., German, D., and Kerrigan, D. (2013) Managing uncertainty: a grounded theory of stigma in transgender health care encounters. *Social Science and Medicine*, 84: 22–29.

Preves, S. (2002) Sexing the intersexed: an analysis of sociocultural responses to intersexuality. *Signs: Journal of Women in Culture and Society*, 27(2): 523–556.

Preves, S. (2003) *Intersex and Identity: The Contested Self*. Piscataway, NJ: Rutgers University Press.

Prigerson, H., Shear, K., Frank, E., Beery, L., *et al.* (1997) Traumatic grief: a case of loss-induced trauma. *American Journal of Psychiatry*, 154(7): 1003–1009.

Provencher, D. (2007) *Queer French: Globalization, Language, and Sexual Citizenship in France*. New York, NY: Routledge Press.

Pruden, H. (2013) *Two-Spirit Resource Directory. National Confederacy of Two-Spirit Organizations and the NorthEast Two-Spirit Society*. Retrieved from: www.nativeyouthsexualhealth.com/2sdirectory.php

Pusch, R.S. (2005) Objects of curiosity: transgender college students' perceptions of the reactions of others. *Journal of Gay and Lesbian Issues in Education*, 3(1): 45–61.

Qadiry, T. (2012) The Afghan Girls Who Live as Boys. *BBC News*. Retrieved from: www.bbc.co.uk/news/magazine-15262680

Quinodoz, D. (1998) A fe/male transsexual patient in psychoanalysis. *International Journal of Psychoanalysis*, 79(10): 95–111.

Rabbinical Assembly (RA) (2016) *Resolution Affirming the Rights of Transgender and Nonconforming People*. Retrieved from: www.rabbinicalassembly.org/story/resolution-affirming-rights-transgender-and-gender-non-conforming-people

Rachlin, K. (2002) Transgender individuals' experiences of psychotherapy. *International Journal of Transgenderism*, 6(1).

Rachlin K. and Lev, A.I. (2013) Challenging cases for experienced therapists. *Journal of Gay and Lesbian Mental Health*, 15(2), 180–199.

Raj, R. (2002) Towards a trans-positive therapeutic model: developing clinical sensitivity and cultural competence in the effective support of transsexual and transgendered clients. *The International Journal of Transgenderism*, 6(2).

Raj, R. (2008) Transforming couples and families: a transformative therapeutic model for working with the loved-ones of gender-divergent youth and trans-identified adults. *Journal of GLBT Family Studies*, 4(2): 133–163.

Ramirez, S., Glover, J., Ohlde, C., Mercer, R., *et al.* (2001) Relationship of numbing to alexithymia, apathy, and depression. *Psychological Reports*, 88(1): 189–200.

Rassin, E. (2003) The White Bear Suppression Inventory (WBSI) focuses on failing suppression attempts. *European Journal of Personality*, 17(4): 285–298.

Rawlinson, G.E. (1976) The significance of letter position in word recognition. Unpublished PhD Thesis, Psychology Department, University of Nottingham, UK.

Rayner, K., White, S., Johnson, R.L., and Liversedge, S.P. (2006) Raeding wrods with jubmled lettres: there is a cost. *Psychological Science*, 17(3): 192–193.

Reck, J. (2009) Homeless gay and transgender youth of color in San Francisco: "No one likes street kids"—even in the Castro. *Journal of LGT Youth*, 6(2–3): 223–242.

Reddy, G. (2005) *With Respect to Sex: Negotiating Hijra Identity in South India*. Chicago, IL: University of Chicago Press.

Reicherzer, S., Patton, J., and Glowiak, M. (2011) *Counseling Transgender Trauma Survivors*. Retrieved from: www.counseling.org/Resources/Library/VISTAS/2011-V-Online/Article_97.pdf

Reicherzer, S. and Spillman, J. (2012) A multiple case study examination of resiliency factors for Mexican and Mexican-American transsexual women. *International Journal of Transgenderism*, 13(3): 147–164.

Reisner, S., Gamarel, K., Nemoto, T., and Operario, D. (2014) Dyadic effects of gender minority stressors in substance use behaviors among transgender women and their non-transgender male partners. *Psycholology of Sexual Orientation and Gender Diversity*, 1(1): 63–71.

Reisner, S., Greytak, E., Parsons, J., and Ybarra, M. (2015) Gender minority social stress in adolescence: disparities in adolescent bullying and substance use by gender identity. *Journal of Sex Research*, 52(3): 243–256.

Reisner, S., Perkovich, B., and Mimiaga, M. (2010) A mixed methods study of the sexual health needs of New England transmen who have sex with nontransgender men. *AIDS Patient Care and STDS*, 24(8): 501–513.

Reitz, N. (2017) The representation of trans women in film and television. *Cinesthesia*, 7(1).

Richards, C., Bouman, W., Seal, L., Barker, M., Nieder, T., and T'Sjoien, G. (2016) Non-binary or genderqueer genders. *International Review of Psychiatry*, 28(1): 95–102.

Richmond, K., Burnes, T., and Carroll, K. (2012) Lost in trans-lation: interpreting systems of trauma for transgender clients. *Traumatology*, 18(1): 45–57.

Riley, E., Wong, W., and Sitharthan, G. (2011) Counseling support for the forgotten transgender community. *Journal of Gay and Lesbian Social Services*, 23(3): 395–410.

Riley, E.A., Clemson, L., Sitharthan, G., and Diamond, M. (2013) Surviving a gender-variant childhood: the views of transgender adults on the needs of gender-variant children and their parents. *Journal of Sex and Marital Therapy*, 39(3): 241–263.

Risman, B.J. (2004) Gender as social structure: theory wrestling with activism. *Gender and Society*, 18(4): 429–450.

Risner, D. (2009) What We Know about Boys Who Dance: The Limitations of Contemporary Masculinity and Dance Education. In J. Fisher and A. Shay (eds) *When Men Dance: Choreographing Masculinities across Borders* (pp.57–77). New York, NY: Oxford University Press.

Roberts, L.F., Brett, M.A., Johnson, T.W., and Wasserug, R.J. (2017) A passion for castration: characterizing men who are fascinated with castration, but have not been castrated. *Journal of Sexual Medicine*, 5(7):1669–1680.

Roberts, S.L. and Sedley, B. (2016) Acceptance and Commitment Therapy with older adults: rationale and case study of an 89-year-old with depression and generalized anxiety disorder. *Quarterly Journal of Experimental Psychology*, 15(1): 53–67.

Roen, K. (2010) Transgender theory and embodiment: the risk of racial marginalization. *Journal of Gender Studies*, 10(3): 253–263.

Roland, C.B. and Burlew, L.D. (eds) (2017) *Counseling LGBTQ Adults throughout the Life Span*. Retrieved from: www.counseling.org/docs/default-source/default-document-library/counseling-lgbtq-adults-throughout-the-life-span-final.pdf?sfvrsn=2

Roscoe, W. (1991) *The Zuni Man-Woman*. Albuquerque, NM: University of New Mexico Press.

Roscoe, W. (1998) *Changing Ones: Third and Fourth Genders in Native North America*. New York, NY: St. Martin's Press.

Rothschild, B. (2000) *The Body Remembers: The Psychophysiology of Trauma and Trauma Treatment*. New York: W.W. Norton.

Rowe, C., Santos, G., McFarland, W., and Wilson, E. (2015) Prevalence and correlates of substance use among trans female youth ages 16–24 years in the San Francisco Bay Area. *Drug and Alcohol Dependence*, 147: 160–166.

Rowson, E. (1991) The effeminates of early Medina. *Journal of the American Oriental Society*, 111(4): 671–693.

Rubin, G. (1992) Of Catamites and Kings: Reflections on Butch Gender and Boundaries. In J. Nestle (ed.) *The Persistent Desire: A Femme-Butch Reader*. Los Angeles, CA: Alyson Publications.

Russell, S.T., Ryan, C., Toomey, R.B., Diaz, R.M., and Sanchez, J. (2011) Lesbian, gay, bisexual, and transgender adolescent school victimization: implications for young adult health and adjustment. *Journal of School Health*, 81: 223–230.

Saks, B. (1998) Transgenderism and dissociative identity disorder: a case study. *The International Journal of Transgenderism*, 2(2).

Sandoz, E. and Dufrene, T. (2013) *Living with Your Body and Other Things You Hate: How to Let Go of Your Struggle with Body Image Using Acceptance and Commitment Therapy*. Oakland, CA: New Harbinger.

Sandoz, E., Wilson, K., and Dufrene, T. (2010) *Acceptance and Commitment Therapy for Eating Disorders: A Process-Focused Guide to Treating Anorexia and Bulimia*. Oakland, CA: New Harbinger.

Schechter, L.S. (2016) *Surgical Management of the Transgender Patient*. Philadelphia, PA: Elesevier.

Scheff, T. (2000) Shame and the social bond: a sociological theory. *American Sociological Association*, 18(1): 84–99.

Scherrer, K.S. (2008) Coming to an asexual identity: negotiating identity, negotiating desire. *Sexualities*, 11(5): 621–641.

Schilt, K. (2010) *Just One of the Guys: Transgender Men and the Persistence of Gender Inequality*. Chicago, IL: University of Chicago Press.

Schilt, K. and Westbrook, L. (2009) Doing gender, doing heteronormativity: "gender normals," transgender people, and the social maintenance of heterosexuality. *Gender and Society*, 23(4): 440–464.

Schleifer D. (2006) Make me feel mighty real: gay female-to-male transgenderists negotiating sex, gender, and sexuality. *Sexualities*, 9(1): 57–75.

Schwartz, P. (1988) A case of concurrent multiple personality disorder and transsexualism. *Dissociation*, 1(2): 48–51.

Scott, R. (1973) *The Transvestite Memoirs of the Abbé de Choisy and the Story of the Marquise/Marquis de Banneville*. London: Peter Owen Publishers.

Sell, I. (2001) Not man, not woman: psychospiritual characteristics of a western third gender. *Journal of Transpersonal*, 33(1): 16–36.

Selvaggi, G. Dhejne, C., Landen, M., and Elander, A. (2012) The 2011 WPATH standards of care and penile reconstruction in female-to-male transsexual individuals. *Advances in Urology*, doi: 10.1155/2012/581712

Sennott, S. (2011) Gender disorder as gender oppression: a transfeminist approach to rethinking the pathologization of gender non-conformity. *Feminisms: Feminist Therapies in the 21st Century*, 34(1–2): 93–113.

Serano, J. (2010) The case against autogynephilia. *International Journal of Transgenderism*, 12(3): 12, 176–187.

Serano, J. (2016) *Whipping Girl: A Transsexual Woman on Sexism and Scapegoating of Femininity* (2nd ed.). Berkeley, CA: Seal Press.

Sevelius, J. (2009) "There's no pamphlet for the kind of sex I have": HIV-related risk factors and protective behaviors among transgender men who have sex with non-transgender men. *Journal of the Association of Nurses in AIDS Care*, 20(5): 398–410.

Shazer, S., Dolan, Y., Korman, H., Trepper, R., McCollum, E., and Berg, I.K. (2012) *More Than Miracles: The State of the Art of Solution Focused Brief Therapy*. New York, NY: Routledge.

Sheerin, J.M. (2009) Transgender Individuals' Experiences in Therapy and Perception of the Treatment Experience. Master's thesis, Smith College, Northampton, MA. Retrieved from: https://scholarworks.smith.edu/theses/1144

Shiloh, R., Schwartz, B., Weizman, A., and Radwan, M. (1995) Catatonia as an unsual presentation of posttraumatic stress. *Psychopathology*, 28(6): 285–290.

Shimizu, M. and Sakamoto, S. (1986) Depersonalization in early adolescence. *The Japanese Journal of Psychology and Neurology*, 40(4): 603–608.

Shipherd, J.C., Green, K.E., and Abramovitz, S. (2010) Transgender clients: identifying and minimizing barriers to mental health treatment. *Journal of Gay and Lesbian Mental Health*, 14(2): 94–108.

Siebler, K. (2012) Transgender transitions: sex/gender binaries in the digital age. *Journal of Gay and Lesbian Mental Health*, 16(1): 74–99.

Sierra, M. and Berrios, G. (1998) Depersonalization: neurobiological perspectives. *Biological Psychiatry*, 44(9): 898–908.

Silva-Santisteban, A., Raymond, H., Salazar, X., Villayzan, J., *et al.* (2012) Understanding the HIV/AIDS epidemic in transgender women of Lima, Peru: results from a sero-epidemiologic study using respondent driven sampling. *AIDS and Behavior*, 16(4): 872–881.

Simeon, D. and Abugel, J. (2006) *Feeling Unreal: Depersonalization Disorder and the Loss of the Self.* New York, NY: Oxford University Press.

Simeon, D., Knutelska, M., Nelson, D., and Guralnik, O. (2003) Feeling unreal: a depersonalization disorder update of 117 cases. *The Journal of Clinical Psychiatry*, 64(9): 990–997.

Simons, L., Schrager, S., Clark, L., Belzer, M., and Olson, J. (2013) Parental support and mental health among transgender adolescents. *Journal of Adolescent Health*, 53(6): 791–793.

Singer, J.L. (1975) *The Inner World of Daydreaming*. New York, NY: Harper and Row.

Singer, J.L. and Antrobus, J.S. (1970) *Imaginal Processes Inventory*. Princeton, NJ: Educational Testing Service.

Singer, J.L. and Schonbar, R.A. (1961) Correlates of daydreaming: a dimension of self-awareness. *Journal of Consulting Psychology*, 25(1): 1–6.

Singh, A. (2013) Transgender youth of color and resilience: negotiating oppression and finding support. *Sex Roles*, 68(11–12): 690–702.

Singh, A. and Burnes, T. (2010) Shifting the counselor role from gatekeeping to advocacy: ten strategies for using the competencies for counseling with transgender clients for individual and social change. *Journal of LGBT Issues in Counseling*, 4(3–4): 241–255.

Singh, A., Hays, D.G., and Watson, L.S. (2011) Strength in the face of adversity: resilience strategies of transgender individuals. *Journal of Counseling and Development*, 89(1): 20–27.

Singh, A. and McKleroy, V. (2011) "Just getting out of bed is a revolutionary act": the resilience of transgender people of color who have survived traumatic life events. *Traumatology*, 17(2): 34–44.

Siverskog, A. (2014) "They just don't have a clue": transgender aging and implications for social work. *Journal of Gerontological Social Work*, 57(2–4): 386–406.

Skinta, M. and Curtin, A. (2016) *Mindfulness and Acceptance for Gender and Sexual Minorities: A Clinician's Guide to Fostering Compassion, Connection and Equality Using Contextual Strategies*. Oakland, CA: Context Press.

Skinta, M. and D'Alton, P. (2016) Mindfulness and Acceptance for Malignant Shame. In M. Skinta and A. Curtin (eds) *Mindfulness and Acceptance for Gender and Sexual Minorities: A Clinician's Guide to Fostering Compassion, Connection and Equality Using Contextual Strategies* (pp.88–107) Oakland, CA: Context Press.

Slabbekoorn, D., Van Goozen, S., Gooren, L., and Cohen-Kettenis, P. (2001) Effects of cross-sex hormone treatment on emotionality in transsexuals. *International Journal Transgenderism*, 5(3).

Sloan, D.M. (2004) Emotion regulation in action: emotional reactivity in experiential avoidance. *Behaviour Research and Therapy*, 42: 1257–1270.

Smith, B. and Horne, S. (2007) Gay, lesbian, bisexual and transgendered (GLBT) experiences with earth-spirited faith. *Journal of Homosexuality*, 52(3–4): 235–248.

Smith, E., Jones, T., Ward, R., Dixon, J., Mitchell, A., and Hillier, L. (2014) *From Blues to Rainbows: Mental Health and Wellbeing of Gender Diverse and Transgender Young People in Australia*. Melbourne: The Australian Research Centre in Sex, Health, and Society.

Smith, L.C., Shin, R.Q. and Officer, L.M. (2012) Moving counseling forward on LGB and transgender issues: speaking queerly on discourses and microaggressions. *The Counseling Psychologist*, 40(3): 385–408.

Smith, Y., Van Goozen, S., Kuiper, A., and Cohen-Kettenis, P. (2005) Sex reassignment: outcomes and predictors of treatment for adolescent and adult transsexuals. *Psychological Medicine*, 35(1): 89–99.

Soheilian, S.S. and Inman, A.G. (2009) Middle Eastern Americans: the effects of stigma on attitudes toward counseling. *Journal of Muslim Mental Health*, 4(2): 139–158.

Spade, D. (2006) Undermining Gender Regulation. In Mattilda aka S.M. Bernstein Sycamore (ed.) *Nobody Passes: Rejecting the Rules of Gender and Conformity*. Emeryville, CA: Seal Press.

Speedlin, S., Milligan, K., Haberstroh, S., and Duffey, T. (2016) *Using Acceptance and Commitment Therapy to Negotiate Losses and Life Transitions*. Vistas Online. Retrieved from: www.counseling.org/knowledge-center/vistas/by-subject2/vistas-families/docs/default-source/vistas/article_121cc024f16116603abcacff0000bee5e7

Sperber, J., Landers, S., and Lawrence, S. (2005) Access to health care for transgendered persons: results of a needs assessment in Boston. *International Journal of Transgenderism*, 8(2/3): 75–91.

Spiegel, D. and Cardena, E. (1996) Diagnostic Issues, Criteria and Comorbidity of Dissociative Disorders. In L. Michelson and W. Ray (eds) *Handbook of Dissociation: Theoretical Empirical and Clinical Perspectives* (pp.227–250). New York, NY: Plenum Press.

Stark, E. and Flitcraft, A.H. (1988) Women and children at risk: a feminist perspective of child abuse. *International Journal of Health Services*, 18(1): 97–118.

Steelman, S. and Hertlein, K. (2016) Underexplored identities: attending to asexuality in therapeutic contexts. *Journal of Family Psychotherapy*, 27(2): 85–98.

Steinberg, M. (1991) The Spectrum of Depersonalization: Assessment and Treatment. In A. Tasman and S. Goldfinger (eds) *American Psychiatric Press Review of Psychiatry*, Vol. 10 (pp.223–247). Arlington, VA: American Psychiatric Association.

Sternberg, R.J. (2007) Triangulating Love. In T.J. Oord (ed.) *The Altruism Reader: Selections from Writings on Love, Religion and Science* (pp. 331–347). West Conshohocken, PA: Templeton Press.

Stincombe, A., Smallbone, J., Wilson, K., and Kortes-Miller, K. (2017) Healthcare and end-of-life needs of lesbian, gay, bisexual, and transgender (LGBT) older adults: a scoping review. *Geriatrics*, 2(1).

Stitt, A. (2013) Gender ego: comparative models of transgender identity acquisition. *Hohonu*, 11: 21–25.

Stitt, A. (2014) The cat and the cloud: ACT for LGBT locus of control, responsibility and acceptance. *Journal of LGBT Issues in Counseling*, 8(3): 282–297.

Stotzer, R. (2014) Law enforcement and criminal justice personnel interactions with transgender people in the United States: a literature review. *Aggression and Violent Behavior*, 19(3): 263–277.

Strosahl, K.D. and Robinson, P.J. (2017) The Mindfulness and Acceptance Workbook for Depression (2nd ed.). Oakland, CA: New Harbinger Publications, Inc.

Stryker, S. and Bettcher, T.M. (2016) Introduction: trans/feminism. *Transgender Studies Quarterly*, 3(1–2): 5–14.

Sullivan, L. (1990) *From Female to Male: The Life of Jack Bee Garland*. Boston, MA: Alyson Books.

Suyemoto, K. (1994) Therapists' Conceptualizations of the Function and Meaning of "Delicate Self-Cutting" in Female Adolescent Outpatients. Retrieved from: Electronic Doctoral Dissertations for UMass Amherst, https://scholarworks.umass.edu/dissertations/AAI9434537

Tabaac, A., Perrin, P., and Benotsch, E. (2017) Discrimination, mental health, and body image among transgender and gender-non-binary individuals: constructing a multiple mediational path model. *Journal of Gay and Lesbian Social Services*, 30(1): 1–16.

Tait, R. (2005) A Fatwa for Transsexuals: One Woman's Courage in Appealing to the Late Ayatollah Khomeini Has Made Tehran the Unlikely Sex Change Capital of the World. *Salon*, July 28. Retrieved from: www.salon.com/2005/07/28/iran_transsexuals

Talusan, M., Provenano, B., Rodriguez, M., Solis, M., and Swartz, A. (2017) Unerased: Counting Transgender Lives. *Mic.com*. Retrieved from: https://unerased.mic.com

Tamagawa, M. (2016) Same sex marriage in Japan. *Journal of GLBT Family Studies*, 12(2): 160–187.

Tamagawa, M. (2017) Coming out of the closet in Japan: an exploratory sociological study. *Journal of GLBT Family Studies*, 14(5): 488–518.

Tando, D. (2016) *The Conscious Parent's Guide to Gender Identity: A Mindful Approach to Embracing Your Child's Authentic Self*. Avon, MA: Adams Media.

Taylor, V. and Rupp, L.J. (2004) Chicks with dicks, men in dresses: what it means to be a drag queen. *Journal of Homosexuality*, 46(3–4): 113–134.

Teasdale, J.D., Moore, R.G., Hayhurst, H., Pope, M., Williams, S., and Segal, Z.V. (2002) Metacognitive awareness and prevention of relapse in depression: empirical evidence. *Journal of Consulting and Clinical Psychology*, 70: 275–587.

Testa, R.J., Jimenez, C.L., and Rankin, S.S. (2014) Risk and Resilience During Transgender Identity Development: The Effects of Awareness and Engagement with Other Transgender People on Affect. *Journal of Gay and Lesbian Mental Health*, 18(1): 31–46.

TGEU (2018) *Trans Murder Monitoring. Transgender Europe and Carsten Balzer.* Retrieved from: https://transrespect.org/en/map/trans-murder-monitoring

The Trevor Project (2019) *National Survey on LGBTQ Mental Health.* New York, NY: The Trevor Project. Retrieved from: www.thetrevorproject.org/survey-2019/?section=Introduction

Tompkins, A.B. (2014) "There's no chasing involved": cis/trans relationships, "tranny chasers," and the future of sex-positive trans politics. *Journal of Homosexuality*, 61(5): 766–780.

Tonic Housing (2019, June) Retrieved from: www.toniclivng.org.uk/about-tonic

Towle, R.B. and Morgan, L.M. (2006) Romancing the Transgender Native: Rethinking the Use of the "Third Gender" Concept. In S. Stryker and S. Whittle (eds) *Transgender Studies Reader* (pp.666–684). New York, NY: Routledge.

Tracy, K. (1990) The Many Faces of Facework. In H. Giles and W.P. Robinson (eds) *Handbook of Language and Social Psychology* (pp.219–226). London: John Wiley and Sons.

Trans Lifeline (2019) Trans Lifeline's Peer Support Hotline. Retrieved from: www.translifeline.org/hotline

Tsemberis, S. (2010) *Housing First: The Pathways Model to End Homelessness for People with Mental Illness and Addiction Manual.* Center City, MN: Hazelden Publishing.

T'Sjoen, G., Van Caenegem, E., and Wierckx, K. (2013) Transgenderism and reproduction. *Current Opinion in Endocrinology, Diabetes and Obesity*, 20(6): 575–579.

Turner, S.S. (1999) Intersex identities: locating new intersections of sex and gender. *Gender and Society*, 13(4): 457–479. Sage Publications.

Union for Reform Judaism (URJ) (2015) *Resolution on the Rights of Transgender and Gender Non-Conforming People.* Retrieved from: https://urj.org/what-we-believe/resolutions/resolution-rights-transgender-and-gender-non-conforming-people

Vale, K., Johnson, T., Jansen, M., Lawson, B., *et al.* (2010) The development of standards of care for individuals and a male-to-eunuch gender identity disorder. *International Journal of Transgenderism*, 12(1): 40–51.

Valentine, D. (2007) *Imagining Transgender: An Ethnography of a Category.* Durham, NC: Duke University Press.

Van Borsel, J., De Cuypere, G., Rubens, R., and Destaerkem, B. (2000) Voice problems in female-to-male transsexuals. *International Journal of Language and Communication Disorders*, 35(3): 427–442.

Van Borsel, J., De Cuypere, G., and Van den Berghe H. (2001) Physical appearance and voice in male-to-female transsexuals. *Journal of Voice*, 15(4): 570–575.

van de Grift, T.C., Elaut, E., Cerwenka, S.C., Cohen-Kettenis, P.T. and B. Kreukels, B.P.C. (2018) Surgical satisfaction, quality of life, and their association after gender-affirming surgery: a follow-up study. *Journal of Sex and Marital Therapy*, 44(2): 138–148.

Van de Poll, M.E. and van Goozen, S.H.M. (1992) Hypothalamic Involvement in Sexuality and Hostility: Comparative Psychologic Aspects. In D.F. Swaab, M.A. Hofman, M. Mirmiran, R. Ravid, and F.W. Van Leeuwen (eds) *The Human Hypothalamus in Health and Disease*, Vol. 93 (pp.343–361). Amsterdam, Netherlands: Elsevier.

Vanderburgh, R. (2007) *Transition and Beyond: Observations on Gender Identity.* Portland, OR: Q Press.

Vanderburgh, R. (2008) Appropriate therapeutic care for families with pre-pubsecent transgender/gender-dissonant children. *Child and Adolescent Social Work Journal*, 26(2): 135–154.

Virupaksha, H., Muralidhar, D., and Ramakshrina, J. (2016) Suicide and suicidal behavior among transgender persons. *Indian Journal of Psychological Medicine*, 38(6): 505–509.

Visnyei, K., Samuel, M., Heacock, L., and Cortes, J. (2014) Hypercalcemia in a male-to-female transgender patient after body contouring injections: a case report. *Journal of Medical Case Reports*, 8(71).

Walch, S.E., Sinkkanen, K.A., Swain, E.M., Francisco, J., Breaux, C.A. and Sjoberg, M.D. (2012) Using intergroup contact theory to reduce stigma against transgender individuals: impact of a transgender speaker panel presentation. *Journal of Applied Social Psychology*, 42(10): 2583–2605.

Wallace, P. (2010) Finding self: a qualitative study of transgender, transition, and adulterated silicone. *Health Education Journal*, 69(4): 439–446.

Wallien, M. and Cohen-Kettenis, P. (2008) Psychosexual outcome of gender-dysphoric children. *Journal of the American Academy of Child and Adolescent Psychiatry*, 47: 1413–1423.

Walling, D., Goodwin, J., and Cole, C. (1998) Dissociation in a transsexual population. *Journal of Sex Education and Therapy*, 23(2): 121–123.

Walser, R. and Westrup, D. (2007) *Acceptance and Commitment Therapy for the Treatment of Post-Traumatic Stress Disorder and Trauma-Related Problems: A Practitioner's Guide to Using Mindfulness and Acceptance Strategies*. Oakland: New Harbinger.

Ware, S. and Marshall, Z. (2014) Disabilities and Deaf Culture. In L. Erickson-Schroth (ed.), *TransBodies, Trans Selves: A Resource for the Transgender Community* (pp.54–61). New York, NY: Oxford University Press.

Watts, A. (2015) The World as Just So. In *Out of Your Mind: Essential Listening from the Alan Watts Audio Archives*. Louisville, CO: Sounds True.

Wegner, D.M. (1994) Ironic process of mental control. *Psychological Review*, 101: 34–52.

Wegner, D.M. and Zanakos, S. (1994) Chronic thought suppression. *Journal of Personality*, 62(4): 615–640.

Wegner, D.M., Schneider, D.J., Carter, S.R., and White, T.L. (1987) Paradoxical effects of thought suppression. *Journal of Personality and Social Psychology*, 53(1), 5–13.

Weinberg, M.S. and Williams, C.J. (2010) Men sexually interested in transwomen (MSTW): gendered embodiment and the construction of sexual desire. *Journal of Sex Research*, 47(4): 374–383.

Weiss, R. (1980) Strategic Behavioral Marital Therapy: Toward a Model for Assessment and Intervention. In J.P. Vincent (ed.) *Advances in Family Intervention, Assessment and Theory*, Vol. 1.(pp.229–271). Greenwich, CT: JAI Press.

Weitzman, G., Davidson, J., and Phillips, R.A. (2012) *What Professionals Should Know about Polyamory*. National Coalition for Sexual Freedom. Retrieved from: https://ncsfreedom.org/images/stories/PolyPaper/72548_NCSF_2012poly7.pdf

Wenzlaff, R. and Wegner, D. (2000) Thought suppression. *Annual Review of Psychology*, 51(1): 59–91.

Westbrook, J. (2016) Beautiful Boxer. *Transgender Universe*, Mar 11. Retrieved from: http://archive.transgenderuniverse.com/2016/03/11/beautiful-boxer/

Wetherell, J.L., Petkus, A.J., McChesney, K., Stein, M.B., *et al.* (2009) Older adults are less accurate than younger adults at identifying symptoms of anxiety and depression. *Journal of Nervous and Mental Diseases*, 197(8): 623–626.

Wheeler D.P. and Dodd, S.J. (2011) LGBTQ capacity building in health care systems: a social work imperative. *Health and Social Work*, 36(4): 307–309.

White, C. and Goldberg, J. (2006) Expanding our understanding of gendered violence: violence against trans people and their loved ones. *Canadian Woman Studies*, 24(1–2): 124–127.

Whittle, S., Turner, L., and Al-Alami, M. (2007) Engendered Penalities: Transgender and Transsexual People's Experience of Inequality and Discrimination. Wetherby, UK: Equalities Review.

Wight, J. (2011) Facing gender performativity: how transgender performances and performativity trouble facework research. *Kaleidoscope: A Graduate Journal of Qualitative Communication Research*, 10, article 6.

Williams, B. and Poijula, S. (2002) *The PTSD Workbook: Simple, Effective Techniques for Overcoming Traumatic Stress Symptoms*. Oakland: New Harbinger.

Williams, J.M.G., Duggan, D.S., Crane, C., and Hepburn, S. (2011) Modes of Mind and Suicidal Processes: The Potential Role of Mindfulness in Changing Minds. In R.C. O'Connor, S. Platt, and J. Gordon (eds) *International Handbook of Suicide Prevention: Research, Policy and Practice*. Hoboken, NJ: Wiley-Blackwell.

Williams, N. (2002) The imposition of gender: psychoanalytic encounters with genital atypicality. *Psychoanalytic Psychology*, 19(3), 455–474.

Wilson, I., Griffin, C., and Wren, B. (2005) The interaction between young people with atypical gender identity organization and their peers. *Journal of Health Psychology*, 210(3): 307–315.

Wilson, K.G. and Murrell, A.R. (2004) Values Work in Acceptance and Commitment Therapy: Setting a Course For Behavioral Treatment. In S.C. Hayes, V.M. Follette, and M.M. Linehan (eds) *Mindfulness and Acceptance: Expanding the Cognitive-Behavioral Tradition* (pp.120–151). New York, NY: Guilford Press.

Witten, T.M. (2003) Life course analysis—the courage to search for something more: middle adulthood issues in the transgender and intersex community. *Journal of Human Behavior in the Social Environment*, 8(2–3): 189–224.

Witten, T.M. (2014a) It's not all darkness: robustness, resilience, and successful transgender aging. *LGBT Health*, 1(1): 24–33.

Witten, T.M. (2014b) End of life, chronic illness, and trans-identities. *Journal of Social Work in End-of-Life and Palliative Care*, 10: 34–58.

Witten, T.M. (2015) Spirituality, Faith, and Religion: The Transgender and Gender Nonconforming Experience. In A. Singh and L. Dickey (2016) *Handbook of Trans-Affirmative Counseling and Psychological Practice*. American Psychological Association.

Witten, T.M. (2016) Aging and transgender bisexuals: exploring the intersection of age, bisexual sexual identity, and transgender identity. *Journal of Bisexuality*, 16: 58–80.

Witten, T.M. and Eyler, A.E. (2012) Transgender and Aging: Beings and Becomings. In T.M. Witten and A.E. Eyler (eds) *Gay, Lesbian, Bisexual and Transgender Aging: Challenges in Research, Practice and Policy* (pp.187–269). Baltimore, MD: Johns Hopkins University Press.

Wolfradt, U. and Neumann, K. (2001) Depersonalization, self-esteem and body image in male-to-female transsexuals compared to male and female controls. *Archives of Sexual Behavior*, 30(3): 301–310.

Wood, J.V., Perunovic, W.Q.E., and Lee, J.W. (2009) Positive self-statements: power for some, peril for others. *Psychological Science*, 20, 860–866.

World Health Organization (2018) *International Statistical Classification of Diseases and Related Health Problems* (11th revision). Retrieved from: https://icd.who.int/browse11/l-m/en

WPATH (2011) *Standards of Care for the Health of Transsexual, Transgender, and Gender Nonconforming People*, Version 7. World Professional Association for Transgender Health. Retrieved from: www.wpath.org/publications/soc

Wu, C., Forbes, E., and Jarvi, K.A. (2017) Clomiphene citrate rescue of spermatogenesis in men with infertility while remaining on finasteride: a case report. *Canadian Urological Association Journal*, 11(3–4): 122–123.

Wyss, S. (2004) 'This was my hell': the violence experienced by gender nonconforming youth in US high schools. *International Journal of Qualitative Studies in Education*, 17(5): 709–729.

Xavier, J. (2000) Final Report of the Washington, DC Transgender Needs Assessment Survey. Retrieved from: doi: 10.13140/RG.2.2.23988.65924

Yarhouse, M.A. and Carrs, T.L. (2012) MtF transgender Christians' experiences: a qualitative study. *Journal of LGBT Issues Counseling*, 6(1): 18–33.

Yep, G (2003) The violence of heteronomitivity in communication studies: Notes on injury,healing, and queer world-making. *Journal of Homosexuality, 45*(2–4): 11–59.

Zandvliet, T. (2000) Transgender Issues in Therapy. In C. Neal, and D. Davies (eds) *Pink Therapy 3: Therapeutic Perspectives on Working with Lesbian, Gay, and Bisexual Clients* (pp.176–189). Buckingham/Philadelphia: Open University.

Zarling, A. and Berta, M., (2017) An Acceptance and Commitment Therapy approach to partner aggression. *Partner Abuse*, 8(1): 89–109.

Zedelius, C. and Schooler, J. (2015) The richness of inner experience: relating styles of daydreaming to creative processes. *Frontiers in Psychology*, 6: 2063.

Zettle, R.D. (2004) ACT with Affective Disorders. In S. Hayes and K. Strosahl (eds) *A Practical Guide to Acceptance and Commitment Therapy* (pp. 77–102). New York, NY: Springer.

Zettle, R.D. (2007) *Act for Depression: A Clinician's Guide to Using Acceptance and Commitment Therapy for Treating Depression*. Oakland, CA: New Harbinger Publications.

Ziegler, K.R. and Rasul, N. (2014) Race, Ethnicity, and Culture. In L. Erickson-Schroth (ed.) *Trans Bodies, Trans Selves: A Resource for the Transgender Community* (pp.40–53). New York, NY: Oxford University Press.

Zikić, O., Cirić, S., and Mitković, M. (2009) Depressive phenomenology in regard to depersonalization level. *Psychiatria Danubina*, 21(3), 320–326.

# Subject Index

Subheadings in *italics* indicate figures and tables.

# Author Index